YALE LAW LIBRARY SERIES IN
LEGAL HISTORY AND REFERENCE

Also by David B. Oppenheimer

Comparative Systemic Racism
(co-edited with Kristen Barnes)

The Global #MeToo Movement
(co-edited with Ann Noel)

Comparative Equality and Anti-Discrimination Law:
Cases, Codes, Constitutions, and Commentary
(with Sheila R. Foster, Sora Han, and Richard T. Ford)

The Ubiquity of Positive Measures for Addressing Systemic
Discrimination and Inequality: A Comparative Global Perspective

Patt v. Donner: A Simulated Trial File for Teaching Civil Procedure
(with Molly Leiwant, Rebecca Schonberg, and Sam Wheeler)

Comparative Perspectives on the Enforcement and Effectiveness
of Antidiscrimination Law: Challenges and Innovative Tools
(co-edited with Marie Mercat-Bruns and Cady Sartorius)

The Great Dissents of the Lone Dissenter:
The Dissenting Opinions of Justice Jesse W. Carter
(co-edited with Allan Brotsky)

Whitewashing Race: The Myth of a Color-Blind Society
(with M. Brown, M. Carnoy, E. Currie, T. Duster, M. Shultz, and D. Wellman)

Rowe v. Pacific Quad—Problems, Teaching Notes and Casefile
(with Frederick Moss)

THE DIVERSITY PRINCIPLE

The Story of a Transformative Idea

DAVID B. OPPENHEIMER

Yale

UNIVERSITY PRESS

New Haven and London

Published with support from the Lillian Goldman Law Library,
Yale Law School.
Published with assistance from the foundation established in memory of
Amasa Stone Mather of the Class of 1907, Yale College.

Yale University Press books may be purchased in quantity for
educational, business, or promotional use. For information, please
e-mail sales.press@yale.edu (U.S. office) or sales@yaleup.co.uk
(U.K. office).

Set in Janson type by IDS Infotech Ltd.
Printed in the United States of America.

Library of Congress Control Number: 2025948082
ISBN 978-0-300-27989-4 (hardcover)

A catalogue record for this book is available from the British Library.

Authorized Representative in the EU: Easy Access System Europe,
Mustamäe tee 50, 10621 Tallinn, Estonia, gpsr.requests@easproject.com

10 9 8 7 6 5 4 3 2 1

For Marcy, for everything

THE DIVERSITY PRINCIPLE

People with different backgrounds, experiences, and viewpoints benefit from engaging with each other. That's why it's important for people who are insiders to expand their circles to include outsiders, and vice versa. The experience of being an outsider is often influenced by age, religion, ethnicity, gender, race, language, disability, economic class, and other forms of identity. Compared with groups that are more homogeneous, diverse groups do a better job of solving problems, making discoveries, teaching and learning from each other, and improving democratic discourse.

Contents

The Diversity Principle Timeline   ix

INTRODUCTION: Two Hundred Years of Valuing Diversity   1

PART I. THE DIVERSITY PRINCIPLE AND THE RISE
OF THE MODERN RESEARCH UNIVERSITY

1.   Upending the Traditional University   23
2.   Liberty, Equality, Diversity   35
3.   Liberty and Diversity at Harvard   50
4.   Harvard's "Jewish Problem"   60

PART II. THE DIVERSITY PRINCIPLE'S INFLUENCE
ON FREEDOM OF SPEECH AND ACADEMIC FREEDOM

5.   The Marketplace of Ideas   67
6.   Boycotts, Quotas, Diversity, and Segregation   79
7.   The Fight over the Meaning of "Excellence"   101
8.   The Open Universities in South Africa   110
9.   The Four Foundations of Academic Freedom   119

PART III. THE DIVERSITY PRINCIPLE IS
EMBRACED BUT THEN REJECTED BY
CONSERVATIVE SUPREME COURT JUSTICES

10. The Legal Brief That Rewrote Affirmative Action Law   133
11. Diversity and the *Bakke* Case   146
12. The Supreme Court's Long Embrace and Turnabout Rejection
    of the Diversity Principle   161

PART IV. THE DIVERSITY PRINCIPLE'S
BENEFITS ARE RECOGNIZED AND
CHAMPIONED BY EDUCATORS, BUSINESS
LEADERS, AND SCIENTISTS

13. Diversity Science   187
14. The Business Case for Diversity   201
15. Diversity and Backlash in Europe   220

PART V. THE WAR AGAINST DIVERSITY

16. From Diversity to DEI   233
17. The War on Diversity   247

POSTSCRIPT   269

Notes   271
Bibliography   383
Acknowledgments   385
Index   389

The Diversity Principle Timeline

1810   Wilhelm von Humboldt founds the University of
            Berlin with policies based on encouraging freedom
            of inquiry and including outsider views through the
            inclusion of Catholics and Jews.

1852   Publication (posthumously) of Humboldt's *Limits of
            State Action*, which articulates the diversity principle.

1859   Publication of *On Liberty* by John Stuart Mill and
            Harriet Taylor Mill, with an epigraph quoting
            Humboldt on the importance of diversity and an ar-
            gument for the importance of diversity in learning
            and in democratic discourse.

1867   John Stuart Mill's address to the students of
            St. Andrews, setting forth the importance of the
            diversity principle in higher education.

1869   Publication of *The Subjection of Women* by Harriet
            Taylor Mill and John Stuart Mill, linking gender
            discrimination and the costs of restricting
            diversity.

1869   Charles Eliot is hired as president of Harvard College
            and begins to implement the diversity principle for
            the purpose of encouraging a "clash of ideas" fueled
            by mixing insider and outsider voices.

1871   Oxford and Cambridge end their exclusion of
            Catholics, Jews, and other "nonconformists."

1910s–1920s John Dewey, Oliver Wendell Holmes, Jr., and Felix Frankfurter collaborate in promoting the educational views of Humboldt and in founding the American Civil Liberties Union, which will become an advocate for academic freedom and diversity.

1911 Publication of Charles Eliot's essay "Diversity in Family, College, and State" endorsing the diversity principle as a foundation of higher education.

1919 Meetings between Oliver Wendell Holmes, Jr., Felix Frankfurter, Learned Hand, and Harold Laski convince Justice Holmes to follow the guidance of the Mills' *On Liberty* in interpreting the U.S. First Amendment to encourage a marketplace of ideas.

1920s Beginning of the "Don't Buy Where You Can't Work" boycott campaign, which will inspire Dr. Martin Luther King, Jr., in his advocacy for racial quotas and affirmative action.

1940s Thurgood Marshall, Pauli Murray, and Erwin Griswold collaborate on legal theories for ending segregation in higher education. Murray advances the argument that Black children will benefit from integration because of the educational benefits of diversity.

1948 Harvard admissions office begins actively recruiting Black students.

1950s Martin Luther King, Jr., and Thurgood Marshall take disparate positions on the merits of direct action and racial quotas, contributing to the development of arguments in support of affirmative action.

1950s Harvard faculty endorses the diversity principle in agreeing to the move from merely admitting Black students who apply to actively recruiting them.

1950s Frankfurter, Griswold, and Chief Justice Albert van der Sandt Centlivres of South Africa collaborate on the role of racial diversity and academic freedom in resisting apartheid in South African higher education.

1957 Publication of *The Open Universities in South Africa* by Centlivres and others, asserting the diversity principle as justifying the right of a university to exercise its academic freedom to admit Black students.

1957 Justice Frankfurter relies on *The Open Universities in South Africa* in his opinion in *Sweezy v. New Hampshire*, supporting the right of a college/university under the First Amendment to select students free of state interference.

1960s Harvard expands its diversity admissions policies, increasing its recruitment of Black, Latino, and Asian American students.

1973 Archibald Cox writes an amicus brief in *DeFunis v. Odegaard*, setting forth the diversity principle as the foundation of what will be called the "Harvard Plan."

1974 Justice Lewis Powell reads the Cox brief and notes his approval of the diversity principle as a justification for considering race in college/university admissions.

1977 *Regents of the University of California v. Bakke* reaches the Supreme Court, where Justice Powell instructs his law clerk that he wants to rely on Cox's diversity argument. An amicus brief filed by Harvard, Columbia, Stanford, and Penn copies and attaches a 1,031-word excerpt from the 1974 Cox brief, calling it the "Harvard College Admissions Program."

1978 *Bakke* case decided. Justice Powell's opinion endorses the diversity principle as a justification for a college/university exercising its freedom under the First Amendment to consider race as a factor in admission. Powell appends the "Harvard College Admissions Program" to his opinion as a model diversity admissions policy.

1980s–1990s Origins and growth of the "business case for diversity" as evidence continues to mount supporting the diversity principle.

2000s The business case for diversity is increasingly expressed as a case for "Diversity, Equity, and Inclusion."

2003 Powell opinion embracing the diversity principle is reaffirmed in Justice Sandra Day O'Connor's majority opinion in *Grutter v. Bollinger*.

2016 Powell and O'Connor opinions embracing the diversity principle are reaffirmed in Justice Anthony Kennedy's opinion in *Fisher v. University of Texas*.

2023   Powell opinion is overruled in *Students for Fair Admis-
            sions, Inc. v. Harvard* and *v. the University of North
            Carolina*, as an ideologically divided Supreme Court
            rejects the diversity principle as "amorphous" and
            without evidentiary support.

2023–25   Multiple conservative leaders and organizations wage
            war on diversity, attacking Diversity, Equity, and In-
            clusion programs at companies and colleges/universi-
            ties, minority scholarships, Critical Race Theory,
            teaching children about racism and exclusion, poli-
            cies adding women and minorities to corporate
            boards, and other diversity initiatives.

2025   President Donald Trump makes the war on diversity a
            central goal of the first hundred days of his second
            term.

Introduction

Two Hundred Years of Valuing Diversity

THIS IS THE STORY of a transformative idea and the people who nurtured it. The idea is the diversity principle: that people with different backgrounds, experiences, and viewpoints benefit from engaging with each other, which is why it's important for people who are "insiders" to expand their circles to include "outsiders," and vice versa. The experience of being an outsider is often determined by age, religion, ethnicity, gender, race, language, disability, economic class, and other forms of identity. Compared with groups that are more homogeneous, diverse groups do a better job of solving problems, making discoveries, teaching and learning from each other, and improving democratic discourse. Many people seem to believe this view originated in the 1970s with the policy of affirmative action in college admissions. That's what I thought too, until I began researching this book.

On the last day of October 2022, the U.S. Supreme Court heard two cases that the Court had merged: one challenged the admissions policies at Harvard University, the other at the University of North Carolina. The complaints were the same: both universities considered students' race when making admissions decisions. Lawyers for the schools told the Court that race was one of many factors admissions officers took into account and that they did so because they wanted to enroll a diverse student body. Justice Clarence Thomas claimed to be flummoxed by this line of argument. Regarding diversity, he stated, "I don't have a clue what it means."[1]

What did Justice Thomas mean? Could he really not know what diversity means? We know from his earlier opinions what he has written about the idea of racial diversity. He thinks the whole notion that diversity matters is vague and intellectually meaningless, and he rejects the premise that students and teachers benefit from studying in a racially diverse environment. Rather, he sees racial diversity as an aesthetic preference of white academics, who want to see some Black and brown faces in their (our) classrooms.

Few, then, were surprised when Justice Thomas and his five fellow conservatives handed down their decision the following June: the schools had lost. Race-based affirmative action at colleges and universities could no longer be justified by a preference for racial or ethnic diversity. The ruling was a decisive break with long-standing precedent. The Court overturned forty-five years of law set forth in opinions authored by three conservative justices appointed by Republican presidents: Lewis Powell, Sandra Day O'Connor, and Anthony Kennedy. Each had held that colleges and universities were permitted to consider an applicant's race and ethnicity if the purpose was to enroll a diverse student body. The 2023 decision rejected this rationale, holding that diversity was too "amorphous" an idea to justify considering race in admissions decisions.

Most of the media response focused on the ruling's immediate effects on highly selective (or "elite") universities—and on the high school students vying to attend them. But as the ruling's repercussions begin to be felt in many areas outside college admissions, it's increasingly clear that something even bigger was at stake: the idea that diversity, especially racial and ethnic diversity, has value. Since the 1990s, it has been commonplace for companies, educational institutions, and cultural organizations to affirm their commitment to diversity. In 2022 every company in the Fortune 100 touted its diversity program on its website. The chairman of the Joint Chiefs of Staff argued that racial diversity in the upper echelons of the military is essential for national security, a stance that earned military academies a special exemption from the Court's affirmative action ban. By 2022, more than one hundred selective colleges and universities had told the Supreme Court that they consider racial and ethnic diversity essential to the education of their students.

As a law professor whose work centers on inequality and racial discrimination, I had been skeptical about the diversity principle. I strongly supported efforts to enroll more students from groups who had been historically excluded. But as a rationale for affirmative action, I found myself sympathetic to Justice Thomas's view that diversity was more about giving white students the benefit of racially mixed classes than about addressing systemic racism. Where had this idea even come from? To answer that question, I began a research journey that took me from diversity skeptic to diversity admirer.

I began by looking into Justice Powell's majority opinion in the 1978 *Bakke* case, the case where the Supreme Court first held that a university may use the goal of racial diversity to justify an affirmative action policy. When I dug into Powell's opinion, I found something astounding: the heart of his diversity argument, found in an appendix describing how Harvard used diversity in making admissions decisions, had been copied word-for-word—essentially cut and pasted—by the authors of a brief submitted in the *Bakke* case, who copied it from a legal brief written four years earlier by Archibald Cox, the great American lawyer who had served as U.S. solicitor general, Harvard Law professor, and Watergate special prosecutor. How did Cox end up with a defining role in our understanding of diversity? Remarkably, we can thank Richard Nixon.

Regarding diversity, Nixon had no idea what forces he was putting in motion. On October 16, 1973, it was revealed that he had taped his conversations in the Oval Office, tapes that would eventually prove that he had ordered a cover-up of the burglary of the Democratic National Committee offices in the Watergate complex. Cox, who had been named as a special prosecutor tasked with investigating the Watergate affair, immediately subpoenaed the recordings relevant to his investigation, but the president resisted, citing executive privilege. Four days later, after Cox refused to drop the subpoenas, Nixon ordered Attorney General Elliot Richardson to fire him. Richardson resigned instead.[2] Nixon gave the same order to Deputy Attorney General William Ruckelshaus, and he too resigned. Finally, Nixon turned to Robert Bork, the solicitor general, and Bork complied.

Cox's firing—and the chain of resignations that preceded it—would become known as the Saturday Night Massacre.[3] It set in motion the impeachment process that led to Nixon's resignation.[4] In its ruling that the tapes were not protected from subpoena, the Supreme Court helped define and limit the scope of executive privilege.[5]

Much has been written about Cox's work as the Watergate special prosecutor and about the Saturday Night Massacre. But Nixon's firing of Cox had an even greater impact in an unrelated area of law and social change, which has been almost entirely unacknowledged. Cox was central to the development of what I call the diversity principle—the idea that diversity contributes to better learning and teaching, better thinking, better science, better business practices, and better democratic engagement. He didn't invent this idea, which originated in the nineteenth century. But by putting it in front of the Supreme Court, he paved the way for the embrace of diversity in America (and beyond) in recent years. This book tells how the diversity principle was formed and grew and how it has profoundly changed our world for the better. As the late Columbia University psychology professor Katherine Phillips put it, diversity "makes us smarter."[6]

After he was fired, Cox returned to Harvard. In early November, the president of Harvard, Derek Bok, asked him to write an *amicus curiae* brief in a case challenging affirmative action in university admissions.[7] Such "friend of the court" briefs are commonly filed by organizations, institutions, and industry groups with the aim of persuading the Supreme Court to see the case as they see it. They can be highly influential: justices often adopt amici arguments in their opinions. Cox's brief argued that under the First Amendment, which has a special role in protecting academic freedom, a university had the right to consider an applicant's race or ethnicity if its goal was to admit a broadly diverse student body; the brief contended that such diversity was central to a modern university's purpose.[8]

Since Cox articulated it fifty years ago, this argument has become widely accepted to the point that it has fundamentally changed society, first in the United States and ultimately worldwide. Most people today recognize that a multitude of voices, especially the voices of outsiders, affects how we understand the world. We make better decisions in business, civil discourse, science, and other areas when people of different backgrounds and experiences participate in those decisions.

Numerous scientific studies support the truth of Cox's argument. But when he was drafting Harvard's amicus brief in 1973, the prevailing views about decision-making favored homogeneity, and the men to whom he was presenting his argument, most of them white Protestants, were not inclined to accept it. That it seems self-evident today testifies to his argument's brilliance.

At the time Cox wrote his brief, many American colleges and universities had only recently begun giving members of racial and ethnic minority groups a boost in admissions, as a part of their efforts to take "affirmative action" to address racism.[9] Harvard had begun actively recruiting Black students in 1948, and at first only a few other top schools had followed.[10] The Civil Rights Movement of the late 1950s and early 1960s inspired a wave of institutions to begin to implement affirmative action policies.[11] The assassination of Martin Luther King, Jr., in 1968 provoked a second wave.[12] But most of these policies were premised on the need for social justice for Black and Hispanic Americans. They aimed to remedy a long history of discrimination against such applicants and to correct for the effects of a broader societal racism that made Black and Hispanic children more likely to receive a substandard K–12 education. In advocating for a diverse student body, Cox took a dramatically different approach.

Cox's 1974 brief anticipated Justice Thomas's questions about the meaning and educational benefits of diversity. He described how Harvard had long attempted to enroll a mix of students who would engage in what the college's former president Charles Eliot had called the "clash of ideas." Harvard wanted students who had grown up in different environments, from big northeastern cities to western farms—and thus brought different experiences to classroom discussions and late night gatherings. It wanted scientists and playwrights; liberals and conservatives; future captains of ships, industry, and politics; athletes and activists—and those at the intersections of all of the above. Harvard had begun actively recruiting Black students (and later Hispanic students) of various backgrounds because the faculty and admissions staff recognized that these students had unique experiences that were meaningfully different from those of most white Americans. They believed Harvard would be a richer place if these students were part of its community. But unless the admissions committee actively sought them out, very few would be admitted.

This book traces the history of the principle at the heart of the Cox brief: that diversity—including racial and ethnic diversity—adds value in education, civic engagement, science, and commerce and that it is inextricable from the freedom of thought on which the modern university is founded. Cox's brief played a critical role in promoting this idea. But the idea itself can be traced back much further.

The diversity principle was put into action by Wilhelm von Humboldt, in his role as the head of the Prussian Ministry of Education. Humboldt is best known as a linguist and diplomat, but his most important accomplishment may be the reforms he instituted in 1810 as the founder of the University of Berlin—now named Humboldt University after Wilhelm and his brother Alexander, the explorer and botanist.[13] Prior to Humboldt, European universities taught entirely by lecture. The professor explained; the students memorized. There was no connection between research and teaching or learning. Humboldt conceived of a university where scholars and students mixed teaching, learning, and experimenting. Together, they would learn by doing and create new knowledge through experience.[14] He believed the best way to accomplish this goal was to bring together all kinds of people with diverse experiences and views—what he called a "Mannigfaltigkeit der Situationen" (variety of situations).[15] In keeping with these principles, he opened the University of Berlin to Catholics and Jews, outsiders in nineteenth-century Prussia.[16]

Wilhelm von Humboldt remains a well-known figure in linguistics, philosophy, political science, and the history of diplomacy. But his wife, Caroline, who in her lifetime was revered by Goethe as "the most important woman of the age," had until recently been largely forgotten.[17] (Her views on sexual freedom have recently led to a renewed interest in her in Germany.) She was the host of the leading intellectual and artistic salons of Berlin, Paris, Rome, and Vienna. At her insistence, the Humboldts strived for equality in their marriage, which included a commitment to sexual openness that led Wilhelm to welcome her lovers into their home and to muse about his own gender identity. Caroline was an important influence on Humboldt's thinking about the importance of diversity.

Humboldt's views on education had a profound effect on the British philosopher John Stuart Mill and his partner (and later wife) Harriet Taylor Mill, who collaborated on his most significant works. *On Liberty*, their best-known book, begins by quoting Humboldt on the value of diversity and goes on to describe it as a prerequisite for freedom in both education and politics, expanding the scope of the diversity principle beyond the university. Had it been written today, the book might have been titled *On Liberty and Diversity*. Following Humboldt, the Mills argued that diversity was essential to learning. They rejected the idea that a professor could challenge students by simulating different points of view, as American law schools sometimes try to do via the "Socratic method."[18] This is not, they wrote, "the way to do justice to the arguments, or bring them into real contact with [a student's] own mind. . . . He must be able to hear them from persons who actually believe them; who defend them in earnest, and do their very utmost for them. He must know them in their most plausible and persuasive form; he must feel the whole force of the difficulty which the true view of the subject has to encounter and dispose of."[19]

The Mills' commitment to diversity was not only theoretical. They supported the campaign to open Oxford and Cambridge to Catholics, Jews, and other nonconformists (meaning those who would not conform to the tenets of the Anglican Church), a campaign that finally succeeded in 1871. They were among the era's leading advocates of women's rights, and their 1869 book *The Subjection of Women* remains an important feminist text. They supported the abolition of slavery, equality for formerly enslaved persons, universal suffrage, home rule for Ireland, and proportional representation to permit minority political parties to enter Parliament.[20]

Humboldt and the Mills advocated for the rights of minorities, but their remarks on diversity tended to focus on the value of exposure to different viewpoints, not on the benefits for minority populations. Today, some opponents of affirmative action seize on this distinction between diversity of opinions and diversity of identities. Why is it necessary, they ask, to incorporate members of marginalized groups to ensure that diverse viewpoints are represented? Isn't it offensive to claim that all white people, or all men, share the same opinions? And, for that matter, isn't it offensive to claim that all Black people, or all women, see things alike? A critic might ask if I am conflating two different meanings of diversity—viewpoint diversity and identity diversity.

Like Justice Thomas's question about what diversity means, these are fair questions that deserve answers. What Humboldt and the Mills recognized is that our viewpoints *are* the product of our identities, backgrounds, and experiences. As John Stuart Mill put it in his 1867 address at the University of St. Andrews: "Improvement consists in bringing our opinions into nearer agreement with facts; and we shall not be likely to do this while we look at facts only through glasses coloured by those very opinions. But since we cannot divest ourselves of preconceived notions, there is no known means of eliminating their influence but by frequently using the differently coloured glasses of other people: and those of other nations, as the most different, are the best."[21] In the context of the time, Catholics and Jews were people "of other nations," just as women and members of ethnic and racial minorities are today.

Thus, while it's certainly not the case that every Black American has the same views (just compare Justice Thomas with his colleague Justice Ketanji Brown Jackson), most Black Americans experience life in America in ways that differ importantly from the experience of most white Americans, and it is in part the viewpoints they've developed from their experiences as Black Americans that contributes to the diversity of a classroom, boardroom, or science lab. This is why Humboldt and the Mills wanted Catholics and Jews admitted to Oxford, Cambridge, and the University of Berlin.

As for Justice Thomas, he too brings a diverse viewpoint based on his personal experiences with racism as a Black American. For proof, one need look no further than his passionate dissent in the Supreme Court's 2003 case *Virginia v. Black*, which concerned the legality of Virginia's prohibition of cross burning. Most members of the Court, all of them white except for Thomas, considered cross burning a form of protected political speech under the First Amendment—even though, in this case, it was done on a Black family's lawn. Thomas, reflecting his own experience, described it as primarily a form of intimidation and thus outside of free speech protections. "One cannot burn down someone's house to make a political point," he wrote, "and then seek refuge in the First Amendment."

The work of translating the ideas of Humboldt and the Mills to an American context fell to a young chemistry professor, Charles Eliot, who served as president of Harvard College from 1869 to 1909 and was the best-known educator of his time.[22] After a few years of teaching at Harvard, Eliot spent two years traveling in Europe, where he was exposed to the recently reformed Humboldt-inspired German universities.[23] He returned home, began teaching at the Massachusetts Institute of Technology, and wrote an influential article in the *Atlantic Monthly* arguing for a similar experiential approach to higher education in the United States.[24] This article so impressed the board of directors at Harvard that they appointed him president at the age of 35.[25]

As president, Eliot put his ideas into operation, opening the university to women (albeit through founding a separate women's college, Radcliffe) and to Catholics, Jews, and Black Americans.[26] The year after Eliot's presidency ended, Edwin Slosson wrote in *Great American Universities*, "The aim of Princeton is homogeneity. Harvard's ideal is diversity. The Harvard students are gathered from all over the world, admitted under all sorts of conditions, and given the most diversified training." The following year Eliot wrote, "I cannot imagine greater diversity than there is in Harvard College. It is not superficial; it is deep. It is shown in the variety of races, religions, households from richest to poorest, and in the mental gifts and ambitions [of our students and faculty]."[27] To Eliot, diverse identities and diverse viewpoints went hand in hand.

The diversity Eliot created at Harvard fostered friendships like that of the elderly Boston Brahmin and Supreme Court Justice Oliver Wendell Holmes, Jr., and the young Jewish radicals Felix Frankfurter and Harold Laski, then instructors at Harvard Law.[28] When anti-war activists were convicted of sedition for speaking out against World War I and their appeals reached the Supreme Court, Frankfurter and Laski urged Holmes to reread *On Liberty* and apply it to create a broad protection for free speech.[29] Despite his disdain for anti-war activists, Holmes—a decorated and wounded Civil War hero—was persuaded. He applied a Mills-like analysis that argued for protecting what came to be called a "marketplace of ideas" and so began reframing how we think about the First Amendment.[30] (The precise phrase was first used by the Court several years later in an opinion by Justice William O. Douglas).[31] That opened the door for Frankfurter to further broaden the First Amendment's scope a generation later by defining academic freedom to include a college's right to select a racially diverse student body.[32]

While this view of academic freedom worked its way through the courts, the U.S. Civil Rights Movement was heating up. From the 1920s through 1960s, activists and civil rights lawyers debated which were the best arguments for ending segregation in public schools and universities. Most of their positions relied on arguments about social justice and equality; segregation was both illegal and immoral. But several key segregation cases raised a diversity argument as well, pointing out that segregated schools failed Black students not only by offering inferior education but by depriving Black children of the opportunity to learn with white children. That argument emerged out of a collaboration between Erwin Griswold and Thurgood Marshall, with Marshall's views influenced by Pauli Murray.[33] As head counsel of the National Association for the Advancement of Colored People (NAACP), Marshall developed the litigation strategy that led to the *Brown v. Board of Education* decision in 1954. He later became the first Black U.S. solicitor general (succeeding Archibald Cox) and the first Black justice on the U.S. Supreme Court.[34] Griswold, who was white, was the dean of Harvard Law School from 1946 to 1967, when he stepped down to succeed Marshall as U.S. solicitor general.[35]

At the NAACP, Marshall brought a series of cases in the late 1940s challenging the segregation of public university law schools in Oklahoma and Texas, with Griswold serving as an expert witness on legal education.[36] Griswold also wrote an influential amicus brief relying on the diversity principle, arguing that when Black law students could not enroll at white universities, they were denied the opportunity to learn from and with their white counterparts.[37] The Supreme Court endorsed this argument, though it largely relied on other grounds to order the universities to desegregate.[38]

Marshall is celebrated today for inventing the idea of strategic litigation—and as perhaps the greatest American lawyer of the twentieth century. Some of his most important legal strategies were first formulated by Pauli Murray, a queer Black woman lawyer who would probably identify today as transgender. Murray was intimately familiar with inequity and exclusion. She was denied entry to the University of North Carolina Law School because she was Black; ostracized at Howard Law—where she finished first in her class—because she was a woman; and denied entry to an advanced degree program at Harvard Law, to which she had earned a scholarship, again because of her sex. She later wrote a legal treatise that Marshall would call "the bible of the civil rights movement" and co-founded the National Organization of Women, though she quickly resigned because NOW ignored the plight of women of color (a term she used fifty years before it became popular). She helped found the Women's Rights Project at the American Civil Liberties Union (ACLU) and partnered with Ruth Bader Ginsburg on their pathbreaking work on gender equality.

Much of the diversity argument framed by Marshall, Murray, and Griswold in the desegregation cases—and by Frankfurter in the academic freedom cases—was drawn from a collaboration with the anti-apartheid movement in South Africa, where the Mills-inspired case for racial diversity was made at the two South African universities that actively resisted apartheid. One of the leaders of this resistance was the chief justice of South Africa, Albert van der Sandt Centlivres, who also served as the chancellor of the University of Cape Town (UCT).[39] Before apartheid was established beginning in 1949, UCT had been racially integrated, and the university leadership fought hard to keep it that way.[40] As he and his colleagues battled the apartheid government, Centlivres exchanged ideas and received encouragement and support from both Frankfurter and Griswold.[41]

In 1957, Centlivres co-authored a book titled *The Open Universities in South Africa*, which argued that academic freedom for a university consisted of "four essential freedoms": that the state not interfere with a university's decisions regarding who will teach, what to teach, how to teach, and whom to teach.[42] The book traced the history of academic freedom and its destruction across much of Europe under Naziism and argued that "racial diversity within the university is essential to the idea of a university in a multi-racial society."[43] Within months of its publication, Frankfurter cited its four principles in a concurring opinion in *Sweezy v. New Hampshire*, a McCarthy-period decision that helped define the contours of academic freedom in the United States.[44] These principles later entered the mainstream of judicial opinion on academic freedom and formed part of the justification for considering race in U.S. college and university admissions.

Frankfurter and Griswold were joined in their admiration of Centlivres by many Harvard Law faculty, including Archibald Cox. Cox was a Frankfurter protégé who, at his mentor's urging, had clerked for Frankfurter's good friend Judge Learned Hand.[45] When a group of Harvard Law faculty wrote to Centlivres to support his call for integrated universities as set forth in *The Open Universities in South Africa*, Cox was among those who signed the letter.[46]

After he was fired by Solicitor General Bork on September 20, 1973, Cox returned to Harvard. He had been gone only five months, but it was too late in the year to assign him any classes. Instead, his friend and former student Derek Bok, now Harvard's president, asked Cox to draft an amicus curiae brief in the case of *DeFunis v. Odegaard*, then pending before the Supreme Court.[47] Marco DeFunis had applied to the University of Washington Law School and been rejected. He sued the university, claiming that it had given preference to applicants of color and that he was denied admission because he was white.

Cox was a brilliant choice for the assignment. He was among the most celebrated appellate lawyers of his time and had represented the United States in cases before the Supreme Court as solicitor general under John F. Kennedy and Lyndon B. Johnson. He had been a law professor at Harvard since 1945, when Harvard had to decide how to select students from the growing number of applications fueled by the GI Bill.[48] This debate took place in the shadow of the despicable 1920s Jewish quota, in which Harvard's president Abbott Lawrence Lowell, over the objections of his predecessor Charles Eliot, had moved to limit the number of Jewish students at Harvard—a policy he cynically couched in the language of diversity.[49] Now, Cox was part of a new postwar generation of faculty who rejected the Jewish quota and debated the role of diversity in selecting a student body. Some favored the "meritocratic" option of relying exclusively on test scores or test scores and grades. But the majority supported considering scores and grades alongside other factors, to create classes of students who could bring diverse backgrounds and experiences to campus.[50]

For his brief in *DeFunis*, Cox gathered a team of Harvard lawyers and wrote a brief that tracked the arguments made in *The Open Universities in South Africa*. It channeled the views of Humboldt and the Mills, traced through Eliot, Holmes, Frankfurter, Marshall, Murray, Griswold, and of course Centlivres. The question, Cox wrote, was not about applicants' equal rights but about how much deference the Court should afford a university in selecting its students, given the First Amendment's protection of academic freedom. Pointing to Harvard's policy, which reflected a preference for high scores and grades along with student body diversity as a model, he argued that "a farm boy from Idaho can bring something to Harvard College that a Bostonian cannot offer. Similarly, a black student can usually bring something that a white person cannot offer."[51] (The recently retired head of Harvard College admissions had in fact grown up on a farm in Idaho, as had Cox's Harvard-educated son-in-law.)

The Cox/Harvard brief in *DeFunis* stood alone. Many amici briefs were filed on behalf of the University of Washington, but no others primarily argued that the Supreme Court should uphold the UW admission plan based on the importance of admitting a diverse group of students. The Cox argument drew positive reviews from *Newsweek* and the *New York Times* and a withering critique by the University of Chicago law professor Richard Posner, a conservative icon.[52] But Marco DeFunis had been admitted to UW Law by court order pending the resolution of his case. When it became clear that he would graduate regardless of what they decided, the justices dismissed the case as moot.[53]

Before the *DeFunis* case was dismissed, the Cox brief had come to the attention of Justice Lewis Powell, and he was intrigued. He marked it up heavily, underlining the explanation of Harvard's diversity policies, and added the *Newsweek* and *New York Times* clippings to his file on the case.[54] Four years later, he found an opportunity to revisit it.

In 1977, the question of university admission policies again came before the Court, in the case of *Regents of the University of California v. Bakke*.[55] Allan Bakke, a white man, had sued the University of California Davis Medical School after being denied admission. He claimed that the school's policy of reserving sixteen places out of one hundred for disadvantaged minority students had violated his right to equal protection under the Fourteenth Amendment. The University of California hired Cox to represent it in the Supreme Court and included his diversity argument in its brief.[56] Powell dusted off his *DeFunis* file and told his clerk that he wanted to use the diversity argument advanced by Cox in the *DeFunis* case.[57]

The Supreme Court decision was evenly split. The four more-conservative members of the Court, plus Powell, held that reserving a specific quota of seats for non-white students violated U.S. equality law.[58] But the four more-liberal members, again joined by Powell, held that race and ethnicity could be used as a *factor* in admissions decisions under certain circumstances.[59] Powell's opinion thus became the opinion of the Court. It closely tracked Cox's brief for Harvard in the *DeFunis* case, even taking a thousand-word excerpt in which Cox described the Harvard admissions system, which had been spliced into another amicus brief filed by Harvard, Columbia, Stanford, and Penn, and appending it to the Court's decision as a model of how to use diversity as a factor in making admissions decisions—a cut and paste job.[60] If diversity was central to a university's mission, Powell wrote, then such a plan would be protected under the university's academic freedom rights guaranteed by the First Amendment.[61]

Powell viewed his opinion in the *Bakke* case as the most important of the more than five hundred opinions he delivered during his fifteen years on the Court.[62] Legal commentators would eventually agree—but they didn't at first.[63] Critics on the left were disappointed that it banned racial quotas, while those on the right considered it an unprincipled compromise that would permit quota-like (or quota-light) policies and bring little change.[64] With few exceptions, Powell's central point, linking academic freedom and the importance of diversity to teaching and learning, went unappreciated.[65]

But that changed. The *Bakke* decision was handed down in 1978; a decade later, selective colleges and universities were beginning to appreciate its depth. If at first they simply read it as permission to use race or ethnicity as a "plus factor" in admissions decisions, over time they began to appreciate how the quest for diversity in their student body was linked to the value of all kinds of diversity in the classroom and throughout the university community.[66] In reevaluating their mission, universities looked to the plan outlined by Cox and Powell as a guidepost. By the time the Supreme Court reconsidered affirmative action in its 2022–23 term, most selective colleges and universities in the United States were following the "Harvard Plan" or something like it.[67]

Of course, not everyone believed that racial and ethnic diversity contributed to the quest for knowledge. In the North as well as the South, some universities were late to integrate, with white alumni often arguing in favor of the segregated status quo. As late as 1986, the year after Michelle Obama graduated from Princeton, an alumni group still vocally argued for keeping Princeton male and homogeneous.[68]

Meanwhile, many supporters of equal rights for Black Americans and other minority groups opposed placing diversity at the center of anti-racism because they thought it didn't go far enough. Instead, they called for affirmative action quotas, reparations, or other explicitly race-based remedies for the country's long history of slavery, Jim Crow, anti-Black violence, and discrimination. Like Justice Thomas, some dismissed diversity policies as primarily benefiting white students by exposing them to a few Black people—a marketing tool rather than a real path toward change.[69]

As the twentieth century sped toward the twenty-first, American corporations were casting about for an alternative to affirmative action in their hiring and marketing. In 1970, not one of America's fifty largest companies mentioned diversity in its annual report. By 2000, nineteen companies in the Fortune 50 were describing themselves as committed to diversity.[70] And in 2022, all fifty had diversity commitments on their websites.[71] In 1986, when *Black Enterprise* listed the "25 Best Places for Blacks to Work" sixteen of the twenty-five described their policies as "affirmative action" programs.[72] Twenty years later, the magazine published a similar report, but this time it was titled "The 40 Best Companies for Diversity."[73] None of the descriptions referred to affirmative action.[74] This turn to diversity as a corporate policy reflected what came to be called "the business case for diversity."[75]

The business case for diversity would sound familiar to anyone who has read the Cox brief in *DeFunis* or the Powell opinion in *Bakke*. The initial argument was that in a multiracial and multicultural society, which itself is part of a global marketplace, a company that maintains a diverse workforce can better appeal to customers from different backgrounds.[76] But over time, the case expanded as business leaders found that by bringing together employees with a variety of experiences and points of view, their companies were positioned to make better decisions and became more successful.[77]

The business case for diversity began with a trickle of papers and proposals by industrial psychologists, human relations specialists, and corporate trainers, starting around the same time as colleges and universities were adopting the Harvard Plan. As more and more schools began to understand diversity as central to higher education, more and more businesses recognized that they, too, could benefit from it.

For most of its history, the idea that diversity improves learning was an unproven theory. While some found the argument persuasive, others reasoned that homogeneous groups work better together because of their shared experiences and values. Beginning in the 1980s, scientists began putting these arguments to the test, asking whether the assertion that diversity improves learning, decision-making, scientific discovery, commerce, and democratic discourse was supported by evidence.

Although the first scholarly papers on diversity were drawn from theory and then from qualitative studies, quantitative studies soon followed.[78] Most of the data confirmed the principle that diversity contributes to success in education and commerce. Diverse classrooms produced more knowledge, diverse workforces were more productive, and diverse companies more profitable.[79] A recent wave of studies shows that scientists working in diverse settings make more discoveries.[80] As the Mills put it, "the only way in which a human being can make some approach to knowing the whole of a subject, is by hearing what can be said about it by persons of every variety of opinion, and studying all modes in which it can be looked at by every character of mind. No wise man ever acquired his wisdom in any mode but this; nor is it in the nature of human intellect to become wise in any other manner."[81]

My colleague Victoria Plaut, a professor of law and psychology at Berkeley, is one of the central figures in the field now known as "diversity science." The late Columbia business school professor Katherine Phillips, whose work helped bring diversity science into the public eye, is another. In an influential article on diversity science published in *Scientific American*, Phillips explained that "being with similar others leads us to think we all hold the same information and share the same perspective. This perspective ... is what hinders creativity and innovation."[82] Diversity, she continued, "encourages the search for novel information and perspectives, leading to better decision-making and problem-solving." Exposure to diversity "can change the way you think" and "makes us smarter."[83]

The growth of empirical evidence confirming the benefits of diversity resembles what occurred in the field of climate science. In the 1970s, a handful of scientists began reporting that higher levels of CO_2 in the earth's atmosphere appeared to be causing changes that could affect our climate. Many responded skeptically, even with derision. But over time, the evidence increased to the point that there is now scientific consensus that burning carbon has induced climate change. Deniers exist, but they are increasingly isolated. The same can be said about evidence for the benefits of diversity. There are still holdouts, some honestly skeptical and others ideologically motivated. But the scientific research is increasingly moving toward consensus on the benefits of diversity—even as the courts are running in the other direction.

In 2003, the business case for diversity was brought into the legal debate over diversity in higher education.[84] Barbara Grutter, a white woman, applied to the University of Michigan Law School and was rejected. She sued the university, claiming that its diversity admissions policies, which resembled the Harvard policies approved in *Bakke*, violated her equality rights and that absent the diversity policies she would have been admitted. The university relied on the Powell opinion in *Bakke* in arguing that while it considered each applicant as an individual, it sought to admit a "critical mass" of Black and Hispanic students so that they would not be isolated within the law school.[85] This concern with preventing the isolation of students from marginalized groups is also found in the Cox brief in *DeFunis* and the Powell opinion in *Bakke*.[86]

The Court again split down the middle. In a companion case (*Gratz v. Bollinger*), the Court held by a 5–4 vote that Michigan's undergraduate admissions system was closer to the quota system disallowed in *Bakke* than to the Harvard diversity plan.[87] But in *Grutter*, the Court held in favor of the law school, again by 5–4. The swing vote was Justice O'Connor, whose majority opinion reaffirmed the Powell opinion in *Bakke*. The Constitution, she wrote, "does not prohibit the law school's narrowly tailored use of race in admissions decisions to further a compelling interest in obtaining the educational benefits that flow from a diverse student body."[88]

Here again, amicus curiae briefs were highly influential—but they did not come from educators and university administrators. Instead, Justice O'Connor highlighted a brief from retired military leaders and two from major corporations: one filed by General Motors and another signed by 3M and other leading businesses. Each of these companies recognized the business case for diversity and looked to universities like UM to produce a diverse group of future business leaders.[89] The retired military leaders made a similar plea: without a diverse group of officer candidates, the U.S. military would end up segregated by rank, with a largely white officer corps leading largely non-white enlisted soldiers and sailors.[90]

These briefs reflect a broader trend: by the early 2000s, American corporate and military leaders had rejected the received wisdom that "great minds think alike" and embraced diversity as a core value. Many companies developed diversity offices and began insisting that their suppliers and subcontractors also commit to diversity. More recently, some of these companies have invested meaningful resources in Diversity, Equity, and Inclusion (DEI) policies and have begun to insist that their foreign subsidiaries and suppliers also commit themselves to diversity. Corporate leaders increasingly justify spending stockholder funds on diversity efforts not only for reasons of social responsibility but for profit. As more and more empirical studies support the value of diversity in many areas of life and work, the business case for diversity has moved from the fringe to the center.[91]

It has also begun to reach across the globe. In recent years the diversity principle has returned to its European roots with the development of the "Diversity Charter."[92] This began as an effort to get French companies and state offices to take diversity into account in hiring, marketing, and other decision-making.[93] It was seen from the beginning as an American-influenced effort, but with a French twist: there would be no explicitly race-conscious policies and no attempts to measure success.[94]

In part because of that twist, some viewed the charter as cost-free virtue signaling.[95] Others insisted it was meant to serve as a cultural force and that efforts to compel legal compliance would weaken its support. A similar disagreement between proponents of voluntary reform and those who favored legal enforcement had been an important part of the debate over civil rights laws in the United States in the 1940s and 1950s.[96]

If measured by its acceptance by businesses and state offices across Europe, the charter was overwhelmingly successful, especially as a tool to address gender inequality. It quickly spread to every European Union member state except Malta.[97] And its proponents turned out to be right: it did contribute to a cultural shift in Europe and, for example, led to the passage of laws requiring gender quotas in selecting public officials and company board members.[98] John and Harriet Mill would have been pleased. The charter's articulation of the benefits of diversity could have been torn from the pages of *On Liberty*.

It is not incidental that two of the leading figures in diversity science are minority women. Dr. Plaut is Latina and Dr. Phillips was Black. The history of the diversity principle—from its origins in nineteenth-century

Prussia to present-day psychology research—is full of thinkers whose lives are testaments to the ideas they promulgated.

Wilhelm von Humboldt's mother was a Huguenot, a member of a small Protestant minority in his native Prussia. His exposure to the ideas of French and German radicalism, romanticism, Judaism, and Catholicism at the salons hosted by his wife, Caroline, helped him to see the value of outsider viewpoints, as did his own experiences of sexual and gender fluidity.

Harriet Taylor Mill and John Stuart Mill were both shut out of Oxford and Cambridge—John because he was a Unitarian, Harriet because she was a woman. John credited Harriet with opening his eyes to ideas that he wouldn't have otherwise considered and with helping shape the argument that voices from diverse backgrounds and experiences, including from gender, racial, and religious minorities, are essential to a robust marketplace of ideas. Along the way, she helped shift him from reformer to radical.

Pauli Murray drew on her own experiences of exclusion to make the case for inclusion. Rejected by the University of North Carolina and Harvard Law and marginalized at Howard and NOW, she developed hard-earned insights into the importance of racial and gender diversity and how they intersect that made their way into some of the most important Supreme Court cases of the twentieth century.

A chain of influence runs from Humboldt through the Mills to Eliot, Frankfurter, and Murray and on to the work of twenty-first-century researchers like Plaut and Phillips. Humboldt opened his university's doors to people of other faiths so that their different viewpoints would contribute to scholarly advancement. The Mills took that principle into the public square, arguing that an educated citizenry needed access to diverse perspectives. In the United States and South Africa, scholars drew upon it to fight pervasive racial injustice and make the case for academic freedom. And over the last few decades, scientists and economists have shown that diversity's benefits extend far beyond the classroom into the boardroom and the laboratory.

Today, however, the expansion of these benefits is under threat. In its 2023 decision rejecting a diversity justification for affirmative action, the new conservative Supreme Court majority overruled four decades of precedent to reject the diversity principle and embrace a view of equality in which any effort to address racial inequality is itself racist.[99]

It is naïve to think the Court will stop with elite colleges and universities. As I write this on the eve of President Donald Trump's second inauguration, conservative advocacy groups already have corporate DEI programs in their sights. Attempts to hire and promote women and people of color and add them to corporate boards are being blamed for everything from bank failures to wildfires and airplane crashes.[100] Efforts to draw voting districts to facilitate the election of people of color are being targeted as racist against whites.[101] Laws prohibiting discrimination are at risk of being found discriminatory based on this warped concept in which any awareness of racism is equated with racism itself.

The end of diversity in admissions is simply the leading edge of a larger war against diversity. As he returns to the White House, President Trump and the governors of two of our largest states—Texas and Florida—have already declared such a war, and many states are joining in banning a host of DEI efforts, prohibiting discussion of racism at public universities, and suing companies to close their DEI offices.[102] They are supported by well-funded and influential lobbying groups, all trying to turn back the clock to a time when straight white Christian men sat at the top of an unquestioned social hierarchy.

Diversity alone won't solve the problem of racial injustice, and it isn't the only tool we can use to make our society more inclusive. But neither is it a simple aesthetic preference, as Justice Thomas would have it. Diversity is an essential ingredient for a robust intellectual and political culture. Without it, we stand to lose a great deal—so many perspectives, so many discoveries. In many cases, we won't even know that they're missing. We are where we are because at critical moments in history people in Europe, North America, Africa, and elsewhere theorized from experience that outsider voices help us understand our world better. All of us living today have benefited from the diversity principle, whether or not we're willing to recognize its impact. Before we abandon it, we should understand its history. The chapters that follow tell that story through the lives of those who nurtured and grew the diversity principle.

PART I

The Diversity Principle and the Rise of the Modern Research University

CHAPTER ONE

Upending the Traditional University

ILHELM VON HUMBOLDT WAS a diplomat, educator, linguist, and a shining light of the German Enlightenment. He is best known today as the inventor of modern linguistics and the designer of the modern research university. Less appreciated is that in the latter role, as founder of the University of Berlin, he brought to life our contemporary understanding of the benefits of diversity in higher education.

Born in 1767 to an aristocratic family, Humboldt grew up between two genteel homes, one in a village near of Berlin and the other in the heart of the city.[1] It was a good time for a wealthy, curious young man to be living in Berlin, then the capital of a newly ascendant Prussia. The Seven Years' War had recently ended, beginning an era of peace and intellectual ferment in the city. King Friedrich II encouraged scientists, artists, and scholars from all over Europe to come to Berlin. Many did, joining a small but thriving community of Huguenots—French-speaking Calvinists who had been driven out of the Catholic kingdoms to the west. As Elector of Brandenburg, Frederick's great-grandfather had issued an edict encouraging Huguenot refugees to settle in the region, promising freedom of worship and plentiful land.

Wilhelm's mother was a Huguenot, and she had her sons home-schooled by prominent Enlightenment tutors, who fostered in Wilhelm an early love of languages and the classics.[2] He benefited greatly from his mother's approval—in sharp contrast to his restless, rebellious brother, Alexander, who dreamed of becoming an explorer.[3] What would come of Alexander's dreams of exploration? Colin Thubron writes, "Alexander von Humboldt was the pre-eminent scientist of his time. Contemporaries spoke of him as second in fame only to Napoleon."[4] When he returned from his explorations in Central and South America, he inspired the twenty-two-year-old Charles Darwin to set sail on his own voyage.[5] Darwin called Alexander the "greatest scientific traveler who ever lived."[6] As to Wilhelm, he is the lesser-known brother, but his influence on how we teach and learn may have been even more important.

As a student Wilhelm became an active member of Berlin's leading intellectual, scientific, and literary salon, led by the prominent Jewish couple Markus and Henriette Herz. Markus led the scientific discussions, Henriette the intellectual and literary. She attracted many of the great writers and philosophers of the era, including Friedrich and Dorothea von Schlegel (the daughter of the German Jewish philosopher Moses Mendelssohn), Immanuel Kant, and Friedrich Schiller.[7] Dorothea von Schlegel and Henriette Herz would later spend two years in Rome with Wilhelm and his wife, Caroline, when he was the Prussian ambassador to the Vatican.[8]

Humboldt's biographer Paul Sweet describes his relationship with Henriette as a "passion," hinting at an affair.[9] It may have whet his appetite for strong, independent, and passionate women, like his beloved wife, Caroline. Whatever else, we know that the relationship with Henriette led to a lifelong romance with philosophy, and his romance with Caroline led to a lifetime of passion and desire.

When Wilhelm was twenty-two and completing his studies, revolution broke out in France. He traveled to Paris, arriving soon after the storming of the Bastille, and stayed several months to observe and admire the revolution and its immediate aftermath.[10] In the years that followed he returned often to Paris, where he became a celebrated public intellectual and in time a leading diplomat.

Soon after Wilhelm's return home from revolutionary France he married Caroline von Dacheröden, a member of a "friendship circle" he had formed alongside his closest friend, Carl George von La Roche, to share their intimate thoughts and feelings with a small group of contemporaries. Sweet writes that when Wilhelm returned from France, Caroline was engaged to La Roche but switched her affections when

Wilhelm rejoined the group.[11] Another Humboldt biographer, Monika Wienfort, claims that La Roche and Caroline were never engaged, although La Roche had declared his love for her.[12] La Roche said he considered Wilhelm a better partner for Caroline; the three remained close throughout their lives.[13]

Wilhelm attended university only briefly, studying law just long enough to pass his exams, which allowed him to enter the Prussian civil service at the age of 23 in 1790. He rose through the ranks with extraordinary speed but grew bored. After just over a year's service, he asked for a leave to pursue his intellectual ambitions full-time. He spent 1791 and 1792 at one of his wife's family's estates writing *The Limits of State Action*, his most important book, which is celebrated today as an early call for individual liberty and a critique of conformity.[14] (Soon after its posthumous publication fifty years later it would strongly influence John Stuart Mill and Harriet Taylor Mill as they wrote *On Liberty*.)[15] Then, at age 27, already married with two children, Humboldt moved with his family to the university town of Jena.[16]

This move placed Humboldt at the center of Europe's literary, artistic, and philosophical scene. Ten years earlier, the University of Jena had come under the patronage of the liberal reformer Duke Karl Augustus, who invited the famed poet and playwright Johann Wolfgang von Goethe to lead the university.[17] Goethe, in turn, began attracting the leading figures of what would become German romanticism. Rejecting the cold rationalism of the Enlightenment, the romantics emphasized individual subjectivity. Under Goethe's leadership, the University of Jena became known as "the romantic university," and it aimed to help students develop personal wisdom and experience, or *Bildung*.[18]

The word *"Bildung"* is not easy to translate into English. The concept includes self-knowledge through intellectual and moral development, cultural literacy, maturity, and the attainment of good judgment.[19] The German legal scholar Gözde Böffel likens it to the development of emotional intelligence. In the spirit of German romanticism, *Bildung* involved a personal journey of learning through experience, which required both freedom to experiment and exposure to many competing viewpoints.[20] Andrew Valls writes that *Bildung* relies heavily on the concept of individuality. Long before he arrived in Jena, Humboldt was already writing about the importance of *Bildung*: as *The Limits of State Action* tells us, "that on which the whole greatness of mankind ultimately depends is the individuality of energy and self-development."[21] An ideal education would thus expose students to varied experiences that would build character and draw out their individuality.

Much of what Humboldt would bring to the University of Berlin was cultivated in Jena. Goethe was soon joined by his close collaborator Friedrich Schiller, whom Humboldt knew from the Herz salon. Goethe and Schiller disagreed about nearly everything—an intellectual rivalry that both men found invigorating.[22] Andrea Wulf writes,

> Goethe described himself as a hard-headed realist, as someone who gained knowledge through the observation of nature. Schiller, by contrast, called himself an "idealist." Inspired by his intense study of Kant's philosophy, Schiller believed that our knowledge of so-called reality was perceived through existing categories in our mind—such as time, space and causality. Goethe insisted that he had come to his conclusions by *looking* at plants—an empirical and scientific approach—while Schiller said that the "idea" of a leaf had existed already in Goethe's mind. Goethe "gets too much from the world of senses," Schiller had told a friend, "whereas I get things from the soul." The discussion was combative but also inspiring, and both agreed that neither had won the argument. The competition between realism and idealism, between object and subject, Goethe later said, was the foundation on which they sealed their connection.[23]

Schiller and Goethe were happy to welcome an erudite young aristocrat and his talented and independent wife. Wilhelm and Caroline became particularly close friends with Schiller and his wife, Charlotte, further bringing Wilhelm into the center of German romanticism in Jena.[24] Humboldt generally sided with Schiller in his philosophical debates with Goethe. Again, from Wulf: "As Schiller paced up and down, Wilhelm dissected deliberately and precisely. He had a knack for pinpointing a problem or awakening a nascent idea in others. Like Schiller, Wilhelm von Humboldt had also studied Kant's philosophy—so intensely, in fact, that his younger brother Alexander had worried that he would 'study himself to death.' Both Schiller and Humboldt were fascinated by the concept of self-determination."[25] Wilhelm's time in Jena would influence all his later work as a diplomat and educational reformer.[26]

The intimacy of the salon made it an ideal space for the work of *Bildung*. Humboldt identified the root of human development not in reason, as his Enlightenment tutors might have encouraged, but in *Sinnlichkeit*, a term typically translated in English as "sensuality."[27] Kris Pangburn cites Humboldt's biographer Paul Sweet as cautioning "against this simple translation, however, noting that there are elements of 'sensuousness' and 'sensuality' in it, but neither of these English words is encompassing enough. Instinctual urges, animal drives, the feeling for beauty, and above all creative power are part of it."[28]

The Humboldts considered sexual experimentation an important part of one's *Bildung*. Sweet writes that when Wilhelm went about "choosing his intimate companions, including his wife, he would select those who believed as he did in freedom to explore life."[29] Caroline was known to be a brilliant thinker in her own right—Goethe called her "the most important woman of the age"—and she and Wilhelm had what they described as an equal marriage that left them free to form outside emotional and sexual attachments.[30] Sweet writes that Wilhelm "abhorred domination of the husband over wife."[31] They endeavored to be gender and sexual equals.[32]

The Humboldts freely experimented with sexual partners and gender roles. Caroline had numerous affairs.[33] Her circle of close friends included a young man named Wilhelm Theodor von Burgsdorff, who became her lover, followed the Humboldts to Jena, and lived with them for nearly two years—first in Jena and then, at Wilhelm's invitation, in Paris. In 1798, Caroline took a month-long vacation to a spa with Burgsdorff with Humboldt's approval, which left her, in Sweet's words, "ecstatic." When Burgsdorff broke up with her, she took up with the family's young tutor.[34] Sweet writes that it "was the essence of Caroline's and Wilhelm's idea of marriage that it should not be based on constraint. Each should be free."[35] Their third child was named Theodor, and their contemporaries suspected that Burgsdorff was the father.[36] Their next son was named Gustav, allegedly after Gustav von Schlabrendorff, another lover.[37]

Caroline's commitment to marriage equality has made her a celebrated figure in twenty-first century Germany. She is perhaps getting the attention she has long deserved as an influencer. Wilhelm's encouragement of her sexual freedom has been described by Hazel Rosenstrauch as evidence of his deep love for her, relying in part on his proclamation that if she were to leave him for another man he would have to be happy, because his love for her meant that anything that added to her happiness added to his.[38]

Wilhelm was an enthusiastic patron of sex workers, recording each experience in his diaries. He wrote approvingly of the homosexual relationships common among friends in ancient Greece. He also maintained close friendships with women and was thrilled when they called him "sister." Sweet writes, "To play the feminine role sometimes certainly suited his inclinations. . . . In an introspective moment, he had written, 'In my feelings there is much that is feminine. It has been said to me more than once that one can talk with me as with a woman, and [his friend Therese Forster] wrote to me not long ago that she would like to call me sister. I do not find it untrue.'"[39] In 1790 he wrote to Caroline, "There is so much female in my feelings."[40] The Humboldts' open marriage, their experiments with polyamory and belief that having multiple lovers helped them further their *Bildung*, and Wilhelm's gender nonconformity all contributed to his appreciation of the importance of diversity in building human character and judgment.

In late 1796, Humboldt's mother died, leaving him and his brother a substantial inheritance.[41] Alexander used his share to begin his scientific travels, which would ultimately earn him a reputation as one of the most important scientists of the nineteenth century. Wilhelm moved his growing family (including Burgsdorff) to Paris, where they would stay for nearly four years.[42] There, he prospered as a public intellectual, frequenting meetings of the group that would become the Académie Française and publishing numerous essays on philosophy, politics, and linguistics.[43] Embracing the then novel idea that field research should support scholarship, he traveled through the Basque country to study the Basque language, changing forever how language is studied. In an interview recorded in 2023, Noam Chomsky stated, "Humboldt was, first of all, a great linguist who recognized some fundamental principles of language that even today are only beginning to be understood. But in the social and political domain, he was not only the founder of the modern research university, but one of the founders of classical liberalism."[44]

In 1802, the thirty-six-year-old Humboldt returned to the Prussian civil service, this time in a position that gave recognition to his now celebrated intellect: ambassador to the Vatican. Caroline thrived in Rome and earned a place at the center of a much-admired intellectual and artistic community. The Humboldt home was a celebrated salon, and Wilhelm continued his life as a public intellectual, publishing frequently across a range of fields.[45]

In January 1809, Humboldt reluctantly returned to Berlin from Rome to take up the leadership of the Prussian Ministry of Education;

he'd have preferred to have stayed with Caroline in Rome, writing her that "managing a crowd of scholars was not much better than having a troop of traveling actors in one's charge."[46] After less than two years he returned to diplomacy, serving as ambassador to Vienna and Britain.[47] Yet his time in the ministry, though brief, was consequential for two major reforms: he initiated a universal public education system that emphasized teacher training, critical thinking, and experiential learning, and he founded the University of Berlin, now named Humboldt University after Wilhelm and his brother Alexander.[48] Between early 1809 and the end of 1810 he had founded the University of Berlin with a new and radical model of university education, hired fifty-two staff members, of whom approximately half were professors, and enrolled over 250 students.[49]

How could he have accomplished so much in so little time? First, Humboldt had the full support of the king and the royal family. He had only agreed to return from Rome with their support assured. Second, he had the support of the other ministers, to whom he was a respected figure as a diplomat and philosopher. Third, the ideas he put in place at the university—academic freedom, research, the emphasis on *Bildung*, and the clash of ideas—were already in play among others of influence, including the philosophers Immanuel Kant and Johann Gottlieb Fichte. And fourth, he was not only remarkably well known, but equally remarkably knowing; most of the fifty-two staff and faculty he hired were people whom he already knew.[50]

In creating the University of Berlin, Humboldt drew on his experience at Jena and his Enlightenment and romantic ideals to bring radical reforms to secondary and university education. He encouraged the faculty and students to teach and learn experientially and to challenge each other's ideas. Before Humboldt, university students studied by memorizing lectures.[51] There was little room for them to pursue their own ideas and interests or to share them with others. As the historian Johan Östling writes, "The eighteenth-century university was intellectually dormant, it was constrained by nepotism and class privileges, and it provided an education that was scholastic and pedantic, at best encyclopedic."[52] Humboldt had students study through experiment and experience, learning by doing alongside their professors. The University of Berlin became the blueprint for the modern research university, a model that is now ubiquitous.[53] In 1851, the philosopher Arthur Schopenhauer wrote, "Before the time of Humboldt, all learning was directed to one end—to qualify a man for a particular profession. But since his time, general cultivation has been regarded as an end in itself. . . . Before his time, the students had to drink in what the professor imparted to them, and repeat it again; they were not called upon to think for themselves. But this is precisely what Humboldt demanded."[54]

As the sociologist Manuela Boatca explains, "The German system of higher education in particular has shaped the modern definition of the Western university during a decisive period in its history. The reforms of the early 19th century initiated by Wilhelm von Humboldt, which centered on the unification of research and teaching in state-sponsored institutions, prompted the restructuring of higher education throughout Europe."[55] Johan Östling writes, "Here, Bildung and scholarship were more important than mechanically teaching long-established material; here was a dynamic connection between the production and the dissemination of knowledge; here academic freedom was given a broader and firmer meaning. The first modern university had been born."[56] The historian Anthony Grafton writes that "scholars of all sorts continue to find cause for respect and anger in his idea of the university as a place where research must be at the center of the teacher's work."[57]

Faculty at the University of Berlin were expected to be scholars, scientists, and teachers, pursuing their own knowledge even as they shared it with their students. Both students and faculty were charged with learning by doing and were encouraged to follow their interests wherever they led. As Paul Sweet writes, "The Humboldtian schema provided the students exceptional freedom to pursue learning according to their own inclinations."[58] Only through self-directed exploration, Humboldt believed, could students achieve their full potential.

The "imperative of self-development [*Bildung*] was the guiding principle in Humboldt's theories," writes Gözde Böffel.[59] "The first condition for achieving this development is freedom ('*Freiheit*'), intimately connected with the second condition of 'variety of situations' ('*Mannigfaltigkeit der Situationen*'), which is what was later translated as 'diversity.'" Moreover, "for Humboldt, diversity, including diversity of experience and exposure to different cultures, ideas, backgrounds and religions, was necessary to develop maturity, wisdom, . . . emotional intelligence and good judgment."[60]

Humboldt also recognized that safeguarding this freedom to explore ideas required protecting scholars and students from state interference—far from a theoretical concern, given that he founded his university just four years after Napoleon's forces had taken Berlin. Independence from the state was part of a concept of academic freedom that continues to undergird our understanding of the idea today.[61] And recognizing that financial as well as legal pressure could easily compromise this freedom, Humboldt insisted that the university have a substantial independent endowment, raised from regional landowners.[62] Like so many educators turned university fund-raisers, in this he failed; the university would be dependent on funding by the state.

Freedom of thought and inquiry were essential elements of Humboldt's approach to education, but they weren't sufficient to create the learning environment he sought. As Östling explains, Humboldt "argued not only for the importance of research, but also for the idea that teaching should be characterized by active dialogic creation that included both students and teachers."[63] He wanted the classrooms at the University of Berlin to be less like silent temples to received wisdom and more like the intellectually vibrant, freewheeling salons he'd attended in Jena and hosted in Rome, a place of lehrfreiheit (freedom to teach) and lernfreiheit (freedom to study). *Bildung* could not proceed without being fed. "Even the most free and self-reliant of men," he wrote, "is hindered in his development, when set in a monotonous situation."[64]

The German philosopher Meike Siegfried traces the concept of diversity in higher education to this vision of dialogue among students and teachers with different backgrounds, experiences, and interests:

> Thinking about diversity in the educational space of the university does not begin with the appearance of the topic on the educational policy agenda, nor with the demand for a power- and society-critical reflection on cognitive processes and mediation processes in higher education in the 1960s—it begins at the moment when the university is thought of as a place of communal activity, enlivened by an inner polyphony that needs the encounter of different speaker positions, views, questions and attitudes. Wilhelm von Humboldt already thinks of the university as such a place.[65]

It's fair to ask why Humboldt saw the benefits of diversity with such clarity that he put it at the center of his reforms. The answer is suggested by his own life. He grew up in a Huguenot family in a city where Huguenots were a minority.[66] He joined a salon of Jewish intellectuals. He befriended some of the most creative thinkers of his time, including

Kant, Schiller, and Goethe. He lived in Paris when it was the intellectual and cultural crossroads of Europe. He engaged with the leaders of the Catholic Church in Rome in his role as the Prussian ambassador. His career was a series of firsthand lessons in the intellectual and cultural benefits of exposure to many voices, including voices that were silenced in his home country.

Humboldt's philosophy of education was also heavily influenced by his peers in the romantic movement, who emphasized the importance of individuality. But as the libertarian essayist George H. Smith notes, it also carries forward the imprint of his early tutoring in what we now call classical liberalism. Humboldt, Smith writes, points out "the synergistic relationship between freedom and cultural diversity on the one hand, and individuality on the other hand—resulting in what we may call a spontaneous cultural order. Freedom and a diversity of situations breed individuality; and individuality, in turn, generates even more freedom and diversity, which promote, in turn, even greater individuality—and so on, indefinitely. This mutual and reciprocal causation is the engine of cultural progress, as new talents are developed, new relationships are formed, and new ideas are discovered."[67]

In an era when many Europeans were beginning to embrace nationalism, Humboldt made the case that diversity favored free inquiry because it allowed people with different backgrounds, experiences, and points of view to learn from each other. He wrote that from "mutual cooperation of its different single members, ... each is enabled to participate in the rich collective resources of all the others."[68] To ensure that an expansive range of viewpoints was represented, Humboldt opened the university's doors to a diverse group of outsiders, including Catholics and Jews, and to members of different social classes.[69] Otherwise, following the eighteenth-century decree by Frederick the Great banning Catholics from public life and the long reign of German anti-Semitism, the faculty and student body would have been all Protestant.[70]

Sweet writes, "It was [Humboldt's] conviction that in an educational system focused on *Bildung*, no attention should be paid to the predilections of a particular caste. The notion that there ought to be a different kind of education for the children of the nobility than for other children 'must be obliterated.'"[71] The same principle applied to religious background. Böffel writes, "Humboldt refers to religion being one aspect of variety [and] strived for equality of different religions. For example, he aimed for a 'fusion' ... of the Jews with the rest of the citizens."[72]

The university's diversity was as noteworthy as it was short-lived. Beginning in 1870, a schism over papal infallibility forced Catholics out (though only until 1878), and the Nazis' rise to power in 1933 would bring the expulsion of Jewish students and faculty from all German universities, as well as from most other cultural life, even before the death camps were built.[73] When Germany was divided after World War II, the university found itself on the East German side of Berlin, where ideological conformity reigned. With the university closed to diversity of voices and experiences, the ideal of *Bildung* was disrupted. But at its best, the university educated a diverse and influential range of thinkers. Felix Mendelssohn, Karl Marx, W. E. B. Du Bois, Albert Einstein, Angela Davis, and the twentieth-century Hasidic leader Rebbe Menachem Mendel Schneerson all brought their backgrounds and viewpoints there.[74]

Humboldt himself would fall victim to changing political tides. After founding the University of Berlin, he left his post in 1812 and spent nearly ten more years in diplomacy, representing Prussia as ambassador in Vienna and London and as a negotiator for the two treaties of Paris and the Congress of Vienna. But he was becoming a lonely voice for liberal ideals.[75] As Prussia (and his beloved Caroline) turned more conservative, his stances against anti-Semitism and in favor of democratic process left him increasingly isolated.[76] In 1816 Caroline wrote to him that "you pride yourself on never leaving the Jews. It is the only fault I know about you."[77] Of his time abroad, a colleague complained, "One never sees Humboldt's name mentioned any more except when paired with a Frenchman or a Jew. It is really disgraceful."[78] In 1819, he either retired or was dismissed from the civil service. He retreated to his family estate and lived out his life as an independent scholar, publishing papers on linguistics that continue to be influential.[79]

But Humboldt's theory of education would persist. Americans studying in Germany in the 1820s returned home "amazed," as the Colgate professor Leo Rockwell put it in a 1950 address to the American Association of University Professors.[80] So were university administrators. By the latter half of the nineteenth century, institutions like the University of Michigan, Cornell, and Johns Hopkins were all emulating the German model.[81] It is now the dominant model of higher education in the United States, where universities are structured around the idea that faculty have great freedom to teach and conduct research as they choose, and students are free to study by exploration, without compulsory drill by recitation.[82] Richard Hofstadter and Walter Metzger write that "if one were to single out the chief German contribution to the American conception of academic freedom, it would be the assumption that academic freedom, like academic searching, *defined* the true university."[83]

Experience was the path, *Bildung* the goal. This demanded free rein to inquire, the essence of academic freedom, and the participation of many voices. In *The Limits of State Action*, Humboldt wrote that "the grand, leading principle, towards which every argument hitherto unfolded in these pages directly converges, is the absolute and essential importance of human development in its richest diversity."[84] John Stuart Mill and Harriet Taylor Mill were so impressed by Humboldt's paean to diversity that they chose this line as the epigraph of *On Liberty*.[85] Their work would play a pivotal role in the development of the meaning of diversity as we know it today.

CHAPTER TWO

Liberty, Equality, Diversity

J OHN STUART MILL WAS born into a family of intellectual and religious nonconformists. His father, James Mill, had graduated from the University of Edinburgh and was licensed as a minister in the Church of Scotland, but he disavowed church doctrine, rejecting the Anglican faith in favor of the freedom-affirming Unitarian Church. Instead of leading a congregation, he took work as a tutor and devoted himself to writing.[1] In 1805, James married Harriet Burrow, age 27. John was born the following year, followed by eight siblings over the next eighteen years.

James Mill wasted little time in beginning his son's education. When John was three years old, his father began teaching him Greek, beginning with *Aesop's Fables*. He added math a few years later, then Latin. The younger Mill seems to have been an eager student. By age 12, he was supplementing his father's lessons in history and political science with differential calculus and other higher mathematics.

Looking back on his unusual education in his *Autobiography*, Mill observed:

> Most boys or youths who have had much knowledge drilled into them, have their mental capacities not strengthened, but overlaid by it. They are crammed with mere facts, and with the opinions or phrases of other people, and these are accepted as a substitute for the power to form opinions of their own: and thus the sons

of eminent fathers, who have spared no pains in their education, so often grow up mere parroters of what they have learnt, incapable of using their minds except in the furrows traced for them. Mine, however, was not an education of cram. My father never permitted anything which I learnt to degenerate into a mere exercise of memory. He strove to make the understanding not only go along with every step of the teaching, but, if possible, precede it. Anything which could be found out by thinking I never was told, until I had exhausted my efforts to find it out myself.[2]

Even as the young Mill continued his studies of Plato and Aristotle, he was put in charge of teaching his younger siblings. He soon discovered that teaching was an advanced form of learning. He fully embraced the idea of learning by doing, following unawares in the path of Humboldt, whom he would later come to revere.

Mill also received inspiration from his godfather, James Mill's good friend Jeremy Bentham.[3] Bentham was another of the shining lights of the Enlightenment, the philosopher regarded as the founder of utilitarianism.[4] He facilitated Mill's brief experiences with formal education, including a year at the Faculté des Sciences in Montpellier, France, that Mill would later call the happiest in his life, and a few years at the school Bentham helped found, University College London. UCL did not require its students or faculty to take the Anglican oaths, unlike Oxford and Cambridge, which thereby excluded Unitarians as well as Catholics and Jews.[5] On Bentham's urging, Mill began studying under John Austin, who originated the theory of legal positivism.[6] Mill would, in his turn, be godfather to the mathematician and philosopher Bertrand Russell, part of a great intellectual lineage from Bentham to Mill to Russell.

Harriet Hardy was born in October 1807, the daughter of a surgeon.[7] Unlike many girls, she was educated, though entirely at home.[8] On March 14, 1826, just five months after her eighteenth birthday, Harriet married the twenty-nine-year-old John Taylor, a successful wholesale pharmacist.[9] By 1831 they had three children.[10] In his *Autobiography*, Mill describes Taylor as an "upright, brave, and honourable man, of liberal opinions and good education, but without the intellectual or artistic tastes which would have made him a companion" for Harriet.[11] The economist and political philosopher Friedrich Hayek, whose work is revered across a wide spectrum, including many conservatives and classical liberals in our own time, edited the letters John and Harriet exchanged during their long, scandalous affair and subsequent marriage. Hayek thus served in effect as Harriet's biographer. He agrees with Mill's assessment of Taylor and adds that the Scottish writer and political theorist Thomas Carlyle, then a friend of Mill's, was "though perhaps less fair ... probably also not quite wrong" in describing Taylor as "an innocent dull good man."[12]

The exact circumstances under which John and Harriet met are unknown. One theory is that Taylor invited Mill to dinner because of Harriet's and John's mutual interest in women's rights.[13] Hayek, however, believes they were introduced by the radical Unitarian minister William J. Fox, then serving as the legal guardian of two teenage sisters, Sally and Eliza Flowers. Hayek reports that John "fancied" Eliza, but Fox was already sleeping with her. To distract John from his interest in Eliza, Fox introduced John to Eliza's best friend—Harriet Taylor. If this is true, the gambit worked. Soon the four of them were regularly seen about town together.[14] The historian Pratinav Anil writes of Harriet's and John's first meeting, "By all accounts, it was a remarkable encounter. Reporting on what transpired, Jane Carlyle [Thomas Carlyle's wife] observed 'that a young Mrs. Taylor, tho' encumbered with a husband and children, had ogled John Mill so successfully that he was desperately in love.' ... Harriet was drawn less to what [the diarist] Caroline Fox ... described as his 'exquisitely chiselled countenance' than his dazzling mind."[15]

The infatuation was immediate and fruitful. Harriet, who had previously written only poetry, began to draft and publish essays on her and John's mutual interests, especially education and the role of women, anticipating arguments that would appear in *On Liberty*. The equality she felt in her relationship with John helped her reach new intellectual heights, and the two began a collaboration that, by John's account, would last from 1831 until her death in 1858.[16]

In 1832, Harriet informed her husband of the relationship; he insisted that she cut it off.[17] Initially, she did, writing to Mill that they must stop seeing each other.[18] She moved with her children to Paris for six months to cement the separation, but Mill followed her there, and the affair resumed. By the time they returned to London, Taylor seems to have acquiesced. Mill visited Harriet at her home nearly every day, with her husband accommodating their time together by dining twice a week at his London club.[19] John and Harriet were often seen in public together, attending concerts and lectures and vacationing in Europe.[20] They were particularly fond of the south of France.[21]

Their intellectual partnership was also flourishing. According to John, while Harriet's contributions to his 1843 treatise *A System of Logic* were confined to the "minuter matters of composition," by 1848, when *The Principles of Political Economy* was published, Harriet was playing a significant role in developing ideas and shaping arguments.[22] "The chapter of the Political Economy which has had a greater influence on opinion than all the rest, that on 'the Probable Future of the Labouring Classes' is entirely due to her," John wrote in his autobiography. "In the first draft of the book that chapter did not exist."[23] This contribution went uncredited at the time. John wrote implausibly that he would have dedicated the essay to her but for her "dislike of publicity."[24]

John Taylor died in 1849.[25] Two years later, Harriet Taylor married John Stuart Mill, a step they undertook with some ambivalence.[26] British marriage law had been liberalized somewhat since Harriet's marriage to Taylor, and Unitarian ministers could now officiate at weddings.[27] But the doctrine of coverture was still in force, stripping married women of legal selfhood.[28] When women married, their bodies and property were held to belong to their husbands.[29] Except under extenuating circumstances, only men could petition for divorce, and then only rarely.[30] In 1851, the year of their marriage, Mill published a public statement on marriage noting his and Harriet's disapproval of "the whole character of the marriage relation as constituted by law."[31] Having "no means of legally divesting myself of these odious powers," he wished to "put on record a formal protest against the existing law of marriage, in so far as conferring such powers, and a solemn promise never in any case or under any circumstances to use them."[32]

Marriage may have had practical benefits for the Mills, but it did nothing to repair their reputations. It only made their long affair seem more scandalous. Having turned away from friends who disapproved of the match, the Mills spent most of their marriage in relative isolation.[33] By then, both John and Harriet suffered from ill health, including tuberculosis.[34] Feeling that they were writing on borrowed time, they worked furiously on material that would become pillars of the Western intellectual canon: *On Liberty, Representative Government,* John's *Autobiography, Utilitarianism,* and *The Subjection of Women.*[35] In the fall of 1858, accompanied by Harriet's daughter, Helen, the Mills set off for the south of France to live and work in a more hospitable climate. But before they arrived, Harriet developed a cough and fever. By the time they reached Avignon on November 3, she was gravely ill.[36] She died that evening.[37]

Mill wrote to a friend: "It is doubtful if I shall ever be fit for anything, public or private, again. The spring of my life is broken."[38] Harriet was buried in Avignon, and Mill purchased a house overlooking the cemetery. He spent part of every year there, visiting her grave several times a day accompanied by Helen, who later became a noted feminist writer and activist in her own right. John and Harriet are now buried there side by side.[39]

Harriet Taylor Mill's role in John Stuart Mill's writings is heavily contested. He viewed her as a genius; some of his friends believed he was blinded by love.[40] But scholars increasingly credit Harriet with many of the insights—and at least some of the writing—that cemented her husband's legacy as perhaps the most important political theorist of the nineteenth century. Why is her contribution significant? Their collaboration itself provides an example of the value of diversity in producing some of the greatest works of political theory in the English language. An account of the dispute, and why I consider Harriet a co-author, follows this chapter as an appendix.

The Mills' most enduring work is *On Liberty*, published in 1859, the year after Harriet's death.[41] They first drafted it as a short essay but spent months and then years in conversation, "bringing it out from time to time, and going through it *de novo*, reading, weighing, and criticising every sentence" until it had evolved into a multichapter volume.[42] Profoundly important in its own time, it continues to influence how we think about state power and individual rights. Its discussions of free speech and the dangers posed by powerful majorities have inspired generations of liberals and conservatives alike.

The book's publication coincided with the founding of the Liberal Party in Britain, and the two became inextricably linked.[43] As *On Liberty* gained readers, the success of the Liberal Party grew. Mill himself joined Parliament as a Liberal in 1865.[44] Three years later, the party came to power under the leadership of Mill's friend William Gladstone, who would dominate British politics for nearly three decades. Even today, the Liberal Party's successor, the Liberal Democrats, mark a change in leadership by having the outgoing leader turn over his or her copy of *On Liberty* to the incoming leader as the party's "book of office."[45]

On Liberty begins with an epigraph from Humboldt's *The Sphere and Duties of Government* (now translated as *The Limits of State Action*): "The grand leading principle, towards which every argument unfolded in these pages directly converges, is the absolute and essential importance of human development in its richest diversity."[46] In his autobiography, Mill credits Humboldt with articulating *On Liberty*'s "leading thought."[47] Mill's biographer Richard Reeves finds in his politics a theory of self-improvement that closely echoes Humboldt's *Bildung*. "At the heart of [Mill's] liberalism," Reeves writes, "was a clearly and repeatedly articulated vision of a flourishing human life—self-improving, passionate, truth-seeking, engaged and colourful—which it was the job of individuals to cultivate, and the duty of society to promote."[48] Mill thus "had a lifelong thirst for dissent, heterodoxy, and for the collision of opposing views."[49] Mill's respect for dissent led to his statement that "the great thing was to consider one's opponents as one's allies; as people climbing the hill on the other side."[50]

One might argue that *On Liberty* would be better titled *On Liberty and Diversity*. The Mills repeatedly stress the importance of outsiders' voices, an argument that today would be called an expression of the diversity principle. The warnings against government power that inspire so many liberals, traditional conservatives, and libertarians today were rooted in the Mills' fear that majoritarian tyranny might quash those voices. For the Mills, this fear extended beyond the realm of government:

> Protection … against the tyranny of the magistrate is not enough: there needs protection also against the tyranny of the prevailing opinion and feeling; against the tendency of society to impose, by other means than civil penalties, its own ideas and practices as rules of conduct on those who dissent from them; to fetter the development, and, if possible, prevent the formation, of any individuality not in harmony with its ways, and compel all characters to fashion themselves upon the model of its own.[51]

The Mills argued that viewpoint diversity and outsider voices are crucial to the search for truth, because discussions among people with different perspectives help us overcome the limitations of our own experience. They believed the core of higher education should be collecting a diverse group of individuals with genuinely different views and backgrounds so that their ideas can grow as they learn from each other. In one of the book's most frequently quoted passages, they wrote, "If all mankind minus one, were of one opinion, and only one person were of the contrary opinion, mankind would be no more justified in silencing

that one person, than he, if he had the power, would be justified in silencing mankind."[52] Less commonly quoted is their staunchly utilitarian
justification for this defense of free speech: "The peculiar evil of silencing the expression of an opinion is, that it is robbing the human race;
posterity as well as the existing generation; those who dissent from the
opinion, still more than those who hold it. If the opinion is right, they
are deprived of the opportunity of exchanging error for truth: if wrong,
they lose, what is almost as great a benefit, the clearer perception and
livelier impression of truth, produced by its collision with error."[53] Given
that no theory or philosophy is perfect on its own, "other ethics than any
which can be evolved from exclusively Christian sources must exist side
by side with Christian ethics to produce the moral regeneration of mankind."[54] Although the phrase "marketplace of ideas" was a half-century in
the future, *On Liberty* remains one of the most eloquent articulations
of the idea that a competition of viewpoints moves humanity closer to
the truth.

On Liberty also offers an important rejoinder to those who would
separate viewpoint diversity from what we today call identity diversity—
factors such as race, ethnicity, religion, culture, or gender. As much as
we may claim otherwise, the Mills argue, our views are products of our
environment:

> The world, to each individual, means the part of it with which
> he comes in contact; his Party, his sect, his church, his class of
> society: the man may be called, by comparison, almost liberal
> and large-minded to whom it means anything so comprehensive
> as his own country or his own age. Nor is his faith in this collec-
> tive authority at all shaken by his being aware that other ages,
> countries, sects, churches, classes, and parties have thought, and
> even now think, the exact reverse. He devolves upon his own
> world the responsibility of being in the right against the dissen-
> tient worlds of other people; and it never troubles him that mere
> accident has decided which of these numerous worlds is the ob-
> ject of his reliance, and that the same causes which make him a
> Churchman in London, would have made him a Buddhist or
> a Confucian in Pekin.[55]

Lived experience creates diverse viewpoints, and these are best represented by those with the experience to back them up. "There are many

truths," the Mills write, "of which the full meaning *cannot* be realized, until personal experience has brought it home."[56] Hearing professors lecture about various points of view is

> not the way to do justice to the arguments, or bring them into real contact with [the student's] own mind. He must be able to hear them from persons who actually believe them; who defend them in earnest, and do their very utmost for them. He must know them in their most plausible and persuasive form; he must feel the whole force of the difficulty which the true view of the subject has to encounter and dispose of.[57]

In the political realm, the Mills argued, the voices of minorities are not fully heard unless they are heard from the mouths (or pens) of the minorities themselves. "In the absence of its natural defenders, the interest of the excluded is always in danger from being overlooked; and, when looked at, it is seen with very different eyes from those of the persons whom it directly concerns."[58] Mill's book *Considerations on Representative Government* (1861), also likely drafted with Harriet, carried forward some of these ideas. In it, they argue that proportional representation, first proposed a few years earlier by the English political theorist Thomas Hare, partly solves the problem of potential tyranny of the majority by allowing minority voices to be heard. It assigns particular importance to political representation for racial minorities.[59]

As Mill's star rose, he rebuffed numerous entreaties to run for political office. Encouraged by Gladstone, he relented in 1865, with some unusual conditions. He would make it clear in his campaign that he did not wish to join Parliament, would not canvass or incur expenses to run, and would not attempt to support the interests of his constituency. He put forth his positions, which included universal suffrage, full equality for women, proportional representation and home rule for Ireland, and a ban on laws limiting the rights of non-Anglicans (including Jews, Catholics, and Muslims), but he refused to state his own religious views. Disregarding the normal campaigning customs of his time, he seldom attended public meetings with potential constituents. He was nonetheless elected.[60]

In Parliament, Mill kept to his word: he supported women's rights, universal suffrage, the rights of Black people in British colonies, Irish home rule, proportional representation, and the rights of non-Anglicans to religious liberty.[61] In 1866 he presented the first bill in the British Parliament calling for women's suffrage, accompanied by a petition circulated by feminist leaders that had garnered over 1,500 signatures.[62] The following year he proposed an amendment to a voting reform act to substitute the word "person" for "man," thus allowing some women to vote.[63] It gained significant but insufficient support. His speech to the Parliament in its favor became part of the canon of the suffrage movement in Britain and the United States.[64] The feminist essayist Mary Harrington calls Mill "the first male feminist."[65]

Only a few months after Mill's election, news arrived of a rebellion in Jamaica, Britain's largest Caribbean colony.[66] Though slavery had been abolished, Black Jamaicans still faced living standards far below those of white British colonists, and high poll taxes prevented the vast majority of them from voting.[67] In October 1865, a rebellion of Black farmers in Morant Bay was violently put down by the colonial governor, John Eyre. His troops killed hundreds of Black people, including women and children, and tortured hundreds of others. Eyre declared martial law, clearing the way for hundreds more to be executed, including one of the colony's few mixed-race elected representatives.[68]

Amid the outrage this caused in Britain, a group of British Liberals formed the Jamaica Committee, which called for Eyre to be tried for murder. Mill led the committee, joined by several other members of Parliament as well as prominent figures like Charles Darwin, whose book *On the Origin of Species* had been published the same year as *On Liberty*.[69] They were countered by the Eyre Defence Committee, whose members included Charles Dickens, Alfred Lord Tennyson, and Mill's now former friend, Thomas Carlyle.[70] A grand jury declined to indict Eyre, despite widespread acknowledgment of his responsibility for the massacre; a civil lawsuit against him was decided in his favor.[71] The next year, Jamaica was put even more firmly under Crown control.[72] As the then Liberal-aligned *Spectator* put it, even as middle-class and upper-class Britons began to accept the broadening of the franchise to the working class, they remained deeply invested in brutal racial hierarchies that devalued Black life at home and in the colonies. "We pardon Eyre," the magazine wrote, "because his error of judgment involves only negro blood, which would have otherwise been in our nation's eyes simply unpardonable."[73]

Mill was hardly an anticolonial hero. Before joining Parliament, he had a long career with the East India Company, and he supported a policy sometimes described as "benevolent despotism" toward those he described as "barbarians," a group that included Indians.[74] Still, his advocacy for Eyre's prosecution helped doom his 1868 election bid, a rematch with the Conservative (and noted bookseller) W. H. Smith.[75]

While some today see Mill primarily as a libertarian or even the father of libertarianism, his brief parliamentary career reveals a nuanced relationship with political power. *On Liberty* suggests that the Mills, like Humboldt, were not only worried about state power but equally apprehensive about the power of social pressure to impose conformity. To the Mills, liberty meant freedom not only from state coercive power but also from social pressure to be like others. Just as Humboldt sought positions in government, Mill was willing to participate in the power of the state when it served his policy goals.

After his election loss, Mill remained an important voice in British politics. He had been denied, as a "nonconformist" who would not swear fealty to the Anglican Church, the opportunity to study at Oxford and Cambridge, England's most prestigious universities, and he supported the admission of Catholics, Jews, and members of other minority religions.[76] The exclusion of nonconformists from Oxford and Cambridge had begun in 1581 and continued for nearly three centuries. Legislation passed in 1854 and 1856 permitted them to attend and graduate but limited their privileges as students.[77] They were, in effect, second-class citizens. Mill pushed Parliament to repeal all religious tests at the two universities and provide for full (male) equality, which it finally did in 1871, two years before his death.[78] He vocally opposed other laws discriminating against nonconformists, especially Jews, and supported a series of bills that would have allowed Jews to serve in Parliament (each of which failed in the House of Lords). He strongly opposed an 1870 bill that would have excluded Jewish children from state-funded schools, calling it "odious."[79]

By the end of the nineteenth century, Catholics and Jews finally had the same rights as any other citizen of the United Kingdom, at least according to the law.[80] The same could not be said of women. Harriet Taylor Mill was, like her husband, a Unitarian, but even if she were Anglican, she would have been excluded from all British institutions of higher education due to her sex.[81] Women wouldn't be admitted to the University of London, until 1868.[82] They couldn't attend Oxford or Cambridge until well into the twentieth century.[83]

To the Mills, this state of affairs was unconscionable. *The Subjection of Women*, published in 1869 and, according to John, largely the work of

Harriet and her daughter, Helen, contains yet another call for diversity as essential to democracy.[84] Yet its language is unusually strident even for John, who hardly shied from conflict. The essay presents the subjection of women as an extreme example of "the law of force," which permits men to enslave women just as whites had enslaved Black people.[85] (The United Kingdom did not abolish slavery until 1838.)[86] It draws parallels between the reasoning used to maintain Black slavery and that which depicted women as unfit for the work, education, and lives of men. Responding to the argument that treating women differently from men is merely "natural," Harriet and Helen ask, "was there ever any domination which did not appear natural to those who possessed it? . . . Did not the slaveowners of the United States maintain the same doctrine[?] . . . Did they not call heaven and earth to witness the domination of white men over the black is natural, that the black race is by nature incapable of freedom, and marked out for slavery?"[87] Richard Reeves notes that unlike most liberals of his time, "Mill consistently denied that there were any inherent differences between races."[88] He held the same view of women and wrote, with Harriet and Helen, that the "law of force" that allows their subjugation harms society at large: "The loss to the world, by refusing to make use of one-half of the whole quantity of talent it possesses, is extremely serious."[89] Equality would bring more diverse voices to the public sphere, allowing women to share their talents and experiences and providing a "stimulus" to the "intellect of men by the competition."[90]

The 1865 election that sent Mill to Parliament coincided with another. The students of St. Andrews in Scotland elected him rector, head of the university, a position he would also hold for three years.[91] His inaugural address is best known as the (probable) origin of the familiar aphorism "Bad men need nothing more to compass their ends, than that good men should look on and do nothing."[92] But it also emphatically articulates his beliefs, gathered over a lifetime, on the importance of diversity. "The proper business of a University," he told the students, is "not to tell us from authority what we ought to believe, and make us accept the belief as a duty, but to give us information and training, and help us to form our own belief in a manner worthy of intelligent beings."[93] Warning against "one-sided" models of education—the ones Humboldt had shattered in Germany—Mill urged students to seek out interlocutors from different backgrounds and to learn from the outlooks that had been unconsciously shaped by those backgrounds:

Improvement consists in bringing our opinions into nearer agreement with facts; and we shall not be likely to do this while we look at facts only through glasses coloured by those very opinions. But since we cannot divest ourselves of preconceived notions, there is no known means of eliminating their influence but by frequently using the differently coloured glasses of other people: and those of other nations, as the most different, are the best.[94]

As the United States emerged from its brutal Civil War, Mill cheered the result. He was a lifelong abolitionist and had fiercely defended the Union, an unpopular stance in England, where the mills depended on Southern cotton—but one that had earned a *New York Times* endorsement for his Parliamentary bid.[95] Abraham Lincoln had praised *On Liberty*, and it was referenced in the Congressional debates over the Fourteenth Amendment.[96] Yet even as slavery was legally abolished and the passage of the Fourteenth and Fifteenth amendments made Black Americans full citizens, a vicious backlash to Black progress was brewing. To many white Americans, the diversity Mill espoused was not a route to moral and intellectual truth but an existential threat. It was in this heated atmosphere that Charles Eliot took the reins at Harvard College. An admirer of Mill and Humboldt, Eliot was determined to bring the clash of ideas to Harvard. His path would be far from smooth.

Appendix

Harriet Taylor Mill's role in John Stuart Mill's writings is contested among scholars.[97] Mill repeatedly asserted that she co-authored many of his works, including *On Liberty*; some (mostly male) scholars find it unlikely, though they are increasingly isolated.

By John's account, he collaborated with Harriet from 1831 until her death in 1858.[98] He wrote in his *Autobiography*,

My wife and I were working together at the "Liberty." I had first planned and written it as a short essay in 1854. It was in mounting the steps of the Capitol, in January, 1855, that the thought first arose of converting it into a volume. ... After it had been written as usual twice over, we kept it by us, bringing it out from time to time, and going through it *de novo*, reading, weighing, and criticising every sentence. Its final revision was to have been a work of the winter of 1858–59, the first after my retirement. ... That hope and every other were frustrated by the most unexpected and bitter calamity of her death.[99]

Further regarding Harriet's role, he wrote,

When two persons have their thoughts and speculations completely in common; when all subjects of intellectual or moral interest are discussed between them in daily life, and probed to much greater depths than are usually or conveniently sounded in writings intended for general readers; when they set out from the same principles, and arrive at their conclusions by processes pursued jointly, it is of little consequence in respect to the question of originality, which of them holds the pen; the one who contributes least to the composition may contribute most to the thought; the writings which result are the joint product of both, and it must often be impossible to disentangle their respective parts, and affirm that this belongs to one and that of the other. In this wide sense, not only during the years of our married life, but during many of the years of confidential friendship which preceded, all my published writings were as much her work as mine; her share in them constantly increasing as years advanced.[100]

Although the modern trend is to credit John Stuart Mill's attribution of Harriet Taylor Mill as his co-author and collaborator, the case remains uncertain.[101] Harriet's biographer Dale Miller frames the issue this way in the *Stanford Encyclopedia of Philosophy*:

Harriet Taylor Mill (1807–1858) poses a unique set of problems for an encyclopedist. The usual approach to writing an entry on a historical figure, namely presenting a straightforward summary of their major works and then offering a few words of appraisal, is not available. This is because she worked in such close collaboration with John Stuart Mill that it is exceedingly difficult to disentangle their contributions to the products of their joint effort. In attempting to assess Taylor Mill's philosophical career, one encounters sharply conflicting reports about her ability from people who knew her, contradictory evidence about her role in authoring several books and essays, and widely varying judgments about how much influence she exerted on Mill's thought and work.[102]

After John's death, scholars recognized that she might have played an important role in his work, but by 1900 that view had faded. Through the early twentieth century, scholars' dominant view of Harriet was negative, critical, and misogynistic. But in compiling the Mills' correspondence in 1951, F. A. Hayek accepted John's attribution of Harriet as a co-author.[103] In the 1970s, and increasingly in the 1980s and 1990s, scholars began to regard Harriet as worthy of study separately from John and then began to make the case that the two were—as John insisted—properly regarded as co-authors.

This shift was largely catalyzed by the work of Alice Rossi, Phyllis Rose, and Gail Tulloch.[104] It began in 1970 with the publication of a volume of essays edited by Rossi, a feminist scholar, activist, and co-founder (with Pauli Murray) of the National Organization of Women. As the prominent Harriet Taylor Mill scholar Jo Ellen Jacobs writes,

> What a breath of fresh air it was when, in 1970, Alice Rossi edited *Essays on Sex Equality by John Stuart Mill and Harriet Taylor.*
> ... Rossi believes, as I do, that Harriet's works need to be studied in order to make an accurate assessment of her work or her influence on John. "None of the Mill scholars have examined the essays collected in this volume for clues to the kind of relationship John and Harriet tried to maintain in their years together. Nor has due allowance been made, in my judgment, for Mill's own intellectual toughness. Mill was not a man to be easily influenced and won over by an idea or person."[105]

The historian Evelyn Forget writes that Rossi "claimed that the 1851 essay, *The Enfranchisement of Women*, was primarily Taylor's work, citing a letter from Mill to Taylor in February 1849 referring to a pamphlet on the topic she had nearly completed, and noting that the content of the article paralleled Taylor's 1831 essay on the topic."[106]

Phyllis Rose also contributed to the growing chorus of recognition. Her 1983 book *Parallel Lives: Five Victorian Marriages* analyzed the power relations in the marriages of prominent couples of the era, including an extensive description of the Mills' relationship.[107] "Harriet made the decisions," Rose writes. "Harriet ran the show. . . . They were a perfect intellectual team" in which Harriet "was the executive."[108] Then in 1989, Gail Tulloch published *Mill and Sexual Equality*, in which she argued that Harriet's influence on John's views of gender equality was apparent in her individual work.[109]

Others who have contributed to the view that Harriet was John's coauthor for *On Liberty* include Susan Groag Bell (1990), Marilyn Yalom (1990), Virginia Allen (1997), Jo Ellen Jacobs (2002), Cécile Tougas and Sara Ebenreck (2000), Evelyn Forget (2003), Mariana Szapuová (2006), Meneka Philips (2018), and Helen McCabe (2023).[110] Each advanced the argument by pointing to ways in which Harriet's voice emerges.

Bell, for example, raises the point that skeptics of Harriet's role had ignored "the exchange of letters between Mill and Harriet Taylor, published [by Hayek] in 1951, [from which] we have long known how instrumental Harriet was in editing and censoring Mill's work."[111] She cites a passage from John's *Autobiography* in which he wrote, "In all that concerned the application of philosophy to the exigencies of human society and progress, I was her pupil, alike in boldness of speculation and cautiousness of practical judgment."[112]

Hayek discusses a letter to Harriet in June 1831 from her friend Eliza Flower, in which Eliza asks Harriet whether it was John or Harriet who authored a letter on Lord Byron in the *Edinburgh Review*. The answer, it turns out, was neither, but the question tells us that one of Harriet's closest friends saw John's and Harriet's writing as similar in style, content, and point of view.[113]

In 2021 three scholars from the Karlsruhe Institute of Technology—Christoph Schmidt-Petri, Michael Schefczyk, and Lilly Osburg—used machine learning to analyze 270 texts written by John, Harriet, or both. They concluded that John was not the sole author of *On Liberty*, with Harriet the likely principal author of chapter 3 and parts of chapter 5 and a contributor to other parts of the book.[114] Chapter 3, on the importance of self-development, follows in the footsteps of Humboldt and his focus on the importance of *Bildung*.[115] But the Schmidt-Petri team opposed crediting Harriet as a co-author because they further concluded that she was unhappy with parts of the text and would not have wanted to be identified with it.[116] And so the debate continues.

CHAPTER THREE

Liberty and Diversity at Harvard

I F CHARLES WILLIAM ELIOT had gotten his way, he might have been a historical footnote. Instead, he became the most transformative leader in the history of America's most prestigious university.

Eliot was born in 1834 into a family of Unitarian abolitionists that produced several leading intellectual figures before, during, and after his life, including the founders of Washington University in St. Louis and Reed College in Oregon and the poet T. S. Eliot.[1] Following the typical path for elite Bostonians, he studied at Harvard, graduating in 1853, and returned the following year to teach math and chemistry. In 1858, he was promoted to assistant professor and married his first wife, Ellen Derby Peabody. They settled in Cambridge and quickly had four children—all boys, only two of whom would reach adulthood.[2]

As a young assistant professor, Eliot was eager for change. He criticized Harvard's traditional approach to teaching science and sought a curriculum that would integrate new developments and a more applied approach to using scientific discoveries.[3] He hoped his critiques would lead to an appointment to the distinguished Rumford Professorship in chemistry. Instead, in 1863, the position went to a rival.[4] Smarting from the rebuff, he took the inheritance he had received from his wealthy grandfather and moved his family to Europe. There he would witness firsthand an entirely new way of teaching and learning. Eliot spent a year in Paris, studying the French universities and marveling at French society, and then moved to the University of Marburg in Germany. Eliot visited several German universities, met with leading chemists whose work he had read and admired, and got to observe the Humboldt model in person.[5]

In 1865, he returned to Boston as a chemistry professor at the newly established Massachusetts Institute of Technology (which would move from Boston to its current home in Cambridge in 1916).[6] MIT's founder, William Barton Rogers, was also a chemist, and his vision for the school emphasized the direct experimentation and hands-on learning that Eliot had admired in Germany.[7] MIT's charter had been signed in April 1861, only two days before the Battle of Fort Sumter inaugurated the American Civil War, and the school wouldn't begin holding classes until the war ended.[8] But it had been in the works for decades.[9] The mid-nineteenth century had seen an explosion of new technologies and rapid industrialization. There was a growing understanding that the available forms of post-secondary education—on the one hand, classics-focused schools like Harvard, set up primarily to train ministers and businessmen; on the other, narrowly targeted and less prestigious vocational programs—would not suffice in the new industrial economy. Rogers garnered enthusiastic backing for the school not only from scientists but from Boston industrialists disappointed with Harvard's lackluster science departments. MIT was one of the first institutions in the country to offer a comprehensive science education. To Eliot, it was a breath of fresh air.

The problems with the American educational system went beyond institutes of higher learning. In Germany, Eliot had been deeply impressed not only by the universities but by the quality of the secondary schools, another Humboldt reform. While American secondary schools focused on teaching Latin, Greek, and morality, German schools taught analytical science and math skills that would prepare their graduates for either the university or industry. Sensing that Americans were no longer content with the state of their higher education, Eliot set out to propose reforms after the German model.[10]

His opportunity came in the form of a long article spanning the February and March 1869 issues of the *Atlantic Monthly*—then as now a leading forum for discussing social issues.[11] Taking the position of parents of secondary school children, Eliot begins:

> What can I do with my boy? I can afford, and am glad, to give
> him the best training to be had. I should be proud to have him
> turn out a preacher or a learned man; but I don't think he has

the making of that in him. I want to give him a practical education; one that will prepare him, better than I was prepared, to
follow my business or any other active calling. The classical
schools and the colleges do not offer what I want. Where can I
put him? Here is a real need and a very serious problem. The
difficulty presses more heavily upon the thoughtful American
than upon the European. He is absolutely free to choose a way
of life for himself and his children; no government leading-
strings or social prescriptions guide or limit him in his choice.
But freedom is responsibility.[12]

He follows this with a devastating critique of the science and technology
instruction at the country's top colleges and universities: Harvard, Yale,
Columbia, Dartmouth, Brown, and the University of Michigan. The way
the schools have organized these programs, he complains, makes them
less demanding than the traditional classics-oriented program of study.
They attract less motivated students and offer a less serious curriculum.[13]
Rather harshly, he charges that "all the scientific schools of the country,
whether connected with colleges or not, have suffered from the fact, that
boys and young men who, from lack of wit or vigor, were found incom-
petent to pursue the usual classical studies of the preparatory school or
the college, turned to the loosely organized scientific schools as safe har-
bors for their laziness or stupidity."[14]

Eliot then turns to Rensselaer Polytechnic Institute (RPI), praising
its four-year advanced program in science and technology, which required no Latin or Greek but did include English, French, and philosophy requirements in addition to science and math. But he reserves his
greatest praise for his own institution, MIT, whose prescribed course of
study and high expectations of its students he describes in detail. MIT's
liberal curriculum, he maintains, differs importantly from that of technical schools that train students in only one discipline. He believes the
more appropriate comparison is a school like Harvard. MIT was demanding, and its name would carry prestige.[15]

In part II of the article, Eliot calls for broad improvements in secondary education, with richer curricula and less emphasis on Greek, and
then returns to the need to improve science education at both the colleges and the technical schools through the adoption of a broad liberal
arts curriculum that includes science and technology.[16] The country's
reputation is at stake:

Americans must not sit down contented with their position
among the industrial nations. We have inherited civil liberty, social mobility, and immense native resources. The advantages we
thus hold over the European nations are inestimable. The question is, not how much our freedom can do for us unaided,
but how much we can help freedom by judicious education. We
appreciate better than we did ten years ago that true progress in
this country means progress for the world. In organizing the new
education, we do not labor for ourselves alone. Freedom will be
glorified in her works.[17]

Across the Charles River from MIT, the businessmen on Harvard's
board of overseers read Eliot's article with great interest. They were so
impressed with his ideas for reforming the American educational system
that they asked him for a meeting and then abandoned their long practice of appointing clergymen to make him Harvard's president. Eliot was
thirty-five. He would stay in the job for forty years.[18]

As the board had hoped, Eliot's reforms dramatically changed Harvard's future. He refocused the college's curriculum away from religion
and toward the physical and social sciences (though he failed in his re-
peated efforts to merge Harvard with MIT).[19] He created or transformed
the professional and graduate schools in medicine, law, and arts and sciences. He revitalized the campus buildings. He created the "Harvard
Annex," which offered women college-level educational opportunities
even though they could not receive a Harvard degree. A few years later,
in 1894, he chartered Radcliffe College as a degree-granting institution
for women.[20]

Scholars disagree about the extent to which these measures were directly inspired by the Humboldtian reforms Eliot observed while visiting
German universities. His first biographer, Henry James (a nephew of the
novelist), wrote that the German model had no appeal to Eliot and that
those who claimed his reforms were based on that model only did so to
criticize him.[21] Emily Levine, a historian of education at Stanford, holds
that Humboldt's influence on Eliot was indirect: Levine points to Johns
Hopkins, founded in 1876, as the first American university inspired by
the Humboldt model and argues that Eliot made Humboldt-like reforms
at Harvard only after he observed Johns Hopkins's success.[22] She is not
incorrect, but Eliot was involved with Johns Hopkins from its founding.[23] How did his Harvard differ from Johns Hopkins? The Humboldt

model emphasized graduate education, with professors and students working together to produce scholarship and new knowledge. This was very much the idea at Johns Hopkins, whose founders at first did not even want to offer an undergraduate program.[24] If we focus less on the divide between graduate and undergraduate education and more on Eliot's broad approach to reform, he looks much more like a Humboldt disciple.

One of his most significant reforms, for example, was allowing undergraduates to choose their own course of study.[25] At most schools, under the English classical system that Harvard embraced before Eliot, students followed a prescribed sequence of classes.[26] Under the Humboldt model, they had few required courses beyond what would today be considered a general education curriculum. Eliot allowed Harvard students to choose "electives," following their interests where they led, a freedom they exercised with enthusiasm, as Eliot had intended.[27]

The Jesuit educator John O'Connor argues that Humbolt's vision was critical to Eliot's reforms even before Johns Hopkins was founded. "For Charles Eliot," O'Connor writes, "the old ways and the old curriculum were too narrow, elementary, or superficial. There was insufficient attention to the German university ideals of free teaching, study, and research. There was insufficient attention to the technical and practical. The American colleges were too sectarian, too undemocratic. Their faculty psychology was faulty; their philosophy, wanting."[28] Eliot believed that "spontaneous diversity of choice" provided "an invaluable addition to human freedom," and he saw the friction between his modern system and the old classical method as part of a philosophical war between the tyranny of the aristocratic past and the freedom of a democratic future.[29] During Eliot's tenure, the sociologist Jerome Karabel writes, "student freedom grew dramatically; having little taste for regulating students, [Eliot] cut the length of the student rulebook from forty pages to five while radically increasing the number of courses offered."[30] It was not only undergraduates who stood to benefit from this latitude.[31] Like Humboldt, Eliot promoted a system that allowed professors the "freedom to investigate, as well as to teach, new things."[32] He wished to recruit brilliant, research-minded faculty, combine the liberal arts school with professional and graduate schools, and foster an "atmosphere of scholarship and freedom favorable to good teaching and research."[33]

With academic freedom, of course, came the possibility of conflict—which Eliot welcomed. Like Humboldt and the Mills, he believed that the clash of ideas was the heart of a university education. It exposed students' biases and preconceptions and helped them see the world through the eyes of others.[34]

Regarding academic freedom, he exclaimed that "a university is the last place in the world for a dictator. Learning is always republican. It has idols, but not masters."[35] On individuality and diversity, in words that could have come from Humboldt, he stated, "For the individual, concentration, and the highest development of his own peculiar faculty, is the only prudence. But for the State, it is variety, not uniformity, of intellectual product, which is needful."[36]

This embrace of conflict—especially in the classroom—represented a significant shift in Harvard's culture. Henry James writes that before Eliot took over the presidency, "it was still bad form, as it had been when Eliot was an undergraduate, for a student to enter into unnecessary conversation with a teacher."[37] Such strict hierarchy clashed with Eliot's Unitarian beliefs, which stressed equality and freedom of thought. As Harvard's president, he held that professors should respect students' opinions as much as their own.[38]

James's biography emphasizes Eliot's respect for diversity of opinion in the classroom and among his colleagues.[39] He was open-minded, especially in response to others' criticisms of his proposed reforms. Like Mill, he regarded his critics as collaborators climbing the same hill from different sides. James wrote that "when a man disagreed or opposed squarely and openly, Eliot respected him and liked him the better."[40] Eliot wrote extensively about the value in differences of opinion, a view that James saw as following the Mills' philosophy: "The exemplary generosity with which Eliot accommodated himself and his work to opposition and disagreement showed how genuinely he believed what John Stuart Mill . . . and his own Unitarians preached."[41]

Eliot's affinity for the Mills appears often in his writing and speeches and in his view of the canon of a liberal education. He had long argued that a five-foot shelf of books could contain all the works one needed to be an educated person.[42] When he stepped down as Harvard's president, he was challenged by the publisher P. F. Collier & Son to create this shelf, a collection known today as the Harvard Classics. Unsurprisingly, he included *On Liberty* and Mill's *Autobiography*.[43]

Like the Mills, Eliot recognized that diverse viewpoints arose from diverse backgrounds. In his inaugural speech, he described Harvard as a place for the poor as well as the rich, for the sons of professional men, traders, mechanics, and farmers.[44] Recognizing that the sons of mechanics and farmers might need assistance paying Harvard's tuition, he developed a generous scholarship program. As Karabel writes, "To be sure, the university's mission was to train an elite, but it was to be an elite drawn from all segments of society."[45]

Thirty-one years after that inaugural speech, Eliot still took pride in Harvard's socioeconomic diversity. In a speech in 1900 welcoming Harvard's incoming freshmen—a class that included the future president Franklin D. Roosevelt—Eliot termed it a common error to believe that Harvard was only for the rich, and he promised the incoming students that they would learn much from each other because they came from many different backgrounds. Over 40 percent of that class came from public schools.[46]

As the former Harvard president Neil Rudenstine writes, Eliot

> expanded the conception of diversity, which he saw as a defining feature of American democratic society. He wanted students from a variety of "nations, states, schools, families, sects, and conditions of life" at Harvard, so that they could experience "the wholesome influence that comes from observation of and contact with" people different from themselves. He wanted students who were children of the "rich and poor" and of the "educated and uneducated," students "from North and South, from East and West," students belonging to "every religious communion, from the Roman Catholic to the Jew and the Japanese Buddhist."[47]

During Eliot's tenure, Harvard would take steps toward that vision, matriculating the children of immigrants, students from minority religions, and—though in small numbers—Black students.

When Eliot was named president, there were a handful of Black students in the professional schools: the first Black students graduated from Harvard Law School and the Harvard School of Dental Medicine in 1869.[48] But Harvard College had never awarded an undergraduate degree to a Black person. Eliot wanted to change that, but his move to enroll Black students generated backlash.[49] The historian Samuel Eliot Morison reports that "Southerners avoided Harvard after the Civil War because it admitted Negroes on the same terms as whites, allowing them to eat at Memorial Hall, room in college dormitories, and participate in debating and athletic contests."[50] Eliot, who would also court scandal by inviting a Catholic priest to give a sermon at the Harvard chapel, seems to have taken this in stride.[51] His correspondence files include an exchange with a Southern descendant of "Harvard men" whose colleague was sending his sons to Yale because he did not want them exposed to Black Americans being treated as equals.[52] Eliot, in reply, confirmed Harvard's equal treatment of all students regardless of race.[53] To another such complaint, he replied that many Southerners were sending their sons to Johns Hopkins or Princeton.[54]

One of Harvard's handful of Black undergraduates was the future sociologist and NAACP co-founder W. E. B. Du Bois, who credited Eliot's reforms with transforming Harvard. It had become, he wrote, "no longer simply a place where rich and learned New England gave the accolade to the social elite. It had broken its shell and reached out to the West and to the South, to yellow students and to black. . . . [Eliot and others] sought to make Harvard an expression of the United States."[55] After earning bachelor's and master's degrees at Harvard, Du Bois studied at the University of Berlin (now Humboldt University) with Eliot's encouragement before returning to Harvard for his PhD.

Du Bois may have been struck by the similarities between the two schools. Eliot does not appear to have used the term "*Bildung*," but in eliminating curricular requirements, encouraging a clash of ideas, and opening the university to outsider voices to broaden students' exposure to a range of ideas, he instituted at Harvard the same principles on which Humboldt had built the University of Berlin. To Eliot, as to the Mills and Humboldt, diversity was a tool for strengthening both the individual intellect and the broader political community: "For the individual, concentration, and the highest development of his own peculiar faculty, is the only prudence. But for the State, it is variety, not uniformity, of intellectual product, which is needful."[56] As Rudenstine writes, "[Eliot] saw that an inclusive vision of higher education not only would benefit individual students, but also would serve the needs of a society strongly reliant on a wide variety of citizens who would have to learn to live together if the nation's democratic institutions were to function effectively and if its ideals were to be realized."[57]

But diversity also meant something to Eliot that it did not to Humboldt. The European concept of diversity was primarily about nationality —then a novel concept—and religious identity. In the United States, where Reconstruction quickly gave way to a brutal retrenchment of white supremacy, any real discussion of diversity could not avoid race. In a 1911 essay titled "Diversity in Family, College, and State," Eliot moves seamlessly from diversity of viewpoint to diversity of race, religion, and class—what we might today call diversity of background or identity:

> Can you imagine a greater diversity of human capacity, disposition, taste, and personal ambition than exists in Harvard College? I cannot. The diversity is wide; and it is not superficial, but deep. Think of the variety of races brought together in Harvard College; of the variety of religions represented here; and of the variety of households,—every kind of household from the poorest to the most luxurious, with every sort between.[58]

In identifying racial, religious, and class differences as sources of "deep" diversity—and speaking about them alongside viewpoints like "taste" and "personal ambition"—Eliot presents the two forms of diversity, background and viewpoint, as inextricable.

Eliot's paean to diversity wouldn't seem out of place in a speech delivered by a college president today. But other writings show that while Eliot seems to have genuinely welcomed viewpoint diversity, when it came to race, nationality, and gender, he was often unable—or unwilling—to see his own rhetoric through to its logical endpoint. Only two years before the publication of "Diversity in Family, College, and State," Eliot had caused outrage—not least among Harvard's Black students and alumni—by defending racial segregation and opposing intermarriage during a tour of the South. In an assessment lauding Eliot's influence, published by the *New York Times* shortly after his death, and relying on quotes from his speeches and writings, the *Times* revealed some of the contradictions in his views over his long life as an influential public figure. For example, he had asserted that the United States benefited from having a "heterogeneous" population, but "assimilation" was going too far. In the early twentieth century he would, like many American elites, become a full-throated advocate of eugenics—though only briefly. And even though he had started the Harvard Annex and signed the diplomas of women graduates from Radcliffe, he made no secret of his belief that women were intellectually inferior.[59]

Still, by the time Eliot stepped down as president in 1909, Harvard had become significantly more diverse in both viewpoint and background. In 1910, the year after Eliot's presidency ended, Edwin Slosson wrote in *Great American Universities*, "The aim of Princeton is homogeneity. Harvard's ideal is diversity. The Harvard students are gathered from all over the world, admitted under all sorts of conditions, and given the most diversified training."[60] Jerome Karabel reports that in 1908 Harvard College had twenty-nine Black students and sixty foreign students, and that

> by the standards of the Big Three [Harvard, Yale, Princeton], Harvard was remarkably heterogeneous under Eliot; in 1908, his last full year in office, public school students constituted 45 percent of the freshman class, and one student in six was either Catholic (9 percent) or Jewish (7 percent). A further sign of Harvard's cosmopolitanism was its openness to blacks, immigrants, and foreigners. A homogeneous New England college when Eliot studied there in the 1850's, Harvard had by the early 1900s become genuinely diverse, a place where the "collision of views" that Eliot valued so highly was powerfully reinforced by the sheer variety of students.[61]

How important were Eliot's contributions? Karabel describes him as

> the nation's leading college president ... dubbed "First Citizen of the Republic" by Theodore Roosevelt ... revered by both his peers in higher education and his fellow citizens. When he retired in 1909 after forty years of service, he had succeeded not only in transforming Harvard, but in changing the definition of a great university. No college president, before or since, has exerted a greater impact on the shape and character of American higher education.[62]

Not all of Eliot's reforms survived his departure. His successor, Abbott Lawrence Lowell, reined in Eliot's elective system and became notorious for his efforts to kick Black students out of Harvard's dorms and dining halls and to institute a quota for Jewish students. Still, in his forty-year tenure, Eliot transformed Harvard into a model of a great university that has been emulated around the world. As the historian of education W. B. Carnochan writes, "American higher education has never been the same after him."[63]

CHAPTER FOUR

Harvard's "Jewish Problem"

CHARLES ELIOT HOPED to be succeeded as Harvard president by Louis Brandeis, a celebrated public interest lawyer and legal scholar who was known as "the people's lawyer."[1] "I am a Unitarian," Eliot explained. "It would please me to be followed by a Jew."[2] But instead, the board of overseers chose Abbott Lawrence Lowell—a notorious racist and opponent of virtually everything Eliot believed in.[3]

By the time of his inauguration in 1909, Lowell had clashed with Eliot for more than a decade over one of the major public policy issues of the late nineteenth and early twentieth centuries: immigration. Lowell was active in the Immigrant Restriction League, a lobbying organization founded in 1894 to advocate legislation to preserve what it saw as America's Anglo-Saxon character.[4] In 1912, while serving as Harvard's president, he was named an honorary vice president of the League.[5] Lowell believed in the superiority of Anglo-Saxon "values and customs" and thought immigrants from eastern and southern Europe, mostly Russian and Polish Jews and Polish and Italian Catholics, would dilute "the stock" of the white race.[6] He supported the total exclusion of Chinese immigrants on the basis of their alleged inability to assimilate and the right of southern states to deny the vote to Black Americans.[7] His vocal anti-Semitism disturbed even his close friends.[8]

Those feelings came to the fore when Louis Brandeis was nominated for the Supreme Court in 1916. Eliot strongly supported the selection, as did the vast majority of the Harvard Law faculty.[9] Lowell, however, helped lead a campaign against Brandeis that was widely understood to be anti-Semitic. Confirmed after a bruising fight, Brandeis was characteristically generous about Lowell's opposition to his candidacy, attributing it to class bias rather than anti-Semitism: "Men like A. Lawrence Lowell who had been blinded by privilege, who have no evil purpose, and many of whom have distinct public spirit, but whose environment—or innate narrowness—have obscured all vision and sympathy with the masses . . . [are] subjects for sympathy."[10]

Eliot, by that time, was coming to believe that immigrants had made America great: "We need them, . . . whether they are Jews or Gentiles, Greeks or Barbarians, literate or illiterate, skilled or unskilled, children or adults."[11] This represented a shift: like many turn-of-the-century white intellectuals, he had been an enthusiastic supporter of the racist eugenics movement. As late as 1911, he was quoted in the *New York Times* as saying that "the mixture of races" would create "an inferior breed."[12] But by 1921, Eliot had embraced the emerging theory of cultural pluralism. "The United States," he wrote, would benefit from being "a country of many races, many religions, and many varieties of human nature, forming one liberty-loving stable democracy."[13]

Lowell, as president of Harvard, was deeply offended by the way Eliot's reforms had liberalized the university. Eliot had ended the requirement that students attend chapel—and although, like Harvard's previous presidents, Eliot was a Unitarian, he had brought in chaplains from other Protestant denominations and even once scandalously permitted a Catholic priest to lead a service at the on-campus chapel.[14] Lowell had led the opposition to Eliot's curricular reforms, including his decision to abandon a required course of study in favor of electives, and as president Lowell sought to distance Harvard from Radcliffe College.[15] In his view, the right students for Harvard were those who were already part of the social elite.[16]

On taking office Lowell began a purge of homosexual students and ordered that Black students no longer be permitted to live in the freshman dorms or eat in the college dining halls.[17] The issue lay quietly for a while, but when a Black student publicized his exclusion from the freshman dorms in 1922, Eliot, still an important public figure as president emeritus, sided with the student.[18] So did many of Harvard's white students and alumni, and their protests ultimately forced Lowell to back down—but not before the issue made the national press.[19] W. E. B. Du

Bois, a founder of the NAACP and Harvard BA, MA, and PhD, linked Lowell to the resurgent Ku Klux Klan, which Lowell had refused to condemn.[20] Membership in the Ku Klux Klan was reaching its zenith in the 1920s. At a time when the entire U.S. population was only a little over one hundred million, the Klan claimed four million members.[21] In turn, the Klan's "Imperial Wizard," Hiram Evans, published an essay calling out Eliot's belief in diversity as at best naïve, arguing that "diverse races never have lived together in such harmony."[22]

Unlike Eliot's prejudices, Lowell's never abated. In 1927, the governor of Massachusetts asked Lowell to lead a commission examining the case of Nicola Sacco and Bartolomeo Vanzetti, Italian immigrants who had been convicted of murder and sentenced to death despite substantial evidence they were innocent. Their trial, in Boston, had been widely condemned as marked by anti-Italian, anti-immigrant, anti-Catholic, and anti-anarchist bias.[23] After Lowell concluded that the trial had been fair and that the two were guilty, the state sent them to the electric chair. It later emerged that Lowell had written his report before the commission even heard from the defense lawyers. Decades later, the Commonwealth of Massachusetts would apologize for framing them.[24] In the 1930s, Lowell would also refuse to condemn Adolf Hitler. Under his influence, Lowell's friend and successor, James B. Conant, president from 1933 to 1953, welcomed Nazi leaders to Harvard as late as 1934 and invited Nazi academics to the Harvard tercentenary celebration in 1936, which was held on Rosh Hashanah.[25]

Incongruously, despite his racism, Lowell was committed to academic freedom. During World War I, he resisted calls to purge German subjects from the curriculum, and when the radical young law professor Harold Laski spoke out in support of the Boston police strike, Lowell supported his right to free speech even though he disagreed with Laski's position. When it appeared that the Harvard overseers might demand Laski's firing, Lowell declared that if they did so, he himself would resign.[26]

The biggest clash between Eliot and Lowell stemmed from the presence of Jewish students at Harvard. As Jewish immigration rose in the early twentieth century, so did Jewish enrollment at Harvard and other elite colleges. By 1918, 20 percent of Harvard's freshman class were Jewish. In 1922, when the proportion reached 21.5 percent, Lowell moved to reduce their number, arguing that the presence of so many Jewish students would make Harvard unappealing to the upper-class white Protestants whom he favored.[27] Karabel writes that Lowell's view of Jews at Harvard is aptly summed up by a letter he wrote to the Harvard philosophy professor William Earnest Hocking, in which he stated, "The summer hotel that is ruined by admitting Jews meets its fate, not because the Jews it admits are of bad character, but because they drive away the Gentiles."[28] Lowell claimed that a high percentage of Jewish students were dismissed from Harvard for cheating. When he learned that his claim was false, he refused to believe it and decided his own administration was lying to him.[29]

In 1922, Lowell instructed the admissions committee to impose a quota limiting the acceptance of Jews each year. Professor Henry Pennypacker, the committee chair, refused to institute a quota without a clear instruction from the faculty. Lowell proposed that the faculty adopt a 15 percent Jewish quota. The faculty refused, but it gave Lowell a partial victory by instructing the admissions committee to take racial and national origin into account in its decision-making.[30]

Following objections from the public and Harvard's board of overseers, as well as second thoughts from faculty members, Lowell was forced to return to the full faculty for another vote. At the next faculty meeting, the earlier vote was rescinded, a proposal to impose a quota failed, and the faculty agreed to appoint a special committee to study the matter. This decision implicitly recognized Lowell's main argument that Harvard had a "Jewish problem." Charles Eliot, now in his late eighties, had one more fight left in him. He joined with a few influential faculty and board members in lobbying the committee to reject the quota. In this they were joined by the public, the press, Harvard's students, and many Harvard alumni.[31] After a year, the committee released its report, unanimously recommending no change in admission policies and affirming Harvard's commitment to "equal opportunity for all regardless of race or religion."[32]

But Lowell wasn't done. The committee had approved measures to admit more students from the South and West, which Eliot and his allies worried would be used as a subterfuge to exclude Jewish applicants, most of whom came from large Eastern cities.[33] To Lowell's delight and Eliot's consternation, a separate committee on class size recommended that Harvard's freshman class be limited to one thousand students, thus requiring the admissions committee to be more selective. When that committee's report went to the board of overseers in January 1926, the board sided with Lowell. A few days later, the faculty further agreed that the admissions committee should gather information about applicants' character and fitness. The admissions committee now had approval to limit class size, apply a subjective test of character, and provide a preference for geographic diversity. That fall the Harvard admissions committee quietly began using these new policies to reduce the number of Jewish students. There would be no *de jure* quota, but there would be a *de facto* one. That year, and for many years to follow, Jewish students made up only about 15 percent of each freshman class. Lowell had won.[34]

The anti-Semitic admissions policies adopted in 1926 were defended, in part, as a commitment to regional diversity. And they did encourage applicants like the "farm boy from Idaho" who would enroll at Harvard, rise to be its dean, and become a symbol of diversity in the *Bakke* case. But the benefit of greater regional diversity came entirely at the expense of Jewish students. The predominantly upper-class white Protestants Lowell favored were admitted in the same numbers as before. It was a distortion of Harvard's tradition under Eliot of making room for students of all races and religions and encouraging students to learn from each other's differences. Contemporary critiques of the diversity justification for affirmative action sometimes mistakenly assert that Harvard's diversity policies were invented to justify the Jewish quota, but those critiques are simply wrong.[35] Harvard's admissions policies favoring diversity predated the Jewish quota by over fifty years; the quota defied that tradition. Eliot's policies of opening Harvard to everyone would begin to be restored after World War II. In the meantime, the Harvard Law School faculty carried the diversity torch forward—moving debates about the relationship between diversity, free speech, and equality out of the academy and into the courts.

PART II

The Diversity Principle's Influence on Freedom of Speech and Academic Freedom

CHAPTER FIVE

The Marketplace of Ideas

OLIVER WENDELL HOLMES, JR., was both a Civil War and civil liberties hero whose life spanned much of U.S. history.[1] He shook hands with the nation's sixth president, an elderly John Quincy Adams, and with the thirty-fifth, the young John F. Kennedy.[2] He served for thirty years on the Supreme Court, where he would transform our understanding of the First Amendment by cementing the "marketplace of ideas" as a cornerstone of U.S. constitutional law. But the patrician Holmes would likely have never become a free speech champion if not for some unlikely friendships that led him to embrace the diversity principle.

Holmes grew up in Boston and Cambridge in a celebrated family. His father, Oliver Wendell Holmes, Sr., coined the term "Boston Brahmin" to poke fun at New England's upper crust, and both father and son fit the bill. Born in a home just north of Harvard Yard, on what is now the campus of Harvard Law School, Holmes, Sr., was one of the best-known figures of his time, famous both as a man of letters and as a dean and professor of medicine at Harvard. He had studied medicine in Paris at a time when the French were creating a science of medicine not yet appreciated in the United States, and his scholarly work on germ theory was controversial and pathbreaking. The Holmeses hosted a literary salon, regularly entertaining writers like Ralph Waldo Emerson, Nathaniel Hawthorne, and Herman Melville, and they helped to found the *Atlantic Monthly*.[3]

Holmes's mother, Amelia Lee Jackson, was an outspoken abolition-ist.[4] But until his son joined the Union army, Holmes, Sr., believed aboli-tionists were demanding too much of the South and that the end of slavery could be achieved peacefully through reasoned discourse.[5] In an infamous moment in Harvard history, he admitted three Black students to the medical school in 1850, only to expel them after students, faculty, and alumni protested.[6] A subsequent faculty resolution concluded "that the intermixing of the white and black races in their lecture rooms is dis-tasteful to a large portion of the class and injurious to the interests of the school."[7] One of the three students was Martin Delany, co-publisher with Frederick Douglass of the important abolitionist newspaper the *North Star*. Delany was a well-known essayist, novelist, and political ac-tivist, and an early (perhaps the first) advocate of Black nationalism.[8] Lincoln described him as "extraordinary."[9] During the Civil War, he would serve as the first Black officer in the U.S. Army.[10]

Holmes, Jr., (hereafter just Holmes) was nine years old when his father expelled Delany and his Black classmates. Several years later, after graduat-ing from the "prep school" Andover, he enrolled at Harvard himself, gradu-ating just as the Civil War began. He volunteered over his father's objections and was trained as an officer, rising to the rank of major and surviving three serious wounds. When the war ended, he enrolled at Harvard Law. Follow-ing just one year there (then the norm) and another as a law clerk, he moved to London to continue his studies.[11] While there, he met John Stuart Mill, then a member of Parliament, and later wrote in his diary that he saw Mill as a great thinker and admired *On Liberty* but found him a dull lunch compan-ion.[12] Holmes would return to England regularly to participate in the work of legal scholars examining the law as an instrument of social policy.

Back in Boston, Holmes practiced admiralty and commercial law while continuing to work as an independent legal scholar. Just fifteen years out of law school, he published a collection of lectures, *The Com-mon Law*, that has become part of the legal canon.[13] It famously begins with a statement at the heart of legal realism: "The life of the law has not been logic: it has been experience."[14] He rejected the popular formalistic approach that treated law as if it were a field of engineering or mathe-matics, arguing instead that law reflects social (and especially judicial) views of public policy, prevailing morality, and social prejudice. He be-lieved that because law is a product of experience, it changes as society changes. His views were seen as an application of Mill's views, and he helped give birth to a new movement in jurisprudence—legal realism.[15]

Holmes's theory put him in opposition to the legal formalists, led by Harvard's transformative dean Christopher Columbus Langdell. Langdell believed that law is a logical system that could be scientifically discerned by studying the text of legal cases. He is hence credited with inventing the "case method" approach to studying law.[16]

Despite disagreeing with Holmes over the fundamental meaning of law, Langdell did not object when the Boston lawyer Louis Brandeis worked with Harvard's president, Charles Eliot, to raise an endowment to recruit the obviously brilliant Holmes to a professorship at Harvard Law. In the fall of 1882, Holmes closed his practice and joined the faculty, where he remained for just a few weeks.[17]

Why weeks? Shortly after joining the Harvard Law faculty, Holmes was offered a seat on Massachusetts Supreme Judicial Court, where his grandfather Charles Jackson had served. He abandoned his new position to join the court before the semester ended, a decision that irritated several of his faculty colleagues. He would serve as an associate justice on the Massachusetts court and then as chief justice until 1902, when he was appointed to the U.S. Supreme Court.[18] He would be joined there in 1916 by his friend Louis Brandeis, who had helped arrange his short-lived faculty appointment at Harvard Law.

Holmes's opinions for the Massachusetts court were regarded as leading the country in privacy, defamation, and labor law.[19] He supported the right of workers to strike and call for boycotts. He put into practice his belief that the law should be understood in its social context. In a 1937 tribute to Holmes's service on the Massachusetts court, the state attorney general James Ronan (who would himself soon be appointed to the Massachusetts high court) wrote that Holmes

recognized that the result of the blind following of precedents may be failure and confusion, even from the logical point of view, when the reason behind the precedent is dead. His conception of the law was as of a living and growing thing,—living, because therein "as in a magic mirror we see reflected not only our own lives, but the lives of all men that have been"; growing, by minute and interstitial steps, guided by the social forces of the community. ... Conventional Boston and more conservative members of the Bar looked somewhat askance at certain of his views; and certain of his opinions concerning boycotts and strikes led the more conservative to regard him as unsafe.

Time has brought generous recognition of the greatness of his judicial work here.[20]

On the U.S. Supreme Court, Holmes's record on civil liberties is decidedly mixed. He wrote the majority opinion in *Buck v. Bell*, which upheld a Virginia law that required mentally disabled people to be forcibly sterilized, writing that "three generations of imbeciles are enough."[21] And in a series of decisions in March 1919, Holmes—a veteran who disdained war resisters—wrote unanimous opinions affirming convictions under the Espionage Act that sent several people to prison for opposing America's entry into World War I.[22]

The teens and twenties of the 1900s were a time of great social conflict that forced the United States to reexamine the First Amendment's free speech guarantees. The repression of speech became increasingly controversial when framed against the fight over immigration, the revival of the movement for Black civil rights by organizations like the NAACP, and the movement for women's suffrage, then reaching its apex. Conflicts between labor and big business led to the suppression of labor unions, as well as the political minorities assumed to be behind them—socialists, communists, and anarchists, mostly from eastern or southern Europe.[23]

All of this came to a head in 1917 when the United States declared war on Germany. Many Americans had resisted U.S. entry into the war, arguing that intervention in what they considered a European matter would only harm the country and its citizens. War opposition was common among farmers, workers, miners, small business owners, German and Irish Americans, and others on the left. Many viewed American intervention as part of a Wall Street plot.[24] The Socialist Party of America was particularly vocal, passing a resolution decrying American entry into the war and encouraging young men to resist the draft. Anti-intervention sentiment reached a climax in the summer of 1917, when the government faced widespread draft resistance, labor strikes, public demonstrations, and press criticism.[25] Interventionists, meanwhile, charged the war's opponents with being lackeys of the German government.[26]

The Wilson administration took a hard line with the war resisters. In June 1917, Congress passed the Espionage Act, which outlawed any speech or activity intended to harm the United States or its military, including efforts to interfere with the draft. The Sedition Act of 1918 broadened the law, rendering illegal any speech that could be construed as critical of the government or the military.[27] The first cases challenging convictions under these acts reached the Supreme Court in 1919, resulting in four free speech opinions by Holmes.

The first to be decided, on March 3, was *Schenck v. United States.* Charles Schenck had been convicted of violating the Espionage Act after he distributed leaflets to draftees encouraging them to resist the draft. Holmes's majority opinion upheld Schenck's conviction and established what became known as the "clear and present danger" test for deciding whether a particular speech is constitutionally protected: "The question in every case is whether the words used are used in such circumstances and are of such a nature as to create a clear and present danger that they will bring about the substantive evils that Congress has a right to prevent. It is a question of proximity and degree."

The second case, *Frohwerk v. United States,* was decided a week later. The defendants in *Frohwerk* were convicted of conspiring to violate the Espionage Act by publishing twelve articles in the *Missouri Staats Zeitung,* a German-language newspaper, that were meant to cause "disloyalty, mutiny, and refusal of duty" in the military. Holmes held that the conviction did not violate the First Amendment, reasoning that although the paper had not apparently made "any special effort to reach men who were subject to the draft"—thus distinguishing the case from *Schenck*— "it is impossible to say that it might not have been found that the circulation of the paper was in quarters where a little breath would be enough to kindle a flame and that the fact was known and relied upon by those who sent the paper out."[28]

The same day, the Court upheld the conviction of the Socialist Party leader, former presidential candidate, and famed orator Eugene Debs for attempting to cause "insubordination, disloyalty, and refusal of duty" in military forces and for obstructing recruiting by delivering a public speech. Holmes, again writing for the majority, found that the conviction did not violate the First Amendment, reasoning: "The main theme of the speech was Socialism, its growth, and a prophecy of its ultimate success. With that we have nothing to do, but if a part or the manifest intent of the more general utterances was to encourage those present to obstruct the recruitment service and if in passages such encouragement was directly given, the immunity of the general theme may not be enough to protect the speech."[29] Five weeks later, Debs entered federal prison, from which he again ran for president in 1920 and earned nearly a million votes—3.4 percent of the total.[30]

In each of these cases, Holmes read the First Amendment as granting the government great latitude to suppress anti-war speech. Then, over the summer of 1919, his view began to change.[31] In the Court's next free speech case, *Abrams v. United States*, the defendants had also been convicted of violating the Espionage Act by urging resistance to the war. They had published two leaflets (also described as articles or pamphlets), one in English and one in Yiddish, that criticized President Woodrow Wilson and the United States government, praised the recent Russian Revolution, and called on workers to participate in a general strike to protest the war. "There is only one enemy of the workers of the world," one read, "and that is CAPITALISM."[32] The majority, applying the same logic Holmes had applied in the March cases, affirmed the convictions, writing that "the plain purpose of [the defendants'] propaganda was to excite, at the supreme crisis of the war, disaffection, sedition, riots, and, as they hoped, revolution, in this country for the purpose of embarrassing and if possible defeating the military plans of the government in Europe."[33]

But Holmes dissented, writing an opinion that would pave the way for the First Amendment jurisprudence of the modern era, with its broad protections of controversial and unpopular speech. It articulates one of the most important values in American democracy, protection of diversity. Its most famous lines seem to channel the Mills:

> The ultimate good desired is better reached by free trade in ideas—that the best test of truth is the power of the thought to get itself accepted in the competition of the market, and that truth is the only ground upon which their wishes safely can be carried out. That at any rate is the theory of our Constitution. It is an experiment, as all life is an experiment. . . . I think that we should be eternally vigilant against attempts to check the expression of opinions that we loathe and believe to be fraught with death, unless they so imminently threaten immediate interference with the lawful and pressing purposes of the law that an immediate check is required to save the country.[34]

How important was Holmes's move from the majority to the dissent? It is widely regarded as a turning point in American constitutional law. Thomas Healy, a scholar who has written the definitive history of the Holmes dissent, relates that after the opinion was circulated among the justices, but three days before it was announced, three of his fellow justices called on Holmes at his home to beg him to withdraw it for the good of the country.[35] Holmes stood his ground.

What caused Holmes's shift? Why did he move from a narrow construction of the First Amendment in *Schenck*, *Frohwerk*, and *Debs* to a civil libertarian position in *Abrams?* A number of leading scholars, including Healy, Geoffrey Stone, Irene Ten Cate, and David Rabban, have attempted to explain his change of heart. They report that during the summer of 1919, Holmes was influenced by a lively set of exchanges about the Mills' views on the value of outsiders' voices as set forth in *On Liberty*. The conversation included a diverse group of legal thinkers—Learned Hand, Zechariah Chafee, Felix Frankfurter, and Harold Laski. They concluded that the views of outsiders were important to preserving democracy.[36]

By nearly any measure, 1919 was a dreadful year in U.S. history. Mass strikes were met by state violence. White mobs attacked Black communities in dozens of cities across the country, murdering hundreds in what became known as the "Red Summer." Tens of thousands died from the third wave of the "Spanish Flu." Anti-communist panic spread in the wake of Russia's October Revolution, inaugurating the first "Red Scare." In November, after a number of bombings carried out by Italian anarchists, the Department of Justice, under Attorney General A. Mitchell Palmer, carried out the notorious "Palmer raids" against immigrants suspected of radical leanings and deported more than ten thousand suspected socialists and communists.

Healy writes,

> The events of 1919 changed Holmes. A contrarian with a love of books and a fondness for debate, he was troubled by the wave of persecution that swept the country once the dangers of war had passed. He was especially troubled when that wave threatened to engulf two of his own friends, a legal scholar named Felix Frankfurter and a British political theorist named Harold Laski. . . . In 1919, they were young academics (Frankfurter was 37, Laski 26) still making names for themselves.[37]

Felix Frankfurter was a Jewish immigrant from Austria who had attended City College of New York and Harvard Law School, graduating in 1906.[38] It is commonly reported (perhaps apocryphally) that he earned the second-highest grade point average in the law school's history, just behind Louis Brandeis.[39] Frankfurter worked briefly in Washington, where he befriended Holmes, and then, at Brandeis's urging, joined the Harvard Law faculty in 1914 at the age of 32.[40]

Harold Laski, also Jewish, was born in England to parents who had immigrated from eastern Europe. He quickly distinguished himself among the intellectual elite, attending University College London (where Mill had studied) and Oxford (where Mill wasn't eligible to study) before going on to lecture at McGill and Harvard, and to help found the New School for Social Research in New York. He lived in North America for only a few years before returning to England in 1920, where he became a professor at the London School of Economics, a leader of the Labour Party, and a leading Marxist activist. But his brief time in the United States was enough to cement a decades-long friendship with Holmes. Healy describes Laski and Holmes—one a Jewish Marxist from Britain, the other a New England WASP and lifelong Republican—as an "odd couple."[41] Holmes, writes Healy,

> believed loosely in free markets, thrifty habits, big business, and the prerogative of the ruling class, but mainly he believed that strong ideological commitments were both foolish and dangerous. And he had no taste for political involvement. . . . Laski, on the other hand, lived and breathed politics. . . . His views were just to the right of Marx—he was a militant suffragist and a revolutionary syndicalist. . . . By the time Laski met Holmes he had tempered his militancy. He gave up violent protests in favor of the lecturer's podium and remade himself into a scholar and public intellectual.[42]

Laski considered Holmes one of the greatest legal thinkers alive, and he admired Holmes's "openness" to his ideas and those of his fellow "young intellectuals." Holmes "received their ideas with the courtesy, admiration and speculative curiosity accorded to honored guests." Holmes, for his part, valued Laski's "astounding erudition." "If there was one thing Holmes valued more than any other, it was intellectual firepower," writes Healy, "and Laski's arsenal was loaded." Holmes described Laski as "one of the most learned men I've ever met of any age."[43] But their connection ran deeper. Holmes and his wife, Fanny, had adopted an orphaned relative, a girl, but never had biological children. Holmes referred to Laski as "my son." More than a decade after the fateful summer of 1919, Laski would return from England to celebrate Holmes's ninetieth birthday; the justice excitedly told his maid, "My boy will be here Saturday."[44] Healy writes that "Laski was the son he never had."[45]

It was at Laski's request that Holmes reread *On Liberty* in the summer of 1919. Laski was then twenty-five years old, Holmes seventy-eight.[46] The timing was perfect for Holmes to revisit the book and rethink his approach to liberty under the First Amendment.

Laski also introduced Holmes to another young free speech advocate, Zechariah Chafee. Chafee, like Holmes, was from an old New England family, the Chafees of Rhode Island. He had joined the law school faculty three years after graduating, and by 1919 he was a full professor, thirty-five years old, and regarded as an expert on free speech.[47] Laski, Frankfurter, and Chafee, Healy writes,

> were also part of a circle of younger intellectuals who worshiped Holmes for his willingness to uphold progressive labor legislation despite his own doubts about the wisdom of such laws. This circle, which included two of the founding editors of *The New Republic*, Herbert Croly and Walter Lippmann, published tributes to Holmes, feted him with parties and dinners, and passed around his opinions like sacred texts. Holmes was buoyed by the admiration of these acolytes, believing he was finally receiving the recognition he had long desired as nothing less than the "greatest jurist in the world." He also developed a genuine affection for the "young lads," as he called them, treating Frankfurter and Laski like the sons he never had. So when the two men came under attack for their "radical" views—Frankfurter for his support of labor unions, Laski for his socialist leanings—Holmes sprang to their defense. He wrote to the president of Harvard, where both men taught, and sought help from the Harvard Law School alumni association. He also began to rethink his stance on the First Amendment, an endeavor his young friends encouraged. For more than a year, they waged an intense behind-the-scenes campaign to strengthen Holmes's appreciation for free speech. They fed him books on political liberalism, wrote him long letters on the value of tolerance and engaged him in impassioned debates.[48]

While the efforts of Laski, Frankfurter, and Chafee may have been the tipping point, Healy locates the beginning of Holmes's free speech

evolution in a conversation with Judge Learned Hand in the summer of
1918.[49] Hand had been a U.S. District Court judge in New York for
nearly ten years and was on the cusp of being appointed to the Court of
Appeals, where he would serve until 1961.[50] His fifty-two years of judicial
service were widely admired, and he was often described as the greatest
American judge to never sit on the Supreme Court.[51] Although Hand
came from a conservative, well-to-do family that traced its roots to the
Mayflower, he became an ardent defender of civil liberties.[52]

In the summer of 1918, Holmes and Hand, two of the most respected judges in the country, found themselves on the same train to
New England.[53] They had crossed paths before—Hand had played a role
in founding *The New Republic*, of which Holmes had been an early supporter—but did not know each other well. Yet their conversation that
day, and the exchange of letters that followed sharing their thoughts
about the First Amendment, would shape modern free speech jurisprudence, and thereby American democracy, for the next century.[54]

Hand had recently had his opinion in an Espionage Act case, *Masses
v. Patten*, overturned by the Second Circuit Court of Appeals. His decision would have allowed *The Masses*, a prominent socialist magazine, to
continue publishing even though it "condemned the war and praised
people who took vigorous measures in opposition to it," writes legal
scholar David Bogen. "Hand held the [Espionage] Act was not violated
by speech unless the speaker urged others that it was their duty or in
their interest to violate the Act."[55] Holmes had read and admired Hand's
opinion in *Masses* and told him so in a letter.[56] The admiration seems to
have been mutual—according to Healy, Hand "worshiped the justice
more than any other man except his late father."[57]

In one of a series of letters after the train ride, Hand wrote to
Holmes: "Opinions are at best provisional hypotheses, incompletely
tested. The more they are tested, after the tests are well scrutinized, the
more assurance we may assume, but they are never absolutes. So we must
be tolerant of opposite opinions or varying opinions by the very fact of
our incredulity of our own."[58] As Bogen points out, this "was virtually the
same argument in favor of free speech Holmes had read in Mill's book
years earlier, but this time from a judge in the midst of dealing with the
greatest speech controversy of his time."[59]

Holmes's shift toward robust free speech protections was thus the
product of a diversity of voices and views from disparate backgrounds,
coming together to persuade him that outsider voices needed protection

from state interference, the essence of Humboldt's and the Mills' views. This intellectual gathering was a study in the power of diversity, illustrating how the development of the idea that diversity creates value came from a series of experiments in diversity itself, including experiential, religious, and lived diversity. First there was the collaboration between Holmes and a group of young progressive intellectuals, including Chafee, Laski, Hand, Frankfurter, and other contributors to *The New Republic*. Though all were men and would today be considered white, they ranged from age 25 to 78, came from immigrant Jewish families and old stock white Protestant backgrounds, and ranged ideologically from Marxist to Democratic to Republican. That collaboration led Holmes to change his views on the First Amendment and adopt the Mills' perspective on the importance of free expression: that interactions among people with diverse experiences and perspectives will produce better ideas, and ultimately the best test of truth. The collaboration between Holmes and *The New Republic* gang was proof of that very concept.

Another outsider, Louis Brandeis, joined Justice Holmes in his *Abrams* dissent. Brandeis had advocated for Holmes's hiring at Harvard, and the two would be close friends for another fifty years—yet another example of diversity. Brandeis was accustomed to being an outsider. He grew up as the child of immigrants and was the only Jew in his class at Harvard Law School.[60] He was known in Boston as "the people's attorney" because so much of his practice was pro bono.[61] His appointment to the Supreme Court in 1916 was among the most controversial in the Court's history. Opponents claimed he was too liberal, but many observers thought the opposition was mostly based on his religion.[62] For twenty-three years he was the Court's most consistent voice for civil liberties and the rights of labor. He would step down just as his friend and protégé Felix Frankfurter was taking his own seat on the Court.[63]

Rodney A. Smolla writes,

> The Holmes dissent in *Abrams* is often paired with the concurring decision of Justice Louis Brandeis in *Whitney v. California*. . . . Together, the Holmes and Brandeis opinions comprise the seminal texts in the canon that now includes hundreds of decisions by the Supreme Court of the United States interpreting the core of the American free speech tradition. Phrases such as the "marketplace of ideas" or "free trade in ideas" or "competition of the market" are ubiquitous in Supreme Court opinions.

Even when these literal phrases are not used, the concept of a marketplace of ideas permeates judicial discourse on the meaning of the First Amendment. Opinions invoking the marketplace metaphor—literally or conceptually—number over one hundred, and opinions that rely on the concept, at least in passing, are double that number.[64]

Thus the diversity principle formulated by Humboldt and the Mills found its way into the work of a Boston Brahmin and a child of Jewish refugees and then—through their overlapping friendships with a gaggle of Republicans, Democrats, and socialists from diverse backgrounds—entered the mainstream of American constitutional law and American values. Men who were Protestants, Catholics, and Jews were joined in the next generation by men and women of diverse races and ethnicities who would carry forward this now mainstream idea from the First Amendment and apply it to the anti-slavery Thirteenth Amendment and the pro-equality Fourteenth Amendment.

CHAPTER SIX

Boycotts, Quotas, Diversity, and Segregation

OR MANY WHITE AMERICANS, the 1920s were an age of prosperity, as the post–World War I boom created new jobs and opportunities in the growing industrial cities. But for Black Americans, the twenties were a time of great hardship. Membership in the KKK reached its zenith at four million, nearly 4 percent of the entire U.S. population.[1] From the records of the Tuskegee Institute, we know that at least 281 Black Americans were lynched between 1920 and 1929.[2] Although the "Great Migration" was well underway, most Black Americans still lived in the rural South, where they faced Jim Crow laws and crushing poverty.[3] Conditions were only marginally better in the urban North and Midwest.[4]

But the 1920s were also the era of the Harlem Renaissance, a flowering of arts and culture. The decade saw the rise of a thriving Black press, increasing enrollment in Black colleges, and a growing Black middle class.[5] The NAACP, founded in 1909, had by 1920 over ninety thousand members in three hundred local chapters.[6] The National Urban League, founded the year after the NAACP, was also growing rapidly. The period described as the nadir was coming to an end.[7]

As demands for racial justice grew, advocates adopted a variety of tactics that reflected different approaches to achieving equality. The NAACP, speaking for the growing Black middle class, pressed its case for equality as a legal right, seeking anti-lynching legislation, anti-discrimination legislation, and an end to state-supported segregation.[8] Black churches and unions were more militant, using strikes and boycotts to demand racial quotas, proportional representation, and reparations.[9] Behind the scenes, advocates engaged in fierce debates over strategy and goals. It is here that the subject of diversity arose, both as a legal basis for desegregation and as a value the movement would advocate. The discussions would resonate for decades, foreshadowing the twenty-first century's debates over reparations, remedies, and affirmative action.

Three twentieth-century Black American civil rights leaders brought the diversity principle into the heart of civil rights law. The first was a minister, the second a lawyer, the third both. The first, Rev. Dr. Martin Luther King, Jr., preached the benefits of diversity for Black Americans, for poor Americans of all races, and, in time, for the soul of our country. His nonviolent direct action boycott campaigns against segregation and in favor of reparations and racial quotas profoundly changed how Americans viewed civil rights. The second, Thurgood Marshall, was chief counsel of the NAACP Legal Defense Fund. His legal strategy dismantled segregation law; it was premised on an argument about the educational and social benefits of diversity for Black children. His success led to his appointment as the first Black Solicitor General and then the first Black Supreme Court Justice. The third was Pauli Murray, a queer Black woman who would probably identify today as a transgender man. Over a decade before Dr. King's rise to leadership, Murray was advocating for Gandhian nonviolent civil disobedience through boycotts, sit-ins, and front-of-the-bus protests. It was Murray who persuaded Marshall to change his litigation strategy challenging segregation to incorporate the diversity principle. She helped Ruth Bader Ginsburg formulate her theory of sex discrimination law. She was a behind-the-scenes strategist for some of the most important developments in civil rights law in the 1940s to 1980s, before becoming an Episcopal priest.

The boycott—a cousin to the labor strike—was a popular form of protest against streetcar segregation in the late nineteenth century.[10] As growing numbers of Black Americans left the South in the Great Migration, boycotts became a useful tool against private businesses. Many of these campaigns began with support from the Black press. In 1929 the *Chicago Whip* called for a boycott under the banner "Spend Your Money Where You Can Work."[11] With the support of churches to supply picketers, the campaign targeted "five and dime" stores, the Walmarts of the twentieth century. Under the pressure of the boycott, stores located in

Black neighborhoods started hiring Black employees, obtaining some two thousand jobs for Black workers in Chicago alone.[12]

In the early 1930s, New York's *Amsterdam News* took up the call, re-naming the campaign "Don't Buy Where You Can't Work." Picketers first targeted Harlem's largest department store, Blumstein's.[13] They then moved on to major national chains like Woolworths and the A&P gro-cery stores.[14] Within a few years, campaigns had spread nationwide.[15] In 1934, NAACP co-founder W. E. B. Du Bois endorsed the boycotts in the organization's magazine, *The Crisis*.[16]

From one perspective, the boycotts were simply demands to stop discrimination. From another, they were demands for proportional representation—racial quotas. In two cases, one from the 1930s, one from the 1940s, the Supreme Court would hold that the former were permissi-ble while the latter were not. It is unfortunate that these cases have been largely forgotten by legal historians, since they reflect an important divide about remedying racism that would ultimately drive a wedge between the NAACP and more militant Black leaders, including Dr. King.[17]

The first case arose in 1936 in Washington, D.C., when the New Negro Alliance began picketing at a Sanitary Grocery Company store lo-cated in a Black neighborhood, demanding that it hire Black workers.[18] Critically, the Alliance did not demand proportional hiring, only that they stop discriminating. Their signs read, "Do Your Part! Buy Where You Work! No Negroes Employed Here!"[19]

Was their picketing protected by law? Until the labor law reforms of the 1930s, union picketing was generally illegal. But in 1932, Congress had passed the Norris-LaGuardia Anti-Injunction Act, protecting peaceful labor picketing. Whether it applied to civil rights picketing was uncertain.

In response to the boycott, the store sued the picketers in the U.S. District Court, and the court issued an injunction ordering them to stop. The Alliance appealed to the U.S. Court of Appeals, which upheld the order. But the Supreme Court ruled that the dispute between the Alliance and the grocery company was a labor dispute protected by the Norris-LaGuardia Act.[20] The majority opinion noted that the picketers were not committing or asking the store to commit any illegal act, and it held that "race discrimination by an employer may reasonably be deemed more unfair and less excusable than discrimination against work-ers on the ground of union affiliation."[21]

The team representing the Alliance included the young Thurgood Marshall, who had graduated from Howard Law six years earlier and joined the legal staff of the NAACP.[22] Marshall grew up in Baltimore, a segregated city with limited opportunities for Black students and workers, and attended segregated schools—the Colored High and Training School followed by Lincoln University and Howard, both historically Black institutions. He had hoped to attend the University of Maryland Law School, but it was closed to Black students. Marshall joined the bar in 1933 and was heading the NAACP legal office by 1938. (In 1940 he created the NAACP Legal Defense Fund as a separate entity to represent the NAACP in court.)[23] He would go on to lead the NAACP to dozens of historic court victories.[24] *New Negro Alliance v. Sanitary Grocery Company* (1938) was his first—and a major Supreme Court win for the movement.

The Sanitary Grocery Company case prompted many more "Don't Shop Where You Can't Work" campaigns across the country, increasingly in smaller cities and in the South. Documented examples include Newark (1938), Dayton (1938), Youngstown (1939), Evansville, Indiana (1939), Houston (1939), Memphis (1939), Kansas City (1939), Oakland (1939), Berkeley (1940), Jackson, Tennessee (1940), Rock Hill, South Carolina (1940), Lockland, Ohio (1941), Newport News (1941), and Alliance, Ohio (1941).[25] The boycotts paused in 1941, when the United States entered World War II, but picked up again after the war ended. The most consequential would take place in Richmond, California.

Richmond is a mid-sized city on San Francisco Bay, north of Berkeley and Oakland. Both the city and its Black population had grown exponentially during the war, as Black migrants from the South came to work in the Kaiser Shipyards, building hundreds of "Victory Ships" for the U.S. Navy and merchant marine. Overall, an estimated fifty thousand Black Americans migrated from the South to Richmond, Oakland, and Berkeley between 1942 and 1945.[26]

When the Lucky Stores chain opened a market in 1947 in a largely Black Richmond neighborhood, but with no Black employees, a local civil rights group, the Progressive Citizens of America, began to picket the store and asked Black customers to boycott until the store agreed to hire Black employees in proportion to their clientele. The store sought an injunction against the picketing, arguing that the Lucky Stores picketers, unlike those in the Sanitary Grocery Company case, were demanding proportional hiring—racial quotas.[27] Proportional hiring, the company argued, is discriminatory and thus unlawful, and picketing to demand an unlawful objective is not protected by either the Anti-Injunction Act or the First Amendment.

It was an astonishing argument. During the war, President Roosevelt had used his war powers to create a federal Fair Employment Practices Commission (FEPC) and authorized it to require non-discriminatory hiring in war industries, including Richmond's shipyards. But when the war ended, Congress—facing Southern resistance—defunded the FEPC, and it was disbanded.[28] California would not prohibit racial discrimination in employment until 1959.[29] The federal Civil Rights Act was further away still. No one was arguing with any force that Lucky's decision not to hire Black clerks violated the law, but Lucky argued that a demand that the company affirmatively hire Black employees *was* unlawful.[30]

Nonetheless, in the spring of 1947, the state trial court in Richmond agreed with the market chain's argument and issued an injunction prohibiting picketing at the store.[31] A few weeks later, the Richmond civil rights leaders John Hughes and Louis Richardson returned to the store to picket, holding signs reading "Lucky Won't Hire Negro Clerks in Proportion to Negro Trade—Don't Patronize."[32] They were arrested, tried for criminal contempt, convicted, and sentenced to $20 fines plus two days in jail.[33] The local NAACP supported the defendants, but Thurgood Marshall and the national NAACP wanted nothing to do with them. Marshall would later change his view, but in the 1940s he was arguing that all discrimination—including discrimination in favor of Black workers—should be illegal. Under his leadership, the NAACP thought any demand for proportional representation conflicted with a demand for non-discrimination.[34]

In the California Supreme Court and then the U.S. Supreme Court, the convictions were affirmed.[35] The unanimous opinion for the Supreme Court was written by Felix Frankfurter, who had followed in Holmes's footsteps and ascended to the high court in 1939.[36] "The conceded purpose of the picketing in this case—to compel the hiring of Negroes in proportion to Negro customers—was unlawful even though pursued in a peaceful manner," Frankfurter wrote. "Having violated a valid injunction, petitioners were properly punishable for contempt. 'The controlling points,' according to the decision of the Supreme Court of California, 'are that the injunction is limited to prohibiting picketing for a specific unlawful purpose, and that the evidence justified the trial court in finding that such narrow prohibition was deliberately violated.' "[37]

The Sanitary Grocery and Lucky Stores cases made it clear that the Supreme Court was willing to affirm the legitimacy of protesting discrimination but not to approve demands for proportional hiring. Such demands nonetheless persisted and would become a critical part of Dr. King's campaign for racial justice in the last six years of his life. This was an important part of a larger conflict between King and Marshall throughout the civil rights era. King embraced militant nonviolent conflict and quota hiring, while Marshall sought change through strategic litigation and legislative reform.[38]

King was no stranger to boycotts: he had been thrust into the leadership of the Civil Rights Movement in 1956 with the Montgomery bus boycott, and his most important desegregation campaign—the Birmingham campaign of 1963—was organized around a boycott of Birmingham's segregated businesses.[39] In 1962, King and the Southern Christian Leadership Conference, which he led, began a nationwide campaign demanding the proportional hiring of Black workers by local businesses, backed up by boycott threats.[40] Named "Operation Breadbasket," the program reached back to the "Don't Shop Where You Can't Work" movement and looked forward toward the 1964 Civil Rights Act, which would prohibit racial discrimination in employment while permitting, but not requiring, preferential hiring and promotion of Black workers.[41] Between 1962 and his assassination in 1968, Dr. King worked relentlessly to bring this proportional hiring/boycott program to cities across America.[42]

Operation Breadbasket organizers demanded basic employment data from companies that revealed "the total number of workers in each job category compared with the number of black workers in these same jobs."[43] Employers with a low proportion of Black workers would be asked to correct the imbalance or face a boycott. As the Operation Breadbasket guidelines explained, "Basically the demands are for a percentage of the jobs comparable to numbers of black people in the city and the volume of business done in the black ghetto. . . . For instance, if the black population is 20% of the population of the city, then 20% black employment would be a fair representation in the company. This might need to be modified, however. . . . For example, if the company does 30% of its business in the black community, and even though the population is only 20% black, a guideline of 30% might be a more appropriate basis for demands."[44] The Chicago-based Borden Company was a case in point. Only twenty-three of the company's 435 employees were Black. In 1966, Operation Breadbasket organizers demanded that the company hire another sixty-four Black employees to raise their total to precisely 20 percent, about equal to Chicago's Black population according to the most recent census.[45]

At that point, Operation Breadbasket had recently expanded to Chicago as part of a larger movement to bring civil rights campaigns to the

North. The Chicago operation was led by King's longtime aide Jesse Jackson, who eventually took over the entire national effort after King's assassination in 1968.[46] The Congress of Racial Equality (CORE) had begun a similar campaign in 1962, specifically demanding "compensatory hiring."[47] According to Terry Anderson, the organization "won concessions from a few employers in Denver, Detroit, Seattle, Baltimore, and a number of cities in New York and California."[48]

Compared to the rest of King's life's work, Operation Breadbasket has gotten relatively little attention. Why? Perhaps the best answer was supplied by King himself in his book *Why We Can't Wait*, written in the wake of the 1963 Birmingham campaign: "Whenever this issue of compensatory or preferential treatment for the Negro is raised, some of our friends recoil in horror. The Negro should be granted equality, they agree; but he should ask for nothing more."[49]

Some have used King's calls for equality—especially his "I Have a Dream" speech—to argue that, were he alive, he would oppose race-conscious affirmative action. But the full text of that speech makes clear that he viewed reparations as essential for his "four little children" to "live in a nation where they will not be judged by the color of their skin but by the content of their character."[50]

> In a sense we've come to our nation's capital to cash a check. When the architects of our republic wrote the magnificent words of the Constitution and the Declaration of Independence, they were signing a promissory note to which every American was to fall heir. This note was a promise that all men—yes, Black men as well as white men—would be guaranteed the unalienable rights of life, liberty and the pursuit of happiness. It is obvious today that America has defaulted on this promissory note insofar as her citizens of color are concerned. Instead of honoring this sacred obligation, America has given the Negro people a bad check, a check which has come back marked insufficient funds.
>
> But we refuse to believe that the bank of justice is bankrupt. We refuse to believe that there are insufficient funds in the great vaults of opportunity of this nation. And so we've come to cash this check, a check that will give us upon demand the riches of freedom and the security of justice.[51]

The following year, in *Why We Can't Wait*, King again uses the principle of reparations to demand affirmative action–type programs:

Few people consider the fact that, in addition to being enslaved for two centuries, the Negro was, during all those years, robbed of the wages of his toil. No amount of gold could provide an adequate compensation for the exploitation and humiliation of the Negro in America down through the centuries. Not all the wealth of this affluent society could meet the bill. Yet, a price can be placed on unpaid wages. The ancient common law has always provided a remedy for the appropriation of the labor of one human being by another. This law should be made to apply for American Negroes. The payment should be in the form of a massive program by the Government of special, compensatory measures which could be regarded as a settlement in accordance with the accepted practice of common law. Such measures would certainly be less expensive than any computation based on two centuries of unpaid wages and accumulated interest.[52]

In 1967, six months before his assassination, King testified before the Kerner Commission, a presidential fact-finding group examining the causes of Black unrest. He read into the record the section from *Why We Can't Wait* that proposed massive government programs in education, health care, employment, and housing as "compensatory consideration for the handicaps [Black Americans have] inherited from the past. It is impossible to create a formula for the future which does not take into account that our society has been doing something special against the Negro for hundreds of years."[53]

King then told the Kerner Commission about a conversation he had had with the prime minister of India, Jawaharlal Nehru, in which Nehru explained why members of lower castes were given preferences in university admissions and public employment. Asked if this was discrimination, Nehru answered that if so, it was nonetheless justified as an act of atonement. King testified: "America must seek its own way of atoning for the injustices she has inflicted on her Negro citizens [not for] atonement's sake, ... [but as a] way to bring the Negro standard to a realistic level. ... The moral justification for special measures for Negroes is rooted in the robberies inherent in the institution of slavery."[54]

Thurgood Marshall would eventually come to agree with King that affirmative action measures were necessary to remedy the ongoing problem of racial inequality. But at the time of the Sanitary Grocery Company case and in the 1930s and 1940s as he began to plan the litigation strategy that would lead to the Supreme Court striking down school segregation in *Brown v. Board of Education*, Marshall pursued the formalist ("color-blind") argument that any discrimination at all by the state violated the Fourteenth Amendment's guarantee of "equal protection of the law." With this as his guiding principle, Marshall began to plan his litigation strategy to end segregation.

Marshall's strategy was to first focus on graduate education, where Black students excluded from white universities had few alternatives and where desegregation might be less emotionally volatile than in hotels, restaurants, workplaces, or neighborhood schools. The NAACP would take on a series of cases, each building on those before, with the goal of getting courts to agree that if a state offered a particular graduate program to whites, then under *Plessy v. Ferguson* (which established the doctrine of "separate but equal") it must also do so for Blacks. This was a step toward convincing them that not only must a program be offered but it must be equal to the graduate education white students received.

The strategy began in 1938, with NAACP litigation against the University of Missouri Law School, which refused to admit Black students. In that case, *Missouri ex rel. Gaines v. Canada*, the Supreme Court held that public universities must offer Black students an education equal to that of white students.[55] But what made an education equal?

In the early 1940s, Marshall and the NAACP answered this question by pointing to tangible evidence that states were systematically providing fewer resources to Black schools—assigning them shabby, outdated textbooks, for example, and allowing classrooms to fall into disrepair. But the legal scholar Pauli Murray considered this way of defining inequality much too narrow. Her argument for desegregation, which would eventually be embraced by Marshall as a key part of the NAACP's legal strategy, was much more comprehensive. At its heart was the diversity principle.

Like Marshall, Murray had been born in Baltimore, but while Marshall enjoyed a stable middle-class upbringing, Murray's early life was marked by tragedy.[56] When she was three, her mother died of a cerebral hemorrhage; her father was then institutionalized for depression in a segregated state hospital, where he would ultimately be beaten to death by a white guard. Murray was taken in by her grandmother and aunt in Durham, North Carolina.[57] Her upbringing gave her a deep personal understanding of what it felt like to live under racial apartheid. Her grandmother had been born in slavery; her grandfather had worked with

Frederick Douglass and Harriet Tubman and fought in the Union army.[58] Durham was intensely segregated. The biographer Kathryn Schulz writes, "From the moment Murray understood the system, she actively resisted it. Even as a child, she walked everywhere rather than ride in segregated streetcars, and boycotted movie theaters rather than sit in the balconies reserved for African-Americans."[59] She would spend the rest of her life challenging restrictive norms.

After graduating from high school in 1926, Murray moved to New York City to attend the all-women Hunter College, part of the celebrated tuition-free City University of New York system that had also educated Felix Frankfurter.[60] After graduating from Hunter, one of four Black students in a class of 247, she began a series of road trips around the country—sometimes "riding the rails" by sneaking into freight cars on long-distance trains. During these trips she presented herself as a boy, and many scholars believe she would likely identify today as a transgender man or nonbinary person.[61] According to the Pauli Murray Center, "Murray self-described as a 'he/she personality' in correspondence with family members. For years, Murray requested—and was denied—testosterone injections and hormone therapy, as well as exploratory surgery to investigate their reproductive organs, believing that they may have been intersex and had undescended testis."[62] (The Pauli Murray Center uses the gender-neutral pronoun to describe Murray. Because Murray used the female pronoun, I use it here except in quotation.) Murray's doctors examined her to investigate whether she was what they termed a "pseudo-hermaphrodite."[63] Kathryn Schulz writes, "Sometimes, Murray seemed to regard herself as a mixture of genders. 'Maybe two got fused into one with parts of each sex,' she mused at one point, 'male head and brain (?), female-ish body, mixed emotional characteristics.' More often, though, she identified as fundamentally male: 'one of nature's experiments; a girl who should have been a boy.'"[64] In her twenties, Murray married a man but quickly realized it was a mistake; for the rest of her life, she would openly date women.[65] Rather than identifying as a lesbian, however, she "regarded her 'very natural falling in love with the female sex' as a manifestation of her inner maleness."[66]

In 1938, Murray applied to graduate school at the University of North Carolina. On December 12 of that year, the Supreme Court held in *Gaines* that Missouri could not exclude Black students from its flagship university's law school.[67] Nonetheless, two days later, the UNC president Frank Graham wrote to Murray, "I'm sorry, but the constitution and the laws of the state of North Carolina prohibit me from admitting one of your race."[68] Murray sought the help of the NAACP to overturn UNC's decision, but Marshall rejected her plea because he did not regard her as a good subject for a test case enforcing the recent Missouri decision.[69] Murray suspected that Marshall considered her too leftist to be a good plaintiff.[70] She wrote to President Roosevelt and First Lady Eleanor Roosevelt asking them to intervene.[71] They didn't, but Eleanor Roosevelt did write back, beginning a lifelong correspondence that would in time become a close and enduring friendship. Forty years later, UNC would offer Murray an honorary degree, but because the university was still resisting orders to desegregate, she declined.[72]

In 1940, inspired by Gandhi's use of nonviolent civil disobedience in India, Murray decided to challenge Virginia's segregation laws. She boarded a Greyhound bus, and when she insisted on riding in the white section, she was arrested, convicted, and fined.[73] The NAACP considered appealing her conviction, but Marshall again did not want to use Murray as a test case. She believed his decision was influenced by the press coverage of the incident, which had described her as a young man based on her dress and appearance.[74]

Despite considering Murray a troublesome plaintiff, Marshall clearly recognized her talent and drive. In 1941, on his recommendation, Murray enrolled at Howard University law school, the leading Black law school in the country.[75] She was one of just two women in the school, and the other soon dropped out. As the sole woman student in her class, she was isolated and unwelcome. Not only was she never called on in class; when she tried to speak, she was drowned out by her fellow students' laughter. Despite this treatment, she earned the top grade in every one of her courses, finished at the top of her class, and was named valedictorian.[76]

Marginalized within the law school, Murray looked elsewhere for allies. She found one in Howard's history department. Caroline Ware, a white woman, helped Murray begin to develop her ideas about the diversity principle.[77] In her autobiography Murray acknowledged the insight she gained from Ware's point of view: "Through Dr. Ware I became increasingly conscious of the damage racial discrimination inflicted upon white as well as black people. Once I was surprised to hear her say that white people were being deprived of a vastly enriching experience by racial segregation. 'My constitutional rights are being violated,' she told me, 'when I am prohibited by segregation laws from associating with my friend and am compelled to sit in a separate car!' "[78]

Through her discussions with Ware, Murray began to formulate the argument that the Fourteenth Amendment, which prohibits race discrimination by state entities, ought to apply to sex discrimination as well as, and in combination with, race discrimination. She was beginning to articulate the principles of what Kimberlé Crenshaw would famously term "intersectionality." Murray called it "Jane Crow."[79] As her biographer Sarah Azaransky writes, "Murray distinguished Jane Crow from white women's and black men's concerns, 'for within this framework of "male supremacy" as well as "white supremacy," the Negro woman finds herself at the bottom of the economic and social scale.' "[80] The discrimination she experienced as a Black woman was not just doubled but compounded.[81]

Twenty-five years later, Murray would bring that argument to a woman she had helped hire to lead the ACLU Women's Rights Project: Ruth Bader Ginsburg. Meanwhile, however, Jane Crow hindered her educational progress. In her final year of law school at Howard, Dean William Hastie encouraged Murray to apply for the Harvard Law JSD program, which provided a doctorate in law. The law faculty was debating whether to end Harvard's exclusion of women, and Murray seemed a perfect test case: it was a long-standing tradition to provide a full scholarship for Harvard's JSD program to the student finishing at the top of the class at Howard Law.[82] But when Murray submitted her application, Harvard rejected her because of her sex.[83] She appealed on the grounds that since she couldn't change her sex, the faculty would need to change its policy. Still, the faculty stood its ground.[84] Even when Murray persuaded not only Eleanor Roosevelt but also President Roosevelt (a Harvard graduate) to intervene, Harvard's president, James B. Conant, refused to be moved.[85]

As a Berkeley Law professor, I relish what happened next: Murray turned her eyes west and enrolled in the Master of Laws (LLM) program at Berkeley.[86] By 1944, Berkeley had a long tradition of admitting white women and Black men but had admitted few Black women.[87] To the university's shame, Murray was shunned by her fellow students and many of the faculty. But in her living quarters at the International House, located at the edge of campus, she felt at home.[88] Her roommates included a second-generation Japanese American who had been interned for three years in Arizona, a Jewish refugee from Germany whose extended family had died in the Holocaust, a fifth-generation Mexican American, a naturalized Chinese American, and a white American raised in China.[89] Murray's biographer Patricia Bell-Scott writes that "Murray and her friends had thought-provoking, heart-to-heart discussions about the similarities and differences" in their experiences with racism and decided to organize a panel to share what they had learned with campus groups.[90] Again, Murray was recognizing the value of perspectives that differed from her own.

Working with Professor Barbara Armstrong, one of the designers of the U.S. Social Security system and the first woman to serve as a law professor at a major U.S. university, Murray completed a thesis on sex discrimination in employment.[91] When it was published in the *California Law Review*, it became the first law review article published on sex discrimination in employment, and the first authored by a Black woman.[92] Murray received her LLM from Berkeley in 1945, passed the California bar exam, and was licensed to practice law in California. But she soon returned east, settling in New York to help care for her aunt.[93]

While at Howard, Murray had begun studying Gandhian nonviolent civil disobedience and had led sit-ins at local D.C. coffee shops. She began working with the pacifist leader Bayard Rustin and with him co-founded the Congress on Racial Equality. In June 1946 Rustin included Murray in a working group on the issue of segregation called the "Journey of Reconciliation." Murray's commitment to nonviolent direct-action protest and her willingness to test the constitutionality of segregation laws made her an obvious candidate for inclusion. In addition to working with Rustin, Murray was joined by Ella Baker, a civil rights leader and fellow North Carolinian.[94] According to Troy Saxby, "the group made plans for an interracial group to tour the South on Interstate buses, taking up seats that defied segregated seating customs and giving lectures on pacifism along the way."[95] Over Murray's and Baker's strong objections, the group decided to allow only Black men to participate, because "mixing races and sexes would possibly exacerbate an already volatile situation."[96]

Yet even as she was being pushed aside by her fellow civil rights activists, Murray's ideas were beginning to take hold. In 1946, Ada Lois Sipuel applied to the law school of the University of Oklahoma, an all-white school and the only public law school in the state.[97] She was denied admission because she was Black. Thurgood Marshall and the NAACP represented her in a suit that eventually made it to the Supreme Court as *Sipuel v. Board of Regents of the University of Oklahoma*.[98] As he prepared for the case, Marshall relied in part on a memo Murray had prepared in 1944 for a civil rights legal seminar at Howard, in which she set forth a

legal strategy for overturning *Plessy v. Ferguson*, the 1896 case that announced the doctrine of "separate but equal" racial segregation.[99] Her
professor, Spottswood Robinson (or in some tellings Leon Ransom), was
a colleague of Marshall's at the NAACP, and, recognizing the argument's
brilliance, gave Marshall a copy.[100]

Murray's memo, titled "Should the Civil Rights Cases and *Plessy v.
Ferguson* Be Overruled?," was years ahead of its time. It argued that the
Fourteenth Amendment, which provides for equal protection of the laws,
and the Thirteenth Amendment, which bans slavery, provide independent bases for banning segregation. Along with the 1866 and 1867 Civil
Rights Acts passed to enforce them, the amendments were intended to
remove all vestiges of slavery, including Jim Crow laws.[101]

The following year, at Berkeley, she would expand on the argument
from the Howard paper, arguing that the Thirteenth Amendment prohibits private housing discrimination as a remnant of slavery.[102] In the
1940s, this argument was too radical to be taken seriously. But in 1968,
the Supreme Court agreed that the Thirteenth Amendment prohibited
private housing discrimination, overruling ninety years of precedent.[103]

Murray's 1944 paper asserted that the "separate but equal" doctrine
violates the Fourteenth Amendment, which bans states from denying
equality to their citizens, because the very idea of segregation is incompatible with equality. This conflicted with the strategy at the NAACP,
where Marshall's approach was to chip away at *Plessy* by showing that the
southern states were not actually providing equal accommodations and
therefore not complying with the decision. Murray's view was radically
different: stop seeking compliance with *Plessy* and show that compliance
is impossible. Her reasoning was built on the diversity principle: Black
children in segregated schools would never get an equal education even
if the facilities and budgets were equal, because integration—Black and
white children learning together—was a necessary component of equality. Her focus was on the harm of exclusion and the benefits of diversity
for Black children, who would receive an equal education only if they
were educated alongside white children.[104]

Murray would get to make this argument to a court in 1946 on behalf of the American Jewish Congress, arguing in an amicus curiae brief
that a California law segregating Mexican American children deprived
the children of equal protection of the laws because the enforced separation of any racial, ethnic, or religious minority is humiliating to the
group classified as inferior.[105]

Finally, Murray argued that in addition to the Thirteenth and Fourteenth amendments, Congress's power to regulate interstate commerce meant that it could ban segregation and discrimination nationwide.[106] This argument was similarly prophetic. In 1964, when Congress passed the most important civil rights bill since Reconstruction, it based its action not on the Fourteenth Amendment but on the Commerce Clause of the Constitution.

Marshall applied Murray's arguments in the *Sipuel* case. Instead of arguing that a separate Black law school would be unequal under the Fourteenth Amendment simply because the facilities or faculty would be inferior, he called on an old friend, Dean Erwin Griswold of Harvard Law School.[107] Griswold had grown up in a privileged white family in the then-affluent Cleveland suburb of East Cleveland, Ohio.[108] His father was the lead partner in a commercial law firm.[109] His parents had met at Oberlin College, an elite and almost entirely white liberal arts college, which Griswold also attended before continuing to Harvard Law.[110] He graduated with both an LLB (the degree that led to legal practice) and an SJD (the law school equivalent of a PhD), briefly entered private practice, and then spent five years as a special assistant to the U.S. attorney general in the solicitor general's office before returning to Harvard as a professor in 1934. In 1946 he was named dean, a position he held for twenty-one years.[111]

Griswold has been portrayed in popular media as unsympathetic to women's participation in law.[112] In 1950, he famously asked the first twelve women admitted to Harvard Law how they could justify taking the place of a man.[113] He was still asking the question in 1956, when the incoming class included Ruth Bader Ginsburg.[114] In 1944, he was on the faculty, though not yet dean, when Harvard Law refused admission to Pauli Murray because of her sex, even though she had finished first in her class at Howard.[115] But Griswold had also lobbied the Harvard administration to open the law school to women, and he would enthusiastically support Ginsburg's appointment to the bench.[116]

Marshall asked Griswold to serve as an expert witness on the question of whether a separate Oklahoma law school for Black students could ever be equal to the all-white school.[117] Griswold took the train from Boston to Tulsa and testified about the importance of diversity to legal education, explaining that "students by themselves, not individually, but in groups of varying sizes, actually provide the largest amount of legal education . . . [and] that process is not possible without a student body of

substantial size, containing students from varying backgrounds and different elements in society."[118] This testimony was the basis for an assertion in the amicus brief filed in *Sipuel* by the National Lawyers Guild:
"One of the most important aspects of legal training is the opportunity
for discussion, debate and exchange of ideas. This becomes meaningless
unless a class or student body is composed of persons having different
and varied backgrounds and divergent views and attitudes toward current
affairs, politics and other subjects."[119] The brief, which relied on Griswold's testimony, could have come straight from Humboldt, the Mills,
Eliot, or Murray.

It is worth noting the difference between how Marshall and Murray
described the diversity principle and how Justice Powell would use it
thirty years later in the *Bakke* case. Murray, Marshall, and Griswold focused on the value of diversity to Black students attending white universities. For Powell, deciding in 1978 whether affirmative action was unfair
to white applicants, the value proposition was flipped; he seemed largely
concerned with the value of diversity to white students. This would be a
key critique of Powell's *Bakke* opinion.

The NAACP victory in *Sipuel* led to the Court's orders two years later
in *McLaurin v. Oklahoma State Regents for Higher Education*, desegregating
the University of Oklahoma Law School, and the better-known *Sweatt v.
Painter*, which desegregated the University of Texas Law School.[120]

In *McLaurin*, a unanimous Court invalidated the University of Oklahoma's policy of restricting Black graduate students' use of the library,
classrooms, and school cafeteria, concluding that it prevented "the intellectual commingling of students" and limited Black students' ability "to
engage in discussions and exchange views with other students," thereby
handicapping their "pursuit of effective graduate education."[121] In the
Texas case, which Marshall argued in the Supreme Court, Griswold co-
authored an amicus brief with six other law professors on behalf of the
Committee of Law Teachers Against Segregation in Legal Education.[122]
Following in the footsteps of Humboldt and the Mills, they argued that
if Texas "afforded equal placement opportunities for every graduate; if it
overcame every other difficulty, Texas (colored) would still not be equal.
For the segregated plan misses the whole purpose of a modern law
school."[123] The practice of law is inherently human, the professors maintained, and a lawyer whose training limited his interactions with a significant part of society would be at a professional disadvantage, less able to
"sense the drives, interests (and weaknesses) of those with whom he

deals—whether as witnesses, negotiators, judges, clients or opponents."[124]
Worse, limiting students' exposure to others limited their exposure to
ideas:

> In classifying the students at the two schools by the test of color,
> Texas effectively eliminates much of the cross-fertilization of
> ideas. When a law student is forced to study and talk the shop
> talk of justice and equity with a segregated handful, he is circum-
> scribed in the effort to achieve any real understanding of justice
> or equity. . . . The method of legal education depends entirely
> upon that thrust and parry of diverse ideas which cannot exist
> among a handful of segregated students.[125]

The Court accepted the argument. It unanimously ruled that the Texas
plan was unconstitutional under the Fourteenth Amendment. Chief
Justice Fred Vinson's majority opinion tracked the diversity language of
the amicus brief:

> The law school, the proving ground for legal learning and prac-
> tice, cannot be effective in isolation from the individuals and in-
> stitutions with which the law interacts. Few students and no one
> who has practiced law would choose to study in an academic vac-
> uum, removed from the interplay of ideas and the exchange of
> views with which the law is concerned. The law school to which
> Texas is willing to admit petitioner excludes from its student
> body members of the racial groups which number 85% of the
> population of the State and include most of the lawyers, wit-
> nesses, jurors, judges and other officials with whom petitioner
> will inevitably be dealing when he becomes a member of the
> Texas Bar. With such a substantial and significant segment of so-
> ciety excluded, we cannot conclude that the education offered
> petitioner is substantially equal to that which he would receive if
> admitted to the University of Texas Law School.[126]

And so in 1950, one hundred forty years after Humboldt first articulated the importance of diversity in higher education, ninety-two years
after the Mills embraced Humboldt's argument and expanded it as a cornerstone of liberty, and eighty-one years after Eliot began to put that argument into effect at Harvard—all to the effect of admitting previously

excluded Catholics and Jews—the U.S. Supreme Court adopted it as a reason for ending racial segregation. The Court would expand the point four years later in *Brown v. Board of Education*, when it ruled that separate schools could never be equal because segregation of Black children was a badge of inferiority—the argument Murray had made a decade earlier in her *Plessy* paper.[127] The unanimous Court, citing the Oklahoma and Texas cases, adopted the language about the importance of students being able "to engage in discussions and exchange views with other students" and recognized that integration fosters equality through the sharing of experiences.[128]

By the time *Brown* was decided, Thurgood Marshall and Murray were friends. Marshall liked to open their conversations by saying, "I know what the law says, Pauli, but tell me something different."[129] He acknowledged drawing on Murray's paper for his winning argument in *Brown*—which didn't prevent most scholars from ignoring her contributions—and credited her with writing "the bible" of the Civil Rights Movement, a compilation of all forty-eight states' segregation and civil rights laws in a volume over a foot thick.[130] The publication allowed civil rights lawyers to compare rights across state lines, previously almost impossible.[131] The ACLU bought and distributed nearly one thousand copies.[132]

Marshall, Murray, and Griswold cemented diversity's place at the center of civil rights law. Marshall would continue to direct the NAACP Legal Defense Fund until 1961, when President Kennedy named him to the U.S. Court of Appeals. In 1965, President Johnson named him solicitor general, taking over from Archibald Cox; in 1967, Johnson nominated him to the Supreme Court and named Griswold to take Marshall's place as solicitor general.[133] (Griswold, in turn, stepped down as dean and professor at Harvard and as a member of the U.S. Civil Rights Commission.)

Murray would continue to break down barriers. In 1956, Lloyd K. Garrison—the great-grandson of the abolitionist William Lloyd Garrison, and one of the experts cited in the law professors' amicus brief in *Sweatt v. Painter*—recruited Murray to join the famed New York law firm Paul, Weiss, Rifkind, Wharton and Garrison, where he was a name partner.[134] She became the first Black woman lawyer to join a major Wall Street law firm. Her foray into corporate law was brief, but consequential—at Paul, Weiss she met Irene Barlow, who became her life partner, a relationship that would continue until Barlow's death in 1973. Murray left the firm after four years, first to serve as a law professor in Ghana, then to enter the doctoral program in law at Yale, where she became the first Black person to earn a Yale JSD (the degree she had sought twenty years earlier at Harvard and ten years earlier at the University of North Carolina).[135]

During her time at Yale, Murray began publishing articles on "Jane Crow" sex and race discrimination. She would spend the rest of her legal career working to bridge the gaps between civil rights for racial minorities and women's rights.[136] She wrote a report for the President's Commission on the Status of Women that addressed the divisions among women's rights advocates over the desirability of an Equal Rights Amendment. Murray tried to bridge the divide by proposing a strategy modeled on the successful litigation campaign of the Black Civil Rights Movement.[137] She spoke out against the exclusion of women speakers at the March on Washington in 1963 and against A. Philip Randolph's decision to hold a pre-march press conference at the National Press Club, knowing that women reporters were barred from attending.[138]

The following year, when Congress was considering striking sex discrimination from the proposed 1964 Civil Rights Act, Murray wrote a memo that was credited with saving the provision—a tremendously consequential move given that the Act would provide the basis for outlawing sex discrimination in employment.[139] The Civil Rights Act, conceived as a law forbidding racial discrimination in both public and private accommodations and employment, faced intense opposition from segregationists.[140] Two days before the House vote on Title VII of the bill, Congressman Howard Smith had offered an amendment to insert "sex" as a protected class.[141] Historians believe that Smith, a segregationist from Virginia, may have proposed the amendment as a poison pill to sink the bill, and according to National Public Radio the proposal elicited "peals of raucous laughter" in the House.[142] The event became mockingly known as Ladies Day—but the amendment passed.[143] When the bill reached the Senate, however, Minority Leader Everett Dirksen, who was key to moving the bill through the chamber, said he would try to remove the mention of "sex."[144]

Murray drafted a memo defending the inclusion of "sex" as a protected class, which she and a network of women activists sent to every congressperson as well as to First Lady "Lady Bird" Johnson.[145] Murray's cover letter noted that opponents of the amendment intended "to intimidate women from speaking out on this issue on the ground that by doing so they will endanger the larger civil rights legislation. As both a Negro and a woman, I feel this point of view is erroneous."[146]

In her memo, Murray, channeling Harriet Taylor Mill, pointed out that the women's rights and anti-slavery movements were historically connected. Women and Black people, she wrote, held "strikingly similar positions in American society," and women had experienced discrimination "comparable to the inequalities imposed upon minorities," based on similar faulty logic.[147]

> As in the Negro problem, most men have accepted as self-evident, until recently, the doctrine that women had inferior endowments in most of those respects which carry prestige, power, and advantages in society, but that they were, at the same time, superior in some other respects. The arguments . . . have been about the same: smaller brains, scarcity of geniuses and so on. . . . The myth of the "contented women," who did not want to have suffrage or other civil rights and equal opportunities, had the same social function as the myth of the "contented Negro."[148]

Murray then addressed the question of "interrelatedness"—what we today call "intersectionality."

> If there is no "sex" amendment, in accordance with the prevailing patterns of employment *both* Negro and white women will share a common fate of discrimination, since it is exceedingly difficult for a Negro woman to determine whether or not she is being discriminated against because of race or sex. These two types of discrimination are so closely intertwined and so similar that Negro women are uniquely qualified to affirm their interrelatedness. A strong argument can be made for the proposition that Title VII without the "sex" amendment would benefit Negro males primarily and thus offer genuine equality of opportunity to only *half* of the potential Negro work force.[149]

Dahlia Lithwick described Murray as "on edge" until she received a note from Lady Bird's secretary, which said that Mrs. Johnson had shared the memo with her husband and that the "sex" amendment would remain in Title VII.[150] The measure passed the Senate and was signed into law on July 2, 1964.[151]

After receiving her JSD degree from Yale in 1965, Murray joined the national office of the American Civil Liberties Union, where she wrote briefs on race and sex discrimination.[152] She and her fellow ACLU counsel Dorothy Kenyon advanced an argument that sex discrimination violates the Fourteenth Amendment, paving the way for the creation of the ACLU Women's Rights Project, directed by a young lawyer named Ruth Bader Ginsburg. Ginsburg would use the Murray-Kenyon argument in her groundbreaking Supreme Court argument in *Reed v. Reed*, which led the Court to hold in 1971 that the Fourteenth Amendment applies to sex discrimination. Although Murray had by then left the ACLU, Ginsburg recognized her contribution, listing her as co-counsel on the Supreme Court brief.[153]

While at the ACLU, Murray began talking with the feminist writer Betty Friedan about the need for a national women's rights organization. Their conversations led to the founding in 1966 of the National Organization of Women.[154] Murray had a vision that NOW would be an NAACP for women.[155] But the leadership's lack of attention to the concerns of poor women and women of color led her to resign within a year. In her resignation letter, she wrote: "And since, as a human being, I cannot allow myself to be fragmented into Negro at one time, woman at another, or worker at another, I must find a unifying principle in all of these movements to which I can adhere."[156] But Murray struggled to find a role in which she could integrate these intersecting elements of her activism. In 1967, she was considered for the position of general counsel of the Equal Employment Opportunity Commission but was rejected after an FBI report described her as too radical, based in part on her political activities and in part on her defiance of gender norms.[157] In 1968, while still at the ACLU, Murray took a position as a professor at Brandeis University as the first director of its Afro-American studies program. She received tenure there in 1970 but clashed repeatedly with Black students, who she felt were too exclusionary of white allies.[158] She was becoming increasingly involved in the Episcopal Church, and when her life partner, Irene Barlow, died in 1973, Murray left Brandeis to enroll as a student again, at the General Theological Seminary.[159] In 1977, she was the first Black woman to be ordained as an Episcopal priest.[160] She served a congregation in Baltimore, where she was born.[161]

On March 28, 1979, Murray delivered a sermon, titled "Challenge of Nurturing the Christian Community in Its Diversity," that celebrated "the vision of a new earthly society in which diversity is valued and which is so structured as to encourage each individual to develop to the fullness of his or her own potential. This vision of the possibility of a new earth and a new human being gives the hope that fuels our efforts toward social change. . . . It foresees a society in which differences of race or sex or ethnic background will be affirmed and celebrated."[162]

Murray died in 1985 having played an enormously influential role in the development of American civil rights law. She pioneered the integration of the diversity principle into civil rights.[163] In 2012 she was canonized by the Episcopal Church.[164] During her lifetime, she could never escape inequity and exclusion on account of her race, her sex, and her gender expression—often at the intersections of all three. Although her contributions to civil rights law went woefully underappreciated, she was perhaps the most creative U.S. constitutional law scholar of the twentieth century. Her experience of serial exclusion as a gender-nonconforming Black woman helped her reimagine the meaning of the Fourteenth and Thirteenth amendments and strengthen the strategy for fighting segregation that would be adopted by Thurgood Marshall and the NAACP. It helped her persuade Congress to prohibit sex discrimination in employment in the 1964 Civil Rights Act. And it helped her articulate the concept of intersectional discrimination that plays such a central role in equality law today. At the core of her legal scholarship and advocacy was an understanding that equality and diversity are inextricably linked—an insight that shapes our understanding of both ideas today.

CHAPTER SEVEN

The Fight over the Meaning of "Excellence"

ITH THE END OF World War II, Harvard's undergraduate enrollment briefly swelled with returning veterans and then fell. In 1950 it accepted nearly two-thirds of applicants. But given the postwar baby boom, it was clear that applications would soon be rising, and they did. By 1967, Harvard was accepting fewer than one in five applicants. Today it accepts fewer than one in twenty-five.[1]

This explosion of applications set off a debate among the faculty: How should the university decide which students should be admitted? Two positions emerged. One side preferred a strictly quantitative approach, relying on the Scholastic Aptitude Test (now known simply as the SAT). As more and more students applied to Harvard, the admissions committee kept raising the minimum score needed to get in. Dean of Admissions Fred Glimp reported that "in the Class of 1956, 90 percent of our students came from the top 12 to 14 percent . . . but in the Class of 1965 the same proportion of the Class came from the top 3 or 4 percent." While many on the faculty wanted to continue in this vein, others thought Harvard's quantitative threshold was already high enough. They preferred to select from the top 5–10 percent those who would make up an interesting and diverse class.[2] In the words of Wilbur Bender, who served as dean of admissions and financial aid from 1952 to 1960, this

was the fundamental question facing the faculty in the decades after
World War II:

> Should the ultimate goal of Harvard's admission effort be to
> come as close as possible to a student body all of whom would
> have outstanding academic ability, all of whom would be, as one
> member of the special faculty committee put it, in the top 1 per-
> cent, or even better, the top half of 1 percent, of American Col-
> lege students? ... Or should we consciously aim for a student
> body with a somewhat broader range of academic ability, per-
> haps the top 5 percent of American college students, a student
> body deliberately selected within this range of ability to include
> a variety of personalities, talents, backgrounds and career goals?[3]

Three Harvard deans, all favoring diversity, played an outsize role in
this debate. Thanks to their efforts, Harvard became significantly more
diverse throughout the postwar years—even before the widespread adoption of affirmative action programs. The admissions compromise they
helped broker was taken up by other colleges—and ultimately endorsed
by the Supreme Court from 1978 until 2023.

The first of the three deans, Wilbur J. Bender, grew up in Goshen,
Indiana, and spent his first two years of college at a small religious institution near his home before transferring to Harvard. After graduating
from Harvard College in 1927, he became an advocate for opening the
university to more low-income students. He served in the Navy during
World War II, returned to Harvard to counsel veterans taking advantage
of the GI Bill, and was appointed as dean of the College in 1947. In 1952
he was made dean of admissions and financial aid, a position he held until
1960.[4]

As someone who had come to Harvard from outside the New England prep school pipeline and spent years counseling veterans from many
backgrounds, Bender firmly believed that Harvard's strength lay in its diversity. He wanted to admit brilliant students, but he thought the school
should be more than a proving ground for future professors.[5] In addition
to the "top 1 percent" whom he expected to continue on to graduate
school and enter academia, he wanted the freshman class also to include
future business leaders and future government leaders like Teddy and
Franklin Roosevelt.[6] He extolled the diversity of Harvard's incoming
classes as a mix of these groups and others, opposed a narrow approach

to admissions, and warned that Harvard would become a rich, upper-middle-class enclave unless it expanded its scholarships.[7]

Bender was succeeded as dean of admissions and financial aid by Fred L. Glimp, who had worked under Bender as an admissions officer. Glimp had grown up on a farm in Idaho, joined the U.S. Army Air Corps out of high school, serving until the end of the war, and then submitted a long-shot application to Harvard. He was accepted, and he excelled, earning his bachelor's degree in 1950 and then studying at Cambridge University on a Fulbright scholarship. He returned to Harvard in 1954 to work in the admissions office. Like Bender, Glimp was deeply committed to diversity in Harvard College admissions. Drawing on his own experience as a "farm boy from Idaho" and a war veteran, he aimed to attract a wide variety of applicants to Harvard and to make sure the College could provide sufficient financial resources for them to attend.[8]

In advocating for diversity, Glimp embraced Bender's arguments and added two more. First, he argued, students and faculty would have a better educational experience if the students attending the College came from all regions of the country, all walks of life, and all economic classes, bringing with them unique backgrounds and talents. Second, he was deeply skeptical of the value of high school grades and test scores as an indicator of future success, especially among students from "seriously disadvantaged backgrounds, from rural areas, and from blue-collar families," who "would be cut out disproportionately" if Harvard relied solely on numerical evaluation for admissions. Raising the numerical threshold for admission might also cause the admissions committee to overlook students with "unusual personal strengths," who would have blossomed at Harvard. In the report he wrote upon leaving the admissions office in 1967, Glimp noted that "a careful review of the academic records of Harvard students shows that in almost every class the low-scoring students receive their degrees about as frequently as high-scoring students, and that a higher proportion of the low-scoring students achieve honor degrees than most laymen would expect. . . . In two of the last seven graduating classes, for example, the man whose secondary school grades and test scores combined to predict for him the lowest academic record in the class graduated magna cum laude."[9]

By 1967 a compromise had emerged. It was agreed that the very top SAT-scoring applicants would be favored and that there would be a reduction in private school and legacy admissions, but also that among those in the top 10 percent of SAT takers, diversity would be an important consideration.[10]

Glimp's report, submitted as he was moving to a new role as dean of Harvard College, was an elegant paean to diversity in all its forms. Because of its importance to Archibald Cox's brief in the *DeFunis* case, which became the Harvard Plan and provided parts of the text of Lewis Powell's majority opinion in *Regents of the University of California v. Bakke*, I quote from it here at length.

> The basic question confronting the Committee was how to choose among many more highly qualified applicants than we have room to accept—highly qualified not only in terms of objective indices of academic promise, and the often helpful comments of teachers about their students' intellectual characteristics, but also in an unusual range of non-academic talents, backgrounds, and personal strengths, styles and promise. The Committee's response has been to seek variety in making its choices. This has seemed important in part because it is consistent with the educational mission of the College, in part because it adds a critical ingredient to the effectiveness of the educational experience here. The Committee's notion of the educational mission of the College has continued to be the historical one— that in addition to the relative handful of men whose intellectual potential will seem extraordinary to the Faculty (presently perhaps as many as 150 men in a class) we have tried to admit men who seemed likely to be promising and effective in the long run in a variety of areas—law, politics, public service, teaching and research, business, writing and other creative arts, medicine and so on. The effectiveness of our students' educational experience has seemed to the Committee to be affected as importantly by a wide variety of interests, talents, backgrounds and career goals as it is by a fine faculty and our libraries, laboratories and housing arrangements. . . .
>
>   . . . The personal styles and expectations of the students we admit should make Harvard College a conglomeration of many colleges rather than a single one. We want the scholars and scientists who tend to think of the College as a particular department of the Faculty, maybe even as an individual member of the Faculty, or more broadly as a California Institute of Technology (though I am aware that this shorthand does violence to the heterogeneity of the CalTech student body). We need the unusually

able, busy students who ran their secondary schools as intellectual or activist leaders—and many of whom will join forces here in the *Crimson* or the Harvard Undergraduate Council, or whatever, and some of whom will do their best to run or change or *be* the College. We need those whose style is that of the long distance runner, who won't stop working or trying when a reasonable man would, and whose expectation is of a long road of challenges. We need the less precocious high school leaders whose "popularity" and performance seem to grow out of good instincts and concern, whose energy and drive may often be associated (in the special sociology of a socially mobile America) with unusual efforts in athletics or in after-school employment, and who expect Harvard to be a place for a collegiate living and learning and the making of warm friendships—all on some sort of assumption that this broad course can lead them to full and useful lives. We need the promising men from the rural areas and the slums, the men who have very little idea what Harvard is but assume it is "good" and that some combination of what the College offers and the interests and the hopes they bring to it will be worthwhile. These men not only have—and often realize—the greatest opportunity for growth during their undergraduate years, but they represent to their classmates, in a way no instruction can, the difference between the degree of performance that grows out of sheer effort and ability and the component that rests on the accrued advantages of status. We need the talented writers and artists and musicians who will think of the College as a sometimes stimulating, sometimes diverting setting for a Juilliard or a writers' workshop. We need the students who come to the College out of a traditional association with it and who approach the broad experiences of the College with expectations that grow out of their understanding of the traditions. And we need the men who care deeply about helping others in an individual personal sense, the kind of men who participate in the incessant reshaping of the efforts of Phillips Brooks House, doing what they feel they ought to do despite the jibes of those who call them do-gooders from one side and the worries of those who think them overly activist on the other. And of course we need Radcliffe, with its own conglomeration of styles and expectations.

It is not just that a diverse heterogeneity in the College is stimulating to the Faculty, or more exciting to contemplate than a homogenous undergraduate academy, or more relevant to liberal education—though each of these points is important enough to bear a good deal of the weight of the argument. It is the effects of diversity on students' experiences. A broad diversity in the College affords a student enough variety and choice of emphasis and style to preserve his self-respect or humility, or both at different times, and to engage his own interests while he meets the generally high standards and expectations of the College and his fellow students. In short, diversity gives him the choice of enough variety to be himself and to enjoy himself while making the often painful effort to become a man of enough breadth and depth to stand a chance of making a difference in the quality and worth of human life.[11]

Glimp's report was written as affirmative action programs were just beginning nationally, before they had become controversial. It touches only glancingly on race. But racial diversity was becoming an important part of Harvard's approach to admissions, largely through the efforts of the third member of this trio, the man Glimp replaced in 1967 as dean of the College: John U. Monro.

Monro had served as director of admissions and financial aid prior to Bender, becoming dean of the College in 1958. He had graduated from Harvard in 1935 and then served in World War II, earning a Bronze Star as a naval officer. Like Bender, he returned to Harvard after the war to counsel incoming veterans.[12] In 1950, three years after Bender began as dean of the College, Monro was named director of financial aid.[13] In 1958, he became dean of the College.[14] At that point, Monro was dean of the College, Bender was dean of admissions and financial aid, and Glimp was working with Bender in admissions (and would succeed him in 1960). Monro remained dean of the College until 1967.[15] Thus, for most of the period 1947–67, the two key positions of dean of Harvard College and dean of admissions and financial aid were held by Bender, Glimp, or Monro.

For understanding the role race and ethnicity played in Harvard's commitment to diversity, Monro was the most important of the three deans. His contribution has not received its due recognition, perhaps because he left Harvard at the height of his career to move to a college that gets far less attention. It was Monro who evoked the nineteenth century to bring racial diversity back into Harvard's core values. The struggle against racism was fundamental to who he was.

In 1948, Monro began organizing summer recruiting trips, first to Chicago and then to the South, to persuade Black students to apply to Harvard. He joined the board of directors of the National Scholarship Service and Fund for Negro Students (NSSFNS), and even as he was rising to his position as dean of Harvard College he was spending more and more of his time focused on improving educational opportunities for Black Americans.[16]

In 1949, Monro recommended that Harvard identify promising Black high school seniors and offer them financial assistance, proposing a goal of ten Black recruits per freshman class.[17] He believed the best way to meet that target was to work with Black leaders in major metropolitan areas. In 1953 he persuaded Harvard to partner with the NSSFNS. Black enrollment figures rose, and by the late 1950s, as many as half of the college's Black applicants said they had worked through the NSSFNS.[18] Between 1948 and 1960, ninety-five Black students entered Harvard.[19]

In 1962, Monro attended a conference of the American Teachers Association where he met the organization's president, Lucius Pitts. Pitts was nearing the end of his first year as president of Miles College, a historically Black college in Birmingham, Alabama, and he invited Monro to visit.[20] On September 4, 1963, Monro arrived at Miles for a faculty workshop. It happened to be the day a federal court order requiring the desegregation of Birmingham's schools took effect. Five Black students at three schools faced violent crowds and empty classrooms. With violence in the air, an armed guard patrolled Miles.[21] Less than two weeks later, on September 15, a Ku Klux Klan bomb would kill four Black girls—fourteen-year-olds Addie Mae Collins, Denise McNair, and Carole Robertson, and eleven-year-old Cynthia Wesley—in the basement of Birmingham's Sixteenth Street Baptist Church.[22]

During his visit, Monro met with Pitts and about fifteen others in a different church basement to discuss a statement, intended for the mayor, regarding the school desegregation disaster. Suddenly they heard a loud explosion. A bomb had gone off at the nearby home of Arthur Shores, the attorney leading the desegregation case. Monro found himself walking up the hill to Shores's house with Pitts and an angry Black crowd. He later wrote that the experience gave him a "first-hand look at the fury, and unity, and determination of the city's Black community."[23]

He pledged to help develop a new freshman studies program at Miles College.[24]

For the rest of the year, Monro returned to Miles every month to plan the freshman studies program. He also committed to directing the English section of a pre-college workshop developed by Pitts. In the summer of 1964, Monro helped start a tutoring program that organized Birmingham elementary-school students into ten teams, each taught by one Harvard student and one Miles student.[25]

Inspired by his summer at Miles, Monro continued his efforts to support civil rights and Black students at Harvard, including endeavors to help fund the *Southern Courier*, a Harvard student newspaper that provided coverage of civil rights.[26] Enrollment of Black students continued to increase, with forty-two Black freshmen entering Harvard in 1965, putting the College well ahead of its Big Three rivals: that year Yale admitted twenty-three Black freshmen, Princeton twelve.[27] The same year, the dean of Harvard Law, Erwin Griswold, launched the first affirmative action program at an American law school.[28]

Much has been written about the origins of affirmative action at American colleges and universities. Many historians trace these policies back to the student unrest of the late 1960s. The sociologists Lisa Stulberg and Anthony Chen make a convincing case that at many highly selective schools, steps toward affirmative action began earlier in the decade, as educators found themselves inspired by the morally compelling nonviolent Civil Rights Movement.[29] But well before the reforms of the 1960s, John Monro was exhorting admissions directors, faculty, and other administrators to lead, not follow, the struggle for inclusion of Black Americans in the nation's top colleges and universities.

As Harvard Law began its affirmative action efforts, Monro continued to work on the Miles College freshman studies program, eventually becoming a trustee at Miles. By the summer of 1965 he had molded his teaching around the needs of Miles students, including a reading list that featured several Black authors. At a College Board conference later that summer, he would push his fellow educators to include works by Black authors on their syllabi. Monro agreed to return to Miles the next summer to direct the entire pre-college workshop, including the social studies and math sections. The following winter, Pitts invited him to run the freshman studies program. Monro accepted and decided to relocate to Alabama.[30]

On March 9, 1967, Monro announced that he was leaving Harvard to become director of freshman studies at Miles.[31] When asked why he would move from the nation's most prestigious university to a small, historically Black college in the Deep South, he replied, "Well, I decided that my job at Harvard is like being a shock absorber in a Rolls Royce. But the really serious issues today are being faced by blacks, and I want to be part of that."[32] The following year, Harvard enrolled fifty-one incoming Black freshmen. By 1970 there would be ninety-eight.[33] Bender and Glimp helped carry on Monro's legacy, ensuring that a commitment to racial and ethnic diversity became a defining part of Harvard's mission.

Archibald Cox had a front-row seat in the faculty debate around Harvard's admissions policies. In 1973 he would draw on that experience to write the brief that described what became the Harvard Plan. His inspiration for that brief came not only from Cambridge but also from South Africa, where a white supremacist government continued to enforce its system of apartheid and where academics resisting those efforts were developing a Holmes-like legal argument that connected racial diversity and academic freedom—an argument that would change the course of American law.

CHAPTER EIGHT

The Open Universities in
South Africa

THE ARGUMENT THAT UNIVERSITIES should be permitted to take race into account in the quest for a racially diverse student body and that they have a right to do so under the principles of academic freedom—that is, the argument made by Archibald Cox and endorsed by Justice Powell—did not originate in America. It was first fully articulated in the late 1940s by two South African scholars defending the University of Cape Town's diversity admissions policies. These arguments made their way into American First Amendment academic freedom doctrine long before the *Bakke* case. On at least three critical occasions, as Harvard's leadership was struggling with how to expand the admissions process to admit more Black students, two of the South African proponents of the "academic freedom to obtain diversity" argument interacted with Dean Erwin Griswold and President Nathan Pusey, Justice Felix Frankfurter, Frankfurter's protégé Archibald Cox, and other key figures at Harvard.

In 1948, Thomas Benjamin ("T. B.") Davie resigned as the dean of the faculty of medicine at the University of Liverpool to return to his native South Africa, having been recruited to serve as principal and vice-chancellor at the University of Cape Town (UCT), a role analogous to that of an American university president.[1] He thus became the academic leader of the country's most prestigious university at a fateful historical moment.

Just months after his arrival, elections brought the white supremacist National Party into power. Its leaders began systematically segregating every aspect of life, banning Black and other non-white persons from most occupations, from voting, and from living in or even visiting white neighborhoods. Non-white Africans were denied freedom of movement, speech, and assembly. In 1959, after a decade of resistance by university leaders, non-white students were banned from attending universities with white students.[2] From his selection as principal until his death in 1955, Davie, who was white, actively opposed apartheid and worked to prevent apartheid laws from taking effect at UCT.[3] In his formal installation address in March 1948, he announced that a university flourishes only in "an atmosphere of absolute intellectual freedom," signaling that UCT would be on a "collision course" with the apartheid supporters favored to win the May 1948 election and take power.[4] Davie had seen how universities failed in the absence of academic freedom. As the UCT professor and historian of apartheid Howard Phillips writes, Davie's ideas about academic freedom were "much influenced by the fate of this freedom in the universities of Nazi Germany and the Iron Curtain countries."[5]

Two years under apartheid sharpened Davie's views on academic freedom.[6] In a 1950 graduation address at the University of Witwatersrand, he articulated his four principles of academic freedom: a university must have "freedom from external interference in (a) who shall teach, (b) what we teach, (c) how we teach and (d) whom we teach."[7] He declared that "our lecture theaters and laboratories shall be open to all who, seeking higher knowledge, can show that they are intellectually capable of benefiting by admission to our teaching."[8] He gave a slightly reformulated version of these principles in February 1953 as "four essential freedoms of a university—to determine for itself on academic grounds who may teach, what may be taught, how it shall be taught, and who may be admitted to study."[9]

That fall, Davie took his views on tour in the United States. On a grant from the Carnegie Corporation, Davie spent September through December touring U.S. universities to discuss the relationship between race and academic freedom.[10] One of his stops was Harvard, where he discussed these topics with the university's new president, Nathan Pusey, and with the law school dean, Erwin Griswold.[11] The conversation with Griswold was an opportunity for the two men to share their developing ideas of how racial exclusion offended principles of academic freedom, a subject then foremost in Davie's thoughts. For Griswold, it had been just five years since he testified as an expert witness for Thurgood Marshall in one of the NAACP's cases against University of Oklahoma, asserting that integration is vital to a university's success because students with different backgrounds and experiences learn from one another.[12] Two years after that, Griswold had made the argument again as a co-author of an amicus curiae brief in the pathbreaking case *Sweatt v. Painter*, which had relied on the diversity principle in ordering the end of segregation at the University of Texas law school.[13]

Davie, meanwhile, was resisting apartheid in higher education in South Africa by arguing that it was essential for students of all races to study together and that a university had a right under the principle of academic freedom to select its students without government interference. Griswold was making almost the same arguments in resisting segregation in the United States. Clearly the two men had a lot to discuss.

Davie's connection with the Carnegie Corporation was facilitated by a young grant-maker, Alan Pifer, who had begun working at Carnegie earlier that year and soon after had met Davie on a trip to South Africa.[14] Pifer would rise up the ranks and eventually serve as the foundation's president for fifteen years, from 1967 through 1982.[15] Under his leadership, Carnegie focused on social and racial justice and education, including programs to build a practice of public interest law addressing South African apartheid.[16] For much of that time, he also served on Harvard's governing board and was thus perfectly positioned to help bring Davie's views on academic freedom and anti-racism to Harvard just as the university was formulating its approach to diversity in admissions.[17]

In his diary of his U.S. trip, Davie noted that Griswold had met Davie's partner in his anti-apartheid work, Albert van der Sandt Centlivres, while on his own Carnegie travel grant, and had a very high opinion of him.[18] Centlivres was the chief justice of South Africa. During Davie's term as principal of the University of Cape Town, Centlivres served as chancellor, a position roughly equivalent to the chair of the board of trustees or regents at an American university.[19]

Griswold and Centlivres first met in 1951 at a legal convention in Sydney, Australia, and they began a long-distance conversation about diversity and academic freedom that would grow to include several influential American lawyers, judges, and legal scholars, including Supreme Court Justice Felix Frankfurter.[20] Davie, sadly, would not stay long in that conversation. He passed away in 1955, only two years after his visit to the States.[21] In a memorial address shortly after his death, the vice chancellor of the University of Liverpool said of Davie's Cape Town years:

> He had a task to perform: the defence of freedom within his University, the upholding of the ideal that Universities should be open to all, irrespective of race, colour, or creed, who can profit by the education they offer. Single-handed, if need be, he set himself to fight that fight; and he fought to the end. . . . Those who have read them know that his pronouncements on the fundamental nature of a University are among the noblest utterances of academic statesmanship.[22]

Centlivres would carry Davie's legacy forward. As chief justice of South Africa from 1950 to 1957, he was at the center of several important cases challenging apartheid, including an epic battle between the courts and Parliament over Parliament's right to remove thousands of non-white voters from Cape Town's voting rolls.[23]

But Centlivres's most important contribution to the fight against apartheid came in his role as chancellor of UCT. When the National Party took power, party leaders immediately began to implement their apartheid policies in many areas of life, but not in higher education.[24] Although the future prime minister D. F. Malan had announced a month before the 1948 election that "we want apartheid as far as our educational institutions are concerned, more particularly in our universities," the first important legislative push to segregate higher education did not come until 1957.[25] That year, the National Party introduced a "University Education Bill" that would require UCT and the University of Witwatersrand ("Wits") to stop admitting non-white students.[26] As the government cracked down on the resulting campus protests, Centlivres waded in to protect his students. Albie Sachs, then a student activist at UCT and later Nelson Mandela's lawyer and a member of the Constitutional Court after the end of apartheid, credited Centlivres with preventing him from being arrested or worse.[27]

In January 1957, with the University Education Bill on the horizon, UCT held a conference with representatives from UCT and Wits, led by their chancellors, to discuss resistance to the bill.[28] The participants agreed to publish a short book explaining their position on "open universities" in South Africa.[29] "Open" universities were defined as those that "admit non-white students as well as white students and aim, in all academic matters, at treating non-white students on a footing of equality with white students, and without segregation."[30]

From January 28 through February 2, 1957, an editorial committee prepared the book for publication. On February 4, Centlivres as chancellor at UCT and Richard Feetham as chancellor at Wits completed and dated the preface, and the booklet, titled *The Open Universities in South Africa*, was rushed to press.[31] Centlivres sent a copy to his friend Justice Frankfurter.[32]

The book begins by asserting that government imposition of apartheid "is an unwarranted interference with university autonomy and academic freedom."[33] The authors argue that their universities' existing policy of "academic non-segregation provides the conditions under which the pursuit of truth may best be furthered," the same idea Humboldt and the Mills had articulated decades earlier.[34] To those thinkers, influenced by the aftermath of religious wars in Europe and the birth of nationalism, non-segregation meant welcoming Jews, Catholics, and other religious minorities along with foreigners and, at least for the Mills, women. In twentieth-century South Africa, it meant welcoming those of other races. Thus, the authors write, "[we] believe that racial diversity within the university is essential to the ideal of a university within a multiracial society."[35]

Echoing the U.S. Supreme Court opinions in *Sweatt v. Painter* and *Brown v. Board of Education*, the book continues by rejecting "the claim that separate but equal university facilities can be provided. This claim ignores those factors in university life that matter most, namely the factors that cannot be assessed in physical or monetary terms."[36] Citing T. B. Davie, the authors write that "it is the business of a university to provide that atmosphere which is most conducive to speculation, experiment and creation. It is an atmosphere in which there prevail 'the four essential freedoms' of a university—to determine for itself on academic grounds who may teach, what may be taught, how it shall be taught, and who may be admitted to study."[37] They continue, "Nowadays it is almost axiomatic that a university should be more diverse in its membership than is the community in which it exists. This diversity itself contributes to the discovery of truth, for truth is hammered out in discussion, in the clash of ideas. . . . There is a salutary discipline in teaching a group whose members are capable of scrutinizing facts from different angles because of their different backgrounds."[38]

Carrying forward the Mills' arguments, they note how important it was that Oxford and Cambridge opened themselves to non-Anglican

Christians, Catholics, and Jews.[39] Such diversity, they write, benefited the entire student body, Anglican and nonconformist, white and non-white alike: "When young men and young women enter an open university in a multiracial society, it may be expected that during their university careers they will have the opportunity not only of equipping themselves professionally, but also of preparing themselves to be useful members of a multiracial society. Understanding, tolerance, sympathy, a capacity for seeing the other man's point of view—all these are different ways of expressing the same fundamental fact."[40]

Most importantly, the authors identify the fundamental part that diversity in its own right takes in the process of learning:

There is no substitute for the clash of mind between colleague and colleague, between teacher and student, between student and student. It is here that is found, in its most intense form, the stimulus of the new, the exciting and the different. It is here that the half-formed idea may take shape, the groundless belief be shattered, the developing theory be tested by the criticisms of one's fellows. It is here that controversy develops, and out of controversy, deeper understanding. For challenge is as essential to knowledge as to life. This is why discussion may be most fruitful when it begins with disagreement, and when it is conducted between persons from different environments, holding different beliefs, and approaching problems from different standpoints. For knowledge is not advanced through conformity: without the continuous need to defend his convictions from the attacks of the unconvinced, the sceptic, or even the heretic, the individual has little protection against the dangers that his own prejudices may bring into his own thinking.[41]

Finally, the authors consider whether South Africa can protect academic freedom by creating separate but equal universities for white and non-white students. To answer this question, they turn to the experience of the United States, citing *McLaurin v. Oklahoma State Regents*, a companion case to *Sweatt v. Painter* and *Sipuel v. Oklahoma*, to argue that separate universities are inherently unequal.[42] Centlivres surely discussed all three cases with his friend Erwin Griswold, who had written an amicus brief in *Sweatt* and testified as an expert witness in *Sipuel*, arguing both times that a legal education that failed to give its students opportunities to learn from peers "from varying backgrounds and different elements in society" was no education at all.[43]

The Centlivres book did not persuade the National Party to abandon its plan to impose apartheid at UCT and Wits. Although the 1957 University Education Bill failed for a combination of political and procedural reasons, the National Party reached its objective in 1959 with the Extension of University Education Act, which made it "a criminal offence for a non-white student to register at a hitherto open university without the written consent of the Minister of Internal Affairs."[44] In response, on March 13, 1959, Centlivres gave an address at UCT on university apartheid during what he described as a "protest meeting."[45] Quoting Davie's 1950 speech at the graduation ceremony at Witwatersrand, Centlivres drew a direct line between academic freedom and racial diversity: "'in a university this means our freedom from external interference in (a) who shall teach, (b) what we teach, (c) how we teach, and (d) whom we teach.' What the last implies is that 'our lecture theatres and laboratories shall be open to all who, seeking higher knowledge, can show that they are intellectually capable of benefiting by admission to our teaching and are morally worthy of entry into the close intimacy of great brotherhood which constitutes the wholeness of a university.' "[46]

Centlivres's speech was printed and distributed globally, with copies going to Justice Frankfurter, President Nathan Pusey at Harvard, and members of the Harvard Law faculty.[47] Eleven days later, Frankfurter wrote to Centlivres, "It does not require a poet's imagination to realize with what a heavy heart, even [if] an easy conscience, you find yourself in the contest in which you are engaged for a cause that has brought down upon you the full force of your government. You must let me tell you the pride, bordering almost on reverence, with which I salute your championship of the cause of free men everywhere."[48]

Pusey also wrote to Centlivres, thanking him for the copy of his "remarkable address on 'university apartheid' . . . a splendid and courageous statement on an issue which has to be fought out again and again if universities are to mean what their name implies."[49] The following day, nineteen members of the Harvard Law faculty sent their own letter, expressing their "admiration and respect for the steadfast effort you are making to preserve the tradition of a free and open university."[50] Many of the signers had met Centlivres in 1955, when he visited Harvard to attend the Chief Justice John Marshall bicentennial symposium on the rule of law.

Erwin Griswold was traveling in Australia and unable to sign the faculty letter, but he wrote Centlivres separately to endorse its contents and express his admiration for the chancellor's courage. In a letter to Justice Frankfurter discussing the Centlivres publication and the Harvard faculty letter, Griswold said he believed the letter had been drafted by the law professor Paul Freund.[51] Two years later, Freund was offered the position of solicitor general by President Kennedy.[52] He declined and suggested that Kennedy appoint Archibald Cox, which he did.[53] Cox, who had signed the faculty letter supporting Centlivres's anti-apartheid work, famously emphasized civil rights in selecting the cases he would argue personally.[54]

Even after the fight to keep the South African universities integrated was lost in 1959, Centlivres continued to argue for diversity as an element of academic freedom.[55] On May 6, 1959, he delivered the first annual T. B. Davie Memorial Lecture on Academic Freedom.[56] Again invoking Davie's resistance to apartheid and his four principles of academic freedom, he added that the university's function in a multiracial society is "to reflect in the composition of its student body the multiracial picture of the society it serves."[57]

Centlivres continued to draw direct comparisons between South Africa and the United States. In June 1961 he published an article entitled "We Fight for Our Rights" in which he drew a comparison between "the wave of McCarthyism which swept over the United States of America a few years ago" and South Africa's challenges to university autonomy.[58] Once again tracing the history of university autonomy back to Cambridge and Oxford, where men of different religions were allowed to study beginning in the mid-1800s, he wrote: "The universities of the Western World, having been freed from the control of the Church, resisted every attempt by the State to substitute its control for that of the Church."[59] In discussing the importance of academic freedom, Centlivres quoted Griswold, "the learned and greatly respected dean of the Harvard Law School," who had said in a speech in New York that "from South Africa . . . comes one of the most balanced and thoughtful statements on the need for an atmosphere of freedom in a university" before quoting a passage from *The Open Universities in South Africa*.[60]

In 1966, the University of Cape Town invited Senator Robert F. Kennedy to South Africa to deliver an address at UCT's "Day of Reaffirmation of Academic and Human Freedom."[61] He was hosted in Cape Town by Margaret Marshall, vice president of the National Union of South African Students, who would subsequently emigrate to the United

States to escape political persecution for her anti-apartheid activism.[62] Marshall would serve as general counsel to Harvard from 1992 to 1996 and then as chief justice of Massachusetts.[63] In 1984 she married the *New York Times* journalist Anthony Lewis, a friend of Archibald Cox's who played a role in bringing insights from the South African anti-apartheid fight to the United States.[64]

At UCT, Kennedy spoke about the need to work for freedom for all people, in the United States, South Africa, and across the globe. The address became known as the "Ripple of Hope" speech, and it is regarded by many as Kennedy's greatest.[65] In the most famous passage, he asserted:

It is from numberless diverse acts of courage such as these that the belief that human history is thus shaped. Each time a man stands up for an ideal, or acts to improve the lot of others, or strikes out against injustice, he sends forth a tiny ripple of hope, and crossing each other from a million different centers of energy and daring those ripples build a current which can sweep down the mightiest walls of oppression and resistance.[66]

Kennedy also highlighted the courage of Chancellor Centlivres, who attended the event.[67] He would pass away three months later.[68] The following year, Erwin Griswold would give the Day of Affirmation speech, honoring Centlivres as a "great South African whose friendship I was proud to hold":

In the course of my life I have been privileged to know many great legal figures, but there has been none who stands higher in my regard than Chief Justice Centlivres. He was a true South African, a great lawyer, a fine gentleman, whose work here, in and out of the law, will provide a long monument.[69]

The argument that universities should be permitted to take race into account in the quest for a racially diverse student body—and that this is a right protected by academic freedom—would not win favor in South Africa until the fall of apartheid in the 1990s. But it would make its way into American law, becoming central to the way courts interpreted academic freedom and laying the groundwork for a series of Supreme Court opinions that would place Harvard's diversity admissions plan at the center of the growing legal debate.

CHAPTER NINE

The Four Foundations of
Academic Freedom

A s A YOUNG PROTÉGÉ of Oliver Wendell Holmes, Felix Frankfurter helped persuade his mentor to adopt the Mills' view of the importance of experiential diversity in promoting democracy. Forty years later, as an Associate Justice of the Supreme Court, Frankfurter would contribute to this insight and serve as a connection point between the South African book on open universities, diversity, and the American meaning of academic freedom under the First Amendment. His protégé Archibald Cox would use Frankfurter's views and the South African argument on diversity and academic freedom to draft the Harvard Plan, which defined the ways in which diversity would thereafter be understood. Just as Holmes's life spanned meetings with both John Quincy Adams and John F. Kennedy, Frankfurter's connections with Holmes and Cox would connect the early twentieth-century view of the First Amendment to the twenty-first-century application of diversity.

Frankfurter was born in Austria and immigrated to the United States with his family at the age of 11. He attended New York City public schools, including the City College of New York when it was regarded as one of the top colleges in the country, and then Harvard Law School, where he graduated first in his class.[1] It is often said, though impossible to verify, that he graduated with the second-highest grade point average in the school's history, the highest having been earned a generation earlier by Louis Brandeis, who would become Frankfurter's mentor, friend, and supporter.[2] Upon graduating in 1905, Frankfurter entered into the first of several professional relationships that would put him at the center of American law and politics, through close associations not only with Holmes and Brandeis, but with Franklin Roosevelt, Henry L. Stimson, and two of his former students, Erwin Griswold and Archibald Cox.[3]

Stimson served as secretary of war under the Republican William Howard Taft (from 1911 to 1913) and the Democrats Franklin D. Roosevelt and Harry S. Truman (from 1940 to 1945, throughout the United States' participation in World War II). In between, he was Herbert Hoover's secretary of state from 1929 to 1933.[4] In today's hyper-partisan era, such a career is hard to imagine. Frankfurter went to work for him in 1905, when Stimson was the U.S. attorney for the Southern District of New York under Theodore Roosevelt, charged with overseeing Wall Street and bringing antitrust cases during the trust-busting years of the Progressive Era. Frankfurter, an assistant U.S. attorney working on antitrust cases, then followed Stimson to the War Department during the run up to World War I. While in New York he began a lifelong friendship with Learned Hand, then just beginning a distinguished career as a federal judge.

In 1914, at Brandeis's urging, Frankfurter was offered a professorship at Harvard Law School.[5] He was thirty-two years old. He would teach at Harvard for the next twenty-five years. The two men remained close throughout Frankfurter's tenure at Harvard, and after Brandeis was appointed to the Supreme Court in 1916, he paid Frankfurter a regular stipend in exchange for conducting research.[6] Frankfurter was thus close with the Court's two leading voices for a Mills-inspired view of free speech under the First Amendment. Holmes's service on the Court ended in 1932.[7] In 1939 Frankfurter was himself appointed to the Court, succeeding Benjamin Cardozo and joining his friend and mentor Brandeis for just two weeks before Brandeis stepped down because of ill health.[8] Frankfurter would serve for twenty-two years.

While at Harvard, Frankfurter was often involved in central issues of public policy. In the War Department he served as Judge Advocate General, deciding issues of military justice, until 1917, when President Wilson appointed him to the President's Mediation Committee. In that role he investigated labor disputes, becoming sympathetic toward labor unions and progressive/radical groups protesting unfair or unsafe working conditions. In 1920, having returned to Harvard, he helped found the American Civil Liberties Union and participated in legal cases on behalf of non-citizens being deported for having left-wing political views, earning himself the enmity of the FBI's founding director, J. Edgar Hoover.[9]

Nor was Frankfurter's involvement with the ACLU without controversy at Harvard. Some conservative alumni and members of the Harvard board fought to push him out of the school because of his advocacy for labor.[10] Brandeis at one point told Frankfurter that Harvard was "really gunning for" him, because he was a "dangerous man."[11] He persuaded Holmes to write to Harvard's president, A. Lawrence Lowell, in Frankfurter's defense.[12] The intervention worked to protect Frankfurter but not his friends. In 1921, Zechariah Chafee was called before the Harvard board of overseers and forced to defend his writings in support of Holmes's dissent in *Abrams v. United States*, where Holmes adopted a Mills-influenced view of the First Amendment.[13]

To the surprise of many, President Lowell acted as Chafee's defense counsel.[14] Lowell, Chafee, and Frankfurter had little in common; Lowell was a notorious anti-Semite and had sparred with Frankfurter—who was Jewish—over Lowell's campaign to impose a Jewish quota on admissions. Yet Lowell defended Chafee, seen as Frankfurter's alter ego, because he felt that the board had no right to interfere in faculty affairs and academic freedom.[15] Ultimately, a panel of state and federal judges convened by the Harvard board decided by a single vote to retain Chafee.[16] Though it was Chafee on trial, many believed that Frankfurter was the real target. *The Nation*, while praising the result, noted that the "real scheme" had been to drive Frankfurter from Harvard.[17]

Harold Laski was not as fortunate. He too was attacked by Frankfurter's opponents, with greater success. Lowell informed him that he would not be fired, but he would never be promoted from his position as an instructor. He returned home to England, took a professorship in law at the London School of Economics, and later led the Labour Party and educated a generation of Labour MPs.[18]

In 1927, Frankfurter again put himself in the center of controversy by writing an article for the *Atlantic Monthly*—later published as a book—attacking the convictions of the Italian immigrants and suspected anarchists Nicola Sacco and Bartolomeo Vanzetti on charges of bank robbery and murder.[19] Frankfurter argued that a careful review of the trial revealed that the two were framed. He demonstrated that the facts could not have been as the prosecution claimed and that the judge had prejudged the case and made several bigoted remarks about the defendants. Their convictions were widely condemned worldwide, persuading the governor of Massachusetts to appoint a three-man commission, led by President Lowell of Harvard, to conduct a pre-execution review of the case.[20] Frankfurter, perhaps because Lowell had stood up for him when alumni called for his firing, assured others that Lowell would be fair.[21] But in a decision that remains controversial to this day, the committee found the trial fair and the judge unbiased.[22] Frankfurter felt (and Laski agreed) that Lowell had allowed class loyalty to outweigh logic and justice.[23] The executions were carried out in August 1927.[24]

Reflecting on the decision in a letter to Roscoe Pound, dean of Harvard Law School, Frankfurter wrote: "To have seven years of systematic perversion of the machinery of justice validated by the authority of the President of Harvard University, when in fact he himself unwittingly is part and parcel of the social forces which help to explain the conviction and forthcoming execution of two innocent men, does too far-reaching violence to my notions of law and justice to enable me to rid myself of a sense of personal responsibility for such a wrong."[25] Years later, Frankfurter described Lowell as unable to cast off the yoke of his class affiliation: "He was incapable of doing what men have done, namely, say their crowd was wrong. You have to transcend the warm feeling of familiarity and reject that warm feeling in a spontaneous loyalty that transcends to greater loyalties, abstract virtues, truth and justice."[26] These remarks bring to mind John Stuart Mill's address to the students at St. Andrews University, when he warned them against too strong an identification with their social class and urged them to seek diversity among those they consulted in forming opinions.[27]

With the election of Franklin D. Roosevelt in 1932, Frankfurter became a close advisor to the president. His expertise in administrative law helped Roosevelt move his New Deal agenda through legal challenges (though not without considerable roadblocks), and many individuals from his long list of former students and protégés received key administration appointments.[28] When Justice Cardozo died in the summer of 1938, the president nominated Frankfurter to the Court.[29] The appointment was controversial: opponents saw Frankfurter as too close to the president, too liberal, and not American enough (a euphemism for Jewish).[30] But he was confirmed and took his seat in January 1939.[31]

Although he was politically liberal, on the Supreme Court Frankfurter was a leading advocate of judicial restraint.[32] His many years working in the executive branch gave him faith in executive power and left him skeptical about the power or wisdom of the federal judiciary to interfere with legislative or executive authority.[33]

Still, Justice Frankfurter was more than willing to use the law's muscle to support academic freedom, which he told Chief Justice Earl Warren was his "chief concern" when serving on the Harvard Law faculty.[34] As a young law professor, he had helped convince Oliver Wendell Holmes to embrace free speech and experiential diversity as essential for a democratic society. His experience coming under fire from Harvard alumni had taught him the particular importance of protecting free expression in a university setting.[35] And his teaching style, which he brought with him to the bench, included confronting discussants with diverse ideas to challenge the logic of their assertions.[36]

That teaching style had been shaped in large part by his friend John Dewey, the country's leading proponent of education reform. Dewey had been educated at Johns Hopkins University, the first university in the United States to adopt the Humboldt method. It had done so in part on the advice of Charles Eliot, who recommended Daniel Coit Gilman to the founding board as Johns Hopkins's first president. Like Eliot, Gilman had visited the German universities as they were adopting Humboldt's reforms and returned to the United States as a convert.[37]

Under Gilman's influence, Dewey became a leader in progressive education, firmly committed to diversity and experiential learning.[38] In 1899, as one of the first professors at the University of Chicago, he published *The School and Society*, which argued that students learn best when exposed to "a number of different personalities" and that education requires the "diverse thoughts and deeds of many persons."[39] Dewey's strong advocacy for civil rights included racial diversity, because, he wrote, "the intermingling in the school of youth of different races, differing religions, and unlike customs creates for all a new and broader environment."[40] A broader environment makes possible a new point of view: "Experience has to be formulated in order to be communicated. To formulate it requires getting outside of it, seeing it as another would see it."[41] He understood racial integration as both a question of justice for Black Americans and an important tool for improving learning for all students, white and Black alike, as well as for educating them about democracy.[42] Dewey's commitment to the Humboldt model of education, to civil rights for Black Americans, and to the importance of diversity is inseparable from his close friend Felix Frankfurter's critical role in defining academic freedom. In 1926, Dewey would take over from Charles Eliot the role of honorary president of the Progressive Education Network.[43]

In 1920, Dewey and Frankfurter collaborated to help found what would become the ACLU.[44] Frankfurter later served on the committee that planned Dewey's seventieth birthday celebration.[45] Both he and Holmes—who had read and admired Dewey's *German Philosophy and Politics*, which discusses Humboldt's influence on education and the founding of the University of Berlin—contributed remarks to be read at the party.[46] Frankfurter would later demonstrate his commitment to racial diversity by becoming the first Supreme Court justice to hire a Black law clerk, William Coleman, in 1948.[47]

Frankfurter's interest in diversity and its link to non-discrimination grew with his connection to Albert van der Sandt Centlivres. The two began corresponding in 1952, when Centlivres wrote to Frankfurter to thank him for having asked Erwin Griswold to send Centlivres a copy of an important U.S. Supreme Court decision (the *Youngstown Steel* case, which had overturned President Truman's seizure of the steel industry during a labor strike).[48] Later that year, Griswold wrote to Frankfurter that, at Frankfurter's suggestion, he had sent Centlivres a copy of Holmes's *The Path of the Law*. The letter suggests that the three men were discussing an essay or judicial opinion by Centlivres, for which Frankfurter was making editorial suggestions.[49] The correspondence continued in 1953, the year Griswold met with T. B. Davie, the principal of the University of Cape Town and an apartheid opponent, with Frankfurter asking Centlivres to meet with an American journalist visiting South Africa and noting that "the problems of South Africa are receiving a great deal of attention in this country."[50]

Frankfurter finally met Centlivres in person in 1955, when Centlivres traveled to the United States to participate in the Chief Justice John Marshall bicentennial symposium on the rule of law, which included among its sixteen papers contributions by Frankfurter, Griswold, and Centlivres.[51]

When *The Open Universities in South Africa* was published in February 1957, Centlivres sent a copy to Frankfurter, who was by that point a friend.[52] Frankfurter received the book as he was preparing for the March 5, 1957, oral argument in *Sweezy v. New Hampshire*, a case concerned with academic freedom in the United States.[53] Given his experiences with repression of his own speech and that of his close friends, Frankfurter was acutely sensitive to questions of academic freedom. He viewed teachers and professors as the "priests of our democracy" and wanted to protect them as Lowell had done.[54] The *Sweezy* case gave him an opportunity to expand that umbrella of protection.

Six years earlier, in 1951, at the height of Senator Joseph McCarthy's campaign against suspected communists, the state of New Hampshire had passed a law authorizing the state attorney general to investigate "subversive persons."[55] Paul Sweezy, a writer, magazine editor, and socialist who had given an invited lecture at the University of New Hampshire, was called before the state attorney general and asked about himself, his friends, his colleagues, his association with the Progressive Party and with its 1948 presidential candidate, Henry Wallace, and the lecture Sweezy had given at the university.[56] Sweezy freely answered questions about himself, but he refused to "name names"—to testify about the political views or memberships of others—or to discuss his university lecture. The First Amendment, he argued, gave him the right to refuse to answer these questions.[57]

"If the very first principle of the American constitutional form of government is political freedom," Sweezy argued to New Hampshire's attorney general, "which I take to include freedoms of speech, press, assembly, and association—then I do not see how it can be denied that these investigations are a grave danger to all that Americans have always claimed to cherish. No rights are genuine if a person, for exercising them, can be hauled up before some tribunal and forced under penalties of perjury and contempt to account for his ideas and conduct."[58]

Sweezy's argument fell on deaf ears. He was cited for contempt, tried, convicted, and sentenced to jail until he agreed to answer the attorney general's questions. The New Hampshire Supreme Court had affirmed his conviction, and now his case was before the United States Supreme Court.[59] He was represented by Thomas Emerson, a law professor at Yale, who had joined Griswold on the Committee of Law Teachers' amicus brief in the *Sweatt v. Painter* case, arguing that the importance of diversity to learning made university segregation a deprivation of equality.[60]

On June 17, 1957, the decision was announced.[61] A plurality opinion (fewer than five, but more than the dissenters) by Chief Justice Earl Warren, joined by Justices Hugo Black, William O. Douglas, and William J. Brennan, concluded that "there unquestionably was an invasion of petitioner's liberties in the areas of academic freedom and political expression—areas in which government should be extremely reticent to tread."[62] But rather than decide the case on those grounds, the plurality chose a narrower path, reversing Sweezy's conviction because the New Hampshire legislature had delegated authority to the attorney general too broadly.[63] It was a victory for Paul Sweezy, but not for free speech or academic freedom.[64]

Frankfurter, in a concurring opinion, abandoned his usual view that the Court should favor narrow rulings over broad ones. He began with a detailed description of the inquiry to which Sweezy was subjected:

> Among the matters about which petitioner was questioned were: details of his career and personal life, whether he was then or ever had been a member of the Communist Party, whether he had ever attended its meetings, whether he had ever attended meetings that he knew were also attended by Party members, whether he knew any Communists in or out of the State, whether he knew named persons with alleged connections with organizations either on the United States Attorney General's list or cited by the Un-American Activities Committee of the United States House of Representatives or had ever attended meetings with them, whether he had ever taught or supported the overthrow of the State by force or violence or had ever known or assisted any persons or groups that had done so, whether he had ever been connected with organizations on the Attorney General's list, whether he had supported or written in behalf of a variety of allegedly subversive, named causes, conferences, periodicals, petitions, and attempts to raise funds for the legal defense of certain persons, whether he knew about the Progressive Party, what positions he had held in it, whether he had been a candidate for Presidential Elector for that Party, whether certain persons were in that Party, whether Communists had influenced or been members of the Progressive Party, whether he had sponsored activities in behalf of the candidacy of Henry A. Wallace, whether he advocated replacing the capitalist system with another economic system, whether his conception of socialism involved force and violence, whether, by his writings and actions, he had ever attempted to advance the Soviet Union's "propaganda line," whether he had ever attended meetings of the Liberal Club at the University of New Hampshire, whether the magazine of which he was co-editor was "a Communist-line publication," and whether he knew named persons.

Petitioner answered most of these questions, making it very plain that he had never been a Communist, never taught violent overthrow of the Government, never knowingly associated with Communists in the State, but was a socialist believer in peaceful change who had at one time belonged to certain organizations on the list of the United States Attorney General (which did not include the Progressive Party) or cited by the House Un-American Activities Committee. He declined to answer as irrelevant or violative of free speech guarantees certain questions about the Progressive Party and whether he knew particular persons. He stated repeatedly, however, that he had no knowledge of Communists or of Communist influence in the Progressive Party, and he testified that he had been a candidate for that Party, signing the required loyalty oath, and that he did not know whether an alleged Communist leader was active in the Progressive Party.[65]

It is not hard to imagine Frankfurter remembering his own experience of alumni trying to have him dismissed from his Harvard professorship because of his "radical" views and his religion.[66] At another time or place he might easily have found himself convicted, like Sweezy, because of his views and outsider status. In standing up for Sweezy he was standing up for diversity of the sort he had helped bring to Harvard, to Washington, and to the Supreme Court.

Turning to the importance of protecting academic freedom more generally, Frankfurter quoted extensively from *The Open Universities in South Africa*:

In a university, knowledge is its own end, not merely a means to an end. A university ceases to be true to its own nature if it becomes the tool of Church or State or any sectional interest. A university is characterized by the spirit of free inquiry, its ideal being the ideal of Socrates—"to follow the argument where it leads." This implies the right to examine, question, modify or reject traditional ideas and beliefs. Dogma and hypothesis are incompatible, and the concept of an immutable doctrine is repugnant to the spirit of a university. The concern of its scholars is not merely to add and revise facts in relation to an accepted framework, but to be ever examining and modifying the framework itself.

Freedom to reason and freedom for disputation on the basis of observation and experiment are the necessary conditions for the advancement of scientific knowledge. A sense of freedom is also necessary for creative work in the arts which, equally with scientific research, is the concern of the university. . . .

. . . It is the business of a university to provide that atmosphere which is most conducive to speculation, experiment and creation. It is an atmosphere in which there prevail "the four essential freedoms" of a university—to determine for itself on academic grounds who may teach, what may be taught, how it shall be taught, and who may be admitted to study.[67]

Frankfurter concluded that the New Hampshire inquiry and contempt conviction had violated Sweezy's First Amendment rights to freedom of speech and association. In the process, he brought T. B. Davie's four essential elements of academic freedom within the protection of the First Amendment.[68] When the opinion was published, Frankfurter immediately sent a copy to Chief Justice Centlivres.[69] Centlivres responded by sending Frankfurter a clipping from the *Cape Times:* the opinion and its link to the anti-apartheid movement had been covered in the South African press.[70]

A decade after *Sweezy,* and two years after Frankfurter's death in 1965, the Supreme Court relied on his concurrence in deciding another academic freedom case. In *Keyishian v. New York Board of Regents* (1967), the Supreme Court held by a 5–4 vote that Harry Keyishian and other faculty members from the University of Buffalo, which had been merged into the State University of New York, were improperly dismissed for refusing to sign a "loyalty oath" affirming that they were not, and had never been, members of the Communist Party.[71] In ruling against the regents, Justice Brennan explained:

Our Nation is deeply committed to safeguarding academic freedom, which is of transcendent value to all of us, and not merely to the teachers concerned. That freedom is therefore a special concern of the First Amendment, which does not tolerate laws that cast a pall of orthodoxy over the classroom. . . . The classroom is peculiarly the "marketplace of ideas." The Nation's future depends upon leaders trained through wide exposure to that robust exchange of ideas which discovers truth "out of a multitude of tongues, [rather] than through any kind of authoritative selection." *United States v. Associated Press*. In *Sweezy v. New Hampshire*, we said: "The essentiality of freedom in the community of American universities is almost self-evident. . . . Teachers and students must always remain free to inquire, to study and to evaluate, to gain new maturity and understanding; otherwise our civilization will stagnate and die."[72]

Sweezy and *Keyishian* affirmed that academic freedom allows colleges and universities to make room for diverse outsider voices and unpopular opinions, that doing so is an important part of an institution's autonomy, and that the state should not interfere in it without a compelling reason. As Justice Frankfurter put it—quoting Centlivres, Davie, and Feetham, channeling Humboldt and the Mills, following in the footsteps of Eliot and Holmes, Murray, Marshall and Griswold, and lighting the path forward for Cox: "It is the business of a university to provide that atmosphere which is most conducive to speculation, experiment and creation. It is an atmosphere in which there prevail 'the four essential freedoms' of a university—to determine for itself on academic grounds who may teach, what may be taught, how it shall be taught, and who may be admitted to study."[73]

The Diversity Principle Is Embraced but Then Rejected by Conservative Supreme Court Justices

The Legal Brief That Rewrote
Affirmative Action Law

B Y THE 1970S, THE idea of separate but equal schools for Black and white students had been fully discredited, thanks in part to arguments about the importance of diversity in the classroom. The principles of academic freedom articulated in apartheid South Africa, which Justice Frankfurter had relied on in his *Sweezy* decision, were well established in First Amendment law. But the task of knitting those two legal threads together—arguing that academic freedom gives universities the right to use race and ethnicity as factors in admissions in order to reap the benefits of diversity—fell to Frankfurter's protégé Archibald Cox.

It's hard to imagine a lawyer better suited to frame this position than Cox. He almost seemed born to teach and practice law: his father and grandfather were both prominent lawyers, and his wife's grandfather was James Barr Ames, once the dean of Harvard Law.[1] Following in his father's footsteps, Cox studied at Harvard College and then Harvard Law School, graduating in 1937, where he was among the last students Felix Frankfurter would teach before joining the Supreme Court in 1939. Frankfurter was so impressed with Cox that he arranged for him to clerk with his old friend Learned Hand, by then a notable public figure and a distinguished judge on the powerful Second Circuit Court of Appeals.[2]

After his clerkship and a brief stint in private practice, Cox joined the legal staff of the solicitor general's office, then served as assistant solicitor of labor during World War II. When the war ended, he returned briefly to private practice and then, in 1945, joined the faculty of Harvard Law School.[3] He thus had an inside view of the postwar faculty debate over admissions policy, as he and his colleagues tried to decide how much to rely on grades and test scores and how much to consider other factors.

At Harvard, Cox continued to pursue his interest in labor law. To the delight of Dean Griswold, he was a prolific scholar and an inspiring teacher. His scholarship had a consequential effect in shaping U.S. Supreme Court decisions at a time when labor law cases were an important part of the Court's docket. Through the 1950s, he worked closely with Senator John F. Kennedy to reform the country's existing labor laws, which had largely been passed during the New Deal, and he earned a reputation as a skilled presenter to Congressional committees.[4]

When Kennedy ran for president, Cox helped him gather a "brain trust" of academics, many of them from Harvard, to advise him on policy.[5] After the election, Kennedy named Cox solicitor general.[6] He thus became the first of three consecutive solicitors general to figure prominently in the history of diversity; he would be succeeded by Thurgood Marshall, who was in turn succeeded by Erwin Griswold. Griswold would be succeeded as dean of Harvard Law by Derek Bok, a Cox protégé, who would go on to serve two stints as president of Harvard. Bok was one of the leading scholars and activists supporting the diversity justification for race-conscious admissions.[7]

As solicitor general, Cox chose cases to argue with an eye toward advancing civil rights for Black Americans, while trying to argue narrowly—as Frankfurter had taught him—so as to bring as many justices as he could along with him. He slowly moved the Court to broaden its view of equal protection by opening the door to challenges to segregation in private businesses and in housing. He helped persuade the Court to embrace federal control over the drawing of electoral districts, leading to the novel "one person one vote" standard of apportionment, and to confirm the constitutionality of the 1964 Civil Rights Act and the 1965 Voting Rights Act.[8] When he stepped down in 1965, he was widely regarded as one of the greatest solicitors general and Supreme Court advocates in U.S. history—a reputation that remains.

After stepping down, Cox returned to Harvard, teaching constitutional law, labor law, and labor arbitration, and accepting invitations to argue important cases before the Supreme Court, often on a pro bono basis. He might have happily remained in Cambridge, but history was not done with him. In 1973, Attorney General Elliot Richardson persuaded Cox to return to Washington as a special prosecutor charged with investigating the burglary and attempted wiretapping of the Democratic National Committee offices in the Watergate hotel and apartment complex.[9]

Within a few months, Cox had uncovered a far-reaching scandal. President Nixon was suspected of ordering the DNC burglary during his 1972 re-election campaign and then attempting to cover it up, of taking millions of dollars in illegal campaign contributions, of ordering policy changes as a quid pro quo for some of those illegal contributions, of lying on his taxes, and of compiling a list of enemies whom he subjected to illegal harassment.[10] Congress conducted a parallel investigation, but it was ultimately Cox's calm, reasoned defense of the rule of law that persuaded the American public of President Nixon's involvement in the Watergate burglary cover-up.

Once it was revealed that President Nixon had taped his Oval Office conversations, including those in which he and his aides discussed the burglary, Cox insisted, with judicial support, that the tapes be provided to the Watergate grand jury.[11] On October 20, 1973, when it became apparent that Cox would not stand down, Nixon ordered Attorney General Elliot Richardson to fire him. Richardson refused and resigned instead. Nixon then ordered Richardson's principal deputy and acting attorney general, William Ruckelshaus, to fire Cox. Ruckelshaus, too, refused the order and resigned. Finally, Nixon turned to the Justice Department's third-in-command, Solicitor General Robert Bork, who carried out the president's order—an act that may have contributed to his rejection by the Senate, fourteen years later, when President Ronald Reagan nominated him to the Supreme Court.[12] The chain of resignations, culminating in Cox's firing, ignited a firestorm of public protest and came to be known as the Saturday Night Massacre.[13] Within a year the Supreme Court would order Nixon to release the tapes, and he would resign under threat of impeachment.[14]

Cox again returned to Cambridge, where his old friend and former student Derek Bok, by then the president of Harvard, asked him to use his suddenly free time to draft an amicus brief in a case pending in the Supreme Court.[15] The case was *DeFunis v. Odegaard*, a challenge to the University of Washington Law School's use of race in admissions.[16] Cox became the brief's principal author.

Like Allan Bakke, whose case would reach the Court four years later, Marco DeFunis was a white applicant to a public university professional school who believed he had been rejected in favor of a less qualified non-white candidate because of affirmative action. After he won in the trial court, DeFunis was allowed to begin law school while waiting for the appellate courts to act.[17] The Supreme Court had taken the case to decide whether the University of Washington had violated DeFunis's right to equal protection; did the law school's affirmative action program discriminate against him based on his race?

Cox brought in three young Harvard legal staffers as co-authors on the brief. Daniel Steiner, age 29, was in his third year as Harvard's general counsel; he would look back at his work on the Harvard diversity model as one of the highlights of his career.[18] James Sharaf, then in his mid-thirties, was assistant general counsel. James Bierman, age 28, was an assistant dean of the law school and associate director of admissions and financial aid.

According to Bierman, by 2024 the sole living co-author, Cox met regularly with the three of them, as well as with several Harvard professors and administrators, to discuss the workings and evolution of the Harvard College admissions process.[19] Many of those Cox consulted were among his closest friends. They included Derek Bok as well as Walter Leonard, Bok's special assistant, who had served as the assistant director of admissions at the school of law from 1969 to 1971, designed the law school's affirmative action admissions program, and worked with Bok on developing the university's affirmative action hiring program.[20] The former Harvard Law School dean Albert Sacks and the law professor and constitutional law scholar Paul Freund also took part, as did Anthony Lewis, a *New York Times* columnist and close friend of Cox's who was visiting at Harvard Law School as a lecturer.[21]

Bierman doesn't recall Fred Glimp personally participating in these discussions, at least those held at the law school. But whether Glimp was in the room or not, his story certainly was. The brief's famous line—"A farm boy from Idaho can bring something to Harvard College that a Bostonian cannot offer. Similarly, a black student can usually bring something that a white person cannot offer"—probably refers both to Glimp, the farm boy from Idaho who was admitted to Harvard College on a scholarship and rose to become its dean, and to Cox's son-in-law, Robert Hart, another Idaho farm boy who had degrees from Harvard.[22]

The other thirty-one amicus briefs filed in the case focused on whether discrimination in favor of minorities should be treated differently from discrimination against majorities. This was the central point of Dr. King's *Letter from Birmingham Jail*, justifying civil disobedience against segregation laws.[23] The University of Washington and its many amici supporters—including over fifty law school deans and a slate of civil rights organizations led by the Mexican American Legal Defense and Education Fund, the Puerto Rican Legal Defense and Education Fund, and the American Civil Liberties Union—all argued that the long history of discrimination against Black, Asian, and Hispanic Americans and the continuing disadvantages they faced justified "benign classification" to help them overcome these hurdles.[24] In a brief written principally by Erwin Griswold, who had just left his position as solicitor general, the Association of American Law Schools argued that the use of race in law school admissions was permissible because of the state's interest in opening access to the bar to minority groups—though as one might expect given Griswold's arguments in the *Sipuel* and *Sweatt v. Painter* cases, it also made a diversity argument in passing.[25] The Council on Legal Education Opportunity made a similar argument about minority underrepresentation in the bar and added that the use of race in admissions was necessary to prevent the number of Black and Hispanic students from being so small that they were racially isolated.[26] The American Bar Association (ABA) argued that the use of race was necessary to address the need for Black lawyers to serve Black communities.[27] The Law School Admission Council argued that the use of race was necessary to address the public need for more minority lawyers; it also contended that minority students with lower numerical qualifications were nonetheless well qualified for law school and that their grades and test scores often reflected historical discrimination.[28]

Each of these arguments has its merits, particularly given the historical circumstances. It was less than a decade since the 1964 Civil Rights Act had taken effect (the bill had given the South a one-year "grace period" to comply) and also less than a decade since President Johnson had made a plea for affirmative action in his graduation speech at Howard University:

> Freedom is not enough. You do not wipe away the scars of centuries by saying: Now you are free to go where you want, and do as you desire, and choose the leaders you please. You do not take a person who, for years, has been hobbled by chains and liberate him, bring him up to the starting line of a race and then say,

"you are free to compete with all the others," and still justly believe that you have been completely fair. Thus it is not enough
just to open the gates of opportunity. All our citizens must have
the ability to walk through those gates. This is the next and the
more profound stage of the battle for civil rights. We seek not
just freedom but opportunity. To this end equal opportunity is
essential, but not enough, not enough. Men and women of all
races are born with the same range of abilities. But ability is not
just the product of birth. Ability is stretched or stunted by the
family that you live with, and the neighborhood you live in—by
the school you go to and the poverty or the richness of your surroundings. It is the product of a hundred unseen forces playing
upon the little infant, the child, and finally the man.[29]

The argument of the many amici supporting the University of
Washington was that Black applicants had been held back—socially, eco-
nomically, academically—and to simply compare their grades and test
scores to those of white applicants was to perpetuate the discrimination
they had experienced. In 1974, selective colleges and universities were
just beginning to recognize the pervasiveness of this discrimination and
to design affirmative action programs to counter it, increasing the number of Black students, and soon after Asian American and Hispanic students, on their campuses.

But Cox and his co-authors took a different approach. Rather than
present affirmative action programs as a remedy for racial discrimination, their brief relied on the diversity principle: racial and ethnic diversity benefits the university and its students, and it is protected by the
principle of academic freedom under the First Amendment. Over many
lunches, with subsequent drafting and redrafting, Cox and his team
traced the history of Harvard's admissions practices as the university expanded its commitment to diversity, hoping to convince the Court that a
diversity justification for using race in admissions was both intellectually
powerful and legally permissible. Cox carefully reviewed the faculty debates, the final reports to the fellows of Harvard College by its admissions deans William Bender (in 1960) and Fred Glimp (in 1968), and the
existing law of equal protection (which Cox had helped create) and of academic freedom (to which his mentor Frankfurter had made essential
contributions). He almost certainly consulted *The Open Universities in
South Africa*, too, which was closely connected with Griswold and Frank-

furter; the latter had quoted its text extensively in his *Sweezy* opinion, which Cox cited in his brief. Channeling Humboldt, the Mills, Eliot, Murray, and the South African apartheid resisters, Cox and his co-authors urged the Court to conclude that as a matter of academic freedom, the University of Washington must have discretion to use race as a factor in deciding whom to admit, with the goal of creating a racially diverse student body.

I found the brief startling. It sets forth the diversity justification for using race in admissions in strikingly familiar language—familiar because the appendix to Justice Powell's majority opinion in *Bakke*, decided four years later, was simply lifted verbatim from the heart of Cox's brief. When Powell took this excerpt and made it an appendix to his opinion, he also elevated Cox's description of diversity-based admissions at Harvard into a blueprint for other selective colleges to follow. The race-conscious, holistic admissions system described in the brief became known as the Harvard Plan. The plan was not written by a Harvard faculty committee or by the Harvard admissions staff, but by a Harvard professor with the help of his three co-counsel.

Here is the 1,031-word excerpt from the brief in which Cox formulates the Harvard Plan. Between this and the *Bakke* appendix there is only one change: in the two places where Cox uses the phrase "25 years," the *Bakke* appendix substitutes "30 years."[30]

Excerpt from the Cox brief in the DeFunis case, as cut and pasted into the brief filed by Harvard, Columbia, Stanford, and Penn in the Bakke case as an appendix titled "Harvard College Admissions Program" and subsequently appended to Justice Powell's opinion in *Bakke*, leading to it being commonly called the "Harvard Plan."

For the past 30 years, Harvard College has received each year applications for admission that greatly exceed the number of places in the freshman class. The number of applicants who are deemed to be not "qualified" is comparatively small. The vast majority of applicants demonstrate through test scores, high school records and teachers' recommendations that they have the academic ability to

---

continued

do adequate work at Harvard, and perhaps to do it with distinction. Faced with the dilemma of choosing among a large number of "qualified" candidates, the Committee on Admissions could use the single criterion of scholarly excellence and attempt to determine who among the candidates were likely to perform best academically. But for the past 30 years, the Committee on Admissions has never adopted this approach. The belief has been that, if scholarly excellence were the sole or even predominant criterion, Harvard College would lose a great deal of its vitality and intellectual excellence, and that the quality of the educational experience offered to all students would suffer. Final Report of W. J. Bender, Chairman of the Admission and Scholarship Committee and Dean of Admissions and Financial Aid, pp. 20 *et seq.* (Cambridge, 1960). Consequently, after selecting those students whose intellectual potential will seem extraordinary to the faculty — perhaps 150 or so out of an entering class of over 1,100 — the Committee seeks — "variety in making its choices. This has seemed important . . . in part because it adds a critical ingredient to the effectiveness of the educational experience [in Harvard College]. . . . *The effectiveness of our students' educational experience has seemed to the Committee to be affected as importantly by a wide variety of interests, talents, backgrounds and career goals as it is by a fine faculty and our libraries, laboratories and housing arrangements.*" Dean of Admissions Fred L. Glimp, Final Report to the Faculty of Arts and Sciences, 65 Official Register of Harvard University No. 25, 93, 10105 (1968).

The belief that diversity adds an essential ingredient to the educational process has long been a tenet of Harvard College admissions. Fifteen or twenty years ago, however, diversity meant students from California, New York, and Massachusetts; city dwellers and farm boys; violinists, painters and football players; biologists, historians and classicists; potential stockbrokers, academics and politicians. The result was that very few ethnic or racial minorities attended Harvard College. In recent years, Harvard College has expanded the concept of diversity to include students from disadvantaged economic, racial and ethnic groups. Harvard College now recruits not only Californians or Louisianans, but also blacks and Chicanos and other minority students. Contemporary conditions in the United States mean that, if Harvard College is to continue to offer a first-rate education to its students, minority representation in the undergraduate body cannot be ignored by the Committee on Admissions.

In practice, this new definition of diversity has meant that race has been a factor in some admission decisions. When the Committee on Admissions reviews the large middle group of applicants who are "admissible" and deemed capable of doing good work in their courses, the race of an applicant may tip the balance in his favor just as geographic origin or a life spent on a farm may tip the balance in other candidates' cases. A farm boy from Idaho can bring something to Harvard College that a Bostonian cannot offer. Similarly, a black student can usually bring something that a white person cannot offer. The quality of the educational experience of all the students in Harvard College depends in part on these differences in the background and outlook that students bring with them.

In Harvard College admissions, the Committee has not set target quotas for the number of blacks, or of musicians, football players, physicists or Californians to be admitted in a given year. At the same time the Committee is aware that, if Harvard College is to provide a truly heterogeneous environment that reflects the rich diversity of the United States, it cannot be provided without some attention to numbers. It would not make sense, for example, to have 10 or 20 students out of 1,100 whose homes are west of the Mississippi. Comparably, 10 or 20 black students could not begin to bring to their classmates and to each other the variety of points of view, backgrounds and experiences of blacks in the United States. Their small numbers might also create a sense of isolation among the black students themselves, and thus make it more difficult for them to develop and achieve their potential. Consequently, when making its decisions, the Committee on Admissions is aware that there is some relationship between numbers and achieving the benefits to be derived from a diverse student body, and between

continued

numbers and providing a reasonable environment for those
students admitted. But that awareness does not mean that the
Committee sets a minimum number of blacks or of people from
west of the Mississippi who are to be admitted. It means only
that, in choosing among thousands of applicants who are not only
"admissible" academically but have other strong qualities, the
Committee, with a number of criteria in mind, pays some attention
to distribution among many types and categories of students.

The further refinements sometimes required help to illustrate the
kind of significance attached to race. The Admissions Committee,
with only a few places left to fill, might find itself forced to choose
between A, the child of a successful black physician in an academic
community with promise of superior academic performance, and B,
a black who grew up in an inner-city ghetto of semi-literate parents
whose academic achievement was lower, but who had demonstrated
energy and leadership, as well as an apparently abiding interest in
black power. If a good number of black students much like A, but
few like B, had already been admitted, the Committee might prefer
B, and vice versa. If C, a white student with extraordinary artistic
talent, were also seeking one of the remaining places, his unique
quality might give him an edge over both A and B. Thus, the critical criteria are often individual qualities or experience not dependent upon race but sometimes associated with it.

By the time the *DeFunis* case reached the Supreme Court, Marco
DeFunis was in his final year of law school. At oral argument, the lawyers
for the University of Washington were asked what would happen if the
Court ruled in their favor shortly before Mr. DeFunis was scheduled to
graduate. When they assured the justices that he would be allowed to
graduate whatever the ruling, the Court dismissed the case as moot.
Cox's brief might have fallen by the wayside, his arguments about race
and academic freedom irrelevant to a Court that had ruled on the legal
doctrine of standing rather than tackling the case on its merits.

But Justice Powell's files reveal that the Cox brief remained very
much on his mind.[31] Buried in his file on *DeFunis* is a memo from his law
clerk John C. Jeffries, Jr., now a distinguished professor at the University

of Virginia, suggesting he pay particular attention to the "brief by Archibald Cox for Harvard College." Powell had added a red check mark over Cox's name.[32] He had also been following the public debate about affirmative action, which had begun heating up as the *DeFunis* case was pending. Anthony Lewis devoted his *New York Times* column of March 3, 1974, to promoting the diversity principle, specifically quoting the Cox/ Harvard brief. Powell clipped the column and added it to his *DeFunis* file.[33] He did the same with a *Newsweek* article by Jerrold K. Footlick that also highlighted the diversity argument.[34]

Four years later, when the *Bakke* case arrived at the Court, Powell remembered the Cox brief.[35] His *Bakke* files include a memo dated August 29, 1977, to Powell from Bob Comfort, one of his law clerks, that extensively discusses the diversity rationale for race-conscious admissions, repeatedly cites as authority the "Brief for Harvard College in *DeFunis*," and specifically refers to the "Idaho farm boy" analogy.[36] The memo concludes by suggesting that the diversity argument offers "the best opportunity for taking a middle course."[37] Powell underlined that phrase and added in the margin, "This is the position that appeals to me. Use *DeFunis*."[38]

The Cox brief from *DeFunis* has received remarkably little attention, and Cox's role in drafting the Harvard Plan is rarely acknowledged. I believe the oversight can be attributed to two mysteries.

The first mystery is the amicus brief jointly filed by Harvard, Columbia, Stanford, and Penn in the *Bakke* case. That brief lifted the 1,031-word excerpt from Cox's *DeFunis* brief that we now call the Harvard Plan, but it did so without attribution. An appendix to the *Bakke* brief describes it simply as the "Harvard College Admission Program."[39] This is the document that Justice Powell appended to his opinion, and thus the four-university *Bakke* brief is generally described as the source of the Harvard Plan, though it was merely a cut-and-paste from the earlier brief. The two briefs share a co-author, the Harvard general counsel Daniel Steiner, who may have decided that no attribution was necessary. And Cox himself may have approved the unattributed cut-and-paste. By then he was Supreme Court counsel for the defendant University of California in the *Bakke* case. Cox and Steiner may have agreed that this would put the two arguments in front of the Court as alternatives, with Cox arguing for a racial justice justification on behalf of the University of California and Steiner arguing for a diversity justification on behalf of Harvard, Penn, Stanford, and Columbia. Even so, I find the lack of attribution mysterious.

Second, the brief is exceedingly hard to find. I learned of its existence from a footnote in a 1974 law review article about the *DeFunis* case by Richard Posner, the great conservative legal scholar from the University of Chicago (who, until his retirement from the bench in 2017, simultaneously served as a law professor and a judge on the United States Court of Appeals for the Seventh Circuit). Posner's article largely focused on rebutting the substantive equality arguments made by the University of Washington and its supporters: that affirmative action was a necessary remedy to our long history of discrimination against Black Americans. But he also argued that racial diversity does not justify race-conscious college admissions. Since this was written in 1974, prior to the brief by the four elite universities in the *Bakke* case, my first reaction was to ask, "Why would he bother to refute an argument that hadn't yet been made?" That is, who and what was Posner refuting? He wrote that "a frequently suggested basis for preferential treatment is the desire to increase the diversity of the student body in the hope of thereby enhancing the quality of the students' educational experience."[40] Despite the word "frequently," he cited only one source: the Harvard brief in the *DeFunis* case. I had never heard of this brief and decided I needed to read it. It turned out to be harder to find than I could have imagined.

My first step was to log on to Westlaw, the legal database that provides copies of every brief filed in the U.S. Supreme Court. It took only a minute to find the many briefs in the *DeFunis* case, and yes, there was a brief filed by Harvard University on behalf of its Center for Law and Education. I eagerly pulled it up and began reading. It was a good brief, but as I read it I became confused. Where was the discussion of diversity? Nowhere in this brief. I concluded there must have been two Harvard briefs, but a further search revealed that if there were two briefs, Westlaw had published only one of them.

This was peculiar. Why would Westlaw leave out one of the briefs? But I wasn't concerned. I logged on to LexisNexis, Westlaw's chief rival, confident I would find it there; I did not. Just like Westlaw, LexisNexis had the brief from the Harvard University Center for Law and Education, but nothing else from Harvard.

Fortunately, my office is just steps from one of the world's great law libraries. The Berkeley Law Library, I knew, held hard copies of every brief filed in the U.S. Supreme Court. It might be dusty, but it would be there. I phoned the library to ask if someone there could pull the briefs from the *DeFunis* case. The answer was stunning. The library had stopped collecting the hard-copy briefs and now relied exclusively on Westlaw and LexisNexis. If it wasn't online, it might as well not exist.

I was still sitting in my office in a state of shock when the phone rang a few minutes later. It was I-Wei Wang, one of our amazing librarians. Was I looking for the briefs in the *DeFunis* case? Yes. Well, it turned out that the legal historian Ann Fagan Ginger, on behalf of the Council on Legal Education Opportunity, thinking in 1974 that the case might be historically important, had published the record of the case, including the full set of briefs, as a three-volume set.[41] The briefs were delivered to my office ten minutes later. (I've since learned from Professor Ron Levin at Washington University that the brief is also included in *Landmark Briefs and Arguments of the Supreme Court of the United States,* edited by Philip Kurland and Gerhard Casper.)[42]

The full set confirmed what I suspected: there were two Harvard briefs. One was filed by the Harvard University Center for Law and Education and was available online. The other was filed on behalf of the president and fellows of Harvard College by Archibald Cox. Once I read it and realized that it was the source of the Harvard Plan, I searched for recognition of its role. I found a few references to Cox's having written a brief for Harvard, but nothing on its importance.[43] Why the brief is not included on Westlaw or Lexis is still a mystery, but the omission has surely been a factor in the lack of recognition Cox deserves for this work.

CHAPTER ELEVEN

Diversity and the *Bakke* Case

OUR YEARS AFTER THE dismissal of the *DeFunis* case, the diversity principle found its champion at the Supreme Court in the unlikely voice of Justice Lewis Powell and his lonely controlling opinion in *Regents of the University of California v. Bakke.*[1] Why lonely? Before Powell weighed in, the Court was split 4–4, with the liberals embracing affirmative action and conservatives looking to forbid it. No other justice would join the reasoning of Powell's opinion. Why controlling? By creating five votes on the two central issues presented, Powell's opinion determined the outcome of the case.[2] Why unlikely? Because, surprisingly, it came from a justice who was an opponent of racial integration and a critic of the universities that stood to benefit from the ruling.

As Marco DeFunis was preparing to graduate from the University of Washington, Allan Bakke was applying to the medical school at the University of California, Davis.[3] At thirty-four, Bakke was older than most applicants, which may have hurt his chances of admission.[4] But his scores on the Medical College Admission Test (MCAT) were above the 90th percentile in science, math, and verbal ability—better than the UC Davis average.[5] The first year he applied, he was rejected despite an interview in which he received a good assessment. The following year, he was rejected again, after the faculty admissions chair interviewed him and gave him a low ranking. But this time, an assistant to the dean of admissions offered him advice on how to challenge the medical school's minority admissions program, which reserved sixteen of the class's one hundred spots for minority group members from disadvantaged backgrounds. The program had been adopted after the school found that under its regular admissions program, it was enrolling no Black, Chicano, or American Indian students and very few Asian Americans.[6]

Bakke learned that some of the students admitted through the special admissions program had lower grades and MCAT scores than he did. Although these scores alone were not dispositive, they influenced the admission committee's decisions. Bakke sued, claiming that he would have been admitted if not for the special admissions program and that he had thus been rejected because of his race, in violation of law. A state trial court ruled in his favor, and the California Supreme Court affirmed, ordering him admitted to the medical school.[7] The case would soon end up in the hands of Archibald Cox.

After completing the amicus brief in *DeFunis*, Cox spent the spring 1974 semester on sabbatical as the Visiting Pitt Professor of American History and Institutions at the University of Cambridge. He then returned to Harvard and resumed his teaching schedule.[8] Three years later, when the *Bakke* case was accepted for review, the University of California asked him to represent it before the Supreme Court. In his argument, he presented the university's position that the Civil Rights Act and the Constitution did not prohibit public universities from considering race when admitting students and that there were good reasons to permit the university to continue doing so. The special admissions program, he wrote, served "the purposes of: (i) 'reducing the historic deficit of traditionally disfavored minorities in medical schools and in the medical profession,' (ii) countering the effects of societal discrimination; (iii) increasing the number of physicians who will practice in communities currently underserved; and (iv) obtaining the educational benefits that flow from an ethnically diverse student body."[9]

In my view, and that of four of the nine justices, these were all good justifications. A long-standing pattern of discrimination by the American Medical Association and all but a handful of American medical schools had left the country with very few Black or Hispanic/Latino medical doctors.[10] Societal discrimination had prevented most Black and Latino students from qualifying for medical school without special consideration. Most who did get in went on to practice medicine in poor minority communities, which were desperately underserved. If five justices had agreed, the *Bakke* case would have produced a vigorous defense of race-conscious affirmative action, as would occur in the employment field a year later.[11] But in education, it was not to be.

The Supreme Court rendered a splintered decision. Eight of the justices believed the case was about racial equality, but they were divided as to the proper outcome. The four more conservative justices—Chief Justice Burger and Associate Justices William Rehnquist, Potter Stewart, and John Paul Stevens—thought that any consideration of race by the university would violate the 1964 Civil Rights Act. The four more liberal justices—Associate Justices Thurgood Marshall, William Brennan, Byron White, and Harry Blackmun—thought that benign consideration of race to address prior systemic inequality was permitted under the Civil Rights Act and the Fourteenth Amendment to the Constitution. Powell was the tie-breaker.[12]

Lewis Powell was an unlikely supporter of race-conscious affirmative action. A Virginian by birth, he spent most of his career practicing corporate law in a large Richmond firm; when he was nominated to the Court in 1971, he was on eleven corporate boards.[13] But he found time to crisscross the country speaking against civil rights demonstrators and in support of unfettered markets.[14] He singled out Martin Luther King, Jr., as a danger to society, tagging him an opponent of civil order, democracy, and capitalism.[15] During the 1950s and 1960s, as many Virginia cities were fighting against school integration, he served on the Richmond school board, chairing it from 1952 to 1961, and the Virginia Board of Education from 1961 to 1969, often speaking in moderate terms while quietly delaying compliance with *Brown v. Board of Education*. In an era when many Southerners preached massive resistance to desegregation, Powell preferred passive resistance, waiting until the Supreme Court lost its appetite for enforcing the ruling. He saw compelled integration as unwarranted and dangerous.[16] The appropriate path to integration, he argued, was to allow white students to voluntarily attend Black schools if that was their preference (it almost uniformly wasn't) but to keep Black students out of white schools.[17] Under his leadership, Richmond schools remained 99.99 percent segregated. When he stepped down from the Richmond school board in 1961, seven years after the *Brown* decision, the city had twenty-three thousand Black students—of whom exactly two were attending school with whites.[18]

Prior to his appointment to the Court, Powell was a sought-after speaker who worked closely with the U.S. Chamber of Commerce.[19] From 1964 to 1965, when the American Bar Association was seen as a moderately conservative organization, he served as its president, where he worked to reduce the scope of proposals for providing federally financed legal services for the poor.[20] Two months before his nomination to the Supreme Court, he was hired by the Chamber of Commerce's education chair to draft a memorandum on how to counter what he and the Chamber saw as a rising tide of anti-business views among the American public.[21] The memo helped inspire the Chamber's growing participation in strategic litigation, the movement to fund an interlocking group of conservative think tanks that have become increasingly influential in American life, and the founding of the Federalist Society, which now wields enormous influence over judicial appointments and conservative legal doctrine.[22] Powell was thus responsible for two documents that would fundamentally alter American society: the 1971 Chamber of Commerce memo, now universally known as the Powell Memo, and the 1978 *Bakke* opinion. My Berkeley Law colleague Asad Rahim, in a brilliant excavation of Powell's papers, has shown that the two opinions are inextricably linked.[23]

As Rahim explains,

> Beginning in the mid-1960s, when he was an education official in Virginia, Powell became consumed by a suspicion that White and Black radicals, influenced by communists, had teamed up to plot a revolution that would dismantle capitalism and overthrow American democracy. According to Powell, the effort to foment insurrection was being executed on two fronts. Black "militant leaders" like Martin Luther King Jr. and the Black Panthers used civil disobedience to sow discord in the streets, and White militants—represented by the New Left—sought to radicalize "an ever-increasing number of white middle-class Americans" by corrupting the intellectual climate of the nation's universities. Powell specifically warned audiences that left extremists aimed to "establish the campus as the principal base of revolution."[24]

Powell was alarmed by the popularity on campuses of what he viewed as radical perspectives on race, imperialism, and capitalism. Leftist professors and student activists, he believed, were pushing their views on vulnerable students—vulnerable because they were forced to listen to radical views while being denied opportunities to hear moderate and conservative perspectives.

Powell believed that leftists were successful not because they had
the most compelling ideas but instead because "young extrem-
ists, professing to be 'liberals,' deny free speech to those with
whom they disagree." . . . After initially advocating for the expulsion of radical students and for stripping tenure from professors
who aided them, Powell eventually concluded that the best strategy to defeat radical leftists was to push for more intellectual diversity in the nation's universities. . . . As he argued before he
joined the Court, if college students were exposed to a robust exchange of ideas, the great majority of them would naturally
come to see the inherent wisdom of free market capitalism and
the greatness of time-honored American institutions. In Powell's
view, radicalism was born of ignorance, and ignorance, at least
on college campuses, was born from a lack of exposure to competing ideas.[25]

In at least partial agreement is the legal scholar Anders Walker, who
saw Powell's hostility toward the Civil Rights Movement—particularly
toward Dr. King—as related to his fear that the United States would suc-
cumb to communism and his general lack of sympathy toward Black
Americans and poor Americans. Looking closely at Powell's speeches and
judicial opinions about civil rights, Walker concludes that Powell believed that Black poverty was, bizarrely, a *positive* form of American diversity, that Black Americans were no more likely to be the victims of
discrimination than white Americans, and that white Americans should
be viewed as multiple minorities, including Irish, Mexicans, and Chinese
who had suffered as much as Black Americans.[26]

It should come as no surprise that when Powell was nominated to
the Court by Richard Nixon (after his two preferred candidates had been
deemed unqualified by the ABA), he faced opposition from civil rights
leaders in his home state of Virginia. But as a well-regarded lawyer, former ABA president, and Southern moderate, he sailed through the confirmation process.[27]

When the *Bakke* case reached the Court, Justice Powell parted from the
eight justices who saw the case as a matter of racial justice. Instead, he
saw the problem of selective admissions in terms of academic freedom.
He agreed with the four more conservative members that a racial quota
was impermissible under the Fourteenth Amendment: because Allan

Bakke had no opportunity to compete for the sixteen seats reserved for minorities, he had been deprived of equal treatment under the law.[28] Powell thus provided the fifth vote for upholding Bakke's claim of discrimination. But he also provided a fifth vote for the more liberal justices, agreeing with them that race could sometimes be considered as a "plus factor" in admissions decisions.[29]

Powell rejected the liberal justices' view that race could be used to counter long-standing societal discrimination, even the playing field, or bring more physicians into underserved minority communities, which often lacked adequate medical care. The only reasoning he accepted for permitting race to be considered under some circumstances was the Millsian argument about diversity he had encountered in Cox's brief in *DeFunis*—which matched the description of the Harvard Plan in the brief filed by Harvard, Columbia, Stanford, and Penn. Powell took the 1,031-word appendix from the four-university *Bakke* brief, which had been cut and pasted from Cox's brief in the *DeFunis* case, and appended it to his opinion.[30]

Powell was persuaded by the Cox argument that the goal of attaining student body diversity justified the use of race as a factor in deciding whom to admit.[31] His explanation connected the dots between the Mills, Holmes, Brandeis, Frankfurter, and the South African apartheid resisters:

> The fourth goal asserted by petitioner is the attainment of a diverse student body. This clearly is a constitutionally permissible goal for an institution of higher education. Academic freedom, though not a specifically enumerated constitutional right, long has been viewed as a special concern of the First Amendment. The freedom of a university to make its own judgments as to education includes the selection of its student body. Mr. Justice Frankfurter summarized the "four essential freedoms" that constitute academic freedom:
>
> "It is the business of a university to provide that atmosphere which is most conducive to speculation, experiment and creation. It is an atmosphere in which there prevail 'the four essential freedoms' of a university—to determine for itself on academic grounds who may teach, what may be taught, how it shall be taught, and who may be admitted to study." *Sweezy v. New Hampshire*, 354 U. S. 234, 263 (1957) (concurring in result).
>
> Our national commitment to the safeguarding of these freedoms within university communities was emphasized in *Keyishian*

v. Board of Regents, 385 U. S. 589, 603 (1967): "Our Nation is deeply committed to safeguarding academic freedom which is of transcendent value to all of us and not merely to the teachers concerned. That freedom is therefore a special concern of the First Amendment. . . . The Nation's future depends upon leaders trained through wide exposure to that robust exchange of ideas which discovers truth 'out of a multitude of tongues, [rather] than through any kind of authoritative selection.' *United States v. Associated Press*, 52 F. Supp. 362, 372" [Learned Hand, J.] . . .

. . . Thus, in arguing that its universities must be accorded the right to select those students who will contribute the most to the "robust exchange of ideas," petitioner invokes a countervailing constitutional interest, that of the First Amendment. In this light, petitioner must be viewed as seeking to achieve a goal that is of paramount importance in the fulfillment of its mission.[32]

In a footnote, Powell cites a 1977 statement on diversity by William Bowen, a scholar of diversity admissions and the president of (the once highly exclusionary) Princeton University:

The president of Princeton University has described some of the benefits derived from a diverse student body: "[A] great deal of learning occurs informally. It occurs through interactions among students of both sexes; of different races, religions, and backgrounds; who come from cities and rural areas, from various states and countries; who have a wide variety of interests, talents, and perspectives; and who are able, directly or indirectly, to learn from their differences and to stimulate one another to reexamine even their most deeply held assumptions about themselves and their world. As a wise graduate of ours observed in commenting on this aspect of the educational process, 'People do not learn very much when they are surrounded only by the likes of themselves.'"[33]

Powell then turns to the question of whether the establishment of an admissions quota is the only way to ensure a racially diverse student body, concluding that it is not. As proof, he points to the segment of the Cox *DeFunis* brief that he now describes as "the Harvard College program." "In such an admissions program," he concludes,

race or ethnic background may be deemed a "plus" in a particular applicant's file, yet it does not insulate the individual from
comparison with all other candidates for the available seats. The
file of a particular black applicant may be examined for his potential contribution to diversity without the factor of race being
decisive when compared, for example, with that of an applicant
identified as an Italian-American if the latter is thought to ex-
hibit qualities more likely to promote beneficial educational
pluralism. Such qualities could include exceptional personal talents, unique work or service experience, leadership potential,
maturity, demonstrated compassion, a history of overcoming disadvantage, ability to communicate with the poor, or other qualifications deemed important. In short, an admissions program
operated in this way is flexible enough to consider all pertinent
elements of diversity in light of the particular qualifications of
each applicant, and to place them on the same footing for consideration, although not necessarily according them the same
weight. Indeed, the weight attributed to a particular quality may
vary from year to year depending upon the "mix" both of the
student body and the applicants for the incoming class.

   This kind of program treats each applicant as an individual
in the admissions process. The applicant who loses out on the
last available seat to another candidate receiving a "plus" on the
basis of ethnic background will not have been foreclosed from all
consideration for that seat simply because he was not the right
color or had the wrong surname. It would mean only that his
combined qualifications, which may have included similar non-
objective factors, did not outweigh those of the other applicant.
His qualifications would have been weighed fairly and competi-
tively, and he would have no basis to complain of unequal treatment under the Fourteenth Amendment.[34]

In sum, Cox, drawing on more than one hundred fifty years of intellectual history beginning with Humboldt and the Mills, drafted a brief
describing Harvard's approach to diversity admissions. Four years later,
lawyers for Harvard and three other universities lifted it word-for-word
and made it an appendix to a brief arguing that Harvard's approach was
justified. Powell took the appendix and made it the central argument of
his opinion endorsing Harvard's approach. Court decisions are often a

collaboration between lawyers and judges. But here it seems closer to say that the key elements of Powell's opinion in the *Bakke* case were essentially ghostwritten by Archibald Cox.

The reaction to Justice Powell's opinion was initially underwhelming. A *Washington Post* article the next day was headlined, "Bakke Decision May Change Very Little."[35] Most observers thought Powell had found a middle ground by prohibiting quotas while endorsing the use of race as a plus factor. Few engaged with Powell's comments on the importance of ensuring a diverse student body or with his argument that diversity was an essential element of academic freedom.[36] Among the exceptions was Harvard law professor Laurence Tribe.[37] Another exception was Vincent Blasi, a law professor at the University of Michigan, who noted that the diversity justification was "the key feature" of Powell's decision and wrote that the "Bakke precedent should pose little difficulty for those special admission programs that are founded on the premise that, because of their skills and special backgrounds, certain minority-race applicants represent a valuable resource which an educational institution primarily concerned with the quality of its dialog ought to draw upon."[38] Among conservative scholars, Guido Calabresi and Robert Bork of Yale also recognized the potential of the diversity argument but found it unconvincing.[39]

Even the in-depth studies of *Bakke* that emerged later gave little room to the diversity principle. In *The Bakke Case: The Politics of Inequality* (1979), Joel Dreyfuss and Charles Lawrence allot only five paragraphs to the Harvard approach to diversity.[40] Bernard Schwartz, who published a comprehensive examination of the decision ten years after it was issued, treats the goal of diversity as merely a means to the end of providing preferences to minority students.[41] "Though the Davis program was invalidated," he writes, "the Powell opinion permits admissions officers to operate programs which grant racial preferences—provided that they do not do so as blatantly as was done under the sixteen-seat 'quota' provided in Davis. . . . The result has been that *Bakke* has, in practice, served to license, not to prohibit, race-conscious admissions programs."[42] In *The Bakke Case: Race, Education and Affirmative Action* (2000), the political scientist Howard Ball similarly describes Powell's opinion as a compromise that permits considerations of race, while failing to describe either the underlying diversity rationale or the question of academic freedom.[43]

The word "diversity" does not even appear in the index of the 1994 biography of Justice Powell written by his former clerk John C. Jeffries,

Jr.[44] It was Jeffries who, while serving as Powell's law clerk in 1974, had recommended that Powell read Cox's brief in the *DeFunis* case.[45] But Jeffries's discussion of how Powell came to embrace the diversity principle takes all of five pages in a 562-page biography, and he describes the opinion as a "middle course" rather than a new approach to admissions. Writing sixteen years after the *Bakke* decision, Jeffries views the difference between Harvard's program to foster diversity and UC Davis's program to counteract racial disadvantage as "more form than substance."[46] "Harvard," he writes, "was simply Davis without fixed numbers."[47] His view in 1994 was that for Powell, "diversity was not the ultimate objective but merely a convenient way to broach a compromise."[48]

Jeffries has more recently reported that when the decision came out, "reviews of the intellectual craft of Powell's opinion were largely negative and sometimes scathing."[49] Jeffries quotes from articles written in 1978 and 1979 by eight leading legal scholars across the political spectrum, all of whom found the opinion seriously problematic.[50] Ronald Dworkin wrote in the *New York Review of Books* that "the argumentative base of [Powell's] opinion is weak. It does not supply a sound intellectual foundation" and "may not be sufficiently strong in principle to furnish the basis for a coherent and lasting constitutional law of affirmative action."[51] John Hart Ely, writing the foreword to the *Harvard Law Review* issue on the 1977–78 Supreme Court term, says nothing about diversity but complains that "Justice Powell forgets that he is not being asked to devise an affirmative action program but rather to rule on the constitutionality of the one the California officials had devised."[52] Antonin Scalia, then a professor at the University of Chicago, described the opinion as "thoroughly unconvincing as an honest, hard-minded, reasoned analysis of an important provision of the Constitution" and predicted that it would lead universities to adopt informal quotas and dishonestly cloak them in the excuse that they were pursuing diversity.[53] Guido Calabresi called the opinion a "compromise that undermines candor and honesty."[54]

Of the eight scholars cited by Jeffries, a few recognized the diversity argument as central to the opinion, but none saw it as transformative, and some found it ridiculous. Only two even mentioned academic freedom.[55] And yet for forty-five years, the ruling that the diversity justification was protected by academic freedom was the controlling law, embraced by nearly all selective colleges and universities in the United States. While affirmative action in higher education remains controversial among the general public, most university faculty and administrators today view diversity and inclusion as among their institutions' essential values. Meanwhile, the *Bakke* opinion is Justice Powell's best known. When he stepped down in 1987 after fifteen years on the Court, he was asked which opinion was his most important. Without hesitation, he named *Bakke*.[56]

It would have been easy for Powell simply to join the other four conservatives and end affirmative action in university admissions then and there. Why would a conservative judge who resisted school integration and considered American colleges and universities breeding grounds for radicalism instead decide to put diversity at the center of American higher education? Why would he write an opinion that satisfied almost no one and yet in time changed the way Americans and others beyond our shores think about racial equality and inclusion? To understand the opinion, it is useful to consider it alongside the influential memo he wrote for the Chamber of Commerce several years before *Bakke*.

On August 11, 1971, just two months before his nomination to the Supreme Court, Powell wrote a memo for Eugene Sydnor, education director for the U.S. Chamber of Commerce.[57] Just as his opinion in *Bakke* was his most important contribution to American society as a judge, the "Powell Memo" was his most important as an advocate. He advised Sydnor that to save American democracy, the Chamber would have to get more involved in politics and law reform and become an active voice for American business interests before the Supreme Court. Campus radicals, Powell argued, had gained too much control over education, the media, and public opinion, and the business community had to fight back. He suggested that business interests could counter the liberalism of U.S. academics by establishing conservative think tanks and other institutions that would challenge liberal views and bring a pro-business viewpoint to public policy debates.[58] Powell expressed his deeply conservative views in terms that verge on the apocalyptic. Here is how he begins:

> No thoughtful person can question that the American economic system is under broad attack....
>
> ...We are not dealing with sporadic or isolated attacks from a relatively few extremists or even from the minority socialist cadre. Rather, the assault on the enterprise system is broadly based and consistently pursued. It is gaining momentum and converts....
>
> ...The most disquieting voices joining the chorus of criticism come from perfectly respectable elements of society: from

the college campus, the pulpit, the media, the intellectual and literary journals, the arts and sciences, and from politicians. In most of these groups the movement against the system is participated in only by minorities. Yet, these often are the most articulate, the most vocal, the most prolific in their writing and speaking. . . .

. . . The overriding first need is for businessmen to recognize that the ultimate issue may be survival—survival of what we call the free enterprise system, and all that this means for the strength and prosperity of America and the freedom of our people. . . .

. . . Strength lies in organization, in careful long-range planning and implementation, in consistency of action over an indefinite period of years, in the scale of financing available only through joint effort, and in the political power available only through united action and national organizations. . . .

. . . A priority task of business—and organizations such as the Chamber—is to address the campus origin of this hostility. Few things are more sanctified in American life than academic freedom. It would be fatal to attack this as a principle. But if academic freedom is to retain the qualities of "openness," "fairness" and "balance"—which are essential to its intellectual significance—there is a great opportunity for constructive action. The thrust of such action must be to restore the qualities just mentioned to the academic communities. . . .

. . . Perhaps the most fundamental problem is the imbalance of many faculties. Correcting this is indeed a long-range and difficult project. Yet, it should be undertaken as a part of an overall program. This would mean the urging of the need for faculty balance upon university administrators and boards of trustees.

The methods to be employed require careful thought, and the obvious pitfalls must be avoided. Improper pressure would be counterproductive. But the basic concepts of balance, fairness and truth are difficult to resist, if properly presented to boards of trustees, by writing and speaking, and by appeals to alumni associations and groups. . . .

. . . The national television networks should be monitored in the same way that textbooks should be kept under constant surveillance. This applies not merely to so-called educational programs (such as "Selling of the Pentagon"), but to the daily "news analysis" which so often includes the most insidious type of criticism of the enterprise system. Whether this criticism results from hostility or economic ignorance, the result is the gradual erosion of confidence in "business" and free enterprise. . . .

. . . Business must learn the lesson, long ago learned by labor and other self-interest groups. This is the lesson that political power is necessary; that such power must be assiduously cultivated; and that when necessary, it must be used aggressively and with determination—without embarrassment and without the reluctance which has been so characteristic of American business.

As unwelcome as it may be to the Chamber, it should consider assuming a broader and more vigorous role in the political arena. . . .

. . . American business and the enterprise system have been affected as much by the courts as by the executive and legislative branches of government. Under our constitutional system, especially with an activist-minded Supreme Court, the judiciary may be the most important instrument for social, economic and political change.

Other organizations and groups, recognizing this, have been far more astute in exploiting judicial action than American business. Perhaps the most active exploiters of the judicial system have been groups ranging in political orientation from "liberal" to the far left.

The American Civil Liberties Union is one example. It initiates or intervenes in scores of cases each year, and it files briefs amicus curiae in the Supreme Court in a number of cases during each term of that court. Labor unions, civil rights groups and now the public interest law firms are extremely active in the judicial arena. Their success, often at business' expense, has not been inconsequential.

This is a vast area of opportunity for the Chamber, if it is willing to undertake the role of spokesman for American business and if, in turn, business is willing to provide the funds. . . .

. . . It hardly need be said that the views expressed above are tentative and suggestive. The first step should be a thorough study. But this would be an exercise in futility unless the Board of Directors of the Chamber accepts the fundamental premise of this paper, namely, that business and the enterprise system are in deep trouble, and the hour is late.[59]

The Powell Memo was initially confidential, but after Powell was confirmed to the Court, it was leaked by the investigative reporter and columnist Jack Anderson.[60] It was then circulated among conservative organizations and potential donors, for whom it served as a blueprint for countering liberalism.[61] The memo catalyzed the establishment of several conservative think tanks as well as the founding of the Federalist Society.[62] Along with the newly litigation-oriented Chamber of Commerce, these institutions have fought back against the liberalization of American society since the 1970s, often effectively and much to the dismay (and envy) of liberal scholars and activists.[63] The think tanks have become enormously influential in the development of pro-business neoliberalism, while the Federalist Society has changed the face of the American judiciary, giving us highly activist judges who are far to the right of both general public opinion and the legal profession.[64] Of the nine members of the current U.S. Supreme Court, six are associated with the Federalist Society.[65]

These institutions have been substantially funded by large amounts of money coming from a small group of very conservative donors.[66] But from Powell's point of view, they demonstrated the power of diversity and academic freedom, the values he would embrace in his *Bakke* opinion.

Scholars seeking to explain Powell's vote in *Bakke* have posited that he was by nature a mediator, looking for compromises everyone could live with. In this sense, they say, he was a true moderate—his generation's version of the politically liberal but judicially conservative Justice Frankfurter.[67] This argument finds support in the trajectory of the diversity cases following *Bakke*, where first Justice Sandra Day O'Connor and then Justice Anthony Kennedy would slip out of their conservatism to provide the tiebreaking vote to preserve universities' freedom to use race in making admissions decisions to promote diversity. Others have argued that, as a former school board chair, Powell saw himself as the "education justice," with a greater understanding of higher education than his colleagues possessed, and that he didn't want the state interfering with educators' judgments unless it was unavoidable.[68]

These explanations, however, are inconsistent with the evidence that Asad Rahim and Anders Walker have unearthed regarding Powell's lack of sympathy for Black Americans and his strong feelings about battling campus radicalism.[69] The evidence supports Rahim's view that Powell was focused on creating greater ideological diversity on campuses as a way of countering student and faculty radicals, whom he viewed as a great danger to American society.[70]

It's possible that Powell softened in his years on the Court. In an interview with the journalist Bill Moyers at the time of Powell's retirement in 1987, he defended diversity admissions by addressing diversity of identity, not of ideology: "I do think—and I think the majority of the court felt—that universities had a perfectly legitimate, indeed substantial, if not compelling interest in having diversity in the student body in our society. It's a part of education, to be in class with people with different backgrounds, both in terms of economic or social or ethnic, from different parts of the country. I think that's a part of being educated."[71]

Whether or not he had his own reasons for endorsing the diversity justification for considering race in admissions, Powell was not the creative thinker who gave us the rule permitting diversity admissions; that was Cox. Or perhaps it's more accurate to say that Cox took the work of dozens of thinkers before him, from Humboldt to Murray to Centlivres, molded it to fit the problem of the exclusion of Black Americans from top universities, and then proposed it to the Court, where Powell accepted it. Considered in this light, Powell's views are far less important than the long chain of ideas that propelled diversity into our jurisprudence.

CHAPTER TWELVE

The Supreme Court's Long
Embrace and Turnabout Rejection
of the Diversity Principle

I MMEDIATELY AFTER THE *BAKKE* decision, few university faculty or admissions officers appreciated the significance of Justice Powell's focus on diversity as a justification for considering race or ethnicity in making admissions decisions. The term "affirmative action" had come into use in 1961, when the presidential advisor Hobart Taylor, Jr., inserted it into President Kennedy's Executive Action on non-discrimination in employment.[1] University leaders had adopted the term later in the decade as they developed policies to recruit more Black and Hispanic students. Most of these early efforts were described in racial justice terms. Few mentioned racial diversity and academic freedom as a legal basis for allowing schools to use race in admissions, and none had developed the argument as thoroughly as Cox did in his *DeFunis* brief, Centlivres in his South African open universities book, or Justice Powell in his *Bakke* opinion.[2]

Although most commentators saw Powell's opinion as simply a compromise allowing the use of race as a plus factor but without quotas, there were a few exceptions.[3] Even before the *Bakke* decision, a few educational leaders had begun speaking about the value of student body diversity, sometimes linking it to racial diversity. Wilbur J. Bender's advo-

cacy of diversity at Harvard had received significant press attention following his 1960 final report.[4] Anthony Chen and Lisa Stulberg have
found evidence that by 1962 Columbia, Princeton, Amherst, and Duke
were using the diversity rationale for recruiting Black and other minority
students even before *DeFunis*.[5] But these were outliers.

Even as they first appeared at many universities, affirmative action
programs already faced political headwinds. Just two years after *Bakke*,
Ronald Reagan ran for president on a platform that highlighted his opposition to affirmative action.

Reagan had gotten his start in politics as an opponent of civil rights.[6]
Campaigning for Barry Goldwater during his 1964 presidential bid, he
praised the candidate for his courage in opposing the 1964 Civil Rights
Act, which Reagan framed as a violation of "individual rights."[7] (That is,
the right to discriminate.) That same year, Californians were voting on
Proposition 14, a ballot initiative to overturn California's housing discrimination law and legalize racial discrimination in housing across the
state.[8] In praise of this initiative, Reagan declared his support for "upholding the right of a man to dispose of his property or not dispose of it
as he sees fit."[9] When the Voting Rights Act was proposed (and passed) in
1965, Reagan opposed it. Years later, he would condemn it as "humiliating to the South."[10] Running for California governor in 1966, Reagan
centered his campaign on his opposition to the Free Speech movement
at Berkeley, which was closely linked to the Civil Rights Movement.[11]
Once in office, he spoke out again in support of housing discrimination,
publicly opposed the 1968 Fair Housing Act, and asserted that "if an individual wants to discriminate against Negroes or others in selling or
renting his house . . . he has a right to do so."[12]

But Reagan truly became a hero for civil rights opponents during his
1980 presidential campaign. To make it clear to white voters where he
stood, his first campaign stop after his nomination was at the county fairground adjoining Philadelphia, Mississippi, previously famous as the
town where three civil rights workers—James Chaney, Andrew Goodman, and Michael Schwerner—were murdered by the local police and
the Ku Klux Klan on June 21, 1964, two days after the Senate passed the
1964 Civil Rights Act after breaking the Southern senators' sixty-day fili-
buster, the longest in Senate history.[13] Though the campaign claimed the
choice of venue was coincidental, Reagan used the fairground venue to
proclaim his support of "states' rights," the code words for opposing desegregation and supporting discrimination.[14] It was one of many racist

dog whistles he would use to appeal to white Southerners throughout his campaign, and it worked—his resistance to civil rights enforcement and affirmative action helped drive him to victory.[15]

As soon as he took office, Reagan began to dismantle federal support for affirmative action and disable the federal agencies responsible for civil rights enforcement.[16] To head the Civil Rights Division of the U.S. Department of Justice, he appointed William Reynolds, a corporate lawyer with no civil rights experience, who considered affirmative action unfair to "innocent whites."[17] Under Reynolds's leadership, the Justice Department intervened in numerous affirmative action and school desegregation cases, always on the side of white objectors.[18] Some scholars attribute the move from corporate affirmative action programs to corporate diversity programs (and now DEI programs) to President Reagan's success in making the term "affirmative action" toxic.[19]

Even before Reagan took office, proponents of race-conscious admissions began bracing for further legal challenges. A year after the *Bakke* decision, in July 1979, the Rockefeller Foundation brought together leading civil rights lawyers and legal scholars for a two-day discussion of *Bakke* as well as the more recent *Weber* case, in which the Court had upheld affirmative action by private employers making decisions about hiring and promotions.[20] Archibald Cox contributed a paper, titled "Minority Admissions After *Bakke*," in which he explained that colleges could be confident that race-conscious admissions programs would withstand legal attacks as long as they (1) emphasized diversity of all sorts, not just racial or ethnic diversity, (2) considered and articulated the educational value of racial and ethnic diversity for the general student body, (3) avoided fixed targets or quotas, and (4) evaluated applicants on a case-by-case basis, with minority status a plus but with no one barred from consideration based on race.[21] Cox would once again prove prescient.[22] He came as close as a lawyer could hope to get to anticipating the Court's subsequent decisions. In three key cases, *Grutter*, *Gratz*, and *Fisher* (discussed below), the Court reaffirmed the argument of the Cox brief in *DeFunis*, as set forth by Justice Powell in *Bakke*. Not until 2023 did it reverse direction, as we will see, holding that the value of diversity does not justify any use of race in college admissions—except for our military academies.[23]

Appreciation of Powell's opinion grew over time. Beginning in the early 1980s, selective colleges began to focus their admissions practices not on remediating past or present racial discrimination, but on admitting a diverse class.[24] Most selective American colleges and universities eventually adopted variations of the Harvard Plan, highlighting the value of diversity in improving the education offered to all their students.[25] In 1997, the Association of American Universities, a consortium of sixty-two leading research universities, affirmed its support for diversity-informed admissions policies "that take many factors and characteristics into account—including ethnicity, race, and gender."[26] Medical and nursing schools similarly shifted their admissions policies toward the "Experiences-Attributes-Metrics" model, which allowed them to consider candidates' backgrounds alongside metrics like MCAT scores and grade point averages.[27] In this process, educational institutions substituted diversity for affirmative action: they moved away from recruiting and admitting minority group members for racial justice purposes and instead committed to admitting more diverse groups of students to capture the educational benefits of diversity. They did so against a background of increasing research into the benefits of diversity and in the shadow of opposition to affirmative action.[28]

As schools increasingly embraced diversity-focused admissions policies, their lawyers—and constitutional scholars generally—grew nervous. They regarded the Powell opinion as a fragile basis for these important and controversial policies. Many scholars preferred to think of affirmative action policies as justified by the need to address past and continuing discrimination, feeling this was a far stronger justification than diversity.[29] They worried about what the legal scholar William Van Alstyne called the "obvious instability of the decision."[30]

A case brought against the University of Texas in 1992 seemed to confirm their skepticism. That year, a white woman named Cheryl Hopwood failed to win admission to the University of Texas Law School—the school that had been required to begin admitting Black students in the 1950s by the decision in *Sweatt v. Painter.* Hopwood and three white men who had also been rejected sued the university for discrimination, claiming that Black and Latino students with lower grades or lower scores on the Law School Admission Test had been admitted instead of them.[31]

Hopwood and her co-plaintiffs technically prevailed in the U.S. District Court in a complicated decision, but they were awarded only nominal damages of one dollar each. The judge found that the university had stopped overtly discriminating against Black and Latino students, but only recently; it was still under the supervision of the U.S. Department of Education because of its failure to admit significant numbers of non-white students.[32] The court noted that well into the 1960s, "Mexican American students were segregated in on-campus housing and assigned to a dormitory known as the 'barracks,' as well as excluded from membership in most university-sponsored organizations."[33] Until the mid-1960s, the board of regents had prohibited Blacks from living in or visiting white dormitories.[34]

The trial court seemed to take a particular delight in noting that "in 1982, Assistant Secretary of Education Clarence Thomas informed Governor Clements that the Texas Plan was deficient because the numeric goals of black and Hispanic enrollment in graduate and professional programs were insufficient to meet Texas's commitment to enroll those minority students in proportion to the representation among graduates of the state's undergraduate institutions."[35] In other words, during his time at the Department of Education, Thomas was not just supporting a racial quota but demanding one. Twelve years later, by the time of the 1994 *Hopwood* decision, Thomas had left the Department of Education and was a justice of the U.S. Supreme Court, where he was a vocal opponent of affirmative action. His former colleagues at the Department of Education were still in court, trying to push the university to admit more non-white students.[36]

The witnesses heard by the District Court included the deans of law at Stanford, Michigan, Louisiana State, and Minnesota, as well as students and faculty at Texas. The court found that "the benefit to the law school educational experience derived from a diverse student population is substantial" and concluded that "according to the evidence presented at trial, without affirmative action the law school would not be able to achieve this goal of diversity."[37] Applying the Powell opinion from *Bakke*, the court ruled that the university was permitted to use race in its admissions process.

But it went on to find that at the time Hopwood applied, the law school had deviated from the Harvard Plan by reviewing applications from minority students separately from those of white students. This violated the rights of the white applicants under the Equal Protection Clause of the Constitution. By the time of trial, however, the law school had changed its system and eliminated the separate lines of evaluation. Moreover, the court found it unlikely that Hopwood and the three other plaintiffs would have been admitted even under an evaluation system that did not consider race. They were thus awarded damages of one dollar for the violation that the university had since repaired, and they were urged by the court to reapply.[38]

The plaintiffs instead appealed to the Fifth Circuit Court of Appeals, the court that sits between the federal district court and the Supreme Court. That court reversed the trial court's decision, rejecting both the trial court's view and Justice Powell's opinion in *Bakke* that the benefits of a diverse student body could justify using race in making admissions decisions.[39] The critical lines of the decision rejected the authority of Justice Powell's opinion as the opinion of a single justice, and thus not the holding of the Court:

> We agree with the plaintiffs that any consideration of race or ethnicity by the law school for the purpose of achieving a diverse student body is not a compelling interest under the Fourteenth Amendment. . . .
>
> In Bakke, the word "diversity" is mentioned nowhere except in Justice Powell's single-Justice opinion. . . . Thus, only one Justice concluded that race could be used solely for the reason of obtaining a heterogenous student body.[40]

Civil rights groups looked expectantly to the Supreme Court to reaffirm Powell's opinion in *Bakke*, reversing the Circuit Court decision. The alternative, affirming the Circuit Court, would end the diversity justification for using race in admissions. The university petitioned for review in the Supreme Court, supported by the U.S. solicitor general and a number of amici briefs urging the Court to take the case.[41]

To the shock of most informed court watchers, the Court denied review, allowing the ruling to stand.[42] The decision to allow a Circuit Court decision to stand does not affect cases outside that circuit, meaning that as of 1996, diversity was not a permissible basis for using race in admissions in Texas, Mississippi, and Louisiana, but it was still arguably proper in the remaining forty-seven states. It would take another seven years of fierce debate over affirmative action before the Supreme Court decided to reaffirm the Powell opinion.

Complicating that debate was the belief of many liberals that diversity was a weak justification for race-conscious admissions, based on their view that its purpose was to give white students the benefits of interacting with Black students rather than benefiting Black students themselves or increasing their representation on campus. Advocates and policymakers began brainstorming other methods of getting schools to admit more minority candidates, ones that would not rely on such shaky legal footing.

In Texas, the *Hopwood* decision led to an innovative legislative solution, the 1997 "Top 10 Percent Plan." Under the plan, any students who finish in the top 10 percent of their high school class may attend any public university in Texas.[43] (The plan was later modified to carve out an exception for the University of Texas's overcrowded flagship campus in Austin; as of 2023, students are guaranteed admission there if they finish in the top 6 percent of their class.)[44] Because most Texas high schools are *de facto* racially segregated, supporters of the plan expected that it would guarantee the university system significant racial and ethnic diversity.[45] But their expectations were largely dashed. White students were sufficiently favored by higher family incomes, positive stereotyping, and other advantages that they were more strongly represented at the top of the class even in schools where they were a minority.[46] Although educators viewed it as a failure, the plan was politically popular, and versions of it were later adopted in other states.[47]

One such state was California. A few months after the Supreme Court declined to hear the *Hopwood* case, California voters passed an amendment to the State Constitution prohibiting consideration of race, sex, or ethnicity in state university admissions, state employment, and state contracting. This effectively ended race-based affirmative action at the country's top-rated public university, the University of California.[48] Similar voter initiatives succeeded in Washington in 1998, Michigan in 2006, and Nebraska in 2008.[49] Florida's ban, in 1999, came via executive order, but it had the same outcome.[50]

Behind each of these initiatives, and a few that failed, was Ward Connerly, a multiracial American businessman who passionately opposed both race-based and gender-based affirmative action.[51] A charismatic campaigner who purportedly had himself benefited from affirmative action programs for minority contractors, he has had a profound impact on American law.[52]

Connerly argued that any consideration of race violated the principle of equality. He linked this view to the line from Martin Luther King's "I Have A Dream" speech in which King looked forward to the day when all Americans would "not be judged by the color of their skin but by the content of their character."[53] Connerly insisted that the 1964 Civil Rights Act requires a "color-blind" approach to university admissions, government contracting, and employment. Even tracking racial statistics, he believed, was wrong.[54] His argument drew significant attention partly because it was simple and appealing to those who were inclined to oppose affirmative action, partly because it was made by a successful businessperson of color, and partly because of his close friendship with Governor Pete Wilson, who campaigned with him in favor of his proposed ban.[55]

It mattered little that King's "I Have A Dream" speech also called for reparations or that he supported employment quotas to create jobs for Black workers. In part because of people like Connerly, King's militancy is largely forgotten, and he is now best remembered for a misreading of his most famous speech.[56] Connerly's voter initiatives succeeded in California and elsewhere, giving further impetus to efforts to define diversity broadly, using factors like family income, social class, parental education, and high school attended in addition to (and sometimes instead of) race and ethnicity.

Connerly's Michigan initiative was a direct response to the Supreme Court's next consideration of race and diversity. In a pair of cases from 1995 and 1997 that reached the Supreme Court together in 2002, challenging the admissions policies of the University of Michigan, the Court reaffirmed both conclusions from Justice Powell's opinion in *Bakke:* quotas were not permitted, but race could be considered in order to increase diversity. These decisions reaffirmed and expanded Powell's endorsement of the diversity principle.[57]

One of the Michigan cases (*Gratz v. Bollinger*) concerned the university's undergraduate admissions program, in which applicants who were Black, Hispanic, or Native American were given additional points in a mathematical model that largely decided who would be admitted. In a 5–4 decision written by Chief Justice William Rehnquist, the Court held that a point system was the functional equivalent of a quota system and therefore unconstitutional.[58] But the companion case (*Grutter v. Bollinger*) challenged the UM law school admissions policy, which was modeled on the Harvard Plan. Here, the Court again split 5–4, but Justice O'Connor switched sides and wrote the majority opinion, finding that the law school's admissions plan was permissible because of the importance of the educational benefits of diversity. She further found that the law school could consider the number of non-white students enrolled in order to maintain a "critical mass" of students from minority identity groups, thus avoiding racial isolation and tokenism, a problem identified by Cox in the brief that became the Harvard Plan.

O'Connor began her majority opinion by reaffirming Justice Powell's opinion in *Bakke* and describing UM's admissions policy in terms reflecting Cox's thinking (and that of those who had influenced him):

The hallmark of that policy is its focus on academic ability coupled with a flexible assessment of applicants' talents, experiences, and potential "to contribute to the learning of those around them." . . . The policy aspires to "achieve that diversity which has the potential to enrich everyone's education and thus make a law school class stronger than the sum of its parts." The policy does not restrict the types of diversity contributions eligible for "substantial weight" in the admissions process, but instead recognizes "many possible bases for diversity admissions." The policy does, however, reaffirm the Law School's longstanding commitment to "one particular type of diversity," that is, "racial and ethnic diversity with special reference to the inclusion of students from groups which have been historically discriminated against, like African-Americans, Hispanics and Native Americans, who without this commitment might not be represented in our student body in meaningful numbers." By enrolling a "critical mass of minority students," the Law School seeks to "ensur[e] their ability to make unique contributions to the character of the Law School."

The policy does not define diversity "solely in terms of racial and ethnic status." Nor is the policy "insensitive to the competition among all students for admission to the Law School." Rather, the policy seeks to guide admissions officers in "producing classes both diverse and academically outstanding, classes made up of students who promise to continue the tradition of outstanding contribution by Michigan Graduates to the legal profession."[59]

Turning to Powell's *Bakke* opinion, O'Connor wrote,

Justice Powell grounded his analysis in the academic freedom that "long has been viewed as a special concern of the First Amendment." Justice Powell emphasized that nothing less than the "'nation's future depends upon leaders trained through wide exposure' to the ideas and mores of students as diverse as this

Nation of many peoples" (quoting *Keyishian v. Board of Regents of Univ. of State of N.Y.*). In seeking the "right to select those students who will contribute the most to the 'robust exchange of ideas,' a university seeks 'to achieve a goal that is of paramount importance in the fulfillment of its mission.'" Both "tradition and experience lend support to the view that the contribution of diversity is substantial."[60]

Expanding on the relationship between diversity and academic freedom, O'Connor channeled Humboldt, the Mills, and Eliot:

> We have long recognized that, given the important purpose of public education and the expansive freedoms of speech and thought associated with the university environment, universities occupy a special niche in our constitutional tradition. . . . In announcing the principle of student body diversity as a compelling state interest, Justice Powell invoked our cases recognizing a constitutional dimension, grounded in the First Amendment, of educational autonomy. "The freedom of a university to make its own judgments as to education includes the selection of its student body." *Bakke, supra.* From this premise, Justice Powell reasoned that by claiming "the right to select those students who will contribute the most to the 'robust exchange of ideas,'" a university "seek[s] to achieve a goal that is of paramount importance in the fulfillment of its mission" (quoting *Keyishian v. Board of Regents of Univ. of State of N. Y., supra*). Our conclusion that the Law School has a compelling interest in a diverse student body is informed by our view that attaining a diverse student body is at the heart of the Law School's proper institutional mission, and that "good faith" on the part of a university is "presumed" absent "a showing to the contrary."[61]

Law professor Devon Carbado finds eight benefits of diversity identified in the O'Connor opinion: "diversity to promote speech and the robust exchange of ideas, diversity to effectuate the inclusion of underrepresented students, diversity to change the character of the school, diversity to disrupt and negate racial stereotypes, diversity to facilitate racial cooperation and understanding, diversity to create pathways to leadership, diversity to ensure democratic legitimacy, and diversity to prevent racial isolation and alienation."[62]

Amicus briefs supporting the university once again played an important role. But unlike in *Bakke*, the most influential briefs were not those filed by educators (of which there were many) but those from former military leaders and leading American businesses.[63] The amici who signed the military brief described themselves as "former high-ranking officers and civilian leaders of the Army, Navy, Air Force, and Marine Corps, including former military-academy superintendents, Secretaries of Defense, and present and former members of the U.S. Senate."[64] The two corporate briefs united sixty-six leading American businesses, in sectors that included banking, technology, the automotive industry, pharmaceutical manufacturing, biotechnology, aviation, and energy.[65] Both groups argued that it was important to the strength of the country's national defense and economy that universities train a diverse group of future leaders.

Justice O'Connor relied on the military and corporate briefs to emphasize that the benefits of diversity went beyond its impact on the university to the very heart of the country's economy and security. Racial diversity in higher education, she found, is essential to the integration of the officer corps, the training of white and minority officers, and the creation of an "effective, battle-ready fighting force."[66] The military brief cautions that the "stark disparity" in the 1960s and 1970s "between the racial composition of the rank and file and that of the officer corps fueled a breakdown of order that endangered the military's ability to fulfill its mission."[67] With this breakdown came a loss of confidence in the fairness and integrity of the military as an institution. Since most military officers are graduates of either the service academies or Reserve Officers' Training Corps (ROTC) programs at universities, the consideration of race in those settings is key to building and maintaining confidence in the institution itself and to ensuring that future officers are equipped to command a racially diverse military. A racially homogeneous educational setting, the brief concluded, does not support this mission.[68] Retired high-ranking military officials would file similar amicus briefs in both *Fisher v. University of Texas* and the Students for Fair Admissions cases against Harvard and UNC, a testament to the enduring benefits and necessity of diversity in the military.[69]

The corporate briefs in *Grutter* similarly argue that diversity in higher education is key to ensuring the cross-cultural competence of the labor force, a necessity of doing business in a global marketplace.[70] Without such competence, businesses are ill-equipped to satisfy multifarious customer bases and establish productive working relationships with international business partners.[71] Here again, Justice O'Connor drew attention to these briefs as a reason for continuing to allow universities to consider race in building a diverse student body.

Like Justice Powell before her, O'Connor was an unlikely savior of diversity-based admissions. When President Reagan named her to the Court in 1981, she was seen as a reliably conservative vote.[72] In previous cases involving affirmative action, she had criticized the use of race in government selection decisions. She was part of a five-member majority in the three major affirmative action cases the Court heard between 1981 and her 2003 opinion in *Grutter*. The first was a 1986 decision condemning a plan to protect non-white teachers from layoffs by making an exception to a school district's seniority policy.[73] The second was a 1989 decision rejecting a city ordinance that required the city's contractors to subcontract at least 30 percent of their work to minority-owned businesses.[74] The third was a 1995 decision rejecting an affirmative-action-in-contracting program adopted by the federal Department of Transportation and the Small Business Administration.[75] Given her votes in those cases, there was little reason to expect her to save a program that considered race as a factor in college admissions decisions. But she did.

Among liberal academics, *Grutter* drew mixed reactions. While most were pleased that they (we) could consider race and ethnicity in admissions, they were unhappy with diversity as a justification. Most hoped that the Court would permit race-conscious affirmative action either as a form of reparations or as a remedy for past and continuing discrimination. That the diversity justification had been put forward by two conservative justices, Powell and O'Connor, added to their discomfort. Among academics, basing affirmative action on diversity drew skepticism from both the left and the right. Conservatives thought diversity admissions was a destructive and unconstitutional policy of liberal social engineering relying on stereotypes about Black Americans and other minority group members. Liberals thought it was a conservative compromise designed to improve the education of white students with little regard for Black students' success.

Justice O'Connor concluded her majority opinion with the hope that in another twenty-five years, affirmative action programs would no longer be needed.[76] Many read this to mean that diversity had been cemented as a legitimate factor in admissions for at least a generation. It was not to be.

Just a few years after the *Grutter* decision, a wealthy businessman named Edward Blum decided to use his millions—and his ability to raise millions more from right-wing donors—to bring a series of legal challenges that almost seemed designed to undermine the success of Black Americans in education, politics, and business.[77] Although his first efforts were unsuccessful, he has ultimately had a profound impact on American law and society.[78] Blum persuaded the Supreme Court to gut the Voting Rights Act and to condone efforts to reduce the voices of Black voters through gerrymandering and voter suppression.[79] He has taken the lead in challenging policies and laws intended to promote diversity on corporate boards.[80] He sued successfully to reduce the number of Black and Hispanic children admitted to Houston's programs for gifted children.[81] And he managed to bring four cases to the Supreme Court challenging the *Grutter* and *Bakke* holdings favoring diversity admissions.[82] In the first two, against the University of Texas, he narrowly failed to achieve his goal.[83] With a change of tactics, he succeeded. In cases Blum brought against Harvard and the University of North Carolina, the Court voted 6–3 to reverse its holdings in *Fisher, Grutter,* and *Bakke.* As of June 2023, diversity no longer justifies the consideration of race in college or university admissions—except at our military academies.[84]

In an interview with the British news and opinion website UnHerd in May 2023, shortly before the Harvard and UNC cases were decided, Blum described his ultimate goal in challenging affirmative action policies: "My great hope is that the opinion that comes out of these two Supreme Court cases provides the US with a legal doctrine that can be applied with regards to employment, to fellowships and scholarships, to voting and contracting issues, and that ... the justices give us something that not only applies to higher education, but also to other, very important areas of American life."[85]

Blum began his attacks on affirmative action in higher education by searching for a white student who had been rejected by the University of Texas and was willing to serve as a plaintiff in a challenge to the university's admissions program.[86] He found Abigail Fisher, the daughter of a friend. Most students at UT are admitted through the "Top 10 Percent Plan," by which any high school seniors graduating in the top 10 percent of their class may attend any UT campus (or, for UT Austin, the top 6 percent).[87] The plan relies on the fact that because most Texas high schools are in effect racially segregated, the top 10 percent at largely minority high schools will include many students of color. As Justice Ruth

Bader Ginsburg put it, "Texas' percentage plan was adopted with racially segregated neighborhoods and schools front and center stage."[88]

Fisher, who had good but not great grades and test scores, did not graduate in the top 10 percent of her high school class.[89] But UT also admitted a small number of students outside the top 10 percent using a holistic review process, modeled on the Harvard Plan, that included race and ethnicity as factors. Blum argued (on Fisher's behalf) that as a white person, Fisher was discriminated against by the holistic review process. The case reached the Supreme Court twice. In 2013, the Court returned it to the lower courts for additional fact-finding, holding that before a college or university could use race as a factor in admissions, it must prove that no race-neutral alternatives would achieve the desired result. In 2016, in an opinion by Justice Kennedy, the Court upheld UT's diversity admissions plan, reaffirming the Powell opinion in *Bakke* and the O'Connor opinion in *Grutter*.[90]

Kennedy, like Powell and O'Connor, was an unlikely savior of diversity-based admissions. He was a Reagan appointee, like O'Connor, and was considered a reliably conservative vote.[91] In 1989 and 1995, he joined with O'Connor in the five-member majority opposed to race-based affirmative action in government contracting.[92] And in *Grutter*, he was one of the four dissenters prepared to reject the Powell opinion from *Bakke*.[93] When *Fisher* was first heard in 2013, Kennedy wrote the majority opinion sending it back to the trial court for further fact-finding.[94]

In that case, known as *Fisher I*, Kennedy had articulated a starting point based on a long line of civil rights decisions:

> Distinctions between citizens solely because of their ancestry are by their very nature odious to a free people, and therefore are contrary to our traditions and hence constitutionally suspect. Because racial characteristics so seldom provide a relevant basis for disparate treatment, the Equal Protection Clause demands that racial classifications be subjected to the most rigid scrutiny. To implement these canons, judicial review must begin from the position that any official action that treats a person differently on account of his race or ethnic origin is inherently suspect. Strict scrutiny is a searching examination, and it is the government that bears the burden to prove that the reasons for any racial classification are clearly identified and unquestionably legitimate.[95]

Given Kennedy's skepticism of distinctions made on the basis of race, most observers expected that the Court would ultimately reject the Texas admissions program.

Among the amici briefs in *Fisher I* was a brief by thirteen universities of every size and from every region describing how they now follow the Harvard Plan, entitled "Holistic Review Of Individual Applications Allows Consideration Of How Each Individual Student Can Contribute To The Diversity Of The Student Body."[96] The amici described their admissions policies post-*Bakke* as compliant with the Harvard Plan. Applicants from minority groups were not evaluated separately from white candidates, nor were seats in any entering class reserved for applicants of a particular race or ethnicity. Rather, the amici considered race or ethnicity as one factor among many used to ensure that their classes are diverse across multiple dimensions. These factors included, but were not limited to, the life experiences, accomplishments, and talents of each applicant. The schools considered whether the applicant was the first in the family to attend college, whether languages other than English were spoken at home, and whether the applicant came from a disadvantaged background.[97] Some of these factors correlated with race and ethnicity, as members of racial or ethnic minority groups were more likely than white applicants to come from disadvantaged families, but the categories were treated as distinct.

A second brief in *Fisher* made much the same point on behalf of another group of ten universities known for their strong science and technology programs.[98] The amici described how they have adopted holistic, individualized admissions policies that consider race as only one, nondeterminative factor.[99] They regarded these holistic admissions policies as essential to achieve educational diversity both within their student bodies and within specific disciplines, programs, and areas of study. The brief argued that educational diversity was especially important to these private research universities because people of color and women have long been significantly underrepresented in science, technology, engineering, and mathematics.[100]

To the surprise of most court observers, when the case returned to the Court in 2016 as *Fisher II*, Justice Kennedy wrote a plurality opinion reaffirming the decisions and reasoning of *Grutter* and *Bakke*.[101] It was within a university's academic freedom, Kennedy wrote, to consider race as a factor in admissions in order to achieve the educational benefits of diversity if racially neutral methods were insufficient.

Kennedy found that the University of Texas had engaged in extensive outreach efforts to African American and Hispanic students, establishing three new scholarship programs, opening new regional admissions centers, increasing its recruitment budget by $500,000, and organizing over one thousand recruitment events. The university had also tried to increase diversity by giving applicants' socioeconomic background more weight in admissions. But none of these measures was sufficient in achieving a student body that was racially and ethnically diverse.[102] Kennedy noted that when race-conscious admissions were banned in Texas after *Hopwood* and before *Grutter*, the University of Texas had admitted no more than 309 African American students in each freshman class of approximately seven thousand students, about 4.4 percent, even though African American Texans had then constituted some 12 to 13 percent of the state's recent high school graduates.[103]

In light of these facts, Justice Kennedy found that the University of Texas's affirmative action admissions policy was "narrowly tailored" and thus permitted.[104] He concluded the opinion by noting that a university was owed great deference "in defining those intangible characteristics, like student body diversity, that are central to its identity and educational mission."[105]

Justice Samuel Alito wrote a fifty-page dissent, almost three times longer than Kennedy's opinion, arguing that UT Austin's use of race as a factor in admissions decisions was unconstitutional and commenting that the majority had sided with the university "simply because it is tired of this case."[106] Curiously, he challenged the university's race-conscious admissions plan because it allegedly discriminated against Asian American students: "UT decided to use racial preferences to benefit African-American and Hispanic students because it considers those groups 'underrepresented minorities.' ... Even though UT's classroom study showed that more classes lacked Asian-American students than lacked Hispanic students, ... UT deemed Asian-Americans '*overrepresented*' based on state demographics" (emphasis original).[107] By repeatedly referencing Asian American students, the Alito dissent was nodding to Blum's next set of challenges to affirmative action, which were already making their way through the federal court system.

Following the decision in *Fisher I*, Edward Blum had switched tactics. While he continued to fund the *Fisher II* litigation, he was also placing advertisements seeking Asian American students denied admission to

Harvard, the University of North Carolina, and the University of Wisconsin.[108] In 2014 he brought suits against Harvard and the University of North Carolina, claiming that both universities were discriminating against Asian Americans in their admissions process, though he declined to name a student as a plaintiff, suing instead in the name of a non-profit organization he established, Students for Fair Admissions (SFFA).[109] The two cases were merged in the Supreme Court. The theory of his cases was that universities were discriminating against Asian American students in evaluating their applications and that the proper remedy should be to stop considering racial diversity as a factor in admissions decisions.[110] That this is a non sequitur didn't seem to bother him.

Harvard, of course, had a long history of using diversity as a factor in admissions, but the University of North Carolina had adopted its diversity admissions policies quite recently. Chartered in 1789, UNC is the oldest public university in the United States.[111] It did not admit Black students for more than one hundred sixty years. In response to *Missouri ex rel. Gaines v. Canada*, 305 U.S. 337 (1938), which held that the state of Missouri was required to provide comparable educational facilities for Black students or otherwise integrate them in its existing white law schools, North Carolina established a separate law school for Black students, now known as the North Carolina Central University School of Law, rather than allow them to enroll at UNC.[112] That same year, UNC denied admission to Pauli Murray because she was Black.[113] Her rejection letter read: "Under the laws of North Carolina, and under the resolutions of the Board of Trustees of the University of North Carolina, members of your race are not admitted to the University. It has long been the social policy of the State to maintain separate schools for the whites and Negroes."[114]

It would be another thirteen years before the first Black students enrolled at UNC. They were five Black men—Harvey Beech, James Lassiter, J. Kenneth Lee, Floyd McKissick, and James Robert Walker—who entered the UNC School of Law in 1951 following the federal court order in *McKissick v. Carmichael*.[115] That year, Pauli Murray tried again to seek admission at the UNC School of Law, this time to earn a doctorate, but she was again turned down.[116] Even after *Brown*, Black enrollment at UNC remained low for years; there were four Black freshmen in 1960 and eighteen in 1963.[117]

Recent enrollment of Black students at UNC remains shockingly low. In 2019, when the population of North Carolina was 22.2 percent

Black, Black students comprised only 8.1 percent of UNC's undergraduate population.[118] The amicus brief from the NAACP Legal Defense and Educational Fund in the Harvard/UNC case noted that the problem was especially acute for Black male students: "From 2009 until at least 2017, UNC enrolled, at most, 125 Black men in an incoming first-year class of over 4,000 students—thus making Black men approximately 2.8 percent of the incoming class as compared to about 11 percent of the state's population. In 2021, there were only 95 Black men enrolled in a first-year class of over 4,500 students, representing just 2 percent of the class."[119]

Following a two-year stay pending the decision in *Fisher II*, the case against Harvard filed by the Students for Fair Admissions went to a three-week bench trial before the federal district court in Boston in October 2018.[120] *SFFA v. UNC* had a similar trajectory: SFFA filed suit in November 2014, and the case was tried in federal court in October 2021.[121] What's peculiar about these lawsuits is that neither identified any student who was denied admission at Harvard or UNC; there is no Marco DeFunis, Allan Bakke, Barbara Grutter, or Abigail Fisher. Despite outreach efforts to find Asian American plaintiffs, SFFA cites only a single unnamed Asian American student who was denied admission to Harvard in its 120-page complaint.[122] It did not find any Asian American applicant to pit against UNC; its unnamed applicant was white.[123]

Despite the lack of an actual Asian American applicant claiming exclusion from Harvard and UNC, the district courts in Massachusetts and North Carolina allowed the cases to go forward.[124] In both instances, the parties engaged in extensive discovery. In the *Harvard* litigation, discovery lasted about twelve months, during which SFFA reviewed over 160,000 student admissions files.[125] SFFA hired Peter Arcidiacono, an economist and professor at Duke University, as an expert witness in both cases.[126] Both SFFA and the universities relied on statistical evidence to determine whether Harvard's and UNC's admissions policies discriminated against Asian American students. In the *Harvard* litigation, SFFA alleged that the university discriminated against Asian American applicants by assigning them lower personal rating scores than those of white applicants who were similarly situated. SFFA claimed that, absent discrimination, Harvard would have enrolled a class that was 28 percent Asian American instead of 24 percent Asian American, as in the class actually enrolled.[127] In the *UNC* litigation, SFFA adopted a broader strategy, claiming that UNC–Chapel Hill's consideration of race in admissions was not narrowly tailored because it failed to consider race merely as a "plus"

factor and ignored race-neutral alternatives that, SFFA asserted, could result in a diverse student body.[128]

It would be an understatement to describe the judicial opinions generated by these cases as lengthy. In the aggregate, they are far longer
than this book. The district court decisions alone were eighty-one pages
in the *Harvard* case and eighty-eight in the *UNC* case.[129] The Supreme
Court decision ran 237 pages.[130] Both district courts ruled in favor of the
universities, finding that their admissions practices were narrowly tailored as required by the Constitution and fully compliant with the precedents in *Fisher, Grutter,* and *Bakke.* Judge Allison D. Burroughs for the
District Court of Massachusetts wrote:

> The statistics themselves are alone not enough to cause the
> Court to conclude that Harvard has engaged in improper inten-
> tional discrimination where Harvard has shown that its admis-
> sions policy uses race only in a permissible and narrowly tailored
> way. . . . Even assuming that there is a statistically significant dif-
> ference between how Asian American and white applicants score
> on the personal rating, the data does not clearly say what ac-
> counts for that difference. In other words, although the statistics
> perhaps tell "what," they do not tell "why," and here the "why" is
> critically important. Further, by its very nature, the personal
> score includes, and should include, aspects of an applicant and
> his or her application that are not easily quantifiable and there-
> fore cannot be fully captured by the statistical data.[131]

Similarly, Judge Loretta C. Biggs of the Middle District of North
Carolina found that "the University engages in a highly individualized,
holistic admissions program that is narrowly tailored in that it considers
race flexibly as only a 'plus factor' among many factors for each and every
applicant and race is not a defining feature in any of its admissions decisions."[132] Moreover, Judge Biggs concluded, "because race is so interwo-
ven in every aspect of the lived experience of minority students, to ignore
it, reduce its importance and measure it only by statistical models as SFFA
has done, misses important context [and obscures] racial barriers and obstacles that have been faced, overcome and are yet to be overcome."[133]

Both courts held that race-neutral alternatives would not produce
the educational benefits of diversity that both Harvard and UNC sought
as well as their existing race-conscious policies did. Expert testimony in

the *UNC* litigation showed that "more than 100 race-neutral simulations, including socioeconomic status plans, high school top X percent plans, [and] geography-based simulations" all yielded a less diverse student body.[134] Eliminating consideration of race in Harvard's admissions policies "would cause the African American representation at Harvard to decline from approximately 14% to 6% of the student population and Hispanic representation to decline from 14% to 9%."[135] Over four years, an estimated one thousand African American and Hispanic students who would otherwise have enrolled would be denied admission under a race-neutral plan.[136] The court noted that "Harvard's current admissions policy does not result in underqualified students being admitted in the name of diversity—rather, the tip given for race impacts who among the highly-qualified students in the applicant pool will be selected for admission to a class that is too small to accommodate more than a small percentage of those qualified for admission."[137]

The First Circuit Court of Appeals upheld the *Harvard* decision in November 2020.[138] In most eras of American legal history, the case would have gone no further. But the Supreme Court took both cases, skipping an appeals court review of the *UNC* case, and in June 2023 it reversed the trial courts' judgments and overruled forty-five years of precedent, holding by a 6–3 vote that diversity is not a compelling reason to consider race in admissions decisions. That was all it ruled. There was no broad ruling about the use of race or the value of diversity outside of college admissions. But it was enough to destabilize not only higher education but education at all levels, as well as much of American government and business.

The majority opinion, written by Chief Justice John Roberts, described the goal of diversity as "commendable" but simultaneously dismissed the proposition that colleges and universities measurably benefit from racial diversity as "not sufficiently coherent" and "amorphous."[139] Roberts further found—contradicting the district court findings—that there was insufficient evidence supporting the assertion that diversity improved learning. (There was, of course, a great deal of evidence of the benefits of racial diversity provided by the colleges and by amici, and the dissents cited it.) The sole exception the Court noted was for military academies, which could, for now, continue their race-conscious admissions practices. As Justice Ketanji Brown Jackson put it, Black and Hispanic students were "welcome in the bunker, not the boardroom."[140]

The Court relied on the plaintiff's arguments—which had been rejected by the district courts and appellate court—to find that the diversity admissions plans only benefited Black and Hispanic students and in so doing discriminated against Asian American applicants.[141] There is a procedural rule that binds the Supreme Court to accept lower courts' findings of fact unless they are "clearly erroneous," a rule the majority disregarded.[142]

In a concurring opinion, Justice Thomas continued the theme of his questions at oral argument, complaining that the term "diversity" was meaningless except as a code word for racial preferences and an excuse to discriminate. Thomas was especially critical of the universities' arguments that their diversity admissions practices considered multiple factors, some of which benefited white and Asian American applicants. He wrote of the diversity admissions policies as if race were the only thing the schools considered under such policies, and only to the benefit of Black and Hispanic applicants.[143] But he did not speak for the majority. His opinion concurred with Chief Justice Roberts's opinion for the Court, but Justice Thomas spoke alone in expressing his more radical view of diversity-based admissions.

While Roberts and Thomas claimed that diversity was only an excuse for discrimination, the dissenting opinion by Justice Jackson, the Court's newest member, described diversity in terms that Archibald Cox would have appreciated:

> UNC has developed a holistic review process to evaluate applicants for admission. ... Students are *not* required to submit demographic information like gender and race. UNC considers whatever information each applicant submits using a nonexhaustive list of 40 criteria grouped into eight categories: "academic performance, academic program, standardized testing, extracurricular activity, special talent, essay criteria, background, and personal criteria."
>
> Drawing on those 40 criteria, a UNC staff member "evaluat[es] ... engagement outside the classroom; persistence of commitment; demonstrated capacity for leadership; contributions to family, school, and community; work history; [and] unique or unusual interests." Relevant, too, would be "relative advantage or disadvantage, as indicated by family income level, education history of family members, impact of parents/guardians in the home, or formal education environment; experience of growing up in rural or center-city locations; [and his] status as

child or step-child of Carolina alumni." The list goes on. The process is holistic, through and through.

So where does race come in? According to UNC's admissions-policy document, reviewers may also consider "the race or ethnicity of any student" (if that information is provided) in light of UNC's interest in diversity. And, yes, "the race or ethnicity of *any* student may—or may not—receive a 'plus' in the evaluation process depending on the individual circumstances revealed in the student's application." Stephen Farmer, the head of UNC's Office of Undergraduate Admissions, confirmed at trial (under oath) that UNC's admissions process operates in this fashion.

Thus, to be crystal clear: *Every* student who chooses to disclose his or her race is eligible for such a race-linked plus, just as any student who chooses to disclose his or her unusual interests can be credited for what those interests might add to UNC. The record supports no intimation to the contrary. Eligibility is just that; a plus is never automatically awarded, never considered in numerical terms, and never automatically results in an offer of admission. There are no race-based quotas in UNC's holistic review process. In fact, during the admissions cycle, the school prevents anyone who knows the overall racial makeup of the admitted-student pool from reading any applications.

More than that, every applicant is also eligible for a diversity-linked plus (beyond race) more generally. And, notably, UNC understands diversity broadly, including "socioeconomic status, first-generation college status . . . political beliefs, religious beliefs . . . diversity of thoughts, experiences, ideas, and talents."[144]

In addition to the carveout for the military academies, the majority opinion emphasized that colleges remain free to consider diversity factors other than race and ethnicity, and it left open an interesting opportunity for college admissions officers and applicants of color. Chief Justice Roberts wrote, "nothing in this opinion should be construed as prohibiting universities from considering an applicant's discussion of how race affected his or her life, be it through discrimination, inspiration, or otherwise."[145] It remains to be seen whether selective colleges will continue to seek diversity by putting a high value on applicants who can articulate how their experiences of race and racism have given them a perspective that will benefit the school's educational goals.

One more observation about the Harvard/UNC majority decision seems noteworthy. Chief Justice Roberts, in his majority opinion, suggested that a new test may apply to practices that are race-blind but nonetheless produce racial/ethnic diversity. He warned colleges and universities that if they try to get around the decision by devising other means of admitting racially diverse student bodies, the Court will stop them. Abandoning earlier precedents, he suggested that race-blind admissions policies that were intended to produce racial diversity—or perhaps even race-blind policies that, regardless of intent, have the effect of producing racial diversity—may also violate civil rights laws.[146] This comment seemed to assume bad faith by America's educators and to take an extremely broad view of the meaning of "reverse discrimination," an odd position for a court that has been very skeptical of discrimination claims by women and people of color. The journalist Chris Williams of *Above the Law* has suggested that this position could endanger law school admissions policies that favor U.S. military veterans, because Black Americans are overrepresented—increasingly so—in the military.[147]

Of the ninety-three amicus briefs the Court received, sixty supported Harvard and UNC–Chapel Hill. Two briefs, filed on behalf of eighty-four Asian American advocacy groups, including the Asian American Legal Defense and Education Fund and the Asian Americans Advancing Justice non-profit organization, rejected the argument that Asian American students do not benefit from diversity-informed admissions policies.[148] Thousands of Harvard students and alumni from a variety of racial and ethnic backgrounds submitted an amicus brief in which they noted the educational benefits of diverse classrooms, commenting on "the deep appreciation professors and classmates showed for their unique perspectives" and describing "how the diverse community of students reduced their feelings of isolation" and "how on-campus diversity helped prepare them for working and living in this nation's pluralistic society."[149] As in *Grutter* and *Fisher*, the universities defending their admissions programs gathered support from amici representing a wide range of stakeholders: other universities, including Historically Black Colleges and Universities (HBCUs); educators (including a brief from law school deans that I authored); school boards and administrators; bar associations and civil rights organizations; labor unions; professional associations of psychologists; high-ranking military officials; media and broadcasting entities; members of Congress; attorneys general and governors of U.S. states;

leading technology and communications firms; scientists; faith-based institutions; and over 1,200 social science researchers.[150] The breadth and depth of the amicus briefs filed in the *Harvard* and *UNC* cases reflect the enduring and wide acceptance of the proposition that diversity has benefits in education and beyond.

Yet the Supreme Court disregarded the long history of precedents written by conservative judges who joined liberals to protect race-conscious admissions—much as it had done in the *Dobbs* case the previous year, when it overturned fifty years of constitutional law protecting abortion. Ironically, even as the Court was departing from history and precedent to deny the educational value of diversity, a growing body of scholarship was strengthening the empirical evidence that diversity benefits learning, teaching, and decision-making in the classroom and beyond.

PART IV

The Diversity Principle's Benefits Are Recognized and Championed by Educators, Business Leaders, and Scientists

CHAPTER THIRTEEN

Diversity Science

ILHELM VON HUMBOLDT, John and Harriet Mills, Charles Eliot, and those they influenced all advocated for diversity on the basis of theory and personal observation. They believed exposure to the voices of outsiders would improve individual character (*Bildung*), teaching and learning, scientific inquiry, and civil discourse. But they had no proof. Instead, they relied on what we might call creative speculation, or what Malcolm Gladwell might call a "hunch."[1]

Others disagreed. They believed homogeneity improved decision-making, wealth-building, and social cohesion. Some who held this view were nationalists or racial supremacists, but others were interested in what today we call "cultural fit." As a recent article in the *Harvard Business Review* put it, "On a homogenous team, people readily understand each other and collaboration flows smoothly, giving the sensation of progress. Dealing with outsiders causes friction, which feels counterproductive."[2]

In recent decades, researchers have used the tools of modern social science to test out these theories. Their vast and growing body of research has largely validated the diversity principle. Companies make higher profits when their workforces and boards are more diverse; students learn more when they study in diverse classrooms and live in diverse student communities; scholarly journals select more impactful papers for publication when their editorial boards are more diverse; doctors trained in diverse groups provide better medical care; and diverse scientific research teams are more effective. The once popular idea that homogeneity benefits decision-making because it reduces conflict is being upended by the evidence. It appears that Eliot was right to rebuild Harvard to emphasize the clash of ideas by seeking the voices of outsiders—and that universities across the country were right to follow his lead. Although dealing with outsiders does cause friction, and even though that friction sometimes feels counterproductive, it's actually positively productive.

Not every study supports the proposition that diversity produces value. Scientific inquiry rarely produces 100 percent certainty. But the growing body of evidence is impossible to ignore. The growth in consensus on the benefits of diversity tracks a similar phenomenon in climate science. In the 1970s, a handful of scientists began reporting that the earth's atmosphere appeared to be changing in response to increased carbon levels, and they warned that the change could affect our climate. Many were skeptical, some even derisive. But over time the evidence mounted to the point that there is now a scientific consensus that burning carbon has induced climate change. There are still deniers, but they are increasingly isolated. The same is true of diversity. Some of the holdouts are honestly skeptical of the benefits of diversity, and some are ideologically motivated. But even as the courts move away from their long-standing deference to universities on the subjects of diversity and academic freedom, the scientific research increasingly affirms the universities' positions.

Two psychology professors, Katherine Phillips and Victoria Plaut, stand out for their pathbreaking work in the emerging field of diversity science. Phillips, who died of breast cancer in 2020 at the age of 47, produced more than one hundred studies investigating the benefits of diversity in commerce, teaching and learning, science, and civic engagement.[3] Her research brought her to the conclusion for which she is best remembered; as the title of an article she published in *Scientific American* put it, "Diversity Makes Us Smarter."[4] Plaut, who is my colleague at Berkeley, popularized the term "diversity science."[5] Her work extended Phillips's research, demonstrating that reaping the benefits of diversity is not possible without an additional focus on equity and inclusion (now collectively known as DEI).

A Black woman who grew up in a predominantly Black neighborhood of Chicago, Katherine Phillips was a living testament to the value of diversity. As a third grader, she was chosen for her academic excellence "to attend a nearly all-white magnet school" in a nearby neighborhood.[6] In the words of her husband, Damon Phillips, she was "the product of an attempt by policymakers to create a more diverse educational setting."[7] Over time it became clear to Phillips that these childhood experiences deeply influenced her career trajectory, and this realization informed her desire to understand the impact of these efforts.

In a *New York Times* retrospective on Phillips's work, Stacy Cowley writes:

> In a videotaped talk at Columbia in 2015, Professor Phillips spoke of her early background in straddling social groups in Chicago and as a college track and field athlete. "My life in the middle led me to a question: What small change can we make as individuals to capture the benefits of diversity?" ... The answer she arrived at was to fight the impulse to seek out commonalities with those we encounter and instead "embrace your differences" by talking about contrasting life experiences. "The environment you will create will be one where difference is normal. ... If you create that kind of environment in your organizations, in your schools, in your families, you will find that the value of diversity is there for you to capture."[8]

After graduating from the University of Illinois at Urbana-Champaign with a degree in psychology, Phillips went on to earn a doctorate in organizational behavior from Stanford's Graduate School of Business in 1999. She joined the faculty at the Kellogg School of Management at Northwestern in 2006 and became the first Black woman to receive tenure there.[9] She co-directed and founded Northwestern's Center on the Science of Diversity, whose goal, she wrote on her LinkedIn page, is "to bring together scholars who share a common interest in the challenges and opportunities associated with social diversity. ... Understanding the barriers and opportunities associated with creating diverse social environments that are positive, sustainable settings for productive exchange is an objective worthy of rigorous scientific inquiry."[10]

In 2011, Phillips moved to Columbia University, where she became the first Black woman to receive tenure at Columbia Business School.[11] She led the Sanford C. Bernstein & Co. Center for Leadership and Ethics and was a mentor to scores of scientists and students.[12] "Kathy not only influenced scholarly thought on the topic" of diversity, wrote the Academy of Management, "but she also worked to make the Academy of Management more inclusive. She was an amazing supporter of junior scholars including women of color."[13] The Academy called her "one of the most recognizable and powerful voices on organizational diversity research."[14]

Phillips is best known for demonstrating that identity diversity and viewpoint diversity are linked, and that they help groups of all kinds make better decisions. Her work assessed the benefits of race, sex, and gender diversity on group problem-solving—for example, how well a group solves a fictional murder mystery.[15] She showed that the experiences and viewpoints of diverse group members get us out of our comfort zones and push us to consider a wider range of ideas. She also found that diverse groups are more than the sum of their parts. Because these groups have a more robust exchange of ideas, their members generate ideas they would not have otherwise considered. The lesson, she wrote, is that "when we hear dissent from someone who is different from us, it provokes more thought than when it comes from someone who looks like us. ... When disagreement comes from a socially different person, we are prompted to work harder. Diversity jolts us into cognitive action in ways that homogeneity simply does not."[16] In a sense, Phillips supplied empirical proof for Mill's 1867 speech to the students at St. Andrews, that people from different backgrounds wear "differently coloured glasses ... and those of other nations, as the most different, are the best [at exposing us to the benefits of diversity]."[17]

Just as Phillips was making waves in the world of organizational psychology, other researchers were examining the diversity principle's impact in higher education. At the time *Bakke* was decided in 1978, arguments supporting diversity in higher education had begun to reflect their American context, taking into account the country's history of racial discrimination and linking diversity with academic freedom under the First Amendment. But they otherwise resembled the arguments made by Wilhelm von Humboldt two centuries earlier—long on theory and observation, but short on empirical data. In the run-up to the 2003 *Grutter* decision, however, that began to change.

When the *Grutter* case went to trial, the lawyers for the University of Michigan asked law school deans to testify about their personal experience with the benefits of diversity. The deans emphasized that the "active, Socratic teaching" practiced in law schools relies on a classroom of students "drawing on a broad range of backgrounds and experiences which are personal."[18] As one former dean put it, this method of teaching involves "direct and often painful dialogue between students who are forced by the method to confront and make explicit their deepest unexamined convictions about legal issues."[19] The Court noted that the dean "testified that racial heterogeneity improves the classroom dynamic even in classes 'far removed from issues traditionally associated with race' such as insurance."[20]

But unlike Thurgood Marshall, for whom Erwin Griswold testified in strikingly similar terms fifty years earlier, the lawyers in *Grutter* could back up their witnesses' claims with empirical data. The flood of research on higher education diversity began in 1998, when William Bowen and Derek Bok published *The Shape of the River: Long-Term Consequences of Considering Race in College and University Admissions.*[21] Bok was a former president of Harvard, Bowen a former president of Princeton. (It was Bok, as president of Harvard, who asked his mentor Archibald Cox to write the amicus brief in *DeFunis*.) They oversaw a multiyear study that followed the progress of over eighty thousand students from twenty-eight selective colleges and universities over thirty years. The study concluded that the evidence was overwhelming that affirmative action had worked: Black students admitted to selective colleges had done well both in school and in life after school. While the Bowen and Bok study focused mostly on the benefits of affirmative action, not of diversity per se, the study showed that the presence of Black students at the universities in the study contributed not only to their own success but to the success of their white peers. White students especially felt that the diversity they experienced helped them get along better with students of other races.[22]

In 2002, a longitudinal study published in the *Harvard Education Review* offered more evidence. Patricia Gurin, Eric Dey, Sylvia Hurtado, and Gerald Gurin found that "informal interaction among different racial and ethnic groups during the college years benefits students' academic and social growth."[23] Diversity improved their ability to think critically and solve problems more readily and to value diverse perspectives. The authors also devoted much of their paper to reviewing dozens of other studies published between 1993 and 2000, noting that "across these different approaches and different samples of students and faculty, researchers have found similar results showing that a wide variety of individual, institutional, and societal benefits are linked with diversity experiences."[24]

In *Grutter*, Justice O'Connor relied in part on these findings to uphold the diversity rationale for race-conscious admissions, writing in her majority opinion that "numerous studies show that student body diversity promotes learning outcomes, and better prepares students for an increasingly diverse workforce and society, and better prepares them as professionals."[25] Since the *Grutter* decision, the pace of diversity research has only increased. The following year, a 2004 study examining the interaction of 357 Black and white students at three universities showed that white students saw participation by Black students as adding novel ideas in group discussions; in addition, "positive effects on integrative complexity were found when the groups had racial-and-opinion-minority members and when members reported having racially diverse friends and classmates."[26] That is, racial diversity led to better decision-making and problem-solving. A 2005 study replicated these results on a larger scale. Data from more than four thousand students at nine universities showed that students who learned in diverse classrooms had better analytical problem-solving skills and complex thinking skills.[27]

Researchers have proposed multiple explanations for why diversity helps groups—and individual members of those groups—think better. One 2005 meta-analysis showed that diversity had a positive effect on cognitive complexity in group discussions of controversial topics (two examples tested were the death penalty and child labor) because non-white students brought a different perspective to the discussion.[28]

Katherine Phillips's work suggests that diversity also brings benefits beyond the novel perspectives that people with different backgrounds may contribute. In 2006, she found that members of diverse groups were more likely to share dissenting views. In homogeneous groups, individuals with dissenting views were less comfortable giving their opinions. This is unfortunate, she wrote, because introducing a dissenting view into a conversation should lead the group to consider alternatives and seek more information, which should be beneficial for decision-making. This study contributed to the growing body of evidence that surface-level diversity that is easily identifiable (such as racial and gender diversity) is beneficial to groups.[29]

Another study by Phillips, published in 2009, revealed that the discomfort people feel in groups with those they perceive as "other" may be a key to understanding why diverse groups are better at problem-solving.[30] In this case, the homogeneous groups consisted of members of fraternities and sororities at a midwestern university. When a non-member was added to the group, the group performed better in a murder mystery task. The performance gains did not result from the new group member's ideas, but from the original members' reaction to the new member's presence. Groups with out-group newcomers were more willing to change their initial opinions than were socially homogeneous groups. Interestingly, groups with out-group newcomers felt less confident in their decisions— even though their results were more accurate—and felt they worked together less effectively than groups with in-group newcomers. "Lacking the social threat of allying with an out-group member," Phillips explained, "oldtimers in socially homogeneous groups were less motivated to reconcile the clash of opinions between themselves and other group members, resulting in subpar performance."[31] The "mere presence" of diversity in a group creates awkwardness, and the need to diffuse this tension leads to better group problem-solving.[32]

In addition to helping students learn to think critically and solve problems, exposure to diversity also increases intellectual engagement, improves intellectual and personal self-confidence, and enables students to integrate multiple perspectives, according to a 2016 meta-analysis by the sociologists Richard Pitt and Josh Packard.[33] A 2005 study conducted at the University of Michigan showed that "students with more experiences with diversity, particularly enrollment in diversity courses and positive interactions with diverse peers, are more likely to score higher on academic self-confidence, social agency, and critical thinking disposition."[34]

These benefits begin well before college. A 2019 study published in *Applied Developmental Science* examined 526 students in the third grade through the fifth grade in thirty-five urban public elementary schools. The study showed—as Pauli Murray predicted—that "classroom diversity was positively related to teachers' reports of child social competence and teacher-child closeness and negatively related to child-reported depression."[35]

Despite this weight of empirical evidence, the diversity principle has its detractors. In 2014, Professor Peter H. Schuck of Yale Law School wrote that "the premises underlying the diversity rationale for race-based affirmative action are empirically tenuous and theoretically implausible."[36] That same year, the conservative scholar-activist Abigail Thernstrom asserted that "the entire edifice of [affirmative action] is built on a purely speculative promise that 'diversity' will bring educational benefits."[37] Two years later, ignoring thousands of studies, the economist Thomas Sowell voiced a particularly acerbic version of this skepticism: "Nothing so epitomizes the politically correct gullibility of

our times as the magic word 'diversity.' The wonders of diversity are pro-
claimed from the media . . . and confirmed in the august chambers of the
Supreme Court of the United States. But have you ever seen one speck
of hard evidence to support the lofty claims?"[38]

The answer to Sowell's question, for those of us who have looked, is
yes, a great deal. Diversity skeptics are increasingly finding their ideas re-
futed by evidence—sometimes in embarrassingly public fashion. In 2022,
four scholars conducted a study of the flagship law reviews at the top
twenty law schools in the United States to examine whether the adoption
of diversity selection policies for student editor positions had affected the
quality of the law reviews. They did so in the shadow of lawsuits against
the Harvard and New York University law reviews by white former editors
who claimed that diversity selection policies had weakened the reviews'
quality and thus damaged the former editors' reputations.[39] The findings
did damage their reputations, but not in the way the former editors anticipated. Using the accepted method of assessing law review quality—the
number of subsequent articles and cases that used the articles published by
the law review as authoritative sources—the study's authors found that over
the five years following the adoption of diversity policies for selecting
editors, the quality of the articles published by the law reviews with more
diverse editorial boards went up by an average of 23 percent.[40] Back in the
days when the white former editors were in charge, the lack of diversity
among their editorial teams led them to select and edit articles that
resulted in fewer citations than they'd have had if they had diversified.

Another way diversity contributes to the public good is by improving our
civic engagement. Interacting with people who come from different
backgrounds, have different lived experiences, hold different views, and
identify with different racial, ethnic, and gender groups helps make people better and more respectful listeners and more open to the ideas of
others.[41]

A 2006 meta-analysis of five hundred studies concluded that positive
intergroup contact reduces prejudice.[42] Other research has shown that
cross-racial interactions had strong positive effects on racial and cultural
engagement; students who attended institutions where they were engaged
in cross-racial interactions showed greater improvements in their knowledge and ability to get along with people of different races or cultures than
did students who had fewer cross-racial interactions.[43] In medicine, a 2019
meta-analysis of studies investigating diversity and health care concluded

that "patients generally fare better when care was provided by more diverse teams. Professional skills-focused studies generally find [that diversity contributes to] improvements to innovation, team communications
and improved risk assessment."[44] The same year, a different study of
racial bias among a group of over three thousand non-Black medical
students showed that "the quality of contact [by non-Black medical stu-
dents] with Black people during medical school predicted non-Black physicians' more positive explicit attitudes and less negative implicit bias
against Black people 2 years later. These findings highlight the role that
interracial contact can play in reducing racial health disparities."[45]

Diversity also helps maintain our democracy. Another longitudinal
study showed that students who regularly encounter people of other
races and ethnicities are more likely to vote and less likely "to perceive
value differences with other racial/ethnic groups. In short, substantial interaction with diverse peers has the effect of providing students with
many opportunities to learn how to resolve conflict and practice democratic skills."[46] Analyzing that longitudinal study, the education professor
Mark Engberg noted that diversity improved "those skills and disposi-
tions that underlie a pluralistic orientation: the ability to see multiple
perspectives; the ability to work cooperatively with diverse people; the
ability to discuss and negotiate controversial issues; openness to having
one's views challenged; and tolerance of others with different beliefs."[47]
He concludes, "For those institutions that take seriously their commitment to turning out graduates who possess the pluralistic skills and dis-
positions needed in today's increasingly diverse workforce and society,
this study has shown that a diverse student body coupled with formal and
informal opportunities to engage in diversity experiences is key to
achieving these goals."[48] A 2011 meta-analysis of multiple studies conducted by Nicholas Bowman produced similar findings, demonstrating
that "diversity experiences are associated with increases in civic attitudes,
behavioral intentions, and behaviors, and the magnitude of this effect is
greater for interpersonal interactions with racial diversity than for curricular and cocurricular diversity experiences."[49]

One important area of civic engagement where diversity has been
proven to matter is in juries, one of the foundations of American democracy,
from which women and Black Americans had long been excluded from participation. The results of that exclusion, including the illegitimate convictions of falsely accused Black defendants, are a national disgrace. Katherine
Phillips reports that a key study by the social psychologist Samuel Sommers,

found that racially diverse groups exchanged a wider range of information during deliberation about a sexual assault case than all-white groups did. In collaboration with judges and jury administrators in a Michigan courtroom, Sommers conducted mock jury trials with a group of real selected jurors. Although the participants knew the mock jury was a court-sponsored experiment, they did not know that the true purpose of the research was to study the impact of racial diversity on jury decision-making. Sommers composed the six-person juries with either all white jurors or four white and two Black jurors. As you might expect, the diverse juries were better at considering case facts, made fewer errors recalling relevant information and displayed a greater openness to discussing the role of race in the case. These improvements did not necessarily happen because the Black jurors brought new information to the group—they happened because white jurors changed their behavior in the presence of the Black jurors. In the presence of diversity, they were more diligent and open-minded.[50]

A study of jury verdicts from 2012 showed that these dynamics have real-world consequences. Analyzing felony trials in Florida between 2000 and 2010, the researchers found that "(i) juries formed from all-white jury pools convict black defendants significantly (16 percentage points) more often than white defendants, and (ii) this gap in conviction rates is entirely eliminated when the jury pool includes at least one black member. The impact of jury race is much greater than what a simple correlation of the race of the seated jury and conviction rates would suggest."[51]

Diversity, the research makes clear, is critically important for the health of our campuses and our democracy. But it isn't a panacea. For institutions to realize the benefits of diversity, they must also focus on equity and inclusion.

Victoria Plaut has been a trailblazer in this regard. A Latina whose mother grew up in Colombia, Plaut never felt she fully belonged to just one culture. From a young age, she said, she "had an interest in understanding the experiences of marginalized communities, and as a student, she sought to build a body of research that would help create more equitable and inclusive environments."[52] She earned a BA in psychology from Harvard in 1996, a master's degree in social psychology from the Lon-

don School of Economics and Political Science in 1997, and a PhD in
social psychology from Stanford in 2003, and she taught at the University of Georgia and the College of the Holy Cross in Worcester, Massachusetts, before her appointment in law and psychology at Berkeley in
2010. In 2022 she was appointed vice-provost.[53]

Initially, Plaut thought inclusion to be primarily of importance to
members of majority groups—demonstrating to whites and men that
they, too, benefited from being part of a diverse group. In 2008, she designed an experiment to study white students' reactions to diversity policies that either emphasized or eliminated language describing the benefit
of diversity policies for whites as well as people of color, and she found
that the language asserting benefits for whites increased white support.
She thus proposed that policies that emphasized "All Inclusive Diversity"
would gain wider acceptance.[54]

But in time she saw that white people and people of color often don't
derive value from diversity in the same way or to the same extent.
Whites profit from the ideas and participation of others, but people of
color benefit from their inclusion only if they are represented in sufficient numbers to avoid social isolation. Their numbers have to reach a
critical mass before they can have truly equal voices and opportunities.[55]
Otherwise, women and people of color often become tokens, formally
included but substantively marginalized, while the advantages of diversity are co-opted. Plaut's insights are being broadly adopted by businesses committed to diversity. As Johnny Taylor, chief executive of the
Society for Human Resource Management, told the *Washington Post*, "we
underestimated that inclusion was the real challenge."[56]

In a 2018 paper, Plaut brings home the problem of diversity without
equity or inclusion through the story of a white male student who complained that his classes lacked racial diversity even though he had paid
for a classroom experience that included Black students. For him, diversity was strictly about his own benefit.[57] Plaut and her co-authors found
that white students were, as theorized, more sympathetic to the view that
diversity aids whites by adding students of color to their classrooms than
to the view that diversity addresses policies and practices of exclusion
that unfairly disadvantage students of color. Justice Thomas makes the
same point in his dissent in the Michigan case, when he describes diversity as whites' aesthetic preference for a few Black faces in the room.[58]

Bias, too, can interfere with the outcomes of diversity, as a 2004 paper
by Katherine Phillips demonstrates. Phillips theorized that being perceived

as an expert should increase one's influence on a group. But possessing expertise may not be enough to get one perceived as an expert. Given men's and women's social roles and the lower performance expectations often held for women, women may be less likely than men to confidently contribute their expertise. Phillips found that women described as experts in a mixed-gender setting were seen as less capable than men. The benefits of diversity were undermined by social prejudice.[59]

Findings like these emphasize the importance of programs that promote equity and inclusion. Plaut's 2014 *Scientific American* article popularized an important study conducted a few years earlier by Gregory Walton and Geoffrey Cohen, in which they asked half of a group of one hundred incoming students to read testimonials from more senior students who wrote about experiencing social difficulties in their first year and worrying that perhaps they did not belong at the school but eventually gaining confidence that they belonged.[60] The other half (the control group) were given unrelated information about changing social and political attitudes. Three years after the intervention, the researchers checked the students' progress. Being in either group made little difference to the white students, but Black students in the experimental group were doing "significantly better academically than their peers in the control group—cutting in half the average achievement gap between racial groups seen at the start of the study."[61]

Workshops and education programs focused on race can help ensure that the rewards of diversity are realized for all students. One study concluded that participation as a first-year student in a multicultural education program promotes democratic sentiments and citizenship practice.[62] Another showed that students who participated in diversity workshops as undergraduates were more cooperative, generous, and civically engaged after graduation and that they demonstrated better leadership skills than those who did not participate. These effects did not depend on the participants' race or ethnicity, gender, and institutional affiliation.[63]

This finding responds to a concern raised by Chief Justice Roberts in the oral argument in *Fisher v. Texas*, in which he asked, "What unique perspective does a minority student bring to a physics class?" Some recent papers are beginning to answer that question.

A 2015 study published in the *Journal of Labor Economics* analyzed the ethnic identity of U.S.-based authors in over 2.5 million scientific papers published between 1985 and 2008; the analysis showed that diversity contributes to the quality of scientific papers: "Greater homophily is associated with publication in lower-impact journals and with fewer citations. Meanwhile, papers with authors in more locations and with longer reference lists get published in higher-impact journals and receive more citations. These findings suggest that diversity in inputs by author ethnicity, location, and references leads to greater contributions to science as measured by impact factors and citations."[64]

A 2022 paper in the *Proceedings of the National Academy of Sciences* reported that the authors examined over six million papers published in medical science journals since 2000 and found that those written by mixed-gender teams are "more novel and highly cited."

> The publications of mixed-gender teams are substantially more novel and impactful than the publications of same-gender teams of equivalent size. The greater the gender balance on a team, the better the team scores on these performance measures. These patterns generalize across medical subfields. Finally, the novelty and impact advantages seen with mixed-gender teams persist when considering numerous controls and potential related features, including fixed effects for the individual researchers, team structures, and network positioning, suggesting that a team's gender balance is an underrecognized yet powerful correlate of novel and impactful scientific discoveries.[65]

These papers tell us what should already be clear from the studies of learning: in scientific inquiry, diversity matters. Research teams that are mixed in gender, race, ethnicity, and other forms of identity do more impactful scientific work. When we erect barriers to participation in science, technology, engineering, and mathematics (STEM) by women and people of color, we slow the progress of science.

This vast body of research has been noticed in the corporate world. Over the past several decades, growing numbers of executives have become convinced that diversity is a driver of business success. In the next chapter I will discuss the "business case for diversity," which has led some companies to make substantial investments in programs to recruit, hire, and retain employees and executives from marginalized backgrounds. But as in academia, the empirical evidence on the side of diversity hasn't stopped opponents of these policies, who, emboldened by the UNC and Harvard decisions, have turned their attention toward rolling them back.

Critics of diversity science sometimes muddy the waters by combining critiques of three related issues. The first is the diversity principle, which I hope this chapter has established as having been verified by decades of scientific inquiry on the heels of two centuries of reasoned speculation. The second is DEI policies, which attempt to apply the diversity principle by transforming how workplaces, universities, and other institutions operate. There are sometimes serious problems with DEI programs that justify caution and skepticism about the impact of DEI programs in some instances, but they do not undermine the findings of diversity science. The third is diversity training, which is sometimes offered as a means of implementing DEI policies. There can be serious problems with diversity training efforts, which will be considered in the next chapter. But shortcomings in the implementation of DEI measures cannot justify abandoning the findings of diversity science.

CHAPTER FOURTEEN

The Business Case for Diversity

I N 1986, *BLACK ENTERPRISE* magazine published a list of the "25 Best Places for Blacks to Work."[1] Sixteen of the twenty-five companies proudly described their "affirmative action" programs, which gave Black candidates a boost in hiring and promotions.[2] Twenty years later, the magazine published a similar report but titled it "The 40 Best Companies for Diversity."[3] None of the descriptions in the 2006 article referred to "affirmative action" programs.[4] In 2009 the magazine *Affirmative Action Register*, founded in 1974 to help companies comply with their civil rights obligations, changed its name to *Insight Into Diversity*.[5]

The turn away from affirmative action and toward diversity was driven by politics, but it also reflected a change in how companies perceive their role as employers. Older approaches to hiring and promoting employees from minority groups focused on legal compliance; companies tried to conform to executive orders by Presidents Kennedy and Johnson and the passage of the 1964 Civil Rights Act, which prohibited employment discrimination and mandated affirmative action by government contractors, which included most large companies. But by the 1990s and 2000s, encouraged by the Reagan and Bush administrations' strong opposition to affirmative action and civil rights enforcement, companies' goals had shifted. Diversity became a business strategy—a factor in a company's success. These new policies relied on empirical studies that people like Katherine Phillips had done in the 1980s and 1990s, work that would inspire a torrent of studies investigating whether diversity might have similar benefits in the corporate world. That body of research laid the foundation of what is now known as the business case for diversity, which companies embraced with enthusiasm.[6] In 1970, not one member of *Fortune*'s list of the fifty largest companies in the United States mentioned diversity in its annual report.[7] By 2000, twenty-two did.[8] By 2022, all fifty would tout their commitment to diversity.[9]

As colleges and universities were adopting the Harvard Plan, as framed and described by Cox and endorsed by Powell's opinion in *Bakke* and O'Connor's opinion in *Grutter*, American corporations were looking for an alternative approach to inclusion in their hiring and marketing. As the acceptance of diversity as central to higher education grew, so did the business case for it. This began with a trickle of papers and proposals by industrial psychologists, human relations specialists, and corporate trainers. Although the first papers were drawn from theory, qualitative and quantitative studies soon followed.[10] Most confirmed the Mills' assertion that diversity contributed to success—in commerce as well as education. The principles that led diverse classrooms to produce more knowledge also led diverse work teams to produce better results. Companies with diverse leadership were more innovative, productive, and profitable.[11] Socially responsible investing produced results at least as good as traditional investing.[12] And a recent wave of studies in the STEM fields of hard science reveals that scientists working in diverse settings make more discoveries.[13] As the Mills put it, "the only way in which a human being can make some approach to knowing the whole of a subject, is by hearing what can be said about it by persons of every variety of opinion, and studying all modes in which it can be looked at by every character of mind. No wise man ever acquired his wisdom in any mode but this; nor is it in the nature of human intellect to become wise in any other manner."[14]

The business case for diversity should be familiar to anyone who has read the Cox brief in *DeFunis* or its later restatements by Powell and O'Connor. Companies that bring together employees with diverse experiences and viewpoints will make better decisions.[15] And in a multiracial, multicultural society, companies need to hire and train employees who can work effectively with all kinds of people, in all kinds of settings, to succeed in a broader marketplace.[16]

Among the earliest and most influential advocates for diversity as a business strategy were Roosevelt Thomas at Harvard Business School and Morehouse College and the team of Price Cobbs, Lennie Copeland, and Lewis Griggs in California's Silicon Valley. In 1988, ten years after the

Bakke decision, Copeland and Griggs, working closely with Cobbs, produced a training film, *Valuing Diversity*, asserting that a diverse workforce helps a company improve its profitability.[17] It was distributed to human relations managers at several large Silicon Valley companies. The same year, Copeland expanded her argument in a two-part article in the journal *Personnel*. She recalls that when she first used the phrase "valuing diversity," she was advised that no one would understand it and she should find another term.[18] But within a year, it was being adopted across the corporate world.[19]

Roosevelt Thomas began the 1980s at Harvard Business School, leaving in 1983 to become dean of the business school at Atlanta University and then, a few years later, a professor at Morehouse College, a leading HBCU.[20] In 1984, he began a consulting practice in diversity management and also established an institute that was eventually named the American Institute for Managing Diversity.[21] In 1990, he published an influential article in the *Harvard Business Review* titled "From Affirmative Action to Affirming Diversity," in which he argued that companies should increase their hiring of Black workers not to further social policy but to improve their bottom line.[22]

Copeland's and Thomas's articles called for changes in how we thought about women and minorities in the workplace, moving away from a model based on affirmative action and compliance with non-discrimination law and toward a business-management model that embraced diversity as a way of making companies more innovative, productive, and successful.

By 2024, most large American companies were at least paying lip service to diversity, and many seemed seriously committed to being diverse across a wide range of identities. In a 2020 survey of 125 chief executive officers (CEOs), 96 percent said they considered diversity a personal strategic priority.[23] Business leaders value diversity because the outsider voices it brings in lead to better decision-making. But they increasingly recognize that it's not enough to bring people from marginalized communities in the door; they need to find ways to make those employees feel they belong there. Some have taken it as their responsibility to provide equity in their workforce and other corporate endeavors. As a result, businesses increasingly seek not only diversity, but diversity, equity, and inclusion—DEI.

Three leading sociologists, the late Lauren Edelman from Berkeley, Frank Dobbin from Harvard, and Alexandra Kalev from Tel Aviv University, have taken the lead in tracing the development of the business case for diversity from its beginnings in affirmative action to the advent of DEI. Building on a wealth of qualitative and quantitative data, they have demonstrated that personnel managers, the precursors of today's human resources and DEI officers—were the major drivers of anti-discrimination law compliance.[24] In the 1970s, these managers developed a series of policies designed to foster compliance with the new civil rights laws, including open job posting, job test validation, the appointment of equal employment officers, the development of best practices in hiring and assessment, and—notably—affirmative action hiring and promotion for women and minorities.[25] It was personnel managers who took the demands for fair hiring—demands that emerged in the "Don't Buy Where You Can't Work" campaigns and Martin Luther King's boycotts, and hiring mandates that were codified in the 1964 Civil Rights Act—and turned them into functioning workplace policies. While in the 1960s this sometimes meant quota hiring, by the 1970s it far more often meant policies designed to recruit more women and minorities and remove the barriers that made it harder for them to compete equally for jobs and promotions.

In the 1980s and early 1990s, as attacks on affirmative action and civil rights enforcement rose, personnel managers recognized that if they became defined as "affirmative action" officers, their careers would be in trouble. So they redefined themselves. Borrowing from the language and reasoning of the *Bakke* decision and embracing the business case for diversity asserted in articles by Copeland, Thomas, and others, they shifted the justification of their work from compliance with civil rights laws to diversity management.[26] They eventually came to see themselves as engaged in a purely business function for which legal compliance was an afterthought.[27]

By 2003, when the *Grutter* case came before the Supreme Court, most American corporate leaders accepted the idea that diversity was important to their success. Many companies developed diversity offices and began insisting that their suppliers and subcontractors also commit to diversity. Of the three amicus curiae briefs Justice O'Connor cited in her majority opinion as highly influential, two were from major corporations—one filed by General Motors, the other by 3M and other leading businesses. The briefs cited emerging evidence that diverse workforces are more productive and have higher profits; that diversity efforts help companies increase their global footprint and attract and retain top talent; and that diverse teams are less prone to "groupthink" and produce more new ideas and innovations than homogeneous teams.[28] The corporations that submitted briefs in *Grutter* looked to universities like Michigan to bring them diverse groups of future leaders.[29]

The studies cited in the *Grutter* briefs were the leading edge of a tsunami of studies demonstrating that diversity is good for business. In 2019, that evidence was collected in a compendium of nearly one hundred studies, published by UC Berkeley Center for Equity, Gender, and Leadership at the Haas Business School (my across-the-parking-lot neighbors on campus).[30] It includes reports published between 1991 and 2019 by institutions ranging from the United Nations and the World Bank to McKinsey and Company and Morgan Stanley. It cites numerous studies published in business, economics, and psychology journals worldwide.

One of the leading sources of data on the business case for diversity has been an independent, global non-governmental organization (NGO) called Catalyst.[31] For more than twenty years, it has been a well-regarded source relied on across the spectrum of commentators on diversity science.[32] In a series of groundbreaking reports between 2004 and 2013, it carefully set out the link between gender diversity and business success. The 2004 report, the first of its kind, examined data from Fortune 500 companies with average revenues of $13.5 billion and found that companies and even whole industries with higher representation of women on management teams had substantially better financial performance across several metrics.[33]

In 2007, Catalyst found that companies with more women on their boards of directors outperformed those with fewer women on three key financial measures: return on equity (53 percent higher), return on sales (42 percent), and return on invested capital (66 percent).[34] The 2011 report, which looked at corporate performance between 2004 and 2008, said that companies with three or more women on their boards outperformed companies with no women directors by 46 percent.[35]

Catalyst's 2013 report synthesized evidence from empirical studies and identified "four pillars of the business case" for diversity: talent, innovation and group performance, reputation and responsibility, and financial performance. The report revealed that diverse organizations are more successful at recruiting and retaining talent and that inclusive workplaces maximize talent and productivity. It also identified the links between diversity and greater innovation, creativity, and complex problem-solving. It showed that gender-diverse boards are linked to better corporate reputation, better corporate governance, better financial performance, and increased corporate social responsibility. Although the report primarily focused on gender diversity, it noted that "beyond gender, other dimensions of diversity are also found to be good for business: race, board member background, LGBT identity, and nationality."[36]

In 2015, the consulting firm McKinsey and Company examined "proprietary data sets for 366 public companies across a range of industries" and found that companies in the top quartile for racial, ethnic, and gender diversity were more likely to have above-average financial returns.[37] The more diverse the company, the better the returns, an insight that was confirmed in a 2017 study by the same authors.[38]

In the world of venture capital, according to a 2018 article in the *Harvard Business Review*, "diversity significantly improves financial performance on measures such as profitable investments at the individual portfolio-company level and overall fund returns." The difference in outcomes could not be explained by how promising the recipient companies were when they received the funds. Instead, the authors attribute the difference to the period "when the investors helped shape strategy, recruitment, and other efforts critical to a young company's survival and growth."[39] Homogeneous partnership in a startup firm reduced an "investment's comparative success rate by 26.4% to 32.2%."[40] Meanwhile, "Venture capital firms that increased their proportion of female partner hires by 10% saw, on average, a 1.5% spike in overall fund returns each year and had 9.7% more profitable exits [taking the company public or otherwise selling it off and exiting the investment at a profit] (an impressive figure given that only 28.8% of all VC investments have a profitable exit)."[41]

A 2020 report by FP Analytics on the power of women to transform male-dominated industries pointed to "gender-lens investing" as an effective tool for supporting female entrepreneurs and promoting gender equality.[42] The report noted that companies "that were founded by women, have women in leadership and board positions, support women-inclusive corporate practices, and/or provide products or services that positively impact women and improve their status and living conditions" contribute to equalizing the status of women in business; in addition, the report indicated that greater gender diversity in male-dominated industries is strongly linked to better economic performance.[43]

In 2019, a headline on the World Economic Forum website described the evidence behind the business case for diversity as "overwhelming."[44] In adopting diversity policies (and later, diversity, equity, and inclusion policies), corporate leaders were partly motivated by the growing empirical evidence that diversity is good for business—but also by other internal and external pressures. Internally, pressure came from both the top and the bottom. Employee demand drove businesses to seek diversity, as companies that spurned such efforts found it harder to retain women employees, and top executives became convinced that diversity was both a good way to increase profits and a positive social good.[45] Externally, businesses came under pressure from Wall Street, advocacy groups, and the government to become more diverse. The Reverend Jesse Jackson's Operation Push offers a compelling example of how the movement for affirmative action morphed into today's workplace diversity efforts. Operation Push grew out of Operation Breadbasket, the campaign begun by Martin Luther King, Jr., to use boycotts and picketing to compel employers to hire Black workers. In 1966, King asked Jackson to move to Chicago and set up an Operation Breadbasket office there. Jackson led several boycott campaigns—some within Chicago, some national—designed to increase the representation of Black workers in important industries. In the wake of King's assassination and a conflict over tactics, Operation Breadbasket became Operation Push, and Jackson over time persuaded major employers to become partners with his campaign and work with him to increase diversity in their operations. Today, Operation Push works with large companies in New York, Atlanta, Chicago, Oakland, and Silicon Valley to assist their diversity efforts. Confrontation has largely given way to cooperation.

Companies today are as likely to feel pressure to diversify from business partners and institutional investors as from civil rights groups. The Council of Institutional Investors, a non-profit advocate for investment integrity, regards as proper corporate governance a policy that "boards should be diverse, including such considerations as background, experience, age, race, gender, ethnicity, and culture."[46]

In 2022, BlackRock, Inc., with more than $8.68 trillion in assets under management, publicly stated that it is "interested in diversity in the board room as a means to promoting diversity of thought and avoiding 'groupthink'" and suggested "that boards should aspire to 30% diversity of membership and [we] encourage companies to have at least two directors on their board who identify as female and at least one who identifies as a member of an underrepresented group."[47] The 30 percent aspiration, adopted by a number of companies, is based in part on findings that multiple candidates from outsider groups are necessary to disrupt biases.[48] In

2021, Vanguard, with $7.2 trillion of assets under management, stated that "diversity of thought, background, and experience, as well as of personal characteristics (such as gender, race, and age), meaningfully contributes to the ability of boards to serve as effective, engaged stewards of shareholders' interests," and it supported efforts to require companies to make progress in diversifying their boards.[49] In 2020, Northern Trust, which manages $1.3 trillion in assets, stated that it had "set a standard that all boards" of U.S. companies should "be at least 20% female" and "have at least one ethnically/racially diverse director."[50] For many top investment firms, the rise of Environmental, Social, and Governance (ESG) investment strategies has been heavily focused on DEI. As of 2020, more than $16 trillion in assets were held by investors and investment advisors employing ESG strategies.[51] For perspective, the total value of the U.S. stock and bond markets is around $100 trillion.

In the legal industry, a campaign begun internally by lawyers has now been imposed externally by their clients. The campaign can be traced to a 1987–88 study commissioned by the Bar Association of San Francisco (BASF) and performed by the University of California, Berkeley, which showed that "racial and ethnic minority lawyers encountered profound disadvantages within the workplace."[52] In response, the executive director of BASF, Drucilla Ramey, lobbied her association to take action.[53] They adopted a set of "Goals and Timetables for Minority Hiring and Advancement," with aspirational targets set every five years. The first five-year target timetable, announced in 1989, aimed for 15 percent of associates and 5 percent of partners to be lawyers of color by 1995. BASF has revisited the goals and timetables every five years since then to evaluate the progress being made.[54] Other leading bar groups have done the same.

In 2016, under pressure from large consumers of legal services as well as influential local bar associations, the American Bar Association adopted Resolution 113, aimed at making the legal profession better reflect the diversity of America and at supporting minority-owned law firms.[55] The ABA considers race/ethnicity, gender, LGBTQ+ status, and disability status as diversity factors. It has adopted three goals: "increase diversity at all levels within the legal profession which will make the legal field a more appealing profession for diverse individuals"; "[increase] the number of diverse attorneys and remediate the issues of implicit bias in the legal profession"; and "encourage corporate clients to use a Model Diversity Survey in procuring and evaluating legal service providers."[56]

The Model Diversity Survey gives corporate clients real-time access to any law firm's diversity demographic data submitted in response to the Model Diversity Survey.[57] That same year, the winning idea of a contest called the *Women in Law Hackathon* was the "Mansfield Rule," which measured "whether law firms have affirmatively considered at least 30% women, lawyers of color, LGBTQ+ lawyers, and lawyers with disabilities for leadership and governance roles, equity partner promotions, formal client pitch opportunities, and senior lateral positions."[58] The Mansfield Rule, named for the first woman admitted to the practice of law in the United States, is inspired by the National Football League's Rooney Rule, which applies a similar standard to teams interviewing coaching candidates.[59]

Independently of the ABA, many companies have begun requiring their outside law firms to reach certain diversity goals. In 2017, Facebook required that women and ethnic minorities "account for at least 33 percent of law firm teams working on its matters."[60] Firms must also show that they "actively identify and create clear and measurable leadership opportunities for women and minorities . . . includ[ing] serving as relationship managers and representing Facebook in the courtroom." Colin Stretch, then Facebook's general counsel, said that "firms typically do what their clients want, and we want to see them win our cases and create opportunities for women and people of color. We think the firms are ready—our articulation gives not just permission but a mandate."[61]

Companies like Hewlett-Packard were more stringent, saying that failure to comply with its diversity requirements for outside counsel would lead to a 10 percent holdback of fees—but with a one-year grace period.[62] The drugmaker Novartis AG requires its outside counsel to commit that "at least 30% of billable associate time and 20% of partner time will be provided by women, racially or ethnically diverse professionals, or members of the LGBT community"; otherwise, 15 percent of its total fees will be withheld.[63] These efforts to export their diversity policies to suppliers of legal services have become an important part of corporate diversity efforts.

In the past few years, the rise of the Black Lives Matter movement and the growing awareness of the long history of police killings of Black Americans have led to what some have called a racial "reckoning" or "awakening." In 2020, following the George Floyd murder, corporate statements of support for diversity initiatives surged. Not all of this support was meaningful. Some is mere window dressing or "virtue signaling";

some is sincere but ineffective. But clearly there is greater recognition that without affirmative efforts to address bias, including implicit (or unconscious) bias, and to address systemic (or structural) racism, we will continue to see wide disparities between the opportunities and achievements of white Americans and persons of color, with especially large disadvantages for Black Americans. For context, consider how vast the earnings gap is between full-time year-round white workers and Black workers who have earned a bachelor's degree or above—their median annual earnings are $111,600 for white men, $85,170 for Black men, $82,270 for white women, and just $75,410 for Black women.[64] In essence, Black women pay an annual penalty of over $36,000 because of their race and gender.

As noted in the prior chapter, discussions of diversity sometimes conflate three related issues, the diversity principle, diversity—or more recently DEI—management, and diversity training. As we have seen, the diversity principle has been upheld by decades of scientific inquiry following on the heels of two centuries of reasoned speculation. DEI policies attempt to apply the diversity principle by reforming (sometimes transforming) how workplaces, universities, and other institutions operate. There can be serious problems with DEI programs, which I will discuss here. These problems can affect the impact of DEI programs in some instances, but they do not negate the findings of diversity science or diminish the business case for diversity. The same is true of diversity training, which is sometimes provided to implement DEI policies. Diversity training efforts can be flawed, but to reject the findings of diversity science or the legitimate goals of DEI programs because they can be ineffective, or even counterproductive, is to throw out the baby with the bathwater.

The development of corporate diversity practices—particularly diversity training—has been fraught with challenges. Critiques of the business case for diversity often point to studies that demonstrate that diversity training is often ineffective and at times counterproductive. Such studies abound; unless diversity training is combined with institutional support for meaningful inclusion and efforts like mentoring programs, it can be worse than nothing. But diversity training is to the benefits of diversity as driver's ed is to safe driving. We want people to drive safely, and the evidence is inconclusive that driver's ed helps us reach that goal.[65] That's not a reason to abandon the goal, given that an estimated forty thousand Americans—disproportionately young people—die in car accidents each year. Similarly, putting diverse people together and helping them work as a team is far different from putting people in a classroom and telling them that working in diverse teams is useful, let alone putting a group of white men in a room and telling them they are racists and sexists. Even when they are, that hardly seems like a good strategy to convince them of anything. But diversity training as a form of personal insult, while sadly and foolishly counterproductive, is almost certainly less common than the urban myths would have us believe. The best evidence on diversity training suggests that when the goal is helping people become more open to working with and hearing the voices of others, when it's done with empathy instead of hostility, and when it's part of a broader program of support, it moves the needle toward inclusion.

A 2016 review of the literature by the leading social scientists Frank Dobbin and Alexandra Kalev showed that diversity training alone is often ineffective. They found that "two-thirds of human resources specialists report that diversity training does not have positive effects, and several field studies have found no effect of diversity training on women's or minorities' careers or on managerial diversity."[66] In one study reported in the *Harvard Business Review*, for example, experimenters created a diversity training program and assigned it to over three thousand employees of a large global organization. They "found very little evidence that diversity training affected the behavior of men or white employees overall."[67] Where it did, it was "not by much and not for long."[68]

Dobbin and Kalev point to five reasons why diversity training alone is ineffective. First, "short-term educational interventions in general do not change people." Second, some research suggests that "antibias training activates stereotypes." Third, training can inspire "unrealistic confidence in anti-discrimination programs, making employees complacent about their own biases."[69] (On this point, Dobbin and Kalev cite a study in which experimenters described subjects' employers as non-discriminatory; subjects subsequently did not censor their own gender biases, leading Dobbin and Kalev to suggest that "employees who go through diversity training may not, subsequently, take responsibility for avoiding discrimination."[70] Rather, "the presence of workplace diversity programs seems to blind employees to hard evidence of discrimination.")[71] Fourth, some studies suggest that training can leave white employees feeling left out and worried that "they will not be treated fairly."[72] Some critics describe this as "white fragility." Finally, Dobbin and Kalev point out that most people react negatively to efforts to control them. On this point, they report that employees respond more favorably to diversity training when they are told it is being done for a business reason rather than that it is necessary to avoid lawsuits. Ultimately, the authors conclude that "in isolation, diversity training does not appear to be effective." That, however, doesn't mean it should be dismissed entirely: "The trick is to couple diversity training with the right complementary measures."[73]

Implicit bias training can also be useful in sensitizing employees and managers to how our minds activate stereotypes. But if done badly, it too can be counterproductive. Consider the comparison between the state of California's mandates for licensed attorneys and physicians. California attorneys must take seventeen hours of continuing legal education every three years, including two hours of implicit bias training. The implicit bias training is usually taught by experts on bias and can be a meaningful tool in revealing, and perhaps combating, bias. By contrast, the requirement for continuing medical education is that each course (or most of them) contain a section on implicit bias. The result is that physicians who are expert in a specialized field of medicine, and who are mainly interested in teaching about that field, are required also to teach a topic in which they may have no expertise and no interest. This rule was challenged by two physicians, an ophthalmologist and an anesthesiologist, who didn't want to teach implicit bias in order to share their expertise on their respective subjects.[74] Although I'm rarely a fan of the Pacific Legal Foundation, the conservative advocacy group that brought the case, I agree with them here. Asking physicians who know little about bias—and may not think it's even a problem—to teach about it is not the best way to sensitize other physicians to the problem of bias in medicine. And given that implicit bias is demonstrably a huge problem in medicine, when we try to fix it, we should do it in a way that's likely to work.

If diversity training alone is counterproductive, what does work? We know that diversity increases company productivity. But do DEI policies increase workplace diversity? Dobbin and Kalev found that voluntary training programs are less likely to backfire. They found greater success with programs that "tackle not only implicit biases, but structural discrimination." They found that targeted recruitment efforts help bring more employees from marginalized populations into the fold: "five years after a company implements a college recruitment program targeting female employees, the share of white women, black women, Hispanic women, and Asian-American women in its management rises by about

10%, on average. A program focused on minority recruitment increases the proportion of black male managers by 8% and black female managers by 9%."[75] Formal mentoring programs can help these new recruits advance by pairing them with established employees, who sponsor their mentees for "key training and assignments."[76] These programs help mentees build skills and introduce them to new opportunities; they also have an effect on the mentors, who "come to believe that their proteges merit these opportunities—whether they're white men, women, or minorities. That is cognitive dissonance—'Anyone I sponsor must be deserving'—at work."[77] Mentoring programs on average "boost the representation of black, Hispanic, and Asian-American women, and Hispanic and Asian-American men, by 9% to 24%."[78]

Introducing more flexible and less hierarchical structures can also help marginalized employees rise, while promoting a culture that values diversity. When employees are assigned to "self-managed work teams," where they work side by side as equals toward a common goal, the process helps break down stereotypes and leads to more equitable hiring and promotion.[79] Dobbin and Kalev report that "at firms that create self-managed work teams, the share of white women, black men and women, and Asian-American women in management rises by 3% to 6% over five years."[80] Rotating management trainees through departments allows them to try their hand at various jobs and deepens their understanding of the whole organization. This kind of cross-training "exposes both department heads and trainees to a wider variety of people. The result . . . is a bump of 3% to 7% in white women, black men and women, and Asian-American men and women in management."[81]

Creating diversity task forces and hiring managers whose job is to increase diversity also pays dividends. Dobbin and Kalev found that simply having a diversity manager who can question other managers and their decisions "prompts managers to step back and consider everyone who is qualified instead of hiring or promoting the first people who come to mind."[82] "Companies that appoint diversity managers see 7% to 18% increases in all underrepresented groups—except Hispanic men—in management in the following five years."[83]

These findings demonstrate what researchers like Victoria Plaut have found in both higher education and in the workplace: diversity training alone is generally insufficient, but practices that promote inclusion make workplaces more diverse and more productive. In a 2015 paper, she and her co-authors summarized the results of several of their studies: (1) "respondents' perceptions of the diversity practice in their organization were directly related to their levels of engagement at work"; (2) a "trust climate acts as a mediator of the relationship between diversity practices and engagement"; and (3) "the indirect effect of diversity practices on engagement was statistically significant only at high levels of inclusion."[84] Based on these findings, they concluded that when employees feel that they are included, that makes them more engaged and more likely to perform well in their jobs.[85]

Despite the evidence that programs designed to promote diversity, and more recently DEI, can be highly effective, they are controversial and subject to strong pushback from opponents. This should not be surprising. As Upton Sinclair wrote, "It is difficult to get a man to understand something when his salary depends upon his not understanding it." And of course DEI initiatives do disadvantage white men by making them compete on a level playing field. But when white men complain that diversity initiatives make them feel unwanted at companies largely run by white men or protest that their feelings have been hurt, the complaints can be taken with a healthy dose of salt. When they complain about the DEI staff or trainers, who are likely to be women and/or members of racial/ethnic minority groups, it is fair to ask whether the critics' biases—whether conscious or unconscious—contributed to their critique. It cannot be easy for a minority woman—already viewed with distrust implicitly—to work with a group of white men to reduce their biases. Nonetheless, there are plenty of examples of DEI efforts that fall flat and of insensitive DEI officers and trainers who alienate employees and make things worse. To return to the analogy of driver training, even people who should (or do) know better sometimes drive recklessly. That doesn't condemn efforts to teach safe driving or to impose speed limits, even though they don't always work. Similarly, we shouldn't abandon programs designed to reduce drug and alcohol abuse even when they don't eliminate the problem; we should instead study them and find ways to improve them. The same is true of diversity training and other DEI programming.

Another way of attacking the diversity principle is to attack the requirement that university faculty members and job candidates supply "diversity statements." Often mischaracterized and sometimes imposed with a heavy hand, such statements are an easy target. At worst they can be performative, or even McCarthy-like loyalty oaths that violate academic freedom and free speech. In such cases they are properly resisted. But they can also prompt self-examination that may make those of us who teach in universities better scholars, teachers, and mentors, and better friends to our colleagues and allies to our students. They can be a way to get busy people to consider how they interact with others—students, colleagues, staff, or neighbors—who have dramatically different experiences and significantly different views. That includes how a liberal professor should interact with a conservative professor or student. How should these individuals go about finding commonality? Katherine Phillips says they should talk about their differences because they may learn from one another. If we assume even a modicum of good faith, diversity statements can be very useful.

At Berkeley, for example, tenured faculty go through an extensive merit review every three years. We prepare a detailed memo setting out our accomplishments over the prior three years, including the books or papers we've published or are writing, the public lectures we've given, the committees we've served on or led, any pro bono work we've done, any private remunerative work we've done, awards we've won, grants we've received, and what we have planned for the coming years. We attach a review of the courses we've taught, an analysis of our student evaluations, our syllabi, and a teaching dossier. In some years a faculty committee asks experts in our field from outside Berkeley for confidential letters evaluating our scholarship. All these materials are reviewed by a faculty committee, which produces a report and makes a recommendation to the dean. The dean reviews the file and makes a recommendation to the provost, who seeks the advice of a campus-wide faculty senate committee. This may earn us a move up the steps of the "faculty ladder" and a pay increase, or it may not.

The law school gives us the option to include a diversity statement as part of our review materials. We're encouraged to write about how we incorporate the benefits of diversity into our scholarship, teaching, and public service. For me, this is an opportunity to reflect on the role of diversity in my professional life and to share my reflections with my colleagues. It encourages me to challenge myself. Can I adjust my teaching methods to reach more students effectively? Are there learning styles I'm ignoring? Am I making space for diverse views in class discussions? Do I have students who are feeling silenced? If so, how can I help give them a voice? To take a concrete example, why do so few men enroll in my comparative equality law course? Is it the subject matter, or am I somehow signaling that they aren't welcome? What about my scholarship: should I seek more diverse views in the sources I consult? In my line of work, these are important questions, and the diversity statement—again, optional—gives me an opportunity to reflect on them.

I understand that not every institution does this well, and that at some places it's done very badly, though again I think that at least some of the criticism should be viewed skeptically. But even in cases where the statements are abused—where they are used, for example, to enforce ideological purity, effectively reducing diversity—that abuse doesn't justify rejecting the value of diversity, any more than an ineffective driver's ed class should make us doubt the importance of road safety.

One might think that the research demonstrating the benefits of diversity would be enough to persuade companies to diversify their workforces, boards, and executive suites of their own accord. But corporate executives remain overwhelmingly white and male: 89 percent of Fortune 500 CEOs are men, and 79 percent are white men.[86] In the "C-suite" as a whole, 51 percent of the top executives in Fortune 500 companies are white men.[87] Among the Fortune 100, 53.5 percent of board members are white men.[88] As of 2024, white non-Hispanic men made up less than 30 percent of the U.S. population.[89]

While the benefits of diverse boards are increasingly clear, the idea that diversity on corporate boards should be required is controversial. Some argue with the premise that diversity is good for companies.[90] Some accept the premise but consider a legal requirement to be unwarranted interference.[91] And some are irrationally hostile to the very idea that diversity is good for business. A good example of this view can be found in the coverage of the 2023 collapse of the Silicon Valley Bank. Andy Kessler, an opinion writer for the *Wall Street Journal*, wrote: "In its proxy statement, SVB notes that besides 91% of their board being independent and 45% women, they also have '1 Black,' '1 LGBTQ+' and '2 Veterans.' I'm not saying 12 white men would have avoided this mess, but the company may have been distracted by diversity demands."[92] Despite the complete lack of evidence that the bank's leaders were distracted by "diversity demands" and despite the fact that more than half of its members were white men, this trumped-up claim became a right-wing talking point, amplified by Donald Trump, Jr., and Senator Josh Hawley.[93]

Demands for board diversity have led to proposals to require that U.S. companies be transparent about the composition of their boards and take steps to diversify them. Each proposal has been challenged in the courts. In 2021, the Nasdaq stock exchange adopted a "diversify or explain" rule that requires most Nasdaq-listed companies to have at least two "diverse" board members, including at least one director who self-identifies as female and at least one who self-identifies as an "underrepresented minority" or part of the LGBTQ+ community—or else explain why they don't meet that benchmark. Companies must indicate the total number of directors and specify (1) the number of directors who identify as female, male, and non-binary or who did not disclose their gender; (2) the number of directors who are African American or Black, Alaskan Native or Native American, Asian, Hispanic or Latino, Native Hawaiian or Pacific Islander, white, or two or more races or ethnicities, disaggregated by gender identity; (3) the number of directors who self-identify as LGBTQ+; and (4) the number of directors who did not disclose a demographic background.[94] The only mandatory part of the rule is the requirement of transparency. Companies must disclose the identities of their board members, with "chose not to disclose" a permitted option. Those that lack diversity do not have to change their board composition; they are merely required to explain their lack of diversity.

On August 6, 2021, the Securities Exchange Commission, in a divided vote, allowed Nasdaq to implement the proposal. But before the new rule was slated to take effect, the Alliance for Fair Board Recruitment, another organization run by the diversity critic Edward Blum, brought an administrative review action in federal court challenging the rule.[95] Under the Securities Act, such challenges go directly to the United States Court of Appeal.[96] With a choice of where to file, Blum selected the Fifth Circuit Court of Appeals, which has a conservative reputation and a 12–5 Republican majority.[97] Seventeen state attorneys general, led by Attorney General Ken Paxton of Texas, joined in the challenge. Blum and the state AGs argued that the Nasdaq rule discriminates against corporate board members based on the protected classes of race and sex by instituting an unconstitutional "quota" system. The challenge attracted significant opposition among companies subject to the rule, which view it as good for business and good for society.[98] On December 11, 2024, by a vote of 9–8 the full court ruled in Blum's favor, overturning the Nasdaq rule.

In 2018 and 2020, the California state legislature passed laws requiring publicly traded companies incorporated or headquartered in California to diversify their boards.[99] The Underrepresented Communities on

Boards Act (AB 979) required these companies' boards to have a minimum number of directors from an "underrepresented community," a requirement they could fulfill by filling open seats or by adding new seats.[100] The Women on Boards Act (SB 826) required "all publicly held domestic or foreign corporations whose principal executive offices are located in California to have at least one female director on their boards by December 31, 2019, either by filling an open seat or by adding a seat."[101] By the end of 2021, the same corporations were required to have minimum numbers of female directors based on the total size of the board. When the bill was passed in 2018, a quarter of California's publicly held corporations had no women directors on their boards.[102]

Here again, Edward Blum's group, the Alliance for Fair Board Recruitment, filed an action in federal court seeking to overturn the state laws. The conservative advocacy group Judicial Watch also filed two actions in California state court challenging the statutes.[103] In all three cases (each of which is on appeal) the court ruled against the board diversity mandates.[104] In the racial diversity case, the state trial court found that racial disparities in board membership might be attributed to "cultural preferences" rather than discrimination. That is, many boards of directors are all-white because non-white Americans have chosen occupations that leave them unqualified for these positions. Board members, the court noted, are generally selected from top executives, who tend to be white men, and "any robust notion of cultural pluralism requires a factfinder to at least consider the possibility that the presence or absence of a given group in a given industry is the product of benign cultural preferences."[105] In other words, the judge concluded that people of color have chosen not to become business executives and board members because, for cultural reasons, they prefer other lines of work. Left unsaid is that the lines of work the court believes Black Americans prefer offer low pay, low prestige, and little security. As President Trump put it in his 2024 campaign, they prefer "Black jobs." It's hard to imagine better evidence of the continuing existence of racism.

Several other states, including Colorado, Maryland, Illinois, New York, and Washington, have enacted board diversity legislation, and others are considering it. None of the existing statutes, however, mandates a minimum number of female directors; instead, they require disclosures about diversity on the board of directors and, in some instances, senior management. Many of these laws were modeled on California's gender diversity mandates but were changed to "disclosure only" during the legislative process.[106]

Since the time of Wilhelm von Humboldt, the value of diversity has been discussed almost exclusively in the context of education, particularly higher education. But today the diversity principle is as likely to come up in commerce, where it has proved its value over several decades. Yet conservative activist groups—joined by the Trump administration—are beginning to challenge diversity policies as a form of discrimination against white males. Universities' ability to select diverse classes of students has been severely restricted by the Supreme Court, and it seems likely that the same could happen to diversity efforts in business. (For an update on developments in the business case for diversity since January 20, 2025, see the postscript to this book at DiversityPrinciple.com.) In the concluding chapter, I will discuss the growing rejection of the diversity principle in both education and commerce. But first I will examine how the U.S. business case for diversity made its way back to Europe, where it has once again been transformed.

CHAPTER FIFTEEN

Diversity and Backlash in Europe

JOHN AND HARRIET MILL finished the penultimate draft of *On Liberty* while dividing their time between a London suburb and the south of France. Their diversity principle has now returned there, including Avignon, where they are buried.[1] An idea that began in Berlin and London and was refined in Paris, Jena, Rome, and Vienna has come full circle, returning to Europe as part of the movement to improve equality for women and members of minority groups.

The business case for diversity crossed the Atlantic in 2004, when a French public policy think tank proposed that French businesses adopt American-style diversity plans. The initial proposal was the work of two French business leaders and an academic, Laurence Méhaignerie, who has since become a member of Parliament associated with the party of President Macron. Méhaignerie and the business leader Yazid Sabeg, who later served from 2007 to 2012 as minister of equality (*égalité*) under President Sarkozy, prepared a paper for the French think tank the Montaigne Institute, founded (and still run) by Claude Bébéar, CEO of the very successful French insurance company Axa. The paper, titled "Those Left Behind by Equal Opportunity" (*Les oubliés de l'égalité des chances*), examines the problem of workplace discrimination against those the French describe as "visible minorities" and proposes measures to address it.[2] One of the suggestions was to create a voluntary list of practices to which businesses and state bodies would agree. The authors called it a Diversity Charter (*Charte de la Diversité*).

On October 22, 2004, Bébéar presented the diversity charter to the leaders of thirty-five large French companies, who agreed to abide by its provisions.[3] To put it in American terms, they agreed to engage in, and report on, gender- and race-conscious efforts to increase the diversity of their companies.

The Charte de la Diversité was influenced by the growing corporate support for diversity in the United States, as well as the concern of French business leaders that with the adoption of European Union anti-discrimination laws in 2000 and their absorption into French national law, failure to address employment discrimination might have serious consequences.[4] Better to act privately, they agreed, than wait for the state to interfere with their hiring and promotion decisions. In this sense the alternative of a voluntary movement toward diversity in Europe parallels that in the United States, which in the period before the 1964 Civil Rights Act was also offered as a more palatable alternative to the legal enforcement of anti-discrimination law. The timing was perfect: the charter spread through Europe like wildfire and has now been adopted not only by businesses but by governmental bodies in every EU country except Malta. It is now administered out of a bureaucracy funded by the European Commission and located in Brussels.

To some extent, diversity is at the heart of European unity. It is a core value of the EU that its constituent countries maintain their own national identities and that a united Europe is strengthened by their diverse national perspectives. The slogan of the European Union since 2000 is "Unity in Diversity." But diversity, in this context, is understood as national diversity. In the case of gender, non-discrimination was a core value of the original six-nation pact that has become the twenty-seven-member European Union. That movement has been embraced by pan-European feminists and has had significant success. But efforts to address racial discrimination have faced substantial resistance. The proposition that diversity of race, ethnicity, disability, age, sexual orientation, and gender can improve decision-making may not be as readily accepted.

The French diversity charter, the first of its kind in Europe, currently has more than 4,500 signatories, mostly small and medium-sized businesses but also large companies and public institutions.[5] It has inspired similar initiatives across the continent. Belgium now has diversity charters in two languages. The German diversity charter (*Charta der Vielfalt*), adopted in 2006, was created by four large multinational companies with the support of Angela Merkel.[6] Today it is funded by twenty-five companies, including Bayer, Deutsche Bank, Ernst & Young, and Siemens, and by the German state.[7] Most of Europe soon followed.[8]

In 2010, the European Commission created the EU Platform of Diversity Charters for companies to share and exchange information through meetings, seminars, and a yearly conference for signatories featuring lecturers and panels.[9] More than fifteen thousand European businesses and organizations have signed a European diversity charter.[10]

As Viviane Reding, a former vice-president of the European Commission and former member of the European Parliament, explained, these moves were particularly important in the wake of the Great Recession, from which Europe struggled to recover for much of the 2010s:

> To kick-start Europe's growth engine, we must explore all avenues to get Europe's economy back on its feet. . . . It is well established that one such avenue is especially promising: business thrives where diversity is actively pursued. . . . Countless studies have indicated the benefits of a more diverse workforce. . . . Europe must capitalize on its diversity dividend. Diversity is Europe's strong suit, and it's high time to wear it.[11]

When the charter was first proposed, some French critics viewed it as cost-free virtue signaling that would detract from the enforcement of anti-discrimination law. Others thought that as an effort to change corporate culture, even with no legal enforcement behind it, it would help change behavior. This disagreement over voluntary measures versus legal mandates reflects an earlier debate about civil rights laws in the United States. Before the passage of the three major civil rights acts in the 1960s, the Roosevelt, Truman, Eisenhower, and Kennedy administrations all tried to persuade large companies to adopt anti-discrimination policies.[12] And a core premise of the push for corporate diversity in the United States today is that it is about business success, not legal compliance. The critics are undoubtedly correct that, unlike anti-discrimination law, the charters are not enforceable. But does that make them ineffective?

In late 2022 and early 2023, I attended two meetings in Brussels that brought together the national representatives of the twenty-seven diversity charters. I found that every speaker and delegate wanted to address the problem of discrimination, and they all believed that diversity efforts could meaningfully reduce inequality, but none of them spoke about law, except briefly in passing. They all advocated the benefits of diversity as a "best practice," as good policy. If they had ever seen a link between anti-discrimination law and diversity, that link had been broken. In listening to the speakers and talking with the participants, I could hear the voices of Humboldt, the Mills, Eliot, Dewey, Frankfurter, Marshall, Murray, Cox, Phillips, and Plaut. They cited the same tsunami of empirical evidence that had turned the U.S. business case for diversity from a theory to a scientific consensus and that had led to the recognition that diversity is central to success in business, scientific inquiry, and civic engagement.

Susan Danger, until recently the CEO of the American Chamber of Commerce in Europe, describes this shared understanding:

> We rely on diverse perspectives to foster the transatlantic relationship and build a strong, united Europe. It's good for business, and it's the right thing to do. Diversity in leadership is strongly correlated with enhanced team performance and profitability, while companies with greater diversity are more likely to see increased innovation and higher financial returns. . . . Among other initiatives, our member companies develop cultures of inclusion through training and mentoring schemes, use technology to more effectively measure and deliver on diversity goals, and facilitate resource groups to enable their employees to be forces of change. Many companies extend their efforts beyond their office walls to support inclusion and diversity in the communities they live and work in.[13]

Another place where discussions of equality and diversity have affected law and policy across Europe is the law of gender quotas. The EU and many of its member states have adopted "gender parity" programs for democratic institutions (parliaments, city councils, other elected government/state bodies) that go far beyond what's been proposed in the United States. For example, gender parity democracy programs in France, Luxembourg, and Belgium require that at least 50 percent of the candidates running for the European Parliament are women. Other countries impose smaller but still significant quotas: 40 percent in Spain, Slovenia, Greece, Portugal, and Croatia; 35 percent in Poland; 33 percent in Italy.[14] In Romania, the law simply states that no list of candidates may be 100 percent male.[15] For the most part, however, these gender quotas are concerned with equality, not diversity. Their proponents argue that women must be equally represented not because gender diversity improves decision-making but because anything less than half (or 33 or 40 percent) is simply unfairly unequal.

The European Union has also enacted pan-European laws addressing equal pay and work-life balance, intended to promote equality for women. The Court of Justice of the European Union, after initially expressing skepticism about gender-based affirmative action, has embraced it as a proper workplace policy to increase women's participation in the workforce. But these policies are grounded in equality law and policy, not in the diversity principle.

In one area of European life, gender laws do rely on the diversity principle: membership on corporate boards.[16] The countries with the highest percentages of women on corporate boards are Norway (48 percent), France (47 percent), Denmark (43 percent), and Italy (42 percent).[17] The arguments made in support of gender parity on boards combine elements of the equality principle—women face discrimination that must be overcome by affirmative (or "positive") action—with the diversity principle: integrating women onto corporate boards will make the companies stronger because diverse boards lead to greater profits.

Norway was the first country to implement mandatory gender quotas for privately owned, publicly traded companies.[18] It consistently leads the world in the percentage of board seats held by women.[19] Although there was much controversy over the quota laws when they were first enacted, support among directors has increased as the law has been implemented.[20]

The comparative legal scholar Aaron Dhir argues that Norway's cultural and political commitment to egalitarianism helped these quota laws gain acceptance.[21] In surveys he conducted of Norwegian corporate directors, most responded that "quota-induced gender diversity has positively affected boardroom work and firm governance."[22] They reported that women contribute positively to firms by bringing a range of perspectives and experience, independence, outsider status, and greater propensity to engage in "rigorous deliberation, risk assessment and monitoring."[23] Nor did women report feeling stigmatized by quota laws.[24]

In 2012, the European Commission proposed a directive to increase women's presence on the boards of the major European companies to 40 percent by 2020.[25] After a decade of debate, the directive was approved by the European Council and the Parliament in 2022. It provides that at least 33 percent of board members in some cases and 40 percent in others must be women, and it requires member states to implement this into their national law by 2026.[26]

The justification for such mandates, whether in Europe or the United States, is that corporations are creations of the state, which gives them significant legal benefits, including limiting the liability of their owners, in exchange for regulation to protect investors and the public. These regulations include, at a minimum, transparency in matters of general public interest. And since the overwhelming evidence now tells us that diversity is good for corporations, their shareholders, their employees, and society, they should be required to add diversity to their boards not only for their own good but for the good of the entire society.[27]

In addressing racism, however, Europe faces a dilemma. The European Union is composed of multiracial societies with laws prohibiting discrimination, and many European businesses have articulated a strong commitment to promoting diversity. But in much of Europe, the idea that racism is a pervasive problem is dismissed out of hand, and race is not recognized as a legitimate form of identity.

In France, for example, diversity initiatives and the language of diversity are pervasive, yet the very idea of racial or ethnic identity is highly politicized.[28] If you ask a white French government official if racial discrimination is a problem in France, a common response is that—while there may be instances of racism—France is a multiracial society, composed of descendants of people from Europe, Africa, the Middle East, Southeast Asia, the Caribbean, the South Pacific, and so on, and there can be no systemic problem because French universalism, which considers French citizenship the most important marker of identity, has rendered the nation color-blind.[29] If you ask the same question of a Black or Arab French person, on the other hand, the answer is almost always yes. They will describe their personal experiences of discrimination in employment, housing, or police encounters. In a 2023 survey, just over nine of ten Black respondents in France said they faced discrimination.[30] Across Europe, there has been a dramatic rise in hate crimes against Muslims and those thought to be Muslims, as well as an increase in laws that restrict Muslim women from covering their heads or faces in public places.

One impediment to implementing the diversity charter was that many European states are unable to measure their success in addressing racism because they prohibit the collection of racial data in the census and other government surveys. In 2007, the French Parliament passed a law permitting the collection of data for the limited purpose of measuring discrimination, but the Constitutional Court overturned it as

violating the French Constitution.[31] The decision reflects a French co-
nundrum: under French law, defining people by a racial category is forbidden, but in French culture Black people (*les noirs*) are constantly
defined by their race—recognized, exoticized, often repressed and vic-
timized. Black and Arab-appearing young men are routinely profiled and
harassed by the police on the Paris Metro, who single them out for identity checks.[32] Few French Arabs or Blacks attend the top French schools
(*les grandes écoles*) or hold positions of power and influence, despite constituting a large (if imprecisely measured) segment of the population.
France thus has an entrenched system of racism while it refuses to recognize race.

A discussion of European racism could begin anywhere in the past
millennium. But in the context of the diversity principle, a good place to
begin is 1999. That year, to the shock of many, for the first time since the
defeat of Hitler and Mussolini and the death of the Spanish dictator
Francisco Franco, a far-right party won a national election in the heart of
Europe. Jorg Haider led the Freedom Party of Austria (FPO), a neo-Nazi
party, to victory in the Austrian parliamentary election. Haider's unabash-
edly racist platform declared "Austria for Austrians" and called for eject-
ing immigrants who were Muslim or who came from Arab countries.

In response to Haider's election, governments across the European
Union recognized the need to take action against racism and other forms
of discrimination. They considered but abandoned a proposal to expel
Austria from the Union.[33] But in rapid order, the EU unanimously adopted
two directives that formed the backbone of European anti-discrimination
law: the Racial Equality Directive and the Equal Treatment Directive.
These directives joined a gender directive, adopted earlier, to form a troika
of EU anti-discrimination laws.

A "directive" in EU law commits all members of the Union to a set
of legal principles and requires them to adopt those principles in each
country's national law in a form consistent with its legal system. The
three equality directives may thus be enforced through litigation in one
country, administrative tribunals in a second, and a conciliation process
in a third. The year-2000 directives dramatically changed discrimination
law across Europe. Countries that were slow to import the laws were
prodded to move more quickly and then in some cases sued by the European Commission.

As to the French Constitutional Court's ruling that racial data may not
be collected, even to measure discrimination, the French civil rights leader

Patrick Lozes responded, "If you're not counted, you don't count."[34] The French sociologist Laurent Thévenot encapsulated the contradiction: "Statistics by ethnic categories are dangerous because they stigmatize people and are likely to support xenophobic or racist behavior. . . . Statistics by ethnic categories are necessary to fight against discrimination."[35]

Support for the French charter was propelled by the race riots that began in the Paris suburb of Clichy-sous-Bois in 2005 and spread throughout the country. They were sparked by the death by electrocution of two teenagers—Zyed Benna, seventeen, and Bouna Traoré, fifteen, of Mauritanian and Tunisian origin respectively—who were coming home from a football match and fled a police identity stop.[36] Such stops of young French men of color are a common police practice and are currently being reviewed by the Council of State in an action against police racial profiling brought by several French NGOs.[37]

Since the riots, people across Europe have increasingly spoken out against racism and patriarchy and in favor of an equality tied to identity. But for every action there is a reaction. Across Europe, we are seeing a reaction to the movement against racism. It is sometimes expressed, again in a term borrowed from the United States, as "anti-wokeism" and often linked to complaints about American academic views on racism and diversity.[38]

As French people of color have become more vocal in speaking out against racism, the French establishment, including President Macron, the former prime minister Edouard Philippe, and the former education minister Jean-Michel Blanquer, have pushed back with complaints that French intellectuals are embracing American-style theories of racism that, they argue, have no place in France.[39] They have been joined by voices from the right, including the two leading far-right political leaders (and likely 2027 presidential candidates) Marine Le Pen and Eric Zemmour.

Macron, for example, complained in 2020 that French academics were inappropriately borrowing "social science theories that are entirely imported from the United States" that "can only be secessionist and break the French Republic in two."[40] He cautioned that "the Anglo-Saxon traditions are not ours." Similarly, the center-right former president Nicholas Sarkozy, when serving as the interior minister, responded to protests by French citizens of color about racist treatment by suggesting that "if people don't like being in France they only have to leave. We've had more than enough of always having the feeling that we must apologize for being French. We cannot change our laws[,] our habits or our customs because they don't please a tiny minority."[41]

Soon after President Macron's complaints about American academics, his minister of education, Jean-Michel Blanquer, followed this up by claiming that "there is a fight to be waged against an intellectual matrix coming from American universities and intersectional theses, which seek to essentialize communities and identities, at the antipodes of our republican model, which, itself, postulates equality between human beings, regardless of their characteristics of origin, gender or religion. This is the breeding ground for a fragmentation of our society and a vision of the world that converges with the interests of Islamists. This reality has particularly corrupted a significant part of the French social sciences."[42] The *New York Times* reported that a "group of 100 prominent scholars wrote an open letter in *Le Monde* supporting the minister and decrying theories 'transferred from North American campuses.' "[43]

Macron is correct that French academics are influenced by American academics' writings on racism. But he fails to recognize that this influence is very much a two-way street. French intellectuals have contributed significant work on racism, feminism, equality, and colonialism that has been highly influential with U.S. academics—and when France exports ideas, the French president is justifiably proud.

Other political leaders and public figures on the right and center-right are speaking out against "wokeism," asserting that it conflicts with the core French value of universalism because it treats the idea of race as legitimate and significant. Arm in arm with American right-wing activists, they seem obsessed with a term that has emerged from Black slang to become a good candidate for slur of the decade. A conservative French think tank has described "wokeism" as "this new totalitarianism whose name cannot be pronounced," which "endangers social cohesion and destroys all the egalitarian achievements of the last two centuries."[44] Eric Ciotti, president of the French Republicans (a center-right party), compared anti-racism to the reign of terror during the French Revolution, stating that "wokeism is the new terror of the century."[45] The far-right Rassemblement National calls it a "doctrine of deconstruction of our civilization."[46]

Meanwhile, the Black French feminist and anti-racism activist and journalist Rokhaya Diallo, a lecturer and researcher at the Sorbonne and at Georgetown, has been vilified by conservative public figures in terms that recall the U.S. culture wars. A radio call-in participant complained that Diallo was insufficiently grateful to her native France. If "Mrs. Diallo hadn't benefited from all France has to give," the caller said, "I think there's a good chance she would be in Africa, weighing 30 kilos (66 pounds) more and with 15 kids, pounding millet on the ground."[47] The program moderator, the centrist journalist Philippe Rossi, was silent at the time but later apologized for not reacting.

The impact of such attacks was evident in the brief tenure of the French civil rights leader Pap Ndiaye as minister of education. A professor at the elite Institute of Political Science ("Sciences Po"), Ndiaye was a well-known commentator on racism in France. He had studied at the University of Virginia, was well versed in American views on diversity and racism, and was among a handful of well-known French intellectuals of color. He was appointed education minister in May 2022, after Blanquer was dismissed for one too many provocations—a keynote address he gave at an "anti-woke" conference. (Blanquer's next career move was to start an "anti-wokeness" think tank and run unsuccessfully for the National Assembly.)[48]

Ndiaye had tried to distance himself from "wokeism" but was nonetheless castigated for his prior public statements on race and racism. In an interview with Le Monde in December 2017, he had said there is structural racism in France, by which institutions such as the police can maintain racist practices. In June 2020, during the rise of the Black Lives Matter movement in the United States following the murder of George Floyd, Ndiaye declared on the radio station France Inter that he was not surprised by the French authorities' silence on the subject, even as other heads of state across Europe reacted, because "the attitude of denial on police violence in France is classic, and has been used for a very long time."[49] In February 2021, he was quoted in Le Monde explaining that "to be woke is to be aware, vigilant, committed."[50] A few months later he declared in the news magazine M, Le magazine du Monde: "I share the cause of woke activists, the fight for environmental protection, feminism or anti-racism."[51] But he added: "I don't approve of the moralizing or sectarian speeches of some of them. I feel more 'cool' than woke."[52]

Ndiaye's appointment set off a firestorm. Marine Le Pen declared that "this choice to put a man who defends indigenism, racialism and wokeism at the head of our national education system is a terrifying choice for the parents and grandparents that we are."[53] Ndiaye responded, "I am sometimes considered too American in France, a little too 'woke,' a little too influenced by the United States."[54] France was uncomfortable with the idea of race, he asserted: "I can attest to the price we pay when one dares to speak about it."[55] Three months after his appointment, a national poll showed that 62 percent of respondents did not trust him to lead his ministry; the following summer, Macron removed him from the position.[56]

The French backlash against anti-racism and race-conscious identity is part of a pan-European phenomenon that includes the rise of far-right parties in Italy, Spain, Germany, Hungary, France, Austria, Sweden, and elsewhere. All these parties follow a similar script: mocking LGBT people; using angry, dehumanizing rhetoric against Muslims; threatening to expel immigrants from outside Europe; complaining about leftist wokeness; and appealing to Christian nationalism.[57] Just as in the United States, there is a widening gap between educated urbanites and less-educated rural populations. While the large multinational companies across Europe and political leaders in Brussels embrace the diversity charter, increasing numbers of white Christian Europeans reject it as they vote for far-right parties, oppose immigration from outside Europe, and support restrictions on Muslim religious practices. Alice Weidel, a leader of the far-right Alternative for Germany (AfD) Party, complained, "They want to destroy our homeland . . . They want to ban our pork knuckle, our bratwurst, our schnitzel. Well, I'll promise you one thing. They will not take away my schnitzel."[58]

This idea that diversity has value began in the nineteenth century as an approach to learning and was soon linked to the principles of academic freedom and democracy. Support for including the voices of minorities in decision-making and civic discourse was seen as more than a matter of justice or fairness: it was a way to reach better decisions and have more productive discourse. For much of the twentieth century, diversity was entwined with academic freedom, free speech rights, and anti-discrimination law. By the late twentieth century, it had become clear that diversity improves learning, decision-making, scientific inquiry, commerce, and civic engagement. In Katherine Phillips's words, "diversity makes us smarter." Yet the campaign against diversity that is taking root in Europe is also becoming an important force in American politics. The U.S. Supreme Court has overturned forty-five years of precedent to rule that racial/ethnic diversity may not be used by colleges and universities in selecting students because—the majority claims—the idea of diversity is "incoherent" and the diversity principle is unproven. That decision now threatens corporate diversity policies as well as other ways of promoting diversity. The collapse of these policies is particularly tragic given the continuing force of systemic racism in American life, the subject of the next chapter.

PART V

The War Against Diversity

CHAPTER SIXTEEN
From Diversity to DEI

THE DIVERSITY PRINCIPLE is primarily concerned with the benefits of diversity to institutions—universities, business entities, democratic bodies—and through them to the people attached to the institutions. Universities seek diversity because it enhances their principal mission of scholarship and teaching. Businesses promote diversity because it brings greater profits while fulfilling their social responsibility. Democratic institutions embrace diversity because it enhances democratic principles of legitimacy through inclusion. But as Pauli Murray recognized, the diversity principle also impacts equity because it recognizes the value of the voices of outsiders and thus increases their opportunity to become participants in institutions from which they would otherwise be excluded. Wilhelm von Humboldt may have endorsed diversity because it enabled him to found a better university, but for the Catholics and Jews to whom he opened the doors, it enabled their opportunity to participate.

In this century, the embrace of the diversity principle has opened doors for many people who would otherwise have been left outside. But as Dobbin and Kalev found, it is not enough to just open the doors. To gain the benefits of diversity, outsiders must be treated as equals and thus made to feel included. Hence, as corporate, organizational, and academic diversity policies gained in importance, the institutions maintaining these policies began to address not only diversity but also "equity" and "inclusion" (thus "DEI").[1]

The term "equity" has to do with the outcomes of diversity policies. In an equitable organization, women, racial and ethnic minorities, and others with marginalized identities have the same opportunity to achieve as their peers. "Inclusion" refers to how people experience their position within an organization. This is the critical point made by Victoria Plaut. In practical terms, as a 2022 report by the consulting firm McKinsey explained, inclusion concerns "the degree to which organizations embrace all employees and enable them to make meaningful contributions. Companies that are intent on recruiting a diverse workforce must also strive to develop a sufficiently inclusive culture, such that all employees feel their voices will be heard—critical if organizations want to retain their talent and unlock the power of their diverse workforce."[2]

The goals of equity and inclusion are particularly challenging when largely white organizations try to open their doors to Black Americans. There is a growing body of research demonstrating that racism is a systemic part of American society, producing deep-seated inequity and exclusion, hence "systemic racism." What is systemic racism? It is the interrelated system by which Black Americans suffer multiple, compounded disadvantages because they are Black. Overt discrimination contributes to the system but it is only the tip of the iceberg. The system that disadvantages Black Americans includes interrelated and compounding disadvantages and discrimination in housing, education, employment, health care, wealth-building, public services, food, retail pricing, banking, investing, the environment, policing, the criminal justice system, and the political system. To see the full system at work, we must walk in the shoes of Black Americans. And unless it is addressed, Black Americans will continue to be excluded from many of the benefits of diversity policies.

Some discrimination is conscious and intentional. Some white Americans (and others) dislike, fear, or wish to avoid Black Americans, and they will act on their bigotry if given an opportunity. Some white Americans (and others) have deep-seated racial prejudices. They think of Black Americans as lazy, violent, unpatriotic, or dishonest. The number of people who hold these views is astonishingly high.[3] But many who think of themselves as free of prejudice nonetheless treat Black Americans less well than they do white Americans because they see Blacks through the lens of a bias they do not acknowledge. This lens, often described as "unconscious bias," has been measured by social scientists since the 1940s.

This unconscious bias is often described as "implicit bias." Implicit racial bias causes us to apply racial stereotypes without consciously realizing that we're doing it. It is one of a constellation of biases that all people have, which we use to make sense of the world. Other common biases include recency, completion, confirmation, expectation, outcome, projection, and conformity bias.[4] For example, confirmation bias causes us to interpret new evidence as confirming our existing beliefs. Projection bias causes us to assume that our future beliefs will be much like our present ones. These biases make it harder for us to change our views when faced with new evidence. Implicit bias helps explain why people who support equality for Black Americans may still act differently toward them, unconsciously displaying biases that interfere with Black Americans' full participation in society. Unconscious or implicit bias, like overt bigotry and prejudice, contributes to the problem of systemic racism. But there's still more to the story.

Discrimination and disadvantage are not limited to Black Americans, of course. Members of other racial, religious, and ethnic minority groups, women, people with disabilities, Native Americans, LGBTQ people, older people, and others all experience discrimination. Such forms of discrimination are often exacerbated by combined forms of discrimination. Pauli Murray called the combination of race and sex discrimination "Jane Crow." The legal theorist Kimberlé Crenshaw has described the problem as "intersectional" discrimination, which occurs when a person has multiple disadvantaged identities that intersect. The intersection intensifies discrimination. For example, the stereotypes that disadvantage Black women are different and greater than those stereotypes that disadvantage Black men or white women. The stereotypes that disadvantage women in their sixties are different from those applied to men of the same age or to younger women. But Black Americans experience more discrimination than other minority group members undergo, and the ensuing disadvantages are more systematized. I mean no disrespect for others by focusing on the system that especially disadvantages Black Americans.

One way to understand systemic racism is to compare it to another familiar system: American democracy. American democracy is a system of interrelated institutions by which we govern ourselves. It consists of local, state, and national representative governments, which make laws through legislation, execute them through administrative actions, and enforce and interpret them through the judicial system, with checks and balances to prevent any one branch from exercising unchecked power. It requires a free press, free speech, religious freedom, an independent judiciary, a non-political civil service, unbiased prosecutors, respect for the rule of law, multiple institutions of civil society (unions, foundations, NGOs, civic associations), and the right to vote. Voting is the most visible part of American democracy, but it is far from the entire system.

Systemic racism is similar. Overt discrimination is only the most visible part of an interrelated system that includes housing, banking, employment, transportation, education, policing, health care, and voting.

Housing

Most Black Americans live in mostly non-white neighborhoods.[5] Richard Rothstein's brilliant book *The Color of Law* has meticulously described the origins of segregated housing patterns in the United States. Beginning in the 1930s, the federal government promoted segregated housing by designating majority-Black neighborhoods as "blighted" and refusing to guarantee loans in those areas. After World War II, when middle-class whites took advantage of the GI Bill to buy houses in the newly emerging suburbs, the new housing tracts were all-white partly because the government would not lend to developers unless they agreed to limit their sales to whites. In the cities, meanwhile, government lenders and banks insisted that new housing projects be either all-white or all-minority. At the same time, the real estate industry insisted that its brokers keep Black Americans out of white neighborhoods.[6] Most white Americans supported these policies. As late as 1963, only 39 percent of white Americans agreed that Black Americans had a right to live in white neighborhoods.[7] That year, when the California legislature voted to prohibit racial discrimination in housing, the real estate industry led a successful voter initiative campaign to overturn the law, affirmatively legalizing segregation, under the slogan "A man's home is his castle."[8]

After the passage of the 1968 Fair Housing Act,[9] government and real estate industry policies formally changed, but real estate agents continued to steer Black homeseekers away from white neighborhoods, and banks still preferred to lend to whites over equally qualified Black loan applicants; study after study shows that housing discrimination continues today.[10] It is far harder for a Black family to find a home in a white neighborhood than in a non-white neighborhood, and residential segregation is still pervasive.[11]

Segregated neighborhoods do more than separate us. Residential segregation compounds the disadvantage of racism because non-white neighborhoods are far more likely than white neighborhoods to have underfunded and underperforming schools, with inferior facilities and fewer after-school programs, certified teachers, counselors, and advanced placement classes.[12] They are more likely to be located near toxic sites and plants that produce pollution, causing environmental hazards to the residents.[13] Non-white neighborhoods have fewer public services like bus lines, libraries, recreation centers, street lighting, street paving, reliable trash removal, parks, cooling shade from trees, and high-speed internet access; they also have less access to services like health care providers, good supermarkets, healthy food, and neighborhood banks.[14] They are, in other words, comparatively undesirable.

Living in these neighborhoods makes you likely to be less healthy; to be exposed to more toxins; to pay more for food (generally of lower quality); and to have a harder time commuting to a job. Most importantly, living in these neighborhoods makes it more likely that your children will attend underperforming schools. Each of these disadvantages leads to others.

Not only are middle-class white neighborhoods better resourced than middle-class Black neighborhoods, but even poor white neighborhoods are better resourced than middle-class Black neighborhoods. Moreover, the relation between income and neighborhood is skewed in whites' favor. Poor white Americans live in middle-class white neighborhoods at a higher rate than one would predict based on their income, while middle-class Black Americans are more likely to live in poor non-white neighborhoods.[15] As a result, both poor and middle-class Black Americans live in poor non-white neighborhoods, with their relatively inferior services and schools, more frequently than their incomes would lead us to expect.[16]

For white Americans, class is closely related to generational wealth accumulation and social mobility.[17] Although the "American Dream" is based on social mobility, movement is slow for most white Americans.[18] Their children tend to end up in the same income and wealth bracket as their parents; the rich stay rich, the middle class stay middle class, the poor stay poor.[19] But for Black Americans, while the poor stay poor, the children of the middle class and upper middle class tend to drop to lower-income brackets. The reason for this is the compounded disadvantages of systemic racism.[20] In combination, underperforming schools, employment discrimination, more health problems, and less wealth-building drive the children of successful middle-class Black Americans back toward poverty.[21] What about the children of affluent Black Americans? We don't know. There are so few of them that it's hard to make a statistically reliable assessment.

These factors also contribute to Black homelessness. Black Americans are more likely to be one paycheck away from losing their homes to foreclosure or eviction, and once in that situation, they are less likely to catch a break from the bank or landlord.[22] It's not surprising that Black Americans are far more likely to be homeless than white Americans.[23]

Banking, Business, and Wealth

Banks contribute to residential segregation and its compounding disadvantages because they remain reluctant to make mortgage loans for homes in non-white neighborhoods, and when they do, they charge higher interest rates.[24] Nor can Black Americans borrow as much to buy a home as a white family; appraisal companies not only place lower values on homes in non-white neighborhoods but also place lower values on Black-owned homes in middle-class and affluent neighborhoods compared to equivalent (in some cases identical) white-owned homes in the same neighborhoods.[25] At the same time, the values of homes increase more slowly in non-white neighborhoods. Thus, if we compare a white family with a statistically identical Black family, the white family can buy a home that will increase in value more quickly, while paying a lower interest rate on their mortgage. Over time, the white family will build more wealth, in the form of home equity, than the Black family.[26]

There's a feedback loop: banks contribute to residential segregation, and residential segregation leads to inferior banking options. People living in a non-white neighborhood often have access to fewer good banking choices (if any), which means lenders will charge more and provide less.[27] Residents may need to use payday loan shops instead of banks to cash checks or engage in other banking transactions.[28] Having a local bank allows customers to form a trusting relationship with a banker, which provides many benefits over time.[29] For example, when the Small Business Administration began making paycheck protection loans to small businesses in 2020 to help offset the devastating impact of the COVID-19 pandemic on small businesses, business owners who did not have a relationship with a bank were mostly unable to apply.[30] It is thus not surprising that over 40 percent of small businesses owned by Black Americans failed between February and April 2020, compared with under 20 percent of small businesses owned by white Americans.[31]

And even successful Black-owned businesses make less money, which locks them out of the most desirable banking options. Even when Black

Americans start businesses with the same amount of capital, it is likely that when they succeed, their businesses earn substantially less than similarly capitalized white businesses. In part, this occurs because white Americans often prefer to do business with other white Americans and because Black Americans, on average, have less wealth and thus less financial capacity to help support Black-owned businesses.[32] As a result, Black entrepreneurs who set up shop in non-white neighborhoods end up with lower profits, along with reduced access to the financial services available to their white counterparts.

Meanwhile, Black families have to make their wealth stretch further for two reasons. First, the average middle-class Black wage earner has a larger extended family to support than the average white wage earner at the same salary.[33] Second, Black unemployment is higher and Black wages are lower.[34] These differences persist even after one corrects for education.[35] Why? Because employment discrimination is another entry point to the interrelated parts of our system of racism.

Employment Discrimination

When equally qualified Black and white candidates apply for jobs, the white jobseeker is more likely to be interviewed, more likely to be offered a job, and likely to be offered a higher starting wage.[36] Not only do employers, on average, favor whites over Blacks when both candidates are equally qualified, they are even likely to favor less-qualified whites over more-qualified Blacks.[37] In one study, when employers were asked to choose between a Black applicant who just got out of high school and an otherwise identical white applicant who just got out of jail, most selected the white applicant, with the Black high school graduate only half as likely to receive a callback or job offer.[38] When law partners read associates' memos, they're far more likely to find typos if they've been told the author is Black.[39] The unsurprising result of these biases is higher unemployment and lower earnings for Black Americans, causing an enormous wage and wealth gap between Blacks and whites.[40] Recall from chapter 14 the earnings gap between full-time year-round white workers and Black workers who have earned a bachelor's degree or above: their median annual earnings are $111,600 for white men, $85,170 for Black men, $82,270 for white women, and just $75,410 for Black women.[41] The income gap is exacerbated by a retirement savings gap, as Black (and Hispanic) workers are less likely to be covered by employer-sponsored retirement plans.[42]

Although it is tempting to see employment discrimination as a product of conscious bigotry, many decision-makers are unaware of any bias on their part, even as they favor white applicants.[43] The common terms for this are "unconscious bias" or "implicit bias," but in my own writing on this subject I prefer the term "negligent discrimination."[44] We hold negligent drivers responsible for the unintentional accidents they cause, but we seldom hold negligent employers responsible for their unintentional discrimination.

The problem of finding good employment is heightened by the problem of access to transportation.[45] Black Americans and other people of color are more likely to use public transit than white Americans, but the funds spent on public transportation go disproportionately toward service for white neighborhoods.[46] As a result, Black Americans are less likely to have access to public transit, even though they are more likely to need it.[47] Lower earnings and higher costs for car purchases have combined to make Black Americans three times more likely than whites to lack access to a car.[48] Black jobseekers overall have less ability to travel to the areas where jobs are located. The problem is long standing. Fifty years ago, Dr. King described Black access to public transit as a "genuine civil rights issue."[49] In the fifty years since, our infrastructure investments in white neighborhoods and disinvestments in non-white neighborhoods have only worsened the disparities.[50]

If Black jobseekers want to buy a car to assist their job search, they will pay substantially more than a similarly situated white person for the exact same car.[51] They will also pay a higher interest rate on their car loan compared to a white buyer with an identical credit rating.[52] And the streets in non-white neighborhoods where they live are likely to be less well maintained than those in white neighborhoods, meaning their cars are likely to need more maintenance, which will further add to their costs.[53]

Each of these comparisons has been based on equally qualified whites and Blacks, measured by factors like education, work experience, income, and credit score. But of course it's a greater challenge for Black Americans to achieve equality in education, experience, or income.

Education

Inequality in education is an essential part of the system of American racism.[54] As I have noted, Black Americans are far more likely to attend elementary and secondary schools that are underfunded and underperforming, compared with the schools attended by white Americans.[55] The teachers are less likely to have teaching credentials, and the buildings are likely to be older and less well maintained.[56] The facilities are less likely to include science labs, language labs, computer labs, swimming pools, and well-stocked libraries.[57] The schools are likely to have fewer advanced placement classes, fewer college counselors, and more students in each classroom.[58] The teachers are likely to have lower expectations of their Black students and other students of color than of their white students and thus demand less of them, a problem President George W. Bush described as the "soft bigotry of low expectations."[59] Black students are more likely than white students to be disciplined for the same conduct, creating disciplinary and sometimes police records for them as children and putting them in the "school to prison pipeline."[60] And the schools are likely to be even more racially segregated than those in 1954, when the Supreme Court held that racial segregation of public schools violated the U.S. Constitution.[61] Given these inequities, it is hardly surprising that Black Americans are less likely than white Americans to graduate from high school, attend college, or graduate from college.[62]

The current move to eliminate minority scholarships is a particularly insidious way of keeping Black and Latino students from pursuing an education, given that these students are more likely to come from low-income families and thus less likely to be able to self-fund their education. The disappearance of these scholarships also affects Black students from middle-income families, which have less wealth, on average, than middle-class white families.

Moreover, the campaign to end these scholarships rests on a flawed assumption: that in their absence there will be equal resources for low- and middle-income students, which in turn is based on the assumption that most scholarships are "need-based." But most scholarships are "merit" scholarships, and most merit scholarships are tuition discounts used to recruit applicants with high SAT scores so as to raise the college's or university's reputation and U.S. News ranking. Since the SAT notoriously results in lower scores for Black and Latino students compared with white students with similar grades, "merit" scholarships are slanted toward middle-class and affluent whites. Even when need-based and minority scholarships are taken into consideration, white students are more likely to receive scholarships than Black, Latino, or Asian American students.

Policing

Black Americans are likely to be both over-policed and under-protected.[63] They are more likely to be subject to police suspicion but less likely to be taken seriously as crime victims.[64] When we compare how the police treat white Americans and Black Americans engaged in identical conduct, we find that Black Americans are more likely to be stopped by the police, verbally threatened or insulted, searched, arrested, and physically violated.[65] Such treatment is common for Black Americans in non-white neighborhoods, and even more common if they are present in white neighborhoods. All too often, when white kids get in minor trouble with the police, they get reprimanded; when Black kids get in the same kind of trouble, they are arrested.[66]

When Black Americans are arrested, they are more likely than white Americans arrested for identical conduct to be charged, held on bail, tried, convicted, and sentenced to prison instead of probation.[67] They serve longer sentences for identical crimes and are less likely to be paroled.[68] The huge number of Black Americans dragged into the criminal justice system for minor drug offenses cascades through the lives of Black communities. For example, if any member of a family living in public housing, including a child, is accused of criminal conduct, even just getting into a fistfight, the entire family is subject to eviction from their home under the federal Department of Housing and Urban Development's "one-strike policy."[69] In a New York case, a housing authority attempted to evict a mother because she allowed her child to stay overnight at her home so that he could get to an early morning doctor's appointment. The child had been banned from the apartment because he had been accused of drug possession; the housing authority tried to enforce the one-strike policy even though the drug charges had been dropped.[70] In another case, a court found that an allegation of drunkenness was enough to justify eviction, even though the tenant was not arrested or charged with any crime.[71] This rule falls disproportionately on Black families because they are far more likely than white Americans to be arrested for drug possession and status crimes like public intoxication, even though rates of possession and use are similar between Black and white Americans. Black Americans are far more likely to be arrested for conduct for which a white person would simply receive a warning.[72]

Health Care

Black Americans suffer myriad disadvantages in health care, which contribute to higher infant mortality rates and shorter life spans compared to white Americans even when controlling for income.[73] Part of the problem is the scarcity of Black doctors: Black Americans make up 12 percent of the U.S. population but only 5 percent of physicians.[74] There are fewer doctors, dentists, medical offices, care centers, and hospitals in and near non-white neighborhoods, and the hospitals and care centers that do serve these communities are likely to be substandard compared with those serving white communities.[75] When the COVID-19 pandemic reached nursing homes, the reports in the press suggested that the results were uniformly devastating. But nursing homes, like nearly all institutions in America, are heavily segregated, and it turns out that residents of mostly non-white nursing homes were far more likely to be infected and die from the virus than residents of white nursing homes.[76]

Good health requires access to good food, and the non-white neighborhoods where most Black Americans live are "food deserts," with few good markets or other sources of high-quality food. The markets that do exist charge higher prices, meaning that white Americans can buy better food for less.[77] Unsurprisingly, Black families are twice as likely to experience "food insecurity" (a euphemism for hunger) as white families.[78] Black Americans are more likely to live in heavily polluted areas, a factor contributing to many health problems.[79] Moreover, employment discrimination against Black Americans means fewer of them have employer-provided medical insurance.[80]

Health provider prejudice adds to the problem as well. When Black and white Americans with identical symptoms and identical insurance seek medical care, doctors are more likely to recommend aggressive and life-saving care for white patients than for Black ones.[81] The probable explanation is unconscious (or implicit) bias.[82] Whether or not doctors (like teachers, lawyers, judges, and other professionals) feel personally committed to racial equality, they (we all) are influenced by racial stereotypes that are hard to escape. For example, doctors assume that Black patients are less likely to understand their instructions, less likely to follow them, and less likely to exercise good judgment in caring for themselves.[83] The attitudes underlying these pernicious stereotypes are racist, but the stereotypes mostly operate at a subconscious level. Doctors are often unaware of them when making decisions about treatment.

Unconscious stereotyping is not limited to doctors or to lawyers, judges, police, and teachers. It is a pervasive part of American society. It explains why Black Americans are often denied service or given lower-quality service in restaurants, hotels, and entertainment venues and why they are treated with suspicion at retail stores or in business transactions.[84] Criminal defense lawyers commonly observe that it is far easier to persuade a white judge (and most judges are white) to give a defendant another chance when the defendant is white.[85] Unconscious stereotyping does not only occur with white judges who are self-consciously prejudiced. For nearly all judges, the stereotypes they have held all their lives lead them to make different assumptions about Black defendants (or witnesses or jurors) than about white ones. One way of understanding this dynamic is to recognize that white judges (like many white Americans) feel less empathy for Black Americans than for white Americans.[86] They find it harder to put themselves in a Black person's shoes.

Another way to describe this behavior is "profiling." Racial profiling is a part of every Black American's life. It means they are more likely to be treated with suspicion in scores of ways as they go about their lives: "driving while Black," "shopping while Black," "banking while Black," "riding an elevator when Black," or even "walking while Black." All carry a constant risk of a misunderstanding that escalates into police action and, all too often, police violence.[87]

The differentials in how Black Americans are treated show up everywhere. Take the simple act of crossing the street. A recent experiment in Portland, Oregon, involved identically dressed white and Black men standing by a crosswalk as traffic approached. Cars stopped far more frequently for white pedestrians than for Black pedestrians, allowing the white pedestrian to cross but not granting the same courtesy to Black pedestrians.[88] Such incidents may sound trivial until we note that Black American pedestrians are more than twice as likely as white pedestrians to be killed by cars.[89] Well over one hundred thousand pedestrians are treated in emergency rooms every year from traffic accidents, and over six thousand die.[90] A disproportionate share are Black.[91]

Voting

Finally, an important part of systemic racism against Black Americans is the suppression of their votes. The right to vote is the most visible feature of

American democracy. Here, there are good reasons to believe that overt racist intent is at work. In theory, Black men have had the right to vote since the Fifteenth Amendment to the U.S. Constitution was ratified in 1870. But since the end of Reconstruction, white Americans have consistently deprived Black Americans of the right to vote. Although the 1965 Voting Rights Act helped expand that right, we continue to see efforts to keep Black Americans from voting, from the fabricated claims of voter fraud used to justify voter ID laws and restrictions on early voting and Sunday voting to racial gerrymandering. The same purpose underlies the outrageously long lines that are the hallmark of voting in Black neighborhoods.[92]

Like every aspect of systemic racism, voter suppression compounds other elements of disadvantage. Absent suppression, Black Americans would have a greater voice and thus more influence over how much money gets spent on schools and libraries, where they are located, and what they teach. They would have more say on public transit spending and road maintenance—not to mention banking regulation, consumer protection, environmental protection, pollution abatement planning, toxic cleanups, employment discrimination, public and private service denial, health care spending, zoning, and housing discrimination. Each of these is connected to the others. That's how systems work. If Black Americans are kept from voting, they will never have the power to escape the other parts of the system of racism.

I should emphasize that every element of systemic racism that I've identified in this chapter has been thoroughly researched and is abundantly verified by hard data. As Casey Stengel used to say, "You could look it up," and I invite skeptical readers to check the references I've supplied. Given the reality of this pervasive system of racism, it should be clear that the preferred policy of conservatives—strict color-blindness in all admission, hiring, and promotion decisions and the elimination of the equity and inclusion aspects of DEI—can never yield the fairness its supporters claim for it. What opponents of DEI call color-blindness is really willful racism-blindness. Chief Justice John Roberts famously wrote that "the way to stop discrimination on the basis of race is to stop discriminating on the basis of race," but this seemingly commonsense idea ignores the fact that the playing field is so profoundly tilted that such a policy can only preserve inequality. It is as true today as it was when President Lyndon Johnson said these words more than sixty years ago:

Men and women of all races are born with the same range of
abilities. But ability is not just the product of birth. Ability is
stretched or stunted by the family that you live with, and the
neighborhood you live in—by the school you go to and the poverty or the richness of your surroundings. It is the product of a
hundred unseen forces playing upon the little infant, the child,
and finally the man.[93]

The reason DEI is needed is not to offer some remorseful payback
for past discrimination or an overdue apology for our ancestors' long-
abolished practice of slavery. It's needed to remedy present discrimination that harms Black people's lives right now, every day. Combined with
the increasingly persuasive evidence of the value of diversity, the need for
diversity, equity, and inclusion policies should be obvious. Yet we are
nonetheless seeing a growing opposition to the consideration of diversity
in education, commerce, governance, and civic engagement. This war
against diversity threatens to upend two hundred years of progress in our
understanding of how to build a better society. It is the subject of the
next—and final—chapter.

CHAPTER SEVENTEEN
The War on Diversity

IVERSITY MATTERS. It matters because people benefit from
the interaction of people with different backgrounds, experiences, viewpoints, religions, nationalities, races, ethnicities,
ages, cultures, genders, abilities, disabilities, and other forms
of personal identity. It matters because including outsider voices makes us
better at learning, scientific discovery, commerce, and civic engagement.
The understanding that diversity matters has gone from a nineteenth-
century outlier theory, based on speculation and limited observation, to
an empirically established foundation of modern society. The diversity
principle justified the admission of Catholics and Jews to the University
of Berlin, Oxford, and Cambridge in the first half of the nineteenth century. It led a few prominent American universities to begin admitting
Catholics, Jews, Blacks, and other racial and ethnic minorities—as well as
immigrants, the poor, and women—in the mid-nineteenth century. It led
judges, lawyers, and scholars to broaden the U.S. constitutional view of
free speech and academic freedom in the twentieth century, providing a
basis for ending segregation in higher education even before the *Brown v.
Board of Education* decision. It spurred resistance to South African apartheid because it interfered with racial diversity at South African universities. It undergirded the affirmative action programs that, until 2023,
predominated at selective U.S. colleges and universities. It provided the
business case for diversity beginning in the late twentieth century. In the

twenty-first century, the principle expanded further to embrace not only diversity but equity and inclusion.

Proponents of the diversity principle have often paid for their views with social ostracism and worse. Because Wilhelm von Humboldt refused to mute his opposition to anti-Semitism, he was forced to resign his government position and retreat from public life. John Stuart Mill lost his campaign for re-election to Parliament because he opposed the dehumanization of Black Jamaicans. Charles Eliot was targeted by the Ku Klux Klan. Louis Brandeis's appointment to the Supreme Court was nearly upended because he was a Jew who represented poor people and union members. Harold Laski was blocked from a professorship at Harvard because of his support for labor unions. Pauli Murray was blocked from universities, jobs, and government positions because of her gender status, race, and politics. Albert van der Sandt Centlivres was forced to retire from his position of chief justice of South Africa because he opposed apartheid. All stood their ground. Their views entered the mainstream of American law and society because three Republican-appointed conservative Supreme Court justices—Lewis Powell, Sandra Day O'Connor, and Anthony Kennedy—defied expectations and embraced the view that colleges and universities could exercise their academic freedom to consider racial and ethnic diversity in choosing to enroll a diverse group of students.

Now, just as it did with abortion rights in *Dobbs v. Jackson Women's Health*, the U.S. Supreme Court has overruled decades of settled precedent to hold that U.S. colleges and universities may no longer use the goal of diversity as a basis for considering race and ethnicity as positive factors in making admissions decisions. The Court's reasoning ignored the history of the diversity principle and twisted the meaning of constitutional equality. The majority, treating all recognition of race as a form of racism, reasoned that a university seeking a racially diverse student body was no different from the many American colleges and universities that refused to admit Black students until legally compelled to do so in the mid-twentieth century. It pretended that ignoring racism does not perpetuate inequality but instead is a form of anti-racism. The majority joined Chief Justice Roberts in his view that people who encourage integration are indistinguishable from segregationists because they have committed the civic sin of being race-conscious.[1] But "color-blindness" in a society with pervasive systemic racism is not a form of opposition to racism. It is simply racism-blindness.

The changes that the *Students for Fair Admissions* decision forced on
society will be profound. As the first reports are released for the students
entering college in 2024, the number of Black students entering some
highly selective colleges and universities has dropped dramatically, while
at others the drop is smaller or even nonexistent. The Massachusetts Institute of Technology's entering class went from 15 percent Black to just
5 percent, a 67 percent drop.[2] At Amherst College, the freshman class fell
from 11 percent Black in 2023 to 3 percent in 2024, a 73 percent drop.[3]
But at Harvard the drop was only 22 percent, from 18 percent of incoming students to 14 percent, or approximately sixty-five students.[4] At the
University of North Carolina, the number of entering Black students
dropped from 11 percent to 8 percent, a 27 percent drop. At Harvard
Law School the number of Black students in the first year class dropped
from forty-three in 2023 to just nineteen in 2024.[5] But at Yale, Duke, and
Princeton, the number of undergraduate Black students enrolling was essentially unchanged. Within days of reporting their enrollments, all three
universities received letters from Edward Blum notifying them that he
planned to sue them for having defied the Supreme Court.

It's far too early to know why some universities see greater drops
than others or how many Black students will no longer be able to enter
our country's leading colleges and universities. We do know that at the
University of California and the University of Michigan, where voters
imposed bans on race/ethnic affirmative action policies in 1996 and 2006
respectively, the number of Black and Latino students fell dramatically.[6]
Before Michigan banned affirmative action, the percentage of Black students at UM was just over 7 percent; today it is under 4 percent, in a
state where 14 percent of the population is Black. Following California's
1996 ban on affirmative action, the percentage of Black students enrolling at Berkeley and UCLA fell from over 7 percent in 1995 to under 3
percent today.[7] Many commentators, including members of the Court,
have urged colleges and universities to adopt policies favoring students
from lower socioeconomic classes, as many colleges and universities had
long been doing and others will now attempt. But the California and
Michigan experience suggests that this will still dramatically reduce the
number of minority students.[8] And to what end? From the early reports
and the evidence supporting the trial court findings in the Harvard and
UNC cases, it appears that the reductions in students from disadvantaged racial and ethnic minority groups will be largely offset by the admission of more white students from affluent families. The trial courts in

the Harvard and UNC cases found that both schools already recruited students from low-income families. There was no need to choose between race-based and class-based admissions preferences. The schools were using both.

One effect of the Court's decision is that colleges will increasingly pretend that SAT scores provide a reasonable measure of a student's potential or merit. This is both unfair and ironic. In his 2024 book on testing, the Columbia journalism professor Nicholas Lemann dismantles every argument on behalf of the SAT as a selection tool for college admissions. At best, the test predicts a student's first year grades, distinguishing those who come to college fully prepared from those who require a year or two to become equally competitive. Do we really care about a student's first year grades if after that first year lower-scoring students do as well as higher-scoring ones? Moreover, Lemann points to a study by Roy Freedle, published in the *Harvard Educational Review*, showing that small changes in the SAT's questions eliminate the "principal cause of the Black-white score gap," but the test makers have declined to make those changes.[9] It's not that the SAT and other standardized tests have no validity; they are great predictive tools for determining the test taker's parents' income.[10] What a step backward the Court has encouraged us to take.

However reluctantly they may comply, most colleges and universities will probably not resist the Court's decision. It took Yale less than three months to agree with Edward Blum that they would remove all considerations of race from their admissions policies and open their books to him if he would drop his suit. Despite this concession, Blum is now preparing a new suit simply because Yale's enrollment of Black students remained essentially unchanged. At most schools, the number of Black and Latino students will probably drop significantly, but where for some reason they don't, we should expect conservative advocacy groups to aggressively push to reduce their numbers by expanding the meaning of the *SFFA* decision in court. Within days of the decision's announcement, Trump advisor Stephen Miller wrote this to the deans of two hundred U.S. law schools:

> There are those within and outside your institutions who will tell you that you can develop an admissions scheme through pretext or proxy to achieve the same discriminatory outcome. Anyone telling you such a thing is coaching you to engage in illegal

conduct in brazen violation of a Supreme Court ruling, law-breaking in which you would be fully complicit and thus fully liable. You are hereby warned.[11]

Is Miller suggesting that attempts to include more students from low-income families should be treated as illegal if they have the effect of increasing Black enrollment? Heads I win, he claims, tails you lose. Either way, it appears that the ultimate goal is to enroll fewer minority and more white students.

Colleges and universities would ignore the law at their peril. Many will search for race-neutral admissions criteria that provide a degree of racial diversity. The Court has never condemned such plans. In his majority decision in the *SFFA* case, Chief Justice Roberts even encouraged schools to ask applicants to share their lived experience with racism. The dissenters in the *Grutter* and *Fisher* cases argued that colleges and universities should be able to find color-blind methods of increasing racial diversity; they seemed to endorse the view that color-blind admission policies are acceptable even if they are intended to result in increased admissions offers to students of color. But one lesson from the *SFFA* case is that precedent doesn't always matter, nor do facts; the Supreme Court ignored the trial court's factual findings and substituted testimony from the plaintiff's experts that the trial court had rejected, asserting that the admissions plans discriminated against Asian Americans. The Court thus overrode the well-established rule that it may reject trial court findings only if they are clearly erroneous. Did the Court invoke the "clearly erroneous" rule? No, it simply ignored it. As Miller's and Blum's threats suggest, conservative advocacy groups may argue that if a college or university admits large numbers of Black or Latino students, it must be improperly engaged in race-based affirmative action. The Court may soon agree with them, even if it means contradicting Chief Justice Roberts.

In 2021, the Pacific Legal Foundation, a conservative advocacy group, brought just such a case against the school board in Fairfax County, Virginia. The group objected to changes in admissions policy at the highly selective Thomas Jefferson High School (TJ). For many years, admission to TJ was based largely on standardized test scores, with the result that most TJ students came from just a few "feeder" middle schools. Following the murder of George Floyd, the school board reexamined these policies in a series of discussions with their staff and the

public. Several low-income schools were sending no students to TJ, and
the school counted only a handful of Black students in a county that was
over 10 percent Black. The staff proposed several race-conscious admissions plans, each of which the board rejected. The board then adopted a
race-blind admissions plan that dropped the $100 application fee, elimi-
nated a standardized test requirement, encouraged admissions officials to
admit students from low-income and non–English speaking families, and
allocated a portion of the spaces in the incoming class to every middle
school in the county. To ensure that admissions decisions would be race-
blind, the new policy instructed the admissions officials not to consider
race or ethnicity and to mask the names and racial/ethnic identities of all
applicants.[12] This is precisely the kind of plan the conservative dissenters
in *Fisher* and *Grutter* seemed to be endorsing.

One result of the new policy was that the number of Asian American
applicants accepted from low-income families increased exponentially
(from one to fifty-one), although the overall number of Asian American
students went down. The number of white students went up slightly, and
the number of Black and Hispanic students went up dramatically. TJ received one thousand more applications than it had in the prior cycle, and
the mean grade point average of applicants increased. Meanwhile, the
number of students from low-income families and English-learner families rose markedly, and students from all twenty-eight Fairfax County
middle schools were admitted. One might think that supporters of in-
come-based affirmative action and class-based diversity would hail such a
plan, but they were silent.

The federal district court judge ruled in favor of the parents who
challenged the new policy, reasoning that since the board was clearly dis-
tressed by the tiny number of Black students at TJ, had discussed adopting race-conscious policies, and had ultimately adopted a plan that
brought an increase in the number of Black students and a decrease in
the number of Asian American students, their policy must therefore be
race-based and thus illegal. He ordered the school board to scrap the
new admissions plan.[13]

The Fairfax school board appealed to the Fourth Circuit Court of
Appeals and asked it to stay the district court decision pending review.
Such stays are granted to freeze the status quo when it appears that the
party seeking the stay has a high likelihood of prevailing once the case
is heard and when the court determines that retaining the status quo
would do less harm than allowing the decision to go into effect in the

meantime. The court granted the stay, leaving the new policy in place while it heard the case.

Then something unusual happened. In April, 2022, the plaintiff parents and the Pacific Legal Foundation asked the Supreme Court to lift the stay so that the new policy could be tossed out immediately. Within weeks, and without hearing arguments on the matter, three members of the Court—Clarence Thomas, Samuel Alito, and Neil Gorsuch—voted to vacate the stay, which would have forced the board to return to the old admissions policy that admitted only a handful of Black, Latino, and low-income Asian students. By doing this on the "shadow docket," they were attempting to stop the new policy from going into effect without having to ask for briefing on the matter or to write an opinion explaining their reasoning.

On May 23, 2023, the Fourth Circuit voted 2–1 to overrule the district court judge and approve the new policy. Judge Toby Heytens explained this outcome in his concurring opinion:

> Under the policy challenged here, no students are told where they can and cannot go to school based on the color of their skin. No seats are reserved based on race. No points are awarded based on race, nor do evaluators consider race as part of a holistic-review calculus. Instead, this case involves a school whose governing board decided to replace one facially race-neutral policy with another. When it did so, the Board also adopted—by a supermajority vote—a rule saying the admissions process must use only race-neutral methods that do not seek to achieve any specific racial or ethnic mix, balance, or targets. The policy challenged here is not just race-neutral: It is race blind.[14]

In a closely watched decision, the Supreme Court denied review without explanation, leaving the Circuit Court opinion as the governing law, at least for now.

The TJ case makes clear that challenging race-conscious affirmative action is just one step in a broader litigation strategy that aims to prohibit increasing diversity even by race-blind methods. As the law professor Jonathan Feingold warns, this strategy "really is about making it unconstitutional or unlawful for schools to try to remedy racial inequality."[15]

If my experience at UC Berkeley is any indication, the end of race-conscious admissions will not end the stigma of being a minority student.

Berkeley was required to stop considering race in admissions decisions in 1996, and the number of Black and Latino students plummeted. But after nearly thirty years of no racial preferences in admissions, I routinely hear from Black and Latino students that white students are telling them, "You're only here because of affirmative action." A recent *New York Times* article confirmed these observations, quoting a Black student at Berkeley who was told by a white student that "she must have been admitted because she was Black" and that she had been excluded from study groups because "they don't think Black students are smart enough to be in their clubs."[16] Almost three decades after Berkeley eliminated race-based admissions, what should we conclude from this? It's not affirmative action that causes stigma—it's racism.

Even before the Supreme Court struck down race-conscious admissions, politicians in conservative states were working to end diversity programming. By September 2024, lawmakers in twenty-eight states had targeted DEI programs at state colleges and universities, often with assistance from conservative think tanks, including the Goldwater Institute, the Claremont Institute, and the Manhattan Institute, which in turn receive funding from a small but powerful cadre of right-wing donors.[17] They justify their efforts in overtly militaristic terms. Ryan P. Williams, the president of the Claremont Institute, wrote that "America is under attack by a leftist revolution disguised as a plea for justice."[18]

In his first term, President Trump led the charge. In September 2020, he issued an Executive Order that required federal agencies and contractors to end all DEI programs that used the words "white privilege," "systemic racism," "intersectionality," or "unconscious bias."[19] When Trump left office, Governor Ron DeSantis of Florida picked up the campaign. He signed a bill barring the state's colleges and universities from publishing DEI statements or spending money, regardless of the source, on DEI programs.[20] Not to be outdone, in June 2023, Trump declared that if elected president in 2024, he would reinstate his 2020 order and "eliminate all diversity, equity, and inclusion programs across the entire federal government." On the afternoon of President Trump's 2025 inauguration he began fulfilling the promise.[21] Even before Trump's return to the White House, the House of Representatives passed a defense appropriations bill in July 2024 that would have required all branches of the U.S. military to cease all DEI efforts, close all DEI offices, and fire all civilian employees in DEI roles—over the objections of military leaders, who continue to regard diversity as essential to their mission.

Two weeks after the *SFFA* decision was handed down, on July 13, 2023, the attorneys general of thirteen Republican-controlled states wrote to the CEOs of the largest one hundred companies in the country (the Fortune 100) to demand that they immediately cease any policies intended to diversify their workforce or supply chain that include race-based recruiting, hiring, promotion, or contracting. The AGs warned the CEOs that they intended to vigorously prosecute firms that failed to comply.[22] The letter stretched the *SFFA* decision far beyond its actual holding. It read as if the Court had overruled several cases that were not cited in the decision and had prohibited practices that were not before it. Most of these attorneys general came from states that had resisted *Brown v. Board of Education* for two generations. Now, claiming to represent the true spirit of non-discrimination, they sought to enforce the *SFFA* case—by egregiously exaggerating its holding—in just two weeks.

In January 2023, in a move reminiscent of the McCarthy era, the head of Florida's Office of Policy and Budget directed all of the state's colleges and universities to "provide a comprehensive list of all staff, programs and campus activities related to diversity, equity and inclusion and critical race theory."[23] Similar demands were made in Kansas, South Carolina, and Oklahoma.[24] In Oklahoma, for example, Secretary of Education Ryan Walters ordered the state's top higher education official to account for "every dollar" spent on DEI over the last ten years.[25] In South Carolina, legislators asked for information from the state's public colleges and universities concerning their spending on all activities "targeted toward people based on their race, ethnicity, or sexual orientation."[26]

In May 2023, the Texas legislature passed SB 17 which, according to *Texas Monthly*, required the state's institutions of higher education to "prohibit the funding, promotion, sponsorship or support of 'any office of diversity, equity, and inclusion,' or any office that operates under another name but which supports the goals of diversity, equity, and inclusion."[27] At the University of Texas at Austin, the state's flagship campus, just 4.5 percent of the students are Black, compared with a Texas population that is nearly 12 percent Black.[28] In response to SB 17, the university fired at least sixty employees working in DEI and closed both its DEI operations and its Women's Center.[29] In Wisconsin, lawmakers eliminated the University of Wisconsin's program for hiring more diverse faculty members.[30] In Utah, the words "diversity, equity, and inclusion" were ordered removed from any university program name where they appeared.[31] As of July 2024, all DEI programs at Utah's state universities were closed, and a monitoring system was in place to ensure compliance.[32] Texas, Kansas, and Iowa also set up anti-DEI compliance systems.[33]

In Alabama, schools are prohibited from promoting the idea that "slavery or racism are aligned with the founding principles of the United States."[34] Tennessee passed a law banning training to address implicit bias at its universities.[35] And even as the University of North Carolina was defending its diversity admissions policies in the Supreme Court, its new board of trustees was moving to ban "DEI statements"—statements in which candidates describe how they will contribute to the university's diversity efforts—from admissions, hiring, promotion, and tenure assessments.[36] A few months later, North Dakota followed suit.[37] At the University of Missouri, the university voluntarily disbanded its DEI division to avoid being ordered to close it by the legislature.[38] Several states have set up enforcement mechanisms to encourage students to complain if their professors promote DEI, fail to encourage viewpoint and cultural diversity, or teach "hurtful" concepts such as that the U.S. Constitution enabled racism.[39]

One of the ironies of colleges and universities shutting down their DEI offices is that in the wake of *SFFA* they are needed more than ever. As the number of Black and Latino students attending selective colleges drops, the role of DEI offices becomes even more important. From my observation, these are the employees most likely to counsel students (and staff) from minority groups who feel racially isolated, to notice when job searches fail to produce women and minority candidates, and to reach out and question whether the search and selection processes were inclusive. They are the employees most likely to encourage recognition of the considerable benefits of diversity to learning, teaching, experimenting, and engaging, and the ones most likely to have by their presence increased the racial/ethnic diversity among the staff at the college or university. They will be missed.

Like most U.S. businesses, most American colleges are run by white men. As of spring 2023, 72 percent of college presidents in the United States were white, and 67 percent were men.[40] As of 2022, college professors were slightly more likely to be men, two-thirds were white, and just 7 percent were Black.[41] University DEI programs act as anti-discrimination barriers, reducing the bias that exists in hiring and promotion, academic programming, and student services. They provide a refuge for students, staff, and faculty who feel isolated, and they remind the academic community of the importance of inclusion. As in any enterprise, their work is not always productive—an outcome common to every kind of human endeavor—but at their best, they help create an atmosphere of welcome on campuses where people of color (and in many cases women) are still seriously underrepresented in leadership positions as well as in dorms and classrooms.

DEI specialists in human resources consult on hiring and promotions in an effort to keep recruitment and evaluation procedures free from bias. Those in academic affairs give faculty the resources to recognize and eliminate many kinds of bias in the classroom. Those in student services ensure that all students have access to services as well as to teaching and learning materials. If DEI programs are eliminated, these functions are likely to disappear. Fewer women and people of color will be hired and promoted, fewer will have access to learning resources, and fewer tools will be offered to help faculty make their courses fair for all students.

The Pacific Legal Foundation, the conservative advocacy group that sued the Fairfax County school board, is trying to ban the use of DEI statements at the University of California by bringing a federal lawsuit on behalf of John Haltigan, a former assistant professor of psychology at the University of Toronto who alleged that he had decided not to apply for a job at the University of California Santa Cruz because the university required applicants to include a diversity statement.[42]

To be clear, Haltigan was not asked anything about his race or ethnicity in the application, nor was he asked to describe his political views. He was asked how—if at all—his research, teaching, mentoring, and service might contribute to the university's diversity goals, which include viewpoint diversity, experiential diversity, socioeconomic diversity, and a commitment to upward social mobility. He was not rejected based on the content of a diversity statement or for any other reason. Unlike the plaintiffs in *DeFunis*, *Bakke*, *Gratz*, *Grutter*, or *Fisher*, he decided not to apply. We'll never know what might have happened had he actually tried out for the job. Haltigan lost in district court, but his case is under review in the Court of Appeals.

In what might be a deliberate provocation, many opponents of DEI claim to ground their objections in the value of academic freedom. For example, Christopher F. Rufo of the conservative think tank the Manhattan Institute, a recent DeSantis appointee to the New College of Florida board of trustees, argued in a July 2023 *New York Times* op-ed that it "strengthen[s] the values of liberal education" when the governor blocks a university faculty's decision to adopt DEI policies.[43] The point of academic freedom, which even Rufo admits is a core value of the modern university, is to protect faculty from political interference, and he counts DEI as political interference. This argument treats all attempts to address discrimination as discriminatory. It is a variant on the increasingly popular white supremacist claim that it is racist to talk about racism.

When white former members of law reviews at Harvard and NYU sued those schools, claiming that the reviews' new DEI policies diluted the quality of the reviews and thus harmed their reputations as former members, their cases were dismissed for lack of standing. Soon after, an academic study demonstrated that law reviews that adopted DEI policies actually improved the quality of their publications. But in October 2023, Stephen Miller and his America First Legal Foundation—the group that sent warning letters to law school deans just days after the Supreme Court announced its decision in the *SFFA* case—filed a new suit against NYU, again seeking to overturn the law review's DEI policies.[44] As in the Pacific Legal Foundation's suit against UC Santa Cruz, the white male plaintiff in Miller's case was not complaining that he'd been rejected by the law review; he was a first year student allegedly worried that he *would* be rejected if he applied in the future.[45] (And conservatives call liberal students "snowflakes.")

Meanwhile, in the wake of the *SFFA* decision, conservative legislators are taking aim at scholarships designated for members of minority groups, calling them discriminatory. The day of the decision, the attorney general of Missouri instructed public and private colleges and universities in the state to drop all minority scholarships immediately.[46] The leader of Wisconsin's Republican caucus introduced legislation to forbid minority scholarships in that state.[47] Complaints to achieve the same result have been filed in Kansas and Kentucky.[48]

Eliminating minority scholarships is a particularly insidious way to keep Black and Latino students from pursuing an education, because such students are more likely to come from low-income families and thus less likely to be able to self-fund their education. Even middle-class Black families are likely to have less wealth than white families with similar household incomes and to have more extended family members needing financial help.

Moreover, the campaign to end minority scholarships rests on a flawed premise: that in the absence of such scholarships, there will be equal resources for all low- and middle-income students regardless of race or ethnicity. This premise is based on the assumption that most scholarships are "need-based." But as we have seen, a majority of scholarships are "merit" scholarships, tuition discounts used to recruit applicants with high SAT scores. These scholarships are not intended to serve an educational purpose: they are given to improve a college's or university's U.S. News rankings. Since the SAT is notorious for marking Black and Latino students with lower scores compared with white students with similar grades, most "merit" scholarships go to middle-class and affluent white students.[49] Even with the existence of need-based and minority scholarships, affluent white students are already more likely to receive scholarships than Black, Latino, or Asian American students. A July 2024 article in *Inside Higher Ed* reported that "the bulk of scholarship funding in the private scholarship space was going to students in the highest income quartile."[50]

Meanwhile, policymakers and activists are demanding the elimination of broad swaths of the K–12 curriculum dealing with race, based on the claim that learning about racism hurts white students' feelings, makes them feel guilty about their ancestors' racism, spreads discord, or denigrates the nation's Founding Fathers.[51] A study conducted at UCLA School of Law showed that measures limiting teaching about racism now "affect over 22 million public school children, almost half of the country's 50.8 million public school students."[52]

In March 2023, an article in the *Washington Post* reported on a recent finding by the Rand corporation that "nearly one-quarter of a nationally representative sample of 8,000 English, math and science teachers reported revising their instructional materials to limit or eliminate discussions of race and gender." In Iowa, which passed a law forbidding teaching that "the United States of America and the state of Iowa are fundamentally or systemically racist or sexist," a teacher was told by his superintendent that teaching "slavery is wrong" is a stance, not a fact, and he could not include that statement in his lessons. A North Carolina social studies teacher was penalized for having her students read excerpts from Columbus's diaries because a parent complained that reading the diaries made her "White son . . . feel guilty." A Virginia statistics teacher was asked to stop using New York City data on "stop-and-frisk" police encounters disaggregated by race because "it might make children uncomfortable." A twelfth-grade English teacher in Arkansas was forced to explain her decision to offer an optional assignment on Mary Wollstonecraft's *A Vindication of the Rights of Woman*, a foundational text of Western philosophy. Teachers in Missouri, facing increased complaints over *Huckleberry Finn* and *Of Mice and Men*, preemptively decided to cut those books from the syllabus.[53] The *Washington Post* reports that at least one hundred sixty teachers have been fired after being targeted in political debates over their teaching.[54]

These debates aren't only changing what teachers do in their own classrooms. They're influencing curricula across the country. The textbook publisher Studies Weekly, which serves forty-five thousand U.S. schools, revised a first-grade American history textbook to omit a mention of Rosa Parks's race from its coverage of the Montgomery bus boycott, leaving students to wonder why Parks was ordered to move to the back of the bus, why she refused, and why her refusal was heroic. It revised a fifth-grade textbook to omit race from its coverage of the exclusion of Black Americans from juries, simply stating that members of an unspecified "certain group" were barred from jury service.[55] Florida's new teaching standards encourage teachers to tell their students that slavery had certain benefits for enslaved Black Americans because they learned useful skills, as if slavery were a job training program.[56] Governor DeSantis, asked for an example, mentioned blacksmithing.[57] The standards do not encourage teachers to note that many Africans were selectively kidnapped and enslaved precisely because of their existing skills, which included irrigation system design, boat design, and cattle ranching, nor that once enslaved they were forbidden from learning the foundational useful skill of literacy.[58]

The point of these bans seems to be that if we stop learning about racism, it will disappear. But ignorance breeds ignorance. I had a friend—a physician—who developed a small growth on his arm. He suspected it was cancerous, but he didn't want to admit the possibility to himself, so he ignored it. It metastasized to his brain and killed him. So it is with racism: left untreated, it metastasizes.

Some of these new bans are framed as prohibitions of critical race theory. CRT is one of a number of analytical tools used in higher education to examine the role of race and racism in American law and history. Scholars use it to understand why a legal case was decided as it was, why a highway was built where it was, why a bank built a branch where it did, why a political leader took a particular position on an issue. In law schools, it is typically used in conjunction with other legal theories, such as law and economics theory or legal textualism.

In my civil procedure course, for example, I teach a case involving a claim against a Chicago bank for its refusal to make a home equity loan to a Black couple. The bank claimed it made its decision because of a low appraisal of the house's value, but the couple argued it was based on their race. The trial court dismissed the case; the court of appeals reinstated it. My students and I discuss the text of the relevant rule on dismissal of claims, the economic considerations offered to defend the bank's decision, and how racial bias might have influenced the decision, using each of these three analytical tools. We often have robust discussions about whether the trial court decision was racially biased and whether the case should have been dismissed before trial. We consider the relevance of Chicago's long history of redlining and assess whether that adds persuasive force to the couple's claim. In an increasing number of states, I would risk having my tenure revoked and being fired for assigning these materials and leading this discussion.

It is ludicrous to suggest that these approaches to legal reasoning are being taught in elementary schools. What *is* happening is that many K–12 teachers have been exposed to the idea that one way to understand history, literature, current events, and other subjects is to look at the role of racism. These teachers use this approach, along with a multitude of others, to enrich classroom discussion and help their students build critical thinking skills. This is what education is supposed to do: expose students to diverse ideas, approaches, and ways of seeing things. But one effect of such teaching is that young people may learn to recognize how racism influences our lives in unexpected ways. The acknowledgment that racism exists—and matters—is what the CRT bans are intended to prevent. It is another example of willful blindness to racism under the guise of color-blindness.

Does that mean that classroom discussions of racism are always successful? Of course not. Teaching about difficult subjects is challenging, and some teachers are better than others. That's equally true of math, science, or literature. When we entrust our children to teachers discussing difficult issues, we are understandably supersensitive to what happens in the classroom. But we are not helping our children when we charge teachers with calling our children racists or making them uncomfortable simply because they try to expose students to important social issues that are foundational to understanding our country's history. By contrast, we don't complain that teachers are making their students feel bad when they teach our children about drug and alcohol abuse in the hope that they will recognize the warning signs of abuse in themselves and others.

These bans are having a widespread effect on school boards, teachers, school librarians, and textbook publishers.[59] The UCLA Law School CRT tracking project reports that in 2021 and 2022, there were over five hundred documented examples of government anti–anti-racism proposals, many focused on CRT.[60] The Brookings Institution reports that as of November 2021, CRT bans had been passed in Arizona, Idaho, Iowa, New Hampshire, North Dakota, Oklahoma, South Carolina, Tennessee, and Texas.[61] According to *Education Week*, "Since January 2021, 44 states have introduced bills or taken other steps that would restrict teaching critical race theory or limit how teachers can discuss racism and sexism. . . . Eighteen states have imposed these bans and restrictions either through legislation or other avenues."[62]

School libraries are a focus of anti-CRT campaigns. The UCLA report on anti-CRT actions provides examples of targeted library materials:

> The common "divisive concept" tenet that children should not be made to feel distressed, guilty, or anguished on account of their race may manifest in parent requests to ban books such as Toni Morrison's novels *Beloved* and *The Bluest Eye*, Harper Lee's *To Kill a Mockingbird*, or films like 2016's *Hidden Figures*, about three Black women who worked as mathematicians on the U.S.'s first manned orbital space flight in the early sixties, because it contains scenes in which a main character must walk a half mile from her work station to the nearest "Colored Bathroom" across the race- and gender-segregated NASA campus. The Williamson County, Tennessee Moms for Liberty chapter even challenged titles like *Martin Luther King, Jr. and the March on Washington* and *Ruby Bridges Goes to School: My True Story* because children could be "emotionally traumatiz[ed]" and gain negative views of firemen and police officers if taught about "white firemen blasting black children [with a firehose] to the point of bruising their bodies and ripping off their clothes" or Bull Connor siccing attack dogs on civil rights demonstrators in Alabama.[63]

A report from the American Library Association listed over 2,500 books that drew complaints in 2022, most of which were by or about LGBTQ people or people of color.[64] According to PEN America, an anti-censorship advocacy group, in the second half of 2022 about 1,500 books were removed from schools and libraries because of complaints, most of which came from conservative activist groups.[65] In May 2023, Amanda Gorman's beautiful patriotic poem "The Hill We Climb," which was written for and recited at President Joseph Biden's inauguration and which expresses Gorman's love for our country, was removed from the shelves of an elementary school library as unsuitable for young children, following a complaint by a woman associated with the Proud Boys organization. With pitch-perfect irony, the complainant had been photographed standing with the convicted January 6 conspirator Enrique Tarrio wearing a T-shirt with the words "Freedom to Choose."[66]

The anti-CRT movement is affecting higher education as well. Dan Patrick, the lieutenant governor of Texas, has proposed revoking the tenure of University of Texas professors who teach critical race theory in their classes.[67] ProPublica reports that in 2022, after Governor Ron DeSantis signed Florida's "Individual Freedom Act," initially named the "Stop W.O.K.E. Act," the University of Central Florida scrambled to eliminate all sociology courses focused on race or racism.[68]

The war against diversity, further fueled by the *SFFA* decision, will not be limited to the admissions policies at a few elite colleges and universities, and it won't be limited to education. Edward Blum, the conservative activist who bankrolled the cases, has made this quite clear in an interview with UnHerd: "My great hope is that the opinion that comes out of these two Supreme Court cases provides the US with a legal doctrine that can be applied with regards to employment, to fellowships and scholarships, to voting and contracting issues, and that … the justices give us something that not only applies to higher education, but also to other, very important areas of American life."[69]

Blum should be very happy. Following the *SFFA* ruling, corporate diversity efforts are already facing legal challenges. The National Center for Public Policy Research, a conservative advocacy group, sued Starbucks for tying executive pay to diversity efforts, claiming that the policy discriminates against white men, but the case was dismissed.[70] Another conservative group, called Do No Harm, sued the drugmaker Pfizer with the goal of ending its minority fellowship program; that case too was dismissed.[71] Although these lawsuits may initially fail in court, they are having their intended effect: chilling diversity efforts across the corporate world. ZipRecruiter reports that job listings for DEI positions dropped by 63 percent across 2023.[72] Zoom, Google, and Meta are slashing or eliminating their DEI staff and programs, reports Bloomberg News: "As more companies divest from or go quiet on DEI, the unsaid message is that avoiding a lawsuit or angering conservative pundits is more important than addressing the factors that cause their workforces to have low representation of Black and Hispanic employees."[73] Inc.com reports that "many corporate diversity, equity, and inclusion (DEI) programs have been under fire from conservative opponents for the better part of a year, and a growing number of businesses are scaling them back in an apparent response." Employees responsible for DEI programs are "being laid off at double the rate of other employees."[74]

Blum himself has filed several of the most high-profile new cases. In one set of cases, he sued the law firms Perkins/Coie, Morrison & Foerster, and Winston & Strawn for offering fellowships for law graduates of color, demanding that the firms "remove race from consideration when selecting fellows."[75] Each of the firms backed down.[76] Another case targeted a small venture capital fund named the Fearless Fund, which is run by two Black women who make small grants to Black female entrepreneurs. To put this work in perspective, consider the fact that Bloomberg reported in February 2024 that "according to Deloitte, just 1% of investment partners are Black women (up from 0.25% in 2020) and Black female entrepreneurs receive less than 0.1% of all venture capital funding."[77] Even that 0.1 percent is apparently too much for Blum. Although the lawsuit is still pending, the fund's financial backers have been pulling out, dramatically reducing the amount of money it can invest.[78] Blum is also "suing the director of the yet-to-be-built National Museum of the American Latino over an internship program created to increase the number of Hispanics in museum positions."[79]

We should expect many more challenges to corporate diversity policies, prompting companies to pull back voluntarily to escape becoming the targets of litigation.[80] Conservative advocacy groups will continue to bring claims that any program intended to increase minority hiring or promotions violates the rights of white employees. Such was the basis of two orders from the governor of Texas, Greg Abbott. The first, in September 2021, banned DEI training in Texas state agencies and required state contractors, if they continued their own DEI training, to pledge not to promote certain ideas related to race and sex.[81] Then, in February

2023, Abbott instructed state offices that any use of DEI in hiring violated the law.[82] Hiring and promotions of women and people of color will surely drop as a result.

The decision in the *SFFA* case will also be used to block the voluntary efforts now underway to increase the racial, ethnic, and gender diversity of corporate boards—yet another area where Blum is bankrolling litigation.[83] It's easy to foresee that Blum and his colleagues will next argue that even voluntary efforts by companies to diversify their boards are illegal.

It wasn't that long ago that employers resisted the civil rights laws because they thought hiring women and minorities would make them less profitable. We are now moving toward a landscape in which many employers believe—rightly, given the evidence—that they will be more profitable with a diverse workforce or board, yet they will nonetheless be forced to abandon their diversity efforts by the threat of legal action.

Another target will be the military. Recall that in the *Grutter* case, Justice O'Connor's opinion relied in part on an amicus brief submitted by retired military leaders describing the importance of diversity in the officer corps.[84] Chief Justice Roberts exempted military academies from the June 2023 ruling striking down affirmative action at colleges and universities. But in July 2023 and again in June 2024, the House of Representatives tried to override the Court, adding an amendment to the defense appropriations bill requiring the academies to stop using affirmative action.[85] Blum then filed a suit challenging admission policies at West Point, which is now moving through the courts. This flies in the face of the military leaders' brief, which argued that "the importance of maintaining a diverse, highly qualified officer corps has been beyond legitimate dispute for decades."[86] The signers of that brief included "35 top former military leaders, reflecting the highest leadership from all four services: four Chairmen of the Joint Chiefs of Staff; Chiefs of Staff of the Army and the Air Force; Chief of Naval Operations of the Navy; Commandant of the Marine Corps; Medal of Honor recipients; and other military leaders who also serve as university presidents, chancellors, and professors."[87] But the anti-diversity warriors think they know better.

The effects of the *SFFA* ruling continue to ripple outward. The California city of La Cañada Flintridge, where just 1 percent of residents are Black, has sued to enjoin enforcement of a new California law requiring all cities to increase their affordable housing. The city is arguing that affordable housing will bring more Black people to La Cañada Flintridge, and any attempt to increase housing for Black Americans violates the *SFFA* decision.[88] In North Carolina, the sole Black woman on the state supreme court responded to a media inquiry about that court's decision to disband its Commission on Fairness and Equity and the termination of racial equity and bias training throughout the state's courts by describing her own observations of the lack of racial diversity in the state's court system. In response, the state Judicial Standards Commission, an unelected body appointed by the governor, announced that it was investigating her for violating the Code of Judicial Conduct, claiming her remarks undermined the "integrity and impartiality of the judiciary." The commission, which has the authority to remove judges from office, agreed to drop the investigation only after she sued them for violating her free speech rights.[89]

As I complete this manuscript and submit it to the copy editor, President Trump has just returned to office. On the afternoon of his inauguration, he issued an Executive Order ending all federal government DEI efforts. Two days later, all federal DEI employees were placed on leave. By the end of the week, they were notified that they were being fired. On his first day back in the White House, Trump rescinded President Biden's Executive Orders requiring the federal government to consider racial equity and DEI in its operations. On his second day back in office, Trump rescinded all prior Executive Orders providing for DEI efforts by privately owned government contractors, including Executive Order 11246, first ordered by President Lyndon Johnson in 1965, which had been in force for nearly sixty years under eleven presidents. The order required contractors not to discriminate and to take affirmative steps to avoid discriminating. On his third day back in office, the president instructed all federal employees to secretly turn in any co-employee who was surreptitiously engaged in any DEI efforts. Those who failed to turn in their DEI-supporting colleagues would face "adverse consequences." Will we soon have an American Stasi?

The fallout from President Trump's war on DEI will be severe. Employment discrimination will increase; women and people of color—men and women alike—will find it harder to find jobs, hold jobs, be promoted, and be paid fairly. Companies will be less profitable. Science labs will be less productive. Universities will be duller places, with classrooms too homogenized and scholars producing less groundbreaking work. Social alienation will grow. Social cohesion will weaken. Some white men may feel temporarily triumphant, but their children will eventually share in the loss. And to what end? As the iconic Alicia Keys said at the 2025 Grammy Awards, "DEI is not a threat—it's a gift."[90]

As conservatives move to treat as illegitimate any diversity other than viewpoint diversity, ignoring the links that tie viewpoint to experience and identity, some white liberals seem ready to throw in the towel. Across the Fortune 500, companies are scaling back or shelving their DEI programs. The *Wall Street Journal* reports that Boeing, Ford, and Walmart are among the companies cutting back their DEI programs.[91] More will follow.

In an August 2024 essay in the *New York Times*, Stanford professors Paul Brest and Emily Levine argue that DEI programs have failed and should be replaced with programs promoting pluralism.[92] The pluralism projects they describe sound excellent, but they could easily fit within a good program intended to increase diversity and reduce exclusion. In the spirit of my friend the late Christopher Edley, who persuaded President Bill Clinton to support an approach to affirmative action they called "mend it, don't end it," we should not abandon diversity efforts in the face of ideological attacks, nor should we abandon the term. We should work on improving DEI programs. Paying attention to insightful and well-meaning critics is at the heart of the diversity principle. But this is not the time to run away from the core values at the heart of the modern university and increasingly across our society. We should not desert the two hundred plus years of intellectual history and the forty plus years of scientific research demonstrating the importance of diversity.

We thus stand in equipoise. Even as the evidence of the benefits of diversity continues to mount and most of society moves toward acceptance of the diversity principle, conservative courts, politicians, and advocacy groups increasingly block the way. At this point it may be helpful to reflect on the rich intellectual history of the idea of diversity, which over two centuries has taught us that difference helps us learn from one another and make better decisions, broadening our world. Diversity opponents argue that the only legitimate form of diversity is viewpoint diversity, and they mistakenly claim John Stuart Mill in support. But it was the Mills—both of them—who taught us that race, gender, religion, and ethnicity were essential parts of a person's experience and that viewpoint diversity was a product of that experience. As the authors of *The Open Universities in South Africa* wrote in 1957, drawing on the work of Humboldt, the Mills, Eliot, Brandeis, and Holmes, working closely with their friends Frankfurter and Griswold, inspired by Murray and Marshall, and in turn inspiring Cox:

> There is no substitute for the clash of mind between colleague and colleague, between teacher and student, between student and student. It is here that is found, in its most intense form, the stimulus of the new, the exciting and the different. It is here that the half-formed idea may take shape, the groundless belief be shattered, the developing theory be tested by the criticisms of one's fellows. It is here that controversy develops, and out of controversy, deeper understanding. For challenge is as essential to knowledge as to life. This is why discussion may be most fruitful when it begins with disagreement, and when it is conducted between persons from different environments, holding different beliefs, and approaching problems from different standpoints. For knowledge is not advanced through conformity: without the continuous need to defend his convictions from the attacks of the unconvinced, the skeptic, or even the heretic, the individual has little protection against the dangers that his own prejudices may bring into his own thinking. . . . [We thus] believe that racial diversity within the university is essential to the ideal of a university within a multiracial society.[93]

Postscript

For an update on developments in the Trump administration's war against diversity since January 2025, see the postscript to this book at DiversityPrinciple.com.

Notes

Introduction

1. Transcript of Oral Argument at 71, *Students for Fair Admissions, Inc. v. President and Fellows of Harvard Coll. and Univ. of N.C.*, 600 U.S. 181 (2023) (No. 21–707).
2. "1973 Year in Review: Watergate Scandal," United Press International, accessed September 21, 2022, www.upi.com/Archives/Audio/Events-of-1973/Watergate-Scandal.
3. Ken Gormley, "The Saturday Night Massacre: How Our Constitution Trumped a Reckless President," National Constitution Center, October 20, 2015, https://constitutioncenter.org/blog/the-saturday-night-massacre-40-years-later-how-our-constitution-trumped-a-r.
4. Gormley, "Saturday Night Massacre."
5. *United States v. Nixon*, 418 U.S. 683 (1974).
6. Katherine W. Phillips, "How Diversity Makes Us Smarter," *Scientific American*, October 1, 2014, www.scientificamerican.com/article/how-diversity-makes-us-smarter/.
7. Jerome Karabel, *The Chosen: The Hidden History of Admission and Exclusion at Harvard, Yale, and Princeton* (Boston: Houghton Mifflin, 2005), 487–88, 499; Brief for the President and Fellows of Harvard College as Amicus Curiae in Support of Respondents, *DeFunis*, 416 U.S. 312 (No. 73–235).
8. See also David B. Oppenheimer, "Archibald Cox and the Diversity Justification for Affirmative Action," *Virginia Journal of Social Policy and the Law* 25, no. 2 (2018): 157–203.
9. Lisa M. Stulberg and Anthony S. Chen, "The Origins of Race-conscious Affirmative Action in Undergraduate Admissions: A Comparative Analysis of Institutional Change in Higher Education," *Sociology of Education* 87, no. 1 (2014): 39–43.
10. Toni-Lee Capossela, *John U. Monro: Uncommon Educator* (Baton Rouge: Louisiana State University Press, 2012), 55–57; Karabel, *The Chosen*, 213.

11. Karabel, *The Chosen*, 406–7; Stulberg and Chen, "Origins of Race-conscious Affirmative Action," 36–52.

12. Karabel, *The Chosen*, 388–91.

13. "History: The Modern Classic of the Reform University," Humboldt-Universität zu Berlin, last modified March 10, 2023, www.hu-berlin.de/en/about/history.

14. Johan Östling, *Humboldt and the Modern German University* (Lund: Lund University Press, 2018), 23–29, 35–49.

15. Wilhelm von Humboldt, *The Limits of State Action*, trans. John Wyon Burrow (Indianapolis: Liberty Fund, 1993), 11–12. Originally published as *Ideen zu einem Versuch die Grenzen der Wirkamkeit des Staats zu bestimmen*. Originally translated into English as *The Spheres and Duties of Government* (London: John Chapman, 1792, 1854); modern edition Cambridge University Press, 1969, reprinted in the United States in 1993 by Liberty Fund.

16. Alfred Jospe, "Universities," Jewish Virtual Library, accessed February 26, 2023, www.jewishvirtuallibrary.org/universities (opened to Jews); Paul R. Sweet, *Wilhelm von Humboldt: A Biography*, vol. 2, *1808–1835* (Columbus: Ohio State University Press, 1980), 58 (opened to Catholics).

17. Ian F. McNeely, "The Humboldts' Marriage and the Gendering of Intellectual Space," paper presented at the German Studies Association Twenty-Ninth Annual Conference, October 2, 2005, https://hdl.handle.net/1794/1439, citing Gustav Sichelschmidt, *Caroline von Humboldt: Ein Frauenbild aus der Goethezeit* (Droste, 1989), 1.

18. John Stuart Mill, *On Liberty* (Kitchener: Batoche Books, 2021), 34–39.

19. Mill, *On Liberty*, 36.

20. Graham Finlay, "John Stuart Mill on the Uses of Diversity," *Utilitas* 14, no. 2 (2002): 189–218; Nicholas Capaldi, *John Stuart Mill: A Biography* (Cambridge: Cambridge University Press, 2004), 322–27; see further chapter 2.

21. John Stuart Mill, *Inaugural Address at St. Andrews* (London: Longmans, Green, Reader, and Dyer, 1867), 25, https://archive.org/details/inauguraladdresoomillgoog/mode/2up; Finlay, "John Stuart Mill on the Uses of Diversity," 199.

22. Henry James, *Charles W. Eliot, President of Harvard University, 1869–1909*, 2 vols. (Cambridge: Houghton Mifflin, 1930), 1:348.

23. James, *Charles W. Eliot*, 1:159–69.

24. Charles W. Eliot, "The New Education," *Atlantic Monthly*, February 1869, 202–20, www.theatlantic.com/magazine/archive/1869/02/the-new-education/309049/.

25. James, *Charles W. Eliot, President of Harvard University*, 1:193.

26. Karabel, *The Chosen*, 45; James, *Charles W. Eliot*, 2:67.

27. Slosson quote, Edwin Slosson, *Great American Universities* (New York: Macmillan, 1910), 104, https://archive.org/details/greatamericanuniooslosrich/page/104; Eliot quote, "No Equality in Our Institutions—Eliot: Tells Har-

vard Students Uniform Conditions Are Only Possible Under a Despotism," *New York Times*, March 21, 1911, https://timesmachine.nytimes.com/timesmachine/1911/03/21/106724906.pdf.

28. Thomas Healy, "The Unlikely Birth of Free Speech," *New York Times*, November 9, 2019, www.nytimes.com/2019/11/09/opinion/free-speech-holmes-supreme-court.html; Thomas Healy, *The Great Dissent: How Oliver Wendell Holmes Changed His Mind—and Changed the History of Free Speech in America* (New York: Metropolitan Books, 2013), 28–46, 127–31.

29. Healy, *The Great Dissent*, 98–99, 204–5; Oliver Holmes to Harold J. Laski, February 28, 1919, in *Holmes-Laski Letters: The Correspondence of Mr. Justice Holmes and Harold J. Laski 1916–1935*, ed. Mark Dewolfe Howe (Cambridge: Harvard University Press, 1953), 187 ("led by what you have said, I reread Mill on *Liberty* . . .").

30. *Abrams v. United States*, 250 U.S. 616 (1919) (Holmes, J., dissenting); see also Healy, *The Great Dissent*, 204–5.

31. *United States v. Rumely*, 345 U.S. 41, 56 (1953).

32. *Sweezy v. New Hampshire*, 354 U.S. 234 (1957).

33. Thurgood Marshall and Erwin Griswold, Letters between Marshall and Griswold, June 7, 10, 14 and September 22, 1948, Collections of the Manuscript Division, Library of Congress.

34. "Civil Rights Leaders: Thurgood Marshall," NAACP, accessed January 25, 2023, https://naacp.org/find-resources/history-explained/civil-rights-leaders/thurgood-marshall.

35. "Solicitor General: Erwin N. Griswold," U.S. Department of Justice, last modified September 18, 2023, www.justice.gov/osg/bio/erwin-n-griswold.

36. *Sipuel v. Bd. of Regents of Univ. of Okla.*, 332 U.S. 631 (1948); *McLaurin v. Okla. State Regents for Higher Education*, 339 U.S. 637 (1950); See *Sweatt v. Painter*, 339 U.S. 629 (1950); Griswold served as expert witness for Marshall in *Sipuel v. Bd. of Regents of Univ. of Okla.*, 332 U.S. 631 (1948); see Thurgood Marshall and Erwin Griswold, Letters between Marshall and Griswold, June 7, 10, 14 and September 22, 1948, Collections of the Manuscript Division, Library of Congress.

37. Brief for The Committee of Law Teachers Against Segregation in Legal Education as Amici Curiae in Support of Petitioner, *Sweatt*, 339 U.S. 629 (Nos. 20–1199 and 21–707).

38. See *Sweatt*, 339 U.S. at 634–35.

39. "Albert Centlivres, 79, Is Dead; Ex–Chief Justice of South Africa," *New York Times*, September 20, 1966, www.nytimes.com/1966/09/20/archives/albert-centlivres-79-is-dead-exchief-justice-of-south-africa.html.

40. Brian Lapping, *Apartheid: A History* (New York: George Braziller, Inc., 1986), 135; See also Albert van der Sandt Centlivres and Richard Feetham, *The Open Universities in South Africa* (Johannesburg: Witwatersrand University Press, 1957).

41. See chapter 8 for an overview of the relationship between Centlivres, Frankfurter, and Griswold; see also David B. Oppenheimer, "The South African Sources of the Diversity Justification for U.S. Affirmative Action," *California Law Review* 13, no. 32 (2022): 45–49.
42. Centlivres and Feetham, *Open Universities in South Africa*, 11–12.
43. Centlivres and Feetham, *Open Universities in South Africa*, 6.
44. *Sweezy v. New Hampshire*, 354 U.S. 234, 263 (1957).
45. Ken Gormley, *Archibald Cox: Conscience of a Nation* (Reading: Perseus, 1999), 38–40.
46. Letter from Nineteen Faculty of Harvard University to Albert van der Sandt Centlivres, C. J., S. Afr. Sup. Ct., March 31, 1959 (on file with author); see also Oppenheimer, "South African Sources of the Diversity Justification," 49.
47. Derek Bok, email message to author, May 13, 2013 (on file with author); *DeFunis v. Odegaard*, 416 U.S. 312 (1974).
48. HLS News Staff, "Professor Emeritus Archibald Cox Dead at 92," *Harvard Law Today*, May 30, 2004, https://hls.harvard.edu/today/professor-emeritus-archibald-cox-dead-at-92/; Oppenheimer, "Archibald Cox and the Diversity Justification," 174–75.
49. Karabel, *The Chosen*, 86–109.
50. Karabel, *The Chosen*, 166–71, 178–79.
51. Brief for the President and Fellows of Harvard College as Amicus Curiae in Support of Respondents at 16, *DeFunis*, 416 U.S. 312 (No. 73–235).
52. Jerrold K. Footlick, "Justice: Racism in Reverse," *Newsweek*, 1974; Anthony Lewis, "The Legality of Racial Quotas: Who Will Pay for the Injustice of the Past," *New York Times*, March 3, 1974, www.nytimes.com/1974/03/03/archives/the-legality-of-racial-quotas-tough-intellectual-issues.html; Richard A. Posner, "The DeFunis Case and the Constitutionality of Preferential Treatment of Racial Minorities," *Supreme Court Review* 1974 (1974): 7–15.
53. *DeFunis*, 416 U.S. at 319–20.
54. John C. Jeffries, Jr., to Justice Powell, memorandum, February 12, 1974, in *DeFunis v. Odegaard*, Supreme Court Case Files, box 17, Powell Papers, Lewis F. Powell, Jr., Archives, Washington and Lee University School of Law, https://scholarlycommons.law.wlu.edu/casefiles/43/.
55. *Regents of the Univ. of Cal. v. Bakke*, 438 U.S. 265 (1978).
56. Gormley, *Archibald Cox*, 401–2; Brief for Petitioner at 29–44, *Bakke*, 438 U.S. 265 (No. 76–811).
57. Bob Comfort to Justice Powell, memorandum, August 29, 1977, in *Regents of the University of California v. Bakke*, Supreme Court Case Files, box 469–472, pp. 1–9, Powell Papers, Lewis F. Powell, Jr., Archives, Washington and Lee University School of Law, https://scholarlycommons.law.wlu.edu/cgi/viewcontent.cgi?article=1113&context=casefiles.
58. *Bakke*, 438 U.S. at 289–90, 319–20.

59. *Bakke*, 438 U.S. at 326 n.1 (Brennan, J., White, J., Marshall, J., and Black-mun, J., concurring in part and dissenting in part).
60. *Bakke*, 438 U.S. at 321–24.
61. *Bakke*, 438 U.S. at 311–15.
62. Linda Greenhouse, "Powell: Moderation Amid Divisions," *New York Times*, June 27, 1987, www.nytimes.com/1987/06/27/us/powell-moderation-amid-divisions.html.
63. For an overview of eight leading scholars from the left to the right criticizing the *Bakke* opinion, see John C. Jeffries, Jr., "Bakke Revisited," *Supreme Court Review* 2003 (2003): 9–10 (citing articles by Guido Calabresi, Vincent Blasi, Harry T. Edwards, Ronald Dworkin, John Hart Ely, Laurence H. Tribe, Robert H. Bork, and Antonin Scalia).
64. Joel Dreyfuss and Charles Lawrence III, *The Bakke Case: The Politics of Inequality* (New York: Harcourt, 1979), 211–13; Ronald Dworkin, "The Bakke Decision: Did It Decide Anything?," *New York Review of Books*, August 17, 1978, www.nybooks.com/articles/1978/08/17/the-bakke-decision-did-it-decide-anything/.
65. Oppenheimer, "Archibald Cox and the Diversity Justification," 196–97.
66. Oppenheimer, "Archibald Cox and the Diversity Justification," 198–99; William G. Bowen and Derek Bok, *The Shape of the River: Long-Term Consequences of Considering Race in College and University Admissions* (Princeton: Princeton University Press, 1998), 8.
67. For examples of over one hundred colleges and universities embracing diversity admissions systems, see the following three briefs: Brief of Georgetown University et al. as Amici Curiae Supporting Respondents, *Students for Fair Admissions, Inc. v. President and Fellows of Harvard Coll. and Univ. of N.C.*, 600 U.S. 181 (2023) (Nos. 20–1199, 21–707); Brief of Amherst et al. as Amici Curiae Supporting Respondents, *Students for Fair Admissions, Inc. v. President and Fellows of Harvard Coll. and Univ. of N.C.*, 600 U.S. 181 (2023) (Nos. 20–1199, 21–707); Brief of Brown University et al. as Amici Curiae Supporting Respondents, *Students for Fair Admissions, Inc. v. President and Fellows of Harvard Coll. and Univ. of N.C.*, 600 U.S. 181 (2023) (Nos. 20–1199, 21–707).
68. Mario Garcia, "'The Future Princeton Is Whatever Emerges from the Battle Now Joined': The Concerned Alumni of Princeton, 1972–1986," Mudd Manuscript Library Blog, Princeton University, August 9, 2017, https://universityarchives.princeton.edu/2017/08/the-future-princeton-is-whatever-emerges-from-the-battle-now-joined-the-concerned-alumni-of-princeton-1972-1986/; David D. Kirkpatrick, "From Alito's Past, a Window on Conservatives at Princeton," *New York Times*, November 27, 2005, www.nytimes.com/2005/11/27/politics/politicsspecial1/from-alitos-past-a-window-on-conservatives-at.html.
69. See Charles R. Lawrence III, "Two Views of the River: A Critique of the Liberal Defense of Affirmative Action," *Columbia Law Review* 101, no. 4

(2001): 928–76; Carlos J. Nan, "Adding Salt to the Wound: Affirmative Action and Critical Race Theory," *Law and Inequality* 12, no. 2 (1994): 553–72; Alex M. Johnson, Jr., "Defending the Use of Quotas in Affirmative Action: Attacking Racism in the Nineties," *University of Illinois Law Review* 1992, no. 4 (1992): 1043–74; Richard Delgado, "The Imperial Scholar: Reflections on a Review of Civil Rights Literature," *University of Pennsylvania Law Review* 132, no. 3 (1984): 570 n.46.

70. Data on file with the author; see also David B. Oppenheimer, "The Disappearance of Voluntary Affirmative Action from the U.S. Workplace," *Journal of Poverty and Social Justice* 24, no. 1 (2016): 45, https://doi.org/10.1332/175982716x14538098991133.

71. Caroline Colvin, "Once Neglected, DEI Initiatives Now Present at All Fortune 100 Companies," *HR Dive*, July 20, 2022, www.hrdive.com/news/2022-fortune-companies-dei/627651/; for the list of the Fortune 100's public-facing DEI acknowledgment, see also "Fortune 100 (2022) and Public-Facing DEI Acknowledgements," July 19, 2022, https://docs.google.com/spreadsheets/d/1 1OBEAG8yQs3olTDDFwt6PoSy9Lqjk9cWslCc-H_ytyo/edit#gid=0.

72. "In Good Company: 25 Best Places for Blacks to Work," *Black Enterprise*, February 1986, 89–100; Oppenheimer, "Disappearance of Voluntary Affirmative Action," 45.

73. Sonia Alleyne, "The 40 Best Companies for Diversity," *Black Enterprise*, July 1, 2006, www.blackenterprise.com/mag/the-40-best-companies-for-diversity/.

74. Alleyne, "40 Best Companies for Diversity"; Oppenheimer, "Disappearance of Voluntary Affirmative Action," 37–50.

75. See Oppenheimer, "Disappearance of Voluntary Affirmative Action," 43–45.

76. R. Roosevelt Thomas, "From Affirmative Action to Affirming Diversity," *Harvard Business Review* 68, no. 2 (1990): 107–17; Lennie Copeland, "Valuing Workplace Diversity: Ten Reasons Employers Recognize the Benefits of a Mixed Work Force," *Personnel Administrator* 33, no. 11 (1988): 38–40; Lennie Copeland, "Valuing Diversity, Part 2: Pioneers and Champions of Change," *Personnel* 65, no. 7 (1988): 48.

77. Lennie Copeland, "Valuing Diversity, Part 1: Making the Most of Cultural Differences at Work," *Personnel* 65, no. 6 (1988): 54–55; Joanne Miller, "The Business Case for Diversity," *Journal of Education for Business* 71, no. 1 (1995): 7–10.

78. Taylor H. Cox and Stacy Blake, "Managing Cultural Diversity: Implications for Organizational Competitiveness," *The Executive* 5, no. 3 (1991): 45–56, www.jstor.org/stable/4165021.

79. See chapters 13 and 14; Rocío Lorenzo, Nicole Voigt, et al., "How Diverse Leadership Teams Boost Innovation," Boston Consulting Group, January 23, 2018, www.bcg.com/publications/2018/how-diverse-leadership-teams-boost-innovation; Dame Vivian Hunt, Sara Prince, et al., "Delivering Through Diversity," McKinsey and Company, January 8, 2018, www.mckinsey.com/capabilities/people-and-organizational-performance/our-insights/delivering-through-diversity#/.

80. Yang Yang, Tanya Y. Tian, et al., "Gender-Diverse Teams Produce More Novel and Higher-Impact Scientific Ideas," *Proceedings of the National Academy of Sciences* 119, no. 36 (2022): 1–8, https://doi.org/10.1073/pnas.2200841119; Kendall Powell, "These Labs Are Remarkably Diverse—Here's Why They're Winning at Science," *Nature*, June 6, 2018, https://doi.org/10.1038/d41586-018-05316-5.

81. Mill, *On Liberty*, 22.

82. Phillips, "How Diversity Makes Us Smarter."

83. Phillips, "How Diversity Makes Us Smarter."

84. *Grutter v. Bollinger*, 539 U.S. 306 (2003).

85. Brief for Respondents at 2–3, *Grutter*, 539 U.S. 306 (No. 02–241).

86. Brief for the President and Fellows of Harvard College as Amicus Curiae, *DeFunis v. Odegaard*, 416 U.S. 312 (1974) (No. 73–235); *Regents of the Univ. of Cal. v. Bakke*, 438 U.S. 265, 323–24 (1978).

87. *Gratz v. Bollinger*, 539 U.S. 244 (2003).

88. *Grutter*, 539 U.S. at 343.

89. Brief of General Motors Corporation as Amicus Curiae in Support of Respondents, *Grutter*, 539 U.S. 306 (Nos. 02–241, 02–516); Brief of 65 Leading American Businesses as Amicus Curiae in Support of Respondents, *Grutter*, 539 U.S. 306 (Nos. 02–241, 02–516).

90. Consolidated Brief of Lt. Gen. Julius W. Becton, Jr. et al. as Amici Curiae in Support of Respondents, *Grutter*, 539 U.S. 306 (Nos. 02–241, 02–516).

91. See also Victoria C. Plaut, "Diversity Science: Why and How Difference Makes a Difference," *Psychological Inquiry* 21, no. 2 (2010): 77–99, https://doi.org/10.1080/10478401003676501.

92. "Diversity Charters by EU Country," European Commission, accessed April 5, 2023, https://commission.europa.eu/strategy-and-policy/policies/justice-and-fundamental-rights/combatting-discrimination/tackling-discrimination/diversity-and-inclusion-initiatives/diversity-charters-eu-country_en.

93. "La Charte de la diversité," Charte de la Diversité, accessed March 19, 2023, www.charte-diversite.com/charte-de-la-diversite/.

94. Laure Bereni, "'Faire de la diversité une richesse pour l'entreprise': La transformation d'une contrainte juridique en catégorie managériale," *Raisons Politiques* 3, no. 35 (2009): 90–92, https://doi.org/10.3917/rai.035.0087.

95. Anne Rodier, "La crise a favorisé les discriminations au travail," *Le Monde*, March 19, 2013, www.lemonde.fr/economie/article/2013/03/19/la-crise-a-favorise-les-discriminations-au-travail_1849804_3234.html.

96. David B. Oppenheimer, Henry Cornillie, Henry Bluestone Smith, Thao Thai, and Richard Treadwell, "Be Careful What You Wish For: Ronald Reagan, Donald Trump, The Assault on Civil Rights, and The Surprising Story of How Title VII Got Its Private Right of Action," *Berkeley Journal of Employment and Labor Law* 39, no. 1 (2018): 153–55, 171, www.jstor.org/stable/26732547; David Freeman Engstrom, "The Taft Proposal of 1946

and the Making of American Fair Employment Law," *Green Bag* 9, no. 2 (2006): 183; Frank Dobbin, "Washington Outlaws Discrimination with a Broad Brush," in Dobbin, *Inventing Equal Opportunity* (Princeton: Princeton University Press, 2009), 32.

97. "Diversity Charters by EU Country," European Commission.

98. Paolo Gaudiano, "EU Law Set to Increase Gender Diversity on Company Boards," *Forbes*, November 30, 2022, www.forbes.com/sites/paologaudiano /2022/11/30/eu-law-set-to-increase-gender-diversity-on-company-boards/?sh=1b432a6833ea; Drude Dahlerup and Lenita Freidenvall, "Gender Quotas in Politics—A Constitutional Challenge," in *Constituting Equality: Gender Equality and Comparative Constitutional Law*, ed. Susan H. Williams (Cambridge: Cambridge University Press, 2009), 38–40, 30–32, https://doi.org/10.1017/CBO9780511596780.

99. *Students for Fair Admissions, Inc. v. President and Fellows of Harvard Coll. and Univ. of N.C.*, 600 U.S. 181 (2023); see also, *Parents Involved in Cmty. Sch. v. Seattle Sch. Dist. No. 1*, 551 U.S. 701, 748 (2007), "The way to stop discrimination on the basis of race is to stop discriminating on the basis of race" (A school board's decision to promote racial integration is indistinguishable from a school board's decision to promote segregation, since both are using race in making school assignments).

100. John J. Bastiat, "Next Major Airline Crash Caused by Wokeness," *Patriot Post*, February 21, 2023, https://patriotpost.us/articles/95116-next-major-airline-crash-caused-by-wokeness-2023-02-21; "Tucker: People Will Die Because of This," Fox News, 5 min., 47 sec., February 23, 2023, www. youtube.com/watch?v=aBzcoxoUDKg; Julian Mark, "GOP Blames Silicon Valley Bank's Collapse on 'ESG' Policies. Here's What to Know," *Washington Post*, March 14, 2023, www.washingtonpost.com/business/2023/03/ 14/svb-esg-woke-investing/.

101. "Legal Defense Foundation Project on Fair Representation," The Project on Fair Representation, accessed April 5, 2023, https://projectonfairrepresentation.org/; Andrew Gumbel, "Man Behind Gutting of Voting Rights Act: 'I Agonise' over Decision's Impact," *The Guardian*, January 5, 2016, www.theguardian.com/us-news/2016/jan/05/edward-blum-voting-rights-act-civil-rights-affirmative-action; Anemona Hartocollis, "He Took on the Voting Rights Act and Won. Now He's Taking on Harvard," *New York Times*, November 19, 2017, www.nytimes.com/2017/11/19/us/affirmative-action-lawsuits.html.

102. Cheyanne M. Daniels, "New Florida Bill Would Ban Diversity, Inclusion Programs on University Campuses," *The Hill*, March 14, 2023, https:// thehill.com/homenews/state-watch/3900186-new-florida-bill-would-ban-diversity-inclusion-programs-on-university-campuses/; Ryan Chandler, "Bill Would Ban Diversity, Equity and Inclusion at Texas Universities," *KXAN*, February 9, 2023, www.kxan.com/news/texas-politics/bill-would-ban-diversity-equity-inclusion-at-texas-universities/; Bianca Quilantan,

"The New Red Scare for Red States: Diversity Programs," Politico, March 19, 2023, www.politico.com/news/2023/03/19/gop-culture-war-college-dei-florida-texas-00087697.

Chapter One. Upending the Traditional University

1. Paul R. Sweet, *Wilhelm von Humboldt: A Biography*, vol. 1, *1767–1808* (Columbus: Ohio State University Press, 1978), 3–4, 7–8.
2. "Alexander and Wilhelm Von Humboldt," Université Paris Sciences & Lettres, accessed November 21, 2022, http://explore.psl.eu/en/discover/virtual-exhibits/humboldt-brothers-spirit-europe/alexander-and-wilhelm-von-humboldt; Sweet, *Wilhelm von Humboldt*, 1:9.
3. Andrea Wulf, *The Invention of Nature: Alexander von Humboldt's New World* (New York: Vintage Books, 2015), 14–16.
4. Colin Thubron, "'The Invention of Nature,' by Andrea Wulf," *New York Times*, September 25, 2015, www.nytimes.com/2015/09/27/books/review/the-invention-of-nature-by-andrea-wulf.html.
5. Andrea Wulf, *Magnificent Rebels: The First Romantics and the Invention of the Self* (New York: Knopf, 2022), 335.
6. Thubron, "'Invention of Nature,' by Andrea Wulf."
7. Sweet, *Wilhelm von Humboldt*, 1:16–17.
8. Barbara Hahn, "Henriette Herz," Jewish Women's Archive, June 23, 2021, https://jwa.org/encyclopedia/article/herz-henriette.
9. Sweet, *Wilhelm von Humboldt*, 1:19, 33–34.
10. Sweet, *Wilhelm von Humboldt*, 1:57.
11. Sweet, *Wilhelm von Humboldt*, 1:34–35; see also Hazel Rosenstrauch, *Wahlverwandt und Ebenbürtig* (Berlin: AB Die Andere Bibliothek, 2017), 46; Dorothee Nolte, *Wilhelm von Humboldt: Ein Lebensbild In Anekdoten* (Berlin: Eulenspiegel Verlag, 2017), 27.
12. Monika Wienfort, *Verliebt, Verlobt, Verheiratet: Eine Geschichte der Ehe seit der Romantik* (In Love, Engaged, Married: A History of Marriage Since the Romantic Era) (Munich: C.H. Beck, 2014), 57, https://cdn-assetservice.ecom-api.beck-shop.de/product/readingsample/13078526/leseprobe_verliebt-verlobt-verheiratet.pdf; *Beiträge zur Humboldt'schen Familienchronik, Literatur und deutschen Sprache: Abhandlungen der Humboldt-Gesellschaft für Wissenschaft, Kunst und Bildung e.V.* (Contributions to the Humboldt Family Chronicle, Literature, and the German Language: Essays of the Humboldt Society for Science, Art, and Education, registered association) (Band, 2011), 16, www.humboldt-gesellschaft.org/files/Downloads/Abhandlungen/Humboldt_28_Okt_2011_e.pdf.
13. Sweet, *Wilhelm von Humboldt*, 1:34–35.
14. Sweet, *Wilhelm von Humboldt*, 1:31, 83–84, 103; Johan Östling, *Humboldt and the Modern German University: An Intellectual History* (Sweden: Lund University Press, 2018), 42 n.39.

15. Kwame Anthony Appiah, "Symphilosophyzing in Jena," *New York Review*, October 20, 2022, www.nybooks.com/articles/2022/10/20/symphilosophizing-in-jena-german-romantics/; Wilhelm von Humboldt, *The Limits of State Action*, trans. John Wyon Burrow (Indianapolis: Liberty Fund, 1993), xvii.

16. Sweet, *Wilhelm von Humboldt*, 1:83.

17. Wulf, *Magnificent Rebels*, 16–18; Wulf, *Invention of Nature*, 27.

18. Östling, *Humboldt and the Modern German University*, 29.

19. Andrew Valls, "Self-Development and the Liberal State: The Cases of John Stuart Mill and Wilhelm von Humboldt," *Review of Politics* 61, no. 2 (1999): 251–53; Ursula Vogel, "Liberty Is Beautiful: Von Humboldt's Gift to Liberalism," *History of Political Thought* 3, no. 1 (1982): 82–86.

20. Gözde Böffel, "Humboldt's View on Diversity and a Comparison to John Stuart Mill," April 5, 2022 (unpublished memorandum on file with author).

21. Valls, "Self-Development and the Liberal State," 253, quoting from Humboldt, *Limits of State Action*; Christoph Lüth, "On Wilhelm von Humboldt's Theory of *Bildung*," *Journal of Curriculum Studies* 30, no. 1 (1998): 43–59.

22. Wulf, *Invention of Nature*, 27; Wulf, *Magnificent Rebels*, 30.

23. Wulf, *Magnificent Rebels*, 32.

24. Sweet, *Wilhelm von Humboldt*, 1:154.

25. Wulf, *Magnificent Rebels*, 64–65.

26. Appiah, "Symphilosophyzing in Jena." ("Among the luminaries he [Schiller] tapped were Goethe, Fichte, and Wilhelm von Humboldt, whose own vision of individuality later inspired J. S. Mill's *On Liberty*.")

27. Kris Pangburn, "The Vital Organism in the Thought of Humboldt and Mill," in *Life Forms in the Thinking of the Long Eighteenth Century*, ed. Keith Michael Baker and Jenna M. Gibbs (Toronto: University of Toronto Press, 2016), 125–49, 127.

28. Pangburn, "Vital Organism in the Thought of Humboldt," 127.

29. Sweet, *Wilhelm von Humboldt*, 1:39.

30. Ian F. McNeely, "The Humboldts' Marriage and the Gendering of Intellectual Space," *German Studies Association* (2005), citing Gustav Sichelschmidt, *Caroline von Humboldt: Ein Frauenbild aus der Goethezeit* (Düsseldorf: Droste, 1989), 1 (most important woman of the age).

31. Sweet, *Wilhelm von Humboldt*, 1:169.

32. Dorothee Nolte, "Geburtstag Wilhelm von Humboldts: 'So viel Weibliches in mir'" (Wilhelm von Humboldt's 250th Birthday: "So Much Feminine in Me"), *Tagesspiegel*, June 6, 2017, http://www.tagesspiegel.de/gesellschaft/so-viel-weibliches-in-mir-3837373.html.

33. Nolte, "Geburtstag Wilhelm von Humboldts."

34. Sweet, *Wilhelm von Humboldt*, 1:179–80, 227.

35. Sweet, *Wilhelm von Humboldt*, 1:180.

36. Nolte, "Geburtstag Wilhelm von Humboldts."

37. Nolte, *Humboldt: Ein Lebensbild*, 65.

38. Rosenstrauch, *Wahlverwandt und Ebenbürtig*, 24.

39. Sweet, *Wilhelm von Humboldt*, 1:168–69.

40. Nolte, *Humboldt: Ein Lebensbild*, 49.

41. Sweet, *Wilhelm von Humboldt*, 1:173.

42. Wulf, *Invention of Nature*, 44–45.

43. Sweet, *Wilhelm von Humboldt*, 1:203.

44. Noam Chomsky, "Noam Chomsky on Language, Left Libertarianism, and Progress," interview by Tyler Cowen, *Conversations with Tyler*, June 14, 2023, https://chomsky.info/2023614-2/.

45. Sweet, *Wilhelm von Humboldt*, 1:255–56, 258, 267; Wulf, *Invention of Nature*, 45.

46. Paul R. Sweet, *Wilhelm von Humboldt: A Biography*, vol. 2, *1808–1835* (Columbus: Ohio State University Press, 1980), 7.

47. Sweet, *Wilhelm von Humboldt*, 2:85, 277.

48. "Short History," Humboldt-Universität zu Berlin, accessed June 13, 2023, www.hu-berlin.de/en/about/history/huben_html/huben_html#vision.

49. Humboldt-Universität zu Berlin, "Geschichte der Humboldt-Universität zu Berlin," Humboldt-Universität zu Berlin, accessed November 28, 2024, www.hu-berlin.de/de/ueberblick/geschichte/abriss; Östling, *Humboldt and the Modern German University*, 34.

50. Sweet, *Wilhelm von Humboldt*, 2:3–4, 10–11, 24, 56; Östling, *Humboldt and the Modern German University*, 29, 34; Bruno Gebhardt, *Wilhelm von Humboldts Gesammelte Schriften: Erster Band 1802–1810* (Berlin: B. Behr's Verlag, 1903), 139.

51. Sweet, *Wilhelm von Humboldt*, 2:22–23.

52. Östling, *Humboldt and the Modern German University*, 23.

53. Östling, *Humboldt and the Modern German University*, 9–10.

54. Arthur Schopenhauer, "On University Philosophy," in *Parerga and Paralipomena: Short Philosophical Essays*, vol. 1 (Cambridge: Cambridge University Press, 2014), 125–76.

55. Manuela Boatca, "Catching Up with the (New) West: The German 'Excellence Initiative,' Area Studies, and the Re-Production of Inequality," *Human Architecture: Journal of the Sociology of Self-Knowledge* 10, no. 1 (2011): 17–30, 18.

56. Östling, *Humboldt and the Modern German University*, xiii.

57. Anthony Grafton, "Wilhelm von Humboldt," *American Scholar* 50, no. 3 (1981): 371–81, 372.

58. Sweet, *Wilhelm von Humboldt*, 2:68.

59. Böffel, "Humboldt's view on diversity."

60. Böffel, "Humboldt's view on diversity."

61. Valls, "Self-Development and the Liberal State," 257–59; Sweet, *Wilhelm von Humboldt*, 2:18–20; Humboldt, *Limits of State Action*, 27–28.

62. Sweet, *Wilhelm von Humboldt*, 2:58; Gry Cathrin Brandser, *Humboldt Revisited: The Impact of the German University on American Higher Education* (New York: Berghahn Books, 2022), 22, https://doi.org/10.1515/9781800735378.

63. Östling, *Humboldt and the Modern German University*, 38; Peter Josephson, Thomas Karlsohn, and Johan Östling, *The Humboldtian Traditions: Origins*

and Legacies (Leiden: Brill, 2014), 2 ("New knowledge could be tested and developed together with the students").

64. Humboldt, *Limits of State Action*, 10.

65. Meike Siegfried, "Perspektiven auf Diversität—Strategien und Diskurse im Kontext Hochschulbildung" in *Praxishandbuch Habitussensibilität und Diversität in der Hochschullehre*, ed. David Kergel and Birte Heidkamp, trans. DeepL Translator (Wiesbaden: Springer VS, 2019), 23–43, 39.

66. Sweet, *Wilhelm von Humboldt*, 1:3, 7.

67. George H. Smith, "The Culture of Liberty: Wilhelm von Humboldt," Libertarianism.org, October 29, 2013, www.libertarianism.org/columns/culture-liberty-wilhelm-von-humboldt#:~:text=Humboldt%20is%20here%20pointing%20out,call%20a%20spontaneous%20cultural%20order.

68. Humboldt, *Limits of State Action*, 11.

69. Sweet, *Wilhelm von Humboldt*, 2:58 (opened to Catholics); Alfred Jospe, "Universities," Jewish Virtual Library, accessed June 13, 2023, www.jewishvirtuallibrary.org/universities (opened to Jews); Werner Treß (Tress), "Liberale Politik im christlichen Staat? Wilhelm von Humboldt und das Bürgerrecht für die Juden" (Liberal Politics in the Christian State? Wilhelm von Humboldt and Citizenship for the Jews), *Zeitschrift für Religions- und Geistesgeschichte* (Journal for the History of Religion and Intellectual History) 69, no. 2 (2017): 193–207, 197, www.jstor.org/stable/44647381.

70. George Becker, "Educational 'Preference' of German Protestants and Catholics: The Politics Behind Educational Specialization," *Review of Religious Research* 41, no. 3 (2000): 311–27, 318.

71. Sweet, *Wilhelm von Humboldt*, 2:48; Brandser, *Humboldt Revisited*, 22.

72. Böffel, "Humboldt's View on Diversity"; Reinhard Rürup, *Emanzipation und Antisemitismus: Studien zur "Judenfrage" der bürgerlichen Gesellschaft* (Göttingen: Vandenhoeck & Ruprecht, 1975), 31.

73. Becker, "Educational 'Preference' of German Protestants and Catholics," 315–16; "German Jewish Refugees, 1933–1939," United States Holocaust Memorial Museum, accessed June 13, 2023, https://encyclopedia.ushmm.org/content/en/article/german-jewish-refugees-1933–1939; Deborah Dwork and Robert Jan Van Pelt, *Flight from the Reich: Refugee Jews, 1933–1946* (New York: Norton, 2009), 21; "Short History," Humboldt-Universität zu Berlin.

74. "Short History," Humboldt-Universität zu Berlin; "W. E. B. Du Bois Memorial Marker at Humboldt-Universität zu Berlin," Humboldt-Universität zu Berlin, accessed June 13, 2023, www.angl.hu-berlin.de/department/duboismemorial; "Angela Davis," The European Graduate School, accessed June 13, 2023, https://egs.edu/biography/angela-davis/; Eli Rubin, "Studies in Berlin: Science, Torah and Quantum Theory," Chabad.Org, accessed June 13, 2023, www.chabad.org/therebbe/article_cdo/aid/2619782/jewish/Studies-in-Berlin-Science-Torah-Quantum-Theory.htm.

75. Sweet, *Wilhelm von Humboldt*, 2:318–20; Treß, "Liberale Politik im christlichen Staat?," 197.

76. Dorothee Nolte, "Caroline von Humboldt: Die schillernde Gattin des Universitätsgründers" (The Dazzling Wife of the University Founder), *Tagesspiegel*, August 1, 2011, www.tagesspiegel.de/wissen/die-schillernde-gattin-des-universitatsgrunders-1974316.html.

77. Beatrix Novy, "Geheimnisse der Humboldt'schen Ehe" (Secrets of Humboldt's Marriage), *Deutschlandfunk*, October 29, 2009, www.deutschlandfunk .de/geheimnisse-der-humboldtschen-ehe-100.html.

78. Sweet, *Wilhelm von Humboldt*, 2:255.

79. Sweet, *Wilhelm von Humboldt*, 2:341, 343; John E. Joseph, "A Matter of Consequenz: Humboldt, Race and the Genius of the Chinese Language," *Historiographia Linguistica* 26, no. 1–2 (1999): 89–148, 89.

80. Leo L. Rockwell, "Academic Freedom: German Origin and American Development," *Bulletin of the American Association of University Professors* 36, no. 2 (1950): 225–36, 225; Emily J. Levine, *Allies and Rivals: German-American Exchange and the Rise of the Modern Research University* (Chicago: University of Chicago Press, 2021), 7.

81. Levine, *Allies and Rivals*, 7; Richard Hofstadter and Walter P. Metzger, *The Development of Academic Freedom in the United States* (New York: Columbia University Press, 1955), 377.

82. Rockwell, "Academic Freedom," 225–26.

83. Hofstadter and Metzger, *Development of Academic Freedom*, 393.

84. Humboldt, *Limits of State Action*, xvii.

85. Appiah, "Symphilosophyzing in Jena"; see John Stuart Mill, *On Liberty* (Project Gutenberg, 2011), xxviii, eBook, www.gutenberg.org/files/34901/34901-h/34901-h.htm.

Chapter Two. Liberty, Equality, Diversity

1. John Stuart Mill, *Autobiography* (London: Longmans, Green, Reader, and Dyer, 1874), 2–3, https://ia804503.us.archive.org/2/items/a592818300 milluoft/a592818300milluoft.pdf; see throughout: Nicholas Capaldi, *John Stuart Mill: A Biography* (Cambridge: Cambridge University Press, 2004); Richard Reeves, *John Stuart Mill: Victorian Firebrand* (London: Atlantic Books, 2008).

2. Mill, *Autobiography*, 31.

3. Mill, *Autobiography*, 2, 5, 9–10, 55–58.

4. Julia Driver, "The History of Utilitarianism," *Stanford Encyclopedia of Philosophy*, March 27, 2009, https://plato.stanford.edu/entries/utilitarianism-history/.

5. University College London, "Bentham and UCL," accessed June 20, 2023, https://www.ucl.ac.uk/bentham-project/who-was-jeremy-bentham/bentham-and-ucl; Mill, *Autobiography*, 57, 63–64, 176.

6. Nicholas Capaldi, *John Stuart Mill: A Biography* (Cambridge: Cambridge University Press, 2004), 35.

7. "Harriet Taylor (1807–1858)," BBC *History*, 2014, www.bbc.co.uk/history/historic_figures/taylor_harriet.shtml (last visited March 18, 2024); Jo Ellen Jacobs and Paula Harms Payne, eds., *The Complete Works of Harriet Taylor Mill* (Bloomington: Indiana University Press, 1998), xli.

8. "Harriet Taylor (1807–1858)."

9. F. A. Hayek, "Harriet Taylor and Her Circle," in *John Stuart Mill and Harriet Taylor: Their Correspondence and Subsequent Marriage* (Chicago: University of Chicago Press, 1951), 24, https://mises.at/static/literatur/Buch/hayek-john-stuart-mill-and-harriet-taylor.pdf.

10. Hayek, *John Stuart Mill and Harriet Taylor*, 25.

11. Mill, *Autobiography*, 184–220, 185.

12. Hayek, *John Stuart Mill and Harriet Taylor*, 24.

13. Jo Ellen Jacobs, "Chronology," in Jacobs and Harms Payne, *The Complete Works of Harriet Taylor Mill*, p. xlii.

14. Hayek, *John Stuart Mill and Harriet Taylor*, 27–29, 36.

15. Pratinav Anil, "The Love Life of J. S. Mill: The Father of Liberalism Caused Quite the Scandal," UnHerd, May 2023, https://unherd.com/2023/05/the-love-life-of-js-mill/.

16. Mill, *Autobiography*, 184, 240–41.

17. Richard Reeves, *John Stuart Mill: Victorian Firebrand* (London: Atlantic Books, 2008), 83.

18. Jo Ellen Jacobs, *The Voice of Harriet Taylor Mill* (Bloomington: Indiana University Press, 2002), xlii.

19. Richard Reeves, *John Stuart Mill: Victorian Firebrand*, 19.

20. Reeves, *John Stuart Mill: Victorian Firebrand*.

21. Adam Gopnik, "Right Again," *New Yorker*, September 29, 2008, www.newyorker.com/magazine/2008/10/06/right-again.

22. Mill, *Autobiography*, 244–45.

23. Mill, *Autobiography*, 245.

24. Mill, *Autobiography*, 248.

25. Jacobs and Harms Payne, *The Complete Works of Harriet Taylor Mill*, 438.

26. Jacobs and Harms Payne, *The Complete Works of Harriet Taylor Mill*, xliii.

27. David L. Wykes, "The Early Nineteenth-Century Unitarian Campaign to Change English Marriage Law," *Studies in Church History* 59 (2023): 292, https://doi.org/10.1017/stc.2023.16.

28. Emily Ireland, "Re-examining the Presumption: Coverture and 'Legal Impossibilities' in Early Modern English Criminal Law," *Journal of Legal History* 43, no. 2 (2022): 187.

29. Ireland, "Re-examining the Presumption," 187.

30. Sybil Wolfram, "Divorce in England 1700–1857," *Oxford Journal of Legal Studies* 5, no. 2 (1985): 156–57, www.jstor.org/stable/764190.

31. John Stuart Mill, "Statement on Marriage," in *The Collected Works of John Stuart Mill*, vol. 21, 138, https://oll-resources.s3.us-east-2.amazonaws.com/oll3/store/titles/255/Mill_0223-21_EBk_v6.0.pdf.

32. Jacobs, *The Voice of Harriet Taylor Mill*, 165; John Lawrence Hill, "The Father of Modern Constitutional Liberalism," *William & Mary Bill of Rights Journal* 27, no. 2 (2018): 431–99, 476.

33. See, for example, Reeves, *John Stuart Mill: Victorian Firebrand*, 152.

34. Hayek, *John Stuart Mill and Harriet Taylor*, 105; Reeves, *John Stuart Mill: Victorian Firebrand*, 246–47.

35. Reeves, *John Stuart Mill: Victorian Firebrand*, 4, 244–45.

36. Hayek, *John Stuart Mill and Harriet Taylor*, 260–64; Reeves, *John Stuart Mill: Victorian Firebrand*, 260.

37. Mill, *Autobiography*, 250; Reeves, *John Stuart Mill: Victorian Firebrand*, 260.

38. Hayek, *John Stuart Mill and Harriet Taylor*, 264.

39. Hayek, *John Stuart Mill and Harriet Taylor*, 265–66.

40. Hayek, *John Stuart Mill and Harriet Taylor*, 83–87.

41. Hayek, *John Stuart Mill and Harriet Taylor*, 266.

42. Mill, *Autobiography*, 241.

43. Eugenio Biagini, "John Stuart Mill and the Liberal Party," *Journal of Liberal History* 70 (2011), https://liberalhistory.org.uk/wp-content/uploads/2014/10/70_Biagini_John_Stuart_Mill_and_the_Liberal_Party.pdf; Duncan Brack, "Great Liberals," *Journal of Liberal History* (2012), https://web.archive.org/web/20120306015811/http://www.liberalhistory.org.uk/item_single.php?item_id=110&item=history.

44. Capaldi, *John Stuart Mill: A Biography*, 322.

45. Biagini, "John Stuart Mill and the Liberal Party"; Brack, "Great Liberals."

46. John Stuart Mill, epigraph in *On Liberty and Other Essays*, ed. John Gray (Oxford: Oxford University Press, 2008), 5 (quoting Wilhelm von Humboldt, *The Sphere and Duties of Government*).

47. Mill, *Autobiography*, 254–55.

48. Richard Reeves, "Prologue," "Strange Confusion (1826–30)," and "*On Liberty* (1859)," in Reeves, *John Stuart Mill: Victorian Firebrand*, 6, 79, 277–78 (arguing that Mill had absorbed a "German Romantic concept of *Bildung*"). See also Philip Kitcher, "The Left Must Reclaim J. S. Mill: The Progressive Philosopher Has Been Defamed," UnHerd, May 2023, https://unherd.com/2023/05/the-left-must-reclaim-js-mill/.

49. Reeves, *John Stuart Mill: Victorian Firebrand*, 6.

50. Reeves, *John Stuart Mill: Victorian Firebrand*, 347.

51. Mill, *On Liberty and Other Essays*, 9.

52. Mill, *On Liberty and Other Essays*, 21.

53. Mill, *On Liberty and Other Essays*, 21.

54. Mill, *On Liberty and Other Essays*, 57.

55. Mill, *On Liberty and Other Essays*, 22–23.

56. Mill, *On Liberty and Other Essays*, 49.

57. Mill, *On Liberty and Other Essays*, 41.

58. Mill, *On Liberty and Other Essays*, 246.

59. Mill, *Considerations on Representative Government* (1861), in *On Liberty and Other Essays*, 308.
60. Mill, *Autobiography*, 279–84.
61. Mill, *Autobiography*, 286–90, 296.
62. "Presenting the 1866 petition," *UK Parliament*, www.parliament.uk/about/living-heritage/transformingsociety/electionsvoting/womenvote/parliamentary-collections/1866-suffrage-petition/presenting-the-petition/ (last visited March 19, 2024).
63. "Presenting the 1866 petition," *UK Parliament*.
64. Nicholas Capaldi, "Public Intellectual," in Capaldi, *John Stuart Mill: A Biography*, 327.
65. Mary Harrington, "Andrew Tate Is J. S. Mill's Monster," UnHerd, May 2023, https://unherd.com/2023/01/andrew-tate-is-js-mills-monster/.
66. Mill, *Autobiography*, 296.
67. Abigail B. Bakan, "A Labor Force in Transition," in Bakan, *Ideology and Class Conflict in Jamaica: The Politics of Rebellion* (Montreal: McGill-Queen's University Press, 1990), 18–49.
68. Bakan, *Ideology and Class Conflict in Jamaica*, 77, 80–83, 89.
69. Mill, *Autobiography*, 296–97; Frederick Burkhardt et al., eds., *The Correspondence of Charles Darwin*, vol. 14 (Cambridge: Cambridge University Press, 2004), xxiv.
70. Peter Daniel, "The Governor Eyre Controversy," *New Blackfriars* 50, no. 591 (1969): 578, www.jstor.org/stable/43244890.
71. Daniel, "The Governor Eyre Controversy," 579–80.
72. Bakan, *Ideology and Class Conflict in Jamaica*, 91.
73. *Spectator*, June 6, 1868, 665–66, quoted in Bernard Semmel, "The Issue of 'Race' in the British Reaction to the Morant Bay Uprising of 1865," *Caribbean Studies* 2, no. 3 (1962): 14, www.jstor.org/stable/25611713.
74. Beate Jahn, "Barbarian Thoughts: Imperialism in the Philosophy of John Stuart Mill," *Review of International Studies* 31, no. 3 (2005): 600, 607, www.jstor.org/stable/40072091.
75. Mill, *Autobiography*, 311–12.
76. Stuart Jones, "The Abolition of Religious Tests: Some Historical Context," University of Oxford, August 2021. Retrieved from https://openingoxford1871.web.ox.ac.uk/article/abolition-religious-tests-some-historical-context; Reeves, *John Stuart Mill: Victorian Firebrand*, 54; letter from John Stuart Mill to Harriet Taylor Mill dated March 18, 1854, *The Collected Works of John Stuart Mill*, vol. 14, *The Later Letters, 1849–1873, Part I* (Toronto: University of Toronto Press); Capaldi, *John Stuart Mill: A Biography*, 33.
77. Jones, "The Abolition of Religious Tests: Some Historical Context."
78. Jones, "The Abolition of Religious Tests: Some Historical Context"; Capaldi, *John Stuart Mill: A Biography*, 13.

79. Samuel Hollander, "John Stuart Mill and the Jewish Question: Broadening the Utilitarian Maximand," in *Happiness and Utility: Essays Presented to Frederick Rosen* (UCL Press, 2009), 260; Bruce L. Kinzer, "The 1870 Education Bill and the Method of J. S. Mill's Later Politics," *Albion* 29, no. 2 (1997): 223–45, https://doi.org/10.2307/4051811.

80. "Religion in the Nineteenth Century," *UK Parliament*, www.parliament.uk/about/living-heritage/transformingsociety/private-lives/religion/overview/religionc19th-/ (last visited March 20, 2024).

81. Janelle Potzsch, "Harriet Taylor Mill: The Unitarian Background," *Women's Studies* 51 (2021): 32, https://doi.org/10.1080/00497878.2021.1992628; "Leading Women Since 1868," *University of London*, www.london.ac.uk/about/history/leading-women-1868#:~:text=In%201868%2C%20nine%20women%20were,for%20society%20as%20a%20whole. (last visited March 20, 2024).

82. "Leading Women Since 1868," *University of London*.

83. "Women Making History," *University of Oxford*, 2020, www.ox.ac.uk/about/oxford-people/women-at-oxford.; "The Rising Tide: Women at Cambridge," *University of Cambridge*, October 14, 2019, www.cam.ac.uk/stories/the-rising-tide.

84. Mill, *Autobiography*, 263–64.

85. Mill, "The Subjection of Women," in On *Liberty and Other Essays*, 478.

86. "The West Indian Colonies and Emancipation," *UK Parliament*, www.parliament.uk/about/living-heritage/evolutionofparliament/legislativescrutiny/parliament-and-empire/parliament-and-the-american-colonies-before-1765/the-west-indian-colonies-and-emancipation/#:~:text=Under%20pressure%20from%20Westminster%2C%20the,slaves%20on%201%20August%201838. (Last visited March 20, 2024).

87. Mill, "The Subjection of Women," in *On Liberty and Other Essays*, 482–83.

88. Reeves, *John Stuart Mill: Victorian Firebrand*, 340.

89. Mill, "The Subjection of Women," in *On Liberty and Other Essays*, 560–61. See also Victoria Bateman, "Could Mill's Model Mend Capitalism?," UnHerd, May 2023, https://unherddev.wpengine.com/2018/09/hasnt-mills-model-saved-capitalism/

90. Mill, "The Subjecton of Women," in *On Liberty and Other Essays*, 562. See also Bateman, "Could Mill's Model Mend Capitalism?"

91. Mill, *Autobiography*, 306–7.

92. John Stuart Mill, *Inaugural Address at St. Andrews* (London: Longmans, Green, Reader, and Dyer, 1867), 74. Available at https://archive.org/details/inauguraladdresoomillgoog/mode/2up.

93. Mill, *Inaugural Address at St. Andrews*, 81–82.

94. John Stuart Mill, *Inaugural Address at St. Andrews*, 25; Graham Finlay, "John Stuart Mill on the Uses of Diversity," *Utilitas* 14, no.2 (2002): 189–218, 199.

95. Henry Ward Beecher, "John Stuart Mill on Parliamentary Reform," *New York Times*, May 7, 1865, 4.

96. Noah Brooks, "Personal Recollections of Abraham Lincoln," in *The Lincoln Anthology: Great Writers of His Life and Legacy from 1860 to Now*, ed. Harold Holzer (New York: Library of America, 2009), 164, 169 (stating that Lincoln "particularly liked" Joseph Butler's "Analogy of Religion" and John Stuart Mill's *On Liberty*); "Congress Debates the Fourteenth Amendment" in *Congress Register* (1866) (reporting that Representative—and future president—James A. Garfield of Ohio quoted Mill when arguing that the ballot is put into the hands of men not so much to enable them to govern others but to prevent them from being misgoverned by others).

97. Reeves, *John Stuart Mill: Victorian Firebrand*, 228–29.

98. Mill, *Autobiography*, 184, 240–41.

99. Mill, *Autobiography*, 251.

100. Mill, *Autobiography*, 241.

101. See Helen McCabe, *A Companion to Mill* (Hoboken: John Wiley & Sons, 2016), where McCabe argues that John and Harriet should be perceived as a team that works within each other's strengths; Menaka Philips, "The 'Beloved and Deplored' Memory of Harriet Taylor Mill: Rethinking Gender and Intellectual Labor in the Canon," *Hypatia* 33 no. 4 (2018), 626–42 (Philips argues that our concept of what it means to substantively contribute should widen); Helen McCabe, "Harriet Taylor Mill," Cambridge University Press online (2023), www.cambridge.org/core/elements/harriet -taylor-mill/8BB84DAB5B4207187C35A611FA4A6688.

102. Dale E. Miller, "Harriet Taylor Mill," *Stanford Encyclopedia of Philosophy* (The Metaphysics Research Lab, Stanford, 2022), ed. Edward N. Zalta and Uri Nodelman, https://plato.stanford.edu/archives/fall2022/entries/harriet-mill/.

103. Hayek, *John Stuart Mill and Harriet Taylor*, 266.

104. Jo Ellen Jacobs, "'The Lot of Gifted Ladies Is Hard': A Study of Harriet Taylor Mill Criticism," *Hypatia* 9, no. 3 (1994), 147-48 (www.jstor.org/stable/3810192).

105. Jacobs, "'The Lot of Gifted Ladies Is Hard,'" 145.

106. Evelyn L. Forget, "John Stuart Mill, Harriet Taylor and French Social Theory," in *The Status of Women in Classical Economic Thought*, ed. Robert Dimand and Chris Nyland (Elgar, 2003), 285–86.

107. Phyllis Rose, "Harriet Taylor and John Stuart Mill," in *Parallel Lives: Five Victorian Marriages* (New York: Knopf, 1983), 132; Jacobs, "'The Lot of Gifted Ladies Is Hard,'" 148.

108. Rose, "Harriet Taylor and John Stuart Mill," 131 (writing that Harriet "was the executive" and "unhampered by the subtleties and nuance of thought which sometimes impeded Mill, unafraid of inconsistency, she cut crudely, perhaps, but emphatically and practically to important matters").

109. Jacobs, "'The Lot of Gifted Ladies Is Hard,'" 147.

110. Susan Groag Bell, "The Feminization of John Stuart Mill," in *Revealing Lives*, ed. Susan Groag Bell and Marilyn Yalom (Albany: SUNY Press, 1990), 81–92; Virginia Allen, "On Liberty and Logic," in *Listening to Their Voices*, ed. Molly Wertheimer (Columbia: University of South Carolina

Press, 1997), 42–68; Jo Ellen Jacobs, "Harriet Taylor Mill's Collaboration with John Stuart Mill," in *Presenting Women Philosophers*, ed. by Cécile Tougas and Sara Ebenreck (Philadelphia: Temple University Press, 2000), 155–66, and Jo Ellen Jacobs, *The Voice of Harriet Taylor Mill*; Evelyn L. Forget, "John Stuart Mill, Harriet Taylor and French Social Theory," 285–310; Mariana Szapuová, "Women in Philosophy: The Case of Harriet Taylor Mill," *Human Affairs* 2 (2006), 133–43; Menaka Philips, "The 'Beloved and Deplored' Memory of Harriet Taylor Mill," 626–42; Helen McCabe, "Harriet Taylor Mill," Cambridge University Press online (2023).

111.   Groag Bell, "The Feminization of John Stuart Mill," 83.
112.   Groag Bell, "The Feminization of John Stuart Mill," 86.
113.   Hayek, *John Stuart Mill and Harriet Taylor*, 31–32.
114.   Christoph Schmidt-Petri, Michael Schefczyk, and Lilly Osburg, "Who Authored *On Liberty*? Stylometric Evidence on Harriet Taylor Mill's Contribution," *Utilitas* 34, no. 2 (2022): 120–38 (doi:10.1017/S0953820821000339).
115.   Mill, *On Liberty and Other Essays*, 62–82.
116.   Christoph Schmidt-Petri, Michael Schefczyk, and Lilly Osburg, "Who Authored *On Liberty*?," 137–38.

Chapter Three. Liberty and Diversity at Harvard

1.   Walter Graeme Eliot, *A Sketch of the Eliot Family* (New York: Press of Livingston Middleditch, 1887), 91, 109, 111; "Eliot, Charles William," *Encyclopedia Britannica*, 11th ed. (Cambridge: Cambridge University Press, 1911), 9:274. "Eliot's notable family members include: William Greenleaf Eliot, founder of Washington University in St. Louis (1811–1887), Thomas Lamb Eliot, founder of Reed College (1841–1936), T. S. Eliot, poet, essayist, publisher, playwright (1888–1965)."
2.   Henry James, *Charles W. Eliot: President of Harvard University, 1869–1909*, 2 vols. (Cambridge: Houghton Mifflin, 1930), 1:xv, 75–79, 114.
3.   Sonia F. Epstein, "The Fraught Courtship of Harvard and MIT," *The Crimson*, February 18, 2018, www.thecrimson.com/article/2018/2/18/mit-harvard-merger/.
4.   Samuel Eliot Morison, *Three Centuries at Harvard: 1636–1936* (Cambridge: Harvard University Press, 2001), 325.
5.   James, *Charles W. Eliot*, 1:112–16, 135–38.
6.   James, *Charles W. Eliot*, 1:159–61.
7.   Elizabeth Andrews, Nora Murphy, Tom Rosko, "William Barton Rogers: MIT's Visionary Founder," *MIT Institute Archives*, https://web.archive.org/web/20080512091317/http://libraries.mit.edu/archives/exhibits/wbr-visionary/.
8.   Jennifer Chu, "MIT and the Civil War," *MIT News*, February 9, 2012, https://news.mit.edu/2012/hockfield-bpl-civil-war-talk-0209#:~:text=On%20April%2010%2C%201861%2C%20the,start%20of%20the%20Civil%20War.

9. A. J. Angulo, "Speaking of Science," *MIT Technology Review*, December 21, 2010, www.technologyreview.com/2010/12/21/198312/speaking-of-science/.

10. James, *Charles W. Eliot*, 1:97, 355–69.

11. Charles W. Eliot, "The New Education," *Atlantic Monthly*, February 1869, 203–20; Charles W. Eliot, "The New Education II," *Atlantic Monthly*, March 1869, 358–67.

12. Eliot, "New Education," 203.

13. Eliot, "New Education," 203–20.

14. Eliot, "New Education," 220.

15. Eliot, "New Education," 216–19; Amy Marcott, "The Harvard Institute of Technology?," *MIT Technology Magazine*, October 25, 2011, https://www.technologyreview.com/2011/10/25/257542/the-harvard-institute-of-technology/; Hugh Hawkins, *Between Harvard and America: The Educational Leadership of Charles W. Eliot* (New York: Oxford University Press, 1972).

16. Eliot, "New Education II."

17. Eliot, "New Education II," 367.

18. James, *Charles W. Eliot*, 1:vii.

19. Epstein, "Fraught Courtship of Harvard."

20. James, *Charles W. Eliot*, 2:62–63, 67.

21. James, *Charles W. Eliot*, 1:136.

22. Emily J. Levine, *Allies and Rivals: German-American Exchange and the Rise of the Modern Research University* (Chicago: University of Chicago Press, 2021), 40–44, 57–58.

23. John A. O'Connor, "Charles Eliot: An Historical Study," *Loyola University Chicago Dissertations*, June 1970, 1:39–40, https://ecommons.luc.edu/cgi/viewcontent.cgi?referer=&httpsredir=1&article=2045&context=luc_diss.

24. Levine, *Allies and Rivals*, 42, 47.

25. James, *Charles W. Eliot*, 2:64.

26. O'Connor, "Charles Eliot," 18, 36.

27. James, *Charles W. Eliot*, 2:64; Leo L. Rockwell, "Academic Freedom: German Origin and American Development," *Bulletin of the American Association of University Professors* 36, no. 2 (1950): 225–36, 227; O'Connor, "Charles Eliot," 13–15.

28. O'Connor, "Charles Eliot," 16.

29. O'Connor, "Charles Eliot," 23; "Highlights from 367 Years of Harvard Presidents," *Harvard Gazette*, February 11, 2007, https://news.harvard.edu/gazette/story/2007/02/highlights-from-367-years-of-harvard-presidents/.

30. Jerome Karabel, *The Chosen: The Hidden History of Admission and Exclusion at Harvard, Yale, and Princeton* (Boston: Houghton Mifflin, 2005), 40.

31. O'Connor, "Charles Eliot," 29; Rockwell, "Academic Freedom," 227.

32. O'Connor, "Charles Eliot," 29.

33. O'Connor, "Charles Eliot," 17.

34. Karabel, *The Chosen*, 44–45; Neil L. Rudenstine, *Pointing Our Thoughts: Reflections on Harvard and Higher Education, 1991–2001* (Cambridge: Harvard University, 2001).

35. Charles W. Eliot, "Inaugural Address," *Harvard Graduate Magazine* (Boston: Harvard Graduates' Magazine Association, 1903), 12:556–76, 575.
36. Eliot, "Inaugural Address," 563.
37. James, *Charles W. Eliot*, 1:214–15.
38. James, *Charles W. Eliot*, 2:26.
39. James, *Charles W. Eliot*, 1:371.
40. James, *Charles W. Eliot*, 1:349.
41. James, *Charles W. Eliot*, 1:348, 371.
42. James, *Charles W. Eliot*, 1:326–27, 2:194.
43. John Stuart Mill, *On Liberty*, in *The Harvard Classics* 25, ed. Charles W. Eliot (New York: P. F. Collier & Son, 1909).
44. Eliot, "Inaugural Address," 12:556–76.
45. Karabel, *The Chosen*, 40.
46. Karabel, *The Chosen*, 13.
47. Neil L. Rudenstine, "Why a Diverse Student Body Is So Important," *Chronicle of Higher Education*, April 19, 1996, www.chronicle.com/article/why-a-diverse-student-body-is-so-important/; Neil L. Rudenstine, *Pointing Our Thoughts: Reflections on Harvard and Higher Education, 1991–2001* (Cambridge: Harvard University, 2001).
48. There were a few Black students in the professional schools when Eliot arrived. See "Chronology of Major Landmarks in the Progress of African Americans in Higher Education," *Journal of Blacks in Higher Education*, accessed June 21, 2023, www.jbhe.com/features/53_blackhistory_timeline.html.
49. Morison, *Three Centuries at Harvard*, 416–17.
50. Morison, *Three Centuries at Harvard*, 416–17.
51. James, *Charles W. Eliot*, 1:374.
52. Letter from Alex Hamilton to Charles W. Eliot, December 7, 1909 (the original is in the Harvard Archives; a copy is on file with the author. All material from these archives throughout the book are courtesy of the Harvard University Archives).
53. Letter from Charles W. Eliot to Alex Hamilton, December 13, 1909 (the original is in the Harvard Archives; a copy is on file with the author).
54. Letter from Charles W. Eliot to Mr. Johnson, January 23, 1925 (the original is in the Harvard Archives; a copy is on file with the author).
55. Rudenstine, "Why a Diverse Student Body Is So Important"; Neil L. Rudenstine, *Pointing Our Thoughts: Reflections on Harvard and Higher Education, 1991–2001* (Cambridge: Harvard University, 2001).
56. Eliot, "Inaugural Address," 563.
57. Rudenstine, "Why a Diverse Student Body Is So Important"; Neil L. Rudenstine, *Pointing Our Thoughts: Reflections on Harvard and Higher Education, 1991–2001* (Cambridge: Harvard University, 2001).
58. Charles W. Eliot, "Diversity in Family, College, and State," *Harvard Alumni Bulletin* 13, no. 33 (1911): 502–09, 505, https://babel.hathitrust.org/cgi/pt?id=hvd.32044107292138&view=1up&seq=644; originally given as an address at the Harvard Union on March 20, 1911; "NO EQUALITY IN OUR IN-

STITUTIONS—ELIOT; Tells Harvard Students Uniform Conditions Are Only Possible Under a Despotism," *New York Times*, March 21, 1911, https://timesmachine.nytimes.com/timesmachine/1911/03/21/issue.html.

59. "Dr. Eliot Pointed Way to Right Living," *New York Times*, August 29, 1926, https://timesmachine.nytimes.com/timesmachine/1926/08/29/98387721.pdf?pdf.

60. Edwin E. Slosson, *Great American Universities* (New York: Macmillan Company, 1910), 104.

61. Karabel, *The Chosen*, 45.

62. Karabel, *The Chosen*, 39.

63. W. B. Carnochan, *The Battleground of the Curriculum: Liberal Education and American Experience* (Stanford: Stanford University Press, 1993), 2.

Chapter Four. Harvard's "Jewish Problem"

1. Diana Klebanow and Franklin L. Jonas, *People's Lawyers: Crusaders for Justice in American History* (New York: M.E. Sharpe, Inc., 2003), 66.

2. Oliver B. Pollak, "Antisemitism, the Harvard Plan, and the Roots of Reverse Discrimination," *Jewish Social Studies* 45, no. 2 (1983): 113–22, 113, www.jstor.org/stable/4467214, citing Allon Gal, *Brandeis of Boston* (Cambridge: Harvard University Press, 1980), 154; see also "Reveal President of Harvard Favored Brandeis as Successor," *Jewish Daily Bulletin*, December 14, 1930, http://pdfs.jta.org/1930/1930-12-14_1833.pdf.

3. Henry Adams Yeomans, *Abbott Lawrence Lowell, 1856–1943* (Cambridge: Harvard University Press, 1948), 91.

4. Erika Lee, *America for Americans: A History of Xenophobia in the United States* (New York: Basic Books, 2019), 113–15.

5. Jerome Karabel, *The Chosen: The Hidden History of Admission and Exclusion at Harvard, Yale, and Princeton* (Boston: Houghton Mifflin, 2006), 47–48.

6. Karabel, *The Chosen*, 48.

7. Abbott Lawrence Lowell, "The Colonial Expansion of the United States," *Atlantic Monthly*, February 1899, 145–54, 151–52.

8. Yeomans, *Abbott Lawrence Lowell*, 213.

9. David G. Dalin, *Jewish Justices of the Supreme Court: From Brandeis to Kagan* (Waltham: Brandeis University Press, 2017), 47–48.

10. Alpheus Thomas Mason, *Brandeis: A Free Man's Life* (New York: Viking Press, 1956), 505.

11. Eliot quoted in Karabel, *The Chosen*, 48 (citing Marcia G. Synnott, "A Social History of Admissions Policies at Harvard, Yale, and Princeton, 1900–1930" (PhD diss., University of Massachusetts, 1974), 210, https://scholarworks.umass.edu/dissertations_1/575).

12. "NO EQUALITY IN OUR INSTITUTIONS—ELIOT, Tells Harvard Students Uniform Conditions Are Only Possible Under a Despotism," *New York Times*, March 21, 1911, https://timesmachine.nytimes.com/timesmachine/1911/03/21/issue.html.

13. Karabel, *The Chosen*, 49, quoting Eliot.
14. Henry James, *Charles W. Eliot: President of Harvard University, 1869–1909*, 2 vols. (Cambridge: Houghton Mifflin, 1930), 1:374.
15. Karabel, *The Chosen*, 45; Morton Keller and Phyllis Keller, *Making Harvard Modern: The Rise of America's University* (Oxford: Oxford University Press, 2001), 52.
16. Keller and Keller, *Making Harvard Modern*, 32.
17. Keller and Keller, *Making Harvard Modern*, 60; see also Nell Painter, "Jim Crow at Harvard: 1923," *New England Quarterly* 44, no. 4 (1971): 627–34, 627; William Wright, *Harvard's Secret Court: The Savage 1920 Purge of Campus Homosexuals* (New York: St. Martin's Press, 2005), 64.
18. Karabel, *The Chosen*, 101.
19. Charles Puttkammer, "Negroes in the Ivy League" (1962), 14 (unpublished manuscript on file at Harvard University Library; copy on file with author); Painter, "Jim Crow at Harvard," 628.
20. Painter, "Jim Crow at Harvard," 630, citing W. E. B. Du Bois, *Crisis* 24 (1922).
21. Theodore Rosengarten, "The Brotherhood of the Shroud," *New York Times*, April 26, 1987, https://www.nytimes.com/1987/04/26/books/the-brotherhood-of-the-shroud.html; see also Karabel, *The Chosen*, 103.
22. Hiram Wesley Evans, "The Klan's Fight for Americanism," *North American Review* 223, no. 830 (1926): 33–63, 61.
23. Karabel, *The Chosen*, 49–50; see also Stacy Jolna and Washington Post Staff Writers, "Harvard Documents on Sacco-Vanzetti Case May Fuel Controversy on Fairness Issue," *Washington Post*, February 1, 1978, www.washingtonpost.com/archive/politics/1978/02/01/harvard-documents-on-sacco-vanzetti-case-may-fuel-controversy-on-fairness-issue/ee2a139f-b13c-4d9e-aa98-720d491c987d/.
24. "Sacco & Vanzetti: Proclamation," Mass.gov, accessed February 15, 2023, www.mass.gov/info-details/sacco-vanzetti-proclamation.
25. Keller and Keller, *Making Harvard Modern*, 154; Stephen H. Norwood, "Legitimating Nazism: Harvard University and the Hitler Regime, 1933–1937," *American Jewish History* 92, no. 2 (2004): 189–223, 190, 196, www.jstor.org/stable/23887353.
26. Drew C. Pendergrass, "The Boys in Crimson: Boston's Police Strikebreakers," *Harvard Crimson Magazine*, November 10, 2016, www.thecrimson.com/article/2016/11/10/boston-strikebreakers/.
27. Jerome Karabel, *The Chosen*, 75, 89.
28. Karabel, *The Chosen*, 88.
29. Keller and Keller, *Making Harvard Modern*, 48.
30. Karabel, *The Chosen*, 89, 90, citing Marcia Graham Synnott, "A Social History of Admissions Policies at Harvard, Yale, and Princeton, 1900–1930" (PhD diss., University of Massachusetts, 1974), 321–24, https://scholarworks.umass.edu/dissertations_1/575.
31. Karabel, *The Chosen*, 92–93, 100.
32. Karabel, *The Chosen*, 101.

33. Karabel, *The Chosen*, 100–104.
34. Indeed, a decade later, in 1934, the executive secretary of admissions, Anne MacDonald, would carefully write to the Harvard president, James Conant, regarding Harvard's de facto Jewish quota: "The interviews with rejected Hebrews or their relatives are particularly precarious, and one needs to be constantly on the alert. ... For the past ten years, or since *the restriction* [Harvard's unofficial Jewish quota] we have been particularly fortunate in settling these cases," Karabel, *The Chosen*, 168, see also 101–2, 108–9.
35. See, e.g., Alan M. Dershowitz and Laura Hanft, "Affirmative Action and the Harvard College Diversity-Discretion Model: Paradigm or Pretext?" 1 *Cardozo Law Review* 379 (1979).

Chapter Five. The Marketplace of Ideas

1. James J. Ronan, "Oliver Wendell Holmes: A Memorial," Mass.gov, accessed February 3, 2023, www.mass.gov/person/oliver-wendell-holmes-jr; Susan-Mary Grant, *Oliver Wendell Holmes, Jr.: Civil War Soldier, Supreme Court Justice* (New York: Routledge, 2016), 1.
2. Roger Angell, "Old Country," *New Yorker*, September 11, 2006, 32, www.newyorker.com/magazine/2006/09/11/old-country; Robert A. James, "Holmes In Nature and Across Time," review of *The Black Book of Justice Holmes*, ed. Michael Hoeflich and Ross Davies (Clark: Talbot Publishing, 2021), July 2, 2021, https://ssrn.com/abstract=3878975.
3. Silas Bent, *Justice Oliver Wendell Holmes, A Biography* (New York: Vanguard Press, 1932), 23, 31, 34; The Editors, "The Atlantic's Founding," *Atlantic Monthly*, November 1997, www.theatlantic.com/magazine/archive/1997/11/the-atlantics-founding/306206/.
4. Grant, *Oliver Wendell Holmes*, 24–25.
5. Bent, *Justice Oliver Wendell Holmes*, 31.
6. Philip Cash, "Pride, Prejudice, and Politics," in *Blacks at Harvard: A Documentary History of African-American Experience at Harvard and Radcliffe*, ed. Werner Sollors, Caldwell Titcomb, and Thomas A. Underwood (New York: New York University Press, 1993), 22–31, 24, 28.
7. Cash, "Pride, Prejudice, and Politics," 29.
8. Ron Soodalter, "My Soul Is Vexed Within Me," *America's Civil War* 32, no. 1 (2019): 32–39, 34, 35; Ron Soodalter, "The Rise and Fall of Martin Delany, the U.S. Army's Visionary First Black Officer," historynet.com, January 22, 2019, www.historynet.com/the-rise-and-fall-of-martin-delany-the-u-s-armys-visionary-first-black-officer/.
9. Soodalter, "My Soul Is Vexed," 36; Soodalter, "The Rise and Fall."
10. Cash, "Pride, Prejudice, and Politics," 30; Soodalter, "My Soul Is Vexed," 34; Soodalter, "The Rise and Fall."
11. Frederic R. Kellogg, *Oliver Wendell Holmes Jr. and Legal Logic* (Chicago: University of Chicago Press, 2018), 19–20; Ronan, "Oliver Wendell

Holmes"; Felix Frankfurter, "Holmes, Oliver Wendell," in *Dictionary of American Biography* 21, supplement 1, ed. Harris E. Starr (New York: Scribner Press, 1944), 417–27, 419.

12. Thomas Healy, *The Great Dissent: How Oliver Wendell Holmes Changed His Mind—and Changed the History of Free Speech in America* (New York: Metropolitan Books, 2013), 98.

13. Frankfurter, "Holmes, Oliver Wendell," 420.

14. Oliver Wendell Holmes, Jr., *The Common Law* (Cambridge: Harvard University Press, 2009), 3, www.jstor.org/stable/j.ctt13x0kkk.

15. Patrick J. Kelley, "Holmes, Langdell and Formalism," *Ratio Juris* 15, no. 1 (2002): 26–51, 26, https://doi.org/10.1111/1467-9337.00195; Jan Vetter, "The Evolution of Holmes, Holmes and Evolution," *California Law Review* 72, no. 3 (1984): 343–68.

16. Bruce A. Kimball, *The Inception of Modern Professional Education: C. C. Langdell, 1826–1906* (Chapel Hill: University of North Carolina Press, 2009), 5–6, 88–89, 108–9, 140–47, 167, 310.

17. Kimball, *The Inception of Modern Professional Education*, 179; Frankfurter, "Holmes, Oliver Wendell," 421.

18. Ronan, "Oliver Wendell Holmes"; Frankfurter, "Holmes, Oliver Wendell," 422.

19. Frankfurter, "Holmes, Oliver Wendell," 421.

20. Ronan, "Oliver Wendell Holmes."

21. *Buck v. Bell*, 274 U.S. 200, 207 (1927).

22. See *Schenck v. United States*, 249 U.S. 47 (1919); *Debs v. United States*, 249 U.S. 211 (1919); *Frohwerk v. United States*, 249 U.S. 204 (1919).

23. See Geoffrey R. Stone, *Perilous Times: Free Speech In Wartime, From the Sedition Act of 1798 to the War on Terrorism* (New York: Norton, 2004), 135–233.

24. Michael E. Parrish, *Felix Frankfurter and His Times: The Reform Years* (New York: Free Press, 1982), 83.

25. Mark Whalan, *American Culture in the 1910s* (Edinburgh: Edinburgh University Press, 2010), 170; Parrish, *Felix Frankfurter and His Times*, 83; see also Stone, *Perilous Times*, 146–53.

26. Parrish, *Felix Frankfurter and His Times*, 83; see also Stone, *Perilous Times*, 153.

27. Ernest Freeberg, *Democracy's Prisoner: Eugene V. Debs, the Great War, and the Right to Dissent* (Cambridge: Harvard University Press, 2008), 46, 70; Stone, *Perilous Times*, 12.

28. *Frohwerk*, 249 U.S. at 209; *Schenck*, 249 U.S. at 52.

29. *Debs*, 249 U.S. at 212–13.

30. Freeberg, *Democracy's Prisoner*, 255; see also Stone, *Perilous Times*, 12.

31. Oliver Wendell Holmes, "The Black Book," in *The Black Book of Justice Holmes: Text Transcript & Commentary*, ed. Michael H. Hoeflich and Ross E. Davies (Clark: Talbot Publishing, 2021) 1–497, 369; Healy, *The Great Dissent*, 98–99; but see Irene M. Ten Cate, "Speech, Truth, and Freedom: An

Examination of John Stuart Mill's and Justice Oliver Wendell Holmes's Free Speech Defenses," *Yale Journal of Law and Humanities* 22, no. 1 (2010): 35–82, 55 (Holmes's first rereading of *On Liberty* took place in February 1919).

32. *Abrams v. United States*, 250 U.S. 616, 623 (1919).
33. *Abrams*, 250 U.S. at 623.
34. *Abrams*, 250 U.S. at 630–31 (Holmes, J., dissenting).
35. Healy, *The Great Dissent*, 1–2 (the justices were Willis Van Devanter, Mahlon Pitney, and an unrecalled third).
36. See Stone, *Perilous Times*, 198–211; David M. Rabban, "The Emergence of Modern First Amendment Doctrine," *University of Chicago Law Review* 50, no. 4 (1983): 1205–1355, 1208–1209; Healy, *The Great Dissent*, 98–99; Thomas Healy, "The Unlikely Birth of Free Speech," *New York Times*, November 9, 2019; Ten Cate, "Speech, Truth, and Freedom," 35–82; Donald L. Smith, *Zechariah Chafee, Jr., Defender of Liberty and Law* (Cambridge: Harvard University Press, 1986), 94–95.
37. Healy, "The Unlikely Birth of Free Speech."
38. Robert M. Mennel and Christine L. Compston, "Introduction," in *Holmes and Frankfurter: Their Correspondence, 1912–1934*, ed. Robert M. Mennel and Christine L. Compston (Hanover: University Press of New England, 1996), xi—xiii, xii.
39. Bruce Allen Murphy and Arthur Owens, "Felix Frankfurter (1882–1965)," in *Great American Judges: An Encyclopedia*, ed. John R. Vile (Santa Barbara: ABC-CLIO, 2003), 1:264–72, 264; but see Brad Snyder, *Democratic Justice: Felix Frankfurter, the Supreme Court, and the Making of the Liberal Establishment* (New York: Norton, 2022), 154; "Secretary to Justice Brandeis Nearly Ties His Harvard Rank," *Christian Science Monitor*, September 12, 1927, https://archive.org/details/per_christian-science-monitor_1927-09-12_19_243; Brad Snyder, "The Judicial Genealogy (and Mythology) of John Roberts: Clerkships from Gray to Brandeis to Friendly to Roberts," *Ohio State Law Journal* 76, no. 6 (2010): 1149–1243, 1170; James M. Landis, "Mr. Justice Brandeis and the Harvard Law School," *Harvard Law Review* 55, no. 2 (1941): 184–90.
40. Joseph P. Lash, "A Brahmin of the Law: A Biographical Essay," in Lash, *From the Diaries of Felix Frankfurter, With a Biographical Essay and Notes* (New York: Norton, 1975), 3–98, 8, 13.
41. Healy, *The Great Dissent*, 30–32, 35; Kingsley Martin, *Harold Laski (1893–1950): A Biographical Memoir* (New York: Viking Press, 1953), 6.
42. Healy, *The Great Dissent*, 32.
43. Healy, *The Great Dissent*, 33.
44. Healy, *The Great Dissent*, 35.
45. Healy, *The Great Dissent*, 34.
46. Letter from Oliver Wendell Holmes, Jr., to Harold J. Laski, February 28, 1919, in *Holmes-Laski Letters: The Correspondence of Mr. Justice Holmes and*

Harold J. Laski, vol. 1, *1916–1925*, ed. Mark DeWolfe Howe (Cambridge: Harvard University Press, 1953), 186–88, 187; see also Healy, *The Great Dissent*, 98.

47. Healy, *The Great Dissent*, 57, 158; Smith, *Zechariah Chafee, Jr.*,7, 94–95.
48. Healy, "The Unlikely Birth of Free Speech."
49. Thomas Healy, "The Justice Who Changed His Mind: Oliver Wendell Holmes, Jr., and the Story Behind *Abrams v. United States*," *Journal of Supreme Court History* 39, no. 1 (2014): 35–78, 56; Healy, *The Great Dissent*, 111–14.
50. Gerald Gunther, *Learned Hand: The Man and the Judge* (Cambridge: Harvard University Press, 1995), 275–76; see also Healy, *The Great Dissent*, 18–24.
51. Steven Mintz and Sarah McNeil, "The Spirit of Liberty," *Digital History*, accessed March 11, 2023, www.digitalhistory.uh.edu/disp_textbook.cfm?smt ID=3&psid=1199; see also Healy, *The Great Dissent*, 17.
52. Gunther, *Learned Hand*, 11–12.
53. Healy, "Justice Who Changed His Mind," 56; Gunther, *Learned Hand*, 161–62; Kellogg, *Oliver Wendell Holmes Jr. and Legal Logic*, 184–86.
54. Healy, "Justice Who Changed His Mind," 60; Healy, *The Great Dissent*, 18.
55. David S. Bogen, "The Free Speech Metamorphosis of Mr. Justice Holmes," *Hofstra Law Review* 11, no. 1 (1982): 97–189, 133–34.
56. Healy, *The Great Dissent*, 98.
57. Healy, *The Great Dissent*, 17.
58. Bogen, "Free Speech Metamorphosis," 136.
59. Bogen, "Free Speech Metamorphosis,"136–37; see also "To Learned Hand from Oliver Wendell Holmes, Jr., February 25, 1919," in *Reason and Imagination: The Selected Correspondence of Learned Hand*, ed. Constance Jordan (Oxford: Oxford University Press, 2013), 72–74 (documenting Holmes's and Hand's discussion of the *Masses* opinion).
60. Murphy and Owens, "Felix Frankfurter (1882–1965)," 264; but see Snyder, *Democratic Justice*, 154; "Secretary to Justice Brandeis Nearly Ties His Harvard Rank," *Christian Science Monitor*; Snyder, "The Judicial Genealogy (and Mythology) of John Roberts," 1170; Landis, "Mr. Justice Brandeis," 184–90.
61. David G. Dalin, *Jewish Justices of the Supreme Court: From Brandeis to Kagan* (Waltham: Brandeis University Press, 2017), 33–34.
62. Dalin, *Jewish Justices*, 46–48; Ronald G. Shafer, "The First Jewish Justice Was Also the First to Face Confirmation Hearings," *Washington Post*, April 4, 2022, www.washingtonpost.com/history/2022/04/04/louis-brandeis-jewish-confirmation-hearings/.
63. Parrish, *Felix Frankfurter and His Times*, 162–63.
64. Rodney A. Smolla, "The Meaning of the 'Marketplace of Ideas' in First Amendment Law," *Communication Law and Policy* 24, no. 4 (2019): 437–75, 438–39.

Chapter Six. Boycotts, Quotas, Diversity, and Segregation

1. David Pietrusza, "The Ku Klux Klan in the 1920s," *Bill of Rights Institute*, https://billofrightsinstitute.org/essays/the-ku-klux-klan-in-the-1920s. (Last visited March 3, 2024); "History," *United States Census Bureau*, www.census. gov/history/www/through_the_decades/fast_facts/1920_fast_facts.html. (last visited March 28, 2024).

2. "Lynchings: By Race and Year," University of Missouri—Kansas City, accessed December 18, 2017, http://law2.umkc.edu/faculty/projects/ftrials/shipp/lynchingyear.html (statistics provided by the Tuskegee Institute); see also W. E. B. Du Bois, "The Shape of Fear," *North American Review* 223 (1926): 291–304.

3. Isabel Wilkerson, *The Warmth of Other Suns: The Epic Story of America's Great Migration* (New York: Random House, 2010), 9.

4. Theodore Kornweibel, "An Economic Profile of Black Life in the Twenties," *Journal of Black Studies* 6, no. 4 (1976): 307–20, www.jstor.org/stable/2783764.

5. "A New African American Identity: The Harlem Renaissance," National Museum of African American History and Culture, accessed February 18, 2023, https://nmaahc.si.edu/explore/stories/new-african-american-identity-harlem-renaissance.

6. "Our History," National Association for the Advancement of Colored People, accessed July 18, 2023, https://naacp.org/about/our-history.

7. The nadir is commonly measured as the period between 1890 and 1915 or 1920. Note that some historians now persuasively argue that during the nadir a great deal of civil rights advocacy was occurring, leading to the movement that followed; see generally Susan D. Carle, *Defining the Struggle: National Organizing for Racial Justice, 1890–1915* (Oxford: Oxford University Press, 2013); August Meier and Elliott Rudwick, *Along the Color Line: Explorations in the Black Experience* (Urbana: University of Illinois Press, 1976); Glenda Elizabeth Gilmore, "Somewhere in the Nadir of African American History, 1890–1920," National Humanities Center, accessed December 18, 2017, http://nationalhumanitiescenter.org/tserve/freedom/1865-1917/essays/nadir.htm.

8. "NAACP: A Century in the Fight for Freedom, Founding and Early Years," Library of Congress, accessed February 18, 2023, www.loc.gov/exhibits/naacp/founding-and-early-years.html.

9. Du Bois, "The Shape of Fear," 291–304; Gary Massoni, "Perspectives on Operation Breadbasket," in *Chicago 1966: Open Housing Marches, Summit Negotiations, and Operation Breadbasket*, ed. David J. Garrow (Brooklyn: Carlson Publishing, 1989), 179–344; Edward Peeks, *The Long Struggle for Black Power* (New York: Charles Scribner's Sons, 1971), 270; Robert J. Weiss, *"We Want Jobs": A History of Affirmative Action* (New York: Garland Publishing, 1997), 60; Paul D. Moreno, *From Direct Action to Affirmative Action: Fair Employment Law and Policy in America, 1933–1972* (Baton Rouge: Louisiana State University Press, 1997), 33–41.

10. "Map of Jim Crow America," *Florida Atlantic University*, www.fau.edu/artsandletters/pjhr/chhre/pdf/sjc-map-jim-crow-america.pdf (last visited March 28, 2024); *Pleasants v. North Beach & Mission R.R. Co.*, 34 Cal. 586, 587 (1868).

11. Peeks, *Long Struggle for Black Power*, 270; Christopher Manning, "African Americans," The Electronic Encyclopedia of Chicago, accessed February 17, 2023, www.encyclopedia.chicagohistory.org/pages/27.html.

12. Massoni, *Chicago 1966*, 192.

13. Peeks, *Long Struggle for Black Power*, 270–72; Cheryl Lynn Greenberg, "*Or Does It Explode?*": *Black Harlem in the Great Depression* (Oxford: Oxford University Press, 1991), 116.

14. "Boycott," *Atlanta University Center Robert W. Woodruff Library*, accessed March 28, 2024, https://digitalexhibits.auctr.edu/exhibits/show/seekingtotell/asm/boycott.

15. See generally Delores Nason McBroome, "Parallel Communities: African Americans in California's East Bay, 1850–1963" (PhD diss., University of Oregon, 1991), 100–103, published as *Parallel Communities: African Americans in California's East Bay, 1850–1964* (New York: Garland Publishing, 1993), 70–71; Meier and Rudwick, *Along the Color Line*, 316.

16. W. E. B. Du Bois, "Boycotts," *The Crisis: A Record of the Darker Races* 41, no. 9 (1934): 268–69, https://archive.org/details/sim_crisis_1934-09_41_9/page/268/mode/2up.

17. But see Catherine Fisk, "'People Crushed by Law Have No Hopes But From Power': Free Speech and Protest in the 1940s," *Law and History Review* 39, no. 1 (2021): 173–203, https://doi.org/10.1017/S0738248020000498.

18. Peeks, *Long Struggle for Black Power*, 276; William J. Brennan, Jr., Robert L. Carter, William T. Coleman, Owen Fiss, A. Leon Higginbotham, and Martha Minow, "A Tribute to Justice Thurgood Marshall," *Harvard Law Review* 105, no. 1 (1991): 23–76, 35–36, www.jstor.org/stable/1341569.

19. *New Negro Alliance v. Sanitary Grocery Co.*, 303 U.S. 552, 557 (1938).

20. *New Negro Alliance*, 303 U.S. at 554, 559.

21. *New Negro Alliance*, 303 U.S. at 561.

22. William J. Brennan, Jr., Robert L. Carter, William T. Coleman, Owen Fiss, A. Leon Higginbotham, and Martha Minow, "A Tribute to Justice Thurgood Marshall," *Harvard Law Review* 105, no. 1 (1991): 23–76, 35–36, www.jstor.org/stable/1341569; Peeks, *Long Struggle for Black Power*, 277.

23. Juan Williams, *Thurgood Marshall: American Revolutionary* (New York: Three Rivers Press, 1998), 34, 41, 52–53, 59, 61; Mark V. Tushnet, *Making Civil Rights Law: Thurgood Marshall and the Supreme Court, 1936–1961* (New York: Oxford University Press, 1994), 27.

24. "Justice Thurgood Marshall Profile—Brown v. Board of Education Reenactment," United States Courts, accessed February 18, 2023, www.uscourts.gov/educational-resources/educational-activities/justice-thurgood-marshall-profile-brown-v-board.

25. Meier and Rudwick, *Along the Color Line*, 316, table II.

26. Lawrence P. Crouchett, Lonnie G. Bunch III, and Martha Kendall Winnacker, *Visions Toward Tomorrow: The History of the East Bay Afro-American Community, 1852–1977* (Oakland: Northern California Center for Afro-American History and Life, 1989), 45–46, cited in Frederic White, "Justice Carter's Dissent in *Hughes v. Superior Court of Contra Costa County*," in *The Great Dissents of the "Lone Dissenter": Justice Jesse W. Carter's Twenty Tumultuous Years on the California Supreme Court*, ed. David B. Oppenheimer and Allan Brotsky (Durham, NC: Carolina Academic Press, 2010), 59.

27. *Hughes v. Superior Ct. of Cal.*, 339 U.S. 460, 461–63 (1950).

28. Jelani M. Favors, "Race Women: New Negro Politics and the Flowering of Radicalism at Bennett College, 1900–1945," *North Carolina Historical Review* 94, no. 4 (2017): 391–430, 425–26, www.jstor.org/stable/45185396.

29. "Legal Records and Reports," *Civil Rights Department of the State of California*, accessed March 28, 2024, https://calcivilrights.ca.gov/legalrecords/.

30. See David B. Oppenheimer and Margaret M. Baumgartner, "Employment Discrimination and Wrongful Discharge: Does the California Fair Employment and Housing Act Displace Common Law Remedies?," *University of San Francisco Law Review* 23, no. 2 (1989): 145–92, 191, https://heinonline.org/HOL/P?h=hein.journals/usflr23&i=155; see also *Rojo v. Kliger*, 52 Cal. 3d 65, 77 n.6 (1990) (citing article with approval).

31. *Hughes v. Superior Ct. in & for Contra Costa Cnty.*, 186 P.2d 756, 759 (Cal. Ct. App. 1947), *vacated*, 32 Cal. 2d 850, 198 P.2d 885 (1948), *aff'd sub nom. Hughes v. Superior Ct. of Cal.*, 339 U.S. 460 (1950).

32. *Hughes* 339 U.S. 460; Shirley Ann Wilson Moore, *To Place Our Deeds: The African American Community in Richmond, California, 1910–1963* (Berkeley: University of California Press, 2000), 90.

33. *Hughes*, 339 U.S. at 462.

34. Fisk, "'People Crushed by Law,'" 173–203.

35. *Hughes*, 339 U.S. at 469, *aff'd* 32 Cal. 2d 850 (1948).

36. *Hughes*, 339 U.S. at 461; Helen Shirley Thomas, *Felix Frankfurter: Scholar on the Bench* (Baltimore: Johns Hopkins University Press, 2019) 24, 26.

37. *Hughes*, 339 U.S. at 462 (quoting *Hughes*, 32 Cal. 2d at 856).

38. Compare Martin Luther King, Jr., *Why We Can't Wait* (New York: Harper & Row, 1964), 147, 150–51, with Fisk, "'People Crushed by Law,'" 186.

39. Robert Jerome Glennon, "The Role of Law in the Civil Rights Movement: The Montgomery Bus Boycott, 1955–1957." *Law and History Review* 9, no. 1 (1991): 59–112, 60, https://doi.org/10.2307/743660; James A. Colaiaco, "The American Dream Unfulfilled: Martin Luther King, Jr., and the 'Letter from Birmingham Jail,'" *Phylon (1960-)* 45, no. 1 (1984): 1–18, 1, https://doi.org/10.2307/274975.

40. Massoni, *Chicago 1966*, 193.

41. See *United Steelworkers v. Weber*, 443 U.S. 193, 244 (1979); David B. Oppenheimer, "The Disappearance of Voluntary Affirmative Action from the U.S.

Workplace," *Journal of Poverty and Social Justice* 24, no. 1 (2016): 37–50, 39–40, https://bristoluniversitypressdigital.com/view/journals/jpsj/24/1/article-p37.xml.

42. See generally "Operation Breadbasket," Martin Luther King, Jr., Encyclopedia, accessed February 18, 2023, https://kinginstitute.stanford.edu/encyclopedia/operation-breadbasket; see also Martin Luther King, Jr., "Annual Report at the Eighth Annual Southern Christian Leadership Conference Convention" (speech, Atlanta, Georgia, September 28, 1964), Civil Rights Movement Archive, www.crmvet.org/docs/6409_sclc_mlk_rpt.pdf; Martin Luther King, Jr., "Martin Luther King, Jr., President, S. Christian Leadership Conference, on Operation Breadbasket," Interview by Associated Press, July 28, 1967, The King Center, https://web.archive.org/web/20171111160843/http://www.thekingcenter.org/archive/document/mlk-interview-associated-press-operation-breadbasket#; Rev. David Wallace and Rev. Jesse Jackson, "Operation Breadbasket," August 25, 1966 (press release), The King Center, https://web.archive.org/web/20171111194202/http://www.thekingcenter.org/archive/document/operation-breadbasket-0#.

43. Massoni, *Chicago 1966*, 197.

44. Massoni, *Chicago 1966*, 309, 321.

45. Massoni, *Chicago 1966*, 202, 309, 321 (August, 1968 Guidelines for Operation Breadbasket Committees).

46. "Jackson, Jesse Louis," Martin Luther King, Jr., Research and Education Institute, Stanford University, accessed March 28, 2024, https://kinginstitute.stanford.edu/jackson-jesse-louis.

47. Terry H. Anderson, *The Pursuit of Fairness: A History of Affirmative Action* (New York: Oxford University Press, 2004), 76.

48. Anderson, *The Pursuit of Fairness*, 76; see also Weiss, *"We Want Jobs,"* 60.

49. King, *Why We Can't Wait*, 147.

50. Martin Luther King, Jr., "I Have a Dream" (speech, Washington, D.C., August 28, 1963), NPR, www.npr.org/2010/01/18/122701268/i-have-a-dream-speech-in-its-entirety; see generally Denise M. Bostdorff and Steven R. Goldzwig, "History, Collective Memory, and the Appropriation of Martin Luther King, Jr.: Reagan's Rhetorical Legacy," *Presidential Studies Quarterly* 35, no. 4 (2005): 661–90; John Blake, "Why Conservatives Call MLK Their Hero," *CNN*, January 19, 2013, http://www.cnn.com/2013/01/19/us/mlk-conservative/index.html; William J. Bennett, "Civil Rights is the GOP's Mission," *Los Angeles Times*, August 12, 1996, http://articles.latimes.com/1996-08-12/local/me-33453_1_civilrights-movement.

51. King, "I Have a Dream."

52. King, *Why We Can't Wait*, 150–51.

53. Martin Luther King, Jr., "Statement to the National Advisory Commission on Civil Disorders" (speech, Atlanta, Georgia, October 23, 1967) (copy of transcript on file with author).

54. King, "Statement to National Advisory Commission."

55. *Missouri ex rel. Gaines v. Canada*, 305 U.S. 337, 350–51 (1938).

56. Pauli Murray, *Pauli Murray: The Autobiography of a Black Activist, Feminist, Lawyer, Priest, and Poet* (Knoxville: University of Tennessee Press, 1989), 14–15; Williams, *Thurgood Marshall*, 37.

57. Murray, *Pauli Murray*, 11, 14–15, 55–58.

58. Pauli Murray, *Proud Shoes: The Story of an American Family* (Boston: Beacon Press, 1999), 103.

59. Kathryn Schulz, "The Many Lives of Pauli Murray," *New Yorker*, April 10, 2017, www.newyorker.com/magazine/2017/04/17/the-many-lives-of-pauli-murray.

60. Murray, *Pauli Murray*, 64–70, 92.

61. Patricia Bell-Scott, *The Firebrand and the First Lady: Portrait of a Friendship: Pauli Murray, Eleanor Roosevelt, and the Struggle for Social Justice* (New York: Knopf, 2016), 28; Kenneth W. Mack, *Representing the Race: The Creation of the Civil Rights Lawyer* (Cambridge: Harvard University Press, 2012), 211–12.

62. "Pronouns & Pauli Murray," Pauli Murray Center for History and Social Justice, accessed June 27, 2023, www.paulimurraycenter.com/pronouns-pauli-murray.

63. Rosalind Rosenberg, *Jane Crow: The Life of Pauli Murray* (New York: Oxford University Press, 2017), 56–60.

64. Schulz, "Many Lives of Pauli Murray."

65. Murray, *Pauli Murray*, 76–77.

66. Schulz, "Many Lives of Pauli Murray."

67. Murray, *Pauli Murray*, 108, 114–16; Pauli Murray, "Oral History Interview with Pauli Murray," interview by Genna Rae McNeil, Southern Oral History Program, February 13, 1976, https://docsouth.unc.edu/sohp/G-0044/excerpts/excerpt_8638.html.

68. Murray, "Oral History Interview."

69. Rosenberg, *Jane Crow*, 76–77.

70. Kenneth W. Mack, *Representing the Race* (Cambridge: Harvard University Press, 2012), 218–19, www.jstor.org/stable/j.ctt24hhwm.

71. Bell-Scott, *Firebrand and the First Lady*, 52–55.

72. Murray, *Pauli Murray*, 110–13, 128–29.

73. Murray, *Pauli Murray*, 138, 142–46.

74. Mack, *Representing the Race*, 218–19.

75. Murray, *Pauli Murray*, 162, 166, 182; Letter from Pauli Murray to Thurgood Marshall dated April 24, 1974, regarding decision in the *DeFunis* case, mentioning how Marshall recommended Murray for admission to Howard Law School, on file at Schlesinger Collection at Radcliffe library.

76. Murray, *Pauli Murray*, 183, 184, 188; www.law.berkeley.edu/spotlight/pauli-murray-us-mint-american-quarters-program/.

77. Rosenberg, *Jane Crow*, 121–24.

78. Murray, *Pauli Murray*, 199.

79. Murray, *Pauli Murray*, 183.

80. Sarah Azaransky, "Jane Crow: Pauli Murray's Intersections and Antidiscrimination Law," *Journal of Feminist Studies in Religion* 29, no. 1 (2013): 155–60, 156, quoting Pauli Murray, "Why Negro Girls Stay Single," *Negro Digest* 5, no. 9 (1947): 4–8, 5, https://doi.org/10.2979/jfemistudreli.29.1.155.

81. Rosenberg, *Jane Crow*, 122–23.

82. Bell-Scott, *Firebrand and the First Lady*, 148.

83. Murray, *Pauli Murray*, 239.

84. Troy R. Saxby, *Pauli Murray: A Personal and Political Life* (Chapel Hill: University of North Carolina Press, 2020), 128–29.

85. Bell-Scott, *Firebrand and the First Lady*, 148–49.

86. Murray, *Pauli Murray*, 256–57.

87. Ivan Natividad, "Legacy of Berkeley Law's First Black Female Graduate Lives On," *Berkeley News*, July 20, 2020, https://news.berkeley.edu/2020/07/20/legacy-of-berkeley-laws-first-black-female-graduate-lives-on/#:~:text=In%201929%2C%20Annie%20Virginia%20Stephens,to%20graduate%20from%20Berkeley%20Law.

88. Murray, *Pauli Murray*, 258–61.

89. Bell-Scott, *Firebrand and the First Lady*, 178–79.

90. Bell-Scott, *Firebrand and the First Lady*, 179; Rosenberg, *Jane Crow*, 158.

91. Murray, *Pauli Murray*, 262.

92. Bell-Scott, *Firebrand and the First Lady*, 193; Pauli Murray, "The Right to Equal Opportunity in Employment," *California Law Review* 33, no. 3 (1945): 388–433.

93. Murray, *Pauli Murray*, 261–63, 265–69.

94. Saxby, *Murray: A Personal and Political Life*, 146–47.

95. Saxby, *Murray: A Personal and Political Life*, 146–47.

96. Saxby, *Murray: A Personal and Political Life*, 147.

97. Ada Lois Sipuel Fisher, *A Matter of Black and White: The Autobiography of Ada Lois Sipuel Fisher* (Norman: University of Oklahoma Press, 1996), 128–30.

98. *Sipuel v. Bd. of Regents of Univ. of Okl.*, 332 U.S. 631, 632 (1948).

99. Pauli Murray, "Should the Civil Rights Cases and *Plessy v. Ferguson* Be Overruled?" (paper prepared for seminar with Professor Leon A. Ransom), May 1944, Papers of Pauli Murray, 1827–1985, MC 412; T-194; T-245, 1467, Box: 84. Schlesinger Library, Radcliffe Institute; Murray, *Pauli Murray*, 254.

100. Schulz, "Many Lives of Pauli Murray"; Rosenberg, *Jane Crow*, 171.

101. Murray, "Should the Civil Rights Cases and *Plessy v. Ferguson* Be Overruled?"; Rosenberg, *Jane Crow*, 155–57; Rebeka Cabrera, "Pauli Murray: Who Was the Legal Advocate and Civil Rights Champion?" *Teen Vogue*, November 18, 2022; "Pauli Murray's Impact and Innovative Legal Spirit," Pauli Murray Center for History and Social Justice, accessed June 27, 2023.

102. Rosenberg, *Jane Crow*, 155–57.

103. *Jones v. Alfred H. Mayer Co.*, 392 U.S. 409 (1968).

104. Murray, "Should the Civil Rights Cases and *Plessy v. Ferguson* Be Overruled?"

105. Rosenberg, *Jane Crow*, 149–50, 169–71.

106. Murray, "Should the Civil Rights Cases and *Plessy* Be Overruled?" at 56.

107. See *Sipuel*, 332 U.S. 631; Transcript of Record at 523–47 (Testimony of Griswold), *Sipuel*, 332 U.S. 631 (No. 369); Letters between Thurgood

Marshall and Erwin Griswold (June 7, June 10, June 14, and September 22, 1948) (on file with Library of Congress and author).

108. Dennis Hevesi, "Erwin Griswold Is Dead at 90; Served as a Solicitor General," *New York Times*, November 21, 1994, www.nytimes.com/1994/11/21/obituaries/erwin-griswold-is-dead-at-90-served-as-a-solicitor-general.html.

109. "Solicitor General: Erwin N. Griswold," Office of the Solicitor General, U.S. Department of Justice, accessed March 28, 2024, www.justice.gov/osg/bio/erwin-n-griswold.

110. Erwin Griswold, "Oral History Project of the Historical Society of the District of Columbia Circuit," Interview by Victoria L. Radd, United States Courts District of Columbia Circuit, January 13, 1992, transcript, https://dcchs.org/sb_pdf/interview-erwin-griswold/.

111. "Solicitor General," Office of the Solicitor General.

112. Julia Cohen and Betsy West, *My Name Is Pauli Murray* (2021: Amazon Studios), www.amazon.com/My-Name-Pauli-Murray/dp/B09DMPMWCP.

113. I am relying on a conversation with one of those twelve women at a reception at Harvard Law School in 1975, when I was a student there.

114. Lori Keeton, "Ruth Bader Ginsburg: A Pioneer and Champion for Women," American Bar Association, August 20, 2020, www.americanbar.org/groups/gpsolo/publications/gp_solo/2020/july-august/ruth-bader-ginsburg-pioneer-and-champion-women/.

115. Cohen and West, *My Name Is Pauli Murray*.

116. Ruth Bader Ginsburg, "The Changing Complexion of Harvard Law School," *Harvard Women's Law Journal* 27 (2004): 303–8, 306, https://heinonline.org/HOL/P?h=hein.journals/hwlj27&i=307.

117. See *Sipuel*, 332 U.S. 631; Transcript of Record at 523–47 (Testimony of Griswold), *Sipuel*, 332 U.S. 631; Letters between Thurgood Marshall and Erwin Griswold (June 7, June 10, June 14, and September 22, 1948) (on file with Library of Congress and author).

118. Transcript of Record at 534 (Testimony of Griswold), *Sipuel*, 332 U.S. 631 (No. 369).

119. Brief of Amicus Curiae for National Lawyers Guild at 10, *Sipuel*, 332 U.S. 631.

120. *McLaurin v. Okla. State Regents for Higher Education*, 339 U.S. 637, 639 (1950); *Sweatt v. Painter*, 339 U.S. 629, 635 (1950).

121. *McLaurin*, 339 U.S. at 641.

122. Brief for The Committee of Law Teachers Against Segregation in Legal Education, *Sweatt*, 339 U.S. 629.

123. Brief for The Committee of Law Teachers Against Segregation in Legal Education at 44, *Sweatt*, 339 U.S. 629.

124. Brief for The Committee of Law Teachers Against Segregation in Legal Education at 45, *Sweatt*, 339 U.S. 629, quoting Eugene V. Rostow, "Liberal Education and the Law: Preparing Lawyers for Their Work in Our Society," *American Bar Association Journal* 35, no. 8 (1949), 626–29, 628, 629.

125. Brief for The Committee of Law Teachers Against Segregation in Legal Education at 45–46, *Sweatt* 339 U.S. 629.

126. *Sweatt*, 339 U.S. at 634; Lloyd K. Garrison, "Character Training of Law Students from the Point of View of the Law Schools and the Bar." *American Law School Review* 8, no. 7 (1936): 592–607.

127. Murray, "Should the Civil Rights Cases and *Plessy* Be Overruled?"

128. *Brown v. Board of Education*, 347 U.S. 483, 493 (1954).

129. Bell-Scott, *Firebrand and the First Lady*, 339, 355.

130. Schulz, "Many Lives of Pauli Murray"; Bell-Scott, *Firebrand and the First Lady*, 208–9.

131. Bell-Scott, *Firebrand and the First Lady*, 208–9.

132. Murray, *Pauli Murray*, 288–89.

133. "Solicitor General," Office of the Solicitor General.

134. See Brief for The Committee of Law Teachers Against Segregation in Legal Education, *Sweatt*, 339 U.S. 629; *Sweatt*, 339 U.S. 629.

135. Murray, *Pauli Murray*, 311, 318, 342, 422–25; "Pauli Murray College: Our History," Yale College, accessed July 17, 2023, https://paulimurray.yalecollege. yale.edu/subpage-1.

136. Murray, *Pauli Murray*, 362; Pauli Murray and Mary O. Eastwood, "Jane Crow and the Law: Sex Discrimination and Title VII," *George Washington Law Review* 34, no. 2 (1965–1966): 232–56.

137. Cynthia Harrison, *On Account of Sex: The Politics of Women's Issues, 1945–1968* (Berkeley: University of California Press 1988), 126.

138. Bell-Scott, *Firebrand and the First Lady*, 337–38.

139. Leah Rosenbaum and Brianne Garrett, "Meet the Forgotten Woman Who Forever Changed the Lives of LGBTQ+ Workers," *Forbes*, June 26, 2020, www.forbes.com/sites/leahrosenbaum/2020/06/26/pauli-murray-lgbtq-rights-civil-rights-act-title-vii/?sh=86737647620b; Murray, *Pauli Murray*, 355–58.

140. Jo Freeman, "How 'Sex' Got into Title VII: Persistent Opportunism as a Maker of Public Policy," *Law and Inequality: A Journal of Theory and Practice* 9, no. 2 (1991): 163–84, 163; George C. Wallace, "The Civil Rights Movement: Fraud, Sham, and Hoax," July 4, 1964, published in "A Segregationist View of the Civil Rights Movement, 1964," PBS, www.pbs.org/wgbh/americanexperience/features/lbj-wallspeech/.

141. Freeman, "How 'Sex' Got into Title VII," 163.

142. Rosenbaum and Garrett, "Meet the Forgotten Woman"; NPR Staff, "How a Poison Pill Worded as 'Sex' Gave Birth to Transgender Rights," NPR, May 15, 2016, www.npr.org/2016/05/15/478075804/how-a-poison-pill-worded-as-sex-gave-birth-to-transgender-rights.

143. NPR Staff, "How a Poison Pill."

144. Pauli Murray, "Memorandum in Support of Retaining the Amendment to H.R. 7152. Title VII (Equal Employment Opportunity) to Prohibit Discrimination in Employment Because of Sex," 1964. Papers of Pauli Mur-

ray, 1827–1985, MC 412; T-194; T-245, 1485. Box: 86. Schlesinger Library, Radcliffe Institute.

145. Dahlia Lithwick, "Who Was Pauli Murray?," *Slate*, August 31, 2021, https://slate.com/news-and-politics/2021/08/my-name-is-pauli-murray-directors-interview.html.

146. Susan Hartmann, "Pauli Murray and the 'Juncture of Women's Liberation and Black Liberation,'" *Journal of Women's History* 14, no. 2 (2002): 74–75.

147. Murray, "Memorandum in Support of Retaining the Amendment," 4–5.

148. Murray, "Memorandum in Support of Retaining the Amendment," 6–7.

149. Murray, "Memorandum in Support of Retaining the Amendment," 20–21.

150. Lithwick, "Who Was Pauli Murray?"

151. "Civil Rights Act (1964)," National Archives, accessed March 28, 2024, www.archives.gov/milestone-documents/civil-rights-act.

152. Murray, *Pauli Murray*, 363.

153. Bell-Scott, *Firebrand and the First Lady*, 345.

154. Murray, *Pauli Murray*, 365–68; "Pauli Murray Timeline," Pauli Murray Center for History and Social Justice, accessed June 29, 2023, www.paulimurraycenter.com/murray-timeline.

155. Bell-Scott, *Firebrand and the First Lady*, 345.

156. Saxby, *Murray: A Personal and Political Life*, 232.

157. Rosenberg, *Jane Crow*, 304–5.

158. Murray, *Pauli Murray*, 387–88, 390–414.

159. Bell-Scott, *Firebrand and the First Lady*, 357; Murray, *Pauli Murray*, 426–31.

160. Bell-Scott, *Firebrand and the First Lady*, 361.

161. Pauli Murray, "Challenge of Nurturing the Christian Community in Its Diversity," in *Pauli Murray: Selected Sermons and Writings*, ed. Anthony B. Pinn (Maryknoll: Orbis Books, 2006), 209–18.

162. Murray, "Challenge of Nurturing," 210, 215.

163. Bell-Scott, *Firebrand and the First Lady*, 375; "Journey Through the Life of Pauli Murray," from *Pauli Murray's Proud Shoes: A Classic in African American Genealogy*, National Museum of African American History and Culture, accessed July 17, 2023, https://nmaahc.si.edu/explore/exhibitions/pauli-murrays-proud-shoes.

164. Duke Today Staff, "Pauli Murray Named to Episcopal Sainthood," July 14, 2012, https://today.duke.edu/2012/07/saintmurray.

Chapter Seven. The Fight over the Meaning of "Excellence"

1. See Fred L. Glimp, "Final Report to the Faculty of Arts and Sciences," in *Official Register of Harvard* 65 (1968), 103; "Admissions Statistics," Harvard College, accessed February 15, 2023, https://college.harvard.edu/admissions/admissions-statistics.

2. Glimp, "Final Report to the Faculty," 105. Jerome Karabel, *The Chosen: The Hidden History of Admission and Exclusion at Harvard, Yale, and Princeton*

(Boston: Houghton Mifflin, 2006), 268, 615 n.216; see also Wilbur J. Bender, "Report on the Admission and Scholarship Committee for the Academic Year 1959–60" (1961); Wilbur J. Bender, "The Top-One-Percent Policy," *Harvard Alumni Bulletin* 64 (1962): 21–25; Wilbur J. Bender, "Is Too Much of 'The Best' Bad for Harvard?," *Boston Globe*, October 8, 1961, https://bostonglobe. newspapers.com/image/433759793; "Ex-Dean Bender's Valedictory Message," *Harvard Crimson*, October 2, 1961, www.thecrimson.com/article/1961/ 10/2/ex-dean-benders-valedictory-message-pexcerpts-from/.

3. Bender, "Report on the Admission and Scholarship Committee," 56.

4. "Wilbur J. Bender '27 Dies at 65; A Dean at Harvard for 13 Years," *Harvard Crimson*, April 7, 1969, www.thecrimson.com/article/1969/4/7/wilbur-j-bender-27-dies-at.

5. Bender, "Report on the Admission and Scholarship Committee," 67–69 (this portion of the report is on file with the author); see Karabel, *The Chosen*, 252–53.

6. "Ex-Dean Bender's Valedictory Message," *Harvard Crimson*, October 2, 1961, www.thecrimson.com/article/1961/10/2/ex-dean-benders-valedictory-message-excerpts-from; see Karabel, *The Chosen*, 279–85.

7. Bender, "Report on the Admission and Scholarship Committee," 64–65, 67–69 (this portion of the report is on file with the author); Karabel, *The Chosen*, 252–53.

8. Fred Glimp, "Glimpses of a Harvard Half-Century," interview by David McClintick, *John Harvard's Journal*, January 1997, www.harvardmagazine. com/sites/default/files/html/1997/01/jhj.glimpse.html; "Remembering Fred Glimp," *Harvard Gazette*, August 10, 2017, https://news.harvard.edu/gazette/ story/2017/08/remembering-fred-glimp/.

9. Glimp, "Final Report to the Faculty," 104–15; see "Ex-Dean Bender's Vale-dictory Message," *Harvard Crimson*.

10. Karabel, *The Chosen*, 251–93.

11. Glimp, "Final Report to the Faculty," 104–15 (courtesy of the Harvard University Archives).

12. Richard Severo, "John U. Monro, 89, Dies; Left Harvard to Follow Ideals," *New York Times*, April 3, 2002, www.nytimes.com/2002/04/03/us/john-u-monro-89-dies-left-harvard-to-follow-ideals.html; see also Toni-Lee Capossela, *John U. Monro: Uncommon Educator* (Baton Rouge: Louisiana State University Press, 2012).

13. Boisfueillet Jones, Jr., "Monro to Resign July 1 as Dean of College; Glimp Will Be Recommended as Successor," *Harvard Crimson*, March 10, 1967, www.thecrimson.com/article/1967/3/10/monro-to-resign-july-1-as/.

14. Capossela, *John U. Monro*, 65.

15. Capossela, *John U. Monro*, 65, 118–20; see also Jones, "Monro to Resign July 1."

16. Capossela, *John U. Monro*, 55–58.

17. Capossela, *John U. Monro*, 56.

18. Karabel, *The Chosen*, 400–401.

19. Charles Puttkammer, *Negroes in the Ivy League* (1962), 15–16 (unpublished manuscript on file at Harvard University Library; copy on file with author).
20. Severo, "John U. Monro, 89, Dies."
21. Capossela, *John U. Monro*, 91.
22. "16th Street Baptist Church Bombing (1963)," National Park Service, last modified September 19, 2022, www.nps.gov/articles/16thstreetbaptist.htm.
23. Capossela, *John U. Monro*, 92 (quoting John U. Monro's "Miles College Assembly Speech").
24. Capossela, *John U. Monro*, 92.
25. Capossela, *John U. Monro*, 96, 99, 105.
26. Capossela, *John U. Monro*, 108.
27. Karabel, *The Chosen*, 401.
28. See William G. Bowen and Derek Bok, *The Shape of the River: Long-Term Consequences of Considering Race in College and University Admissions* (Princeton: Princeton University Press, 1998), 5.
29. Lisa M. Stulberg and Anthony S. Chen, "The Origins of Race-conscious Affirmative Action in Undergraduate Admissions: A Comparative Analysis of Institutional Change in Higher Education," *Sociology of Education* 87, no. 1 (2014): 36–52, 36.
30. Capossela, *John U. Monro*, 110, 112, 118, 134–35.
31. Capossela, *John U. Monro*, 119–20.
32. Ken Gewertz, "Champion of Disadvantaged, Monro, Dies at 89," *Harvard Gazette*, April 11, 2002, https://news.harvard.edu/gazette/story/2002/04/champion-of-disadvantaged-monro-dies-at-89/.
33. Karabel, *The Chosen*, 403–4.

Chapter Eight. The Open Universities in South Africa

1. Howard Phillips, *UCT Under Apartheid, Part 1: From Onset to Sit-in, 1948–1968* (Auckland Park: Fanele, 2019), 4–6; "Dr. T. B. Davie. In Memoriam Service at Cape Town," *South African Medical Journal* 30 (January 1956): 43–44, https://journals.co.za/doi/epdf/10.10520/AJA20785135_30531; Mamokgethi Phakeng, "The 2022 T. B. Davie Memorial Lecture," University of Cape Town, August 11, 2022, www.news.uct.ac.za/article/-2022–08–11-the-2022-tb-davie-memorial-lecture.
2. Leonard Thompson, *A History of South Africa*, 3rd ed. (New Haven: Yale University Press, 2001), 187; Phillips, *UCT Under Apartheid, Part 1*, 1, 87–126 (discussion of the legalization of racial segregation of public premises, racial disenfranchisement, and labor regulation); Trevor Noah, *Born a Crime and Other Stories* (Johannesburg: Macmillan, 2016), 22–23.
3. Phillips, *UCT Under Apartheid, Part 1*, 6–7; see also Albert van der Sandt Centlivres, "T. B. Davie Memorial Lecture" (speech, May 6, 1959) (the First T. B. Davie Memorial Lecture; on file with the author, courtesy of the library at the University of Cape Town); T. B. Davie, "Address on the Occasion of

the Graduation of the University of Witwatersrand" (speech, December 6, 1950) (transcript available in the UCT Libraries, Special Collections Division, and on file with the author); T. B. Davie, "The Function of a University in a Multi-Racial Society" (speech before the Institute of Race Relations, May 1, 1954) (on file with the author); T. B. Davie, "Education and Race Relations in South Africa" (speech for the Eleventh Hoernlé Memorial Lecture before the Institute of Race Relations, 1955) (on file with the author).

4. Phillips, *UCT Under Apartheid, Part 1*, 2 (citing T. B. Davie, "Inaugural Address on the Occasion of the Installation of T. B. Davie as Principal," March 1, 1948) (transcript available in the UCT Libraries, Special Collections Division, BUZV Collection—Staff); Phillips, *UCT Under Apartheid, Part 1*, 2.

5. Phillips, *UCT Under Apartheid, Part 1*, 6.

6. Phillips, *UCT Under Apartheid, Part 1*, 7.

7. Davie, "Address on the Occasion of the Graduation of the University of Witwatersrand," 7.

8. Davie, "Address on the Occasion of the Graduation of the University of Witwatersrand," 7.

9. Albert van der Sandt Centlivres and Richard Feetham, *The Open Universities in South Africa* (Johannesburg: Witwatersrand University Press, 1957), 11–12 (citing T. B. Davie, "Address to New Students at the University of Cape Town," February 28, 1953).

10. T. B. Davie, "Report on the Tour of Canadian & American Universities by the Principal of UCT Under His Auspices of the Carnegie Corporation of New York, September–December 1953," 1 (on file with UCT Libraries, Special Collections Division, and on file with author); see also Alan Pifer, "Carnegie Oral History Project: Alan Pifer," interview by Brenda Hearing, July 14, 1998, transcript, 274, www.columbia.edu/cu/lweb/digital/collections/oral_hist/carnegie/video-interviews/.

11. T. B. Davie, "Diary of Trip to U.S. Universities, September to December 1953," 5 (on file with author); Davie's visit to Harvard also featured his having lunch with and attending a lecture by Gordon Allport, the pathbreaking professor of psychology who was about to publish his landmark text, *The Nature of Prejudice*; see "Diary of Trip to U.S. Universities," 7. See also Davie, "Report on the Tour of Canadian & American Universities" 27–34; Ken Gewertz, "Nathan Pusey Dies at 94: Harvard's 24th President Served University for Almost Two Decades," *Harvard Gazette*, November 15, 2001, https://news.harvard.edu/gazette/story/2001/11/nathan-pusey-dies-at-94/.

12. See discussion of Marshall and Griswold collaboration in chapter 6; Transcript of Record at 523–547 (Testimony of Griswold), *Sipuel v. Bd. of Regents of the Univ. of Okla.*, 332 U.S. 631 (1948) (No. 369).

13. Brief for the Committee of Law Teachers Against Segregation in Legal Education as Amicus Curiae, *Sweatt v. Painter*, 339 U.S. 629 (1950) (No. 44), republished in *Minnesota Law Review* 34 (1950): 289–387, 319–20; *Sweatt v. Painter*, 339 U.S. 629 (1950).

14. Davie, "Report on the Tour of Canadian & American Universities," 1–3; Letter from Alan Pifer to T. B. Davie, January 11, 1955 (on file with author).

15. "Pifer, Alan J.," Carnegie Corporation Oral History Project, accessed July 5, 2023, www.columbia.edu/cu/lweb/digital/collections/oral_hist/carnegie/video-interviews/.

16. "Past Presidents: Alan Pifer, 1967–1982," Carnegie Corporation of New York, accessed February 15, 2023, www.carnegie.org/about/our-history/past-presidents/#pifer.

17. "Pifer, Alan J.," Carnegie Corporation Oral History Project, transcript.

18. Davie, "Diary of Trip to U.S. Universities," 5.

19. Phillips, *UCT Under Apartheid, Part 1*, 3–4; see generally Davie, "Report on the Tour of Canadian & American Universities," 10–12 (comparing South African university structures to U.S. university structures); Phillips, *UCT Under Apartheid, Part 1*, 4 (describing the relationship between Principal and Chancellor as "akin to that between the Patron and the CEO of a non-government organisation").

20. Letter from Albert van der Sandt Centlivres to Felix Frankfurter, undated ("I was particularly pleased during my visit to Australia last year to make the acquaintance of Dean Griswold") (on file with author); "Legal Convention Opens at Sydney Town Hall," *Sydney Morning Herald*, August 9, 1951, https://trove.nla.gov.au/newspaper/article/18215998; Letter from Erwin Griswold to Felix Frankfurter, April 9, 1959 (discussing Griswold's ongoing correspondence with Centlivres) (on file with author).

21. "Obituary, Dr. T. B. Davie," *Journal of the Royal Society of Arts* 104, no. 4967 (1955): 126–27, 127.

22. "An in Memoriam Address Given in Liverpool Cathedral on 23 December 1955 by the Vice-Chancellor of Liverpool University," *South African Medical Journal* 30 (March 1956): 275–76.

23. Phillips, *UCT Under Apartheid, Part 1*, 3–4; "Albert Centlivres, 79, Is Dead; Ex-Chief Justice of South Africa," *New York Times*, September 20, 1966, https://timesmachine.nytimes.com/timesmachine/1966/09/20/90226322.html?pageNumber=47 (detailing Justice Centlivres's role in overturning the act of Parliament that disenfranchised non-white voters).

24. Thompson, *A History of South Africa*, 197 (noting that Parliament passed the Extension of University Education Act in 1959, though the government came to power in 1948).

25. Phillips, *UCT Under Apartheid, Part 1*, 1.

26. This is also known as the Separate University Education Bill, which was introduced as a public law, improperly, because it affected private interests and thus required input from private parties affected; it was sent back to committee and then eventually passed in 1959 under the title "Extension of University Education Act No. 45," officially establishing separate university colleges for black students and prohibiting them from attending white universities, except under special ministerial permission; see "Academic Apart-

heid," *The Round Table* 50, no. 198 (1960): 134–39, 136–37, https://doi.org/10.1080/00358536008452233.

27. Zoom conversation between Albie Sachs and David Oppenheimer, April 8, 2021 (transcript on file with author).

28. Albert van der Sandt Centlivres and Richard Feetham, *The Open Universities in South Africa* (Johannesburg: Witwatersrand University Press, 1957), iii.

29. Van der Sandt Centlivres and Feetham, *The Open Universities in South Africa*, iii.

30. Van der Sandt Centlivres and Feetham, *The Open Universities in South Africa*, iii.

31. Van der Sandt Centlivres and Feetham, *The Open Universities in South Africa*, iii, iv.

32. Adam Sitze, "The University in the Mirror of Justices," *Yale Journal of Law and the Humanities* 33, no. 1 (2021): 175–222, 217 n.154, https://openyls.law.yale.edu/bitstream/handle/20.500.13051/18176/5_Sitze_University%20in%20the%20Mirror%20of%20Justices_PRINT_20220426.pdf?sequence=1&isAllowed=y.

33. Van der Sandt Centlivres and Feetham, *The Open Universities in South Africa*, 5.

34. Van der Sandt Centlivres and Feetham, *The Open Universities in South Africa*, 5–6.

35. Van der Sandt Centlivres and Feetham, *The Open Universities in South Africa*, 6.

36. Van der Sandt Centlivres and Feetham, *The Open Universities in South Africa*, 7, 41–43; *Sweatt v. Painter*, 339 U.S. 629, 635 (1950); *Brown v. Board of Education*, 347 U.S. 483, 495 (1954).

37. Van der Sandt Centlivres and Feetham, *The Open Universities in South Africa*, 11–12.

38. Van der Sandt Centlivres and Feetham, *The Open Universities in South Africa*, 14–15.

39. Van der Sandt Centlivres and Feetham, *The Open Universities in South Africa*, 13.

40. Van der Sandt Centlivres and Feetham, *The Open Universities in South Africa*, 29.

41. Van der Sandt Centlivres and Feetham, *The Open Universities in South Africa*, 34–35 (quotation reprinted with permission of Witwatersrand University Press).

42. *McLaurin v. Okla. State Regents for Higher Education*, 339 U.S. 637 (1950); *Sweatt v. Painter*, 339 U.S. 629 (1950); *Sipuel v. Bd. of Regents of Univ. of Okla.*, 332 U.S. 631, 631 (1948).

43. Transcript of Record at 534 (Testimony of Griswold), *Sipuel v. Bd. of Regents of the Univ. of Okla.*, 332 U.S. 631 (1948) (No. 369).

44. Brian Lapping, *Apartheid: A History* (New York: George Braziller, 1987), 135.

45. Sipho M. Pityana and Mamokgethi Phakeng, "Renaming Memorial Hall Sarah Baartman Hall," University of Cape Town, December 13, 2018, www.news.uct.ac.za/article/-2018–12–13-renaming-memorial-hall-sarah-baartman-hall. The earlier namesake of the hall was Leander Starr Jameson, a British colonialist who led a raid against Boer colonies in South Africa. The hall was renamed to instead honor a Khoi woman, Sarah Baartman, who was taken from her home and exhibited as a freak show attraction in England and France. Upon her death, European scientists dissected her and called her "the missing link between human and ape." In renaming the hall, UCT hoped to honor Sarah Baartman and "pay homage to the lives that were lost through slavery." Albert van der Sandt Centlivres, "Address by the Chancellor of the University of Cape Town at Jameson Memorial Hall," March 13, 1959, 1 (on file with author).

46. Van der Sandt Centlivres, "Address by the Chancellor of the University of Cape Town at Jameson Memorial Hall," 2.

47. See the following letters sent in response: Letter from Felix Frankfurter to Albert van der Sandt Centlivres, March 24, 1959 (on file with author); Letter from Nathan M. Pusey to Albert van der Sandt Centlivres, March 30, 1959 (on file with author); Letter from nineteen faculty members of Harvard University to Albert van der Sandt Centlivres, March 31, 1959 (on file with author).

48. Letter from Felix Frankfurter to Albert van der Sandt Centlivres, March 24, 1959 (on file with author).

49. Letter from Nathan M. Pusey to Albert van der Sandt Centlivres, March 30, 1959 (on file with author).

50. Letter from nineteen faculty members of Harvard University to Albert van der Sandt Centlivres, March 31, 1959 (on file with author).

51. Letter from Erwin Griswold to Felix Frankfurter, April 9, 1959 (on file with author).

52. Eric Pace, "Paul A. Freund, Authority on Constitution, Dies at 83," *New York Times,* February 6, 1992, https://timesmachine.nytimes.com/timesmachine/1992/02/06/258192.html?pageNumber=91; Paul A. Freund papers, HOLLIS 5999978, Harvard Law School Library, Historical and Special Collections, accessed February 22, 2023, https://id.lib.harvard.edu/ead/law00164/catalog.

53. Archibald Cox, "Archibald Cox: Oral History," interview by Thomas Hilbink, June 20, 2000, transcript of Session 2, www.columbia.edu/cu/lweb/digital/collections/oral_hist/cox/interview.html.

54. Letter from nineteen faculty members of Harvard University to Albert van der Sandt Centlivres, March 31, 1959 (on file with author); Charles J. Ogletree, "[Archibald Cox]," *Harvard Law Review* 118, no. 1 (2004): 14–18, 14, www.jstor.org/stable/4093276; Victor S. Navasky, *Kennedy Justice* (New York: Atheneum, 1971), 292; "About Archibald Cox," Columbia University Libraries Oral History Research Office, accessed July 10, 2023, www.columbia.edu/cu/lweb/digital/collections/oral_hist/cox/about.html (listing

some important civil rights cases that Cox argued and won); Archibald Cox, "Archibald Cox: Oral History," interview by Thomas Hilbink, June 20, 2000, transcript of Session 2, www.columbia.edu/cu/lweb/digital/collections/oral_hist/cox/interview.html; Seth P. Waxman, "Twins at Birth: Civil Rights and the Role of the Solicitor General," *Indiana Law Journal* 75 (2000): 1297–1316, https://scholarship.law.georgetown.edu/cgi/viewcontent.cgi?article=1281&context=facpub; Ken Gormley, *Archibald Cox: Conscience of a Nation* (Reading: Addison-Wesley, 1997), 147.

55. Lapping, *Apartheid: A History*, 135.

56. Van der Sandt Centlivres, "T. B. Davie Memorial Lecture."

57. Van der Sandt Centlivres, "T. B. Davie Memorial Lecture."

58. Albert van der Sandt Centlivres, "We Fight for Our Rights," in *UCT at 150: Reflections*, ed. Alan Lennox-Short and David Welsh (Cape Town: David Philip, 1979), 17.

59. Van der Sandt Centlivres, "We Fight for Our Rights," 17–18.

60. Van der Sandt Centlivres, "We Fight for Our Rights," 19 (discussing Albert van der Sandt Centlivres and Richard Feetham, *The Open Universities in South Africa*); van der Sandt Centlivres, "We Fight for Our Rights," 19.

61. Phillips, *UCT Under Apartheid, Part 1*, 4; Robert F. Kennedy, "Day of Affirmation Address," University of Cape Town, South Africa (speech, June 6, 1966), www.jfklibrary.org/learn/about-jfk/the-kennedy-family/robert-f-kennedy/robert-f-kennedy-speeches/day-of-affirmation-address-university-of-capetown-capetown-south-africa-june-6-1966; Robert C. Byrd, "Robert F. Kennedy, June 6, 1966: Keynote Address: Day of Reaffirmation of Academic and Human Freedom (Cape Town, South Africa)," in *The Senate: 1789–1989*, vol. 3, *Classic Speeches, 1830–1993*, ed. Wendy Wolf (Washington, D.C.: U.S. Government Printing Office, 1994), 709–18, https://archive.org/details/senate17891989clo3robe/page/708/mode/2up.

62. Margaret Marshall, "A Conversation with Margaret Marshall," interview by Linda Greenhouse, Kennedy Library Forums, October 4, 2011, www.jfklibrary.org/events-and-awards/forums/past-forums/transcripts/a-conversation-with-margaret-marshall-kennedy-library-forums.

63. "Women Inspiring Change: Margaret Marshall," Harvard Law School, March 1, 2014, https://orgs.law.harvard.edu/womeninspiringchange/2014/03/01/margaret-marshall/.

64. "Margaret H. Marshall, a Law Partner, Is Wed to Anthony Lewis, a Columnist," *New York Times*, September 24, 1984, https://timesmachine.nytimes.com/timesmachine/1984/09/24/issue.html.

65. Mark Memmott, "Looking Back: RFK's 'Ripple of Hope' Speech in South Africa," NPR, June 30, 2013, www.npr.org/sections/thetwo-way/2013/06/30/197342656/looking-back-rfks-ripple-of-hope-speech-in-south-africa.

66. Kennedy, "Day of Affirmation Address."

67. Kennedy, "Day of Affirmation Address" (see references to "Chancellor" in the speech).

68. "Albert Centlivres, 79, Is Dead."

69. Academic Freedom Committee, *The Open Universities in South Africa and Academic Freedom, 1957–1974: A Review* (Johannesburg: Juta, 1974), 13; Erwin N. Griswold, "Day of Affirmation Address, University of Cape Town" (speech, June 23, 1967) (on file with author).

Chapter Nine. The Four Foundations of Academic Freedom

1. Brad Snyder, *Democratic Justice: Felix Frankfurter, the Supreme Court, and the Making of the Liberal Establishment* (New York: Norton, 2022), 9–10, 13–16, 24.

2. Bruce Allen Murphy and Arthur Owens, "Felix Frankfurter (1882–1965)," in *Great American Judges: An Encyclopedia*, ed. John R. Vile (Santa Barbara: ABC-CLIO, 2003), 1:264–72, 264; but see Snyder, *Democratic Justice*, 154; "Secretary to Justice Brandeis Nearly Ties His Harvard Rank," *Christian Science Monitor*, September 12, 1927, https://archive.org/details/per_christian-science-monitor_1927-09-12_19_243; Brad Snyder, "The Judicial Genealogy (and Mythology) of John Roberts: Clerkships from Gray to Brandeis to Friendly to Roberts," *Ohio State Law Journal* 76, no. 6 (2010): 1149–1243, 1170; James M. Landis, "Mr. Justice Brandeis and the Harvard Law School," *Harvard Law Review* 55, no. 2 (1941): 184–90.

3. Snyder, *Democratic Justice*, 7, 26, 200; Archibald Cox, "Archibald Cox: Oral History," interview by Thomas Hilbink, June 20, 2000, transcript of Session 1, www.columbia.edu/cu/lweb/digital/collections/oral_hist/cox/interview.html.

4. "Biographies of the Secretaries of State: Henry Lewis Stimson (1867–1950)," Office of the Historian, accessed July 19, 2023, https://history.state.gov/departmenthistory/people/stimson-henry-lewis.

5. Snyder, *Democratic Justice*, 27–28, 45–46, 54, 58–61; Bruce Allen Murphy, *The Brandeis/Frankfurter Connection: The Secret Political Activities of Two Supreme Court Justices* (New York: Oxford University Press, 1982), 38–39; Melvin I. Urofsky and David W. Levy, eds., *Letters of Louis D. Brandeis*, vol. 3, *1913–1915* (Albany: State University of New York Press, 1973), 134–36, 209 (letters from Brandeis to Winfred Thaxter Denison, July 12, 1913; Brandeis to Roscoe Pound, July 12, 1913; Brandeis to Pound, November 5, 1913).

6. Snyder, *Democratic Justice*, 72; Murphy, *The Brandeis/Frankfurter Connection*, 38–45.

7. Edmund Fuller, "Oliver Wendell Holmes, Jr.," in *Encyclopaedia Britannica*, last modified March 4, 2023, www.britannica.com/biography/Oliver-Wendell-Holmes-Jr.

8. Snyder, *Democratic Justice*, 332–33; Associated Press, "Justice Brandeis Resigns from Supreme Court Bench," *Burlington Free Press*, February 14, 1939.

9. Snyder, *Democratic Justice*, 85, 89–95 (excerpts of letters expressing Frankfurter's desire for even members of the Industrial Workers of the World to get a fair trial), 123–25, 695–96.

10. Snyder, *Democratic Justice*, 117; H. N. Hirsch, *The Enigma of Felix Frank-furter* (New York: Basic Books, 1981), 67–70.

11. Snyder, *Democratic Justice*, 117 (citing a letter Frankfurter wrote to his wife).

12. Snyder, *Democratic Justice*, 119–20.

13. Hirsch, *The Enigma of Felix Frankfurter*, 70; Harlan Buddington Phillips and Felix Frankfurter, *Felix Frankfurter Reminisces* (New York: Reynal & Co., 1960), 176.

14. Snyder, *Democratic Justice*, 126.

15. Hirsch, *The Enigma of Felix Frankfurter*, 69, 70; see also Abbott Lawrence Lowell, "President's Report, 1916–17," in *Reports of the President and the Treasurer of Harvard College, 1916–17* (Cambridge: Harvard University Press, 1918), 5–27, https://babel.hathitrust.org/cgi/pt?id=nyp.33433076009 350&view=1up&seq=13.

16. Snyder, *Democratic Justice*, 126; Henry Adams Yeomans, *Abbott Lawrence Lowell, 1856–1943* (Cambridge: Harvard University Press, 1948), 319 (listing the judges presiding over the trial). The voting panel here was comprised of eleven men: Francis J. Swayze (justice of the New Jersey Supreme Court), Benjamin Cardozo (judge of the New York Court of Appeals and later a justice of the U.S. Supreme Court), William H. Dunbar (a former law partner of Brandeis), Robert Grant (judge of Probate Court and Court of Insolvency in Boston), Augustus N. Hand (judge of the Southern District of New York and brother to Learned Hand), Julian W. Mack (judge of the Seventh Circuit), Langdon Marvin (a former law partner of Franklin Delano Roosevelt), James M. Morton, Jr. (judge of the District of Massachusetts), William Thomas (of San Francisco), Henry N. Sheldon (retired justice of the Massachusetts Supreme Court), and Jeremiah Smith (of Boston).

17. Snyder, *Democratic Justice*, 125, 126 (citing "Editorial Paragraphs," *The Nation*, August 17, 1921), 324.

18. Snyder, *Democratic Justice*, 125, 126 (citing "Editorial Paragraphs," *The Nation*, August 17, 1921), 324; Edward Shils, "The Career of Harold Laski," *New Criterion*, April 1994, https://newcriterion.com/issues/1994/4/the-career-of-harold-laski.

19. Felix Frankfurter, "The Case of Sacco and Vanzetti," *The Atlantic*, March 1927, www.theatlantic.com/magazine/archive/1927/03/the-case-of-sacco-and-vanzetti/306625/; Felix Frankfurter, *The Case of Sacco and Vanzetti: A Critical Analysis for Lawyers and Laymen* (Boston: Little, Brown, 1927).

20. Annika Neklason, "Sacco and Vanzetti's Trial of the Century Exposed Injustice in 1920s America," *Smithsonian Magazine*, May 27, 2021, www.smithsonian-mag.com/history/sacco-and-vanzettis-trial-century-exposed-injustice-1920s-america-180977843/; "Sacco & Vanzetti: The Lowell Committee," Mass.gov, accessed July 19, 2023, www.mass.gov/info-details/sacco-vanzetti-the-lowell-committee.

21. Snyder, *Democratic Justice*, 173–74.

22.   "Sacco & Vanzetti: The Lowell Committee," Mass.gov, accessed July 19, 2023, www.mass.gov/info-details/sacco-vanzetti-the-lowell-committee.

23.   Letter from Harold J. Laski to Oliver Wendell Holmes, Jr., September 8, 1927, in *Holmes-Laski Letters: The Correspondence of Mr. Justice Holmes and Harold J. Laski*, vol. 2, *1926–1935*, ed. Mark DeWolfe Howe (Cambridge: Harvard University Press, 1953), 968–70, 968; Hirsch, *The Enigma of Felix Frankfurter*, 92–93.

24.   "Sacco & Vanzetti: The Executions & Funeral," Mass.gov, accessed July 20, 2023, www.mass.gov/info-details/sacco-vanzetti-the-executions-funeral.

25.   Hirsch, *The Enigma of Felix Frankfurter*, 92.

26.   Hirsch, *The Enigma of Felix Frankfurter*, 93.

27.   John Stuart Mill, *Inaugural Address at St. Andrews* (London: Longmans, Green, Reader, and Dyer, 1867), 25, https://archive.org/details/inauguralad dresoomillgoog/mode/2up.

28.   Snyder, *Democratic Justice*, 239–63.

29.   Snyder, *Democratic Justice*, 310–11.

30.   Snyder, *Democratic Justice*, 210–18, 239–63, 310–11, 313–28; see also Franklyn Waltman, "Looking Forward," *The Republican*, February 23, 1939, https://chroniclingamerica.loc.gov/lccn/sn88065202/1939-02-23/ed-1/seq-6/; Arthur Hachten, "Anti-Jewish Move Halted at Hearing," *Washington Times*, January 10, 1939, https://chroniclingamerica.loc.gov/lccn/sn84026749/1939-01-10/ed-1/seq-1/.

31.   Snyder, *Democratic Justice*, 313–28.

32.   Hirsch, *The Enigma of Felix Frankfurter*, 183; Snyder, *Democratic Justice*, 393.

33.   Wallace Mendelson, "Mr. Justice Frankfurter on Administrative Law," *Journal of Politics* 19, no. 3 (1957): 441–60, 444–47, www.jstor.org/stable/2126769. See for example Snyder, *Democratic Justice*.

34.   Snyder, *Democratic Justice*, 630; see also Marjorie Heins, *Priests of Our Democracy: The Supreme Court, Academic Freedom, and the Anti-Communist Purge* (New York: New York University Press, 2013).

35.   Snyder, *Democratic Justice*, 117, 630.

36.   Hirsch, *The Enigma of Felix Frankfurter*, 142–53.

37.   Louis Menand, *The Metaphysical Club* (London: HarperCollinsPublishers, 2001), 256–57.

38.   Peter Gibbon, "John Dewey: Portrait of a Progressive Thinker," *Humanities* 40, no. 2 (2019), www.neh.gov/article/john-dewey-portrait-progressive-thinker.

39.   John Dewey, *The School and Society* (Chicago: University of Chicago Press, 1900), 16, 126.

40.   John Dewey, *Democracy and Education: An Introduction to the Philosophy of Education* (New York: Macmillan, 1921), 25–26.

41.   Dewey, *Democracy and Education*, 6; see also Michele S. Moses and Mitchell J. Chang, "Toward a Deeper Understanding of the Diversity Rationale," *Educational Researcher* 35, no. 1 (2006): 6–11, 8.

42. Kelly Vaughan, "Progressive Education and Racial Justice: Examining the Work of John Dewey," *Education and Culture* 34, no. 2 (2018): 39–68, 44–46; Susan D. Carle, "John Dewey and the Early NAACP: Developing a Progressive Discourse on Racial Injustice, 1909–1921," in *Dewey's Enduring Impact: Essays on America's Philosopher*, ed. John R. Shook and Paul Kurtz (Amherst: Prometheus Books, 2011), 249–62, 249; see also Letter from John Dewey to National Kindergarten Association, April 11, 1914, in Larry Hickman, ed., *The Correspondence of John Dewey, 1871–1918* (Charlottesville: Intelex, 2008), letter no. 04876.

43. Craig Kridel and Robert V. Bullough, Jr., "The Educational Context of the Eight-Year Study," in *Stories of the Eight-Year Study: Reexamining Secondary Education in America* (New York: State University of New York Press, 2007), 25–37, 26.

44. Jay Martin, *The Education of John Dewey: A Biography* (New York: Columbia University Press, 2003), 248–49.

45. Gibbon, "John Dewey: Portrait of a Progressive Thinker."

46. Oliver Wendell Holmes, "The Black Book," in *The Black Book of Justice Holmes: Text Transcript & Commentary*, ed. Michael H. Hoeflich and Ross E. Davies (Clark: Talbot Publishing, 2021) 1–497, 385; John Dewey, *German Philosophy and Politics* (New York: Henry Holt, 1915), 78.

47. Snyder, *Democratic Justice*, 511–13.

48. Letter from Albert van der Sandt Centlivres to Felix Frankfurter, undated (on file with author).

49. Letter from Erwin Griswold to Felix Frankfurter, October 6, 1952 (on file with author).

50. Letter from Felix Frankfurter to Albert van der Sandt Centlivres, March 3, 1953 (on file with author); see also "Obituary, Dr. T. B. Davie," *Journal of the Royal Society of Arts* 104, no. 4967 (1955): 126–27, 127, www.jstor.org/stable/41364833.

51. Adam Sitze, "The University in the Mirror of Justices." *Yale Journal of Law and the Humanities* 33, no. 1 (2021): 175–222, 217 n.154. https://openyls.law.yale.edu/bitstream/handle/20.500.13051/18176/5_Sitze_University%20in%20the%20Mirror%20of%20Justices_PRINT_20220426.pdf. See "Program of a Conference Concerning Government Under Law on the Occasion of the Bicentennial of John Marshall," Harvard Law School, 3, 5 (September 22, 1955) (on file with author); see also Arthur E. Sutherland, ed., *Government Under Law: A Conference Held at Harvard Law School on the Occasion of the Bicentennial of John Marshall Chief Justice of the United States, 1801–1835* (Cambridge: Harvard University Press, 1956), 3–34, 398–400, 423–52, 552–55 (transcript of speeches by Centlivres, Frankfurter, and Griswold); Arthur E. Sutherland, ed., *Government Under Law: A Conference Held at Harvard Law School on the Occasion of the Bicentennial of John Marshall Chief Justice of the United States, 1801–1835* (Cambridge: Harvard University Press, 1956), 3–34, 398–400, 423–52, 552–55 (transcript of speeches by Centlivres, Frankfurter, and Griswold).

52. Albert van der Sandt Centlivres and Richard Feetham, *The Open Universities in South Africa* (Johannesburg: Witwatersrand University Press, 1957).

53. "Sweezy v. New Hampshire," accessed July 20, 2023, www.oyez.org/cases/1956/175; *Sweezy v. New Hampshire*, 354 U.S. 234 (1957).

54. *Wieman v. Updegraff*, 344 U.S. 183, 196 (1952); the quoted language is the title of a leading study of academic freedom by Marjorie Heins, *Priests of Our Democracy: The Supreme Court, Academic Freedom, and the Anti-Communist Purge* (New York: New York University Press, 2013).

55. "Joseph R. McCarthy: A Featured Biography," United States Senate, accessed July 20, 2023, www.senate.gov/senators/FeaturedBios/Featured_Bio_McCarthy.htm; *Sweezy v. New Hampshire*, 354 U.S. 234, 236.

56. Louis Uchitelle, "Paul Sweezy, 93, Marxist Publisher and Economist, Dies," *New York Times*, March 2, 2004, www.nytimes.com/2004/03/02/business/paul-sweezy-93-marxist-publisher-and-economist-dies.html; see also Brief for Appellant at 5, *Sweezy v. New Hampshire*, 354 U.S. 234 (1957) (No. 175).

57. *Sweezy v. New Hampshire*, 354 U.S. 234, 239 n. 6, 241 n.7, 244.

58. John Bellamy Foster, "The Commitment of an Intellectual: Paul M. Sweezy (1910–2004)," *Monthly Review*, October 1, 2004, https://monthlyreview.org/2004/10/01/the-commitment-of-an-intellectual-paul-m-sweezy-1910–2004/.

59. *Sweezy v. New Hampshire*, 354 U.S. 234, 244–45, 255.

60. Louis H. Pollak, "Thomas I. Emerson: Pillar of the Bill of Rights," *Yale Law Journal* 101, no. 2 (1991): 321–26, www.jstor.org/stable/796803; *Sweezy v. New Hampshire*, 354 U.S. 234, 235; Brief for The Committee of Law Teachers Against Segregation in Legal Education at 36–40, *Sweatt v. Painter*, 339 U.S. 629 (1950) (No. 44).

61. *Sweezy v. New Hampshire*, 354 U.S. 234.

62. *Sweezy v. New Hampshire*, 354 U.S. 234, 250.

63. *Sweezy v. New Hampshire*, 354 U.S. 234, 253–55.

64. Heins, *Priests of Our Democracy*, 179–82.

65. *Sweezy v. New Hampshire*, 354 U.S. 234, 257–59 (Frankfurter, J., concurring).

66. Compare *Sweezy v. New Hampshire*, 354 U.S. 234, 260 (1957), with Snyder, *Democratic Justice*, 117.

67. *Sweezy v. New Hampshire*, 354 U.S. 234, 262–63, citing van der Sandt Centlivres and Feetham, *The Open Universities in South Africa*, 10–12.

68. *Sweezy v. New Hampshire*, 354 U.S. 234, 261–63, 266–67.

69. See Letter from Albert van der Sandt Centlivres to Felix Frankfurter, June 29, 1957.

70. Letter from Albert van der Sandt Centlivres to Felix Frankfurter, June 29, 1957; Frankfurter's files, physically stored at the U.S. Library of Congress, can also be accessed behind a paywall via ProQuest History Vault, https://proquest.libguides.com/historyvault/lawandsociety. See James Reston, "High Court Decision Put a Strong Stress on Academic Liberty," *New York*

Times, June 19, 1957; Price Day, "Issues of Freedom Elsewhere: A Voice from Africa," *Baltimore Sun*, June 24, 1957; "Court on Freedom in S.A. Universities," *Cape Times*, June 27, 1957. As the case was under consideration, coverage of the book appeared in unsigned stories in the *Philadelphia Tribune* ("Academic Freedom," *Philadelphia Tribune*, February 16, 1957) and the *Chicago Defender* ("African Students Buck Plans for Segregation," *Chicago Defender*, March 9, 1957).

71. *Keyishian v. Bd. of Regents*, 385 U.S. 589, 591–93 (1967).
72. *Keyishian v. Bd. of Regents*, 385 U.S. 589, 603.
73. *Sweezy v. New Hampshire*, 354 U.S. 234, 263 (Frankfurter, J., concurring, quoting from van der Sandt Centlivres and Feetham, *The Open Universities in South Africa*).

Chapter Ten. The Legal Brief That Rewrote Affirmative Action Law

1. Ken Gormley, *Archibald Cox: Conscience of a Nation* (Reading: Addison-Wesley, 1997), 3–5, 31.
2. Gormley, *Archibald Cox*, 38–40.
3. Gormley, *Archibald Cox*, 56–57, 59–60.
4. Gormley, *Archibald Cox*, 63–78, 83–84, 97–111.
5. Gormley, *Archibald Cox*, 112–22.
6. Anthony Lewis, "Cox of Harvard to Be Appointed," *New York Times*, December 28, 1960, www.nytimes.com/1960/12/28/archives/cox-of-harvard-to-be-appointed-accepts-solicitor-generals-office.html.
7. Among the most important works on U.S. affirmative action is William G. Bowen and Derek Bok, *The Shape of the River: Long-Term Consequences of Considering Race in College and University Admissions* (Princeton: Princeton University Press, 1998).
8. Lincoln Caplan, *The Tenth Justice: The Solicitor General and the Rule of Law* (New York: Knopf, 1987), 186–94; Gormley, *Archibald Cox*, 156–57, 161–81.
9. Anthony Ripley, "Archibald Cox Appointed Prosecutor for Watergate," *New York Times*, May 19, 1973, www.nytimes.com/1973/05/19/archives/archibald-cox-appointed-prosecutor-for-watergate-richardson.html.
10. Seymour M. Hersh, "Airline Discloses Illegal Donation to '72 Nixon Drive," *New York Times*, July 7, 1973; Carl Bernstein and Bob Woodward, "FBI Finds Nixon Aides Sabotaged Democrats," *Washington Post*, October 10, 1972; Carl Bernstein and Bob Woodward, "Dean Alleges Nixon Knew of Cover-up Plan," *Washington Post*, June 3, 1973; Eileen Shanahan, "Nixon and the Tax Laws," *New York Times*, December 11, 1973; Paul L. Montgomery, "The Case Against Richard Nixon: A Catalog of Charges and His Replies," *New York Times*, August 9, 1974.
11. Susanna McBee, "Court Battle Set as Nixon Defies Subpoenas," *Washington Post*, July 27, 1973.

12. Kenneth B. Noble, "Bork Irked by Emphasis on His Role in Watergate," *New York Times*, July 2, 1987, www.nytimes.com/1987/07/02/us/bork-irked-by-emphasis-on-his-role-in-watergate.html.

13. "Archibald Cox, Special Watergate Prosecutor, Dies at 92," *New York Times*, May 31, 2004, www.nytimes.com/2004/05/31/us/archibald-cox-special-watergate-prosecutor-dies-at-92.html; Douglas E. Kneeland, "Nixon Discharges Cox for Defiance; Abolishes Watergate Task Force; Richardson and Ruckelshaus Out," *New York Times*, October 20, 1972, https://archive.nytimes.com/www.nytimes.com/learning/general/onthisday/big/1020.html.

14. John Herbers, "Nixon Resigns," *New York Times*, August 8, 1974, https://archive.nytimes.com/www.nytimes.com/learning/general/onthisday/big/0808.html.

15. Derek Bok, email message to author, May 13, 2013, subject line: "I'm hoping you can help me with a research project on the diversity justification for affirmative action" (on file with author).

16. *DeFunis v. Odegaard*, 416 U.S. 312, 314 (1974).

17. *Defunis*, 416 U.S. at 314–15.

18. "Daniel Steiner Dies at 72," *Harvard Gazette*, June 15, 2006, https://news.harvard.edu/gazette/story/2006/06/daniel-steiner-dies-at-72/.

19. James (Jim) N. Bierman, telephone interview with author, June 14, 2016.

20. Sam Roberts, "Walter J. Leonard, Pioneer of Affirmative Action in Harvard Admissions, Dies at 86," *New York Times*, December 16, 2015, www.nytimes.com/2015/12/17/education/walter-j-leonard-pioneer-of-affirmative-action-in-harvard-admissions-dies-at-86.html; Geoffrey D. Garin, "Bok's Tough Bargainer in the Action Office," *Harvard Crimson*, June 13, 1974, www.thecrimson.com/article/1974/6/13/boks-tough-bargainer-in-the-action.

21. Bierman, telephone interview.

22. Bierman, telephone interview.

23. The letter was initially printed in mimeograph form. It was then republished in the *Atlantic Monthly* and in a book by King about the Birmingham campaign. Martin Luther King, Jr., "The Negro Is Your Brother," *Atlantic Monthly*, August, 1963, 78, www.theatlantic.com/magazine/archive/1963/08/the-negro-is-your-brother/658583/.

24. Brief for a Group of Law School Deans as Amici Curiae at 1, *DeFunis*, 416 U.S. 312, republished in *Defunis Versus Odegaard and the University of Washington: The University Admissions Case, The Record*, vol. 2, ed. Ann Fagan Ginger (Dobbs Ferry: Oceana Publications, 1974), 725–56; Brief of Amici Curiae the Mexican American Legal Defense and Educational Fund et al. at 16–34, *DeFunis*, 416 U.S. 312.

25. Brief for the Association of American Law Schools as Amicus Curiae at 14, *DeFunis*, 416 U.S. 312.

26. Brief of the Council on Legal Education Opportunity as Amicus Curiae at 3–4, *DeFunis*, 416 U.S. 312.

27. Brief of the American Bar Association as Amicus Curiae in Support of Respondents at 15–17, *DeFuni*, 416 U.S. 312.
28. Brief of Law School Admission Council Amicus Curiae at 23–26, *DeFunis*, 416 U.S. 312.
29. Lyndon B. Johnson, "Commencement Address at Howard University" (speech, Howard University, June 4, 1965), American Presidency Project, www.presidency.ucsb.edu/documents/commencement-address-howard-university-fulfill-these-rights.
30. *Regents of Univ. of Cal. v. Bakke*, 438 U.S. 265, 321 (1978); Brief of the President and Fellows of Harvard College as Amicus Curiae at 16–17, *DeFunis v. Odegaard*, 416 U.S. 312 (1974) (No. 73–235).
31. Justice Powell's *DeFunis v. Odegaard* File, Box 17, Powell Papers, Lewis F. Powell, Jr., Archives, Washington and Lee University School of Law, Lexington, Virginia, https://scholarlycommons.law.wlu.edu/casefiles/43/ (hereinafter Justice Powell's *DeFunis* archive).
32. John C. Jeffries, Memorandum to Justice Powell, February 12, 1974, in Justice Powell's *DeFunis* archive at 32, https://scholarlycommons.law.wlu.edu/casefiles/43/.
33. Anthony Lewis, "The Legality of Racial Quotas: Who Will Pay for the Injustice of the Past?," *New York Times*, March 3, 1974, www.nytimes.com/1974/03/03/archives/the-legality-of-racial-quotas-tough-intellectual-issues.html (reprinted in Justice Powell's *DeFunis* archive at 45).
34. Jerrold K. Footlick, "Justice: Racism in Reverse," *Newsweek*, 1974 (reprinted in Justice Powell's *DeFunis* archive at 68; identifying Cox as a principal amicus brief author and quoting the language from the Cox brief about the "farm boy from Idaho").
35. Justice Powell's *Regents of University of California v. Bakke* File, Box 469–72, Powell Papers, The Lewis F. Powell, Jr., Archives, Washington and Lee University School of Law, Lexington, Virginia, https://scholarlycommons.law.wlu.edu/casefiles/114/ (hereinafter Justice Powell's *Bakke* archive).
36. Bob Comfort, Memorandum to Justice Powell, August 29, 1977, in Justice Powell's *Bakke* archive, 15–92, https://scholarlycommons.law.wlu.edu/casefiles/114/ (hereinafter Comfort *Bakke* Memo); Comfort *Bakke* Memo at 30–40, 55, 58–61 (pages correspond to the pagination on the memo; appearing as pp. 49–61, 76, 79–82 in pdf format of the archive).
37. Comfort *Bakke* Memo at 58 (page corresponds to the pagination on the memo).
38. Comfort *Bakke* Memo at 58 (page corresponds to the pagination on the memo).
39. Brief of Columbia University et al. as Amici Curiae at Appendix 1, *Bakke*, 438 U.S. 265.
40. Richard A. Posner, "The DeFunis Case and the Constitutionality of Preferential Treatment of Racial Minorities," *Supreme Court Review* 1974 (1974): 1–32, 7.
41. Ginger, *Defunis Versus Odegaard*, 2:725–56.

42. *Landmark Briefs and Arguments of the Supreme Court of the United States: Constitutional Law: 1974 Term Supplement,* ed. Philip B. Kurland and Gerhard Casper (Arlington: University Publications of America, 1975).

43. A 2021 article in the *New Yorker* by Nicholas Lemann and a 2022 *New York Times Magazine* article by Emily Bazelon discuss the importance of the Cox brief. Both rely on my work and on interviews with me. See Nicholas Lemann, "Can Affirmative Action Survive?," *New Yorker,* July 26, 2021, www.newyorker.com/magazine/2021/08/02/can-affirmative-action-survive; and Emily Bazelon, "Why Is Affirmative Action in Peril? One Man's Decision," *New York Times Magazine,* February 15, 2023, www.nytimes.com/2023/02/15/magazine/affirmative-action-supreme-court.html.

Chapter Eleven. Diversity and the *Bakke* Case

1. *Regents of the Univ. of Cal. v. Bakke,* 438 U.S. 265 (1978). Portions of this chapter are substantially drawn from my earlier paper: David B. Oppenheimer, "Archibald Cox and the Diversity Justification for Affirmative Action," *Virginia Journal of Social Policy and the Law* 25, no. 2 (2018): 157–203, 196–98.

2. *Bakke,* 438 U.S. at 269–72.

3. *DeFunis v. Odegaard,* 416 U.S. 312, 317 (1974); *Bakke,* 438 U.S. at 276.

4. Howard Ball, *The* Bakke *Case: Race, Education, and Affirmative Action* (Lawrence: University Press of Kansas, 2000), 208.

5. See *Bakke,* 438 U.S. at 277 n.7; Joel Dreyfuss and Charles Lawrence III, *The* Bakke *Case: The Politics of Inequality* (New York: Harcourt Brace Jovanovich, 1979), 16.

6. Timothy J. O'Neill, *Bakke & the Politics of Equality: Friends and Foes in the Classroom of Litigation* (Middletown: Wesleyan University Press, 1987), 21–27. *Bakke,* 438 U.S. at 272, 276–77 nn. 6 and 8.

7. *Bakke,* 438 U.S. at 277–80 n.7.

8. Ken Gormley, *Archibald Cox: Conscience of a Nation* (Reading: Addison-Wesley, 1997), 394–95.

9. *Bakke,* 438 U.S. at 306.

10. Andrew A. Sorensen, "Black Americans and the Medical Profession, 1930–1970," *Journal of Negro Education* 41, no. 4 (1972): 337–42, https://doi.org/10.2307/2966980.

11. *United Steelworkers v. Weber,* 443 U.S. 193 (1979); see also *Johnson v. Transportation Agency,* 480 U.S. 616 (1987).

12. *Bakke,* 438 U.S. at 269–72, 356–57, 404–6, 421.

13. Louis Kohlmeier, "Justice Powell: For Business, a Friend in Court," *New York Times,* March 14, 1976, www.nytimes.com/1976/03/14/archives/justice-powell-for-business-a-friend-in-court.html.

14. Linda Greenhouse, "Lewis Powell, Crucial Centrist Justice, Dies at 90," *New York Times,* August 26, 1998, www.nytimes.com/1998/08/26/us/lewis-powell-crucial-centrist-justice-dies-at-90.html.

15. Anders Walker, "A Lawyer Looks at Civil Disobedience: How Lewis F. Powell, Jr., Reframed the Civil Rights Revolution," *University of Colorado Law Review* 86, no. 4 (2015): 1229–72, 1230–32, https://heinonline.org/HOL/P?h=hein.journals/ucollr86&i=1281.

16. John C. Jeffries, Jr., *Justice Lewis F. Powell, Jr.* (New York: Charles Scribner's Sons, 1994), 139–73.

17. Asad Rahim, "Diversity to Deradicalize," *California Law Review* 108, no. 5 (October 2020): 1423–86, 1435, https://doi.org/10.15779/Z38NZ80Q8S.

18. Jeffries, *Justice Lewis F. Powell*, 140–41.

19. Rahim, "Diversity to Deradicalize," 1474.

20. For example, the ABA's new Code of Professional Responsibility, adopted in 1969, was seen as a conservative effort to block the growth of public interest law. See, e.g., John F. Sutton, Jr., "How Vulnerable Is the Code of Professional Responsibility," *North Carolina Law Review* 57, no. 4 (1979): 497–518, 497–98, https://heinonline.org/HOL/LandingPage?handle=hein.journals/nclr57&div=42&id=&page=; Harold Brown, "ABA Code of Professional Responsibility: In Defense of Mediocrity," *Valparaiso University Law Review* 5, no. 1 (1970): 95–108, 105–8, https://scholar.valpo.edu/cgi/viewcontent.cgi?article=2076&context=vulr; Jerold Auerbach, *Unequal Justice* (New York: Oxford University Press, 1976), 268–74; Jeffries, *Justice Lewis F. Powell*, 195; Auerbach, *Unequal Justice*, 268–74.

21. Lewis F. Powell, Memorandum to Eugene B. Sydnor, Jr., "Attack on American Free Enterprise System," August 23, 1971, 1, https://scholarlycommons.law.wlu.edu/cgi/viewcontent.cgi?article=1000&context=powellmemo.

22. Evan Mandery, "Why There's No Liberal Federalist Society," *Politico Magazine*, January 23, 2019, www.politico.com/magazine/story/2019/01/23/why-theres-no-liberal-federalist-society-224033/.

23. Rahim, "Diversity to Deradicalize," 1476.

24. Rahim, "Diversity to Deradicalize," 1427.

25. Rahim, "Diversity to Deradicalize," 1427–30.

26. Walker, "Lawyer Looks at Civil Disobedience," 1253–55.

27. Jeffries, *Justice Lewis F. Powell*, 228–33.

28. *Regents of the Univ. of Cal. v. Bakke*, 438 U.S. 265, 289 (1978).

29. See *Bakke*, 438 U.S. at 269–72, 289.

30. *Bakke*, 438 U.S. at 306–16, 321–24. Although the UC Davis brief had included a section on the diversity justification for affirmative action and the amicus brief for the four elite colleges had framed the diversity argument as Cox had developed it in the *DeFunis* case, it was not raised at oral argument, either by Cox or through the justices' questions. We know from Justice Powell's archives that he intended to ask Cox how Harvard went about choosing an Idaho farm boy over a Boston first-family son and whether there was a guarantee of a certain number of seats for farm boys. But he didn't get to this question before time ran out. See Justice Powell's *Bakke* archive, folder 4 (appearing as p. 155 in the pdf format of the archive).

31. See *Bakke*, 438 U.S. at 312.

32. *Bakke*, 438 U.S. at 311–13.

33. *Bakke*, 438 U.S. at 312 n.48.

34. *Bakke*, 438 U.S. at 316–19.

35. Bill Peterson, Nancy Ross, Jack Egan, Helen Dewar, and James L. Rowe, Jr., "Bakke Decision May Change Very Little," *Washington Post*, June 29, 1978, www.washingtonpost.com/archive/politics/1978/06/29/bakke-decision-may-change-very-little/c5a4dd25-93d7-417a-bd56-a1532ac950b3/.

36. But see Guido Calabresi, "Bakke as Pseudo-Tragedy," *Catholic University Law Review* 28, no. 3 (1979): 427–44, 430–31, https://scholarship.law.edu/cgi/viewcontent.cgi?article=2367&context=lawreview; Robert Bork, "The Unpersuasive Bakke Decision," *Wall Street Journal*, July 21, 1978.

37. Laurence Tribe, "Perspectives on Bakke: Equal Protection, Procedural Fairness, or Structural Justice," *Harvard Law Review* 92, no. 4 (1979): 864–77, 864.

38. Vincent Blasi, "Bakke as Precedent: Does Mr. Justice Powell Have a Theory?," *California Law Review* 67, no. 1 (1979): 33, 67.

39. Calabresi, "Bakke as Pseudo-Tragedy," 430–31; Bork, "Unpersuasive Bakke Decision."

40. Dreyfuss and Lawrence, *The Bakke Case*, 126–27, 211–12.

41. Bernard Schwartz, *Behind Bakke: Affirmative Action and the Supreme Court* (New York: New York University Press, 1988), 151–56, https://heinonline.org/HOL/P?h=hein.beal/behbkkeooo1&i=3.

42. Schwartz, *Behind Bakke*, 153–54.

43. Ball, *The Bakke Case*, 122–33.

44. Jeffries, *Justice Lewis F. Powell*, 680.

45. See Justice Powell's *DeFunis v. Odegaard* File, Box 17, Powell Papers, Lewis F. Powell, Jr., Archives, Washington and Lee University School of Law, Lexington, Virginia, https://scholarlycommons.law.wlu.edu/casefiles/43/ (appearing as p. 33 in the pdf format of the archive).

46. Jeffries, *Justice Lewis F. Powell*, 476, 484.

47. Jeffries, *Justice Lewis F. Powell*, 484.

48. Jeffries, *Justice Lewis F. Powell*, 500.

49. John C. Jeffries, Jr., "Bakke Revisited," *Supreme Court Review* 2003 (2003): 1–25, 9, www.jstor.org/stable/3536948.

50. Jeffries, "Bakke Revisited," 9–10 (citing articles by Vincent Blasi, Robert H. Bork, Guido Calabresi, Ronald Dworkin, Harry T. Edwards, John Hart Ely, Antonin Scalia, and Laurence H. Tribe).

51. Ronald Dworkin, "The Bakke Decision: Did It Decide Anything," *New York Review of Books*, August 17, 1978, www.nybooks.com/articles/1978/08/17/the-bakke-decision-did-it-decide-anything/.

52. John Hart Ely, "Foreword: On Discovering Fundamental Values," *Harvard Law Review* 92, no. 1 (1978): 5–56, 12–13 n.47, www.jstor.org/stable/1340566.

53. Antonin Scalia, "The Disease as Cure: 'In Order to Get Beyond Racism, We Must First Take Account of Race,'" *Washington University Law Quarterly* 1979, no. 1 (1979): 147–57, 148, https://openscholarship.wustl.edu/law_lawreview/vol1979/iss1/17.

54. Calabresi, "Bakke as Pseudo-Tragedy," 432.

55. Calabresi, "Bakke as Pseudo-Tragedy," 431 n.15; Bork, "Unpersuasive Bakke Decision."

56. Greenhouse, "Lewis Powell, Crucial Centrist Justice."

57. Rahim, "Diversity to Deradicalize," 1474.

58. Powell, "Attack on American Free Enterprise," 15–19, 24–27.

59. Powell, "Attack on American Free Enterprise," 1–3, 10–11, 15, 19, 21, 25–27, 33–34.

60. Rahim, "Diversity to Deradicalize," 1476.

61. Kim Phillips-Fein, *Invisible Hands: The Making of the Conservative Movement from the New Deal to Reagan* (New York: Norton, 2009), 161.

62. Mandery, "Why There's No Liberal Federalist Society"; see also Phillips-Fein, *Invisible Hands*, 161–65; Linda Greenhouse, "Powell: Moderation Amid Divisions." *New York Times*, June 27, 1987, www.nytimes.com/1987/06/27/us/powell-moderation-amid-divisions.html.

63. Emma Green, "How the Federalist Society Won," *New Yorker*, July 24, 2022, www.newyorker.com/news/annals-of-education/how-the-federalist-society-won.

64. Greg Olear, "How the Court Was Captured (with Sen. Sheldon Whitehouse)," *Prevail*, October 29, 2021, https://gregolear.substack.com/p/how-the-court-was-captured-with-sen; Mandery, "Why There's No Liberal Federalist Society."

65. Olear, "How the Court Was Captured"; see also Green, "How the Federalist Society Won"; David Montgomery, "Conquerors of the Courts," *Washington Post Magazine*, January 2, 2019, www.washingtonpost.com/news/magazine/wp/2019/01/02/feature/conquerors-of-the-courts/; Ben Schreckinger, "'She's Been Groomed for This Moment': Amy Barrett's Supreme Court Preparation Began Early," Politico, September 20, 2020, www.politico.com/news/2020/09/20/amy-coney-barrett-supreme-court-419219.

66. Mandery, "Why There's No Liberal Federalist Society."

67. Jeffries, *Justice Lewis F. Powell*, 180–82.

68. Victoria J. Dodd, "The Education Justice: The Honorable Lewis Franklin Powell, Jr.," *Fordham Urban Law Journal* 29, no. 2 (2001): 683–703, 683, https://ir.lawnet.fordham.edu/ulj/vol29/iss2/9; J. Peter Byrne, "Academic Freedom: A 'Special Concern of the First Amendment,'" *Yale Law Journal* 99, no. 2 (1989): 251–340, 314, www.jstor.org/stable/796588.

69. Rahim, "Diversity to Deradicalize," 1457; Walker, "Lawyer Looks at Civil Disobedience," 1230–43; Anders Walker, "Diversity's Strange Career: Recovering the Racial Pluralism of Lewis F. Powell, Jr.," *Santa Clara Law Review* 50, no. 3 (2010): 647–80, 668–74, https://ssrn.com/abstract=1508581.

70. Rahim, "Diversity to Deradicalize," 1429.

71. Lewis F. Powell, Jr., "Justice Lewis F. Powell, Jr.," interview by Bill Moyers, *In Search of the Constitution*, June 25, 1987, https://billmoyers.com/content/justice-lewis-f-powell.

Chapter Twelve. The Supreme Court's Long Embrace and Turnabout Rejection of the Diversity Principle

1. Nikole Hannah-Jones, "The 'Colorblindness' Trap: How a Civil Rights Ideal Got Hijacked," *New York Times*, March 13, 2024, www.nytimes.com/2024/03/13/magazine/civil-rights-affirmative-action-colorblind.html.
2. See Anthony Chen and Lisa Stulberg, "Before *Bakke:* The Hidden History of the Diversity Rationale," *University of Chicago Law Review Online*, October 30, 2020, https://lawreviewblog.uchicago.edu/2020/10/30/aa-chen-stulberg/ (noting that "race was initially just one of many dimensions of diversity that were on the minds of college and university administrators, but the dramatic struggle over civil rights in 1963 gave race a new, decisive salience").
3. William G. Bowen and Derek Bok, "Historical Context," in Bowen and Bok, *The Shape of the River: Long-Term Consequences of Considering Race in College and University Admissions* (Princeton: Princeton University Press, 1998): 1–14, 8.
4. Wilbur J. Bender, "Is Too Much of 'The Best' Bad for Harvard?," *Boston Globe*, October 8, 1961, https://bostonglobe.newspapers.com/image/433759793/.
5. Chen and Stulberg, "Before *Bakke.*"
6. See David B. Oppenheimer, Henry Cornillie, Henry Bluestone Smith, Thao Thai, and Richard Treadwell, "Be Careful What You Wish For: Ronald Reagan, Donald Trump, the Assault on Civil Rights, and the Surprising Story of How Title VII Got Its Private Right of Action," *Berkeley Journal of Employment and Labor Law* 39, no. 1 (2018): 147–76, 149–52.
7. Juan Williams, "Reagan, the South and Civil Rights," NPR, June 10, 2004, www.npr.org/2004/06/10/1953700/reagan-the-south-and-civil-rights; Pat Horan, "Reagan, Goldwater and Rise of Conservatism," *RealClearHistory*, October 27, 2014, www.realclearhistory.com/articles/2014/10/27/reagan_goldwater_and_rise_of_conservatism_184.html.
8. See Taylor Branch, *Pillar of Fire: America in the King Years, 1963–65* (New York: Simon and Schuster, 1998), 242; Thomas W. Casstevens, *Politics, Housing and Race Relations: California's Rumford Act and Proposition 14* (Berkeley: Institute of Governmental Studies, 1967), 53–67; David B. Oppenheimer, "California's Anti-Discrimination Legislation, Proposition 14, and the Constitutional Protection of Minority Rights: The Fiftieth Anniversary of the California Fair Employment and Housing Act," *Golden Gate University Law Review* 40, no. 2 (2010): 117–27, 124.
9. United Press International, "State Officials at Odds on Proposition 14 Status," *Desert Sun*, May 12, 1966.
10. Matthew Yglesias, "Reagan's Race Record," *The Atlantic*, November 9, 2007, www.theatlantic.com/politics/archive/2007/11/reagans-race-record/46875/.

11. The Free Speech movement began as a campaign to allow pro–civil rights students at University of California, Berkeley, to set up tables in Sproul Plaza urging students to picket Berkeley stores that discriminated against Black workers. See "Chronology of Events: Three Months of Crisis," *California Monthly*, February 1965, https://oac.cdlib.org/view?docId=kt196n983c;NAAN=13030&doc.view=frames&chunk.id=d0e832&toc.depth=1&toc.id=&brand=oac4.

12. Yglesias, "Reagan's Race Record"; Pedro Noguera and Robert Cohen, "Remembering Reagan's Record on Civil Rights and the South African Freedom Struggle," *The Nation*, February 11, 2011, www.thenation.com/article/archive/remembering-reagans-record-civil-rights-and-south-african-freedom-struggle/#:~:text=Reagan%20ascended%20to%20the%20White,the%20White%20House%20violated%20othe.

13. Ian Haney López, *Dog Whistle Politics: How Coded Racial Appeals Have Reinvented Racism and Wrecked the Middle Class* (Oxford: Oxford University Press, 2014), 58 (citing Paul Krugman, "Republicans and Race," *New York Times*, November 19, 2007, www.nytimes.com/2007/11/19/opinion/19krugman.html); "Murder in Mississippi," PBS *American Experience*, accessed March 6, 2023, www.pbs.org/wgbh/americanexperience/features/freedom summer-murder/.

14. Haney López, *Dog Whistle Politics*, 58 (citing Bob Herbert, "Righting Reagan's Wrongs?," *New York Times*, November 13, 2007, www.nytimes.com/2007/11/13/opinion/13herbert.html).

15. Ian Haney-López, "The Racism at the Heart of the Reagan Presidency," *Salon*, January 11, 2014, www.salon.com/2014/01/11/the_racism_at_the_heart_of_the_reagan_presidency/.

16. Michael K. Brown, Martin Carnoy, Elliott Currie, Troy Duster, David B. Oppenheimer, Marjorie M. Schultz, and David Wellman, *Whitewashing Race: The Myth of a Color-Blind Society* (Berkeley: University of California Press, 2003), 184; Frank Dobbin, *Inventing Equal Opportunity* (Princeton: Princeton University Press, 2009), 135–37.

17. Haney López, *Dog Whistle Politics*, 70.

18. Haney López, *Dog Whistle Politics*, 70.

19. See Dobbin, *Inventing Equal Opportunity*, 133–60.

20. See *Bakke, Weber, and Affirmative Action: A Rockefeller Foundation Conference July 12–13, 1979* (New York: Rockefeller Foundation, 1979); *United Steelworkers v. Weber*, 443 U.S. 193, 204–7 (1979).

21. Archibald Cox, "Minority Admissions After *Bakke*," in *Bakke, Weber, and Affirmative Action: A Rockefeller Foundation Conference* (New York: Rockefeller Foundation, 1979), 80–112, 102.

22. *Students for Fair Admissions, Inc. v. President and Fellows of Harvard Coll.*; *Students for Fair Admissions, Inc. v. Univ. of N.C.*, No. 20–199, No. 21–707, 2023 WL 4239254, at *2166 n.4, 2175 (June 29, 2023).

23. *Students for Fair Admissions, Inc. v. President and Fellows of Harvard Coll.*, 161 n.45, 163.

24. Bowen and Bok, *The Shape of the River*, 8–9.
25. See, e.g., Daniel N. Lipson, "Embracing Diversity: The Institutionalization of Affirmative Action as Diversity Management at UC-Berkeley, UT-Austin, and UW-Madison," *Law & Social Inquiry* 32, no. 4 (2007): 985–1026, www.jstor.org/stable/20108738 (interviews of thirty-nine admissions officials from leading public research universities demonstrate deep commitment to diversity in admissions and shift from an affirmative action/racial justice justification for using race to a diversity justification); Michael Bastedo, "Holistic Admissions as a Global Phenomenon," in *Higher Education in the Next Decade: Global Challenges, Future Prospects*, ed. Heather Eggins, Anna Smolentseva, and Hans de Wit (Leiden: Brill, 2021), 91–114 (discussing the implementation of the diversity rationale in higher education admissions systems in Australia, China, England, France, Hong Kong, Ireland, Japan, and South Korea).
26. Judith Rodin, "On the Importance of Diversity in University Admissions" (speech, Washington, D.C., April 14, 1997), https://almanac.upenn.edu/archive/v43/n35/aau.html.
27. Christina J. Grabowski, "Impact of Holistic Review on Student Interview Pool Diversity," *Advances in Health Sciences Education* 23 (2018): 487–98, 489, https://link.springer.com/article/10.1007/s10459-017-9807-9; "Academic Metrics Hold Steady with Holistic Admissions," University of Illinois Chicago, last modified August 8, 2019, https://nursing.uic.edu/news-stories/academic-metrics-hold-steady-with-holistic-admissions/.
28. See chapter 13, "Diversity Science," on the scientific literature supporting the benefits of diversity.
29. See, e.g., William Van Alstyne, "A Preliminary Report on the Bakke Case," *AAUP Bulletin* 64, no. 4 (1978): 286–97, 288–91 (discussing "The Obvious Instability of the Decision"); William J. Bennett and Terry Eastland, "Why Bakke Won't End Reverse Discrimination," *Commentary*, September 1978, www.commentary.org/articles/william-bennett/why-bakke-wont-end-reverse-discrimination-1/.
30. Van Alstyne, "A Preliminary Report on the Bakke Case," 286–97, 288–91.
31. *Hopwood v. Texas*, 861 F. Supp. 551, 553 (W.D. Tex. 1994), *rev'd*, 78 F.3d 932 (5th Cir. 1996).
32. *Hopwood v. Texas*, 555, 583–85 (W.D. Tex. 1994), *rev'd*, 78 F.3d 932 (5th Cir. 1996).
33. *Hopwood v. Texas*, 555 (W.D. Tex. 1994), *rev'd*, 78 F.3d 932 (5th Cir. 1996).
34. *Hopwood v. Texas*, 555 (W.D. Tex. 1994), *rev'd*, 78 F.3d 932 (5th Cir. 1996).
35. *Hopwood v. Texas*, 556 (W.D. Tex. 1994), *rev'd*, 78 F.3d 932 (5th Cir. 1996).
36. "Clarence Thomas Wins Senate Confirmation," *Congressional Quarterly*, 1991, https://library.cqpress.com/cqalmanac/document.php?id=cqal91-1110583.
37. *Hopwood v. Texas*, 571 (W.D. Tex. 1994), *rev'd*, 78 F.3d 932 (5th Cir. 1996).
38. *Hopwood v. Texas*, 557, 572, 579, 582, 583–85 (W.D. Tex. 1994), *rev'd*, 78 F.3d 932 (5th Cir. 1996).

39.   *Hopwood v. Texas*, 78 F.3d 932, 934–35 (5th Cir. 1996), *abrogated by Grutter v. Bollinger*, 539 U.S. 306 (2003).

40.   *Hopwood v. Texas*, 78 F.3d 932, 944 (5th Cir. 1996), *abrogated by Grutter v. Bollinger*, 539 U.S. 306 (2003).

41.   Brief for the United States as Amicus Curiae Supporting Petitioner, *Texas v. Hopwood*, 1996 WL 33467197 (No. 95–1773); Brief of the States of Maryland et al. as Amici Curiae in Support of Petitioners, *Texas v. Hopwood*, 1996 WL 33467196 (No. 95–1773); see also Brief of Amicus Curiae of Texas Law School Deans in Support of Petitioner's Request for Grant of Writ of Certiorari, *Univ. of Tex. L. Sch. v. Hopwood*, 2001 WL 34124798 (No. 00–1609).

42.   *Hopwood v. Texas*, 78 F.3d 932, 944 (5th Cir. 1996), *cert. Denied*, 533 U.S. 929 (2001).

43.   Lindsay Daugherty, Paco Martorell, and Isaac McFarlin, "The Texas Ten Percent Plan's Impact on College Enrollment," *Education Next*, last updated April 22, 2014, www.educationnext.org/texas-ten-percent-plans-impact-college-enrollment/.

44.   "Top 10 Percent Law," *UT News*, last accessed March 6, 2023, https://news.utexas.edu/topics-in-the-news/top-10-percent-law/.

45.   Richard Lempert, "Fisher v. University of Texas: History, Issues, and Expectations," Brookings, December 9, 2015, www.brookings.edu/blog/fixgov/2015/12/09/fisher-v-university-of-texas-at-austin-history-issues-and-expectations/.

46.   See Brief of Amici Curiae Deborah Cohen and 67 Other Professors in Support of Respondents at 25–38, *Students for Fair Admissions, Inc. v. President and Fellows of Harvard Coll.*, 600 U.S. 181 (2023).

47.   Catherine L. Horn and Stella M. Flores, *Percent Plans in College Admissions: A Comparative Analysis of Three States' Experiences* (Cambridge: Civil Rights Project at Harvard University, 2003), 24.

48.   Robert Pear, "In California, Foes of Affirmative Action See a New Day," *New York Times*, November 7, 1996, www.nytimes.com/1996/11/07/us/in-california-foes-of-affirmative-action-see-a-new-day.html.

49.   Ethan Bronner, "U. of Washington Will End Race-Conscious Admissions," *New York Times*, November 7, 1998, www.nytimes.com/1998/11/07/us/u-of-washington-will-end-race-conscious-admissions.html; Tamar Lewin, "Michigan Rejects Affirmative Action, and Backers Sue," *New York Times*, November 9, 2006, www.nytimes.com/2006/11/09/us/politics/09michigan.html; Joe Shaulis, "Affirmative Action Ban Passed in Nebraska, Trailing in Colorado," *Jurist*, November 5, 2008, www.jurist.org/news/2008/11/affirmative-action-ban-passed-in/.

50.   Peter T. Kilborn, "Jeb Bush Roils Florida on Affirmative Action," *New York Times*, February 4, 2000, www.nytimes.com/2000/02/04/us/jeb-bush-roils-florida-on-affirmative-action.html.

51.   Kevin Carey, "A Detailed Look at the Downside of California's Ban on Affirmative Action," *New York Times*, last updated October 18, 2021, www.

nytimes.com/2020/08/21/upshot/00up-affirmative-action-california-study.html.

52. Suzanne Espinosa Solis, "Affirmative Action Critic Used His Minority Status / UC Regent Got No-Bid State Contracts," *San Francisco Chronicle*, May 8, 1995, www.sfchronicle.com/news/article/Affirmative-Action-Critic-Used-His-Minority-3034207.php; see also Lydia Chavez, *The Color Bind: California's Battle to End Affirmative Action* (Berkeley: University of California Press, 1998).

53. Martin Luther King, Jr., "I Have a Dream" (August 28, 1963), www.gilder-lehrman.org/sites/default/files/inline-pdfs/king.dreamspeech.excerpts.pdf; Amy Wallace, "He's Either Mr. Right OR Mr. Wrong: What Drives Ward Connerly in His Crusade to End Affirmative Action?," *Los Angeles Times*, March 31, 1996, www.latimes.com/archives/la-xpm-1996-03-31-tm-53137-story.html; see also Chavez, *The Color Bind*.

54. Darryl Fears, "California Activist Seeks End to Identification by Race," *Washington Post*, July 4, 2003 https://www.washingtonpost.com/archive/politics/2003/07/05/calif-activist-seeks-end-to-identification-by-race/d70f1582-51d4-4670-a9c2-07b2bfcf1a08/; Christopher Byrns, "Political Activist Ward Connerly Speaks on Racial Equality in Higher Education," *Cornell Daily Sun*, November 13, 2015, https://cornellsun.com/2015/11/13/political-activist-ward-connerly-speaks-on-racial-equality-in-higher-education/.

55. Wallace, "He's Either Mr. Right OR Mr. Wrong."

56. David B. Oppenheimer, "Dr. King's Dream of Affirmative Action," *Harvard Latin American Law Review* 21 (2018): 55–86, 59, 82–84.

57. *Grutter v. Bollinger,* 539 U.S. 306, 341 (2003).

58. *Gratz v. Bollinger,* 539 U.S. 244, 252–55, 271–76.

59. *Grutter v. Bollinger,* 539 U.S. 306, 315–16.

60. *Grutter v. Bollinger,* 539 U.S. 306, 324–26.

61. *Grutter v. Bollinger,* 539 U.S. 306, 329.

62. See Devon W. Carbado, "Intraracial Diversity," *UCLA Law Review* 60, no. 5 (2013): 1130–83, 1145–48; see also Reva B. Siegel, "Equality Talk: Antisubordination and Anticlassification Values in Constitutional Struggles over *Brown*," *Harvard Law Review* 117, no. 5 (2004): 1470–1547 (arguing that *Grutter*, while affirming the diversity rationale, expands "the concept of diversity so that it explicitly embraces antisubordination values").

63. In total, twenty-two amicus briefs from educators and educational institutions were filed. See, for example: Brief of the Society of American Law Teachers as Amicus Curiae in Support of Respondents, *Grutter v. Bollinger,* 539 U.S. 306 (2003) (No. 02–241); Brief of American Law Deans Association as Amicus Curiae in Support of Respondents, *Grutter v. Bollinger,* 539 U.S. 306 (2003) (No. 02–241); Brief of Amici Curiae National School Boards Association et al., in Support of Respondents, *Grutter v. Bollinger,* 539 U.S. 306 (2003) (Nos. 02–241, 02–516); Brief of the Leadership Conference on Civil Rights and the LCCR Education Fund as Amici Curiae in Support of Respondents, *Grutter v. Bollinger,* 539 U.S. 306 (2003) (Nos. 02–

241, 02–516); Brief of Amici Curiae Judith Areen, Katharine Bartlett, Michael Fitts, Anthony Kronman, David Leebron, Saul Levmore, Richard Revesz, Kathleen Sullivan, Lee Teitelbaum, and David Van Zandt—in Their Individual Capacities as Deans of, Respectively, Georgetown Law Center, Duke Law School, University of Pennsylvania Law School, Yale Law School, Columbia Law School, University of Chicago Law School, New York University Law School, Stanford Law School, Cornell Law School, and Northwestern University School of Law—in Support of Respondents, *Grutter v. Bollinger*, 539 U.S. 306 (2003) (No. 02–241); Brief of Howard University as Amicus Curiae in Support of Respondents, *Grutter v. Bollinger*, 539 U.S. 306 (2003) (Nos. 02–241, 02–516); Brief of Amici Curiae Massachusetts Institute of Technology et al. in Support of Respondents, *Grutter v. Bollinger*, 539 U.S. 306 (2003) (Nos. 02–241, 02–516); Brief of the American Educational Research Association et al. as Amici Curiae in Support of Respondents, *Grutter v. Bollinger*, 539 U.S. 306 (2003) (No. 02–241); Brief for the Arizona State University College of Law Supporting Respondents, *Grutter v. Bollinger*, 539 U.S. 306 (2003) (No. 02–241); Brief of Amici Curiae of the Coalition for Economic Equity et al. in Support of Respondents, *Grutter v. Bollinger*, 539 U.S. 306 (2003) (No. 02–241); Brief of the University of Pittsburgh et al. as Amici Curiae in Support of Respondents, *Grutter v. Bollinger*, 539 U.S. 306 (2003) (Nos. 02–241, 02–516); Brief of the Harvard Black Law Students Association et al. as Amici Curiae Supporting Respondents, *Grutter v. Bollinger*, 539 U.S. 306 (2003) (No. 02–241); Brief of Harvard University, Brown University, The University of Chicago, Dartmouth College, Duke University, The University of Pennsylvania, Princeton University, and Yale University as Amici Curiae Supporting Respondents, *Grutter v. Bollinger*, 539 U.S. 306 (2003) (Nos. 02–241, 02–516); Brief of Amicus Curiae of the National Education Association et al., in Support of Respondents, *Grutter v. Bollinger*, 539 U.S. 306 (2003) (Nos. 02–241, 02–516); Brief of the Clinical Legal Education Association as Amicus Curiae in Support of Respondents, *Grutter v. Bollinger*, 539 U.S. 306 (2003) (No. 02–241); Brief for the Association of American Medical Colleges et al. as Amici Curiae in Support of Respondents, *Grutter v. Bollinger*, 539 U.S. 306 (2003) (No. 02–241); Brief of Amici Curiae American Council on Education and 52 Other Higher Education Organizations in Support of Respondents, *Grutter v. Bollinger*, 539 U.S. 306 (2003) (No. 02–241); Brief of Amherst et al., Amici Curiae, Supporting Respondents, *Grutter v. Bollinger*, 539 U.S. 306 (2003) (Nos. 02–241, 02–516); Brief of Amicus Curiae Association of American Law Schools in Support of Respondents, *Grutter v. Bollinger*, 539 U.S. 306 (2003) (No. 02–241); Brief of Carnegie Mellon University and 37 Fellow Private Colleges and Universities as Amicus Curiae in Support of Respondents, *Grutter v. Bollinger*, 539 U.S. 306 (2003) (Nos. 02–241, 02–516); Brief of Amici Curiae Columbia University, Cornell University, Georgetown University, Rice University, and Vanderbilt

University in Support of Respondents, *Grutter v. Bollinger,* 539 U.S. 306 (2003) (Nos. 02–241, 02–516); Brief of Amicus Curiae of the School of Law of the University of North Carolina Supporting Respondents, *Grutter v. Bollinger,* 539 U.S. 306 (2003) (No. 02–241); Consolidated Brief of Lt. Gen. Julius W. Becton, Jr., et al. as Amici Curiae in Support of Respondents, *Grutter v. Bollinger,* 539 U.S. 306 (2003) (Nos. 02–241, 02–516); Brief of General Motors Corporation as Amicus Curiae in Support of Respondents, *Grutter v. Bollinger,* 539 U.S. 306 (2003) (Nos. 02–241, 02–516); Brief for Amici Curiae 65 Leading American Businesses in Support of Respondents, *Grutter v. Bollinger,* 539 U.S. 306 (2003) (Nos. 02–241, 02–516).

64. Consolidated Brief of Lt. Gen. Julius W. Becton, Jr., et al. as Amici Curiae in Support of Respondents, *Grutter v. Bollinger,* 539 U.S. 306 (2003). The military brief was filed on behalf of Lieutenant General Julius W. Becton, Jr., Admiral Dennis Blair, Major General Charles Bolden, Honorable James M. Cannon, Lieutenant General Daniel W. Christman, General Wesley K. Clark, Senator Max Cleland, Admiral Archie Clemins, Honorable William Cohen (former Secretary of Defense), Admiral William J. Crowe, General Ronald R. Fogleman, Lieutenant General Howard D. Graves, General Joseph P. Hoar, Senator Robert J. Kerrey, Admiral Charles R. Larson, Senator Carl Levin, Honorable Robert "Bud" McFarlane (National Security Advisor to President Reagan), General Carl E. Mundy, Jr., General Lloyd M. Newton, Lieutenant General Tad J. Oelstrom, Honorable William J. Perry (former Secretary of Defense), Admiral Joseph W. Prueher, Senator Jack Reed, Honorable Joseph R. Reeder, General H. Norman Schwarzkopf, General John M. D. Shalikashvili, General Hugh Shelton, General Gordon R. Sullivan, General Anthony Zinni.

65. The corporate briefs were filed on behalf of General Motors Corporation, 3M, Abbott Laboratories, Alcoa, Inc., Alliant Energy Corporation, Altria Group, Inc., American Airlines, Inc., American Express Company, Amgen Corporation, Ashland Inc., Bank One Corporation, Baxter Healthcare Corporation, The Boeing Company, Charter One Financial, Inc., Chevron Texaco Corporation, The Coca-Cola Company, Coca-Cola Enterprises Inc., DaimlerChrysler Corporation, Deloitte Consulting L.P., Deloitte & Touche LLP, The Dow Chemical Company, Eastman Kodak Company, Eaton Corporation, Eli Lilly & Company, Ernst & Young LLP, Exelon Corporation, Fannie Mae, General Dynamics Corporation, General Electric Company, General Mills, Inc., John Hancock Financial Services, Harris Bankcorp, Inc., Hewlett-Packard Company, Illinois Tool Works Inc., Intel Corporation, Johnson & Johnson, Kaiser Found. Health Plan, Inc., Kellogg Company, KPMG Int'l for KPMG LLP, Kraft Foods Inc., Lockheed Martin Corporation, Lucent Technologies, Inc., Medtronic, Inc., Merck & Co., Inc., Microsoft Corporation, Mitsubishi Motors North America, MSC Software Corporation, Nationwide Mutual Insurance Co., NetCom Solutions International, Nike Inc., Northrop Grumman Corporation, Pepsi

Bottling Group, Inc., PepsiCo Inc., Pfizer Inc., PPG Industries, Inc., Price-waterhouseCoopers LLP, The Procter & Gamble Company, Reebok International, Sara Lee Corporation, Schering-Plough Corporation, Shell Oil Company, Steelcase, Inc., Sterling Financial Group of Cos., United Airlines, Inc., Whirlpool Corporation, Xerox Corporation.

66. Consolidated Brief of Lt. Gen. Julius W. Becton, Jr., et al. as Amici Curiae in Support of Respondents at 27, *Grutter v. Bollinger,* 539 U.S. 306 (2003).

67. Consolidated Brief of Lt. Gen. Julius W. Becton, Jr., et al. as Amici Curiae in Support of Respondents at 28, *Grutter v. Bollinger,* 539 U.S. 306 (2003).

68. Consolidated Brief of Lt. Gen. Julius W. Becton, Jr., et al. as Amici Curiae in Support of Respondents at 27–32, *Grutter v. Bollinger,* 539 U.S. 306 (2003) (Nos. 02–241, 02–516).

69. See, e.g., Brief of Lt. Gen. Julius W. Becton, Jr., et al. as Amici Curiae in Support of Respondents, *Fisher v. Univ. of Tex.,* 579 U.S. 365 (2016) (No. 14–981); Brief for Lt. Gen. Julius W. Becton, Jr., et al. as Amici Curiae in Support of Respondents, *Fisher v. Univ. of Tex.,* 570 U.S. 297 (2013) (No. 11–345); Brief of Adm. Charles S. Abbot et al. as Amici Curiae in Support of Respondents, *Students for Fair Admissions, Inc. v. President and Fellows of Harvard Coll.,* 600 U.S. 181 (2023). In addition, the Department of Defense joined in the amicus briefs for the United States. See Brief for the United States as Amicus Curiae Supporting Respondents, *Fisher v. Univ. of Tex.,* 579 U.S. 365 (2016) (No. 14–981); Brief for the United States as Amicus Curiae Supporting Respondents, *Students for Fair Admissions, Inc. v. President and Fellows of Harvard Coll.,* 600 U.S. 181 (2023).

70. Brief of General Motors Corporation as Amicus Curiae in Support of Respondents at 2, *Grutter v. Bollinger,* 539 U.S. 306; Brief for Amici Curiae 65 Leading American Businesses in Support of Respondents at 2, *Grutter v. Bollinger,* 539 U.S. 306 (2003).

71. Brief of General Motors Corporation as Amicus Curiae in Support of Respondents at 13, *Grutter v. Bollinger,* 539 U.S. 306.

72. Abigail Perkiss, "A Look Back at Sandra Day O'Connor's Court Legacy," *National Constitution Center,* July 1, 2022, https://constitutioncenter.org/blog/a-look-back-at-justice-sandra-day-oconnors-court-legacy.

73. *Wygant v. Jackson Bd. of Educ.,* 476 U.S. 267 (1986).

74. *City of Richmond v. J. A. Crosen Co.,* 488 U.S. 469 (1989).

75. *Adarand Constructors, Inc. v. Pena,* 515 U.S. 200 (1995).

76. *Grutter v. Bollinger,* 539 U.S. 306, 343 (2003).

77. Sarah Hinger, "Meet Edward Blum, the Man Who Wants to Kill Affirmative Action in Higher Education," *American Civil Liberties Union,* October 18, 2018, www.aclu.org/news/racial-justice/meet-edward-blum-man-who-wants-kill-affirmative-action-higher; Malathi Nayak, "California Race, Gender Quotas for Boards Face Legal Test," *Bloomberg Law,* July 13, 2021, https://news.bloomberglaw.com/esg/californias-racial-quota-for-company-boards-hit-with-lawsuit; Nia L. Orakwue and Leah J. Teichholtz, "SFFA

Funded by Large Conservative Trusts, Public Filings Show," *Harvard Crimson*, October 28, 2022, www.thecrimson.com/article/2022/10/28/donors-sffa-conservative-trusts/.

78. Joan Biskupic, "Special Report: Behind U.S. Race Cases, a Little-known Recruiter," Reuters, December 4, 2012, www.reuters.com/article/us-usa-court-casemaker-idUSBRE8B30V220121204.

79. See *Shelby County v. Holder*, 570 U.S. 529 (2013); Anemona Hartocollis, "He Took on the Voting Rights Act and Won. Now He's Taking on Harvard," *New York Times*, November 19, 2017, www.nytimes.com/2017/11/19/us/affirmative-action-lawsuits.html.

80. Malathi Nayak, "California Race, Gender Quotas for Boards Face Legal Test," *Bloomberg Law*, July 13, 2021, https://news.bloomberglaw.com/esg/californias-racial-quota-for-company-boards-hit-with-lawsuit; see also Cydney Posner, "Fifth Circuit Hears Oral Argument on Challenge to Nasdaq Board Diversity Rules—Will the Rules Survive?," *JD Supra*, September 8, 2022, www.jdsupra.com/legalnews/fifth-circuit-hears-oral-argument-on-8046591/.

81. Caroline Hendrie, "Houston Reaches for Diversity Without Quotas," *Education Week*, June 10, 1998, www.edweek.org/leadership/houston-reaches-for-diversity-without-quotas/1998/06.

82. Robert Barnes, "How One Man Brought Affirmative Action to the Supreme Court. Again and Again," *Washington Post*, October 24, 2022, www.washingtonpost.com/politics/2022/10/24/edward-blum-supreme-court-harvard-unc/.

83. David G. Savage, "Conservative Legal Strategist Has No Office or Staff, Just a Surprising Supreme Court Track Record," *Los Angeles Times*, December 22, 2015, www.latimes.com/nation/la-na-supreme-court-strategist-20151222-story.html.

84. *Students for Fair Admissions, Inc. v. President and Fellows of Harvard Coll.*, 600 U.S. 181, 213 n.4 (2023).

85. Freddie Sayers, "Edward Blum: My Battle Against Affirmative Action," UnHerd, May 29, 2023, https://unherd.com/2023/05/edward-blum-my-battle-against-affirmative-action/.

86. Savage, "Conservative Legal Strategist Has No Office or Staff."

87. Emily Bazelon and Adam Liptak, "How Will the Supreme Court Rule on Affirmative Action?," *New York Times Magazine*, December 8, 2015, www.nytimes.com/2015/12/08/magazine/how-will-the-supreme-court-rule-on-affirmative-action.html ("U.T. Austin admits 75 percent of the freshman class based on what's called the Top 10 Percent Plan"); "Top 10 Percent Law," University of Texas at Austin, last accessed August 16, 2023, https://news.utexas.edu/topics-in-the-news/top-10-percent-law/.

88. *Fisher v. Univ. of Tex.*, 570 U.S. 297, 335 (2013) (Ginsburg, J., dissenting).

89. Nikole Hannah-Jones, "What Abigail Fisher's Affirmative Action Case Was Really About," ProPublica, June 23, 2016, www.propublica.org/article/a-colorblind-constitution-what-abigail-fishers-affirmative-action-case-is-r.

90. *Fisher v. Univ. of Tex.*, 579 U.S. 365, 305–06, 314–15, 388 (2016).

91. "Nomination of Anthony M. Kennedy To Be an Associate Justice of the Supreme Court of the United States," *National Archives*, November 11, 1987, www.reaganlibrary.gov/archives/speech/nomination-anthony-m-kennedy-be-associate-justice-supreme-court-united-states; Andrew Cohen, "Anthony Kennedy Was No Moderate," *Brennan Center for Justice*, June 27, 2018, www.brennancenter.org/our-work/analysis-opinion/anthony-kennedy-was-no-moderate.

92. *City of Richmond v. J. A. Croson Co.*, 488 U.S. 469 (1989); *Adarand Constructors, Inc. v. Pena*, 515 U.S. 200 (1995).

93. *Grutter v. Bollinger*, 539 U.S. 306, 387 (2003).

94. *Fisher v. Univ. of Tex.*, 570 U.S. 297 (2013).

95. *Fisher v. Univ. of Tex.*, 570 U.S. 297, 309–10 (2013).

96. See Brief of Brown University et al. in Support of Respondents, *Fisher v. Univ. of Tex.*, 570 U.S. 297 (2013) (No. 11–345).

97. Brief of Brown University et al. in Support of Respondents at 11–12, 16–20, *Fisher v. Univ. of Tex.*, 570 U.S. 297.

98. See Brief of California Institute of Technology et al. as Amici Curiae in Support of Respondents, *Fisher v. Univ. of Tex.*, 570 U.S. 297 (2013).

99. Brief of California Institute of Technology et al. as Amici Curiae in Support of Respondents at 3, *Fisher v. Univ. of Tex.*, 570 U.S. 297 (2013).

100. Brief of California Institute of Technology et al. as Amici Curiae in Support of Respondents at 3, *Fisher v. Univ. of Tex.*, 570 U.S. 297.

101. Only seven justices participated because Justice Scalia had passed away and Justice Kagan recused herself because she had filed an amicus brief in *Fisher I* while serving as solicitor general; the vote was 4–3 in favor of the university.

102. *Fisher v. Univ. of Tex.*, 579 U.S. 365, 383, 385, 388 (2016).

103. Brief for the Black Student Alliance at the University of Texas at Austin et al. as Amici Curiae in Support of Respondents at 12, 17, *Fisher v. Univ. of Tex.*, 570 U.S. 297 (2013); *Fisher v. Univ. of Tex.*, 579 U.S. 365 (2016).

104. *Fisher v. Univ. of Tex.*, 579 U.S. 365, 388 (2016).

105. *Fisher v. Univ. of Tex.*, 579 U.S. 365, 388.

106. *Fisher v. Univ. of Tex.*, 579 U.S. 365, 437.

107. *Fisher v. Univ. of Tex.*, 579 U.S. 365, 397.

108. "Were You Denied Admission to Harvard? It may be because you're the wrong race," *Harvard University Not Fair*, last accessed March 16, 2023, https://harvardnotfair.org; Edward Blum, "Speech Before the Houston Chinese Alliance," Youtube Video, 18:44, www.youtube.com/watch?v=DiBvo-o5JRg ("I needed plaintiffs. I needed Asian plaintiffs"); "Were You Denied Admission to the University of North Carolina? It may be because you're the wrong race," *The University of North Carolina at Chapel Hill Not Fair*, last accessed March 16, 2023, https://uncnotfair.org; Blum, "Speech Before the Houston Chinese Alliance," Youtube Video; "Were

You Rejected from the University of Wisconsin at Madison? It may be because you're the wrong race or ethnicity," *The University of Wisconsin-Madison*, last accessed March 16, 2023, https://uwnotfair.org; Blum, "Speech Before the Houston Chinese Alliance," Youtube Video.

109. Nick Anderson, "Lawsuits Allege Unlawful Racial Bias in Admissions at Harvard, UNC–Chapel Hill," *Washington Post*, November 17, 2014, www.washingtonpost. com/local/education/lawsuits-allege-unlawful-racial-bias-in-admissions-at-harvard-unc-chapel-hill/2014/11/17/b117b966-6e9a-11e4-ad12-3734 c461eab6_story.html.

110. Complaint at 3–6, *Students for Fair Admissions, Inc. v. President and Fellows of Harvard Coll.*, 397 F. Supp. 3d 126 (D. Mass. 2019).

111. "About Us," *The University of North Carolina System*, www.northcarolina. edu/about-us/ (last visited April 5, 2024).

112. Mary Wright, "Mission Accomplished: The Unfinished Relationship Between Black Law Schools and Their Historical Constituencies," *North Carolina Central Law Review* 39, no. 1 (2016): 1–32, 4–5.

113. "Pauli Murray: Birth of an Activist," *University of North Carolina Libraries*, November 3, 2010, https://library.unc.edu/past-exhibits/pauli-murray-birth-of-an-activist/.

114. "Pauli Murray—Members of Your Race Are Not Admitted," *National Humanities Center Resource Toolbox: The Making of African American Identity*, vol. 3, *1917–1968*, last accessed March 16, 2023, https://nationalhumanitiescenter. org/pds/maai3/protest/text1/paulimurray.pdf.

115. "Paving the Way: Carolina's Black Pioneers," *UNC–Chapel Hill*, last accessed March 16, 2023, www.unc.edu/story/bhm/; *McKissick v. Carmichael*, 187 F.2d 949, 953–54 (4th Cir. 1951).

116. Letter from Pauli Murray inquiring about admission to the School of Law at UNC–Chapel Hill, May 17, 1951, https://exhibits.lib.unc.edu/exhibits/ show/womenatunc/barriers/paulimurray; see also Letter from Dean Henry Brandis, Jr., to Pauli Murray, June 6, 1951, https://exhibits.lib.unc. edu/items/show/7295.

117. "First Black Undergraduate Students," *The Carolina Story: A Virtual Museum of University History*, last accessed March 16, 2023, https://museum. unc.edu/exhibits/show/integration/leroy-frasier—john-lewis-bran.

118. Ruth Samuel, "UNC–Chapel Hill Has a Problem Retaining Black Male Students," *University of North Carolina Media Hub*, May 5, 2021, https:// mediahub.unc.edu/unc-chapel-hill-has-a-problem-retaining-black-male-students/.

119. Amici Curiae Brief of the NAACP Legal Defense and Educational Fund, Inc., and the National Association for the Advancement of Colored People in Support of Respondents at 20–21, *Students for Fair Admissions, Inc. v. Univ. of N.C.*, No. 21–707, 2023 WL 4239254 (June 29, 2023).

120. "Federal Court Finds in Favor of Harvard in Admissions Case," *Massachusetts Institute of Technology Office of the General Counsel*, October 1, 2019, https://ogc. mit.edu/latest/federal-court-finds-favor-harvard-admissions-case.

121. Nate Raymond, "University of North Carolina Defeats Challenge to Race-based Admissions Policies," Reuters, October 19, 2021, www.reuters.com/world/us/university-north-carolina-defeats-challenge-race-based-admissions-policies-2021-10-19/.

122. Complaint at 8, *Students for Fair Admissions, Inc. v. President and Fellows of Harvard Coll.*, 397 F. Supp. 3d 126 (D. Mass. 2019).

123. Complaint at 8, *Students for Fair Admissions, Inc. v. Univ. of N.C.*, 567 F. Supp. 3d 580 (M.D.N.C. 2021).

124. See *Students for Fair Admissions, Inc. v. President and Fellows of Harvard Coll.*, 261 F. Supp. 3d 99 (D. Mass. 2017); *Students for Fair Admissions, Inc. v. Univ. of N.C.*, 567 F. Supp. 3d 580 (M.D.N.C. 2021).

125. Daphne C. Thompson, "Admissions Lawsuit Plaintiff Requests Extensive Harvard Records for Discovery," *Harvard Crimson*, May 4, 2015, www.thecrimson.com/article/2015/5/4/race-based-lawsuit-update/; Nancy Leong, "Preliminary Thoughts on the Summary Judgment Motions in the Harvard Affirmative Action Lawsuit," *Take Care Blog*, June 18, 2018, https://takecare-blog.com/blog/preliminary-thoughts-on-the-summary-judgment-motions-in-the-harvard-affirmative-action-lawsuit.

126. *Students for Fair Admissions, Inc. v. President and Fellows of Harvard Coll.*, 397 F. Supp. 3d 126, 158 (D. Mass. 2019); *Students for Fair Admissions, Inc. v. Univ. of N.C.*, 567 F. Supp. 3d 580, 612 (M.D.N.C. 2021).

127. *Students for Fair Admissions, Inc. v. President and Fellows of Harvard Coll.*, 397 F. Supp. 3d 126, 161 n.45, (D. Mass. 2019) (Expert Report of Peter S. Arcidiacono).

128. Complaint at 55, *Students for Fair Admissions, Inc. v. Univ. of N.C.*, 567 F. Supp. 3d 580 (M.D.N.C. 2021).

129. See *Students for Fair Admissions, Inc. v. President and Fellows of Harvard Coll.*, 397 F. Supp. 3d 126 (D. Mass. 2019); *Students for Fair Admissions, Inc. v. Univ. of N. Carolina*, 567 F. Supp. 3d 580 (M.D.N.C. 2021).

130. *Students for Fair Admissions, Inc. v. President and Fellows of Harvard Coll.*, 600 U.S. 181 (2023).

131. *Students for Fair Admissions, Inc. v. President and Fellows of Harvard Coll.*, 397 F. Supp. 3d 126, 203 (D. Mass. 2019).

132. *Students for Fair Admissions, Inc. v. Univ. of N.C.*, 567 F. Supp. 3d 580, 666 (M.D.N.C. 2021).

133. *Students for Fair Admissions, Inc. v. Univ. of N.C.*, 567 F. Supp. 3d 580, 667 (M.D.N.C. 2021).

134. *Students for Fair Admissions, Inc. v. Univ. of N.C.*, 567 F. Supp. 3d 580, 664 (M.D.N.C. 2021).

135. *Students for Fair Admissions, Inc. v. President and Fellows of Harvard Coll.*, 397 F. Supp. 3d 126, 178 (D. Mass. 2019).

136. *Students for Fair Admissions, Inc. v. President and Fellows of Harvard Coll.*, 397 F. Supp. 3d 126, 178 (D. Mass. 2019).

137. *Students for Fair Admissions, Inc. v. President and Fellows of Harvard Coll.*, 397 F. Supp. 3d 126, 178 (D. Mass. 2019).

138. *Students for Fair Admissions, Inc. v. President and Fellows of Harvard Coll.*, 980 F.3d 157, 164 (1st Cir. 2020).

139. *Students for Fair Admissions, Inc. v. President and Fellows of Harvard Coll.*, 600 U.S. 181, 214 (2023).

140. *Students for Fair Admissions, Inc. v. President and Fellows of Harvard Coll.*, 600 U.S. 181, 411 (Jackson dissenting) (2023).

141. *Students for Fair Admissions, Inc. v. President and Fellows of Harvard Coll.*, 600 U.S. 181, 268 (2023).

142. Fed. R. Civ. P. 52(a)(6).

143. *Students for Fair Admissions, Inc. v. President and Fellows of Harvard Coll.*, 600 U.S. 181, 206, 213 n. 4, 253–54, 268–269 (2023).

144. *Students for Fair Admissions, Inc. v. President and Fellows of Harvard Coll.*, 600 U.S. 181, 398–400 (2023).

145. *Students for Fair Admissions, Inc. v. President and Fellows of Harvard Coll.*, 600 U.S. 181, 230 (2023).

146. *Students for Fair Admissions, Inc. v. President and Fellows of Harvard Coll.*, 600 U.S. 181, 230–31 (2023).

147. Chris Williams, "Republicans Say ABA's Diversity Revision Doesn't Go Far Enough," *Above the Law*, January 8, 2025, https://abovethelaw.com/2025/01/republicans-say-abas-diversity-revision-doesnt-go-far-enough/.

148. See Brief of Asian Americans Advancing Justice and 37 Organizations as Amici Curiae in Support of Respondents, *Students for Fair Admissions, Inc. v. President and Fellows of Harvard Coll.*, 600 U.S. 181 (2023); Brief of Amici Curiae Asian American Legal Defense and Education Fund et al. in Support of Respondents, *Students for Fair Admissions, Inc. v. President and Fellows of Harvard Coll.*, 600 U.S. 181 (2023).

149. Brief for Students and Alumni of Harvard College as Amici Curiae in Support of Respondents at 4, *Students for Fair Admissions, Inc. v. President and Fellows of Harvard Coll.*, 600 U.S. 181 (2023).

150. Brief for Amici Curiae HBCU Leaders and National Association of Equal Opportunity in Higher Education in Support of Respondents, *Students for Fair Admissions, Inc. v. President and Fellows of Harvard Coll.*, 600 U.S. 181 (2023); Brief of the National Academy of Educators as Amicus Curiae in Support of Respondents, *Students for Fair Admissions, Inc. v. President and Fellows of Harvard Coll.*, 600 U.S. 181 (2023); Brief of the National Education Association and Service Employees International Union as Amici Curiae in Support of Respondents, *Students for Fair Admissions, Inc. v. President and Fellows of Harvard Coll.*, 600 U.S. 181 (2023); Brief of National School Boards Association et al. as Amici Curiae in Support of Respondents, *Students for Fair Admissions, Inc. v. President and Fellows of Harvard Coll.*, 600 U.S. 181 (2023); Brief of Amici Curiae College Board, National Association for College Admissions Counseling, et al. in Support of Respondents, *Students for Fair Admissions, Inc. v. President and Fellows of Harvard Coll.*, 600 U.S. 181 (2023); Brief of American Council on Education

and 39 Other Higher Education Associations as Amici Curiae in Support of Respondents, *Students for Fair Admissions, Inc. v. President and Fellows of Harvard Coll.*, 600 U.S. 181 (2023); Brief for Admissions and Testing Professionals as Amici Curiae Supporting Respondents, *Students for Fair Admissions, Inc. v. President and Fellows of Harvard Coll.*, 600 U.S. 181 (2023); Brief of Amici Curiae Deborah Cohen and 67 Other Professors in Support of Respondents, *Students for Fair Admissions, Inc. v. President and Fellows of Harvard Coll.*, 600 U.S. 181 (2023); Brief of American Federation of Teachers as Amicus Curiae in Support of Respondents, *Students for Fair Admissions, Inc. v. President and Fellows of Harvard Coll.*, 600 U.S. 181 (2023); Brief of Amici Curiae Deans of U.S. Law Schools on Behalf of Respondents, *Students for Fair Admissions, Inc. v. President and Fellows of Harvard Coll.*, 600 U.S. 181 (2023); Brief of Professors of History and Law as Amici Curiae in Support of Respondents, *Students for Fair Admissions, Inc. v. President and Fellows of Harvard Coll.*, 600 U.S. 181 (2023); Brief for the American Bar Association as Amicus Curiae in Support of Respondents, *Students for Fair Admissions, Inc. v. President and Fellows of Harvard Coll.*, 600 U.S. 181 (2023); Brief of the Washington Bar Association and the Women's Bar Association of D.C. as Amici Curiae in Support of Respondents, *Students for Fair Admissions, Inc. v. President and Fellows of Harvard Coll.*, 600 U.S. 181 (2023); Brief for 25 Diverse, California-Focused Bar Associations et al. as Amici Curiae in Support of Respondents, *Students for Fair Admissions, Inc. v. President and Fellows of Harvard Coll.*, 600 U.S. 181 (2023); Brief of Amici Curiae National Asian Pacific American Bar Association and National LGBTQ* Bar Association in Support of Respondents, *Students for Fair Admissions, Inc. v. President and Fellows of Harvard Coll.*, 600 U.S. 181 (2023); Brief of Amici Curiae National Women's Law Center and 37 Additional Organizations Committed to Race and Gender Equality in Support of Respondents, *Students for Fair Admissions, Inc. v. President and Fellows of Harvard Coll.*, 600 U.S. 181 (2023); Brief of Amici Curiae National Black Law Students Association in Support of Respondents, *Students for Fair Admissions, Inc. v. President and Fellows of Harvard Coll.*, 600 U.S. 181 (2023); Brief of Amici Curiae the American Civil Liberties Union et al. in Support of Respondents, *Students for Fair Admissions, Inc. v. President and Fellows of Harvard Coll.*, 600 U.S. 181 (2023); Brief of the National Education Association and Service Employees International Union as Amici Curiae in Support of Respondents, *Students for Fair Admissions, Inc. v. President and Fellows of Harvard Coll.*, 600 U.S. 181 (2023); Brief for Amici Curiae American Psychological Association et al. in Support of Respondents, *Students for Fair Admissions, Inc. v. President and Fellows of Harvard Coll.*, 600 U.S. 181 (2023); Brief of Adm. Charles S. Abbot et al. as Amici Curiae in Support of Respondents, *Students for Fair Admissions, Inc. v. President and Fellows of Harvard Coll.*, 600 U.S. 181 (2023); Brief in Support of Respondents of Amici Curiae Multicultural Media, Telecom and Internet Council, Inc., et al., *Students for Fair Admissions, Inc. v. President and Fellows of Harvard Coll.*, 600 U.S. 181 (2023); Brief of Bobby Scott, Member of Congress, and 64 other Members of Congress, as Amici Curiae Supporting Respondents, *Students for Fair Admissions, Inc. v. President and Fellows of Harvard Coll.*, 600 U.S. 181 (2023); Brief of Amici Curiae United States Senators and Former Senators Supporting Respondents, *Students for Fair Admissions, Inc. v. President and Fellows of Harvard Coll.*, 600 U.S. 181 (2023); Brief for Massachusetts, California, et al. as Amici Curiae in Support of Respondents, *Students for Fair Admissions, Inc. v. President and Fellows of Harvard Coll.*, 600 U.S. 181 (2023); Brief of Southern Governors as Amici Curiae in Support of Respondents, *Students for Fair Admissions, Inc. v. President and Fellows of Harvard Coll.*, 600 U.S. 181 (2023); Brief for Massachusetts Institute of Technology et al. as Amici Curiae in Support of Respondents, *Students for Fair Admissions, Inc. v. President and Fellows of Harvard Coll.*, 600 U.S. 181 (2023); Brief for Amici Curiae Applied Materials, Inc., et al. in Support of Respondents, *Students for Fair Admissions, Inc. v. President and Fellows of Harvard Coll.*, 600 U.S. 181 (2023); Brief for Major American Business Enterprises as Amici Curiae Supporting Respondents, *Students for Fair Admissions, Inc. v. President and Fellows of Harvard Coll.*, 600 U.S. 181 (2023); Brief of Amici Curiae Individual Scientists in Support of Respondents, *Students for Fair Admissions, Inc. v. President and Fellows of Harvard Coll.*, 600 U.S. 181 (2023); Brief of Faith Organizations as Amici Curiae in Support of Respondents, *Students for Fair Admissions, Inc. v. President and Fellows of Harvard Coll.*, 600 U.S. 181 (2023); Brief of 1,246 American Social Science Researchers and Scholars as Amici Curiae in Support of Respondents, *Students for Fair Admissions, Inc. v. President and Fellows of Harvard Coll.*, 600 U.S. 181 (2023).

Chapter Thirteen. Diversity Science

1. Malcolm Gladwell, *Blink: The Power of Thinking Without Thinking* (New York: Little, Brown, 2007).
2. David Rock, Heidi Grant, and Jacqui Grey, "Diverse Teams Feel Less Comfortable—and That's Why They Perform Better," *Harvard Business Review*, September 22, 2016, https://hbr.org/2016/09/diverse-teams-feel-less-comfortable-and-thats-why-they-perform-better.
3. See "Katherine W. Phillips," Google Scholar, accessed August 7, 2023, https://scholar.google.com/citations?user=LtMuT7IAAAAJ&hl=en.
4. Katherine W. Phillips, "How Diversity Makes Us Smarter," *Scientific American* 311, no. 4 (October 2014): 43–47, https://doi.org/10.1038/scientificamerican1014-42.
5. Victoria C. Plaut, "Diversity Science: Why and How Difference Makes a Difference," *Psychological Inquiry* 21, no. 2 (June 2010): 77–99, https://doi.org/10.1080/10478401003676501.

6. Stacy Cowley, "Katherine W. Phillips, 47, Dies; Taught the Value of Diversity," *New York Times*, February 13, 2020, www.nytimes.com/2020/02/13/business/katherine-w-phillips-dead.html.

7. Cowley, "Katherine W. Phillips, 47, Dies."

8. Cowley, "Katherine W. Phillips, 47, Dies."

9. Sofia Kwon, "Katherine Phillips, Business School Professor, Leaves Lasting Legacy of Workplace Diversity," *Columbia Daily Spectator*, February 19, 2020, www.columbiaspectator.com/news/2020/02/20/katherine-phillips-business-school-professor-and-workplace-diversity-advocate-has-died/; Cowley, "Katherine W. Phillips, 47, Dies."

10. "Katherine W. Phillips," LinkedIn, accessed February 25, 2024, www.linkedin.com/in/katherine-w-phillips-7265831/; "Strength Through Diversity," *Purpose Built Communities*, July 9 2019. https://purposebuiltcommunities.org/podcast/strength-through-diversity/.

11. Cowley, "Katherine W. Phillips, 47, Dies."

12. Cowley, "Katherine W. Phillips, 47, Dies."

13. "Katherine W. Phillips (1972–2020)," *Managerial and Organizational Cognition Division*, 2020, https://moc.aom.org/new-item4/kathyphillips.

14. "Katherine W. Phillips (1972–2020)," *Managerial and Organizational Cognition Division*.

15. Phillips, "How Diversity Makes Us Smarter," 43–47.

16. Phillips, "How Diversity Makes Us Smarter," 43–47.

17. John Stuart Mill, *Inaugural Address at St. Andrews* (London: Longmans, Green, Reader, and Dyer, 1867), 25, https://archive.org/details/inauguraladdresoomillgoog/mode/2up; Graham Finlay, "John Stuart Mill on the Uses of Diversity," *Utilitas* 14, no. 2 (2002): 189–218, 199.

18. Brief for Respondents at 21–26, *Grutter v. Bollinger*, 539 U.S. 306 (2003) (No. 02–241), 2003 WL 402236.

19. Brief for Respondents at 21–26, *Grutter*, 539 U.S. 306 (2003) (No. 02–241), 2003 WL 402236.

20. Brief for Respondents at 24, n.37, *Grutter*, 539 U.S. 306 (2003) (No. 02–241), 2003 WL 402236.

21. William G. Bowen and Derek Bok, *The Shape of the River: Long-Term Consequences of Considering Race in College and University Admissions* (Princeton: Princeton University Press, 1998).

22. Bowen and Bok, *The Shape of the River*, 225–28.

23. Patricia Gurin, Eric Dey, Sylvia Hurtado, and Gerald Gurin, "Diversity and Higher Education: Theory and Impact on Educational Outcomes," *Harvard Educational Review* 72, no. 3 (2002): 330–66, https://doi.org/10.17763/haer.72.3.01151786u134n051 (see abstract).

24. Gurin et al., "Diversity and Higher Education," 333–34.

25. *Grutter*, 539 U.S. at 330, citing Brief for American Educational Research Association et al. as *Amici Curiae*, 3.

26. Anthony Lising Antonio et al., "Effects of Racial Diversity on Complex Thinking in College Students," *Psychological Science* 15, no. 8 (2004): 507–10, https://doi.org/10.1111/j.0956-7976.2004.00710.x.

27. Sylvia Hurtado, "The Next Generation of Diversity and Intergroup Relations Research," *Journal of Social Issues* 61, no. 3 (2005): 595–610, 598–606, https://doi.org/10.1111/j.1540-4560.2005.00422.x.

28. Jeffrey F. Milem, Mitchell J. Chang, and Anthony Lising Antonio, *Making Diversity Work on Campus: A Research-Based Perspective*, Making Excellence Inclusive Initiative (Association of American Colleges and Universities, 2005), 8, https://web.stanford.edu/group/siher/AntonioMilemChang_making diversitywork.pdf. (discussing as examples death penalty and child labor discussions); Antonio et al., "Effects of Racial Diversity on Complex Thinking."

29. Katherine W. Phillips and Denise Lewin Loyd, "When Surface and Deep-Level Diversity Collide: The Effects of Dissenting Group Members," *Organizational Behavior and Human Decision Processes* 99, no. 2 (2006): 143–60, https://doi.org/10.1016/j.obhdp.2005.12.001.

30. Katherine W. Phillips, Katie A. Liljenquist, and Margaret A. Neale, "Is the Pain Worth the Gain? The Advantages and Liabilities of Agreeing with Socially Distinct Newcomers," *Personality and Social Psychology Bulletin* 35, no. 3 (2009): 336–50, https://doi.org/10.1177/0146167208328062.

31. Phillips, Liljenquist, and Neale, "Is the Pain Worth the Gain?," 347.

32. Phillips, Liljenquist, and Neale, "Is the Pain Worth the Gain?," 336.

33. Richard N. Pitt and Josh Packard, "Activating Diversity: The Impact of Student Race on Contributions to Course Discussions," *Sociological Quarterly* 53, no. 2 (2012): 295–320, 295, https://doi.org/10.1111/j.1533-8525.2012.01235.x.

34. Thomas F. Nelson Laird, "College Students' Experiences with Diversity and Their Effects on Academic Self-Confidence, Social Agency, and Disposition Toward Critical Thinking," *Research in Higher Education* 46, no. 4 (2005): 365–87, 365, https://link.springer.com/article/10.1007/s11162-005-2966-1.

35. Christina L. Rucinski et al., "Classroom Racial/Ethnic Diversity and Upper Elementary Children's Social-Emotional Development," *Applied Developmental Science* 25, no. 2 (2021): 183–99, 183, https://doi.org/10.1080/10888691.2019.1576524.

36. Peter H. Schuck, "Assessing Affirmative Action," *National Affairs* 20 (2014): 76–96, 76.

37. Abigail Thernstrom, "Questioning the Rationale for Affirmative Action," *Virtual Mentor* 16, no. 6 (2014): 495–97, 495.

38. Thomas Sowell, "The 'Diversity' Fraud," *Creators*, December 20, 2016, www.creators.com/read/thomas-sowell/12/16/the-diversity-fraud.

39. *Fac., Alumni, & Students Opposed to Racial Preferences v. N.Y. Univ.*, 11 F.4th 68, 73 (2d Cir. 2021), *cert. denied*, 142 S. Ct. 2813 (2022); *Fac., Alumni, & Students Opposed to Racial Preferences v. Harvard L. Rev. Ass'n*, 2019 WL 3754023, at 2 (D. Mass. 2019).

40. Adam Chilton, Justin Driver, Jonathan S. Masur, and Kyle Rozema, "Assessing Affirmative Action's Diversity Rationale," *Columbia Law Review* 122, no. 2 (2022): 331–406, 331, https://columbialawreview.org/content/assessing-affirmative-actions-diversity-rationale/.

41. Michelle Castellanos and Darnell Cole, "Disentangling the Impact of Diversity Courses: Examining the Influence of Diversity Course Content on Students' Civic Engagement," *Journal of College Student Development* 56, no. 8 (2015): 794–811, 805, https://doi.org/10.1353/csd.2015.0089.

42. Thomas F. Pettigrew and Linda R. Tropp, "A Meta-Analytic Test of Intergroup Contact Theory," *Journal of Personality and Social Psychology* 90, no. 5 (2006): 751–83, 766, https://doi.org/10.1037/0022-3514.90.5.751.

43. Nida Denson and Mitchell J. Chang, "Racial Diversity Matters: The Impact of Diversity-Related Student Engagement and Institutional Context," *American Educational Research Journal* 46, no. 2 (2009): 322–53, 336, https://doi.org/10.3102/0002831208323278.

44. L. E. Gomez and Patrick Bernet, "Diversity Improves Performance and Outcomes," *Journal of the National Medical Association* 111, no. 4 (2019): 383–92, 383, https://doi.org/10.1016/j.jnma.2019.01.006; see also Ivuoma N. Onyeador et al., "The Value of Interracial Contact for Reducing Anti-Black Bias Among Non-Black Physicians: A Cognitive Habits and Growth Evaluation (CHANGE) Study Report," *Psychological Science* 31, no. 1 (2020): 18–30, 18, https://doi.org//10.1177/0956797619879139.

45. Onyeador et al., "The Value of Interracial Contact," 28.

46. Hurtado, "The Next Generation," 606.

47. Mark E. Engberg, "Educating the Workforce for the 21st Century: A Cross-Disciplinary Analysis of the Impact of the Undergraduate Experience on Students' Development of a Pluralistic Orientation," *Research in Higher Education* 48, no. 3 (2007): 283–317, 312, https://doi.org/10.1007/s11162-006-9027-2.

48. Engberg, "Educating the Workforce for the 21st Century," 312.

49. Nicholas A. Bowman, "Promoting Participation in a Diverse Democracy: A Meta-Analysis of College Diversity Experiences and Civic Engagement," *Review of Educational Research* 81, no. 1 (2011): 29–68, 29, https://doi.org/10.3102/0034654310383047.

50. Katherine W. Phillips, "How Diversity Makes Us Smarter," *Scientific American*, October 1, 2014, www.scientificamerican.com/article/how-diversity-makes-us-smarter/, citing Samuel R. Sommers, "On Racial Diversity and Group Decision Making: Identifying Multiple Effects of Racial Composition on Jury Deliberations," *Journal of Personality and Social Psychology* 90, no. 4 (2006): 597–612, https://doi.org/10.1037/0022-3514.90.4.597.

51. Shamena Anwar, Patrick Bayer, and Randi Hjalmarsson, "The Impact of Jury Race in Criminal Trials," *Quarterly Journal of Economics* 127, no. 2 (May 1, 2012): 1017–55, 1017 https://doi.org/10.1093/qje/qjs014.

52. Ivan Natividad, "Victoria Plaut Is Berkeley's New Vice Provost for the Faculty," *Berkeley News*, July 1, 2022, https://news.berkeley.edu/2022/07/01/victoria-plaut-is-berkeleys-new-vice-provost-for-the-faculty.

53. Berkeley Law faculty profile, www.law.berkeley.edu/our-faculty/faculty-profiles/victoria-plaut/.

54. Flannery G. Stevens et al., "Unlocking the Benefits of Diversity: All-Inclusive Multiculturalism and Positive Organizational Change," *Journal of Applied Behavioral Science* 44, no. 1 (March 2008): 116–33, https://doi.org/10.1177/0021886308314460. See also Victoria C. Plaut et al., "'What About Me?' Perceptions of Exclusion and Whites' Reactions to Multiculturalism," *Journal of Personality and Social Psychology* 101, no. 2 (2011): 337–53, https://doi.org/10.1037/a0022832.

55. Kyneshawau Hurd and Victoria C. Plaut, "Diversity Entitlement: Does Diversity-Benefits Ideology Undermine Inclusion?," *Northwestern University Law Review* 112, no. 6 (2018): 1605–36, https://scholarlycommons.law.northwestern.edu/cgi/viewcontent.cgi?article=1345&context=nulr.

56. Taylor Telford and Julian Mark, "DEI Is Getting a New Name. Can It Dump the Political Baggage?," *Washington Post*, May 5, 2024, www.washingtonpost.com/business/2024/05/05/dei-affirmative-action-rebrand-evolution/.

57. Hurd and Plaut, "Diversity Entitlement," 1607.

58. *Grutter*, 539 U.S. at 355.

59. Melissa C. Thomas-Hunt and Katherine W. Phillips, "When What You Know Is Not Enough: Expertise and Gender Dynamics in Task Groups," *Personality and Social Psychology Bulletin* 30, no. 12 (December 2004): 1585–98, https://doi.org/10.1177/0146167204271186.

60. Victoria C. Plaut, "Inviting Everyone In," *Scientific American* 311, no. 4 (October 2014): 52–57, https://doi.org/10.1038/Scientificamerican1014-52.

61. Plaut, "Inviting Everyone In," quoting from Gregory M. Walton and Geoffrey L. Cohen, "A Brief Social-Belonging Intervention Improves Academic and Health Outcomes of Minority Students," *Science* 331 (2011): 1447–51, https://doi.org/10.1126/science.1198364.

62. Patricia Gurin, Biren A. Nagda, and Gretchen E. Lopez, "The Benefits of Diversity in Education for Democratic Citizenship," *Journal of Social Issues* 60, no. 1 (2004): 17–34, 20–24, https://doi.org/10.1111/j.0022-4537.2004.00097.x.

63. Nicholas A. Bowman, Nida Denson, and Julie J. Park, "Racial/Cultural Awareness Workshops and Post-College Civic Engagement: A Propensity Score Matching Approach," *American Educational Research Journal* 53, no. 6 (2016): 1556–87, 1576 (table 4), https://doi.org/10.3102/0002831216670510.

64. Richard B. Freeman and Wei Huang, "Collaborating with People Like Me: Ethnic Coauthorship Within the United States," *Journal of Labor Economics* 33, no. 1 (2015): S289-S318, S289, https://doi.org/10.1086/678973.

65. Yang Yang et al., "Gender-Diverse Teams Produce More Novel and Higher-Impact Scientific Ideas," *Proceedings of the National Academy of Sciences of the United States of America* 119, no. 36 (2022): e2200841119, https://doi.org/10.1073/pnas.2200841119.

Chapter Fourteen. The Business Case for Diversity

1. "In Good Company: 25 Best Places for Blacks to Work," *Black Enterprise*, February 1986, 89–102.
2. David B. Oppenheimer, "The Disappearance of Voluntary Affirmative Action from the U.S. Workplace," *Journal of Poverty and Social Justice* 24, no. 1 (2016): 37–50, 45, https://doi.org/10.1332/175982716x14538098991133.
3. Sonia Alleyne, "The 40 Best Companies for Diversity," *Black Enterprise*, July 1, 2006, www.blackenterprise.com/mag/the-40-best-companies-for-diversity/.
4. Alleyne, "The 40 Best Companies for Diversity"; Oppenheimer, "Disappearance of Voluntary Affirmative Action," 45.
5. Insight Staff, "Focus on DEI in Higher Education," Insight into Diversity, September 25, 2023, www.insightintodiversity.com/focus-on-dei-in-higher-education-highlighting-your-work-for-50-years/.
6. Oppenheimer, "Disappearance of Voluntary Affirmative Action," 45; Price Cobbs, Lennie Copeland, and Lewis Griggs, "Valuing Diversity," Griggs Productions, 1988, YouTube, https://youtube.com/playlist?list=PLiJyjSQ4i EzJh-nkgppxDVp5_IFwMbD1O.
7. Research on file with author.
8. Research on file with author.
9. Caroline Colvin, "Once Neglected, DEI Initiatives Now Present at All Fortune 100 Companies," *HR Dive*, July 20, 2022, www.hrdive.com/news/2022-fortune-companies-dei/627651/; see also for the list of the Fortune 100's public-facing DEI acknowledgment: "Fortune 100 (2022) and Public-Facing DEI Acknowledgements," July 19, 2022, https://docs.google.com/spreadsheets/d/11OBEAG8yQs3olTDDFwt6PoSy9Lqjk9cWslCc-H_ytyo/edit#gid=0.
10. Alison M. Konrad, "Special Issue Introduction: Defining the Domain of Workplace Diversity Scholarship," *Group & Organization Management* 28, no. 1 (2003): 4–17, https://doi.org/10.1177/1059601102250013.
11. Rocío Lorenzo et al., "How Diverse Leadership Teams Boost Innovation," Boston Consulting Group, January 23, 2018, www.bcg.com/publications/2018/how-diverse-leadership-teams-boost-innovation (finding that companies with above average leadership diversity produced 19 percent more revenue); Dame Vivian Hunt et al., "Delivering Through Diversity," McKinsey and Company, January 18, 2018, www.mckinsey.com/capabilities/people-and-organizational-performance/our-insights/delivering-through-diversity (finding that companies with executive teams in the top-quartile for gender and

ethnic/cultural diversity are 21 percent and 33 percent, respectively, more likely to have above-average profitability than those in the bottom quartile).

12. Quinn Curtis, Jill Fisch, and Adriana Z. Robertson, "Do ESG Funds Deliver on Their Promises?," *Michigan Law Review* 120, no. 3 (2021): 393–450, https://repository.law.umich.edu/mlr/vol120/iss3/2/; RBC Global Asset Management, *Does Socially Responsible Investing Hurt Investment Returns?* (Royal Bank of Canada, 2019), 16, www.rbcgam.com/documents/en/articles/does-socially-responsible-investing-hurt-investment-returns.pdf.

13. Yang Yang et al., "Gender-Diverse Teams Produce More Novel and Higher-Impact Scientific Ideas," *Proceedings of the National Academy of Sciences* 119, no. 36 (2022): e2200841119, https://doi.org/10.1073/pnas.2200841119; Kendall Powell, "These Labs Are Remarkably Diverse—Here's Why They're Winning at Science," *Nature*, June 6, 2018, www.nature.com/articles/d41586-018-05316-5.

14. John Stuart Mill, *On Liberty* (Kitchener: Batoche Books, 2001), 22.

15. Erik Larson, "New Research: Diversity + Inclusion = Better Decision Making at Work," *Forbes Magazine*, September 21, 2017, www.forbes.com/sites/eriklarson/2017/09/21/new-research-diversity-inclusion-better-decision-making-at-work/?sh=400117174cbf; Vivian Hunt, Dennis Layton, and Sara Prince, "Diversity Matters," McKinsey and Company, February 2, 2015, 9–12, www.mckinsey.com/~/media/mckinsey/business%20functions/people%20and%20organizational%20performance/our%20insights/why%20diversity%20matters/diversity%20matters.pdf.

16. Thomas Helfrich, "How Diversity Can Help with Business Growth," *Forbes*, November 12, 2021, www.forbes.com/sites/forbestechcouncil/2021/11/12/how-diversity-can-help-with-business-growth/.

17. Cobbs, Copeland, and Griggs, "Valuing Diversity"; Oppenheimer, "Disappearance of Voluntary Affirmative Action," 44.

18. Lennie Copeland, email message to author, December 2, 2014 (on file with author); Lennie Copeland, "Valuing Diversity, Part 1: Making the Most of Cultural Differences at Work," *Personnel* 65, no. 6 (1988): 52–59.

19. Lennie Copeland, email message to author, December 2, 2014 (on file with author).

20. Dana Wilkie, "Roosevelt Thomas, Jr., Pioneer in Workplace Diversity, Dies," *Society for Human Resource Management*, May 22, 2013, www.shrm.org/resourcesandtools/hr-topics/behavioral-competencies/global-and-cultural-effectiveness/pages/rooseveltthomas.aspx.

21. "Roosevelt Thomas, Jr.," *Diversity Officer Magazine*, accessed April 3, 2023, https://diversityofficermagazine.com/leadership/roosevelt-thomas-jr/.

22. R. Roosevelt Thomas, Jr., "From Affirmative Action to Affirming Diversity," *Harvard Business Review* 68, no. 2 (1990): 107–17.

23. "Fortune/Deloitte CEO Survey: October 2020 Highlights," Deloitte, www2.deloitte.com/content/dam/Deloitte/us/Documents/CMO/fortune-deloitte-CEO-survey-october-2020-highlights.pdf.

24. Frank R. Dobbin et al., "The Expansion of Due Process in Organizations," in *Institutional Patterns and Organizations: Culture and Environment*, ed. Lynne G. Zucker (Cambridge: Ballinger, 1988), 71–98; Frank Dobbin, *Inventing Equal Opportunity* (Princeton: Princeton University Press, 2009); Lauren B. Edelman, Sally Riggs Fuller, and Iona Mara-Drita, "Diversity Rhetoric and the Managerialization of Law," *American Journal of Sociology* 106, no. 6 (2001): 1589–641.

25. Dobbin, *Inventing Equal Opportunity*; Edelman et al., "Diversity Rhetoric and the Managerialization of Law," 1589–641.

26. Dobbin, *Inventing Equal Opportunity*, 133–60.

27. Edelman et al., "Diversity Rhetoric and the Managerialization of Law," 1591.

28. Brief of 65 Leading American Businesses as Amici Curiae Supporting Respondents at 7 n.5, *Grutter v. Bollinger*, 539 U.S. 306 (2003) (Nos. 02–241, 02–516); Janine S. Hiller and Stephen P. Ferris, "Separating Myth from Reality: An Economic Analysis of Voluntary Affirmative Action Programs," *University of Memphis Law Review* 23, no. 4 (1993): 773–804, 794–95; Federal Glass Ceiling Commission, *A Solid Investment: Making Full Use of the Nation's Human Capital* (Washington, D.C.: The Commission, 1995), https://hdl.handle.net/2027/uc1.31210016330647; John P. Fernandez, *Race, Gender, and Rhetoric: The True State of Race and Gender Relations in Corporate America* (New York: McGraw-Hill, 1999); Taylor H. Cox and Stacy Blake, "Managing Cultural Diversity: Implications for Organizational Competitiveness," *Academy of Management Executive* 5, no. 3 (1991): 45–56, 48–49; See, e.g., Charlan J. Nemeth, "Differential Contributions of Majority and Minority Influence," *Psychological Review* 93, no. 1 (1986): 23–32; Sumita Raghuram and Raghu Garud, "The Vicious and Virtuous Facets of Workforce Diversity," in *Selected Research on Work Team Diversity*, ed. Marian N. Ruderman, Martha W. Hughes-James, and Susan E. Jackson (Washington, D.C.: American Psychological Association, 1996), 155–78; John P. Fernandez, *The Diversity Advantage: How American Business Can Out-Perform Japanese and European Companies in the Global Marketplace* (New York: Lexington Books, 1993), 284–85.

29. Brief of General Motors Corporation as Amicus Curiae Supporting Respondents, *Grutter*, 539 U.S. 306 (2003) (Nos. 02–241, 02–516); Brief of 65 Leading American Businesses as Amici Curiae Supporting Respondents, *Grutter*, 539 U.S. 306 (2003) (Nos. 02–241, 02–516).

30. Navjot Hansra, Kellie McElhaney, and Genevieve Smith, *The Business Case for Gender Diversity: A Research Compendium* (Berkeley: UC Berkeley Haas School of Business Center for Equity, Gender, and Leadership, 2019), https://haas.berkeley.edu/wp-content/uploads/Business-Case-for-Gender-Diversity_EGAL_June-2019.pdf.

31. Catalyst, "Why Diversity and Inclusion Matter," (2020), www.catalyst.org/research/why-diversity-and-inclusion-matter/.

32. "What We Do," Catalyst, accessed October 13, 2024, www.catalyst.org/what-we-do/.

33. Catalyst, *The Bottom Line: Connecting Corporate Performance and Gender Diversity* (2004), www.catalyst.org/wp-content/uploads/2019/01/The_Bottom_Line_Connecting_Corporate_Performance_and_Gender_Diversity.pdf.

34. Lois Joy et al., *The Bottom Line: Corporate Performance and Women's Representation on Boards* (Catalyst, 2007), www.catalyst.org/wp-content/uploads/2019/01/The_Bottom_Line_Corporate_Performance_and_Womens_Representation_on_Boards.pdf.

35. Nancy M. Carter and Harvey M. Wagner, *The Bottom Line: Corporate Performance and Women's Representation on Boards (2004–2008)* (Catalyst, 2011), www.catalyst.org/wp-content/uploads/2019/01/the_bottom_line_corporate_performance_and_womens_representation_on_boards_2004–2008.pdf.

36. Catalyst, *Why Diversity Matters* (July 2013), https://talentfirst.net/wp-content/uploads/2023/12/Catalyst_-Why-Diversity-Matters.pdf.

37. Hunt et al., "Diversity Matters."

38. Hunt et al., "Delivering Through Diversity."

39. Paul Gompers and Silpa Kovvali, "The Other Diversity Dividend," *Harvard Business Review* 96, no. 4 (2018): 72–77, 75, https://hbr.org/2018/07/the-other-diversity-dividend.

40. Gompers and Kovvali, "The Other Diversity Dividend."

41. Gompers and Kovvali, "The Other Diversity Dividend."

42. FP Analytics, *Women as Levers of Change: Unleashing the Power of Women to Transform Male-Dominated Industries* (2020), https://womenasleversofchange.com/.

43. FP Analytics, *Women as Levers of Change.*

44. Vijay Eswaran, "The Business Case for Diversity in the Workplace is Now Overwhelming," World Economic Forum, April 29, 2019, www.weforum.org/agenda/2019/04/business-case-for-diversity-in-the-workplace.

45. Heather Foust-Cummings, Laura Sabattini, and Nancy Carter, *Women in Technology: Maximizing Talent, Minimizing Barriers* (New York: Catalyst, 2008), 2–3, www.catalyst.org/wp-content/uploads/2019/01/Women_in_Technology_Maximizing_Talent_Minimizing_Barriers.pdf.

46. Council of Institutional Investors, "Corporate Governance Policies," 8, March 7, 2022, www.cii.org/files/03_07_22_corp_gov_policies.pdf.

47. BlackRock, *BlackRock Investment Stewardship: Proxy Voting Guidelines for U.S. Securities* (2022), 6–7, https://perma.cc/EW84-PS5S; see also BlackRock, *Our Approach to Engagement on Board Diversity* (2021), 2, https://perma.cc/BL38-SLGS.

48. Stefanie K. Johnson, David R. Hekman, and Elsa T. Chan, "If There's Only One Woman in Your Candidate Pool, There's Statistically No Chance She'll Be Hired," *Harvard Business Review*, April 26, 2016, https://hbr.org/2016/04/if-theres-only-one-woman-in-your-candidate-pool-theres-statistically-no-chance-shell-be-hired.

49. Vanguard, *Proxy Voting Policy for U.S. Portfolio Companies* (2021), 5, https://perma.cc/XLE9-YP7C; Vanguard, *Investment Stewardship: 2020 Annual Report* (2020), 27, https://corporate.vanguard.com/content/dam/corp/advocate/investment-stewardship/pdf/policies-and-reports/2020_investment_stewardship_annual_report.pdf.

50. Northern Trust Asset Management, *Stewardship Report 2020* (2020), 34, https://perma.cc/S3RS-DZL7.

51. Brief of Investors and Investment Advisers as Amici Curiae Supporting Respondent Securities and Exchange Commission at 6–7, *All. for Fair Bd. Recruitment v. SEC*, No. 21–60626 (5th Cir. April 1, 2022); US SIF, *2020 Report on US Sustainable and Impact Investing Tools: 2020 Trends Report Highlights* (2020).

52. San Francisco Bar Association, *2015 Goals and Timetables for Minority Hiring, Advancement, and Retention Report* (2015), 10, www.sfbar.org/wp-content/uploads/2019/09/2015-goals-and-timetables-report.pdf.

53. Drucilla Stender Ramey, "A '70's Woman's View of 40 Years in the Life of the Law," *Golden Gate University Law Review* 47, no. 2 (2017): 145–52, https://heinonline.org/HOL/P?h=hein.journals/ggulr47&i=187.

54. San Francisco Bar Association, *2015 Goals and Timetables*, 10, 76.

55. Brad Smith, "ABA Resolution 113: Creating a Legal Profession That Reflects the Public It Serves," Microsoft, November 22, 2016, https://blogs.microsoft.com/on-the-issues/2016/11/22/aba-resolution-113-creating-legal-profession-reflects-public-serves/; Brad Smith, "Microsoft Women- and Minority-owned Law Firm Legal Spending This Decade Tops $100 Million: Additional Progress Towards a More Diverse and Inclusive Legal Profession," Microsoft, November 1, 2016, https://blogs.microsoft.com/on-the-issues/2016/11/01/microsoft-legal-spending-on-women-and-minority-owned-law-firms-tops-100-million-this-decade-toward-aim-of-more-diverse-and-inclusive-legal-profession/.

56. American Bar Association, "ABA Model Diversity Survey," accessed August 14, 2023, www.americanbar.org/groups/diversity/DiversityCommission/model-diversity-survey/.

57. American Bar Association, "ABA Model Diversity Survey."

58. "An Open Letter from the 2020–2021 Mansfield Law Firms Chairs & Managing Partners," Diversity Lab, accessed August 14, 2023, www.diversitylab.com/mansfield-rule-4-0/.

59. Caren Ulrich Stacy, "44 Law Firms Pilot Version of Rooney Rule to Boost Diversity in Leadership Ranks," Diversity Lab, September 25, 2017, www.diversitylab.com/wp-content/uploads/2015/08/Mansfield-Rule-Press-Release-Updated-9-25-17-Diversity-Lab.pdf.

60. Ellen Rosen, "Facebook Pushes Outside Law Firms to Become More Diverse," *New York Times*, April 2, 2017, www.nytimes.com/2017/04/02/business/dealbook/facebook-pushes-outside-law-firms-to-become-more-diverse.html.

61. Rosen, "Facebook Pushes Outside Law Firms to Become More Diverse."

62. Rosen, "Facebook Pushes Outside Law Firms to Become More Diverse" (discussing Hewlett-Packard as an example).

63. Sam Skolnik, "Novartis Demands Outside Counsel Make Tough Diversity Guarantees," *Bloomberg Law*, February 12, 2020, https://news.bloomberglaw.com/us-law-week/novartis-demands-outside-counsel-make-tough-diversity-guarantees.

64. "PINC-01. Selected Characteristics of People 15 Years and Over, by Total Money Income, Work Experience, Race, Hispanic Origin, and Sex," *United States Census Bureau*, https://www.census.gov/data/tables/time-series/demo/income-poverty/cps-pinc/pinc-01.html#par_textimage_14.

65. Maryam Akbari et al., "Is Driver Education Contributing Towards Road Safety? A Systematic Review of Systematic Reviews," *Journal of Injury & Violence Research* 13, no. 1 (2021): 69–80, https://pmc.ncbi.nlm.nih.gov/articles/PMC8142340/.

66. Frank Dobbin and Alexandra Kalev, "Why Doesn't Diversity Training Work?," *Anthropology Now* 10, no. 2 (2018): 48–55, 49, https://scholar.harvard.edu/files/dobbin/files/an2018.pdf.

67. Edward Chang et al., "Does Diversity Training Work the Way It's Supposed To?," *Harvard Business Review*, July 9, 2019, https://hbr.org/2019/07/does-diversity-training-work-the-way-its-supposed-to.

68. Dobbin and Kalev, "Why Doesn't Diversity Training Work?," 49.

69. Dobbin and Kalev, "Why Doesn't Diversity Training Work?," 50.

70. Emilio J. Castilla and Stephen Benard, "The Paradox of Meritocracy in Organizations," *Administrative Science Quarterly* 55, no. 4 (2010), https://journals.sagepub.com/doi/10.2189/asqu.2010.55.4.543; Dobbin and Kalev, "Why Doesn't Diversity Training Work?," 50.

71. Dobbin and Kalev, "Why Doesn't Diversity Training Work?," 50.

72. Dobbin and Kalev, "Why Doesn't Diversity Training Work?," 50.

73. Dobbin and Kalev, "Why Doesn't Diversity Training Work?," 50–52.

74. "New Lawsuit Challenges California's Mandatory Implicit Bias Training in Healthcare," Pacific Legal Foundation, August 1, 2023, https://pacificlegal.org/press-release/new-lawsuit-challenges-californias-mandatory-implicit-bias-training-in-healthcare/, accessed May 8, 2024; Ronnie Cohen, "California's Mandatory Antibias Training for Doctors Violates Free Speech, Critics Say," *San Francisco Chronicle*, February 23, 2024, www.sfchronicle.com/health/article/california-doctor-anti-bias-training-lawsuit-18681179.php.

75. Frank Dobbin and Alexandra Kalev, "Why Diversity Programs Fail (And What Works Better)," *Harvard Business Review* 94, nos. 7/8 (2016): 52–60, 57, https://hbr.org/2016/07/why-diversity-programs-fail.

76. Dobbin and Kalev, "Why Diversity Programs Fail," 57.

77. Dobbin and Kalev, "Why Diversity Programs Fail," 57.

78. Dobbin and Kalev, "Why Diversity Programs Fail," 57.

79. Dobbin and Kalev, "Why Diversity Programs Fail," 58.

80. Dobbin and Kalev, "Why Diversity Programs Fail," 58.
81. Dobbin and Kalev, "Why Diversity Programs Fail," 58.
82. Dobbin and Kalev, "Why Diversity Programs Fail," 60.
83. Dobbin and Kalev, "Why Diversity Programs Fail," 60.
84. Stephanie N. Downey, Lisa van der Werff, and Victoria C. Plaut, "The Role of Diversity Practices and Inclusion in Promoting Trust and Employee Engagement," *Journal of Applied Social Psychology* 45, no. 1 (2015): 35–44, 39, https://doi.org/10.1111/jasp.12273.
85. Downey et al., "The Role of Diversity Practices and Inclusion," 42.
86. Women Business Collaborative, *Women CEOs in America: Changing the Face of Business Leadership* (2024), 14, https://wbc-a4i-2024.s3.us-east-2.amazonaws.com/2024-WBC-CEO-Report-092304–0658pm-web.pdf. Emma Hinchliffe, "Women CEOs Run 10.4% of Fortune 500 Companies. A Quarter of the 52 Leaders Became CEO in the Last Year," *Fortune* (June 5, 2023), https://fortune.com/2023/06/05/fortune-500-companies-2023-women-10-percent/; Spencer Stuart, *Fortune 500 C-Suite Snapshot: Profiles in Functional Leadership* (December 2023), www.spencerstuart.com/research-and-insight/fortune-500-c-suite-snapshot-profiles-in-functional-leadership.
87. Stuart, *Fortune 500 C-Suite Snapshot*; see also Tina Shah Paikeday, and Nisa Qosja of Russell Reynolds Associates, email messages to author, April 13–14, 2023 (on file with author), regarding RRA Proprietary Analysis, *S&P 100 Leadership Teams* (2022) (n=100 companies, 1,583 executives).
88. Deloitte and the Alliance for Board Diversity, *Missing Pieces: The Board Diversity Census of Women and Minorities on Fortune 500 Boards*, 7th ed. (Deloitte Center for Board Effectiveness, 2023), 11, www2.deloitte.com/content/dam/Deloitte/us/Documents/us-missing-pieces-7th-edition-report.pdf.
89. "Quick Facts," *United States Census Bureau*, www.census.gov/quickfacts/.
90. Andy Kessler, "Who Killed Silicon Valley Bank?," *Wall Street Journal*, March 12, 2023, www.wsj.com/articles/who-killed-silicon-valley-bank-interest-rates-treasury-federal-reserve-ipo-loan-long-term-bond-capital-securities-startup-jpmorgan-bear-stearns-lehman-brothers-b9ca2347; "Ron DeSantis Blames Woke Economics for SVB Collapse," *Fox Business*, YouTube, 57 sec., March 13, 2023, www.youtube.com/watch?v=t-t_h5HsGrA&ab_channel=FoxBusiness.
91. Wall Street Journal Editorial Board, "The Woke NASDAQ," *Wall Street Journal*, December 1, 2020, www.wsj.com/articles/the-woke-nasdaq-11606865986.
92. Andy Kessler, "Who Killed Silicon Valley Bank?"
93. Josh Hawley (@HawleyMO), "So these SVB guys spend all their time funding woke garbage," Twitter (now X), March 13, 2023, https://twitter.com/HawleyMO/status/1635349271632580613; Donald Trump, Jr. (@DonaldJTrumpJr), "SVB is what happens when you push a leftist/woke ideology," Twitter (now X), March 12, 2023, https://twitter.com/DonaldJTrumpJr/status/1634921788068204544; Charlie Kirk (@charliekirk11), "It is a mystery why Silicon Valley Bank collapsed," Twitter (now X), March 10, 2023, https://twitter.com/charliekirk11/status/1634250858362994688?lang=en.

94. U.S. Securities and Exchange Commission, *Release No. 34–92590*, August 6, 2021, 5–6 n.18, www.sec.gov/rules/sro/nasdaq/2021/34-92590.pdf.

95. See "Home," Alliance for Fair Board Recruitment, accessed August 17, 2023, https://fairrecruitment.org/; *All. for Fair Bd. Recruitment v. SEC*, No. 21–60626 (5th Cir. April 1, 2022).

96. 15 U.S.C.A. § 78y(a)(1).

97. Jessica B. Mages, Amy R. Curtis, and Melissa Davis Andrews, "SEC, Nasdaq Square Off Against Challengers to Nasdaq's Board Diversity Rule," *Holland & Knight SECond Opinions Blog*, September 1, 2022, www.hklaw.com/en/insights/publications/2022/09/sec-nasdaq-square-off-against-challengers-to-board-diversity-rule; David Smith, "How Trump Reshaped the Fifth Circuit to Become the 'Most Extreme' US Court," *The Guardian*, November 15, 2021, www.theguardian.com/law/2021/nov/15/fifth-circuit-court-appeals-most-extreme-us.

98. See, e.g., Brief of Ad Hoc Coalition of NASDAQ-Listed Companies as Amicus Curiae Supporting Respondent, *All. for Fair Bd. Recruitment v. SEC*, No. 21–60626 (5th Cir. April 1, 2022), www.akingump.com/a/web/5nWVnuDAafnis54He9JBda/alliance_for_fair_board_recrui_88.pdf.

99. "Diversity on Boards," California Secretary of State, accessed August 17, 2023, www.sos.ca.gov/business-programs/diversity-boards.

100. "Underrepresented Communities on Boards," California Secretary of State, accessed August 17, 2023, www.sos.ca.gov/business-programs/underrepresented-communities-boards.

101. "Women on Boards," California Secretary of State, accessed August 17, 2023, www.sos.ca.gov/business-programs/women-boards.

102. "Women on Boards," California Secretary of State.

103. Judicial Watch, "Closing Arguments Scheduled in California Gender Quota Lawsuit," press release, February 15, 2022, www.judicialwatch.org/closing-arguments-ca-gender-quota/; Judicial Watch, "California Court Opinion Explains Historic Ruling Against Race, Ethnic, LGBT Quotas," press release, April 6, 2022, www.judicialwatch.org/ca-court-opinion-explains-historic-ruling/.

104. *Alliance for Fair Board Recruitment v. Weber*, No. 2:21-CV-01951-JAM-AC, 2023 WL 3481146 (E.D. Cal. May 15, 2023); *Crest v. Padilla*, No. 20STCV37513 (L.A. Superior Ct., April 1, 2022); *Crest v. Padilla*, No. 19STCV27561 (L.A. Superior Ct., May 13, 2022).

105. *Crest v. Padilla*, No. 20STCV37513, slip op. at 17 n.21 (L.A. Superior Ct., April 1, 2022).

106. Michael Hatcher and Weldon Latham, "States Are Leading the Charge to Corporate Boards: Diversify!," *Harvard Law School Forum on Corporate Governance*, May 12, 2020, https://corpgov.law.harvard.edu/2020/05/12/states-are-leading-the-charge-to-corporate-boards-diversify/; Jen Rubin, "Show or Tell: A Roadmap for Board Diversity Laws," *Bloomberg Law*,

June 13, 2022, https://news.bloomberglaw.com/daily-labor-report/show-or-tell-a-road-map-for-board-diversity-laws.

Chapter Fifteen. Diversity and Backlash in Europe

1. See chapter 2.
2. Yazid Sabeg and Laurence Méhaignerie, *Les oubliés de l'égalité des chances* (Institut Montaigne, 2004), www.institutmontaigne.org/publications/les-oublies-de-legalite-des-chances.
3. See "French Diversity Charter," European Commission, accessed August 23, 2023, https://commission.europa.eu/strategy-and-policy/policies/justice-and-fundamental-rights/combatting-discrimination/tackling-discrimination/diversity-and-inclusion-initiatives/diversity-charters-eu-country/french-diversity-charter_en#:~:text=The%20French%20diversity%20charter%20was,inspiring%20similar%20initiatives%20across%20Europe.
4. Laure Bereni, "'Faire de la diversité une richesse pour l'entreprise': La transformation d'une contrainte juridique en catégorie managériale," *Raisons Politiques* 3, no. 35 (2009): 87–105, 90–92, https://doi.org/10.3917/rai.035.0087.
5. "French Diversity Charter," European Commission; "La Charte de la diversité," Charte de la Diversité, accessed August 26, 2023, www.charte-diversite.com/charte-de-la-diversite/ (French).
6. *Voluntary Diversity Initiatives In and For Europe: The Role of Diversity Charters*, European Community Programme for Employment and Social Solidarity, 11, www.iegd.org/pdf/Task 4—Diversity Charters.pdf; see also "About the Diversity Charter," Charta der Vielfalt, accessed February 1, 2024, www.charta-der-vielfalt.de/en/diversity-charter-association/about-the-diversity-charter/.
7. "German Diversity Charter," European Commission, accessed February 28, 2024, https://commission.europa.eu/strategy-and-policy/policies/justice-and-fundamental-rights/combatting-discrimination/tackling-discrimination/diversity-and-inclusion-initiatives/diversity-charters-eu-country/german-diversity-charter_en.
8. Italy and Spain established charters in 2009, followed by Austria and Sweden in 2010, Denmark in 2011, Estonia, Poland, Ireland, Luxembourg, and Finland in 2012, Czechia in 2014, the Netherlands in 2015, Hungry and Portugal in 2016, Croatia, Slovakia, and Slovenia in 2017, Lithuania and Romania in 2018, Cyprus, Greece, and Latvia in 2019, and Bulgaria in 2020. "Diversity Charters by EU Country," European Commission, accessed March 5, 2024, https://commission.europa.eu/strategy-and-policy/policies/justice-and-fundamental-rights/combatting-discrimination/tackling-discrimination/diversity-and-inclusion-initiatives/diversity-charters-eu-country_en.
9. "EU Platform of Diversity Charters," European Commission, accessed June 27, 2019, https://commission.europa.eu/strategy-and-policy/policies/justice-and-fundamental-rights/combatting-discrimination/tackling-discrimination/

diversity-and-inclusion-initiatives/eu-platform-diversity-charters_en; "'United in Diversity—a Common Challenge': EU Diversity Charters' Annual Forum 2019," European Commission, accessed June 28, 2019, https://ec.europa.eu/info/events/united-diversity-common-challenge-2019-may-16_en.

10. Kerensa Keevil, "Strength in Difference: How We're Partnering with Organisations Across Europe to Realise the Power of Diversity and Inclusion," Aga Khan Foundation, January 30, 2023, www.akf.org.uk/strength-in-difference-how-were-partnering-with-organisations-across-europe-to-realise-the-power-of-diversity-and-inclusion/.

11. Viviane Reding, "Time to Reap Europe's Diversity Dividend," in *Corporate Social Responsibility and Diversity Management: Theoretical Approaches and Best Practices*, ed. Katrin Hansen and Cathrine Seierstad (Switzerland: Springer, 2017), v–vii, v, vii, https://doi.org/10.1007/978-3-319-43564-0.

12. David B. Oppenheimer, Henry Cornillie, Henry Bluestone Smith, Thao Thai, and Richard Treadwell, "Be Careful What You Wish For: Ronald Reagan, Donald Trump, The Assault on Civil Rights, and The Surprising Story of How Title VII Got Its Private Right of Action," *Berkeley Journal of Employment and Labor Law* 39, no. 1 (2018): 147–76, 153–55, 171, www.jstor.org/stable/26732547; David Freeman Engstrom, "The Taft Proposal of 1946 and the (Non-) Making of American Fair Employment Law," *Green Bag* 9, no. 2 (2006): 181–202, 183; Frank Dobbin, *Inventing Equal Opportunity* (Princeton: Princeton University Press, 2009), 32.

13. Susan Danger, edited email to author, May 30, 2023 (on file with author).

14. Ionel Zamfir, *Towards Gender Balance in the European Elections: Electoral Quotas—What Can They Achieve?* (Brussels: European Parliament, 2023), 7, www.europarl.europa.eu/RegData/etudes/BRIE/2023/751447/EPRS_BRI(2023)751447_EN.pdf.

15. Pauline Mullet, "Are There Rules to Ensure Parity in European Elections?," *Libération*, March 21, 2019, www.liberation.fr/checknews/2019/03/21/y-a-t-il-des-regles-pour-assurer-la-parite-lors-des-elections-europeennes_1716360/; Pierre Breteau, "European Elections 2019: Why Women Make Up Only a Third of Those Elected to Parliament," *Le Monde*, April 3, 2019, www.lemonde.fr/les-decodeurs/article/2019/04/03/europeennes-pourquoi-les-femmes-ne-representent-qu-un-tiers-des-elus-au-parlement_5445192_4355770.html; Martina Prpic and Samy Chahri, *At a Glance: Women in Parliament* (Brussels: European Parliament, 2017), 2, www.europarl.europa.eu/RegData/etudes/ATAG/2017/599314/EPRS_ATA(2017)599314_EN.pdf. For an overview of measures in Europe on promotion of gender-balance in political decision-making, see Biljana Kotevska and Vera Pavlou, *Promotion of Gender Balance in Political Decision-making* (Luxembourg: European Commission, 2023), www.equalitylaw.eu/downloads/5824-promotion-of-gender-balance-in-political-decision-making.

16. Aaron A. Dhir, *Challenging Boardroom Homogeneity: Corporate Law, Governance, and Diversity* (New York: Cambridge University Press, 2015), 3.

17. Statista Research Department, "Share of Female Directors on Boards in the Financial Services Industry in Europe in 2023, by Country," *Statista*, October 24, 2024, www.statista.com/statistics/1322153/europe-women-on-boards-financial-services-by-country/.

18. Dhir, *Challenging Boardroom Homogeneity*, 76–77; see also Anne Kjølseth Ekerholt, Advokatfirmaet Selmer, and Carmen Di Marino, "Norway," in *Breaking the Glass Ceiling: Women in the Boardroom*, 3rd ed., ed. Tara Giunta and Lianne Labossiere (Paul Hastings LLP, 2013), 94–96.

19. "Gender Statistics Database," European Institute of Gender Equality, accessed August 31, 2023, https://eige.europa.eu/gender-statistics/dgs/indicator/wmidm_bus_bus__wmid_comp_compbm/datatable.

20. Dhir, *Challenging Boardroom Homogeneity*, 113; see also Cathrine Seierstad and Morten Huse, "Gender Quotas on Corporate Boards in Norway: Ten Years Later and Lessons Learned," in *Gender Diversity in the Boardroom*, vol. 1, *The Use of Different Quota Regulations*, ed. Cathrine Seierstad, Patricia Gabaldon, and Heike Mensi-Klarbach (Cham: Springer, 2017), 11–45, 16–17.

21. Dhir, *Challenging Boardroom Homogeneity*, 101, 113.

22. Dhir, *Challenging Boardroom Homogeneity*, 101.

23. Dhir, *Challenging Boardroom Homogeneity*, 101.

24. Dhir, *Challenging Boardroom Homogeneity*, 102.

25. European Commission, *Proposal for a Directive of the European Parliament and of the Council on Improving the Gender Balance Among Non-executive Directors of Companies Listed on Stock Exchanges and Related Measures* (Brussels: European Commission, 2012), 5, https://eur-lex.europa.eu/legal-content/EN/TXT/PDF/?uri=CELEX:52012PC0614&from=EN; European Commission, *Strategic Engagement for Gender Equality 2016–2019* (Luxembourg: Publications Office of the European Union, 2016), 14, https://op.europa.eu/en/publication-detail/-/publication/24968221-eb81-11e5-8a81-01aa75ed71a1.

26. "Gender Equality: The EU Is Breaking the Glass Ceiling Thanks to New Gender Balance Targets on Company Boards," European Commission, November 22, 2022, https://ec.europa.eu/commission/presscorner/detail/en/statement_22_7074.

27. Deloitte and The Alliance for Board Diversity, *Missing Pieces: The Board Diversity Census of Women and Minorities on Fortune 500 Boards*, 6th ed. (Center for Board Effectiveness, 2021), 25, https://static1.squarespace.com/static/5acfa3fc71069926659e2bad/t/60be9dce4637a3474ecf335f/1623104980318/FINAL_Missing_Pieces_Report_Board_Diversity_Census_6th_edition.pdf; U.S. Securities and Exchange Commission, "Comments on NASDAQ Rulemaking: The Nasdaq Stock Market LLC; Notice of Filing of Proposed Rule Change to Adopt Listing Rules Related to Board Diversity," www.sec.gov/comments/sr-nasdaq-2020-081/srnasdaq2020081.htm.

28. Jean Beaman, "Race: A Never-Ending Taboo in France," *Georgetown Journal of International Affairs*, April 1, 2021, https://gjia.georgetown.edu/2021/04/01/race-a-never-ending-taboo-in-france/.

29. Abby LaBreck, "Color-Blind: Examining France's Approach to Race Policy," *Harvard International Review*, February 1, 2021, https://hir.harvard.edu/color-blind-frances-approach-to-race/#:~:text=French%20universalism%20can%20be%20traced,cultural%20distinctions%20or%20historical%20variations; David B. Oppenheimer, "Why France Needs to Collect Data on Racial Identity—In a French Way," *Hastings International and Comparative Law Review* 31, no. 2 (2008): 735–52, https://papers.ssrn.com/sol3/papers.cfm?abstract_id=1236362.

30. Robin Richardot, "Racisme: 91% des personnes noires en métropole se disent victimes de discrimination," *Le Monde*, February 15, 2023, www.lemonde.fr/societe/article/2023/02/15/racisme-91-des-personnes-noires-en-metropole-se-disent-victimes-de-discrimination_6161879_3224.html.

31. Conseil Constitutionnel (Constitutional Council) decision No. 2007–557, November 15, 2007.

32. See "France: Systemic Police Discrimination Requires Reforms," Amnesty International, January 27, 2021, www.amnesty.org/en/latest/news/2021/01/france-systemic-police-discrimination-requires-reforms/

33. Ian Black, "Europe Issues Haider Ultimatum to Austria," *The Guardian*, February 1, 2000, www.theguardian.com/world/2000/feb/01/austria.ianblack; Ian Black and Kate Connolly, "EU leaders Urged to Keep Haider Out," *The Guardian*, January 28, 2000, www.theguardian.com/world/2000/jan/29/ianblack.kateconnolly.

34. David B. Oppenheimer, "Facts Are Essential," *Law.com*, June 11, 2007, www.law.com/nationallawjournal/almID/1181293529767/.

35. Laurent Thévenot, *Droit et Bonnes Pratiques Statistiques en Matiere de Discrimination: Jalons historiques d'un questionnement sur les origines* (INSEE, 2006), 2, www.researchgate.net/publication/238688253_DROIT_ET_BONNES_PRATIQUES_STATISTIQUES_EN_MATIERE_DE_DISCRIMINATION_Jalons_historiques_d'un_questionnement_sur_les_origines_1. (translated by author).

36. "France Police Cleared over Zyed and Bouna 2005 Deaths," BBC News, May 18, 2015, www.bbc.com/news/world-europe-32778505; Didier Lapeyronnie, "Révolte primitive dans les banlieues françaises: Essai sur les émeutes de l'automne 2005," *Déviance et Société* 30 (2006): 431–48, 431, www.cairn.info/revue-deviance-et-societe-2006-4-page-431.htm.

37. "France: Class Action Lawsuit Against Ethnic Profiling Filed over Systemic Racial Discrimination," Amnesty International, July 22, 2021, www.amnesty.org/en/latest/press-release/2021/07/france-class-action-lawsuit-against-ethnic-profiling-filed-over-systemic-racial-discrimination/.

38. Clea Caulcutt, "France's Culture Wars Reignited After Macron Appoints 'Woke' Minister," Politico, May 30, 2022, www.politico.eu/article/france-culture-war-emmanuel-macron-government-woke-minister-pap-ndiaye-education-reform/.

39. Marianne Enault, Sarah Paillou, and David Revault d'Allonnes, "Hommage à Samuel Paty, lutte contre l'islamisme: Blanquer précise au JDD ses mesures pour la rentrée scolaire," *Le Journal du Dimanche*, August 24, 2023, www.lejdd.fr/Politique/hommage-a-samuel-paty-lutte-contre-lislamisme-blanquer-precise-au-jdd-ses-mesures-pour-la-rentree-scolaire-4000971; Caulcutt, "France's Culture Wars."

40. Norimitsu Onishi, "Will American Ideas Tear France Apart? Some of Its Leaders Think So," *New York Times*, February 9, 2021, www.nytimes.com/2021/02/09/world/europe/france-threat-american-universities.html; Camille Stromboni, "Comment Emmanuel Macron s'est aliéné le monde des sciences sociales," *Le Monde*, June 30, 2020, www.lemonde.fr/societe/article/2020/06/30/comment-emmanuel-macron-s-est-aliene-le-monde-des-sciences-sociales_6044632_3224.html.

41. Kim Willsher, "Sarkozy Reaches Out to Far-right Voters," *Guardian*, April 23, 2006, www.theguardian.com/world/2006/apr/24/france.thefarright.

42. Marianne Enault, Sarah Paillou, and David Revault d'Allonnes, "Hommage à Samuel Paty, lutte contre l'islamisme: Blanquer précise au JDD ses mesures pour la rentrée scolaire," *Le Journal du Dimanche*.

43. Onishi, "Will American Ideas Tear France Apart?"; see also "Une centaine d'universitaires alertent: 'Sur l'islamisme, ce qui nous menace, c'est la persistance du déni,'" *Le Monde*, October 31, 2020, www.lemonde.fr/idees/article/2020/10/31/une-centaine-d-universitaires-alertent-sur-l-islamisme-ce-qui-nous-menace-c-est-la-persistance-du-deni_6057989_3232.html.

44. Nadia Geerts, *Le Wokisme: Ce Nouveau Totalitarisme Dont On Ne Peut Prononcer Le Nom* (Brussels: Centre Jean Gol, 2023), www.cjg.be/wp-content/uploads/2023/02/CJG-ETUDE-Wokisme.pdf.

45. Nicolas Truong, "Le 'wokisme,' déconstruction d'une obsession française," *Le Monde*, June 23, 2023 (updated July 24, 2023), www.lemonde.fr/idees/article/2023/06/23/le-wokisme-deconstruction-d-une-obsession-francaise_6178851_3232.html.

46. Truong, "Le 'wokisme,' déconstruction."

47. Jean-Luc Nsengiyumva, "De l'antiwokisme ou l'itération d'un réflexe colonial," *La Revue Nouvelle* 3, no. 3 (2023): 13–23, https://doi.org/10.3917/rn.231.0013.

48. Clea Caulcutt, "French Education Minister's Anti-woke Mission," Politico, October 19, 2021, www.politico.eu/article/macron-education-minister-jean-michel-blanquer-anti-woke/.

49. France Inter, "Pap Ndiaye: 'L'attitude de déni sur les violences policières en France est classique,'" YouTube Video, June 4, 2020, www.youtube.com/watch?v=pW_YGuTVepk.

50. Marie Slavicek, "'Les militants woke s'inscrivent dans une histoire longue de mobilisation politique de la jeunesse,'" *Le Monde*, February 8, 2021, www.lemonde.fr/international/article/2021/02/08/les-militants-woke-s-inscrivent-dans-une-histoire-longue-de-mobilisation-politique-de-la-jeunesse_6069230_3210.html.

51. Mattea Battagla and Sylvie Lecherbonnier, "Pap Ndiaye, un choix symbolique à la tête de l'éducation nationale," *Le Monde*, May 21, 2022, www.lemonde.fr/politique/article/2022/05/21/pap-ndiaye-un-choix-symbolique-a-la-tete-de-l-education-nationale_6127066_823448.html.

52. Battagla and Lecherbonnier, "Pap Ndiaye, un choix symbolique."

53. Felicia Sideris, "Pap Ndiaye: les critiques contre le nouveau ministre de l'Éducation nationale passées au crible," *TF1 Info*, May 21, 2022, www.tf1info.fr/politique/nomination-de-pap-ndiaye-dans-le-nouveau-gouvernement-borne-on-decortique-les-critiques-a-l-encontre-du-nouveau-ministre-de-l-education-nationale-2220499.html.

54. Nicolas Lecaussin, "Monsieur Le Ministre Pap Ndiaye Parle Du Wokisme, De L'anti-Americanisme Et Critique Son Propre Pays," IREF, September 25, 2022, https://fr.irefeurope.org/publications/les-pendules-a-lheure/article/monsieur-le-ministre-pap-ndiaye-parle-du-wokisme-de-lanti-americanisme-et-critique-son-propre-pays/.

55. "En déplacement aux Etats-Unis, Pap Ndiaye pointe 'la puissance de l'extrême droite' en France," *Libération*, September 21, 2022, www.liberation.fr/societe/en-voyage-aux-etats-unis-pap-ndiaye-pointe-la-puissance-de-lextreme-droite-en-france-20220921_FET7LD7IOBD3HDYEGJ2YO2JBXY/.

56. Louis Augry, "62% des Français ne font pas confiance au Ministre De L'Éducation Pap Ndiaye," *BFM TV*, September 1, 2022, www.bfmtv.com/societe/education/62-des-francais-ne-font-pas-confiance-au-ministre-de-l-education-pap-ndiaye_AN-202209010208.html.

57. See, e.g., Sarah Marsh and Petra Wischgoll, "Germans Protest Nationwide After Far-right Meeting on Deportation Plan," Reuters, January 17, 2024, www.reuters.com/world/europe/nazis-no-thank-you-germans-take-streets-call-afd-ban-2024-01-17; Frances D'Emilio, "Italian Leader Tones Down Divisive Rhetoric but Carries on with Pursuit of Far-right Agenda," AP News, August 24, 2023, https://apnews.com/article/meloni-italy-farright-ideology-fascism-d55b333e7ccd40405d03c87fcb6f36ae; Aislinn Laing, "Who Is Spanish Far-right Leader Santiago Abascal?," Reuters, July 21, 2023, www.reuters.com/world/europe/santiago-abascal-who-is-spains-far-right-leader-what-does-he-stand-2023-07-17/; Claudia Chiappa, "Swedish PM Rebukes Far-right Leader Who Said Mosques Should Be Flattened," Politico, November 27, 2023, www.politico.eu/article/swedish-pm-ulf-kristersson-slams-far-right-party-leader-for-suggesting-mosques-should-be-demolished/; Justin Spike, "At CPAC, Hungary's Orban Decries LGBTQ+ Rights, Migration," AP News, May 4, 2023, https://apnews.com/article/cpac-hungary-orban-woke-gender-migration-da47d0febc22d935de0b48fe5e3ad4a6.

58. Rob Schmitz, "Germany's Far-right Party Now Polls Higher Than the Three Parties in Government," NPR, October 7, 2023, www.npr.org/2023/10/07/1204450909/germanys-far-right-party-now-polls-higher-than-the-three-parties-in-government.

Chapter Sixteen. From Diversity to DEI

1. In Britain, where the term "equality" includes the concept of "equity" (or "substantive equality") the phrase is "equality, diversity, and inclusion." There is a move among some U.S. diversity consultants to use the term "belonging" instead of "inclusion." Jennifer Miller, "Why Some Companies Are Saying 'Diversity and Belonging' Instead of 'Diversity and Inclusion,'" *New York Times*, May 13, 2023, www.nytimes.com/2023/05/13/business/diversity-equity-inclusion-belonging.

2. McKinsey Explainers, "What Is Diversity, Equity, and Inclusion?," McKinsey and Company, August 17, 2022, www.mckinsey.com/featured-insights/mckinsey-explainers/what-is-diversity-equity-and-inclusion#/.

3. Sean McElwee, "The Hidden Racism of Young White Americans," PBS *News Hour*, March 24, 2015, www.pbs.org/newshour/nation/americas-racism-problem-far-complicated-think; Jonathan Capehart, "When 'Telling It Like It Is' Exposes 'Lazy' Thinking about Blacks," *Washington Post*, June 30, 2016, www.washingtonpost.com/blogs/post-partisan/wp/2016/06/30/when-telling-it-like-it-is-exposes-lazy-thinking-about-blacks/.

4. See generally Linda Hamilton Krieger, "The Content of Our Categories: A Cognitive Bias Approach to Discrimination and Equal Employment Opportunity," *Stanford Law Review* 47, no. 7 (1995): 1161–1248; Joyce Ehrlinger, Wilson O. Readinger, and Bora Kim, "Decision-Making and Cognitive Biases," in *Encyclopedia of Mental Health*, 2nd ed., ed. Howard S. Friedman (Oxford: Elsevier, 2016), 5–12; Lance D. Reich, "Cognitive Biases Make Judges and Juries Believe Weird Things," *Scitech Lawyer* 10, no. 1 (2013): 5–7.

5. William H. Frey, "Even as Metropolitan Areas Diversify, White Americans Still Live in Mostly White Neighborhoods," Brookings, March 23, 2020, www.brookings.edu/articles/even-as-metropolitan-areas-diversify-white-americans-still-live-in-mostly-white-neighborhoods/; Richard Rothstein, *The Color of Law: A Forgotten History of How Our Government Segregated America* (New York: Liveright, 2017), 6; see generally Douglas S. Massey and Nancy A. Denton, *American Apartheid: Segregation and the Making of the Underclass* (Cambridge: Harvard University Press, 1993) on institutionalized residential segregation; Sean F. Reardon, Lindsay Fox, and Joseph Townsend, "Neighborhood Income Composition by Household Race and Income, 1990–2009," *Annals of the American Academy of Political and Social Science* 660 (2015): 78–97, www.jstor.org/stable/24541828.

6. Rothstein, *Color of Law*, 48, 101–2.

7. Howard Schuman, Charlotte Steeh, and Lawrence Bobo, *Racial Attitudes in America: Trends and Interpretations* (Cambridge: Harvard University Press, 1985), 74–75.

8. See *Mulkey v. Reitman*, 64 Cal.2d 529, 550 (1966) (dissenting opinion), aff'd, *Reitman v. Mulkey*, 387 U.S. 369 (1967); David B. Oppenheimer, "California's Anti-Discrimination Legislation, Proposition 14, and the Constitutional

Protection of Minority Rights: The Fiftieth Anniversary of the California Fair Employment and Housing Act," *Golden Gate University Law Review* 40, no. 2 (2010): 117–27, 124; see also Thomas W. Casstevens, *Politics, Housing and Race Relations: California's Rumford Act and Proposition 14* (Berkeley: Institute of Governmental Studies, 1967), 48.

9. Fair Housing Act of 1968, 42 U.S.C. §§ 3601–3619 (1968).

10. See, e.g., Ann Choi, Bill Dedman, Keith Herbert, and Olivia Winslow, "Long Island Divided," *Newsday*, November 17, 2019, https://projects. newsday.com/long-island/real-estate-agents-investigation/ (finding discrimination among real estate agents in Long Island); Margery Austin Turner, Rob Santos, Diane K. Levy, Doug Wissoker, Claudia Aranda, and Rob Pitingolo, *Housing Discrimination Against Racial and Ethnic Minorities 2012* (Washington, D.C.: U.S. Department of Housing and Urban Development, 2013), www.huduser.gov/portal/publications/fairhsg/hsg_discrimination_2012. html (finding that white homeowners were more likely to be favored and that real estate agents showed minority homeseekers fewer homes and apartments); Emily Krone, "The New Housing Discrimination: Realtor Minority Steering," *Chicago Policy Review*, October 19, 2018, https:// chicagopolicyreview.org/2018/10/19/the-new-housing-discrimination-realtor-minority-steering/; Matthew Hall, Kyle Crowder, and Amy Spring, "Neighborhood Foreclosures, Racial/Ethnic Transitions, and Residential Segregation," *American Sociological Review* 80, no. 3 (2015): 526–49, 544 (finding that the 2007 foreclosure crisis was structured along racial and ethnic lines and led to racial migration patterns that increased residential segregation; that segregation is maintained by discriminatory practices and racially stratified opportunity structures; and that discriminatory lending behaviors and racially targeted predatory lending led to the foreclosure crisis); Reardon et al., "Neighborhood Income Composition," 78–81, 94–95.

11. See Reardon et al., "Neighborhood Income Composition," 94–95.

12. See Linda Darling-Hammond, "Unequal Opportunity: Race and Education," Brookings, March 1, 1998, www.brookings.edu/articles/unequal-opportunity-race-and-education/; Hannah Furfaro, "To Understand Structural Racism, Look to Our Schools," *Seattle Times*, July 14, 2020, www.seattletimes.com/ education-lab/to-understand-structural-racism-look-to-our-schools/; see also Stephen J. Carroll, Cathy Krop, Jeremy Arkes, Peter A. Morrison, and Ann Flanagan, *California K–12 Public Schools: How Are They Doing?* (Santa Monica: Rand, 2005), www.rand.org/pubs/monographs/MG186.html (finding that teachers in primarily minority schools in California are five times more likely to lack credentials compared with teachers in primarily white schools); Alex Dobuzinskis, "U.S. Minority Students Concentrated in High-Poverty Schools: Study," Reuters, September 24, 2019, www.reuters.com/article/us-usa-education-poverty/u-s-minority-students-concentrated-in-high-poverty-schools-study-idUSKBN1WA052 (finding that Black and Hispanic students are concentrated in high-poverty schools with fewer resources); see generally

Jonathan Kozol, *Savage Inequalities: Children in America's Schools* (New York: Crown Publishing, 1991).

13. George Galster and Patrick Sharkey, "Spatial Foundations of Inequality: A Conceptual Model and Empirical Overview," *Russell Sage Foundation Journal of the Social Sciences* 3, no. 2 (2017): 1–33, 5; Robert J. Sampson and Alix S. Winter, "The Racial Ecology of Lead Poisoning: Toxic Inequality in Chicago Neighborhoods, 1995–2013," *Du Bois Review* 13, no. 2 (2016): 261–83, 262–64, 279–80; Vann R. Newkirk II, "Trump's EPA Concludes Environmental Racism Is Real," *The Atlantic*, February 28, 2018, www.theatlantic.com/politics/archive/2018/02/the-trump-administration-finds-that-environmental-racism-is-real/554315/; Michael Ash and T. Robert Fetter, "Who Lives on the Wrong Side of the Environmental Tracks? Evidence from the EPA's Risk-Screening Environmental Indicators Model," *Social Science Quarterly* 85, no. 2 (2004): 441–62, 459–60 (finding that Black Americans tend to live in more polluted areas between and within cities).

14. See, e.g., Michael K. Brown, Martin Carnoy, Elliott Currie, Troy Duster, David B. Oppenheimer, Marjorie M. Schultz, and David Wellman, *Whitewashing Race: The Myth of a Color-Blind Society* (Berkeley: University of California Press, 2003); Guillermo Mayer and Richard A. Marcantonio, "Bay Area—Separate and Unequal," *Race, Poverty & the Environment* 12, no. 1 (Winter 2005/2006): 20–23, www.reimaginerpe.org/node/313; Eric Mann, "Fight for the Soul of the City: The Battle over Buses in Los Angeles," *The Nation*, May 8, 2013, www.thenation.com/article/archive/fight-soul-city-battle-over-buses-los-angeles/ (discussing "transit racism" impacting low-income and minority riders in Los Angeles); Ananya Sen and Catherine Tucker, "Social Distancing and School Closures: Documenting Disparity in Internet Access Among School Children" (unpublished), April 10, 2020, SSRN: 3572922, https://ssrn.com/abstract=3572922 (finding that poor and non-white children still have less access to the internet and that African American children are less likely to have access when high-speed internet is available; and exploring the implications of internet access during the COVID-19 pandemic); Sei-Ching Joanna Sin, "Disparities in Public Libraries' Services Levels Based on Neighborhood Income and Urbanization Levels: A Nationwide Study," *Proceedings of the American Society for Information Science and Technology* 45, no. 1 (2008): 1–12, 1, 9–10, https://asistdl.onlinelibrary.wiley.com/doi/epdf/10.1002/meet.2008.1450450263 (finding that libraries in low-income areas have shorter hours, less staff and programs, and smaller collection sizes); Corinne Ramey, "America's Unfair Rules of the Road," *Slate*, February 27, 2015, https://slate.com/news-and-politics/2015/02/americas-transportation-system-discriminates-against-minorities-and-poor-federal-funding-for-roads-buses-and-mass-transit-still-segregates-americans.html (detailing racially discriminatory issues within transit systems in "most corners of the United States"); Chanjin Chung and Samuel L. Myers, Jr., "Do the Poor Pay More for Food? An Analysis of

Grocery Store Availability and Food Price Disparities," *Journal of Consumer Affairs* 33, no. 2 (1999): 276–96, 292–95; Kelly M. Bower, Roland J. Thorpe, Jr., Charles Rohde, and Darrell J. Gaskin, "The Intersection of Neighborhood Racial Segregation, Poverty, and Urbanicity and Its Impact on Food Store Availability in the United States," *Preventive Medicine* 58 (2014): 33–39; Charlene Barker, Aderson Francois, Rachel Goodman, and Effat Hussain, *Unshared Bounty: How Structural Racism Contributes to the Creation and Persistence of Food Deserts* (New York: New York Law School Racial Justice Project, 2012), 19–21; Alison Hope Alkon and Kari Marie Norgaard, "Breaking the Food Chains: An Investigation of Food Justice Activism," *Sociological Inquiry* 79, no. 3 (2009): 289–305, 293–96 (placing food deserts in the context of institutional racism); Ruqaiijah A. Yearby, "Racial Inequities in Mortality and Access to Health Care: The Untold Peril of Rationing Health Care in the United States," *Journal of Legal Medicine* 32 (2011): 77–91, 87–90.

15. Massey and Denton, *American Apartheid*, 118–45; Michael A. Fletcher, "Poor Whites Live in Richer Neighborhoods Than Middle-class Blacks and Latinos," *Washington Post*, June 24, 2015, www.washingtonpost.com/news/wonk/wp/2015/06/24/poor-whites-live-in-richer-neighborhoods-than-middle-class-blacks-and-latinos/.

16. Fletcher, "Poor Whites Live in Richer Neighborhoods"; Emily Badger, Claire Cain Miller, Adam Pearce, and Kevin Quealy, "Extensive Data Shows Punishing Reach of Racism for Black Boys," *New York Times*, March 19, 2018, www.nytimes.com/interactive/2018/03/19/upshot/race-class-white-and-black-men.html.

17. See generally Melvin L. Oliver and Thomas M. Shapiro, *Black Wealth/White Wealth: A New Perspective on Racial Inequality* (New York: Rutledge, 2006).

18. Badger et al., "Extensive Data Shows" (finding that black men enjoy much less mobility than white men; finding that Blacks in well-off families are more likely to end up further behind than their parents compared to whites; and finding that "there are essentially no such neighborhoods" where poor Black boys do as well as whites).

19. See generally Oliver and Shapiro, *Black Wealth/White Wealth*.

20. Raj Chetty, Nathaniel Hendren, Maggie R. Jones, and Sonya R. Porter, "Race and Economic Opportunity in the United States: An Intergenerational Perspective," *Quarterly Journal of Economics* 135, no. 2 (2020): 711–83, 733 ("Blacks have much lower rates of upward mobility than whites and much higher levels of downward mobility").

21. Galster and Sharkey, "Spatial Foundations of Inequality," 2–6; see also Dalton Conley, *Being Black, Living in the Red: Race, Wealth, and Social Policy in America* (Berkeley: University of California Press, 2010); Badger et al., "Extensive Data Shows"; Chetty et al., "Race and Economic Opportunity," 732–34; see also Oliver and Shapiro, *Black Wealth/White Wealth*, 69–128.

22. Steve Dubbs, "Is Living Paycheck to Paycheck the New Normal for Middle-Class America?," *Nonprofit Quarterly*, February 4, 2019, https://nonprofitquarterly.org/is-living-paycheck-to-paycheck-the-new-normal-for-middle-class-america/ (finding that 24.3 percent of Black households are likely to fall behind on their bills compared to 13.2 percent of all households); Deena Greenberg, Carl Gershenson, and Matthew Desmond, "Discrimination in Evictions: Empirical Evidence and Legal Challenges," *Harvard Civil Rights–Civil Liberties Law Review* 51 (2016): 115–58 (discussing racial discrimination in the rental context, particularly in evictions); Dirk Early, Edgar Olsen, and Paul E. Carrillo, "Analysis: African-Americans Pay More for Rent, Especially in White Neighborhoods," *Chicago Reporter*, October 31, 2018, www.chicagoreporter.com/analysis-african-americans-pay-more-for-rent-especially-in-white-neighborhoods/; see also Meghan E. Irons, "Researchers Expected 'Outrageously High' Discrimination Against Black Renters. What They Found Was Worse Than Imagined," *Boston Globe*, July 1, 2020, www.bostonglobe.com/2020/07/01/metro/blacks-voucher-holders-face-egregious-housing-discrimination-study-says/; Debbie Gruenstein Bocian, Wei Li, Carolina Reid, and Roberto G. Quercia, *Lost Ground, 2011: Disparities in Mortgage Lending and Foreclosures* (Durham: Center for Responsible Lending, 2011), 5 ("African Americans and Latinos were much more likely to receive high interest rate [subprime] loans and loans with features that are associated with higher foreclosures, specifically prepayment penalties and hybrid or option ARMs").

23. See Meghan Henry, Rian Watt, Anna Mahathey, Jillian Ouellette, and Aubrey Sitler, *The 2019 Annual Homeless Report (AHAR) to Congress, Part 1: Point-in-Time Estimates of Homelessness* (U.S. Department of Housing and Urban Development, 2020), 1, www.huduser.gov/portal/datasets/ahar/2019-ahar-part-1-pit-estimates-of-homelessness-in-the-us.html ("African Americans have remained considerably overrepresented among the homeless population compared to the U.S. population"); see also Teresa Wiltz, "'A Pileup of Inequities': Why People of Color Are Hit Hardest by Homelessness," *Stateline*, March 29, 2019, https://stateline.org/2019/03/29/a-pileup-of-inequities-why-people-of-color-are-hit-hardest-by-homelessness/ (discussing the reasons for racial disparities in housing).

24. See Debbie Gruenstein Bocian, Keith S. Ernst, and Wei Li, *Unfair Lending: The Effect of Race and Ethnicity on the Price of Subprime Mortgages* (Durham: Center for Responsible Lending, 2006), 2–9, 11–12, 16–19 (discussing "redlining," which is the "systematic exclusion of neighborhoods of color when marketing or originating home loans"); Bocian et al., *Lost Ground*, 11 ("Research also has shown that place matters, and that higher-priced and subprime loans were more frequent in low-income and minority neighborhoods than in higher-income or predominantly non-Hispanic white neighborhoods").

25. Debra Kamin, "Home Appraised With a Black Owner: $472,000. With a White Owner: $750,000," *New York Times*, August 18, 2022 (updated June

21, 2023), www.nytimes.com/2022/08/18/realestate/housing-discrimination-maryland.

26. See Mike Konczal and Bryce Covert, "This Is the Key to Recovering Black Wealth in America," *The Nation*, January 13, 2015, www.thenation.com/article/archive/key-recovering-black-wealth-america/ (discussing how housing segregation "deprives [B]lack families of the opportunity to build wealth through their homes" in the same way that whites can and how racial segregation in housing depresses the value of black property and maintains redlining practices); see also Oliver and Shapiro, *Black Wealth/White Wealth*, 111.

27. Jacob William Faber, "Segregation and the Cost of Money: Race, Poverty, and the Prevalence of Alternative Financial Institutions," *Social Forces* 98, no. 2 (2019): 819–48, 820–22 (discussing the lack of quality banking and financial services in Black neighborhoods); see also Ozgur Emre Ergungor, "Bank Branch Presence and Access to Credit in Low- to Moderate-Income Neighborhoods," *Journal of Money, Credit and Banking* 42, no. 7 (2010): 1321–49 (finding a significant relationship between branch access and mortgage origination and concluding that an increase in branches in minority neighborhoods would support mortgage originations).

28. Faber, "Segregation and the Cost of Money," 819–48; see generally Jerzy Eisenberg-Guyot, Caislin Firth, Marieka Klawitter, and Anjum Hajat, "From Payday Loans to Pawnshops: Fringe Banking, the Unbanked, and Health," *Health Affairs* 37, no. 3 (2018): 429–37; Neil Bhutta, "Payday Loans and Consumer Financial Health," *Journal of Banking & Finance* 47 (2014): 230–42.

29. See generally Hans Degryse and Steven Ongena, "Distance, Lending Relationships, and Competition," *Journal of Finance* 60, no. 1 (2005): 231–66 (discussing the impact of lender-borrower and bank-borrower distance on pricing of bank loans).

30. See Office of the Inspector General, *Flash Report Small Business Administration's Implementation of the Paycheck Protection Program Requirements* (2020), 4, www.sba.gov/document/report-20–14-flash-report-small-business-administrations-implementation-paycheck-protection-program-requirements (finding that disbursement of funds did not align with requirements to prioritize underserved and rural markets); Aaron Gregg, "Watchdog Faults SBA on Minority-Owned and Rural Small-Business Relief Lending," *Washington Post*, May 8, 2020, www.washingtonpost.com/business/2020/05/08/sba-ppp-ig-report/ (discussing failures by the Small Business Administration to direct private lenders to prioritize minority-owned businesses as Congress intended).

31. Robert W. Fairlie, *The Impact of COVID-19 on Small Business Owners: Evidence of Early-Stage Losses from the April 2020 Current Population Survey* (Cambridge: National Bureau of Economic Research, 2020), 5, 9, 14.

32. See Robert W. Fairlie and Alicia M. Robb, "Why Are Black-Owned Businesses Less Successful Than White-Owned Businesses? The Role of

Families, Inheritance, and Business Human Capital," *Journal of Labor Economics* 25, no. 2 (2007): 289–323, 312 (discussing the role of human capital); Philipp Koellinger and Maria Minniti, "Not for Lack of Trying: American Entrepreneurship in Black and White," *Small Business Economics* 27, no. 1 (2006): 59–79 (discussing how the underrepresentation of Black Americans in entrepreneurship is not the result of "lack of trying" but is due to stronger barriers of entry and higher failure rates); Raphaël Charron-Chénier, Joshua J. Fink, and Lisa A. Keister, "Race and Consumption: Black and White Disparities in Household Spending," *Sociology of Race and Ethnicity* 3, no. 1 (2017): 56–67 (discussing disparities in spending patterns between white and Black households).

33. Anne Helen Petersen, "The Mirage of the Black Middle Class," *Vox*, January 26, 2021, www.vox.com/the-goods/22245223/black-middle-class-racism-reparations.

34. See "Labor Force Statistics from the Current Population Survey," U.S. Bureau of Labor Statistics, accessed September 25, 2023, www.bls.gov/web/empsit/cpsee_e16.htm (finding that Black unemployment was 5.4 percent and white unemployment was 3.0 percent in the second quarter of 2023); Valerie Wilson and William M. Rodgers III, *Black-White Wage Gaps Expand with Rising Wage Inequality* (Washington, D.C.: Economic Policy Institute, 2016), 2–5; Drew DeSilver, "Black Unemployment Rate Is Consistently Twice That of Whites," Pew Research Center, August 31, 2013, www.pewresearch.org/short-reads/2013/08/21/through-good-times-and-bad-black-unemployment-is-consistently-double-that-of-whites/; Paul Solman, PBS *Newshour*, podcast audio, July 15, 2020, at 44:30, www.pbs.org/newshour/show/july-15-2020-pbs-newshour-full-episode; see also Andrew Hacker, *Two Nations: Black and White, Separate, Hostile, Unequal* (New York: Charles Scribner's Sons, 1992), 107–33.

35. Wilson and Rodgers, *Black-White Wage Gaps*, 2–5 (finding that the Black-white wage gap expanded when corrected for education, experience, metro status, and region of residence).

36. Margaret Simms and Marla McDaniel, *The Black-White Jobless Gap* (Washington, D.C.: Urban Institute, 2012), www.urban.org/sites/default/files/publication/29676/901378-The-Black-White-Jobless-Gap.pdf.

37. Devah Pager, Bruce Western, and Bart Bonikowski, "Discrimination in a Low-Wage Labor Market: A Field Experiment," *American Sociological Review* 74, no. 5 (2009): 777–99, 792–95.

38. Devah Pager, "The Mark of a Criminal Record," *American Journal of Sociology* 105, no. 5 (2003): 937–75, 938–39, 957–62.

39. Elie Mystal, "Proof That Typos Are Racist," *Above The Law*, April 17, 2014, https://abovethelaw.com/2014/04/proof-that-typos-are-racist/.

40. See generally Oliver and Shapiro, *Black Wealth/White Wealth*.

41. "PINC-01. Selected Characteristics of People 15 Years and Over, by Total Money Income, Work Experience, Race, Hispanic Origin, and Sex," *United*

States Census Bureau, https://www.census.gov/data/tables/time-series/demo/income-poverty/cps-pinc/pinc-01.html#par_textimage_14.

42. Jacqueline Salmon, "Studies Spotlight Racial, Ethnic Gaps in Retirement Savings," AARP, September 2, 2022, www.aarp.org/retirement/retirement-savings/info-2022/workplace-savings-plans-racial-inequities.html#:~:text=Black%20and%20Hispanic%20workers%20have,in%20life%2C%20according%20to%20researchers.

43. Pager et al., "Discrimination in a Low-Wage Labor Market," 793–95 ("Employers appeared to see more potential in the stated qualifications of white applicants, and they more commonly viewed white applicants as a better fit for more desirable jobs").

44. See David B. Oppenheimer, "Negligent Discrimination," *Penn Law Review* 141, no. 3 (1993): 899–972.

45. See, e.g., Mayer and Marcantonio, "Bay Area," 20–23; Darnell Grisby, "To Fight Racism, Transit Has a Key Role," Bloomberg, July 20, 2020, www.bloomberg.com/news/articles/2020-07-20/the-powerful-role-transit-plays-in-racial-justice (noting that many Black workers are shut out from work opportunities because of limited access to transit and long or impossible commutes).

46. See Grisby, "To Fight Racism" (noting that many districts spend more on improving suburban public transit than extending transit access in inner cities); Alejandro De La Garza, "Covid-19 Has Been 'Apocalyptic' for Public Transit. Will Congress Offer More Help?," *Time*, July 21, 2020, https://time.com/5869375/public-transit-coronavirus-covid/ (noting that people of color make up less than 40 percent of the U.S. population but account for 60 percent of public transit riders); see generally *Labor/Cmty. Strategy Ctr. v. L.A. Cnty. Metro. Transp. Auth.*, 263 F.3d 1041 (9th Cir. 2001), *cert. denied*, 535 U.S. 951 (2002); Juliet Ellis, "End Funding Discrimination in Public Transit," *Race, Poverty, & the Environment* 17, no. 1 (2010): 39, www.jstor.org/stable/41554710 (discussing public transportation in rural and small towns).

47. De La Garza, "Covid-19 Has Been 'Apocalyptic'"; Grisby, "To Fight Racism."

48. Anjali Mahendra, Dario Hidalgo, and Schuyler Null, "Transport and Inequality: Why Disparities in Access Matter in Cities," *City Fix*, August 10, 2020, https://thecityfix.com/blog/transport-inequality-disparities-access-matter-cities-anjali-mahendra-dario-hidalgo-schuyler-null/.

49. Grisby, "To Fight Racism."

50. Grisby, "To Fight Racism."

51. Ian Ayres, "Fair Driving: Gender and Race Discrimination in Retail Car Negotiations," *Harvard Law Review* 104, no. 4 (1991): 817–72, 872.

52. Mark A. Cohen, "Imperfect Competition in Auto Lending: Subjective Markup, Racial Disparity, and Class Action Litigation," *Review of Law and Economics* 8, no. 1 (2012): 21–58; Lisa Rice and Erich Schwartz, Jr., *Discrimination When Buying a Car: How the Color of Your Skin Can Affect Your Car-*

Shopping Experience (Washington, D.C.: National Fair Housing Alliance, 2018), 5.

53. See Sean F. Reardon and Kendra Bischoff, "Income Inequality and Income Segregation," *American Journal of Sociology* 116, no. 4 (2011): 1092–1153, 1100–1101 (discussing the impact of income segregation on the quality of "public goods and local social institutions" in Black communities).

54. Goodwin Liu, "Education, Equality, and National Citizenship," *Yale Law Journal* 116, no. 2 (2006): 330–411.

55. Kozol, *Savage Inequalities*, 119–20, 173–76.

56. Carroll et al., *California K–12 Public Schools*, 68–70, 92–93.

57. Kozol, *Savage Inequalities*, 180, 193, 202; see also Notice of Proposed Settlement, 1, 7, *Williams v. California*, No. 312236 (Cal. Sup. Ct. San Francisco Cty.), www.cde.ca.gov/eo/ce/wc/documents/wmssettlenotice.pdf (detailing successful settlement that required, through state legislation and funding, compliance with standards for school facilities in California).

58. Sophie Quinton, "The Race Gap in High School Honors Classes," *The Atlantic*, December 11, 2014, www.theatlantic.com/politics/archive/2014/12/the-race-gap-in-high-school-honors-classes/431751/; Douglas J. Gagnon and Marybeth J. Mattingly, *Most U.S. School Districts Have Low Access to School Counselors* (Durham: University of New Hampshire Carsey School of Public Policy, 2016), 3–4, https://scholars.unh.edu/cgi/viewcontent.cgi?article=1285&context=carsey; Hammond, "Unequal Opportunity."

59. Ronald F. Ferguson, "Teachers' Perceptions and Expectations and the Black-White Test Score Gap," *Urban Education* 38, no. 4 (2003): 460–507, 493–96, https://doi.org/10.1177/0042085903038004006.

60. Russell J. Skiba, Robert H. Horner, Choong-Geun Chung, M. Karega Rausch, Seth L. May, and Tary Tobin, "Race Is Not Neutral: A National Investigation of African American and Latino Disproportionality in School Discipline," *School Psychology Review* 40, no. 1 (2011): 85–107, 95, 101; "School-to-Prison Pipeline," American Civil Liberties Union, accessed October 5, 2023, www.aclu.org/issues/juvenile-justice/school-prison-pipeline/school-prison-pipeline-infographic; see also U.S. Department of Education, *Protecting Civil Rights, Advancing Equity: Report to the President and Secretary of Education* (Washington, D.C.: Office for Civil Rights, 2015).

61. Gary Orfield, Jongyeon Ee, Erica Frankenberg, and Genevieve Siegel-Hawley, "*Brown* at 62: School Segregation by Race, Poverty, and State," Civil Rights Project at UCLA, May 16, 2016, www.civilrightsproject.ucla.edu/research/k-12-education/integration-and-diversity/brown-at-62-school-segregation-by-race-poverty-and-state; *Brown v. Board of Education*, 347 U.S. 483, 495 (1954).

62. See Joel McFarland, Jiashan Cui, Juliet Holmes, Xiaolei Wang, *Trends in High School Dropout and Completion Rates in the United States: 2019* (Washington, D.C.: National Center for Education Statistics, 2020), https://nces.ed.gov/pubs2020/2020117.pdf.

63. Rod K. Brunson, "Protests Focus on Over-policing. But Under-policing Is Also Deadly," *Washington Post*, June 12, 2020, www.washingtonpost.com/outlook/underpolicing-cities-violent-crime/2020/06/12/b5d1fd26-acoc-11ea-9063-e69bd6520940_story.html.

64. Radley Balko, "There's Overwhelming Evidence That the Criminal Justice System Is Racist. Here's the Proof," *Washington Post*, June 10, 2020, www.washingtonpost.com/graphics/2020/opinions/systemic-racism-police-evidence-criminal-justice-system/.

65. Much literature has been written on this issue. Selected case studies showing this issue include the following: U.S. Department of Justice Civil Rights Division, *Investigation of the Ferguson Police Department* (Washington, D.C.: Department of Justice, 2015), 64–68, 72–75, www.justice.gov/sites/default/files/opa/press-releases/attachments/2015/03/04/ferguson_police_department_report.pdf (detailing the presence of racial bias in the Ferguson police department, including with regard to vehicular stops); Erica L. Smith and Matthew R. Durose, *Characteristics of Drivers Stopped by Police, 2002* (Washington, D.C.: Bureau of Justice Statistics, 2006), 6–7, 9, https://bjs.ojp.gov/content/pub/pdf/cdsp02.pdf (providing racial data for persons stopped while driving by the police); Lynn Langton and Matthew Durose, *Police Behavior During Traffic and Street Stops, 2011* (Washington, D.C.: Bureau of Justice Statistics, 2016), 1, 3, 9–10, https://bjs.ojp.gov/content/pub/pdf/pbtss11.pdf (explaining the differences in perceptions of traffic stops between Black and white drivers and police); Human Rights Watch, "Decades of Disparity: Drug Arrests and Race in the United States," Human Rights Watch, March 2, 2009, www.hrw.org/report/2009/03/02/decades-disparity/drug-arrests-and-race-united-states (explaining the effects of racial bias in drug searches and arrests). Recent coverage includes Pierre Thomas, John Kelly, and Tonya Simpson, "ABC News Analysis of Police Arrests Nationwide Reveals Stark Racial Disparity," ABC News, June 11, 2020, https://abcnews.go.com/US/abc-news-analysis-police-arrests-nationwide-reveals-stark/story?id=71188546 (showing that Black people are ten times more likely to be arrested than white people); Drew DeSilver, Michael Lipka, and Dalia Fahmy, "10 Things We Know About Race and Policing in the U.S.," Pew Research Center, June 3, 2020, www.pewresearch.org/short-reads/2020/06/03/10-things-we-know-about-race-and-policing-in-the-u-s/ (recounting Americans' perceptions about race and policing); Erik Ortiz, "Inside 100 Million Police Traffic Stops: New Evidence of Racial Bias," NBC News, March 13, 2019, www.nbcnews.com/news/us-news/inside-100-million-police-traffic-stops-new-evidence-racial-bias-n980556 (providing an update on racial bias in police traffic stops).

66. See generally "Report to the United Nations on Racial Disparities in the U.S. Criminal Justice System," The Sentencing Project, April 19, 2018, www.sentencingproject.org/publications/un-report-on-racial-disparities/ (describing the factors that disproportionately affect Black youth and thus

result in higher rates of imprisonment, including prosecutorial bias, drug free school zone laws, and poverty); David M. Ramey, "The Social Structure of Criminalized and Medicalized School Discipline," *Sociology of Education* 88, no. 3 (2015): 181–201 (showing that racial minorities are more likely to be over-policed at school and more likely to be imprisoned for school infractions).

67. Carlos Berdejó, "Criminalizing Race: Racial Disparities in Plea-Bargaining," *Boston College Law Review* 59, no. 4: 1187–249, 1189–96; Wendy Sawyer, "How Race Impacts Who Is Detained Pretrial," Prison Policy Initiative, October 9, 2019, www.prisonpolicy.org/blog/2019/10/09/pretrial_race/; see also Timothy Williams, "Black People Are Charged at a Higher Rate Than Whites. What If Prosecutors Didn't Know Their Race?," *New York Times*, June 12, 2019, www.nytimes.com/2019/06/12/us/prosecutor-race-blind-charging.html (describing implicit bias in charging decisions in San Francisco).

68. Berdejó, "Criminalizing Race," 1189; Michael Winerip, Michael Schwirtz, and Robert Gebeloff, "For Blacks Facing Parole in New York State, Signs of a Broken System," *New York Times*, December 4, 2016, https://nyti.ms/2h3m4Xs.

69. Leah Goodridge and Helen Strom, "Innocent Until Proven Guilty?: Examining the Constitutionality of Public Housing Evictions Based on Criminal Activity," *Duke Forum for Law & Social Change* 8, no. 1 (2016): 1–25, 1–2, 5, 11; Wendy J. Kaplan and David Rossman, "Called 'Out' at Home: The One Strike Eviction Policy and Juvenile Court," *Duke Forum for Law & Social Change* 3, no. 1 (2011): 109–38, 110, 135; see, e.g., *Robinson v. Martinez*, 764 N.Y.S.2d 94, 95 (N.Y. App. Div. 2003); *Hoopa Valley Hous. Auth. v. Hunsucker*, No. Ud-13–003/A-13–003 (February 27, 2014); *Hous. Auth. of City of New Haven v. DeRoche*, 962 A.2d 904, 911 (Conn. App. Ct. 2009).

70. See *Robinson*, 764 N.Y.S.2d at 95.

71. See *DeRoche*, 962 A.2d at 911.

72. Christopher Ingraham, "White People Are More Likely to Deal Drugs, But Black People Are More Likely to Get Arrested for It," *Washington Post*, September 30, 2014, www.washingtonpost.com/news/wonk/wp/2014/09/30/white-people-are-more-likely-to-deal-drugs-but-black-people-are-more-likely-to-get-arrested-for-it/; Alan Rosenberg, Allison K. Groves, and Kim M. Blankenship, "Comparing Black and White Drug Offenders: Implications for Racial Disparities in Criminal Justice and Reentry Policy and Programming," *Journal of Drug Issues* 47, no. 1 (2017): 132–42, 137–38; Megan T. Stevenson and Sandra G. Mayson, "The Scale of Misdemeanor Justice," *Boston University Law Review* 98, no. 3 (2018): 731–77, 758–59 (finding that the Black arrest rate is higher than the white arrest rate for most misdemeanor offenses).

73. S. Jay Olshansky, Toni Antonucci, Lisa Berkman, Robert H. Binstock, Axel Boersch-Supan, John T. Cacioppo, Bruce A. Carnes, Laura L. Carstensen, Linda P. Fried, Dana P. Goldman, James Jackson, Martin Kohli, John Rother,

Yuhui Zheng, and John Rowe, "Differences in Real Life Expectancy Due to Race and Educational Differences Are Widening, and Many May Not Catch Up," *Health Affairs* 31, no. 8 (2012): 1803–13, 1806–7. Another study showed a 99 percent higher incidence of breast cancer between white and Black women. Jennifer M. Orsi, Helen Margellos-Anast, and Steven Whitman, "Black–White Health Disparities in the United States and Chicago: A 15-Year Progress Analysis," *American Journal of Public Health* 100, no. 2 (2010): 349–56, 352. Moreover, there are disparate outcomes in maternity. Emily E. Petersen, Nicole L. Davis, David Goodman, Shanna Cox, Carla Syverson, Kristi Seed, Carrie Shapiro-Mendoza, William M. Callaghan, and Wanda Barfield, "Racial/Ethnic Disparities in Pregnancy-Related Deaths—United States, 2007–2016," Center for Disease Control and Prevention, September 6, 2019, www.cdc.gov/mmwr/volumes/68/wr/mm6835a3.htm?s_cid=mm6835a3_w. COVID-19 has exacerbated these disadvantages. See Rodney A. Brooks, "African Americans Struggle with Disproportionate COVID Death Toll," *National Geographic*, April 24, 2020, www.nationalgeographic.com/history/2020/04/coronavirus-disproportionately-impacts-african-americans/; John Eligon, Audra D. S. Burch, Dionne Searcey, and Richard A. Oppel, Jr., "Black Americans Face Alarming Rates of Coronavirus Infection in Some States," *New York Times*, April 14, 2020, www.nytimes.com/2020/04/07/us/coronavirus-race.html; David R. Williams and Lisa A. Cooper, "COVID-19 and Health Equity—A New Kind of 'Herd Immunity,'" *Journal of American Medical Association* 323, no. 24 (2020): 2478–80.

74. "Diversity in Medicine: Facts and Figures 2019," Association of American Medical Colleges, accessed October 7, 2023, www.aamc.org/data-reports/workforce/data/figure-18-percentage-all-active-physicians-race/ethnicity-2018.

75. Vann R. Newkirk II, "America's Health Segregation Problem," *The Atlantic*, May 18, 2016, www.theatlantic.com/politics/archive/2016/05/americas-health-segregation-problem/483219/; Liz Kowalczyk, "Color Line Persists, in Sickness as in Health," *Boston Globe*, December 12, 2017, https://apps.bostonglobe.com/spotlight/boston-racism-image-reality/series/hospitals/.

76. Robert Gebeloff, Danielle Ivory, Matt Richtel, Mitch Smith, Karen Yourish, Scott Dance, Jackie Fortiér, Elly Yu, and Molly Parker, "The Striking Racial Divide in How Covid-19 Has Hit Nursing Homes," *New York Times*, May 21, 2020, www.nytimes.com/article/coronavirus-nursing-homes-racial-disparity.html.

77. Barker et al., *Unshared Bounty*, 6; Angela Hilmers, David C. Hilmers, and Jayna Dave, "Neighborhood Disparities in Access to Healthy Foods and Their Effects on Environmental Justice," *American Journal of Public Health* 102, no. 9 (2012): 1644–54, 1649–50.

78. Christianna Silva, "Food Insecurity in the U.S. by the Numbers," NPR, September 27, 2020, www.npr.org/2020/09/27/912486921/food-insecurity-in-the-u-s-by-the-numbers.

79. Hiroko Tabuchi and Nadja Popovich, "People of Color Breathe More Hazardous Air. The Sources Are Everywhere," *New York Times*, April 28, 2021, www.nytimes.com/2021/04/28/climate/air-pollution-minorities.html; Gabi Velasco, "How Transportation Planners Can Advance Racial Equity and Environmental Justice," *Urban Institute*, August 18, 2020, www.urban.org/urban-wire/how-transportation-planners-can-advance-racial-equity-and-environmental-justice; Oliver Milman, "Robert Bullard: 'Environmental Justice Isn't Just Slang, It's Real,'" *The Guardian*, December 20, 2018, www.theguardian.com/commentisfree/2018/dec/20/robert-bullard-interview-environmental-justice-civil-rights-movement (reporting that Black Americans are more likely to live in polluted environments and are thus more likely to have asthma, cancer, and learning disabilities); see also Vanessa Williams, "Residential Segregation Plays a Role in Coronavirus Disparities, Study Finds," *Washington Post*, August 17, 2020, www.washingtonpost.com/nation/2020/08/17/residential-segregation-plays-role-covid-19-disparaties-study-finds/ (noting that Black Americans are more likely to live in areas with more pollution, increasing their exposure to the coronavirus).

80. Christian E. Weller, "African Americans Face Systematic Obstacles to Getting Good Jobs," Center for American Progress, December 5, 2019, www.americanprogress.org/issues/economy/reports/2019/12/05/478150/african-americans-face-systematic-obstacles-getting-good-jobs/.

81. Khiara M. Bridges, "Implicit Bias and Racial Disparities in Health Care," *Human Rights* 43, no. 3 (2018): 19–20, www.jstor.org/stable/27171264; Joseph V. Sakran, Ebony Jade Hilton, and Chethan Sathya, "Racism in Health Care Isn't Always Obvious," *Scientific American*, July 9, 2020, www.scientificamerican.com/article/racism-in-health-care-isnt-always-obvious/; see also Austin Frakt, "Bad Medicine: The Harm That Comes from Racism," *New York Times*, January 13, 2020 (updated July 8, 2020), www.nytimes.com/2020/01/13/upshot/bad-medicine-the-harm-that-comes-from-racism.html; Rob Picheta, "Black Newborns More Likely to Die When Looked After by White Doctors," CNN, August 20, 2020, www.cnn.com/2020/08/18/health/black-babies-mortality-rate-doctors-study-wellness-scli-intl/index.html.

82. Elizabeth N. Chapman, Anna Kaatz, and Molly Carnes, "Physicians and Implicit Bias: How Doctors May Unwittingly Perpetuate Health Care Disparities," *Journal of General Internal Medicine* 28, no. 11 (2013): 1504–10, 1506–8.

83. Roni Caryn Rabin, "Doctors Are More Likely to Describe Black Patients as Uncooperative, Studies Find," *New York Times*, February 16, 2022, www.nytimes.com/2022/02/16/health/black-patients-doctor-notes-diabetes.html; Kelly M. Hoffman, Sophie Trawalter, Jordan R. Axt, and M. Norman Oliver, "Racial Bias in Pain Assessment and Treatment Recommendations, and False Beliefs About Biological Differences Between Blacks and Whites," *Proceedings of the National Academy of Sciences of the United States of America* 113, no. 16 (2016): 4296–301, 4297–98; Marie V. Plaisime, David J.

Malebranche, Andrea L. Davis, and Jennifer A. Taylor, "Healthcare Providers' Formative Experiences with Race and Black Male Patients in Urban Hospital Environments," *Journal of Racial and Ethnic Health Disparities* 4 (2017): 1120–27.

84. Emily Flitter, "'Banking While Black': How Cashing a Check Can Be a Minefield," *New York Times*, June 18, 2020, www.nytimes.com/2020/06/18/business/banks-black-customers-racism.html; Melissa Repko, "As Black Buying Power Grows, Racial Profiling by Retailers Remains Persistent Problem," CNBC, July 5, 2020, www.cnbc.com/2020/07/05/as-black-buying-power-grows-racial-profiling-by-retailers-remains-a-problem.html.

85. See, e.g., Shaila Dewan and Andrew W. Lehren, "After a Crime, the Price of a Second Chance," *New York Times*, December 12, 2016, www.nytimes.com/2016/12/12/us/crime-criminal-justice-reform-diversion.html; Jeffrey J. Rachlinski and Sheri Lynn Johnson, "Does Unconscious Racial Bias Affect Trial Judges?," *Notre Dame Law Review* 84, no. 3 (2009): 1195–246, 1214–15; Mark W. Bennett, "Unraveling the Gordian Knot of Implicit Bias in Jury Selection: The Problems of Judge-Dominated Voir Dire, the Failed Promise of *Batson*, and Proposed Solutions," *Harvard Law & Policy Review* 4 (2010): 149–71, 162–63; Jerry Kang, Mark Bennett, Devon Carbado, Pam Casey, Nilanjana Dagupta, David Faigman, Rachel Godsil, Anthony G. Greenwald, Justin Levinson, and Jennifer Mnookin, "Implicit Bias in the Courtroom," *UCLA Law Review* 59, no. 5 (2012): 1124–87, 1146–48. Black Americans also are more likely to receive harsher sentences. See, e.g., Traci Burch, "Skin Color and the Criminal Justice System: Beyond Black-White Disparities in Sentencing," *Journal of Empirical Legal Studies* 12, no. 3 (2015): 395–420. Similar outcomes also result with juries. See, e.g., William J. Bowers, Benjamin D. Steiner, and Marla Sandys, "Death Sentencing in Black and White: An Empirical Analysis of the Role of Jurors' Race and Jury Racial Composition," *Journal of Constitutional Law* 3, no. 1 (2001): 171–274, 239–43. For the effects of political affiliation see Alma Cohen and Crystal S. Yang, "Judicial Politics and Sentencing Decisions," *American Economic Journal: Economic Policy* 11, no. 1 (2019): 160–91, 185–86. Note also that defense lawyers have their own racial biases too. See, e.g., Andrea D. Lyon, "Race Bias and the Importance of Consciousness for Criminal Defense Attorneys," *Seattle University Law Review* 35, no. 3 (2012): 755–68, 763–65.

86. L. Song Richardson, "Systemic Triage: Implicit Racial Bias in the Criminal Courtroom," *Yale Law Journal* 126, no. 3 (2017): 862–93, www.yalelawjournal.org/article/systemic-triage-implicit-racial-bias-in-the-criminal-courtroom; James D. Johnson, Carolyn H. Simmons, Amanda Jordan, Lesie MacLean, Jeffrey Taddel, Duane Thomas, John F. Dovidio, and William Reed, "Rodney King and O. J. Revisited: The Impact of Race and Defendant Empathy Induction on Judicial Decisions," *Journal of Applied Social Psychology* 32, no. 6 (2002): 1107–327, https://doi.org/10.1111/j.1559-1816.2002.tb01432.x; Douglas O. Linder, "Juror Empathy and Race," *Tennessee Law Review* 63

(1996): 887–916, https://irlaw.umkc.edu/cgi/viewcontent.cgi?article=1406&context=faculty_works.

87. Sharon LaFraniere and Andrew W. Lehren, "The Disproportionate Risks of Driving While Black," *New York Times*, October 24, 2015, www.nytimes.com/2015/10/25/us/racial-disparity-traffic-stops-driving-black.html; Flitter, "Banking While Black."

88. Tara Goddard, Kimberly Barsamian Khan, and Arlie Adkins, "Racial Bias in Driver Yielding Behavior at Crosswalks," *Transportation Research* 33 (2015): 1–6.

89. Todd Datz, Michael Saunders, and Jillian McKoy, "Racial Disparities in Traffic Fatalities Much Wider Than Previously Known," Harvard T. H. Chan School of Public Health June 7, 2022, www.hsph.harvard.edu/news/press-releases/racial-disparities-traffic-fatalities/; Adam Paul Susaneck, "American Road Deaths Show an Alarming Racial Gap," *New York Times*, April 26, 2023, www.nytimes.com/interactive/2023/04/26/opinion/road-deaths-racial-gap.html; Kiara Alfonseca, "Black, Native, Low-income People More Likely to Be Killed While Walking: Report," ABC News, July 12, 2022, https://abcnews.go.com/US/report-highlights-dangerous-places-walk-america/story?id=86662072#:~:text=Black%20pedestrians%20are%20twice%20as,likely%20to%20be%20fatally%20hit.

90. U.S. Department of Transportation, *Traffic Safety Facts: 2018 Data* (Washington, D.C.: U.S. Department of Transportation, 2020), 2, https://crashstats.nhtsa.dot.gov/Api/Public/ViewPublication/812850.

91. Datz et al., "Racial Disparities in Traffic Fatalities."

92. Danny Hakim and Michael Wines, "'They Don't Really Want Us to Vote': How Republicans Made It Harder," *New York Times*, November 3, 2018, www.nytimes.com/2018/11/03/us/politics/voting-suppression-elections.html; J. Gerald Hebert and Danielle Lang, "Courts Are Finally Pointing out the Racism Behind Voter ID Laws," *Washington Post*, August 3, 2016, www.washingtonpost.com/posteverything/wp/2016/08/03/courts-are-finally-pointing-out-the-racism-behind-voter-id-laws/. Consider also the impacts on voting regulations from the Supreme Court's decision in *Shelby County v. Holder*, 570 U.S. 529 (2013), eviscerating the 1965 Voting Rights Act.

93. Lyndon B. Johnson, "Commencement Address at Howard University" (speech, Howard University, June 4, 1965), American Presidency Project, www.presidency.ucsb.edu/documents/commencement-address-howard-university-fulfill-these-rights.

Chapter Seventeen. The War on Diversity

1. *Parents Involved in Cmty. Sch. v. Seattle Sch, Dist., No. 1*, 551 U.S. 701, 748 (2007).

2. Anemona Hartocollis and Stephanie Saul, "At M.I.T., Black and Latino Enrollment Drops Sharply After Affirmative Action Ban," *New York Times*, August 21, 2024, www.nytimes.com/2024/08/21/us/mit-black-latino-enrollment-affirmative-action.html.

3. Anemona Hartocollis and Stephanie Saul, "At 2 Elite Colleges, Shifts in Racial Makeup After Affirmative Action Ban," *New York Times*, August 30, 2024, www.nytimes.com/2024/08/30/us/black-enrollment-affirmative-action-amherst-tufts-uva.html.

4. Anemona Hartocollis, "Harvard's Black Student Enrollment Dips After Affirmative Action Ends," *New York Times*, September 11, 2024, www.nytimes.com/2024/09/11/us/harvard-affirmative-action-diversity-admissions.

5. Stephanie Saul and Anemona Hartocollis, "Black Student Enrollment at Harvard Law Drops by More Than Half," *New York Times*, December 16, 2024, www.nytimes.com/2024/12/16/us/harvard-law-black-students-enrollment-decline.html; Melissa Korn, "The Colleges Falling Behind on Black Student Enrollment," *Wall Street Journal*, September 9, 2024.

6. John Yang and Cat Wise, "University Makes Major Push for Diversity Without Considering Race, Gender in Admissions," PBS *NewsHour*, October 4, 2022, www.pbs.org/newshour/show/university-makes-major-push-for-diversity-without-considering-race-gender-in-admissions; Stephanie Saul, "Affirmative Action Was Banned at Two Top Universities. They Say They Need It," *New York Times*, August 26, 2022, www.nytimes.com/2022/08/26/us/affirmative-action-admissions-supreme-court.html.

7. Saul, "Affirmative Action Was Banned at Two Top Universities"; Emma Gallegos, "Student Racial Diversity Falters Without Affirmative Action, UC Tells U.S. Supreme Court," *EdSource*, August 26, 2022, https://edsource.org/updates/efforts-to-increase-student-racial-diversity-fails-without-affirmative-action-uc-tells-supreme-court#:~:text=The%20proportion%20of%20Black%20and,and%20nearly%2011%25%20in%201998; Sean Brenner, "How UCLA Has Responded to Proposition 209," *UCLA Newsroom*, June 29, 2023, https://newsroom.ucla.edu/releases/how-ucla-has-responded-to-proposition-209.

8. Mark C. Long and Nicole A. Bateman, "Long-Run Changes in Underrepresentation After Affirmative Action Bans in Public Universities," *Educational Evaluation and Policy Analysis* 42, no. 2 (2020): 188–207, https://doi.org/10.3102/0162373720904433.

9. Nicholas Lemann, *Higher Admissions: The Rise, Decline, and Return of Standardized Testing* (Princeton: Princeton University Press, 2024), 68, 70–71.

10. Liz Mineo, "New Study Finds Wide Gap in SAT/ACT Test Scores Between Wealthy, Lower-Income Kids," *Harvard Gazette*, November 22, 2023, https://news.harvard.edu/gazette/story/2023/11/new-study-finds-wide-gap-in-sat-act-test-scores-between-wealthy-lower-income-kids/.

11. Stephen Miller, Letter to Dean John P. Manning of Harvard Law School, June 23, 2023, https://fingfx.thomsonreuters.com/gfx/legaldocs/gkvlwrdaqpb/America%20First%20Legal%20Warning%20Letter_Harvard.pdf; Lauren Sforza, "Stephen Miller Warns Schools of Lawsuits If They Ignore Supreme Court Affirmative Action Ruling," *The Hill*, July 7, 2023, https://

thehill.com/regulation/court-battles/4078821-stephen-miller-warns-schools-of-lawsuits-if-they-ignore-supreme-court-affirmative-action-ruling/.

12. *Coal. for TJ v. Fairfax Cnty. Sch. Bd.*, No. 1:21CV296, 2022 WL 579809 (E.D. Va. February 25, 2022), rev'd and remanded, 68 F.4th 864 (4th Cir. 2023).

13. *Coal. for TJ*, 2022 WL 579809.

14. *Coal. for TJ v. Fairfax Cnty. Sch. Bd., 68 F.4th 864, 888–89 (4th Cir. 2023).*

15. John Fritze, "Affirmative Action: The Next Legal Battle over Race and Education Has Already Begun," *USA Today*, November 2, 2022, www.usatoday.com/story/news/politics/2022/11/02/affirmative-action-supreme-court-next-legal-battle/10655719002/.

16. Amy Harmon, "How It Feels to Have Your Life Changed By Affirmative Action," *New York Times*, June 21, 2023, www.nytimes.com/2023/06/21/us/affirmative-action-student-experiences.html.

17. Chronicle Staff, "DEI Legislation Tracker," *Chronicle of Higher Education*, July 14, 2023, www.chronicle.com/article/here-are-the-states-where-lawmakers-are-seeking-to-ban-colleges-dei-efforts; Jeannie Suk Gersen, "The Supreme Court Overturns Fifty Years of Precedent on Affirmative Action," *New Yorker*, June 29, 2023, www.newyorker.com/news/daily-comment/the-supreme-court-overturns-fifty-years-of-precedent-on-affirmative-action; Nicholas Confessore, "'America Is Under Attack': Inside the Anti-D.E.I. Crusade," *New York Times*, January 20, 2024, www.nytimes.com/interactive/2024/01/20/us/dei-woke-claremont-institute.

18. Confessore, "America Is Under Attack."

19. Executive Order 13950, 85 Fed. Reg. 60633 (September 22, 2020); Jessica Guynn, "Donald Trump Executive Order Banning Diversity Training Blocked by Federal Judge," *USA Today*, December 23, 2020; www.usatoday.com/story/money/2020/12/23/trump-diversity-training-ban-executive-order-blocked-federal-judge/4033590001/.

20. Jack Stripling, "DeSantis Signs Bill to Defund DEI Programs at Florida's Public Colleges," *Washington Post*, May 15, 2023, www.washingtonpost.com/education/2023/05/15/desantis-defunds-dei-programs-florida-colleges/.

21. Anjali Huynh, "Trump, Crossing Paths with DeSantis, Tries to Outflank Him," *New York Times*, June 30, 2023, www.nytimes.com/2023/06/30/us/politics/trump-desantis-moms-for-liberty.html.

22. Wyatte Grantham-Philips and Geoff Mulvihill, "Fortune 100 Companies Are Getting Swarmed by Republican AGs Using the Supreme Court Affirmative Action as a Lever into the Workplace," *Fortune*, July 15, 2023, https://fortune.com/2023/07/15/affirmative-action-13-republican-attorney-general-letter-corporate-ceos-fortune-100/.

23. Dara Kam, "Florida Is Cleared of Violating a Court Order over the 'Stop Woke Act,'" NPR, January 13, 2023, www.wusf.org/education/2023-01-13/florida-cleared-violating-court-order-stop-woke-act.

24. Jenner & Block LLP, "State Anti-DEI Initiatives Are Gaining Momentum: What Does It Mean for Your Organization?," *JDSupra*, February 24, 2023, www.jdsupra.com/legalnews/state-anti-dei-initiatives-are-gaining-9819065/.

25. Ben Felder, "Walters to Higher Ed Board: Provide Account of 'Every Dollar' Spent on Diversity Training," *The Oklahoman*, January 26, 2023, www.oklahoman.com/story/news/politics/government/2023/01/26/oklahoma-superintendent-education-ryan-walters-wants-every-dollar-diversity-training-accounted/69840233007/.

26. Adrienne Lu, "South Carolina Requests Colleges' DEI Spending, Following Florida and Oklahoma," February 8, 2023, www.chronicle.com/article/south-carolina-requests-colleges-dei-spending-following-florida-and-oklahoma.

27. Dan Solomon, "A Texas GOP Lawmaker Wants to Increase 'Viewpoint Diversity' by Banning Diversity, Equity, and Inclusion in Higher Ed," *Texas Monthly*, December 21, 2022, www.texasmonthly.com/news-politics/texas-dei-schools-bill/; Audra D. S. Burch, "Texas Lawmakers Pass Ban on D.E.I. Programs at State Universities," *New York Times*, May 29, 2023, www.nytimes.com/2023/05/29/us/texas-dei-program-ban.html?searchResultPosition=1.

28. Acacia Coronado, "Texas Ban on University Diversity Efforts Provides a Glimpse of the Future Across GOP-led States," AP News, February 16, 2024, https://apnews.com/article/texas-university-diversity-ban-dei-46e4b6193abe27b6abbdffcd1945cf38.

29. Lily Kepner, "Sources: UT Lays Off at Least 60 Employees Previously in DEI-related Position, Close DCCE," *Austin-Statesman*, April 2, 2024, www.statesman.com/story/news/politics/state/2024/04/02/texas-senate-bill-17-anti-dei-ut-fires-four-staff-related-positions-two-sources-confirm/73179902007/; Johanna Alonso, "'Heartbreaking to Be Collateral' in the Battle over DEI," *Inside Higher Ed*, July 29, 2024, www.insidehighered.com/news/students/diversity/2024/07/29/laid-dei-employee-texas-speaks-out.

30. Erin Gretzinger, "After Months of Political Pressure and a Failed Vote, Wisconsin's Regents Approve Deal on DEI," *Chronicle of Higher Education*, December 14, 2023, www.chronicle.com/article/after-months-of-political-pressure-and-a-failed-vote-wisconsins-regents-approve-deal-on-dei.

31. Courtney Tanner, "Gov. Cox Signs Utah Anti-DEI Bill Prohibiting Diversity Efforts He Once Championed," *Salt Lake Tribune*, January 30, 2024, www.sltrib.com/news/education/2024/01/31/utahs-gov-cox-signs-anti-dei-bill/.

32. Johanna Alonso, "DEI Ban Prompts Utah Colleges to Close Cultural Centers, Too," *Inside Higher Ed*, July 1, 2024, www.insidehighered.com/news/diversity/2024/07/01/onset-anti-dei-law-utah-colleges-close-cultural-centers?mc_cid=2c3673137c&mc_eid=39c6955034; "Utah Bans DEI at Universities and in Public-Sector Employment, the Latest in a String of Similar Statewide

Bans," Crowell, July 7, 2024, www.crowell.com/en/insights/client-alerts/utah-bans-dei-at-universities-and-in-public-sector-employment-the-latest-in-a-string-of-similar-statewide-bans.

33. Maggie Hicks, "New Anti-DEI Legislation Goes into Effect in 4 States," *Chronicle of Higher Education*, July 1, 2024, www.chronicle.com/article/new-anti-dei-legislation-goes-into-effect-in-4-states.

34. Claire Suddath, "Alabama's Anti-DEI Bill Fits Nicely with Its History of School Segregation," Bloomberg, February 29, 2024, www.bloomberg.com/news/newsletters/2024-02-29/alabama-s-anti-dei-bill-fits-nicely-with-its-history-of-school-segregation.

35. Chronicle Staff, "DEI Legislation Tracker."

36. Kendall Tietz, "University of North Carolina Moves to Ban 'Diversity, Equity and Inclusion' Statements in Anti-Woke Backlash," Fox News, February 24, 2023, www.foxnews.com/media/university-north-carolina-moves-ban-diversity-equity-inclusion-statements-anti-woke-backlash.

37. Chronicle Staff, "DEI Legislation Tracker."

38. Liam Knox, "Mizzou Dissolves DEI Office," *Inside Higher Ed*, July 31, 2024, www.insidehighered.com/news/diversity/race-ethnicity/2024/07/31/u-missouri-axes-dei-office-pre-empt-state-mandate

39. Hicks, "New Anti-DEI Legislation"; North Dakota Century Code Chapter 15-10.6, Senate Bill 2247, 68th Legislative Assembly (2023), https://legiscan.com/ND/text/SB2247/2023; see also Mark Walsh, "If Critical Race Theory Is Banned, Are Teachers Protected by the First Amendment?," *Education Week*, June 10, 2021, www.edweek.org/policy-politics/does-academic-freedom-shield-teachers-as-states-take-aim-at-critical-race-theory/2021/06.

40. "Round-up: College Presidents Remain Older, Male and White Despite Diversification Efforts," National Association of Independent Colleges and Universities, April 14, 2023, www.naicu.edu/news-events/headline-news/2023/04/round-up-college-presidents-remain-older-male-and-white-despite-diversification-efforts-april-1.

41. "College Professor Demographics and Statistics in the US," Zippia, accessed October 21, 2023, www.zippia.com/college-professor-jobs/demographics/.

42. Nanette Asimov, "Forced to Submit Diversity Statement, Professor Sues UC over 'Compelled Speech,'" *San Francisco Chronicle*, May 19, 2023, www.sfchronicle.com/bayarea/article/forced-affirm-dei-belief-professor-sues-uc-18109509.php; Conor Friedersdorf, "The Hypocrisy of Mandatory Diversity Statements," *The Atlantic*, July 3, 2023, www.theatlantic.com/ideas/archive/2023/07/hypocrisy-mandatory-diversity-statements/674611/.

43. Christopher F. Rufo, "D.E.I. Programs Are Getting in the Way of Liberal Education," *New York Times*, July 27, 2023, www.nytimes.com/2023/07/27/opinion/christopher-rufo-diversity-desantis-florida-university.html.

44. Adam Chilton, Justin Driver, Jonathan S. Masur, and Kyle Rozema, "Assessing Affirmative Action's Diversity Rationale," *Columbia Law Review* 122, no.

2 (2022): 331–406, 331, https://columbialawreview.org/content/assessing-affirmative-actions-diversity-rationale/; Karen Sloan, "Conservative Group Sues NYU, Claiming Selection of Law Journal Student Staff Discriminates," Reuters, October 19, 2023, www.reuters.com/legal/government/conservative-group-sues-nyu-claiming-selection-law-journal-student-staff-2023–10–19/.

45. Karen Sloan, "NYU Says White Man's Discrimination Suit over Law Review Selection Is 'Half-Baked,'" Reuters, January 30, 2024, www.reuters.com/legal/legalindustry/nyu-says-white-mans-discrimination-suit-over-law-review-selection-is-half-baked-2024–01–30/.

46. Scott Jaschik, "Does the Supreme Court Order Apply to Financial Aid?," *Inside Higher Ed*, July 5, 2023, www.insidehighered.com/news/admissions/2023/07/05/missouri-attorney-general-orders-colleges-drop-minority-scholarships.

47. Ja'han Jones, "After Gutting Affirmative Action, Republicans Target Minority Scholarships," MSNBC, July 4, 2023, www.msnbc.com/the-reidout/reidout-blog/republicans-minority-scholarships-wisconsin-rcna92426.

48. Bradford Betz, "University Slapped with Civil Rights Lawsuit over Racially 'Discriminatory' Scholarships," Fox News, September 19, 2023, www.foxnews.com/us/university-slapped-civil-rights-lawsuit-racially-discriminatory-scholarships; Joseph Ax, "Anti-Affirmative Action Group, Emboldened by US Supreme Court, Targets Scholarship," U.S. News, September 22, 2023, www.usnews.com/news/top-news/articles/2023–09–22/anti-affirmative-action-group-emboldened-by-us-supreme-court-targets-scholarships.

49. Mark J. Drozdowski, "The Hidden Truth Behind Merit Scholarships," bestcolleges.com, November 29, 2023, www.bestcolleges.com/news/hidden-truth-behind-merit-scholarships/.

50. Liam Knox, "Addressing Scholarships' Equity Problem," *Inside Higher Ed*, July 26, 2024, www.insidehighered.com/news/students/financial-aid/2024/07/26/connecting-minority-students-private-scholarships.

51. Divya Kumar, "Judge Stops Enforcement of Stop WOKE Act at Florida Colleges, Universities," *Tampa Bay Times*, November 17, 2022, www.tampabay.com/news/education/2022/11/17/judge-stops-enforcement-stop-woke-act-florida-colleges-universities/ (A federal judge granted a preliminary injunction to block the enforcement of the new Florida law, the "Stop WOKE" Act, prohibiting classroom discussions of race or color that make anyone feel "guilt, anguish or other psychological distress"); Leah Watson, "Lessons Learned from Our Classroom Censorship Win Against Florida's Stop W.O.K.E. Act," American Civil Liberties Union, November 29, 2022, www.aclu.org/news/free-speech/lessons-learned-from-our-classroom-censorship-win-against-floridas-stop-w-o-k-e-act.

52. Taifha Alexander, LaToya Baldwin Clark, Kyle Reinhard, and Noah Zatz, *CRT Forward: Tracking the Attack on Critical Race Theory* (Los Angeles: UCLA

School of Law Critical Race Studies, 2022), 6; https://crtforward.law.ucla.edu/new-crt-forward-report-highlights-trends-in-2021-2022-anti-crt-measures/.

53. Hannah Natanson, "'Slavery Was Wrong' and 5 Other Things Some Educators Won't Teach Anymore," *Washington Post*, March 6, 2023, www.washingtonpost.com/education/2023/03/06/slavery-was-wrong-5-other-things-educators-wont-teach-anymore/.

54. Hannah Natanson, "Her Students Reported Her for a Lesson on Race. Can She Trust Them Again?," *Washington Post*, September 18, 2023, www.washingtonpost.com/education/2023/09/18/south-carolina-teacher-ta-nehisi-coates-racism-lesson/.

55. Sarah Mervosh, "Florida Scoured Math Textbooks for 'Prohibited Topics.' Next Up: Social Studies," *New York Times*, March 16, 2023, www.nytimes.com/2023/03/16/us/florida-textbooks-african-american-history.html/.

56. Solcyre Burga, "Florida Approves Controversial Guidelines for Black History Curriculum. Here's What to Know," *Time*, July 20, 2023, https://time.com/6296413/florida-board-of-education-black-history/.

57. Carolina A. Miranda, "Dear Ron DeSantis: African Blacksmiths Would Like a Word," *Los Angeles Times*, August 5, 2023, www.latimes.com/entertainment-arts/newsletter/2023–08–05/dear-ron-desantis-african-blacksmiths-would-like-a-word-essential-arts-arts-culture.

58. David Hackett Fischer, *African Founders: How Enslaved People Expanded American Ideals* (New York: Simon and Schuster, 2022).

59. Carolyn Thompson and Heather Hollingsworth, "Some School Systems Pause Diversity Programs Amid Pushback," AP News, February 20, 2022, https://apnews.com/article/coronavirus-pandemic-health-business-education-race-and-ethnicity-50c02554ffb341073a1da08e336b6fe4.

60. Alexander et al., *CRT Forward*, 4

61. Rashawn Ray and Alexandra Gibbons, "Why Are States Banning Critical Race Theory?," Brookings, November 2021, www.brookings.edu/blog/fixgov/2021/07/02/why-are-states-banning-critical-race-theory/.

62. Sarah Schwartz, "Map: Where Critical Race Theory Is Under Attack," *Education Week*, June 11, 2021 (updated June 13, 2023), www.edweek.org/policy-politics/map-where-critical-race-theory-is-under-attack/2021/06.

63. Alexander et al., *CRT Forward*, 31.

64. Alexandra Alter and Elizabeth A. Harris, "Attempts to Ban Books Doubled in 2022," *New York Times*, March 23, 2023, www.nytimes.com/2023/03/23/books/book-ban-2022.html.

65. Alexandra Alter, "Book Bans Rising Rapidly in the U.S., Free Speech Groups Find," *New York Times*, April 20, 2023, www.nytimes.com/2023/04/20/books/book-bans-united-states-free-speech.html.

66. Maya Yang, "Florida Mother Behind Ban on Amanda Gorman Poem Has Proud Boys Links," *The Guardian*, May 25, 2023, www.theguardian.com/us-news/2023/may/25/amanda-gorman-poem-ban-parent-proud-boys-daily-salinas.

67. Isaiah Mitchell, "Dan Patrick Proposes Combating Critical Race Theory in Public Higher Education by Phasing Out Professors' Tenure," *The Texan*, February 18, 2022, https://thetexan.news/issues/social-issues-life-family/dan-patrick-proposes-combating-critical-race-theory-in-public-higher-education-by-phasing-out-professors/article_ecdf1be7–3823–505c-8eaf-83a016fcbc27.html.

68. Daniel Golden, "Muzzled by DeSantis, Critical Race Theory Professors Cancel Courses or Modify Their Teaching," ProPublica, January 3, 2023, www.propublica.org/article/desantis-critical-race-theory-florida-college-professors.

69. Freddie Sayers, "Edward Blum: My Battle Against Affirmative Action," UnHerd, May 29, 2023, https://unherd.com/2023/05/edward-blum-my-battle-against-affirmative-action/.

70. Robert Sheen, "Starbuck Lawsuit Dismissal: A Triumph for Corporate Diversity Efforts," *JDSupra*, October 13, 2023, www.jdsupra.com/legal-news/starbucks-lawsuit-dismissal-a-triumph-9978836/.

71. Nate Raymond, "U.S. Appeals Court Weighs Challenge to Pfizer Diversity Fellowship," Reuters, October 3, 2023, www.reuters.com/legal/litigation/us-appeals-court-weighs-challenge-pfizer-diversity-fellowship-2023–10–03/; Caroline Colvin, "Appeals Court Rejects Challenge to Pfizer's Diverse Fellowship Pipeline," *HR Dive*, March 7, 2024, www.hrdive.com/news/pfizer-breakthrough-fellowship-dei-lawsuit/709676/.

72. Sarah Kessler, "D.E.I. Goes Quiet," *New York Times*, January 13, 2024, www.nytimes.com/2024/01/13/business/dealbook/dei-goes-quiet.html.

73. Claire Suddath, "Does DEI Still Matter?," Bloomberg, February 15, 2024, www.bloomberg.com/news/newsletters/2024–02–15/us-companies-cut-diversity-teams-does-dei-matter-in-corporate-america.

74. Bruce Crumley, "Diversity Policy Backlash Drives Cuts to DEI Staff," Inc.com, February 20, 2024, www.inc.com/bruce-crumley/diversity-policy-backlash-drives-cuts-to-dei-staff.html.

75. Douglas Belkin and Erin Mulvaney, "Activist Behind Supreme Court Affirmative Action Cases Is Now Suing Law Firms," *Wall Street Journal*, August 22, 2023, www.wsj.com/us-news/edward-blum-lawsuits-affirmativeaction-law-firms-b8871ab1; Dan Roe, "Is Edward Blum Done Suing Law Firms?," *Law.com*, December 21, 2023, www.law.com/therecorder/2023/12/21/is-edward-blum-done-suing-law-firms/.

76. Roe, "Is Edward Blum Done?"

77. Claire Suddath, "Why Companies Are Scaling Back DEI in America," Bloomberg, February 1, 2024, www.bloomberg.com/news/newsletters/2024–02–01/why-companies-are-scaling-back-dei-in-america.

78. Joshua Q. Nelson, "Firms Face Financial Woes, Conduct Layoffs Due to Litigation Targeting DEI-based Grants: Report," Fox News, February 24, 2024, www.foxnews.com/media/firms-face-financial-woes-conduct-layoffs-litigation-targeting-dei-based-grants-report.

79. Suzanne Gamboa, "Smithsonian Latino Museum Internship Is Targeted by Conservative Legal Activist," NBC News, February 23, 2024, www.nbcnews.com/news/latino/smithsonian-latino-museum-internship-targeted-conservative-legal-rcna140244.

80. Jeff Green, "Businesses Are Quietly Rethinking Their DEI Efforts: Equality," Bloomberg, July 27, 2023, www.bloomberg.com/news/newsletters/2023-07-27/businesses-are-quietly-rethinking-their-dei-efforts-equality.

81. David Martin Davies, "Governor Abbott Declares Diversity, Equity and Inclusion Policies in Hiring Are Illegal," Texas Public Radio, February 14, 2023, www.tpr.org/podcast/the-source/2023-02-14/governor-abbott-declares-diversity-equity-and-inclusion-policies-in-hiring-are-illegal.

82. Kate McGee, "Gov. Greg Abbott Tells State Agencies to Stop Considering Diversity in Hiring," *Texas Tribune*, February 7, 2023, www.texastribune.org/2023/02/07/greg-abbott-diversity-equity-inclusion-illegal/.

83. Jody Godoy, "Activist Behind Harvard Race Case Takes Aim at Calif. Board Laws," Reuters, July 13, 2021, www.reuters.com/legal/legalindustry/activist-behind-harvard-race-case-takes-aim-calif-board-laws-2021-07-13/.

84. *Grutter v. Bollinger*, 539 U.S. 306, 331 (2003); Consolidated Brief of Lt. Gen. Julius W. Becton, Jr. et al. as Amici Curiae in Support of Respondents, *Grutter v. Bollinger*, 539 U.S. 306 (2003) (No. 02–241); see also Brief for the United States as Amicus Curiae Supporting Respondents, *Fisher v. Univ. of Tex.*, 579 U.S. 365 (2016) (No. 14–981).

85. Karoun Demirjian, "House Narrowly Passes Defense Bill, Setting Up Showdown over Social Issues," *New York Times*, July 14, 2023, www.nytimes.com/2023/07/14/us/politics/defense-bill-house-ndaa.html.

86. Brief of Adm. Charles S. Abbot et al. at 5, *Students for Fair Admissions, Inc. v. President and Fellows of Harvard Coll. and Univ. of N.C.*, 600 U.S. 181 (2023) (No. 21–707).

87. Brief of Adm. Charles S. Abbot et al. at 4, *Students for Fair Admissions*, 600 U.S. 181.

88. Emily Hoeven, "This Rich California City Is Using the Affirmative Action Ruling to Stop Affordable Housing," *San Francisco Chronicle*, September 1, 2023, www.sfchronicle.com/opinion/article/la-canada-flintridge-housing-18335041.php.

89. Nate Raymond, "North Carolina Ethics Panel Drops Probe over Justice's Diversity Critique," Reuters, January 17, 2024, www.reuters.com/legal/legalindustry/north-carolina-ethics-panel-drops-probe-over-justices-diversity-critique-2024-01-17/.

90. Alicia Keys, Comments at 2025 Grammy Awards; see Julia Jacobs, "Weeks into Trump's Second Term, Several Artists Alluded to Politics on Stage," *New York Times*, February 3, 2025.

91. Callum Borchers, "They Helped Create DEI—and Even They Say It Needs a Makeover," *New York Times*, December 22, 2024, www.wsj.com/lifestyle/workplace/dei-corporate-creators-program-changes-2db86ed8.

92. Paul Brest and Emily J. Levine, "D.E.I. Is Not Working on College Campuses. We Need a New Approach.," *New York Times*, August 30, 2024, www.nytimes.com/2024/08/30/opinion/college-dei-programs-diversity.html.

93. Albert van der Sandt Centlivres and Richard Feetham, *The Open Universities in South Africa* (Johannesburg: Witwatersrand University Press, 1957), 6, 34–35 (quotation reprinted with permission of Witwatersrand University Press).

Bibliography

To save trees (and perhaps facilitate corrections), the bibliography for this book is being maintained online by the University of California, Berkeley Law Library and may be accessed at https://lawcat.berkeley.edu/record/1317856?v=pdf or at https://doi.org/10.15779/J2/DIVERSITY_PRINCIPLE_ BIBLIOGRAPHY or via the book's website at DiversityPrinciple.com.

Acknowledgments

I began the research that led to this book in the spring of 2012, while on sabbatical. My purpose at the time was to understand the origins of the diversity justification for affirmative action. Once I discovered that Archibald Cox played a key role and that he was able to do so only because he'd been fired by Richard Nixon and Robert Bork in the "Saturday Night Massacre," I was hooked. Nonetheless, I came to the question as a diversity skeptic, concerned that diversity-based affirmative action was mostly an excuse to improve the education of white students by exposing them to small numbers of non-white students. Over the twelve years in which I pursued the project I've discovered that nearly everything I thought I knew about the diversity principle was wrong. Along the way, I have become a diversity admirer.

Between the fall of 2012 and the spring of 2025, I was assisted by more than one hundred fifty research assistants, including University of California, Berkeley, undergraduates, Berkeley law students, and law student and post-doc volunteers from other universities who worked with our Berkeley Center on Comparative Equality and Anti-Discrimination Law. They provided not just research assistance but a level of insight and collaboration that made our many meetings themselves a demonstration of the diversity principle. I could not have done this without them. I hope my records caught all of their names, including Madilyn Abbe, Sumayyah Rose Abuelmaatti, Astrid Ackerman, Christofer Adams, Sarina Alero Tawiah Addy, Nazli Aghazadeh-Wegener, Rishi Neil Ahuja, Nadia Akbari, Marlee Allison, Eric Monek Anderson, Russel Anderson, Yusra Arub, Tomasz Roman Barczyk, J. Alejandro Barrientos, Evan Bell, Veerangna Bhandari, Jona Bocari, Gözde Böffel, Rachel McCarthy Bosley, Victoria Bosley, Timothy Bott, Anna Braunroth, Esteem Brumfield, Loulie Bunzel, Keytoya Burrell, Laiza Cabote, Ernesto Tonatiuh Casillas, Natalie Castaneda, Sindi Cela, Aaron J. Cheung, Megan E. Cistulli, Benjamin Coleman, Henry H. Cornillie, Rachel Corrigan, Emily Daniel-Papi, Chelsea Davis, DeCarol Davis, Rozette Adriano De Castro, Alaina Delsignore,

Lauren Dias, Amyrah Doty, Astrid Duperthuy, Luke Edwards, Taqwa Elhindi, Mona Faham, Amina Fahmy, Julia Fauzia-Whatley, Rye Flores, Rachel Foodman, Satchel Friedman, Elizabeth Fulton, Jeffrey Fung, Claire van Gaalen, Sarah Gallo, Lauren Glasby, Celeste Gomez, Denison Goodrich-Schlenker, Angela Ariana Griffiths, Nina Kumari Gupta, Kenna Guzman, Sara Haji, Shams Al Hajjaji, Adriana Hardwicke, Meghan Harrington, Talia Harris, Priscilla N. Hatton, Emma Heijmans, Alexandra Heller, Katherine Hendrickson, Daniella V. Hernandez, Marianne Hrdlicka, Murtaza Husain, Valerie Jameson, Tomas Johnson, AJ Stone Jonathan, Sydney Judilla, Eric Jung, Arthur Karadzhyan, Mehtab Khan, Nicole Khoury, Jung Kim, Zoe Kleinfeld, Ivette Knapp, Emma Lapinsky, Aaron Lee, Katie Lee, Natalia Ramírez Lee, Michael Andrew Leite-Garcia, Mellori E. Lumpkin-Dawson, Melinda Lu, Masao MacMaster, Kaelyn Mahar, Noa Marks, Nicole Mauri, Katy Ghaleh Mahmoudi, Anissa Medina, Aaron Thomas Murphy, Ariel Murphy, Bianca Torres Murray, Lawrence Myung, Carlos A. Nevarez, Elisabeth Ng, AnVy H. Nguyen, Suaad Nour, Paloma Palmer, Camille Pannu, Lilliana Paratore, Julia Parish, Samantha Parr, Alexis Payne, Javier Perez, Benjamin Porter, Brittany Postle, Lisa Chaiet Rahman, Omeed Rajaee, Melanie L. Ramey, Christina Randall, Zoe Reier, Maria Richards, Edward Richter, Christopher Riley, Sasan Saadat, Isabella Sanchez, Cady Sartorius, Amisha Sethi, Reed Shaw, Sally Sheehan, Yemaj Sheik, S. Candice Shikai, Hudson Gencheng Shou, Lydia Sidhom, Jasleen Singh, Henry Bluestone Smith, Dakota Sneed, Alexandra Solomon, Georgiana Soo, Kaylee Yoshii Spiegelman, Harriet Steele, Audree Steinberg, Marie Talarico, Julie Ann Talbo, Julissa Tapia, Emma Tavangari, Sasha Thomas-Nuruddin, Rukayatu Tijani, Chieh Tung, Naomi Uwaka, Farraj C. Vazquez, Vidya Venugopal, Aaron Voit, Kate Gardner Walford, Gregory Washington, Rachel Weissman, Courtney Christine Whang, Sarah Williams, Rachel Weissman, Xandra Jiepei Xiao, Sophie Xue, Jane Yang, Yao Yang, Elizabeth Yates, Yasir Yetimoglu, Evelyn Yeung, Jasmine Yi, Hailey Yook, Han Hee Yu, Orlando Sanchez Zavala, Ziang Zhou, and Julian Zhu.

At the risk of insufficiently recognizing the important contributions of this long list of students, many of whom went above and beyond, there are three who carried the book forward when I might have faltered, and thus an extra special thank you is due to Isabelle Borchardt, Daniel Myerson, and Devin Shields.

As it was, along the way I was diverted by three editions of a casebook on comparative equality law, a book on comparative remedies for discrimination, and a book on comparative affirmative action, along with law review articles related to this work, including papers on systemic racism, diversity in higher education in South Africa, Archibald Cox and the diversity justification for affirmative action, Dr. King and affirmative action, and voluntary affirmative action. Regarding those law review articles, parts of chapters 6 and 14 previously appeared in David B. Oppenheimer, "The Disappearance of Voluntary Affirmative Action from the US Workplace," *Journal of Poverty and Social Justice* 24, no. 1 (2016): 37–50, © David

B. Oppenheimer 2016. Parts of chapters 7, 10, and 11 previously appeared in David B. Oppenheimer, "Archibald Cox and the Diversity Justification for Affirmative Action," *Virginia Journal of Social Policy and the Law* 25, no. 2 (2018): 157–203, © David B. Oppenheimer 2018. Parts of chapter 12 previously appeared in David B. Oppenheimer, Henry Cornillie, Henry Bluestone Smith, Thao Thai, and Richard Treadwell, "Be Careful What You Wish For: Ronald Reagan, Donald Trump, The Assault on Civil Rights, and The Surprising Story of How Title VII Got Its Private Right of Action," *Berkeley Journal of Employment and Labor Law* 39, no. 1 (2018): 147–76, © David B. Oppenheimer 2018. And parts of chapters 8 and 9 previously appeared in David B. Oppenheimer, "The South African Sources of the Diversity Justification for U.S. Affirmative Action," *California Law Review* 13, no. 32 (2022): 45–49, © David B. Oppenheimer 2022. In addition, I am grateful to and acknowledge permission from The Harvard University Archives to publish material from their collections, Wits University Press to reproduce a quote from *The Open Universities in South Africa*, Susan Danger for providing her quotation on diversity in Europe, and Gözde Böffel for permission to quote from her research memo on Humboldt.

But I always kept coming back to this question: What are the intellectual, cultural, and legal origins of the diversity principle?

In addition to the sources listed in the notes, I consulted with and was frequently put back on my path by conversations and/or correspondence with Haim Abraham, Chris Ambrosi, Susanne Baer, Mark Bell, Jim Bierman, Laura Bourgeois, Emmanuelle Bribosia, Jim Brosnahan, Hannah Buxbaum, Richard Buxbaum, Jozephien Van Caeneghem, Laura Carlson, Erwin Chemerinsky, Vivian Cheung, Price Cobbs, Debbie Collier, Bob Comfort, Lennie Copeland, Sabrina D'Andrea, Erin Delaney, Moira Dustin, Christopher Edley, Michael Feldberg, Catherine Fisk, William Fitzsimmons, Richard Ford, Sheila Foster, Mark Gergen, Fred Glimp, Lewis Griggs, Trina Grillo, Sora Han, Felix Hartmann, Colleen Haas, Robert Haas, Thelton Henderson, Stuart James, Anthony Julius, Panos Kapotas, Gary Kates, Marcy Kates, Michael Kesselbrenner, Bill Kidder, Jennifer Krebs, George Langford, Sophie Latraverse, Taeku Lee, Nicholas Lemann, Marian Lever, David Lieberman, Katerina Linos, Ian F. Haney Lopez, Benedicte Magdelaine, Dania Matos, Jack McNulty, Marie Mercat-Bruns, Carrie Newkirk, Colm O'Cinneide, Karen O'Connell, Alvaro Oliveira, Amy Oppenheimer, Eva Paterson, Marie-Christine Pauwels, Andy Plump, Charles Puttkammer, Sophie Robin-Olivier, Marjolaine Roccati, Isabelle Rorive, Richard Rothstein, Daniel Sabbagh, Albie Sachs, Elaine Sciolino, Marlene Silbert, Kendall Thomas, Charlie Tsunoda, Karen Vandekerckhove, Jan Vetter, Luci Wagner, and Stephanie Wildman.

In the summer of 2022 I co-authored an amicus brief for a group of law school deans in the cases filed by Students for Fair Admissions against Harvard and the University of North Carolina, which helped me realize that it was time to finish the project. Thank you to my co-author on the brief, Jim Bierman, and my six former students who did much of the work on the brief: Loulie Bunzel, Megan Cistulli, Lexi Heller, Daniel Myerson, AJ Stone Jonathan, and Courtney Whang.

Determined to finish, in the fall of 2022 I went on sabbatical again (thank you, Dean Erwin Chemerinsky), moved to Paris and then London, and started writing. Thanks to my Paris landlord (and now friend) Yezid Sayigh and to my host at the Sorbonne, Sophie Robin-Olivier. Thanks to my London hosts Lizzie Barmes and Kate Malleson at Queen Mary University of London and Colm O'Cinneide at University College London. Colm and Sophie were among the founders of our Center on Comparative Equality Law, many of whose members were a frequent source of ideas for further research.

I learned so much from my co-authors on my first book examining racism, *White-Washing Race: The Myth of a Color-Blind Society*, published in 2003 by the University of California Press. My co-authors' insights and voices were often in my head as I worked on this project. Much of our work together is reflected in chapter 16, on systemic racism. A big thank you to the late David Wellman and to Michael Brown, Martin Carnoy, Elliot Currie, Troy Duster, and Marjorie Shultz.

I'm grateful to the many librarians who helped me track down sources, including Doug Avila, Kristie Chamorro, Marci Hoffman, Edna Lewis, Dean C. Rowan, and I-Wei Wang at the Berkeley Law Library, and librarians at the Harvard University Library, the Library of Congress, the British Library, the Schlesinger Library at Radcliffe, and the University of North Carolina library. The bibliography can be found online at the University of California Berkeley Law Library thanks to the efforts of Joe Cera and Kristie Chamorro.

A number of friends and colleagues read parts of the manuscript and saved me various levels of embarrassment. Margie Heins, a First Amendment scholar and a friend for nearly fifty years, helped shape my discussion of academic freedom and pointed out that "you have Immanuel Kant's first name spelled three different ways, none of them correct." Nicholas Lemann kept finding new sources and juicy quotes to pass along. The Enlightenment historian Gary Kates saved me from numerous errors and helped with context and nuance. Richard Rothstein read several early chapters and helped me make my writing more accessible (I hope), as did Elaine Sciolino, Gary Kates, Marion Abbott, my agents Peter Bernstein and Amy Bernstein, and my freelance editor Emma Berry. Marcy Kates, my beloved wife, and Liz Casey, with Margaret Otzel, at Yale University Press read the full manuscript and made it immeasurably better, as did two anonymous peer reviewers at Yale. Bill Frucht, my principal editor at Yale (with his colleague Amanda Gerstenfeld), has an uncanny ability to turn a phrase just slightly and make it sing. He read my work with such care and respect. Thank you, Bill; I hope we get to do this again.

If you enjoyed reading the book all of the above deserve a lot of the credit. If you didn't, that's on me.

Finally, this book is dedicated to my wife, Marcy Kates, the love of my life. I could not have done this without her love and support.

Index

Abbott, Greg, 264, 265
Abrams v. United States, 72–73, 77, 121
academic freedom, 30–31, 54–55, 62,
    124–25, 128–29, 150, 155, 157, 170,
    175, 257–58; diversity and, 117, 118,
    151, 257–58; First Amendment pro-
    tection of, 4, 9, 12, 13, 125, 127–28,
    138, 151; principles of, 11, 111, 114,
    151; in South Africa, 111, 114, 118
Academy of Management, 189–90
affirmative action, 94, 138, 155, 161–64,
    249; business, for, 201, 204; gender-
    based, 167, 223–24; race-based, 1–3,
    4, 85, 86, 166, 167; reparations and,
    85–86; stigma of, 253–54; university
    education, in, 2, 4, 13, 108, 191
Affirmative Action Register, 201
Alabama, 256
Alito, Samuel, 176, 253
Allen, Virginia, 49
Alliance for Fair Board Recruitment,
    217, 218
America First Legal Foundation, 258
American Bar Association (ABA), 137;
    Model Diversity Survey, 208–9;
    Resolution 113, 208
American Civil Liberties Union
    (ACLU), 96, 98–99, 121, 124;
    Women's Rights Project, 10, 99

American Library Association, 263
Ames, James Barr, 133
Amherst College, 162, 249
Amsterdam News, 80
Anderson, Jack, 159
Anderson, Terry, 85
Anil, Pratinav, 37
Anti-Apartheid Movement in South
    Africa, 10, 109, 111–18; Robert
    Kennedy and, 117–18; Centlivres
    and, 112–18, Thomas Benjamin
    Davie and, 110–13, 117; Albie Sachs
    and, 113. *See also* University of Cape
    Town
anti-Semitism, 33, 60–61
anti-wokeism, 227, 228, 229
A&P Grocery Stores, 80
Applied Developmental Science, 193
Arcidiacono, Peter, 178
Arizona, 262
Arkansas, 260
Armstrong, Barbara, 91
Asian Americans, 60, 176–77
Association of American Universities,
    164
Atlantic Monthly, 67, 320 n.23; "The
    Case of Sacco and Vanzetti," 121–22;
    "The New Education," 8, 51–53
Austin, John, 36

Austria, 230, 353 n.8; Freedom Party of Austria (FPO), 226
Azaransky, Sarah, 90

Baartman, Sarah, 311 n.45
Baker, Ella, 91
Bakke. See *Regents of the University of California v. Bakke*
Ball, Howard: *Bakke Case, The*, 154
banks, discrimination and, 238–39
Bar Association of San Francisco (BASF), 208
Barlow, Irene, 96, 99
Basque language, 28
Bayer, 222
Bébéar, Claude, 220–21
Beech, Harvey, 177
Belgium, 221, 223
Bell, Susan Groag, 49
Bell-Scott, Patricia, 90–91
Bender, Wilbur, 101–3, 106, 138, 140, 161–62
Benna, Zyed, 227
Bentham, Jeremy, 36
bias, 197–98, 235; implicit, 212, 234–35, 240, 243–44
Bierman, James, 136
Biggs, Loretta C., 179
Bildung, 25, 26, 27, 30, 31, 32, 33
Birmingham, Alabama, 84, 107
Black, Hugo, 125
Black Americans, 7–8, 218; racial quotas, 81, 82–84; in the 1920s, 79–80; systemic racism and, 234–36, 245
Black Enterprise: "40 Best Companies for Diversity," 14, 201; "25 Best Places for Blacks to Work," 14, 201
Black Lives Matter, 209
Blackmun, Harry, 148
BlackRock, Inc., 207
Blanquer, Jean-Michel, 227, 228, 229
Blasi, Vincent, 154
Bloomberg, 264

Blum, Edward, 173, 174, 176–77, 249, 250, 263, 264, 265; Alliance for Fair Board Recruitment, 217, 218
Blumstein's, 80
boards, corporate, 205–6, 216–19, 224–25, 265
Boatcǎ, Manuela, 30
Boeing, 267
Böffel, Gözde, 25, 30, 32
Bogen, David, 76
Bok, Derek, 4, 11, 134, 135, 136; *Shape of the River, The*, 191
Borden Company, 84
Bork, Robert, 3, 135, 154
Bowen, William, 152; *Shape of the River, The*, 191
Bowman, Nicholas, 195
boycotts, Civil Rights Movement, and the, 80–81, 84–85; Don't Shop Where You Can't Work, and, 80–84; Holmes, and, 69; Jesse Jackson, and, 207; Martin Luther King, and, 84–85, 204, 207; Montgomery Bus, 84, 260; Operation Breadbasket, and, 84–85, 207; Pauli Murray, and, 88; Supreme Court and, 83–84; Thurgood Marshall, and, 86
Brandeis, Louis, 60–61, 69, 77, 120, 248
Brennan, William J., 125, 128–29, 148
Brest, Paul, 267
Brookings Institution, 262
Brown University, 52
Brown v. Board of Education, 9, 87, 96, 114, 148
Buck v. Bell, 70
Bulgaria, 353 n.8
Burger, Warren Earl, 148
Burgsdorff, Wilhelm Theodor von, 27
Burroughs, Allison D., 179
Bush, George W., 241
business case for diversity, 2, 14–15, 16, 171–72, 199, 201–19; corporate boards, 205–6, 216–19, 224–25, 265;

development of, 204–7; earnings gap, 210; in Europe, 220–21, 222–23, 224–25; pillars of, 205

businesses, discrimination and, 238–39

Calabresi, Guido, 154, 155
California, 167; Proposition 14, 162; Underrepresented Communities on Boards Act, 217–18; Women on Boards Act, 218. *See also* University of California
California Law Review, 91
Cambridge University, 7, 36, 44
Carbado, Devon, 170
Cardozo, Benjamin, 120, 122, 315 n.16
Carlyle, Jane, 37
Carlyle, Thomas, 37, 43
Carnegie Corporation, 111, 112
Carnochan, W. B., 59
case method, 69
Catalyst, 205–6
Catholics: discrimination against, 6, 7, 8, 32, 33, 36, 44, 247
Centlivres, Albert van der Sandt, 10, 110, 112–14, 118, 124, 128, 248; "Address by the Chancellor of the University of Cape Town at Jameson Memorial Hall," 116; *Open Universities in South Africa, The*, 10–11, 12, 113–16, 117, 124, 127–28, 138, 267–68; "T. B. Davie Memorial Lecture," 117; "We Fight for Our Rights," 117
Chafee, Zechariah, 73, 75, 121
Chaney, James, 162
Charte de la Diversité, 220–21
Chen, Anthony, 108, 162
Chicago Whip, 80
Chomsky, Noam, 28
Ciotti, Éric, 228
Civil Rights Act (1964), 83, 84, 97, 134, 137, 148, 162, 167, 201
Civil Rights Movement, 80–86, 91, 150
Claremont Institute, 254
classic liberalism, 32

Coal. for TJ v. Fairfax Cnty. Sch. Bd., 251–53
Cobbs, Price, 202; *Valuing Diversity*, 203
Cohen, Geoffrey, 198
Coleman, William, 124
Collins, Addie Mae, 107
Colorado, 218
Columbia University, 52, 162
Comfort, Bob, 143
Conant, James B., 62, 90, 293 n.34
Congress of Racial Equality (CORE), 85, 91
Connerly, Ward, 167–68
Copeland, Lennie, 202, 203; *Valuing Diversity*, 203
Council on Legal Education Opportunity, 137
coverture, 38
Cowley, Stacy, 189
Cox, Archibald, 11, 109, 110, 117, 119, 120, 133–35, 147; *Bakke* representation, 13, 147; *DeFunis v. Odegaard* amicus curiae brief, 3, 4, 5, 11–12, 16, 135–45, 151, 160; "Minority Admissions After *Bakke*," 163; Watergate special prosecutor, 3–4, 135
Crenshaw, Kimberlé, 90, 235
Crisis, The, 80
critical race theory, 260–61
Croatia, 223, 353 n.8
Cyprus, 353 n.8
Czechia, 353 n.8

Danger, Susan, 223
Dartmouth College, 52
Darwin, Charles, 24, 43
Davie, Thomas Benjamin ("T. B."), 110–13, 114; "Address on the Occasion of the Graduation of the University of Witwatersrand," 111
Davis, Angela, 33
Debs v. United States, 71

DeFunis v. Odegaard, 11; *amicus curiae* briefs, 3, 4, 5, 11–12, 16, 135–45, 151
Delany, Martin, 68
Denmark, 224, 353 n.8
DeSantis, Ron, 254, 260, 263
Deutsche Bank, 222
Dewey, John, 123–24; *Democracy and Education,* 123; *German Philosophy and Politics,* 124; *School and Society, The,* 123
Dey, Eric, 191
Dhir, Aaron, 224
Diallo, Rokhaya, 228–29
Dickens, Charles, 43
Dirksen, Everett, 97
discrimination, 234–47; banking, in, 238–39; business, in, 238–39; education, in, 240–41; health care, in, 194–95, 243–44; housing, in, 162, 236–38; intersectional, 98, 235; policing, in, 242; systemic racism and, 234–36; voting. in, 244–45; wealth accumulation, in, 238–39. *See also* employment discrimination; race discrimination; religious discrimination; sex discrimination
diversity, 76–77, 154–55; gender, 205–6, 224–25; identity, 7, 41, 58, 160, 190; national, 57–58, 221; regional, 64; religious, 57, 247; value of, 2, 5, 17, 19, 31, 115, 170–71, 194, 203, 247; viewpoint, 7, 40, 41, 58, 190; war against, 248–68. *See also* business case for diversity
Diversity, Equity, and Inclusion (DEI), 17, 188, 200, 203, 210, 246, 258. *See also* diversity; equity; inclusion
Diversity Charters, 17, 220–21
diversity managers, 213
diversity principle, 1, 2, 4, 5, 6, 9–10, 17, 18, 19, 40, 67, 78, 87, 89, 92, 94, 100, 112, 138, 143, 146, 154, 155, 168, 187, 190, 193, 199, 200, 210, 214, 219, 220, 224, 225, 230, 233, 247, 248, 267, 269

diversity science, 15–16, 187–200, 201, 205; civic interactions and, 194–96; higher education, diversity impact on, 190–94; organizational psychology, 190, 192–93
diversity statements, 214–16, 256
diversity training, 200, 210–12
Dobbin, Frank, 203, 211–13
Dobbs v. Jackson Women's Health, 248
Do No Harm, 263
Douglas, William O., 9, 125
Dreyfuss, Joel: *Bakke Case, The,* 154
Du Bois, W. E. B., 33, 57, 61–62, 80
Duke University, 162, 249
Dunbar, William H., 315 n.16
Dworkin, Ronald, 155

Ebenreck, Sara, 49
Edelman, Lauren, 203
Edley, Christopher, 267
education discrimination, 240–41
Education Week, 262
Einstein, Albert, 33
Eliot, Charles William, 5, 11, 46, 50–59, 60, 61, 63, 69, 123, 187, 248; "Diversity in Family, College, and State," 58; educational reforms at Harvard, 8, 53–59; "Inaugural Address," 55–56, 57; "The New Education," 8, 51–53
Eliot, Ellen Derby Peabody, 50
Ely, John Hart, 155
Emerson, Ralph Waldo, 67
Emerson, Thomas, 125
employment discrimination, 80–81, 82–86, 91, 239–40
Engberg, Mark, 195
Environmental, Social, and Governance (ESG), 208
Episcopal Church, 99, 100
equality, 92, 167, 223–24
Equal Rights Amendment, 97
equity, 188, 196–99, 233, 234
Ernst & Young, 222

Espionage Act, 70, 71, 72

Estonia, 353 n.8

European Commission, 222, 224

European Union: corporate board membership, 224–25; Court of Justice, 224; diversity and, 221; Diversity Charters, 17, 221; Equal Treatment Directive, 226; gender parity programs, 223; Platform of Diversity Charters, 222; Racial Equality Directive, 226; racism in, 225–30

Evans, Hiram, 62

Experiences - Attributes - Metrics model, 164

Eyre, John, 43

Facebook, 209

Fair Employment Practices Commission (FEPC), 82–83

Fair Housing Act (1968), 162, 236

Fearless Fund, 264

Federalist Society, 149, 159

Feetham, Richard, 114; *Open Universities in South Africa, The*, 10–11, 113–16, 117, 124, 127–28, 138, 267–68

Feingold, Jonathan, 253

Fichte, Johann Gottlieb, 29

Finland, 353 n.8

First Amendment, 67, 82, 128; academic freedom, 4, 12, 13, 119, 138, 151; clear and present danger test, 71; free speech clause, 8, 9, 70–73, 75–77, 125

Fisher v. University of Texas, 163, 171, 173–76, 198, 251

Florida, 19, 167, 254, 260; "Individual Freedom Act," 263; Office of Policy and Budget, 255. *See also* University of Central Florida

Flowers, Eliza, 37, 49

Flowers, Sally, 37

Floyd, George, 209

Footlick, Jerrold K., 143

Ford, 267

Forget, Evelyn, 48, 49

Fourteenth Amendment, 46, 78, 90, 95, 99, 148, 150; Equal Protection clause, 12–13, 87, 92, 153, 165, 166

Fox, Caroline, 37

Fox, William J., 37

FP Analytics, 206

France, 24, 223, 224, 230; Diversity Charter, 220–21; racism in, 225–26; Rassemblement National, 228; universalism, 225, 228

Frankfurter, Felix, 119–23, 124, 133; Brandis, and, 120, 121, 151; "The Case of Sacco and Vanzetti," 121–22; Centlivres, and, 10, 110, 112, 114, 116, 117, 124–25, 128; Cox, and, 119, 133, 138; early life, 88; Holmes, and, 9, 73–74, 75, 119, 123, 151; *Hughes* opinion, 83; studies at Harvard, 119–20; *Sweezy* opinion, 11, 126–28, 129, 139, 151

Freedle, Roy, 250

Free Speech movement, 162

Freund, Paul, 117, 136

Friedan, Betty, 99

Friedrich II, 23

Frohwerk v. United States, 71

Garrison, Lloyd K., 96

General Motors, 16, 204

General Theological Seminary, 99

Germany, 230; Alternative for Germany (AfD) Party, 230; *Charta der Vielfalt*, 221–22; education in, 5–6, 28–30, 33, 51; Romanticism in, 25, 32. *See also* University of Berlin

Gilman, Daniel Coit, 123

Ginger, Ann Fagan, 145

Ginsburg, Ruth Bader, 10, 90, 93, 99, 173–74

Gladstone, William, 39, 42

Gladwell, Malcolm, 187

Glimp, Fred, 101, 103, 106, 136, 138; "Final Report to the Faculty," 103, 104–6, 140

Goethe, Johann Wolfgang von, 6, 25, 26, 27, 32

Goldwater, Barry, 162

Goldwater Institute, 254

Goodman, Andrew, 162

Google, 264

Gorman, Amanda: "The Hill We Climb," 263

Gorsuch, Neil, 253

Grafton, Anthony, 30

Graham, Frank, 88–89

Grant, Robert, 315 n.16

Gratz v. Bollinger, 16, 163, 168

Greece, 28, 223, 353 n.8

Griggs, Lewis, 202; *Valuing Diversity,* 203

Griswold, Erwin, 9, 93, 108, 117, 118, 120, 134, 137; Centlivres and, 10, 112, 115, 117; Davie and, 110, 111–12; *Sipuel* testimony, 93–94; *Sweatt amicus curiae* brief, 94–95, 96, 125

Grutter v. Bollinger, 16, 163, 168–72, 173, 174, 190–91, 192, 204–5, 251, 265; *amicus curiae* briefs, 171–72

Gurin, Gerald, 191

Gurin, Patricia, 191

Haider, Jörg, 226

Haltigan, John, 257

Hand, Augustus N., 315 n.16

Hand, Learned, 11, 73, 76, 120, 133

Hare, Thomas, 42

Harrington, Mary, 43

Harvard Business Review, 187, 203, 206, 211

Harvard Classics, 55

Harvard College/University, 1, 8–9, 52, 53, 177, 249; admission policies at, 101–3; educational reforms at, 53–59; under Eliot, 8, 53–59; Harvard Annex, 53; Jewish students at, 11, 62–64, 121; Law School, 10, 56, 64, 108, 249; under Lowell, 11, 60–64; recruitment of Black students, 4–5, 56–57, 107, 108; School of Dental Medicine, 56. *See also* Harvard Plan

Harvard Educational Review, 191, 250

Harvard Plan, 13, 104, 139–42, 143, 145, 151, 152, 164, 165, 175

Hastie, William H., 81, 90

Hawley, Josh, 216

Hawthorne, Nathaniel, 67

Hayek, Friedrich, 36–37, 48, 49

health care, discrimination in, 194–95, 243–44

Healy, Thomas, 72, 73, 74, 75–76

Herz, Henriette, 24

Herz, Markus, 24

Hewlett-Packard, 209

Heytens, Toby, 253

Hocking, William Earnest, 63

Hofstadter, Richard, 34

Holmes, Amelia Lee Jackson, 68

Holmes, Fanny, 74

Holmes, Oliver Wendell, Jr., 9, 67, 68–70, 73–77, 120, 123, 124; *Abrams v. United States* opinion, 72, 77, 121; *Buck v. Bell* opinion, 70; *Common Law, The,* 68; *Debs v. United States* opinion, 71; *Frohwerk v. United States* opinion, 71; *Path of the Law, The,* 124; *Schenck v. United States* opinion, 71

Holmes, Oliver Wendell, Sr., 67–68

homogeneity, 4, 8, 187, 188

Hoover, Herbert, 120

Hoover, J. Edgar, 121

Hopwood v. Texas, 164–66, 167, 176

housing discrimination, 162, 236–38

Howard University: Law School, 10, 89

Huckleberry Finn, 260

Hughes, John, 83

Hughes v. Superior Court, 82–83

Huguenots, 23, 31

Humboldt, Alexander von, 5, 24, 28

Humboldt, Caroline, 6, 18, 24–25, 26, 27, 28, 33

Humboldt, Gustav, 27

Humboldt, Theodor, 27

Humboldt, Wilhelm von, 5–6, 18, 23–33, 187, 248; education reform by, 5–6,

28–30, 33–34; *Limits of State Action, The*, 25, 31, 34, 39–40; as linguist, 28; sexual experimentation by, 27, 28; University of Berlin, founder of, 5–6, 23, 26, 29–30, 32

Humboldt University. *See* University of Berlin

Hungary, 230, 353 n.8

Hurtado, Sylvia, 191

Idaho, 262

Illinois, 218

Immigrant Restriction League, 60

implicit bias, 212, 234–35, 240, 243–44

Inc.com, 264

inclusion, 18, 188, 196–99, 213–14, 233, 234

Inside Higher Ed, 259

insiders, 1

Insight Into Diversity, 201

integration, 92, 148

intersectionality, 90, 98, 235

Iowa, 256, 259, 262

Ireland, 353 n.8

Italy, 223, 224, 230, 353 n.8

Jackson, Jesse, 84–85; Operation Push, 207

Jackson, Ketanji Brown, 7, 180; *SFFA* opinion, 181–82

Jacobs, Jo Ellen, 48, 49

Jamaica, 43

James, Henry, 53, 55

Jameson, Leander Starr, 311 n.45

Jeffries, John C., Jr., 142, 154–55

Jews: anti-Semitism, 33, 60–61; discrimination against, 6, 7, 8, 32, 33, 36, 44, 62–63, 247; quotas for, 11, 63–64, 121

Johns Hopkins University, 53–54, 123

Johnson, "Lady Bird," 97, 98

Johnson, Lyndon B., 96; "Commencement Address at Howard University," 137–38, 245–46

Journal of Labor Economics, 198–99

Journey of Reconciliation, 91

Judicial Watch, 218

juries, 195–96

Kagan, Elena, 335 n.101

Kalev, Alexandra, 203, 211–13

Kansas, 255, 256, 258

Kant, Immanuel, 24, 26, 29, 32

Karabel, Jerome, 54, 56, 59, 63

Karl Augustus, Duke, 25

Kennedy, Anthony, 2, 159, 174, 248; *Fisher I* opinion, 174–75; *Fisher II* opinion, 175–76

Kennedy, John F., 96, 134; Executive Action, 161

Kennedy, Robert F., 117; "Ripple of Hope" speech, 118

Kentucky, 258

Kenyon, Dorothy, 99

Kessler, Andy, 216

Keyishian v. New York Board of Regents, 128–29, 151–52, 170

Keys, Alicia, 267

King, Martin Luther, Jr., 81, 83–84, 148, 207, 240; Birmingham campaign, 84–85; boycotts and, 84–85, 204, 207; civil disobedience, and, 137, 149; "I Have a Dream" speech, 85, 167, 168; Kerner Commission testimony, 86; *Letter from Birmingham Jail*, 137; Montgomery bus boycott, 84; quotas and, 168; reparations, and, 85–86, 168; *Why We Can't Wait*, 85–86

Ku Klux Klan, 62, 79

La Cañada Flintridge, California, 265–66

Landmark Briefs and Arguments of the Supreme Court of the United States, 145

Langdell, Christopher Columbus, 69

La Roche, Carl Georg von, 24–25

Laski, Harold, 9, 62, 73, 74–75, 121, 248

Lassiter, James, 177

Latvia, 353 n.8

Lawrence, Charles: *Bakke Case, The,* 154

Lee, J. Kenneth, 177

legal realism, 68

lehrfreiheit, 31

Lemann, Nicholas, 250

Leonard, Walter, 136

Le Pen, Marine, 227, 229

Levin, Ron, 145

Levine, Emily, 53, 267

Lewis, Anthony, 118, 136, 143

LexisNexis, 144

Liberal Party, 39

libertarianism, 44

libraries, school, 262–63

Lincoln, Abraham, 46, 68

Lithuania, 353 n.8

Lithwick, Dahlia, 98

Lowell, Abbott Lawrence, 11, 59, 60–64, 121, 122

Lozès, Patrick, 227

Lucky Stores, 82–83

Luxembourg, 223, 353 n.8

M, Le magazine du Monde, 229

MacDonald, Anne, 293 n.34

Mack, Julian W., 315 n.16

Macron, Emmanuel, 227, 230

Malan, D. F., 113

Manhattan Institute, 254

Mansfield Rule, 209

March on Washington, 97

marketplace of ideas, 9, 67, 72, 77–78, 128

Marshall, Margaret, 117–18

Marshall, Thurgood, 9–10, 81–82, 83, 86–87, 89, 96, 134, 148; *New Negro Alliance* representation, 81, 82; *Sipuel* representation, 91–92, 93–94

Marvin, Langdon, 315 n.16

Marx, Karl, 33

Maryland, 218

Massachusetts Institute of Technology (MIT), 8, 51, 52, 249

Masses v. Patten, 76

McCabe, Helen, 49

McKinsey and Company, 206, 234

McKissick, Floyd, 177

McKissick v. Carmichael, 177

McLaurin v. Oklahoma State Regents for Higher Education, 94, 115

McNair, Denise, 107

Méhaignerie, Laurence, 220; *Les oubliés de l'égalité des chances,* 220

Melville, Herman, 67

Mendelssohn, Felix, 33

Mentoring programs, 213

Merkel, Angela, 221

Meta, 264

Metzger, Walter, 34

Michigan, 167, 168. *See also* University of Michigan

Miles College, 107, 108, 109

military: academies, affirmative action in, 163, 171, 180, 265; diversity, importance of, 2, 16, 171, 265

Mill, Harriet Burrow, 35

Mill, Harriet Taylor, 6–7, 18, 36–39, 98, 187; contributions to John's works, 39, 46–49; *Enfranchisement of Women, The,* 48; *On Liberty,* 6, 9, 15, 25, 34, 37, 38, 39–42, 44, 46, 49, 55, 73, 75, 202, 220; *Principles of Political Economy, The,* 38; *Subjection of Women, The,* 7, 38, 44–45

Mill, James, 35

Mill, John Stuart, 6–7, 18, 35–36, 37–46, 68, 187, 267; *Autobiography,* 35–36, 38, 39, 40, 46–47, 49, 55; *Considerations on Representative Government,* 38, 42; *Inaugural Address at St. Andrews,* 7, 45–46, 122; *On Liberty,* 6, 9, 15, 25, 34, 37, 38, 39–42, 44, 46, 49, 55, 68, 73, 75, 202, 220; in Parliament, 39, 42–44, 248; *Principles of Political Economy, The,* 38; "Statement on Marriage," 38; *Subjection of Women, The,* 7, 38, 44–45; *System of Logic, A,* 38; *Utilitarianism,* 38

Miller, Dale: *Stanford Encyclopedia of Philosophy*, 47–48
Miller, Stephen, 250–51, 258
Missouri, 258, 260. *See also* University of Missouri
Missouri ex rel. Gaines v. Canada, 87, 88, 177
Monde, Le, 229
Monro, John U., 106–9
Montaigne Institute, 220
Morison, Samuel Eliot, 56–57
Morrison & Foerster, 264
Morton, James M., Jr., 315 n.16
Moyers, Bill, 160
Murray, Pauli, 9, 10, 18, 87–93, 96–100, 177, 233, 235, 248; at ACLU, 10, 90, 96, 99; at Paul Weiss, 96; attendance at Berkeley, 90–92; attendance at Howard, 10, 18, 81–82, 89–93; attendance at Hunter, 88; attendance at Yale, 96–98; boycotts and, 80, 81, 88; "Challenge of Nurturing the Christian Community in Its Diversity," 99–100; civil disobedience and, 89, 91; Eleanor Roosevelt and, 89–90; Episcopal Priesthood, 79–80, 99–100; Gender Identity, 10, 80, 88; "Memorandum in Support of Retaining the Amendment," 97–98; *Pauli Murray*, 89; *Reed v. Reed*, and, 99; Rejection by Harvard Law, 10, 18, 90–93; Rejection by University of North Carolina, 10, 18, 88–89, 97; Ruth Bader Ginsburg, and, 10, 80, 90, 93, 99; "Should the Civil Rights Cases and *Plessy v. Ferguson* Be Overruled?," 92–93; Title VII, and, 97–98; Thurgood Marshall and, 9–10, 80, 87, 89, 91, 93, 94, 96, 268
Muslims: discrimination against, 225

Nasdaq, 217
Nation, The, 121
National Association for the Advancement of Colored People (NAACP), 9, 79–80, 81, 83, 89; Legal Defense Fund, 82, 96, 178
National Center for Public Policy Research, 263
National Museum of the American Latino, 264
National Organization of Women, 10, 99
National Scholarship Service and Fund for Negro Students (NSSFNS), 107
Ndiaye, Pap, 229–30
Nebraska, 167
Nehru, Jawaharlal, 86
Netherlands, 353 n.8
New Hampshire, 262. See also *Sweezy v. New Hampshire*
New Negro Alliance, 81
New Negro Alliance v. Sanitary Grocery Co., 81–82
Newsweek, 12, 143
New York, 85, 88, 91, 96, 218
New York Times, 12, 46, 58, 61, 143, 189, 228, 254, 258, 267
New York University, 258
Nixon, Richard, 3–4, 135, 150
nonconformists, 7, 44
Norris-LaGuardia Anti-Injunction Act, 81, 82
North Carolina, 259, 266. *See also* University of North Carolina
North Carolina Central University School of Law, 177
North Dakota, 256, 262
Northern Trust, 208
Norway, 224
Novartis AG, 209

O'Connor, John, 54
O'Connor, Sandra Day, 2, 159, 172, 248; *Grutter* opinion, 16, 168–72, 192, 204, 265
Of Mice and Men, 260
Oklahoma, 255, 262. *See also* University of Oklahoma Law School

Operation Breadbasket, 84–85, 207
Operation Push, 207
Osburg, Lilly, 49
Östling, Johan, 29, 30, 31
outsiders, 1, 40, 77

P. F. Collier & Son, 55
Pacific Legal Foundation, 212, 251, 257
Packard, Josh, 193
Palmer, A. Mitchell, 73
Pangburn, Kris, 27
Parks, Rosa, 260
Patrick, Dan, 263
Paul, Weiss, Rifkind, Wharton and
    Garrison, 96
Paxton, Ken, 217
PEN America, 263
Pennypacker, Henry, 63
Perkins Coie, 264
Personnel, 203
Pfizer, 263
Philippe, Edouard, 227
Philips, Menaka, 49
Phillips, Damon, 189
Phillips, Howard, 111
Phillips, Katherine, 17, 188–90, 192–93,
    196, 197–98, 215, 230; "How
    Diversity Makes Us Smarter," 4, 15,
    188
Pifer, Alan, 112
Pitt, Richard, 193
Pitts, Lucius, 107, 108
Plaut, Victoria, 15, 17, 188, 196–97, 198,
    213, 234
Plessy v. Ferguson, 87, 92
pluralism, 267
Poland, 223, 353 n.8
policing, discriminatory, 242
Portugal, 223, 353 n.8
Posner, Richard, 12, 144
Pound, Roscoe, 122
Powell, Lewis, 2, 148–50, 155, 160, 248;
    Bakke opinion, 3, 13, 16, 94, 104, 139,
    143, 146, 150–54, 156, 159–60, 161,

163, 164, 166, 168, 169–70, 202; Cox
    brief, knowledge of, 12, 142–43, 323
    n.30; Powell Memo, 149, 156–59
Princeton University, 8, 14, 108, 162, 249
*Proceedings of the National Academy of
    Sciences*, 199
profiling, 244
Progressive Citizens of America, 82
ProPublica, 263
Pusey, Nathan, 110, 111, 116

quotas, 204, 217; gender, 223–24; Jewish,
    11, 63–64, 121; racial, 81, 82–84, 150,
    152, 165, 168

Rabban, David, 73
race discrimination, 10, 79, 81, 82–86,
    90, 235
racism, 218, 248, 259, 260; in Europe,
    225–30; stigma and, 253–54;
    systemic, 229, 234–36, 245
Radcliffe College, 8, 53, 61
Rahim, Asad, 149–50, 159–60
Ramey, Drucilla, 208
Rand Corporation, 259
Randolph, A. Philip, 97
Reagan, Ronald, 162–63
Reding, Viviane, 222
Reed v. Reed, 99
Reeves, Richard, 40, 45
*Regents of the University of California v.
    Bakke*, 3, 12–13, 16, 94, 104, 139, 143,
    146–48, 150–54, 159–60, 161, 163,
    166, 168, 169–70, 173, 174
Rehnquist, William, 148, 168
religious discrimination, 7, 32, 33, 36, 44,
    225
Rensselaer Polytechnic Institute (RPI), 52
Reynolds, William, 163
Richardson, Elliot, 3, 135
Richardson, Louis, 83
Richmond, California, 82–83
Roberts, John, 198, 245, 248; *SFFA*
    opinion, 180–81, 182, 183, 251, 265

Robertson, Carole, 107
Robinson, Spottswood, 92
Rockefeller Foundation, 163
Rockwell, Leo, 33
Rogers, William Barton, 51
Romania, 223, 353 n.8
Romanticism, 25, 32
Ronan, James, 69–70
Roosevelt, Eleanor, 89, 90
Roosevelt, Franklin D., 89, 90, 120, 122
Rose, Phyllis, 48; *Parallel Lives: Five Victorian Marriages*, 48–49
Rosenstrauch, Hazel, 27
Rossi, Alice, 48; *Essays on Sex Equality by John Stuart Mill and Harriet Taylor*, 48
Rossi, Philippe, 229
Rothstein, Richard: *Color of Law, The*, 236
Ruckelshaus, William, 3, 135
Rudenstine, Neil, 56, 57
Rufo, Christopher F., 258
Russell, Bertrand, 36
Rustin, Bayard, 91

Sabeg, Yazid: *Les oubliés de l'égalité des chances*, 220
Sacco, Nicola, 62, 121–22
Sachs, Albie, 113
Sacks, Albert, 136
Sanitary Grocery Company, 81
Sarkozy, Nicholas, 227–28
Saturday Night Massacre, 3, 135
Saxby, Troy, 91
Scalia, Antonin, 155, 335 n.101
Schefczyk, Michael, 49
Schenck v. United States, 71
Schiller, Charlotte, 26
Schiller, Friedrich, 24, 26, 32
Schlabrendorf, Gustav von, 27
Schlegel, Dorothea von, 24
Schlegel, Friedrich von, 24
Schmidt-Petri, Christoph, 49
Schneerson, Menachem Mendel, 33
scholarships, academic, 241, 258–59

Scholastic Aptitude Test (SAT), 101, 103, 241, 250, 259
Schopenhauer, Arthur, 29–30
Schuck, Peter H., 193
Schulz, Kathryn, 88
Schwartz, Bernard, 154
Schwerner, Michael, 162
Scientific American, 15, 188, 198
scientific support for diversity. *See* diversity science
Securities Act, 217
Securities Exchange Commission, 217
Sedition Act (1918), 70–71
self-managed work teams, 213
separate but equal doctrine, 87, 92, 114, 115
sex discrimination, 10, 89, 90, 91, 97–98, 99, 235
Sharaf, James, 136
Sheldon, Henry N., 315 n.16
Shores, Arthur, 107
Siegfried-Laferi, Meike, 31
Siemens, 222
Silicon Valley Bank, 216
Sinclair, Upton, 214
Sinnlichkeit, 27
Sipuel v. Board of Regents of the University of Oklahoma, 91, 93–94, 115, 137
Slosson, Edwin, 8
Slovakia, 353 n.8
Slovenia, 223, 353 n.8
Small Business Administration, 238
Smith, George H., 32
Smith, Howard, 97
Smith, Jeremiah, 315 n.16
Smith, W. H., 44
Smolla, Rodney A., 77–78
Sommers, Samuel, 195–96
South Africa, 10, 110–18, 247; Extension of University Education Act, 116; National Party, 111, 113, 116; University Education Bill, 113, 116. *See also* University of Cape Town; University of Witwatersrand

South Carolina, 255, 262
Southern Christian Leadership
    Conference, 84
Sowell, Thomas, 193–94
Spain, 223, 230, 353 n.8
Spectator, 43
Starbucks, 263
Steiner, Daniel, 136, 143
Stengel, Casey, 245
Stephens, John Paul, 148
Stewart, Potter, 148
Stimson, Henry L., 120
Stone, Geoffrey, 73
strategic litigation, 10, 87
Stretch, Colin, 209
*Students for Fair Admissions, Inc. v.
    President and Fellows of Harvard Coll.,*
    1, 171, 173, 177, 178–84
*Students for Fair Admissions, Inc. v.
    President and Fellows of Harvard Coll.
    and Univ. of N.C.,* 1–2, 180, 249–50,
    251, 255, 265
*Students for Fair Admissions, Inc. v.
    University of N.C.,* 1, 171, 173,
    177–84
Students for Fair Admissions (SFFA),
    177
Studies Weekly, 260
Stulberg, Lisa, 108, 162
Swayze, Francis J., 315 n.16
Sweatt v. Painter, 94–95, 96, 112, 114,
    115, 125, 137, 164
Sweden, 230, 353 n.8
Sweet, Paul, 24, 27, 28, 30, 32
Sweezy v. New Hampshire, 11, 124–28,
    129, 139, 151
Sydnor, Jr., Eugene, 156
systemic racism, 229, 234–36, 245
Szapuová, Mariana, 49

Taft, William Howard, 120
Tarrio, Enrique, 263
Taylor, Helen, 38, 39, 45
Taylor, Hobart, Jr., 161

Taylor, John, 36–37, 38
Taylor, Johnny, 197
Ten Cate, Irene, 73
Tennessee, 256, 262
Tennyson, Alfred Lord, 43
Texas, 19, 256, 262, 264–65; SB 17, 255.
    See also University of Texas
Texas Monthly, 255
Thernstrom, Abigail, 193
Thévenot, Laurent, 227
Thomas, Clarence, 1–2, 7, 165, 181, 197,
    253; *SFFA* opinion, 181; *Virginia v.
    Black* dissent, 8
Thomas, Roosevelt, 202, 203; "From
    Affirmative Action to Affirming
    Diversity," 203
Thomas, William, 315 n.16
3M, 16, 204
Thubron, Colin, 24
Tougas, Cecile, 49
training: diversity, 200, 210–12
transportation, access to, 240
Traoré, Bouna, 227
Tribe, Laurence, 154
Truman, Harry S., 120
Trump, Donald, 18–19, 218, 266;
    Executive Order 11246, 266;
    Executive Order 13950, 254
Trump, Donald, Jr., 216
Tulloch, Gail, 48; *Mill and Sexual
    Equality,* 49

U. S. Constitution: Commerce Clause,
    93; Fifteenth Amendment, 46, 245;
    Thirteenth Amendment, 78, 92. *See
    also* First Amendment; Fourteenth
    Amendment
UCLA School of Law, 259, 262
unconscious bias; 234, 235, 240, 243,
    254. *See also* implicit bias
UnHerd, 173, 263
Unitarians, 35, 36, 55, 60
United States v. Associated Press, 129,
    152

United Steelworkers v. Weber,
163
University College London (UCL),
36, 74
University of Berlin, 5–6, 23, 26, 29–30,
32, 33, 57
University of California, 167, 249;
Davis Medical School, 12, 146.
See also University of California
Berkeley
University of California Berkeley, 90–91,
215, 253–54; Center for Equity,
Gender, and Leadership, 205; Law
Library, 144
University of Cape Town (UCT), 10,
110, 111, 113, 116
University of Central Florida, 263
University of Jena, 25, 26
University of Michigan, 52, 168, 249;
Law School, 16, 168, 190–91
University of Missouri, 256; Law School,
87
University of North Carolina, 1, 88–89,
177–78, 249, 256; Law School, 10.
*See also Students for Fair Admissions,
Inc. v. University of N.C.; Students for
Fair Admissions, Inc. v. President and
Fellows of Harvard Coll. and Univ. of
N.C.*
University of Oklahoma Law School,
94
University of Oxford, 7, 36, 44
University of Texas, 263; Austin,
167, 255; Law School, 94, 95, 164,
176; "Top 10 Percent Plan," 167,
173
University of Washington: Law School,
11, 136–39, 142, 144
University of Wisconsin, 177, 255
University of Witwatersrand (Wits), 111,
113, 116
U.S. Chamber of Commerce, 148, 149,
156, 159
Utah, 255–56

Valls, Andrew, 25
Van Alstyne, William, 164
Vanguard, 208
Vanzetti, Bartolomeo, 62, 121–22
Vinson, Fred, 95
Virginia, 259–60
Virginia v. Black, 8
voting, discrimination in, 244–45
Voting Rights Act (1965), 134, 162, 173,
245

Walker, Anders, 150, 159
Walker, James Robert, 177
Wall Street Journal, 216, 267
Walmart, 267
Walters, Ryan, 255
Walton, Gregory, 198
Wang, I-Wei, 145
Ware, Caroline, 89
Warren, Earl, 123, 125
Washington, 167, 218. *See also* University
of Washington
Washington Post, 259, 260; "Bakke
Decision May Change Very Little,"
154
Washington University (St. Louis),
50
Watergate, 3, 135
wealth, discrimination in accumulation
of, 238–39
Weidel, Alice, 230
Wesley, Cynthia, 107
Westlaw, 144
White, Byron, 148
Whitney v. California, 77
Wienfort, Monika, 25
Williams, Chris, 183
Williams, Ryan P., 254
Wilson, Pete, 168
Wilson, Woodrow, 120
Winston & Strawn, 264
Wisconsin, 255, 258. *See also* University
of Wisconsin
wokeism, 228, 229

Wollstonecraft, Mary: *Vindication of the Rights of Woman, A*, 260
Women in Law Hackathon, 209
Woolworths, 80
World Economic Forum, 206–7
Wulf, Andrea, 26

Yale University, 52, 108, 249, 250

Zemmour, Éric, 227
ZipRecruiter, 264
Zoom, 264